HOLLYWOOD'S EMBASSIES

FILM AND CULTURE SERIES

FILM AND CULTURE

A series of Columbia University Press

Edited by John Belton

For a complete list of titles, see page 505.

HOLLYWOOD'S EMBASSIES

How Movie Theaters Projected American Power Around the World

ROSS MELNICK

Columbia University Press
New York

Columbia University Press
Publishers Since 1893
New York   Chichester, West Sussex
cup.columbia.edu

Copyright © 2022 Columbia University Press
All rights reserved

Library of Congress Cataloging-in-Publication Data
Names: Melnick, Ross, author.
Title: Hollywood's embassies : how movie theaters projected American power around the world / Ross Melnick.
Description: New York : Columbia University Press, [2021] | Series: Film and culture series | Includes bibliographical references and index.
Identifiers: LCCN 2021020183 (print) | LCCN 2021020184 (ebook) | ISBN 9780231201506 (hardback) | ISBN 9780231201513 (trade paperback) | ISBN 9780231554138 (ebook)
Subjects: LCSH: Motion picture theaters—Political aspects. | United States—Foreign relations—20th century. | United States—Foreign relations—21st century. | Civilization—American influences.
Classification: LCC NA6845 .M35 2021 (print) | LCC NA6845 (ebook) | DDC 725.823—dc23
LC record available at https://lccn.loc.gov/2021020183
LC ebook record available at https://lccn.loc.gov/2021020184

Cover design: Milenda Nan Ok Lee
Cover image: *Calcutta* by Dilip Kumar DasGupta. Courtesy of the Library of Congress.

This work was supported by a grant from the Academy Film Scholars Program of the Academy of Motion Picture Arts and Sciences.

CONTENTS

Acknowledgments ix

Introduction: "Shop Windows," "Cultural Embassies," and Hollywood's Global Exhibition   1

PART I.
Europe. When Expansion was Paramount (1923–1993): "Shop Window" Cinemas and the European Expansion of U.S. Film Exhibitors

1. Hollywood's British Invasion and the Battle of Birmingham, 1919–1929   29

2. Hollywood's European Adventure, 1925–1941   48

3. A New Battleground: U.S. Exhibitors Under Nazi Occupation, 1941–1945   64

4. Postwar Europe and the Legacy of Hollywood Cinemas, 1945–1993   76

PART II.
Australasia. Banking on Australasia (1930–1982): Global Banks and U.S. Cinema Ownership in Australia and New Zealand

5. Fox Chases Hoyts: U.S. Cinema Ownership in Australia, 1930–1936   93

6. The Fox Chase in New Zealand and Australia, 1936–1946   116

7. Hollywood and Australasian Cinemas, 1946–1982   129

PART III.
Latin America and the Caribbean. Hollywood in Cinelandia (1927–1973):
U.S. Cinemas and Local Politics in Latin America and the Caribbean

8. Cine Metros y Cine Paramounts, 1926–1941: MGM and Paramount's Latin American Shop Window Cinemas   147

9. Prop(aganda) Window Cinemas, 1933–1945: Ufa, Hollywood, and the Battle for Hearts and Minds Through South American Cinemas During World War II   160

10. Hollywood Cinema Expansion in Postwar South America, 1945–1973   168

11. Caribbean Dreams, 1929–1973: Hollywood Cinemas in Cuba, Jamaica, Puerto Rico, and Trinidad   182

PART IV.
Middle East. Hollywood's Muddle East (1925–1982):
Political Change in Egypt and Israel and the Consequences for Hollywood's Middle Eastern Cinemas

12. Buildings, Ballyhoo, and Boycotts in Egypt, 1925–1947: Alternating Realities at Hollywood's Egyptian Cinemas   209

13. No Meeting in the Middle, 1947–1956: Hollywood Cinemas, Egyptian Revolution, and Israeli Independence   225

14. After the Revolution, 1957–1982: Twentieth Century-Fox, Egypt, and Israel   248

PART V.
Africa. An "Unhappy Image of the United States Before an African Population" (1932–1975): Race, Industry, and Rebellion at Hollywood's African Cinemas

15. MGM and the "Uncrowned King of South Africa," 1932–1937: Hollywood Shop Window Cinemas in a Bitterly Protected Market   269

16. Fox Hunting on the African Continent, 1937–1956: Twentieth Century-Fox and the Struggle for Control of African Cinemas   279

17. A "Royal" Mess: Racial Strife in Colonial Zimbabwe, the Struggle for Independence in Postcolonial Kenya, and the End of Hollywood's Control of South African Cinemas, 1959–1975   293

PART VI.
Asia. Eastern Promises (1927–2013):
Hollywood's Cinemas in China, India, Japan, and the Philippines

18. *Benshi* and Ballyhoo, 1927–1973: Hollywood's Shop Window Cinemas in Japan and the Philippines   333

19. Joining the Global Metro Cub Club, 1936–1973: MGM and Fox's Shop Window Cinemas in India   346

20. China as Hollywood's Final Frontier, 1946–2013: Hollywood's Chinese Cinemas and the End of Hollywood's Exhibition Empires   361

Epilogue: Global Exhibition Flows in Reverse Before the Pandemic, 2013–2019   380

Notes   393
Index   469

ACKNOWLEDGMENTS

I must begin, as I did for my earlier book *American Showman*, by noting that the seeds of *Hollywood's Embassies* were planted almost two decades ago in a graduate silent film seminar taught by Chris Horak at UCLA in 2003. I was one year into my research on Samuel "Roxy" Rothafel when I began noticing that a number of Roxy's former colleagues at the Capitol Theatre in New York were being sent by Loew's to Paris to upgrade the opulent Gaumont Palace. This breadcrumb led me to the Gaumont-Loew-Metro agreement and a thousand more discoveries along the way.

This global research remained largely in the background until 2010 when I arrived at the Bill and Carol Fox Center for Humanistic Inquiry (CHI) at Emory University as a Postdoctoral Fellow and started a captivating year of research that began to reveal the scale and scope of Hollywood's exhibition operations overseas. Now, after a decade of traveling to archives, libraries, and cinemas around the world, *Hollywood's Embassies* is finally complete.

You certainly can't work on a book like this without a tremendous infrastructure of family, friends, colleagues, institutions, and granting bodies that make this kind of work possible.

I must first thank, once more, my mentors at UCLA who trained me and supported this research at its inception: my amazing doctoral committee—Janet Bergstrom, John Caldwell, Steve Mamber, and David Myers—as well as faculty members Chris Horak, Denise Mann, Michael Friend, Jonathan Kuntz, Chon Noriega, and the dearly missed Steve Ricci. Their historiographical training continues to inform my research and writing. Vincent Brook, Nick

Browne, Teshome Gabriel, Kathleen McHugh, and Vivian Sobchack were also essential to that experience.

As mentioned, this project blossomed at the CHI and I must, once again, thank then-CHI director Martina Brownley; associate, now executive, director Keith Anthony; and staff members Colette Barlow and Amy Erbil. CHI colleagues and friends who made a tremendous impact that year include Emory faculty members Deepika Bahri, Yayoi Everett, and Jeffrey Lesser as well as my postdoctoral colleagues Danielle Bobker, Amy Gansell, and Amanda Golden. My conversations with Deepika were invaluable, as was her friendship. Jeff was equally wonderful, and he whet my appetite for my future research on, and visit to, Brazil. Across campus I found a second home and an amazing Film Studies department led by the always incomparable Matthew Bernstein. Matthew has continued to be a constant source of wisdom and, best of all, friendship, ever since. Leslie Taylor and David Pratt took me in when I arrived at Emory and made that incredible year even more special. James Steffens was the kind of librarian/scholar one can only dream of working with. Finally, Benny Hary was an invaluable guide to thinking about cinema in both Egypt and Israel and his friendship and support were even more essential.

As an assistant professor at Oakland University in 2011, I began working on this book in earnest with all of the materials I had gathered at Emory. I thank Kyle Edwards and all of my former colleagues at Oakland in Cinema Studies, Media Studies, and English for the support they provided this project and the students I learned from that year. What an amazing group they were.

In 2012 I began a new position in the Department of Film and Media Studies at UC Santa Barbara. Each and every one of my colleagues has played a pivotal role in supporting me and this book over the past decade. I must first thank Cristina Venegas, who picked me up from the airport when I landed from snowy Detroit and welcomed me to the best academic home one could ask for. I profusely thank my faculty colleagues Peter Bloom, Anna Brusutti, Alenda Chang, Michael Curtin, Mona Damluji, Dana Driskel, Anna Everett, Cynthia Felando, Dick Hebdige, Jennifer Holt, Wendy Jackson, Chris Jenkins, James McNamara, Michael Miner, Lisa Parks, Patrice Petro, Bhaskar Sarkar, Laila Shereen Sakr, Greg Siegel, Naoki Yamamoto, Janet Walker, and Charles Wolfe. What an incredible array of brain power and warmth. Janet encouraged me to travel extensively; Chuck provided methodological genius; Michael and Jen facilitated my global research; and Peter, Bhaskar, and Cristina provided tremendous insights into Africa, South Asia, and Latin America, respectively. I must also thank Greg and Patrice for their constant encouragement and the important questions they have raised along the way. There is simply no chance this book would have been the same without them and all of my amazing colleagues. I'm also eternally grateful to the hardest working staff in the world, Catherine Cox, Kathy Murray, Joe Palladino, Janice Strobach, and

Dana Welch, who made this book and everything else possible. I must also thank Executive Vice Chancellor David Marshall for his tremendous support as dean of Humanities and Fine Arts as well as the wonderful deans that followed him, John Majewski and Mary Hancock. This project has been supported by four different chairs of my department and I thank them for all of their support, big and small. Over the years I've also learned so much from the students in my graduate global film exhibition seminar. Their own research and our innumerable discussions have been central to how I present this book and how I hope it can be useful in and out of the classroom. There is so much about global film exhibition still to discover.

A book like this is inordinately expensive to research and write. I could never have completed it without the tremendous support of several granting bodies at the University of California, Santa Barbara and a number of important external organizations. I thank Emory University once more for the postdoctoral fellowship that jumpstarted this book; the National Endowment for the Humanities for a fellowship that enabled me to take a year away for research and writing; the Academy of Motion Picture Arts and Sciences for an Academy Film Scholars Grant that helped immeasurably to complete this research; and the Theatre Historical Society for a Thomas R. DuBuque Research Fellowship that facilitated research in their archives. UC Santa Barbara supported this research every step of the way. I profusely thank the Academic Senate for several Faculty Research Grants and a Faculty Career Development Award; the Division of Humanities and Fine Arts for the Robert Emmons Award; the Office of Academic Personnel for the Regents' Humanities Faculty Fellowship; the College of Letters & Science for a Regents' Junior Faculty Fellowship; and the Interdisciplinary Humanities Center for a Release Time Award.

There were innumerable libraries, archives, and historical societies around the world who made this book possible: In Australia, Australia Film Institute Research Collection at RMIT University, Cinema and Theatre Historical Society, National Archives of Australia, National Library of Australia, National Film and Sound Archive of Australia, and City of Sydney Archives. In Brazil, Arquivo Centimetro (Ivo Raposo), Arquivo Cinédia (Alice Gonzaga), Arquivo Nacional, Arquivo Público do Estado de São Paulo, Biblioteca do MAM (Museu de Arte Moderna do Rio de Janeiro), Biblioteca Nacional, and Cinemateca Brasileira. In England, British Film Institute, British Library, Cinema Theatre Association, Imperial War Museum Library, and National Archives. In France, La Bibliothèque Nationale de France, La Cinémathèque Française, and Mémorial de la Shoah. In Israel, Historical Archives of the Municipality of Tel Aviv-Yafo and the Tel Aviv Cinematheque Library. In the Netherlands, the Eye Collection Centre at the EYE Film Institute and Stadsarchief Amsterdam. In Italy, Biblioteca Sormani in Milan. In New Zealand, Archives

New Zealand, Auckland War Memorial Library, National Library of New Zealand, and Ngā Taonga Sound & Vision. In Sweden, Bibliotek at the Swedish Film Institute. In the United States, Margaret Herrick Library (AMPAS), National Archives and Records Administration, New York Public Library for the Performing Arts, Stanford University Special Collections and University Archives, Theatre Historical Society of America, Warner Bros. Archive/USC, Wisconsin Center for Film and Theater Research, Wisconsin Historical Society, and the Wolfsonian-FIU as well as many other libraries including those at UCLA, UC Santa Barbara, and USC that enabled this research. I am grateful as well to the innumerable global digital newspaper and magazine repositories including the BNDigital and Hemeroteca Digital Brasileira (Brazil), British Newspaper Archive, Delpher (Netherlands), Gallica (France), Historical Jewish Press (Israel), Media History Digital Library, Newspapers.com, Papers Past (New Zealand), ProQuest Historical Newspapers, Trove (Australia), and many, many others.

I am grateful to *Cinema Journal*, now the *Journal of Cinema and Media Studies*, where portions of chapters 16 and 17 were originally published. Early work on Egypt and Palestine/Israel originally appeared in the *Historical Journal of Film, Radio and Television*. Preliminary work on both China and Cuba first appeared in the edited collection *Hollywood and the Law* (BFI, 2015) and I am grateful to the editors of the collection and BFI for their early support of this research.

I am also deeply grateful to a fantastic group of research assistants who have assisted me over the past eight years. Naomi DeCelles, Hiroumi Kevin Jimbo, Aleah Kiley, Yongli Li, Charlotte Orzel, and Thong Win were all instrumental in that work. I must thank Yongli as well for assistance with Mandarin translations, Hiroumi for translating numerous Japanese articles, Isi Bolozky for research and translation of numerous Hebrew documents, and my good friend Benoit Marchisio for his early assistance with materials from *La Cinémathèque Française*.

One of the greatest joys of writing this book is the number of friends and colleagues I've made along the way. I was so lucky to meet Clément Dassa, who provided me with wonderful memories of his father's work at MGM and his own recollections of Cairo moviegoing. Thank you Clément for your friendship and for allowing me to use here a few of the amazing images from your collection. What can I say about Brazilian film scholar João Luiz Vieira? A renowned scholar of Brazilian film history, a beautiful soul, and a wonderful friend. It was through him that I met the incomparable Ivo Raposo and traveled to Conservatoria all those years ago to visit the amazing Centimetro. An enormous thank you to Ivo for opening his home and his archive to me and for allowing me to use these images here. Experiencing the wonder of the Centimetro was truly one of the most magical cinematic experiences I have ever had. Rafael de Luna Freire and Luciana Correa de Araújo are now longtime friends who have been so generous to share their tremendous knowledge of Brazilian film history and the history of distribution and exhibition therein. It was through Rafael that I met João and through Luciana that I met the great José Inácio de Melo Souza, who helped me to navigate the Sao Paulo archives. Thank you all so much. João and Rafael also connected me to the great Hernani Heffner at the Rio MAM who connected me to the Cinédia archives. Finally, I have to thank my wonderful friend Courtney Brannon Donoghue, who traveled with me during this amazing trip. What an amazing experience it was, and what an incredible group of scholars and friends. Obrigado.

Wherever I traveled over the past decade for this book, I was able to see some of my favorite people: Deb Verhoeven in Melbourne, Ken Roe in London, Benoit Marchisio and Stephan Zaubitzer in Paris, and Kirsten Thompson while still in Wellington. They all provided context, assistance, and friendship—then, there, and now. In the midst of the pandemic, writing these acknowledgments is a rather wonderful time-traveling device. I miss those days!

I do not have enough words of appreciation for the support and encouragement of John Belton, Jennifer Crewe, and Philip Leventhal. This project began under Jennifer's editorial guidance before she became associate provost and director of Columbia University Press. I'm so grateful to have worked with her on this book at its earliest stages and had the great fortune to work with Philip ever since. John and Philip have been there for every new development, every new archive, and every new chapter. So many wonderful meetings at Society for Cinema and Media Studies conferences and lunches in New York as this took shape. Thank you so much for your endless support, guidance, and friendship.

After the significant length of *American Showman*, I promised Jennifer that I would produce a much smaller manuscript next time. For many years, I believed this was possible. However, as every chapter grew with the discovery of new countries, new histories, and new contexts, the book expanded exponentially. When the manuscript was finally completed, I turned to my good friend and amazing colleague Rebecca Prime to help me figure out how to cut this book down to a more manageable size and to make sure that it held together as a cohesive manuscript and not just a series of region-specific sections. Rebecca was a godsend. Her insights, edits, inquiries, and notes shaped this book in so many ways. I miss our conversations by phone and receiving her excellent notes and edits. It's such a privilege and an honor to have someone that brilliant provide guidance on your work. Thank you, Rebecca, for everything. I also thank Patricia Bower for her tremendous copyediting, patience, and inquiries. It made the book infinitely stronger. Another enormous thank you to Marisa Lastres at Columbia University Press for seeing this book through its production.

Beyond all of my great friends at UC Santa Barbara, I'm so grateful to have an amazing group across the country who take my mind off work and yet help shape my research and life in so many ways. I wish I had the space to write a sentence about all of the amazing people below. Please know how much you all mean to me and how much your friendship has helped me, especially during the last years of writing this book. I cannot thank enough Michael Albright; Jaimie Baron; Kymber Blake; Catherine Brougham; Nigel Bruce; Rob Cavanaugh; Steve Charboneau; Jonathan Cohn; Mirasol Enriquez; Chelsea Erin; Bishnupriya Ghosh; Francesca Fabro; Scott Feinberg; Kate Fortmueller; Scott Froschauer; Jason Gendler; Lindsay Giggey; Harrison Gish; Ben Harris; Scott King; Sara Levavy; Mark Lipson; Maja Manojlovic; Cheryl Marx; Rob Meltzer; Jen Moorman; Ahmed Nassef; Jennifer Porst; Aviva Raichelson; A. J. Roquevert; Art, Gigi, and Roxanne Rothfael; Ben Sampson; Mindy Schirn; Sudeep Sharma; Maya Smukler; Katherine Spring; Akilesh Sridharan; Lem Thomas; Kim Tomaselli; Julie Turnock; Ellen Viera; Kristen Warner; Dan Warren; Laurel Westrup; Julia Wright; Saba Zafar; and Christoph Zimny. Some family members are more like friends, especially Alon Borten, James Breitinger, and Memy Melnick. Thanks so much for being both.

So many close, wonderful friends and scholars have provided excellent feedback, questions, and support along the way, including Matthew Bernstein, Emily Carman, Mark Cooper, Manuel Covo, Tom Doherty, Courtney Brannon Donoghue, Kathy Fuller-Seeley, Josh Gleich, Josh Glick, Colin Gunckel, Chris Horak, Sangjoon Lee, Charlie Keil, Rob King, Paul Moore, Paul McDonald, Charles Musser, Mark Quigley, Eric Smoodin, Daniel Steinhart, Deb Verhoeven, Greg Waller, and Mark Williams. Thank you all so much. Over the past number of years, I have also been fortunate to be part of a weekly writing group with scholars Dawn Fratini and Luci Marzola. Coffee writing sessions turned into weekly pandemic Zooms in 2020. I cannot thank them both enough for their perseverance, friendship, and counsel on this project.

As the first draft of this book was nearing completion, in February 2020, my mother-in-law, Neta Bolozky, passed away. Neta was a tireless champion and a towering presence in all of our lives. There has been a deafening silence ever since. My grandparents, Lester and Evy Melnick, my uncle Don Melnick, my friend Eric Mack, and others like Steve Ricci, Edward Branigan, and Teshome Gabriel all sadly passed away during the writing of this book. Along with Neta's passing, there were tremendous losses alongside the gains of the past decade. This book is a tribute to all of them. They are deeply missed.

I am blessed to have the unending support and enormous generosity of my father-in-law, Shmuel; my sister-in-law, Michal, and her husband, Dan; and all of the Bolozkys, Bortens, and Koppelmans around the world.

I must thank my brother, Joshua, and my parents for all of their love and support. I would never have pursued this career without their passion for education, history, culture, and cinema. Our conversations over the past half century have always been about history—familial, political, cultural, and cinematic—and they lit the fire that has kindled and maintained my passion for film, moviegoing, and historiography. As always, *Hollywood's Embassies* was read in draft form by my father, historian Ralph Melnick, who provided key insights and inquiries that helped shape this book in innumerable and important ways. I'm so fortunate to have them all in my life and proud to have been able to follow in their footsteps, even if it took a detour through Hollywood and the tech world to get there. Thank you for everything. My life is full and blessed because of them.

Finally, this book is dedicated to my wife, Noa. Buried inside each page is an invisible set of coffees made, moments shared, movies watched, vacations postponed, plans dashed, and the reality of a decade of writing and research. Anyone who is married to a writer knows the burden it can become. There is no book without Noa. There is nothing without her. I love you.

Thank you for reading *Hollywood's Embassies*. I hope, like my own revelations while writing it, that it opens up new ideas, new territories, and new avenues for discovery. The hardest part about completing a book that brought you such joy is to say good-bye. Fortunately, to you, I can say hello and I hope you enjoy the read, the time travel, the globetrotting, and the complex infrastructure of our world that this research can only begin to open up.

HOLLYWOOD'S EMBASSIES

INTRODUCTION

"Shop Windows," "Cultural Embassies," and Hollywood's Global Exhibition

"The extent of Metro-Goldwyn-Mayer's overseas holdings is not generally appreciated even by those familiar with the company. While the British studio at Borehamwood near London has received much recent publicity and the two London showcase theatres are well-known, the 48 overseas theatres owned and operated by Metro are something of a secret."
—*Variety*, January 1970

"I am bitterly opposed to it. They ought to get out."
—Samuel Goldwyn, on Hollywood's overseas cinemas, as quoted in the *Austin Statesman*, May 1947

The opening night of Twentieth Century-Fox's Royal Cinema in Salisbury, Southern Rhodesia (now Harare, Zimbabwe), on September 7, 1959, was slated to have a picture-perfect Hollywood ending. The country's top politicians were on hand for the debut of the Fox film *South Pacific* (directed by Joshua Logan, 1958), with all proceeds for the local Red Cross. *South Pacific*'s message of racial tolerance, however, was starkly undermined by Fox's South African management team, who had strictly forbidden all "non-Europeans" from attending the opening, in direct opposition to the Southern Rhodesian government's stated policy of "multiracial partnership."

FIGURE 0.1 MGM International Convention, ca. 1953. (Courtesy of Clément Dassa)

Like many other U.S.-operated cinemas overseas, the Royal became a highly contested venue for Hollywood and the U.S. government, which struggled for years to contain the diplomatic and public relations crisis that erupted before and after the premiere. Twentieth Century-Fox's troubled history in Africa—from the politically divisive, whites-only cinemas it operated in Kenya, South Africa, and colonial Zimbabwe to its Egyptian cinemas that were sites of political protest and violence during the 1940s and 1950s—reflects the industrial opportunities and geopolitical complications Hollywood encountered around the world, in Africa, Asia, Australasia, the Caribbean, Europe, Latin America, and the Middle East, during its nine decades of global film exhibition.

Hollywood's Embassies: How Movie Theaters Projected American Power Around the World is the first political, cultural, and industrial history of Hollywood's foreign ownership and operation of hundreds of cinemas in more than three dozen countries from 1923 to 2013. Over the past three decades, numerous scholars such as Ian Jarvie, Richard Maltby, Kristin Thompson, and John Trumpbour have analyzed Hollywood's distribution of films overseas and the complex structure of "Global Hollywood." Despite these invaluable contributions, there has been little research examining how MGM, Paramount,

Twentieth Century-Fox, and Warner Bros. operated hundreds of cinemas (movie theaters) outside of North America, from Argentina to Zimbabwe, to secure distribution for their films and attract local moviegoers to American-style cinemas featuring American studio product. The importance of these Hollywood-owned cinemas and cinema chains for local audiences, and the manner in which they secured international markets for American films, is largely absent from most works focused on the relationship between "Hollywood" films and their global circulation.

Philip Turner's short history of Europe's rebranded MGM Cinemas circuit (which was formed in England in 1991) is a case in point, as Turner overlooks the scale and size of Hollywood's earlier cinema exhibition expansion. He writes that "outside of the original MGM-Loew's production-exhibition arrangement, MGM appears never to have enjoyed the luxury of a worldwide theatre network"—although the company had owned and operated dozens of cinemas throughout the world for half a century, from the 1920s well into the 1970s, from Rio de Janeiro to London to Johannesburg to Mumbai and Manila.[1] Charles Acland's *Screen Traffic*, a seminal work on multiplexes, globalization, and Hollywood overseas, is one of the very few books to reference this earlier history of cinema globalization. Observing that Paramount, Loew's, and Fox had a smattering of foreign theaters in "earlier periods," he concludes that "these precursors pale in comparison to the building and buying of the 1990s."[2] However, by the late 1950s Twentieth Century-Fox alone owned and operated hundreds of cinemas throughout the world, stretching from Lima to Amsterdam to Nairobi to Calcutta to Melbourne and back again.

Neither have scholars reckoned with another striking feature of Hollywood's global machinery: that audiences in major media capitals around the world were as seduced by the hundreds of cinemas owned and operated by MGM, Paramount, Twentieth Century-Fox, Warner Bros., and other U.S. film companies as by the films themselves. As cinema architect S. Charles Lee famously opined, the allure of Hollywood and its exotic "show" began "on the sidewalk," from the first glittering Paramount bulb on the marquee to Warner Bros.' sumptuous lobbies to MGM's deluxe ushers and ballyhoo, to Twentieth Century-Fox's musical fanfare, newsreels, and its short and feature films.[3] As I argue in *American Showman* (Columbia University Press, 2012), a night at the movies was a cohesive and powerfully transporting experience, one that operated as a so-called shop window for American films, industrial practices, and culture and as a "cultural embassy" for Hollywood, selling a very specific American style of entertainment and politics in which American films, stars, and brands were the exotic allure.[4] Maltby argues that Hollywood's global influence and "the act of Americanisation took place in the space between the audience and the screen, in the transient act of consumption of the shadow images of cinema's Great Dark Room."⁵ From 1923 to 2013, Hollywood sold its films, its brand identity, and its ideology to urban moviegoers through these buildings, featuring American technology, management, and cinema policies, some of which actually revealed darker truths, paradoxes, and hypocrisies about the United States that undercut the work of "official" U.S. embassies and consulates operating throughout the world.

Hollywood's Embassies documents and analyzes a history that has either been largely diminished in scholarly importance or, more to the point, is largely unknown. However, historians who have worked on national film exhibition histories—of England, New Zealand, Australia, South Africa, and many other nations—have individually noted the importance of Hollywood exhibitors operating on their home turf. What has remained absent from the previous film historiography, though, is a regional, comparative, and global examination of this transnational phenomenon. As I argue throughout this book, singular analyses of Hollywood's exhibition operations in a particular country (almost) always need to be conducted with larger regional frameworks in mind. Twentieth Century-Fox's exhibition forays in Egypt, for example, directly related to its exhibition operations in Israel and vice versa; Paramount and Loew's/MGM's strategy in France reflected its experience in England; Fox's dominance in Australian and New Zealand exhibition were related to changes in domestic, regional, and global investment banking and, later, by commingled management and executives; Paramount's investment in cinema exhibition in the Caribbean involved multiple countries and interconnected exhibitors, countries, and politics. A regional approach also helps us better understand Hollywood's exhibition interests in West and North Africa, East Asia, South America, and many other regions throughout the world. The more one examines Hollywood's investment in and disruption of local and regional markets, the more evident are the ways in which Hollywood executives, U.S. consular officials, and local political leaders achieved their financial, diplomatic, and political goals. Likewise, Hollywood's hold over local audiences was cemented not only through its on-screen narratives but through the cinemas in which they were shown.

The lacuna in film and media scholarship around this expansive and enormously influential history stems from a variety of factors. First, film (and media) studies, for much of the last half century, has privileged film production and filmmakers over film exhibition and film exhibitors. As Toby Miller, Freya Schiwy, and Marta Hernández Salván note, because "other parts of the cycle—circulating, promoting and showing movies—lack glamour and artistry even as they are extremely profitable," scholars have "tend[ed] to focus on production to the exclusion of distribution and exhibition."⁶ Over the past two decades, however, scholars such as Charles Acland, James Burns, Kathy Fuller-Seeley, Paul Moore, Eric Smoodin, Gregory Waller, and many others have dramatically changed the importance of studying film exhibition as it intersects with local, national, and global affairs. Elsewhere, national and city- and site-specific film exhibition (micro) histories have expanded widely during this same period, with both film and media scholars and architectural historians adding much-needed context to local cinemas and cinema chains. Each year brings us closer to understanding the contours and contexts of film exhibition throughout the world. Still, that "map" is only partially filled and requires decades of additional "cartographers."

Industry trade journals, newspapers, magazines, and many other publications have also historically privileged film production over film exhibition and distribution, even during the vertically integrated studio years. Coverage of Hollywood's distribution overseas since the 1920s has paled compared to the ink local outlets and trade journals devoted to this American film exhibition "invasion" overseas. However, the "trades" *did* cover Hollywood's global exhibition expansion, whether it was in Argentina or colonial Zimbabwe, providing a bread-crumb trail that scholars can use to find more in-depth coverage of this phenomenon and the local response to it. In addition, corporate annual reports, newspapers, and many other documents covered this phenomenon for the nine decades of its growth from 1923 to 2013.

If, as *Variety* noted in January 1970, MGM's 48 global cinemas were "something of a secret," it wasn't a very well-kept one.[7] And if it was a secret to *Variety*—despite its own reporting on this phenomenon for half a century prior—then it was because U.S. trade journals then and now have also focused primarily on the North American market. There was, for example, nothing secret about Twentieth Century-Fox's ownership of 155 cinemas across Africa during the 1950s and 1960s or its ownership of dominant Australian and New Zealand cinema chains from the 1930s to the 1980s. Metro-Goldwyn-Mayer's global brand was, in fact, even more directly sutured onto its foreign cinemas (Metro Theatres/Cine Metros) than Loews Inc.'s domestic chain (Loew's Theatres). In the United States, before the consent decree broke up the Loew's–MGM relationship in 1959, domestic cinemas were named Loew's for the parent company. Overseas, Loew's (and later MGM's) foreign cinemas were named "Metro" after the successful launch of the first Metro Theatre in Johannesburg in 1932. After that, Metro cinemas could be found throughout major cities in South America—three Metros alone dotted Rio de Janeiro—while Paramount's name was emblazoned on palatial cinemas in countries such as Brazil (Cine Paramount) and France (Le Paramount). Beginning in 1938 with the launch of the eponymous Warner Theatre in London, Warner Bros.' name could also be found on cinemas in Havana, Cuba, and, later, through a massive global chain (Warner Bros. International Theatres) that stretched from Portugal to China, managed under the watchful eye of veteran exhibitor Salah Hassanein, who had begun his career four decades earlier working for Twentieth Century-Fox

FIGURES 0.2–0.5 Paramount, Warner Bros., MGM, and Twentieth Century-Fox cinemas around the world. Pictured on pages 6–9 are a program from Le Paramount in Paris (author's collection); a photograph of the Warner Theatre in London (courtesy of Cinema Theatre Association); a Metro Theatre program from Brisbane, Australia (courtesy of Fryer Library); and a photograph of 20th Century Theatre in Johannesburg (Twentieth Century-Fox Annual Report, New York Public Library for the Performing Arts).

FIGURES 0.2–0.5 (*continued*)

in Cairo in the 1940s, the location of Fox's own shop window cinema, the Cairo Palace and MGM's Cinema Metro. RKO, Universal, and United Artists also operated a small number of cinemas in foreign markets.

The significance of Hollywood's forgotten history of owning and operating cinemas around the world comes into full relief in relation to the common perception that Hollywood "lost" or divested its cinemas after the consent decree. This is only true in the United States. The settlement that Paramount

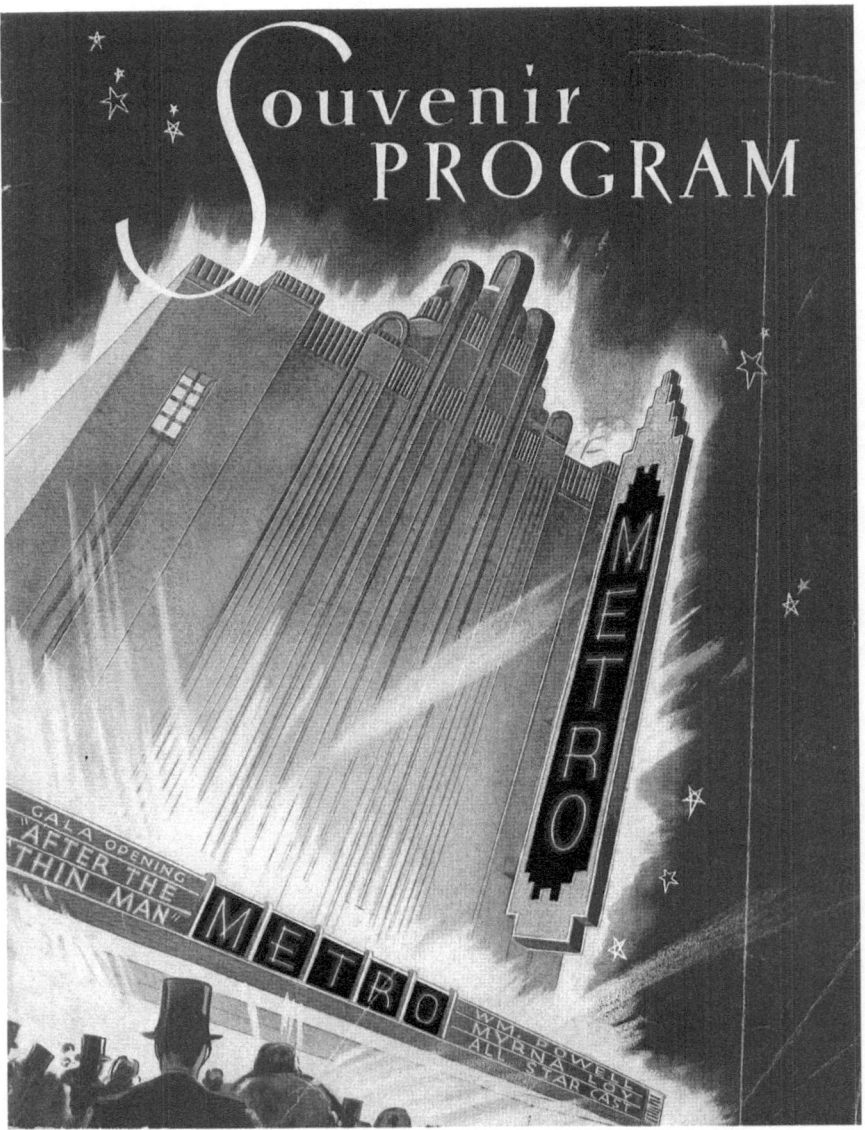

FIGURES 0.2–0.5 (*continued*)

struck with the U.S. Department of Justice, for example, required only that the company "divorce its domestic exhibition business from its production and distribution business."[8] It does not mention Paramount's overseas cinemas. For Twentieth Century-Fox and the others, no such edict of theater/cinema divorcement was required internationally. Thinking through the U.S.

FIGURES 0.2–0.5 (*continued*)

government's desire to use Hollywood to spread American culture and ideology around the world, why would they seek a divestiture of Hollywood's international exhibition operations that would have only benefited local and competitive film industries, cinemas, and chains?

For nine decades, stretching from the silent era to contemporary Hollywood, U.S. film exhibitors maintained a frequently fraught, often lucrative, and at times violent and politically adverse relationship with audiences, distributors, exhibitors, and politicians around the world. These American-run cinemas were, after all, not merely outposts for the exhibition of Hollywood films; they were also "cultural embassies" designed to attract local audiences to American films and moviegoing practices. As Paramount-, Metro-, Warner-, and Fox-owned or -operated cinemas opened around the world, Hollywood not only dominated the content on the screen but increasingly owned the screens as well.

Through archival research conducted in nine countries on four continents, *Hollywood's Embassies* examines the role Paramount played in integrating multiclass and multiracial audiences at their Cine Tacna in Lima, Peru, and the way that child-oriented moviegoing clubs at MGM cinemas in India, Egypt, and Australia cultivated an audience for Hollywood cartoons, newsreels, and feature films even amid nationalization and postcolonial independence. These deluxe cinemas, and hundreds of other American-owned movie houses overseas, helped foster a multigenerational relationship between Hollywood and its international audiences, remembered fondly by former club members like Salman Rushdie in *Midnight's Children* and by Egyptian director Mohamed Khan. Honored in France, boycotted in England, burned in Egypt, or protested in colonial Zimbabwe, this global expansion of American film exhibition highlights the complications and opportunities generated by this first wave of physical global expansion decades before the growth of American-owned theme parks, retailers, and restaurant chains overseas. Each venue—from MGM's movie houses in Calcutta, Cairo, and Buenos Aires, to Fox's cinemas in Adelaide, Alexandria, and Tel Aviv, to Warner Bros.'s deluxe theaters in Havana, London, and Lima, to Paramount's cinemas in Tokyo, Paris, and São Paulo—provides an extraordinary glimpse into the exportation of U.S. cinema practices and how film exhibition played a crucial role in globalizing the lure of and adulation for "Hollywood." Movies distributed by MGM, Paramount, Fox, and Warner Bros. may have introduced global audiences to American culture, but in many international cities these American-run cinemas may have had just as large an impact on the exportation of American cultural and social mythology.

While acknowledging that Hollywood was popular around the world because of the films produced by its U.S. studios, *Hollywood's Embassies* argues these U.S.-owned and -operated movie houses also played a definitive role in that growing affinity (and revulsion) as they acculturated global audiences to American industrial and cultural practices and the overseas marketing of wealth, leisure, consumerism, and "democracy." Hollywood films and stars attracted foreign audiences, but Hollywood's overseas cinemas also provided a crucial opportunity to "enter" the United States through what were veritable "cultural embassies" managed by American executives and outfitted with American technology and accoutrements that provided a quintessentially "American" service experience of cross-class appeal to local audiences. Brand identity and brand loyalty, with Paramount, "Metro" (MGM), Warner, and "20th Century" (Twentieth Century-Fox) cinemas showing company-produced newsreels, shorts, and feature films, featuring the musical fanfare of each Hollywood studio, created a visual, aural, and consumerist appeal to generations of foreign moviegoers. Metro Cub Clubs (MGM) and other child-oriented programs also hooked postcolonial youths in places like Egypt and India just as nationally oriented independence movements and film industry protectionism were ascendant.

Hollywood's marketing of luxury and consumption through these overseas cinemas was, however, often tone deaf to new and ongoing social, cultural, and political pushback and even anger. The story of Hollywood's global cinemas, therefore, is not a simplistic narrative of unidirectional cultural and industrial indoctrination and colonization. It is instead one of hybridity and negotiation, booms and busts, successes and failures, adoptions and repulsions, which all serve as a harbinger of struggles to come in the construction and operation of Cold War–era Hilton Hotels, Walt Disney theme parks, and the proliferation of American restaurant and retail outlets overseas. For the first time, beginning in the 1920s, American multinational multimedia corporations set out to colonize the streetscapes of the world's most important cities. They found local film industries, exhibitors, politicians, and tastemakers struggling to maintain their independence against the money and power of Hollywood and rising local demand for American films *and* these American-owned cinemas. Hollywood, through its foreign cinemas and cinema chains, hoped to secure both its distribution networks and its dominance. It sought to vertically integrate the mind of the global moviegoer, to watch American films in an American cinema in a distinctly American way and context. This success would benefit the continued, multigenerational, and never-ending circulation of Hollywood films and, for the U.S. State and Commerce Departments, a constant flow of American political and consumerist messaging, selling American ideas, products, and (soft) power, especially during fractious and wartime periods. An American-owned cinema operating overseas in a major media capital such as Buenos Aires or Bombay meant gaining a *physical* and not just a metaphorical foothold in a foreign nation. For a company like Fox or MGM, it meant securing a grandiose first-run cinema (or cinema chain) that allowed each company to control the premiere release of its films and its messaging in a foreign and sometimes hostile environment. Set against the backdrops of the rise of fascism in the 1930s, World War II, the Cold War, and other geopolitical contexts, these cinemas were enormously important for Hollywood and the U.S. government. American-owned cinemas, when operating without a locally prohibitive mandate, could transmit U.S.-produced newsreels, shorts, and feature films to local audiences without government filtration or objection. The power of an American-owned and operated "shop window" overseas therefore often became a red line for those concerned about U.S. cultural and industrial hegemony and the loss of local control and power.

Because of the very physical nature of this American exportation overseas, with an American building inside a major capital or city abroad, it was often film exhibition—not film production or distribution—that most challenged issues of nationalism and foreign investment overseas. Film production was transient, contingent, and often temporary, even with the construction of local studios and incentives. Film distribution, too, remained largely invisible to local audiences and still dependent on domestic exhibitors. It was foreign ownership or operation of local cinemas, therefore, that often fomented dissent and anger, from industry boycotts of American films in England to political violence in Egypt. U.S. film distribution overseas was often a less physically obtrusive and obvious form of American soft power extension. As noted by the U.S. State Department's need to gauge the reaction of local governments to a proposed purchase of a local cinema or chain, control over local film exhibition felt to many people around the world like ceding physical control over a domestic market to Hollywood. Restricting the flow of money from these venues back to the United States also did little good as many countries learned that blocking Hollywood film companies from repatriating their distribution profits back to the United States only spurred more local (exhibition) investment. Meanwhile, as U.S. film companies bought local chains and then employed their local workforce to work in Hollywood's overseas cinemas, this only reinforced the sense that the U.S. film industry was "colonizing" the local market and employing its managers to lobby on behalf of Hollywood during times of political, economic, and social protectionism or anti-Americanism.

American cooptation worked in other ways as well, as Hollywood's local cinemas and exchanges purchased acres of advertising space in foreign trade journals and local newspapers. Multipage spreads often accompanied the opening of new Hollywood "shop windows" in foreign markets with MGM and others spending lavishly on full-page advertisements. Foreign trade journals were also compromised in their antagonism toward this foreign invasion of the local film industry by their cozy relations with Hollywood overseas and their executives—American or otherwise—working in these areas. Advertising, and the threat of its loss, also hemmed in local criticism. As Dale Turnbull, former head of the Fox-owned Hoyts circuit in Australia, observed, local trade papers during his era survived only due to the ad revenue they generated.[9]

There were many reasons for the expansion of American film companies into exhibition overseas. In the early to mid-1920s, in nearly every territory around the world, the major American film companies deemed the revenues generated by domestically owned cinemas overseas and the overall quality of those cinemas in terms of décor, technology, and operation to be deficient. That deficiency, they felt, hurt foreign distribution revenues as local cinema operators charged too little for the exhibition of Hollywood's films. American exhibitors like Hugo Riesenfeld and Sid Grauman, traveling to Europe during this era, deemed those cinemas abroad to be severely lacking. Even the opulent cinemas of the era, such as the Gaumont Palace in Paris, did not generate enough by American standards or comparison. As production budgets and corporate overhead grew back in the States, and the U.S. distribution and exhibition market rounded into maturity, Marcus Loew and others recognized that expanding foreign markets was one of the key business development opportunities. The subsequent opening of branch offices around the world spurred MGM and Paramount to seek local showcase cinemas—or "shop window" cinemas—abroad, guaranteeing the premiere exhibition of company films without having to negotiate for playing time or split ticket sales with local exhibitors. The purchase and formation of local cinema chains by Fox, MGM, and Paramount—in Africa, Asia, Australasia, Europe, and Latin America—further enabled American film companies to gain control over their product and additional sources of revenue.

International division heads for the American film companies were convinced these foreign, American-operated cinemas would make these markets more profitable through higher ticket sales and would influence local exhibitors to upgrade their own cinemas through both film trade acclaim and industrial competition. Paramount and MGM's exploitation methods at its shop window cinemas and other U.S.-operated cinema chains were also intended to influence exhibitors from smaller cities and towns across a given country who traveled to these shop window cinemas to see the premiere presentation of a new American film and market those films similarly in their own lobbies, retail stores, and by other means of (cross-)promotion and advertisement.

Technological developments were another reason for this international growth in exhibition. MGM cinemas, for example, were often the first movie houses in a foreign city to feature air-conditioning, which allowed cinemas to stay open (and busy) during the summer months. In other cases, such as Paramount cinemas of the late 1920s, many were the first to install synchronous sound systems in cities such as Tokyo and São Paulo. In the 1950s Fox-owned cinemas brought widescreen cinema to Australia, New Zealand, and other markets before their competitors. In fact, Fox stated that CinemaScope was one of the driving forces behind its 1950s exhibition expansion abroad. The other reason, of course, was the loss of its domestic theater chain and those revenues.

Forced upgrades of local cinemas through this competition was a motivating factor. In the 1920s Paramount's showcase cinema in Paris, Le Paramount, and the Gaumont-Loew-Metro agreement that provided Loew's International with control over Gaumont's French cinemas were both efforts to secure premium venues for distributing Hollywood films but were also obtained to force French exhibitors to match U.S. presentation standards or risk losing customers who were attracted to American-run cinemas and their marketing, presentation, and management techniques. As Marcus Loew noted, "We have no desire to build or own a theatre in any city which is adequately seated and properly equipped theatrically to present pictures as they reasonably should be exhibited." But Loew and others found the globe's most promising territories to be not at all "adequately seated or properly equipped" and instead financially and operationally underwhelming.[10] By directly competing with domestic cinemas, American film companies reasoned that local exhibitors would be forced to upgrade their own presentation standards and, by consequence, their daily ticket prices would lead to greater revenues from foreign cinemas regardless of American ownership or control. Half a century later, Salah Hassenein employed similar logic when he encouraged Warner Bros. to create a new global circuit, Warner Bros. International Theatres (WBIT), in 1987 to expand Hollywood's market share around the world and thus grow its foreign revenues in expanding post–Cold War markets. WBIT hoped to spur the growth of new, more profitable multiplexes for Hollywood films through direct competition with aging local cinemas.

While the shop window cinema model was often used by Paramount, MGM, and Warner Bros. in the early to mid-twentieth century, Fox/Twentieth Century-Fox often sought chain ownership instead. Fox's foreign-owned circuits secured the distribution of Fox films throughout Australia, Kenya, New Zealand, South Africa, and colonial Zimbabwe and funneled money back into Fox's coffers in the United States. In fact, as Dale Turnbull, former director of Fox's Hoyts Theatres and of Twentieth Century-Fox distribution in Australia, notes, he would often be assailed by local Fox staff in Australia for not giving preferable terms to Fox films booked at Hoyts Theatres. Turnbull argued that his job was to make the most money for the benefit of Twentieth Century-Fox in the United States; Fox films in Australia had to negotiate with the Fox-owned Hoyts like all other distributors.[11] (The same was true for WBIT in Taiwan, for example, as the local branch of Warner Bros. there had to negotiate terms with WBIT like any other.[12]) While Fox was primarily invested in whole chain operation in the above markets, it is worth noting that the company did have its own shop window cinemas in foreign markets where it did not own chains in cities such as Amsterdam, Bombay, Lima, and London. As *Hollywood's Embassies* makes clear, the strategy for each company differed from country to country, city to city, and year to year. The flexibility and malleability of this global enterprise can be categorized not by their holistic similarity but by the vast differences in their global operations.

Hollywood's Embassies collates the reasons American film companies built, bought, or leased cinemas overseas. In Tel Aviv, for example, Spyros Skouras proudly noted that the company built its 1957 showcase cinema in Israel for personal and political reasons to help boost the fortunes of the new country through this real estate and entertainment investment and through the cinema's associated office building for doctors and other essential workers. Loew's and Fox, in another example, had very different reasons for investing in Australia. Fox bought Hoyts in 1930, which provided the company with outlets across the country for Fox films as well as substantial exhibition revenues from the many studios they contracted with. MGM, meanwhile, built and bought shop window cinemas in Australia to enable it to secure unfettered access to big city audiences outside of the Hoyts/Greater Union national duopoly.

Hollywood's Embassies argues that each of the four American film companies most involved in foreign exhibition made its own decisions in each market in each country in each decade, often in contrast to one another. Every market was different, which makes this history so fascinating and yet so complex. This variety and complexity are evident in each of the six regions featured in this book in which Hollywood bought, built, leased, or operated cinemas.

Hilton-Managed Hotels and Hollywood-Owned Cinemas

Because there has been comparatively little scholarship on Hollywood's overseas cinemas between 1923 and 2013, because the focus of this work is on *cinemas* rather than on *cinema*, and because this book focuses on Hollywood's collision with local and global politics, culture, and industry, *Hollywood's Embassies* does not have a proper antecedent. The books by Acland, Jarvie, Thompson, Trumpbour, and others provide invaluable context and methodologies, but they do not offer a blueprint for how to conduct this study focused on buildings, not box office.

Instead, I found early inspiration and affinity with some of the through lines and threads of Annabel Wharton's *Building the Cold War: Hilton International Hotels and Modern Architecture*. In her innovative work of architectural and political history, Wharton maps the global expansion of Hilton International Hotels against the United States' postwar, Cold War–era global politics, foreign investments, and diplomacy as she "consider[ed] the inscription of power in the urban landscape."[13] Wharton cites the American technology that Hilton's international hotels featured abroad as examples of the allure and power of American modernity and the faith and fervor of capitalism—"its ice water tapped to individual guest rooms, its direct-line telephones, its radios, its air-conditioning, and, most fundamentally, the architectural form of the building itself"—and of how these buildings became "a space of modern luxury and technological desire, a space that effected, with pomp and prominence, the new and powerful presence of the United States. The building dramatically marked the city with the difference between its traditional culture and desired American modernity and named that desire Hilton."[14]

There is, however, a key distinction between the Paramount, MGM, Warner Bros., and Fox cinemas erected around the world during the interwar period and after and Hilton's international hotels that dotted the globe after World War II. Wharton writes that "the Modern space of the Hilton International hotel was carefully coded as foreign by its decoration. Like the great hotels of the colonial era in the Middle East, the postcolonial Hiltons embodied the cultural values of home veiled with references to the local. Interior design bore the burden of representing the host site."[15] While Hilton Hotels attracted Americans and other tourists through their "foreign" architectural and aesthetic presentation, Hollywood's Metro Theatres, Cine Paramounts, and other overseas "cultural embassies" derived their local allure from their exotic presentation of America. Hilton sold the local to the foreign; Hollywood sold the foreign to the local. The work of American cinema architects like John Eberson, Thomas Lamb, and others attracted local moviegoers by their very American exteriors. Inside, that exotic appeal was often softened by more familiar, indigenous aesthetics through color, design, stage presentations, and even the optics of a racially segregated audience. In this way Hollywood drew in audiences by playing up its own exotic appeal, a reversal of traditional cultural appropriation. Hollywood appropriated itself—and the look of its U.S. cinemas—and brought those designs to world markets.

Hilton's hotels and Hollywood's movie houses overseas shared one key feature: as Wharton writes, the "political role of architecture was, nevertheless, recognized... as advancing American interests abroad." A 1953 *Arts and Architecture* article dubbed "American buildings abroad as the 'architectural calling cards' of the U.S. government."[16] The lockstep advance of U.S.-owned cinemas and hotels abroad even saw the occasional convergence. Egyptian journalist Samir Raafat writes that the world premiere of MGM's *Valley of the Kings* (1955) at the Cinema Metro in Cairo with stars Robert Taylor and Eleanor Parker in attendance "coincided with the festive events that followed the groundbreaking ceremony of the Nile Hilton Hotel on [Cairo's] Tahrir Square. It was on that occasion that Samia Gamal dragged Robert Taylor onto center stage where the American superstar, wearing a tarboush [sic] and belted the traditional way, danced with Egypt's foremost belly dancer before an enthralled audience."[17] In this way, American architecture, fashioned to exoticize both the United States (cinemas) and Egypt (hotels), dramatically announced the design and operational flexibility and marketing of American corporations overseas.

Another notable intersection is how both industries openly embraced their political and ideological function. Conrad Hilton, for example, dubbed his foreign hotels "little Americas" because they "promised an excellent profit as well as world peace through the economic suppression of communism."[18] "That Hilton International hotels were political is not my hypothesis, but

Conrad Hilton's claim," Wharton writes. "Hilton explicitly represented his international hotels as ideological, in the popular sense of ideology as propaganda. He repeatedly reported that Hilton International Hotels were constructed not only to produce a profit, but also to make a political impact on host countries." She cites Hilton's own words at length: "If we really believe in what we are all saying about liberty, about Communism, about happiness, that we, as a nation, must exercise our great strength and power for good against evil. If we really believe this, it is up to each of us, our organizations and our industries, to contribute to this objective with all the resources at our command." Hilton added later that "an integral part of my dream was to show the countries most exposed to Communism the other side of the coin—the fruits of the free world."[19]

Many of the leading figures in Hollywood felt similarly, especially during the Cold War. Arthur Loew argued in 1949, for example, that through the company's cinemas and films, "We are selling America and American democracy overseas."[20] Twentieth Century-Fox president Spyros Skouras was also an ardent anticommunist and saw the expansion of U.S.-operated cinemas abroad as part of a larger struggle against the Soviet Union's geopolitical (out) reach. "From this standpoint," he told *Variety* in 1953,

> it is a Twentieth Century-Fox solemn responsibility... to increase motion picture outlets throughout the free world because... no medium can play a greater part than the motion picture in indoctrinating people into the free way of life and instilling in them a compelling desire for freedom and hope for a brighter future. Therefore, we as an industry can play an infinitely important part in the worldwide ideological struggle for the minds of men and confound the Communist propagandists.[21]

Nor was the U.S. government blind to the political significance of Hollywood's overseas cinemas. Every American cinema bought, built, or leased overseas was tracked and used for social and political engagement by U.S. consular officials. Large-scale purchases, such as Fox's acquisition of the African Consolidated Theatres circuit in Kenya, colonial Zimbabwe, and South Africa, were viewed by the U.S. government as an opportunity to lock down venues for American messaging through news, short, and feature films and to establish political connections and influence. These cinemas, therefore, benefited U.S. tax rolls in their profits and the nation's ideological mission.

Hollywood's Embassies focuses on the industrial structure of Hollywood's overseas exhibition and its effects on, and engagement with, local and global politics and society. Wharton notes that Hilton Hotels in "Istanbul, Cairo, Athens, Berlin, London, Tel Aviv, and Jerusalem altered the cities in which they were built" as "Hilton International produced abroad an icon of

American economic authority."[22] Hollywood's cinemas played a similar role in announcing the economic, political, industrial, and cultural power of the United States. As Ai Lin Chua has argued about the modern cinemas being built in major media capitals,

> Around the world, cinemas of this era were important icons of architectural, technological and cultural modernity—in the cityscape. They were designed to reflect the latest trends in sophistication and glamour. Their flamboyance made them instant landmarks whether in the commercial centres of major cities, or in small towns.... An aura of modernity, luxury, glamour and romance was deliberately cultivated through imposing architecture, attention to detail in the interior fittings, the use of as-yet uncommon new technologies such as elevators, as well as careful marketing.[23]

Hollywood's Embassies examines the iconography and the industry, the meaning and the machinery of American cinemas overseas, how they transformed film exhibition locally and globally, and how they were alternately embraced and rejected as symbols of Hollywood and American culture.

The "Shop Window" and the "Cultural Embassy" Versus Cultural Ambassador / Institute

Two terms are featured throughout this book. The first—the "shop window" cinema—was largely British trade industry nomenclature for a deluxe cinema in a media capital that used the highest level of showmanship to "sell" a picture to local audiences and to persuade other exhibitors to book, market, and present a film in a similar style as the "shop window" in which it first appeared. The second term—"cultural embassy"—is a neologism intended to illuminate the political, industrial, cultural, and diplomatic function of these cinematic "little Americas" that drew local moviegoers to "enter" the United States on foreign soil.

The concept of the "shop window"—akin to a department store window display selling Hollywood merchandise marketed in the American style—would come to dominate the strategy for Paramount and Loew's overseas in the 1920s and would soon become the model for many American-run cinemas around the world. Instead of buying cinemas en masse (a tactic only Fox would later undertake), Paramount and Loew's built shop window cinemas where exhibitors from across a country could see how to "put over" the company's films in smaller, local markets. These opulent movie houses also drummed up interest with the rest of the trade by drawing large crowds attracted by the many features American audiences had come to expect at movie palaces

FIGURES 0.6–0.7 *Kinematograph Weekly* (left) and *Bioscope* (right) outline Paramount/Famous-Lasky's "Shop Window."

during the silent era: large orchestras, ornate décor, well-drilled ushers, the best in projection and lighting, stage shows, and, above all, a reliable but affordable brand of mass entertainment. These shop windows, Hollywood film companies posited, would teach the American presentation method to local exhibitors who would then exhibit Hollywood films in the Hollywood way and thereby increase profits and prestige for the studio. If American presentation standards were to take hold across Europe, for example, along with a corresponding increase in ticket sales and attendance, the studios reasoned it would have to be done by Americans to influence the operations of local exhibitors. Shop window cinemas also benefited distribution as they generated excitement about a prestigious film the same way a Broadway run in New York might spur excitement for that same film when it finally reached Topeka.

The use of "cultural embassy" appropriates the terminology of an official embassy and employs that model in a privatized manner to sell American culture, ideology, messaging, industrial practices, and movies to local audiences. The National Museum of American Diplomacy defines an official American embassy overseas as "the headquarters for U.S. Government representatives serving in a foreign country" in which U.S. embassy staff "interact with representatives of the host government, local businesses, nongovernmental organizations, the media and educational institutions, as well as private citizens to increase understanding of the United States and its policies and to collaborate on shared interests." Official U.S. embassy staff are needed to "analyze the political and economic situation in the host country and report back to the Department of State on issues that affect the United States."[24] Similarly, the manager of a Cine Metro or Le Paramount, in concert with the head of the local branch office, was also charged with "analyz[ing] the political and economic situation in the host country" and reporting back to their managers in the United States. They also kept in touch with local U.S. ambassadors and consular officials, especially during times of political, industrial, and economic trouble. They also sought to engage with the "host government, local businesses, nongovernmental organizations, the media and educational institutions, as well as private citizens." This is precisely the work of Hollywood's exhibition and distribution managers around the world as they sought to engage local political, cultural, and social leaders, market to and with local businesses, and promote American movies and messaging through a multigenerational appeal to local moviegoers.

"While Americans work at embassies and consulates, most of the staff comes from the host country," the National Museum of American Diplomacy notes, and "these employees are essential to the success of any embassy because they know the local culture, have essential skills, or are well connected to government and civil society leaders." These hiring practices were mimicked as well by Hollywood's international cinemas overseas in which managers were sent from the United States to overseas cinemas to lead a team of local workers who helped them translate American practices into local customs and helped pair the exotic nature of an American shop window with workers familiar with local languages, cultures, audiences, and customs. In this way American shop windows abroad sold exoticism on the outside and comfort and familiarity on the inside. Translated to local situations, Hollywood and its cinemas increasingly became entwined in the local context and were patronized as hybridized local but still foreign institutions. These cinemas were therefore unofficial cultural embassies, instrumental to Hollywood and local U.S. consular staffs in selling the promise and allure of America.

Methodology

Wharton observes that "all historians are tourists in a past where they may visit but where they will never belong."[25] I was also a "historical tourist" for this book, researching and writing about more than three dozen countries in the process. This was a daunting effort that required tenacity, a great deal of humility, and a library of contextual readings. I hope to have done justice to the scholars who made my own interventions possible and to the many nations this book examines. With that in mind, I do want to clarify what I address in this book and what I do not. This is a globally oriented book about Hollywood's operations of cinemas and cinema chains overseas. South African film history, for example, is a rapidly growing subject of inquiry for renowned scholars such as Keyan Tomaselli, Jacqueline Maingard, Thelma Gutsche, Ntongela Masilela, Martin Botha, Lucia Saks, and many others. *Hollywood's Embassies* intersects with their research, but this book is not about African film audiences, colonial African films, or African filmmaking or filmmakers and is not an attempt to theorize the reception of Hollywood films in this region (or any other) through ethnographic field work. Those are subjects examined brilliantly by the ongoing work of Didier Gondola, Laura Fair,

James Burns, Charles Ambler, and many others. Therefore, I am not staking a claim to any other subjectivities but instead providing an American perspective on Hollywood's forays throughout the world and analyzing what it tells us, from that perspective, about the need to understand the manifestations of Hollywood's global infrastructure to comprehend the internal and external logics of the American film industry and how that engagement changed how Hollywood conducted its overseas business.

In addition, while I often consulted local-language sources and hired translators and researchers for languages I do not read, this book is, once again, written from a very American, Western-oriented perspective, using many types of English-language and other sources. This is not, therefore, a study of the bottom-up resistance to Hollywood in foreign markets, nor could I possibly hope to reproduce a fully local perspective of Hollywood's incursion and resistance. Instead, *Hollywood's Embassies* is an analysis of the business practices of Hollywood overseas and the resultant political, cultural, and industrial ramifications. Where possible, I attempt to recapture the words, sentiments, exchanges, and protests Hollywood encountered through the voices of those involved. Due to archival and other lacunae, however, this was not always possible. Diplomatic records helped enormously, but they transmit those details and voices in second- and thirdhand fashion, as do the trade journals and newspapers that recount these phenomena.

Over the past decade, though, I have conducted site visits to dozens of libraries and archives around the world in **Australia** (Australia Film Institute Library, Cinema and Theatre Historical Society, National Archives, National Film and Sound Archive, National Library, Sydney and Melbourne Council Archives); **Brazil** (Arquivo Público do Estado de São Paulo, Centimetro, Cinedia, Cinemateca Brasileira, Museu de Arte Moderna do Rio de Janeiro, Prefeitura Municipal de São Paulo); **England** (British Film Institute, British Library, Cinema Theatre Association, Imperial War Museum, and National Archives); **France** (Archives Nationales, Bibliothèque Nationale de France Cinémathèque Française, and Memorial de la Shoah); **Israel** (Municipal Historical Archives of Tel Aviv-Yafo and Tel Aviv Cinematheque); **Italy** (Biblioteca Sormani); **Netherlands** (EYE Institute, Stadsarchief Amsterdam); **New Zealand** (Auckland War Memorial Library, National Archives, National Library, and Nga Taonga Sound & Vision Archive); and the **United States** (Avery Library/Columbia University, Margaret Herrick Library, National Archives and Records Administration, New York Public Library for the Performing Arts, Stanford University Library, Theatre Historical Society, Wisconsin Historical Society, USC Warner Bros. Archives, and Wolfsonian-FIU). In addition, outside researchers were employed to comb records in and order materials from archives and libraries in South Africa (University of the Witwatersrand Library), Sweden (Svenska Filminstitutet), and many other locations. Sometimes, unfortunately, repeated requests for access to government records in places such as Kenya and Zimbabwe went unanswered, despite numerous attempts for access and information over several years.

I also scoured digital newspaper repositories from Australia, Brazil, China, England, France, Israel, Jamaica, New Zealand, and many other nations. The Media History Digital Library, ProQuest Historical Newspapers, and other databases also supplied access to trade and newspaper coverage in the United States and in overseas newspapers and trade journals. Municipal and state archives in places like São Paulo, Sydney, and other cities supplied blueprints, licenses, correspondence, applications, and many other kinds of documentation. Personal papers of architects and film executives, specifically those of Spyros Skouras, were also invaluable, documenting a wide range of international activities that are increasingly difficult to access due to the ongoing consolidation in Hollywood and the growing legal and logistical obstacles to legacy studio archives.

Additional research was derived from the Cinema Treasures website and database, cinema programs and other ephemera were purchased abroad and online, and interviews and meetings were conducted with Clément Dassa, son of former MGM Egypt head Maurice Dassa; Salah Hassanein, former WBIT president; Steve Solot, former senior vice president of the Motion Picture Association in Latin America; and many others that helped filled in the gaps. I am grateful as well for the oral histories conducted and transcribed throughout the world that provided key details and context and for the many books written by cinema historians and family members that provided information, memories, and anecdotes. It took many, many villages and villagers to help me compile the mountains of research needed to complete this book.

History and Chapter Breakdowns

Hollywood's Embassies is organized into six parts focusing on six regions. Although this project commenced as a chronological history with a temporally comparative framework, a regional approach was later adopted to highlight the similarities and differences inherent in Hollywood's work in various countries within the same region and to compare and contrast the work of different studios within those geographies.

The first wave of Hollywood's efforts to operate cinemas abroad began in 1923 and created a series of pitched battles in Europe, South America, Asia, and Africa. The most aggressive campaigns by Paramount in England and by United Artists in South Africa failed, however, when local exhibitors instigated boycotts of each company's films until they ceased buying, leasing, and building local cinemas. Instead of large-scale foreign ownership of cinemas overseas—a tactic only Fox later undertook—what developed over the next nine decades was a series of "shop windows" for the premiere presentation of Hollywood films. Paramount's and Loew's/MGM's shop window cinemas were meant to serve as cinematic showrooms where exhibitors from across a given country could see how to present and advertise the company's films in the American way. These shop windows were routinely among each city's most prestigious cinemas and a place where local moviegoers mingled amidst an atmosphere of hybridized American and indigenous social conventions and theater design.

Part I: Europe

"When Expansion Was Paramount (1923–1993): 'Shop Window' Cinemas and the European Expansion of U.S. Film Exhibitors" focuses on the earliest wave of this activity in the 1920s, when Paramount constructed new cinemas in Paris and London and leased the Cine Coliseum in Barcelona and the China Theatre in Stockholm. Paramount's attempted expansion in Birmingham, England, led to a boycott of the company's films by British exhibitors, however, who feared that Paramount's takeover would herald the end of the British film industry. The company was forced to abandon its large-scale plans in England amid the pushback from native exhibitors and, instead of dominating foreign markets, Paramount focused its expansion on a network of shop window cinemas in major international cities that promoted studio films, higher ticket prices, and American movie palace architecture, equipment, and management techniques. MGM also built its first shop window cinema in London in the 1920s and signed an agreement with Gaumont to operate their numerous cinemas in France, Egypt, Syria, Algeria, Palestine, and Tunisia. Part I includes the transformation of Le Paramount in Paris during World War II when it became a venue for Nazi-approved films—all while its French staff clandestinely used the cinema as a base for the French Resistance—and concludes by tracing the late-twentieth-century expansion of Warner Bros. throughout Europe.

Part II: Australasia

"Banking on Australasia (1930–1982): Global Banks and U.S. Cinema Ownership in Australia and New Zealand" examines Fox's contrast to Paramount and MGM's selective "shop window" model in which the company attempted to dominate English-speaking markets outside the United States through large-scale acquisition. After being pushed by its U.S. bankers (Chase) to acquire a 49 percent interest in England's Gaumont British in 1929, Fox purchased Hoyt's Theatres, the dominant theater chain in Australia, in 1930 from

English, Scottish and Australian Bank, before Chase loaded up even more debt by maneuvering Twentieth Century-Fox to buy a controlling interest in New Zealand's Amalgamated Theatres circuit from the Moodabe family. The Moodabes worked with or for Fox for seven decades and were frequent visitors to the Los Angeles studio, posing for pictures with Shirley Temple and Grace Kelly and conferring with key executives. Their close relationship serves as an important reminder of how American film companies strengthened their bonds with overseas employees, sales offices, and cinemas through global communication and local audience research and by providing foreign subsidiaries and executives with access to stars and studios. Part II explains how U.S. investment banks and financiers facilitated this global expansion.

Part III: Latin America and the Caribbean

"Hollywood in Cinelandia (1927–1973): U.S. Cinemas and Local Politics in Latin America and the Caribbean" analyzes Hollywood's vast expansion in Latin America in the 1920s and 1930s with MGM's forty-four-theater circuit debuting in Brazil in 1927; new "Metro" cinemas built throughout the 1930s; and Paramount, Fox, and Warner Bros.'s operating cinemas in Peru, Cuba, Colombia, and other Latin American countries in the 1940s and 1950s. After the establishment of Empresas Reunidas Metro-Goldwyn-Mayer, Ltda. in Brazil in 1927, MGM expanded its collection of shop window cinemas in the 1930s, specially focusing on Latin America with Cine Metros opening in Argentina, Brazil, Chile, Peru, Puerto Rico, Uruguay, and Venezuela. By the end of the 1940s Lima, Peru had become the only city in the world beside London to have shop window cinemas operated by MGM as well as Paramount, Fox, and Warner Bros. Hollywood maintained cinemas throughout the region in an effort to keep its films flowing to company-owned cinemas as politics and the global film industry grew increasingly complex during the 1950s and 1960s. Part III also focuses on the Caribbean and specifically on prerevolutionary Cuba and its troubled Warner and Paramount cinemas; MGM's foray into a divisive and rebellious Puerto Rico; and MGM and Paramount's efforts to build cinemas in British colonial Trinidad and Jamaica.

Part IV: Middle East

"Hollywood's Muddle East (1925–1982): Political Change in Egypt and Israel and the Consequences for Hollywood's Middle Eastern Cinemas" highlights MGM and Fox's theatrical expansion into Egypt and how geopolitical turmoil would come to entangle U.S. efforts to build cinemas in the Middle East. Despite the immense popularity of the MGM and Fox cinemas in Cairo and Alexandria—with Fox's Cairo Palace and MGM's Metro Theatre patronized by both King Farouk and later by President Gamal Abdel Nasser—the Metro in Cairo was thrice attacked during anti-Western protests in 1945, 1947, and 1952. These cinemas became indelible symbols of the growing Western influence in Egypt and therefore key targets for anti-British, anti-U.S., and anti-Israel protests and violence. Elsewhere, Fox's investment in and operation of the Tel Aviv Cinema was part of Spyros Skouras's efforts to counteract the rise of socialism and communism in the new State of Israel during the Cold War. Part IV examines how Egyptian nationalism actually facilitated Hollywood's expansion throughout Egypt and the Middle East and how Fox's Israeli expansion withered on the vine.

Part V: Africa

"An 'Unhappy Image of the United States Before an African Population' (1932–1975): Race, Industry, and Rebellion at Hollywood's African Cinemas" focuses on Fox's acquisition of the African Consolidated Theatres chain, with 144 cinemas in Kenya, Southern Rhodesia (colonial Zimbabwe), and South Africa in 1956. These cinemas were, not surprisingly, racially segregated and in many cases for whites only—even at the Fox Drive-In in Nairobi. This part highlights the company's troubled history in apartheid South Africa and Colonial Kenya and Zimbabwe and the repercussions the U.S. State Department faced due to Fox's segregated cinemas during the long process of racial integration. This history also examines Hollywood's efforts to expand into West and North Africa and how French colonial power maintained its dominance in the region. This part concludes with the withering of Hollywood's overseas cinema chains as Fox sold its African holdings between 1969 and 1975.

Part VI: Asia

"Eastern Promises (1927–2013): Hollywood's Cinemas in China, India, Japan, and the Philippines" details Hollywood's century-long desire to expand its exhibition holdings throughout Asia in Japan, India, China, and the Philippines. Paramount leased the Hogaku-Za in Tokyo in 1927 as its shop window, and within a few short years Paramount's Japanese circuit merged with local cinema chain Shochiku, providing Paramount with key outlets for its films around the country. In India, MGM opened two of the nation's most opulent cinemas with Metro Cinemas in Bombay (Mumbai) and Calcutta (Kolkata). Although Bombay's Metro was feted upon its opening by the *Times of India*, the *Bombay Sentinel* newspaper and industry trade journal *filmindia* lodged severe protests against the cinema's management, messaging, and movies during the country's colonial and postcolonial period. In China, MGM leased the

Roxy Cinema in Shanghai after World War II and began construction on another cinema just before the Chinese revolution that barred American films (and cinemas) from the country. More than fifty years later, Warner Bros. International Theatres reentered China with a series of joint ventures with local exhibitors including Dalian Wanda. Part VI tracks Warner Bros.'s successes and failures to build cinemas throughout China during the 2000s amid changing foreign investment laws and regulations. With Warner Bros.'s sale of its Chinese cinemas and its Warner-Mycal Cinemas in Japan in 2013, Hollywood exited global exhibition after nine decades of expansion.

※※※

Writing this introduction at the end of my journey—and not at the beginning—my mind drifts back to a singular memory in the spring of 2011 when I had just begun this research. I was a postdoctoral fellow at the Fox Center for Humanistic Inquiry (CHI) at Emory University and was excited to learn that Salman Rushdie, who had a longstanding appointment at Emory, would be presenting a film one evening. Energized by his vivid recollection of the Metro Cub Club at MGM's Metro Theatre in Bombay/Mumbai in his landmark novel, *Midnight's Children*, I stayed after to talk with him, introduced by my CHI colleague, Emory professor Deepika Bahri. Rushdie was patient and interested in my ongoing research, but his eyes twinkled and his body rocked at the mention of the Metro Cub Club. Talking to him that night, and later visiting Ivo Raposo in Brazil, where he built a two-story replica of MGM's Metro-Tijuca in his backyard using that cinema's original seats, chandeliers, and projectors, I could see then and now what Hollywood's "cultural embassies" had meant to the world and why studying these cinemas helps to fill in a missing piece of our global story: how Hollywood sold itself to an increasingly receptive and increasingly Americanized world. In a now precarious moment for theatrical exhibition, this legacy is a reminder of how important cinemas and foreign cinemas once were for Hollywood and the U.S. government.

PART I

EUROPE

When Expansion Was Paramount (1923–1993)
"Shop Window" Cinemas and the European Expansion of U.S. Film Exhibitors

CHAPTER 1

HOLLYWOOD'S BRITISH INVASION AND THE BATTLE OF BIRMINGHAM, 1919–1929

In our vanity we have cherished the illusion that England is the cultural wet-nurse of America; and, failing to detect the condescension with which the polite enthusiasm of our visitors is tempered, we imagine that the Americans who annually seek our shores depart wiser and more civilized than they came. We do not reflect—no doubt because the reflection is unpalatable—that these Americans, visiting us in much the same spirit as that in which a self-made magnate returns to the scenes of his childhood, are rapidly changing the face of England.
—Leonora Lockhart, London, 1930

"Colonialism" is somewhat a dirty word in 1978, but back in the 1920s, when motion pictures were the major form of entertainment, this was not the case. The studio which did more to spread the gospel of top class film exhibition was Hollywood's Paramount Pictures.
—Jan Dalgliesh, *Console*, 1978

Walking along the Boulevard des Capucines in Paris and around Leicester Square in London today, there is little trace of Hollywood's influence on the cinematic architecture of those streets. For nearly half a century, though, from the 1920s to the 1970s, U.S.-owned and -operated cinemas in London and other European cities acted as Hollywood's cinematic and cultural embassies for locals, tourists, and the many ex-pats who flocked to these venues for their American films, décor, showmanship, and a new form of global cosmopolitanism. Entering a Paramount cinema in England or France—like visiting a Disneyworld in Shanghai or Paris decades later—was to find a venue imbued with American branding and entertainment but refined for local consumption and adoption. The foreign was hybridized with the local. Whether at the Paramount in Manchester, England, or Le Paramount in Paris, France, Hollywood's overseas cinemas combined foreign excitement with local comfort in a physical edifice dedicated to selling foreign films and adapted to increasingly nativist and protectionist markets.

Part I, "Europe: When Expansion Was Paramount," examines Hollywood's desire to construct "shop window" or "key" cinemas in major European media capitals during the 1920s; the local response to these "invasions" from local cinemas and regulators eager to preserve national control and identity; Hollywood's continued expansion during the 1930s; the problems and opportunities created by owning foreign real estate and cultural venues during a decade of domestic and global warfare in the 1930s and 1940s; and the postwar and late-twentieth-century desire by U.S. film companies to use their exhibition chains and real estate holdings to maintain distribution control in these increasingly protective and locally productive film markets. Created to maximize revenues from growing European markets; to present company films in premiere, first-run cinemas; to pressure domestic exhibitors to upgrade their cinemas through competition; and to extend the brand awareness of MGM, Warner Bros., and other studios, these European "shop window" cinemas became contested battle grounds for U.S. film companies, local trade organizations, the U.S. State and Commerce Departments, and the local executives caught in between.

In contrast to Hollywood's film distribution to foreign markets, its foreign exhibition practices—how U.S. film companies secured premiere first-run releases for their films through these U.S. owned or operated foreign cinemas—remains understudied.[1] Accordingly, the significance of these cinemas as *cultural embassies*—aesthetic, industrial, social, cultural, and political outposts of U.S. film, ideology, and culture—has yet to be fully explored. Arthur Loew, head of Loew's International, laid out a manifesto for why American cinemas abroad (and locally owned deluxe cinemas in Europe) were essential for the growth of Hollywood: "I have always believed the future of the American motion picture depends upon its progress in foreign markets," he wrote in March 1928. "There is no question but that people of other nationalities would react to motion pictures exactly as Americans do if films were presented in their countries as they are here.... Under equal economic and other conditions, the man in Canton, China, is as great a potential motion picture enthusiast as the man in Canton, Ohio." Loew argued that "the film industry [overseas] is chiefly impeded by poor theatre conditions" and noted that the foreign market still had enormous capacity for growth and would represent one of the only ways to boost annual revenue. "Producers of American motion pictures today depend for their existence upon income from countries outside of the United States," he added. "With the cost of pictures steadily increasing, and with the United States nearly at its peak, the motion picture industry must, of necessity, look to foreign markets for its future existence."[2]

This book begins with a focus on when global exhibition expansion became both paramount and Paramount—when leasing, owning, and operating cinemas overseas was envisioned as a crucial way to secure foreign markets and increase foreign revenues for American films and the companies that distributed them. It was a maturation point and a pivot for the industry that involved a vast network of international executives, lawyers, accountants, branch offices, cinemas, staffs, and investment capital. Analyzing American film distribution overseas in countries such as England, France, Belgium, and the Netherlands without examining these new American-owned and -operated cinemas is to overlook the synchronicity between distribution and exhibition, industry relations, and the soft power opportunities of opening these American cultural embassies across Europe and, later, around the world.

Expansion Is Paramount in the United Kingdom

Over a decade before Loew's Inc. began crafting a global cinema circuit, its founder, Marcus Loew, was already dreaming of an international chain of theaters for his vaudeville acts. Loew hoped to "Encircle the Globe" in 1914 with "a vaudeville circuit that starts west from New York and keeps on going, until it comes back to town after circling the earth."[3] After purchasing the Sullivan and Considine circuit in the United States, Loew traveled to England, South Africa, Australia, and New Zealand to scout additional theaters to buy, build, or lease for his planned global circuit. Loew's international expansion would have to wait until the 1920s, though, when the company was better capitalized through Wall Street investment and able to benefit from its own motion pictures (Metro/MGM), which shipped more easily than vaudeville acts.[4]

Famous Players Films' distribution in England had begun much earlier in 1912 when Adolph Zukor traveled to London with a print of *Queen Elizabeth* (*Les Amours de la Reine Élisabeth*, 1912) and set up a foreign film office for his burgeoning production company in association with World's Films of

London. In 1914 Paramount—the company now distributing Famous Players(-Lasky) films—opened a second office in Liverpool. Emil Shauer was hired as Paramount's foreign manager, and additional film exchanges were opened in Birmingham, Manchester, and Cardiff. Two years later John Cecil Graham was hired as Paramount's new head in England to spearhead Paramount's growth in Europe for the next two decades.[5]

By the end of World War I, flush with Wall Street capital and expanding revenues from an improving global film distribution network and domestic theatrical expansion throughout the United States, Paramount built a new studio for Famous Players-Lasky (FPL) films and planned a chain of British cinemas.[6] A new British company was formed in London in 1919—Famous Players-Lasky British Producers Ltd.—whose chief objectives were to produce, distribute, and exhibit films as well procure the equipment for all three processes. The company was also created to purchase or lease real estate and operate "theatres, palaces and halls, cinematographic shows and exhibitions." Famous Players-Lasky British Producers Ltd. was also established to acquire, merge, or absorb local companies producing, distributing, or exhibiting motion pictures. To ease its way into this foreign market with differing legal, political, and financial laws, the board of directors was composed entirely of British citizens, including a member of Parliament and a Welsh coal millionaire, except for J. C. Graham—the sole American.[7]

Paramount formed another British company, Picture Playhouses, Ltd. (PPL), that was expressly established to "erect theaters and exhibit films along the lines followed by American exhibitors."[8] *Variety* added that these cinemas would be built throughout the United Kingdom with seating capacities of 3,500 to 4,500 seats, making them among the largest cinemas in the world, rivaling the Gaumont Palace in Paris and Paramount's newly acquired Rialto and Rivoli cinemas in New York.[9] PPL capitalized at $5 million and selling stock to the public, planned to build cinemas in London, Manchester, and Glasgow.[10] These cinemas would be, according to the *New York Clipper*, "the first of a series of houses that will be built throughout the country."[11] Through these joint efforts, Famous Players-Lasky British Producers established new production studios in England—buying the former White City studio in Shepherd's Bush for Paramount Pictures' UK productions—while its cousin, PPL, began looking for British cinemas to acquire or real estate where the company could build.

The expansion of PPL could hardly have arrived at a more sensitive time in England. The country was still reeling psychically, financially, and logistically from the toll and toil of World War I. While the victory over the Ottoman Empire promised England new territorial dominion in the Middle East and elsewhere, it also moved the previously isolationist United States further onto the global stage in terms of military, political, industrial, and cultural power. Further, after World War I, U.S. industries found willing markets for their goods in Europe that had previously been purchased from England (and other European countries). American films, books, music, vaudeville, and other entertainment were also increasingly omnipresent after war's end. By mid-1919 there was already a veritable "American Invasion of London," according to *Variety*, in which American actors, plays, managers, and others were all "elbowing British art out of British theatres and music halls."[12]

Worried British cinema owners also gathered together in Glasgow, Scotland, to voice their concern over the growing proliferation of American films in British cinemas and the possibility that U.S. film exhibitors like Paramount might begin operating competitively in England.[13] Sidney Low, writing in London's conservative, partisan weekly *Saturday Review* (of politics, literature, science and art), added that this invasion might destroy the very Britishness of the empire and, more dangerously, loosen the cultural bonds between England and its subjects throughout the world. American films might, Low suggested, create British colonial subjects that were British in title only and American by choice and persuasion. In August 1919 he wrote:

> If our masses at home, and our masses overseas, are so constantly steeped in the American atmosphere, may they not lose a little of their Britannic consciousness?... But if in Melbourne and Toronto, and in Capetown and Calcutta, the majority of persons are always looking at American scenes, familiarising themselves with American society, American institutions, American customs, American standards of life and thought, and even American slang, while of England and the English they see and hear nothing—is it likely their attachment to the old land, and their interest in it, will be maintained?[14]

Low added that the creation of Famous Players-Lasky British Producers Ltd. and PPL was a dangerous new sign that U.S. companies and creators were not only interested in capturing the imaginations of British and colonial subjects from afar but were now setting up shop in England to dominate the local dream factories and their houses of exhibition. Low's response represents the reaction to U.S.-owned or operated cinemas abroad throughout the twentieth century. While the proliferation of American film content was often a concern to local politicians and exhibitors, public demand made it hard to counteract. Thus the need for quotas, tariffs, local exhibition requirements, and other protective measures. U.S. ownership of cinemas abroad, however, was often a red line for those concerned about U.S. cultural and industrial hegemony. Here were U.S. retail and real estate establishments operating—or threatening to operate—on local soil, posing a seemingly direct threat to local exhibitors and their cinemas' national identity. Building cinemas in England threatened not only British cultural pride but the very livelihood of a whole segment of the British economy.

The British film industry was not the only British body concerned by the U.S. invasion. A. E. Newbould, a member of the British Parliament, also advocated on behalf of the Cinematograph Exhibitors Association of Great Britain and Ireland (CEA) in their opposition to U.S. film exhibitors buying, building, or leasing local cinemas. He argued that "whilst the British exhibitor welcomes the American film," local cinema owners were "opposed for obvious reasons to a large circuit of theaters distributed thruout [sic] this country being either owned or directed by an American producing and renting company."[15] Newbould was joined by fellow parliamentarian J. A. Seddon as, *Exhibitors Herald and Motography* noted, the "Anti-American Film Agitation In England" had now taken a most "Serious Turn." "British producers and some of the larger British exhibitors" had now begun a "concerted effort" to influence parliament to stem "the invasion of American producers and to place restrictions around the importation of American films."[16] A discussion of a national boycott of American films was even debated, as was support for official legislation that would bar all American films from being distributed in the United Kingdom. "One has got to look ahead as regards the rising generation," R. A. Pitcairn, director of the New Gallery Kinema in London, explained. "As it is, I am afraid that lots of the children in this country must think there is no other flag or no other country in the world except America and that is a matter of the gravest importance to the public and nation."[17] To allow FPL to open local cinemas, Pitcairn and others argued, would leave the region even more susceptible to American culture.

These suspicions were not entirely unfounded; Richard A. Rowland, president of Metro Pictures and Screen Classics, returned from England and other parts of Europe in 1919 and declared "the foreign field as ripe for American invasion in general" and "for Metro invasion in particular."[18] British film industry trade journals also spread fear about American control of the British market and psyche. *Wid's Daily*, for example, came out against PPL and asked board member David Davies and the company to "capitulate" to these growing concerns.[19] Independent exhibitors, however, especially those in smaller towns, understood that American films already dominated their market and would continue to do so. Few wanted to upend the system by which those films were delivered. Large, competitive exhibitors and trade organizations, recognizing a diminution in their power due to U.S. vertical integration overseas, saw the advancement of Paramount and other U.S. companies through a very different lens.

Instead of a proposed industry boycott, PPL was stymied instead by ongoing postwar cinema building embargoes—as well as a steep rise in construction costs—which did not lessen for another three years after the end of World War I.[20] Maj. William Evans, another director of Famous Players-Lasky British Producers Ltd., argued, "What we need in Great Britain more than anything else at the present time is more theaters—theaters of the type of [New York's] Rivoli and Rialto."[21] A month after Evans's plea, in April 1921, much of the British national construction ban ended. *Wid's Daily* noted that PPL would finally start building "on a rather extensive scale."[22] However, for reasons unknown, PPL did not begin to build at all. Instead, Paramount's British employees remained focused on expanding their film distribution network, exchange facilities, and marketing operations in both mature and developing regions in Europe. That August FPL began "invading France with American films," according to the *Los Angeles Times*, by forming Société Anonyme Française des Films Paramount, which would become the distribution apparatus for Paramount in France as well as the headquarters controlling branch offices in Belgium, Egypt, Turkey and the "French colonies."[23] Exhibition was certainly not off the company's radar, though. Paramount secured the Cine Coliseum in Barcelona in 1923 as a key cinema for Paramount films, the first of many Paramount-operated venues to come.[24]

"Key Theaters" for U.S. Film Companies

The year 1923 proved to be a pivotal one in the American film companies' efforts to transform their industry into a truly global business, to not only distribute their films around the world but to make their deluxe exhibition in major media capitals commonplace and even desired by local cinemagoers. In so doing, these cinemas helped make American films (and culture) a globally desired and normalized cultural product.

After a (presumably British) lessee fell out in late July 1923, FPL, Goldwyn-Cosmopolitan, and a late entry—Loew's Inc.—all vied to make the large and centrally located Tivoli their own London showcase cinema.[25] Marcus Loew arrived in early August 1923 and secured a six-year booking agreement at a "record figure" for the company's Metro films to be given exclusive first-run engagements at the Tivoli.[26] The Tivoli's façade added a large sign that read "The Home of Metro Pictures. Metro Pictures Best in the World." The Tivoli deal enabled Loew's Inc. to secure a three-week exclusive window for each Metro film exhibited there.[27] The Loew's agreement was one of many that had begun to change the cinematic patina of London from decidedly British to one increasingly partnered with, influenced, or controlled by U.S. film companies and culture. The Tivoli's opening program noted that "the Tivoli is an historic name" that would now become "A 'KEY' THEATRE" for Metro Films."[28]

Other companies were also looking to become distributor-exhibitors in England (and other overseas markets). William Randolph Hearst's Cosmopolitan Productions leased the Empire Theatre in London for its films in June 1923, while William Fox leased the city's Palace and began screening Fox films there in September, backed by a seventy-five-piece orchestra.[29] Paramount, boxed out of the Tivoli Theatre it had coveted, secured its own lease of the Pavilion Theatre.[30] Carl Laemmle subsequently leased the Empire Theatre in Leicester Square as London's key cinema for Universal films.[31] By the end of the crucial year of 1923, Fox, Universal, Paramount, MGM, and Cosmopolitan had all secured first-run showcase cinemas in London.

The proliferation of exclusive U.S. film contracts for these British musical/legitimate/variety houses-turned-cinemas not only changed their programming but also brought an American brashness to this still buttoned up interwar city. "LONDON, the aristocratic," *Exhibitors Trade Review* remarked, "is becoming commercial." The revamped Tivoli and Pavilion both now featured large signs lighting up the night sky with advertisements for new American films.[32] Paramount was keen to demonstrate the local approval of these U.S.-operated cinemas, rather than a local boycott, and circulated a press story that the Prince of Wales had hurried to the Pavilion to see *The Covered Wagon*, along with the throngs of other Brits, only to find there were no seats available. "The Prince refused to allow anybody to be disturbed and returned to his car amid the cheers of the crowd," *Variety* reported.[33] The story affirmed the local desire for American films and cinemas and marketed the movie house, as in the United States, as a place where the rich rubbed elbows with the poor. Here, royals and subjects watched together. It was precisely the cross-class, bootstrap mythology Hollywood and the U.S. State Department desired.

The "Shop Window" Policy

Loew's and Paramount had been motivated in part by the poor grosses generated for their films throughout Europe. Many American film executives traced these lackluster ticket sales directly to Europe's lackluster cinemas. Hugo Riesenfeld, the Austrian-born conductor turned manager of Paramount's Rialto, Rivoli, and Criterion cinemas in New York, noted that even large European cinemas like the Gaumont Palace in Paris were "utterly lacking in those facilities and conveniences which help to make films such a success over here."[34] American exhibitor Sid Grauman toured European cinemas in 1924 and commented that the "presentation of motion pictures in Europe is ten years behind America. In neither London nor Paris did I see anything to equal American methods or productions."[35] Richard Maltby and Ruth Vasey note that "the Americans had always seen the large numbers of small and medium-sized cinemas in Europe as a blight upon the territory," and in 1925 they finally tested the viability of buying, leasing, or building large cinemas in Europe to boost their increasingly important but still lagging foreign revenues.[36] This new effort would have at least three benefits: larger profits from larger cinemas charging higher prices; a forced upgrade of older cinemas as a result of direct competition; and, finally, 100 percent of the net profit taken at the ticket windows of U.S.-owned cinemas when showing their own product.

Paramount was still exhibiting its films first at the Pavilion in London but, like Loew's, wanted more control. In May 1925 the company announced the construction of a new Paramount cinema, where "pictures would be presented in a manner which would make [them] known and provide ready-made audiences for the exhibitors when the pictures were generally released. The Paramount," J. C. Graham declared, "will be the firm's 'shop window' and every picture will have the advantage of expert presentation and advertising," often in keeping with the presentation of these films as they were first shown in the United States.[37] The "shop window" concept would come to dominate the European strategy for Paramount and Loew's in the 1920s.

The desire for shop window cinemas was rampant in 1925. Joseph Schenck, heading United Artists, announced plans to open a 3,000-seat cinema in Birmingham, where, he charged, United Artists had "failed to obtain proper prices."[38] Schenck noted that the company was interested in gaining a foothold in Birmingham due to the local terms United Artists had been forced to accept.[39] Laemmle also announced the purchase of the 1,500-seat Briggate Picture House in Leeds in June 1925 for the exhibition of Universal films.[40] Albert Warner told *Bioscope* that his company might also begin building shop window cinemas. W. Gavazzi King, general secretary of the CEA, was increasingly alarmed by the American activity across Europe. "The U.S.A would never permit its picture theatres to be controlled by a foreign power, and it is equally certain that such a situation should never be allowed in this country," he told *Bioscope* in October 1925. "The cinemas are the fortresses of the industry, of which the studios are merely the munition factories. Surrender the British cinemas, and the British film industry will, indeed, cease to exist."[41] A united front of British exhibitors, increasingly concerned about the growing American cinema invasion in and outside of London, moved quickly to force Laemmle to sell his new cinema in Leeds or face a national boycott of Universal films by British exhibitors.[42] Marcus Loew, sensitive to the growing backlash, told *Motion Picture News* in early July:

> We do not intend to build any theatres in England because our films are being properly presented there.... We have no intention of erecting theatres anywhere in the world merely for the purpose of creating a competitive situation. We have no desire to build or own a theatre in any city which is adequately

seated and properly equipped theatrically to present pictures as they reasonably should be exhibited.... Our spirit is not competitive. Our desire is to keep hands-off where things are recognizedly right. And to help with our resources and advice where they are admittedly wrong.[43]

Despite Loew's statement, E.A. Schiller and other Loew's and Jury-Metro-Goldwyn executives in London were already negotiating to purchase London's famed Empire Theatre. Loew's veritable house architect, Thomas W. Lamb, was also in England that summer. Lamb had designed numerous Loew's theaters across the United States, including the Capitol Theatre in New York that had become part of the Loew's chain after the Metro-Goldwyn merger in 1924.[44] Rather than stick with the Tivoli, and various troubling faults in its construction that Loew's would never have been able to overcome, Loew's hoped to build a new modern cinema that would be as opulent as Paramount's forthcoming London showcase and as sumptuous as those deluxe theaters Loew's was building throughout North America.[45] Loew's Inc. and its British subsidiary completed the acquisition of the old Empire by the end of August 1925, one month after Loew pledged not to build in England. *The Times* reported that the new "super cinema" would be designed by Lamb "on the lines of the Capitol Theatre in New York."[46]

Blowback and the U.S. State Department

This American activity alarmed a British exhibition industry already fighting back against block-booking and other American film distribution practices overseas.[47] The following *South Wales News* editorial about the "plight of British films" was among the numerous responses to the proliferation of American films and culture in the United Kingdom: "Stated briefly... for every British film displayed there are nine American. Not content with this state of things, the Americans are actively gaining control of a considerable number of cinemas, and treating them as 'tied homes' for the sale and display of their films. It is not desirable that American sentiments, theories, ideas, and expressions should be allowed to monopolise the attention of British cinema-goers."[48] The pushback was strong enough for the U.S consular in Wales to alert the State Department that a "propaganda campaign against the American film" was already at hand—and growing.[49]

With new Paramount and Loew's cinemas in London, coupled with ongoing key cinema deals between Fox, Universal, and other U.S. film companies, more than one thousand exhibitors from London and its neighboring "home counties" chose to celebrate Trafalgar Day (October 21, which commemorated the British naval victory over the French and Spanish in 1805) by holding a mass protest "against the foreign film yoke." Most were outraged by the block-booking practices of Paramount that they claimed were a restraint of trade and "roundly condemned" the growing "menace of the key theatre." An official resolution was drawn up at the protest that asked the CEA to take "immediate and effective steps to remove the growing evil of block-booking and the control, direct or indirect, by film manufacturers, producers or renters, of cinema theatres throughout this country." While many exhibitors protested against this invasion, British exhibitor Sidney Bernstein, who later modeled his Granada Theatres on American cinema design and industrial practices, noted that the "chief enemy of the British exhibitor" was not the growth of American shop windows but British "laziness." "If we stuck to our business and worked like the Americans," he told the *Daily Express*, "we should be better able to compete with America. We cannot prevent them taking our best brains, but we can refuse to show their worst films."[50]

In December 1925 Loew's formally announced the purchase of London's famed Empire Theatre in Leicester Square, which, in a symbolic move, would be demolished and replaced by a new American-style "Empire" for MGM productions.[51] As one London editor later noted, "The passing of the Empire [is] another step in the Americanization of London."[52] That a British "Empire" was to be torn down and replaced by an American "Empire" was not lost on the film industry or the British trade and popular press.[53] The *Los Angeles Times* noted that with these and other announcements, "Americans are engaged in an intensive campaign to buy up European cinemas and to crowd out local producers," directly linking the construction of American cinemas in Europe to both a greater domination of foreign exhibition and a means by which to further expand and control distribution.[54] The *New York Times* added that MGM's Empire acquisition would be the seventh London cinema now controlled with "American money." "This invasion by American producers has made British film producers nervous," the *Times* reported. "They fear that, as in the United States, producing organizations, after buying up theatres by wholesale, will drive exhibitors out of business."[55] Paramount only exacerbated these concerns when the company announced its plans to build another house—the Carlton Theatre in London—as well as another Paramount Theatre in Brussels, all while it completed the purchase of the old Vaudeville Theatre in Paris.[56] By then E. E. Shauer reported that Paramount's theater circuit had grown to 358 cinemas in the United States and 10 overseas cinemas under its direct control.[57]

Paramount's "Shop Window"

The name of Paramount's first London cinema, perhaps due to local concerns, changed from "The Paramount" to "The Plaza"—removing any named association with the parent U.S. company.[58] Nonetheless, in January 1926, two months before opening, London's *Daily Express* made clear that "the Plaza is an American-owned theatre, controlled by the Famous Players-Lasky Corporation, whose films are celebrated throughout the world under the brand name of Paramount." FPL executives were equally blunt about the purpose of the company's wholly owned shop window cinema: "We shall use the Plaza primarily for 'demonstrating' our own films," FPL's Al Kaufman told the newspaper. "The main object is to show exhibitors exactly how, in our opinion, our films should be presented to the public." Still, he held out an olive branch to British producers: "The pictures shown," he added, would "not be exclusively of the Paramount brand. We estimate that we shall have at least fifteen vacant weeks every year to show other, preferably British, pictures." Kaufman announced that the company *had* chosen a "British picture"—albeit a Paramount release—*Nell Gwynn* to launch the cinema. Kaufman reinforced the idea of the Plaza as "a memorial to the insistence and enthusiasm of Mr. J. C. Graham, the popular European representative of Famous-Lasky, whose desire to have a 'shop-window' for his films brought the theatre into existence."[59]

The use of the term "shop window" was omnipresent, featured again a week later in a *Kinematograph Weekly* article about "Paramount's Super in Regent Street and Jermyn Street." The cinema, the trade journal wrote, was "designed primarily to fill the purpose of a shop window for the Lasky product, it will not only give that organisation's pictures adequate presentation, but act as an object-lesson to all exhibitors who wish to give their cinemas the advantage of the most up-to-date and scientific methods available." The *Kine Weekly* added that the Plaza's director Al Kaufman "differ[ed] from our own super showmen ... in his expressed intention to run the hall so that his ideas shall be copied by others." In that way, the Plaza, like other shop windows to come, was directly constructed and staffed to influence local exhibition practices, to make them more American in both industrial and cultural practice. "It is his aim," the trade journal added, "to put a show to which our Katzs, our Graumans, and our Rothafels may come and study points." Kaufman brought conductor Frank Tours over from New York to arrange the Plaza's music and conduct its forty-five-piece orchestra, installed an American Wurlitzer organ "which has never before been used in Europe," and began a four shows per day policy that, *Kine Weekly* remarked, was "a daring experiment ... and one that will be watched with keen interest."[60] The Plaza's Wurlitzer also eschewed the British custom of burying the organ in the orchestra pit and instead made it and its player highly visible to local audiences up near the stage.

The Plaza was also the first London cinema to feature female ushers, an idea that others like Sid Grauman had used at his Egyptian Theatre in Hollywood but had not yet become a custom in London's more formal settings. The installation of the so-called Tiller Girls performing on stage in Francis Mangan's "divertissements" was also an innovation. Like American movie showmen Sid Grauman, Samuel "Roxy" Rothafel, and others, the Plaza's stage shows would often be produced using themes tied in with the feature films being presented to allow the live performances to enhance the filmed presentations. Kaufman also employed American ballyhoo practices by adorning London buses with advertisements reading "Start Saying Plaza!"[61] Rather than hiding the new cinema's foreignness—numerous journalists of the time remarked that Englishmen had no idea how to pronounce the name "Plaza"—Kaufman and FPL overtly celebrated its foreign visibility.[62]

The Plaza, like many Hollywood-owned shop window cinemas to follow, mixed American techniques with local styles to blend the foreign with the local, the new with the familiar. The selection of British architect Frank Verity, who had designed the Shepherd's Bush Pavilion, the Marble Arch Pavilion, and the Scala Theatre, reinforced Paramount's cross-cultural approach as Verity's name and design aesthetic was familiar to British cinemagoers and thus reduced the foreignness of the Plaza's American operation.[63] England's still rigid class system was also integrated into the design of Verity's Plaza. While most of the theater's seats were well within reach of commoners, the Plaza contained a "Royal Circle" or what *Bioscope* dubbed "millionares' [sic] row," described as a "cosy little circle to seat about eighty people" in "a comfortable easy chair." "There are only three rows," the trade journal added, "and it is easy to predict that at seven shillings and sixpence per seat (tax included) there will never be many unoccupied during any performance."[64]

The *Kine Weekly* noted that the selection of *Nell Gwynn* as its opening film was a "very welcome item of news" and "a shrewd stroke of business ... with a big British winner."[65] In advance of its opening, *Kine Weekly* devoted a full supplemental section to the Plaza titled "Paramount's Shop Window," arguing that in their "magnificent new theatre"—"the latest expression of American principles of equipment and presentation"—"Famous Players have provided London with a new show place ... [that] will intrigue the British exhibitor as the first manifestation in this country of the purely American theory of kinema showmanship. To the public, it promises a revelation of what is achievable in the picture entertainment 'de luxe.'"[66] *Bioscope* added that "London's Palatial Plaza ... Famous-Lasky's Shop Window" has "a 'best' in everything—until something better comes along" and added that at this "'shop-window' for Famous-Lasky pictures,... every picture ... will be 'put over' as it ought to be, and with the aid of music, organ and orchestra, lighting effects and stage settings, the utmost ounce of entertainment value will be given to every picture."[67] The Plaza Theatre program further concretized the relationship between the cinema and Paramount by noting that "Plaza Policy" meant that "the Plaza will be the London home of Paramount productions" and that "the Theatre was conceived and constructed for this purpose by the FAMOUS

PLAYERS LASKY CORPORATION." The Plaza's program also reinforced its "clearance"—preventing any other cinemas in the same zone from screening these films—as "feature films presented at the Plaza each week cannot be seen elsewhere for a period of from three to six months."[68]

A private premiere was held for England's political, social, and cultural elite before it opened to the public in March 1926. Kaufman's guest list included the Prince and Princess Arthur of Connaught and Princess Helena Victoria as well as "representatives of every branch of the social and political life of the capital, with the addition of members of the world of letters, art and drama, and a very full representation of film folks from all parts of Britain, the Continent, and America."[69] The Plaza's opening night confirmed the "glocal" mishmash with American Frank Tours leading the British orchestra in the British national anthem accompanying newsreels and other shorts from British Pathé and Gaumont. H. F. Kessler-Howes, writing in the *Kine Weekly*, remarked, "The big picture is just an item in the programme, and almost as much time is taken up with variety acts and prologues, yet this type of programme is hailed by many as something new. Still, if the Plaza method is successful in the West End, it is safe to prophesy that our other leading kinemas will soon fall into line."[70] Just like American movie palaces of the 1920s, motion pictures were only one part of the Plaza's evening of entertainment. A night at the Plaza for British audiences meant a feature film and an American-style stage show, often in aesthetic or thematic connection with one another—a policy that was in step with such opulent American theaters as the Capitol under Rothafel and Major Edward Bowes or Hollywood's Egyptian Theatre under Sid Grauman.[71]

The Plaza had opened in March 1926 along American lines, with American Simplex projectors, an American Wurlitzer organ, American-style prologues, and, most important, transplanted Americans J. C. Graham serving as managing director and Al Kaufman in charge of operations.[72] The introduction of American "deluxe" entertainment had an immediate impact. Only six months after the Plaza opened, *Bioscope* reported numerous attempts by native exhibitors to copy its stage show and film policy.[73]

The Battle of Birmingham, 1927

Despite Paramount and Loew's expansion efforts, Warner Bros. and United Artists remained reluctant to build, lease, or buy British cinemas and risk alienating their exhibition partners. Instead, both companies signed agreements with London cinemas to hold trade screenings and book first-run engagements on an exclusive basis.[74] "From what I can see," United Artists' Joseph Schenck told *Bioscope*, "any move on the part of producers in the direction of theatre ownership is unwelcome to the British exhibitor, and we are not out to offend, but to please."[75] Schenck had learned this lesson from the furor that had erupted in 1925 after he scouted Birmingham, England, for a new three-thousand-seat theater for United Artists, a project the company was forced to abandon amid the uproar.

Paramount had no such concern and felt emboldened to now expand their influence beyond London's Plaza Theatre. Effecting a plan they first hatched in 1919 with PPL, Paramount sought to secure additional cinemas in the largest British cities and received a riotous response. So began what *Bioscope* later dubbed "the Battle of Birmingham"—a key moment in Hollywood's expansion efforts overseas and one that would come to (re)define the strategies for international exhibition for Paramount as well as MGM and, later, Warner Bros.[76]

In December 1926 Paramount quietly leased the Levy circuit's Scala and Futurist theaters in Birmingham, England, from Sol and Alfred Levy. (Under the agreement, Sol Levy would continue to operate the Scala for Paramount.)[77] The reaction from most British exhibitors was outwardly hostile, and *Motion Picture News* reported that "exhibitors and film renters view the new situation with considerable alarm."[78] The CEA rebuked Paramount's expansion plans by noting that they were "detrimental to the future of the British industry" and would be the subject of an urgent organizational

FIGURE 1.1 Scala in Birmingham, England. (Courtesy of Cinema Theatre Association)

meeting held on January 4, 1927.[79] Councilor G. F. McDonald, former president of the CEA, arrived at Birmingham's Futurist and announced that Midland exhibitors were ready to "fight [the] invasion" and "retaliate with every effective weapon at their command."[80]

The blowback was strong enough to attract the American embassy's attention. U.S. diplomat Homer Brett wrote from England to the U.S. State Department that "purchases of picture theaters by American motion-picture producers have aroused antagonism among the owners and an attempt is being made to organise a boycott against producers who enter into competition with exhibitors." Still, he remained optimistic that the anger would soon die down. Despite newspaper headlines such as the *Nottingham Guardian*'s "An American Invasion," Brett still felt that "the general public, so far as I can observe, remain indifferent to the agitation and would not hesitate to patronize a picture theater because it was American-owned, unless intense propaganda against American films should in the future arouse a sense of national antagonism."[81]

At the CEA Midlands branch meeting in early January 1927 in Birmingham, exhibitors passed a resolution "in the national interest" that agreed to book films only from "producers or renters who did not enter into competition with them as exhibitors."[82] At a concurrent meeting in Liverpool, the Northwest branch of the CEA backed the Midlands boycott of Paramount. W. R. Fuller, general secretary of the CEA, told the *Nottingham Guardian*, "If the exhibitors on this side stand together in this way [through a boycott], it will simply mean that it will not pay the foreign corporations to acquire cinemas here and lose all their other business."[83] The General Council of the CEA backed the national boycott that February. Citing "the American invasion and control" of British cinemas, the CEA requested that the local and national government "act in the matter" to protect Liverpool, Birmingham, and other exhibitors.[84] Paramount countered these angry protests by noting that it was now "willing to sublet [the Futurist] to any British exhibitor who will protect Famous' first run releases and not restrict them on other bookings."[85]

Paramount also found some British exhibitors willing to tolerate their expansion. H. Moorhouse of England's Moorhouse circuit "flatly refused to be a party to the 'absurd boycott'" and *Film Daily* reported that "many others express similar views."[86] The British trade journal *Bioscope* also objected to the boycott, calling the General Council vote "deplorable," and wondered if "the resolution is to be interpreted as a placatory gesture from a benignant mother to an angry child."[87]

Attacks on Paramount and Sol and Alfred Levy continued over the following weeks. In March 1927, F. W. Locke, the past chairman of the northwestern branch of the CEA, wrote that Alfred Levy "draws attention to the fact that big circuits are being built up in this country, and apparently does not think it matters whether they are British, German, French, or American. Well, I along with many other British exhibitors, think it does matter." Locke then swung at Levy's patriotism, with perhaps a nod to the era's rampant antisemitism: "May I appeal to Mr. Levy to be British?" Locke argued that all foreign companies hoping to buy or build theaters in England should be boycotted, including Jury-Metro-Goldwyn.[88]

Fierce discussions were subsequently held between members of the CEA and between the CEA and J. C. Graham, and a compromise was ironed out. Paramount returned the Futurist to the Levys' control in exchange for an end to the CEA boycott and a resumption of Paramount films being booked into British cinemas.[89] Further, *Film Daily* wrote, "Famous will not enter into competition with exhibitors in the future."[90] The CEA boycott was formally withdrawn on March 15, 1927, and an official announcement made on March 24.[91] Instead, Paramount remained focused on its Plaza shop window in London, and the détente between the company and the CEA held. In late April 1927 C. J. North, chief of the Motion Picture Section of the Specialties Division of the Bureau of Foreign and Domestic Commerce, wrote that he had "talked to some of the Famous Players here about [the boycott] on my last trip to New York and they seemed to regard it as a dead issue. I certainly hope so."[92]

A few months later Paramount acquired the La Scala Picture House in Dublin, Ireland, and reopened it on August 1, 1927, as the Capitol, making it the new shop window cinema for Paramount films in Ireland.[93] Five months later *Film Daily* reported in January 1928 that Paramount was once again "actively acquiring theaters in Great Britain, not in the open but through individuals connected with the organization here." The trade journal added, pointedly, that "the British trade is cognizant of the move. This, despite the declaration made by Adolph Zukor in London last May that Paramount had no plans to acquire houses in England."[94] All of this was a prelude to a larger Paramount-owned *and* -branded chain to come in the 1930s.

A New American "Empire"

For the moment, the end of the CEA boycott in March 1927 meant that it was London's West End exhibitors who were most directly affected by U.S. cinema expansion. In addition to the ongoing excitement over Paramount's Plaza, Loew's had finally closed Leicester Square's venerable Empire Theatre in January 1927 to build its own shop window cinema in its place. The symbolism of the demolition of the old Empire—which staged its last performances in January 1927 just as the Battle of Birmingham was heating up—and the construction of a new Empire could not have been more symbolic. The Empire's final night, on January 22, featured Fred and Adele Astaire. "Next week," the *New*

York Times remarked, "wreckers will begin dismantling one of the principal places . . . to make way for an American movie palace."[95]

Harry Portman, who had held a series of management roles in Loew's U.S. southern division, was appointed director of all of Loew's cinemas now operating or under construction in England, France, and Belgium and was made supervisor of the Empire Theatre construction.[96] Two months later Loew's sent Samuel Eckman Jr. from New York to London to assist Portman; support their British distribution arm, Jury-Metro-Goldwyn; help manage the Empire Theatre construction and opening; and avoid the wrath of an increasingly anti-American CEA.[97] Loew's also sent several of its New York employees to London, including Don Albert, the associate conductor of the Capitol Grand Orchestra at the Capitol Theatre, who became the first musical conductor of the Empire. (Albert's tenure at the Empire was a two-month loan from the Capitol.)[98]

The Empire Theatre's opening night on November 8, 1928, was a gala affair with Arthur Loew, Eckman, Norma Shearer, and "ambassadors of every country, members of the Diplomatic Corps, and a host of social personalities" on hand.[99] "The scenes outside the Empire Theatre were extraordinary," the *Daily Film Renter* reported. "Practically from Piccadilly right through to Charing Cross Road traffic was at a standstill, and outside the theatre itself a large force of police had to be called to hold back the huge crowds that thronged Leicester Square."[100] Loew's made a concerted effort to ensure that the opening was as "spiritually British" as possible. The opening film—like the Plaza's selection of *Nell Gwynn*—had British origins. *Trelawney of the Wells*, *Bioscope* reported with some native pride, was created by British author Sir Arthur Wing Pinero, and the cast included Canadian Norma Shearer, British Ralph Forbes, Dublin-born Owen Moore, Australian O. P. Heggie, and other cast members.[101] Despite the appeals to the evening's purported Britishness and fit, J. B. Priestley, writing in the *Saturday Review*, acknowledged the obvious:

> They call it The Empire and it stands exactly where our old acquaintance stood, on the north side of Leicester Square. But let nobody imagine it is the same place. These two Empires have their roots in two different continents, for the old music-hall was essentially European, and the new kinema is undoubtedly American. No, they do not belong to the same age, perhaps not to the same civilization. A social historian might do worse than begin a gigantic study of our times with an artful reference to the fall of the old Empire and the sudden rise of the new.[102]

By 1928 American shop windows had become an accepted part of the London cinema scene and would become evermore so in the 1930s. The successful exportation of American exhibition practices had also produced something imminently more successful than direct competition. With their immensely popular shop window cinemas, Paramount and Loew's had attracted large audiences to these "super cinemas" and thus encouraged domestic exhibitors to copy their design and operation. Sometimes these cinemas even attracted a new breed of exhibitor modeled on the American system. Perhaps no one exemplified this Americanized European exhibitor better than Sidney Bernstein, who formed the Granada Theatres circuit in England. "An American influence permeated all Sidney Bernstein's ideas about cinema operation and showmanship," according to historian Allen Eyles. "He called his 'cinemas' theatres as the Americans did.... Bernstein mixed music hall and film in American-style cine-variety longer and more extensively than any other circuit did in Britain."[103] With exhibitors like Sidney Bernstein at Granada, and other circuits presenting American films at higher ticket prices, American-owned shop windows had helped the U.S. film companies realize their ultimate goal: to transform the way the region presented and consumed motion pictures, thereby expanding the overseas profit potential for Hollywood.

By 1929 American shop window cinemas and the growing American influence on indigenous exhibitors in cities around England helped to develop in patrons what *Kine Weekly* dubbed the "kinema mind," a moviegoing consciousness that had now spurred an intense building boom of large-scale movie houses—all charging higher prices—to generate larger profits for American distributors and their increasingly opulent retailers: British cinemas.[104]

CHAPTER 2

HOLLYWOOD'S EUROPEAN ADVENTURE, 1925–1941

England was certainly not the only target of U.S. film exhibition expansion in Europe. In 1925 Paramount had also purchased the Vaudeville Theatre in Paris in order to extensively renovate and reopen it not as a venue for vaudeville but as a new Paramount "super cinema."[1] Loew's subsequently announced its own five-year agreement with the vertically integrated French Gaumont company that gave Loew's Inc. supervision of Gaumont's distribution, marketing, and exhibition operations.[2] Gaumont-Loew-Metro was established in May 1925 to control the sixteen-cinema Gaumont circuit, which included the famous Gaumont Palace and Madeleine cinemas in Paris.[3] A separate unit, Gaumont-Metro-Goldwyn, was now responsible for the distribution of Metro-Goldwyn and other films in France. Gaumont-Loew-Metro was also in charge of the films' presentation and exploitation in France, Belgium, Switzerland, Egypt, Syria, Algeria, Palestine, and Tunisia, where Gaumont had a strong presence with foreign branches and cinemas.[4] By forming Gaumont-Metro-Goldwyn and Gaumont-Loew-Metro, Loew's could be assured that its distribution, marketing, and exhibition practices would be carried out on three continents while the marketing of MGM films and implementation of Loew's exhibition practices would reach previously untouched regions. E. A. Schiller, general theatre representative of Loew's Inc., and J. Robert Rubin of Metro-Goldwyn sailed to France in 1925 and then to Egypt to supervise the implementation of Loew's exhibition practices at these newly managed Gaumont cinemas.[5]

To further upgrade the décor of the palatial Gaumont Palace in Paris and improve its previously disappointing grosses, Loew's also turned to Schiller to expand the cinema's already well-respected orchestra, place flowers throughout the building, renovate the entire structure inside and out, place curtains over the screen when not in use, and vastly improve its projection, along with "other improvements too numerous to mention."[6] *Bioscope*'s Parisian correspondent noted that after Schiller's subsequent makeover of Gaumont's Madeleine, the cinema was now "drawing a better-class public" and "better business than it ever did before."[7]

New York's Capitol Theatre, owned by Loew's Inc. after the 1924 acquisition of Goldwyn Pictures, provided the talent pool for Loew's continued revamp of the Gaumont Palace. In August 1926 Tommy Dowd, the assistant to Major Edward Bowes, managing director of the Capitol, was sent to Paris for six weeks to "redecorate" MGM's Parisian shop window and instill "American presentation methods."[8] Dowd repainted the interior cream and gold, raised the stage four feet, and increased the size of the considerable orchestra by ten musicians.[9] One year later Dowd was sent back to the Gaumont Palace indefinitely and placed in charge of its orchestra.[10] He was also sent to further replicate the Capitol Theatre's presentation methods. He subsequently remarked, "In Paris there seems to be apparent a general trend to follow our own elaborate form of entertainment.... The large seating capacity of the[se] theatres are testimonial to the fact that the public is receiving this new development with enthusiasm."[11] French approval of Loew's Inc.'s management of the Gaumont cinemas was confirmed when Marcus Loew was awarded La Légion d'honneur (the Legion of Honor) by France in August 1926 for "improving the quality of French amusements both in regard to films and theatrical ventures." (Henry Portman, the American general manager of the Gaumont Palace, was appointed an officer of public education by the French government for his presentation of children's matinees.)[12] By early 1927 Léon Gaumont, following a two-month trip to New York where he met with Marcus Loew, announced that Gaumont—with MGM financing—would build an even larger chain of cinemas throughout France.[13] "As Metro Goldwyn are interested in the Gaumont enterprises," a reporter from *Argus* commented, "American capital is evidently to be invested in exhibition in France."[14] Those new cinemas, *Film Daily* reported, would be "patterned after the Capitol, New York."[15]

Loew's Inc.'s Samuel Eckman would play a central role in Loew's/MGM's operations in Europe over the next two decades. In addition to his work with Portman on the construction of the new Empire Theatre, Eckman oversaw the takeover of several French cinemas, including the Omnia Cinema in Rouen, the Cinema Palace in Angers, the Cameo at Lille, and the Select at Le Havre in late 1927.[16] It was during Eckman's tenure at Gaumont-Metro-Goldwyn that the company distributed Abel Gance's *Napoleon* to the Opera cinema, in conjunction with Société Générale des Films, and presented Gance's three-projector film across the cinema's triptych screen.[17] The film's gross was a record for the cinema.[18] William A. Johnston noted in *Motion Picture News* that the Gaumont Palace was "doing good business under the Loew-Metro management" with its "orchestra, organ and presentation approach" all of "the American style of show."[19]

Eckman's role also extended to Loew's recent acquisition of three additional cinemas in Brussels, Ghent, and Charleroi, Belgium.[20] These purchases, and MGM's new chain of forty-four cinemas in Brazil, were part of a reported $50 million global expansion in which Loew's planned to operate upward of four hundred theaters internationally.[21] None of these interventions went unnoticed, and the spread of U.S. film exhibition ownership abroad continually fomented local industry resentments.[22] "Foreign film factors will naturally resent efforts of rank outsiders to gobble up their theaters," *Film Daily* columnist Red Kann observed, adding that "if the march of progress decrees that American distributors must have their first-run outlets abroad just as they have them here what can be done about it? Perhaps a graceful way out will be that which M-G-M has taken in France. There, at least, both the native and foreign organizations work together on a partnership arrangement."[23] Further evidence of MGM's expansion abroad could be found in Holland, where Loew's already co-owned a theater in Den Haag (The Hague) and now planned a similar takeover of local cinemas under the direction of Eckman and Portman.[24] By September 1927, Loew's was now operating twenty cinemas in Europe.[25] Each new acquisition required massaging local distributor–exhibitor relationships, a key part of their continual work.

Paramount was also active in France. Alongside new Paramount shop windows in London, Tokyo, and other cities, the company now turned its attention to the conversion of the Vaudeville Theatre in Paris into Le Paramount. The opulent shop window cinema opened in Paris on November 24, 1927, with the president of the French Republic, Raymond Poincaré, in attendance along with a "large and brilliant audience, including four Cabinet Ministers, most of the members of the Diplomatic Corps," and others including Marshal Ferdinand Foch, who commanded the allied forces during World War I.[26] Like Paramount's London Plaza, the 1,900-seat "Le Paramount" was also designed by Frank Verity in association with Auguste Bluysen of Paris, providing the cinema with a Paramount aesthetic accompanied by a French flair. Plans were completed by the R. E. Hall & Company of New York, but construction of the cinema was overseen by a Frenchman, M. Simeon Shepard.[27]

Upon the Paramount's debut, Morris Gilbert, writing in the *New York Times*, remarked how much Le Paramount in Paris replicated the 3,500-seat flagship Paramount Theatre in New York City. "Save that smoking is permitted in the

FIGURE 2.1 Le Paramount program, Paris, ca. 1930. (Author's collection)

theatre, Americans can easily forget, in the Paramount, that they are abroad.... The orchestra pit rises and sinks, the lighting effects are spectacular, quite in the Paramount manner, and the program is reminiscent of Times Square."[28] The cinema was also built with the American practice of omitting side boxes that kept patrons separated by class. Le Paramount was, in nearly every way, an American cinema. With American Al Kaufman as its director and Harold Franklin observing from New York, Le Paramount took in more money than any cinema in France in its opening weeks.[29] *Bioscope*'s French correspondent Georges Clarrière commented that "American enterprise in French cinema exploitation is very helpful to the trade in general, and is teaching others in the exhibiting line a lesson they need to learn—i.e. how to house spectators comfortably."[30] Le Paramount had to cater to the public's desire for American films while maintaining a French "mode" of presentation. Early reviews were bullish. Pierre Kefer, for example, writing in the February 1928 issue of *Du Cinéma*, commented that Le Paramount was "without a doubt" the cleanest and most comfortable cinema in Paris and had already acquired the finest cinema audience in the city.[31]

Laemmle, Parufamet, and the American Incursion into Germany

Germany was another highly fertile market for Hollywood during the late silent era as intertitles could be easily translated into German with no concerns (yet) about dubbing versus subtitling. Universal was particularly active here, no doubt in part due to Carl Laemmle's continued familial, cultural, and linguistic ties to his country of origin. In 1925 Universal struck a massive distribution and financing deal with Ufa's (Universum-Film Aktiengesellschaft) 130 cinemas. This arrangement with the cash-strapped Ufa was diverted at the last moment, however, by Paramount and Loew's, who parachuted into Germany and pledged $4 million to Ufa (and Universal) in order for their own films to be distributed throughout the chain with far less screen time for Universal. This offer came in two parts: on one hand, Paramount and Loew's offered much needed cash; on the other, an extortionist deal was submitted in which the two vertically integrated majors threatened to build as many cinemas as Ufa currently held in Germany and fill them with Hollywood films at "cut-rate prices" if Ufa refused their offer. Ufa was left with little choice, both needing the infusion of capital for their ballooning production costs and unable to risk a rival Hollywood-owned cinema chain undercutting their real cash cow—Ufa's 130 cinemas that played Ufa and other films, including those from Hollywood. This tremendously imbalanced deal—the so-called Parufamet agreement between **Par**amount, **Ufa**, and **Met**ro—is often discussed in terms of what it meant for international distribution and the lack of reciprocity on the part of Paramount and Loew's to screen many Ufa titles in the United States. However, it is important to note once again that this agreement was secured in large part due to the rapid growth of Hollywood's overseas exhibition empires and its real estate prowess. It was the threat of Hollywood's overseas cinema building and buying that forced Ufa into this lopsided agreement. Ufa, in its weakened position, capitulated in much the same way other foreign markets would. The company reckoned that it could surrender many of its screens to Hollywood but never the walls that contained them.[32]

Universal did go on to open its own key cinemas in Germany in the years to come. After securing the Rialto Theatre as its London shop window (and later taking over the Rialto in Leeds as well), Universal opened two massive cinemas in Berlin.[33] The first was a 2,500-seat cinema, the Mercedes Palast, on Berlin's Utrechter Straße, and the second, a 4,000-seat cinema in the Neukölln section of Berlin.[34] Real estate was purchased by Universal in May 1926, the theater announced that July, and the new Mercedes Palast opened only months later in October 1926 with *Michael Strogoff* as "the Universal—Film de France special." The theater was operated by Oskar Einstein, Universal's sales agent in Germany, and local theater manager Fred S. Englander and was designed by Fritz Williams, who had also built the Ufa Thurmstrasse Theatre and the Piccadilly as a single-level cinema despite its size.[35] Einstein was a cousin of Carl Laemmle and had been Universal's representative in Berlin since 1911.[36]

Crowds surrounded the opening of the Mercedes Palast, even though the film had previously debuted at the Ufa-Palast am Zoo, and required fifty policemen to escort invited guests into the premiere.[37] The *Universal Weekly* claimed that the "gigantic popular price house" was "the first big theatre built solely for the masses in Germany."[38] *Film Daily* added that the "opening of the Mercedes Palast has led to speculation as to Universal's theater plans in Europe" and reported plans that it might "operate a number of houses throughout Europe" to match its domestic efforts in the United States where "Universal is steadily building up its chain" with "around 200 houses."[39] These two Universal cinemas, rather than portending a foreign growth area for the company, would prove to be aberrations.

Outright control of cinemas on European soil was not the only means by which American exhibition practices were exported. In August 1925 Ufa hired movie palace conductor Erno Rapee, formerly of New York's Capitol and Philadelphia's Fox theaters, to oversee the reopening, management, and musical accompaniment of the Ufa-Palast am Zoo in Berlin, the country's most prestigious cinema, and to manage Ufa's 132 cinema circuit.[40] Ufa also brought over Alexander Oumansky, former head of ballet at New York's Capitol, with whom Rapee had previously worked, to upgrade the Ufa-Palast am Zoo.[41] The *New York Times* commented upon Rapee and Oumansky's debut at the Palast:

> When Berlin's largest motion picture house ... was reopened tonight after having undergone a renovation, its audience seemed to be transported to Broadway, New York. Not only was the feature film an American production but for the first time in Germany a combination of symphony concert, ballet and film was offered. The Americanization of the theatre's methods of presentation has been carried out by its new directors.... The Ufa Palast has been rebuilt according to American ideas.[42]

Rapee added that "this American type of entertainment, the backbone of which I consider the large and well trained orchestra, has won out and is today the customary way picture theatres are being run."[43] Siegfried Kracauer, writing in 1926 of this growing influence, remarked that moviegoing in the city had been changed forever. "The large picture houses in Berlin are palaces of distraction," he argued. "To call them *movie cinemas (Kinos)* would be disrespectful." Indeed, "it is the picture palaces, those optical fairylands, which are shaping the face of Berlin," Kracauer wrote, adding that they had all "adopted the American style of a self-contained show which integrates the film as part of a larger whole."[44] The *New York Times* reported that German newspapers were littered with anger over this "American invasion" of the cinema.[45] By the end of 1926, *Variety* added that "the standardization of the American formula of presentation for film house programs has crept around the globe and is evidenced in almost every country.... England, Germany, France, Australia and South Africa have [all] felt the trend of the times and have their 'de luxe' performances."[46]

Fox, Paramount, and the New Blueprint for Foreign Control

Fox Film Corp. developed a very different global strategy from that of Paramount and Loew's and one that was consistent with William Fox's expansive mergers and acquisition frenzy in the late 1920s in which he bought the West Coast Theatres chain and other large regional circuits, culminating in the short-lived acquisition of a controlling interest in Loew's/MGM in 1929. The pending sale of Loew's to Fox, which the Hoover administration's Justice Department later blocked, gave Fox temporary control of Loew's' growing inventory of European cinemas, which included the Empire in London; nine additional cinemas in Paris, Bordeaux, Lyon, Toulouse, Toulon, Strasbourg, Lille, Le Havre and Rouen, France; and five cinemas in Belgium, with two in Brussels and three others in Charleroi, Liège, and Ghent.[47] To secure Fox's access to many more British cinemas for its films, Fox negotiated a 49 percent interest in the Gaumont-British Picture Corp.[48] While Fox was never able to gain control over the company's board, the *Saturday Review*, in an article titled, "The Americanization of Amusement," commented, "Technically, the control is British; but in fact, control is exercised through a private syndicate in which the Fox Film Company holds a large interest."⁴⁹

Paramount also expanded throughout the late 1920s. Overseas, the company now operated a growing cinema circuit in Europe—in London (Plaza), Paris (Paramount), Barcelona (Coliseum), and Stockholm (China); in Latin America, Havana (Fausto), São Paolo (Cine Paramount), and Mexico City (Teatro Olimipa); and in Asia with Tokyo's Hogaku-Za, which *Variety* dubbed "the model theatre of the Far Eastern show world."⁵⁰ (See parts III and VI for more information on the company's early Latin American and Asian cinemas, respectively.) Throughout the 1920s, Paramount executives cherry-picked key cities where shop window cinemas would secure first-run distribution and exhibition and generate excitement about Paramount films for local exhibitors. Paramount was building a global chain.

In Sweden, for example, Paramount's local subsidiary, Filmaktiebolaget Paramount (Film AB. Paramount), had already taken over the 1,600-seat China Theatre in Stockholm from Svensk Filmindustri, one of Sweden's leading film companies.⁵¹ The theater opened on October 19, 1928, under Paramount's "direktion." Paramount International's house organ, *Paramount Around the World*, noted that the China-biografen (China cinema) was the "finest of all film theatres in Scandinavia" with the "utmost charm and comfort." It was managed by Carl P. York, Paramount's general manager for Scandinavia, with Melville Shauer, head of Paramount's European operations, overseeing.⁵² Sweden's *Filmnyheter* reported that the China-biografen was now "a theater of the kind developed in America in the last decade" and designed with "America's modern cinema architecture" in mind by architect J. Albin Stark, who had "studied American theater architecture" in association with Charles Magnusson.⁵³ In the succeeding years, Film AB. Paramount operated several other cinemas in the region, including the Kinopalaeet in København (Copenhagen), Denmark, by 1930 as well as the Palladium and Drott theaters in Malmö, Sweden, by 1932.⁵⁴

Despite its growing cinema interests in Scandinavia, Paramount's focus remained on adding additional cinemas in England due in large part to the larger grosses in that English-speaking market after the coming of sound. The Frank Verity–designed Carlton Theatre in London's Haymarket section, just a few blocks away from Leicester Square and the Plaza Theatre, had originally opened in April 1927 as a live-performance venue.⁵⁵ It was originally licensed to J. C. Graham, Paramount's British director, though the company did not yet operate it.⁵⁶ The primarily legitimate theater had hosted the London premiere and a five-week engagement of *Wings* on March 26, 1928. Otherwise, it had been the home of musical revues and plays.⁵⁷ In 1930 Paramount purchased the cinema from the Carlton Theatre Company, and it became the second London shop window for Paramount films.⁵⁸ Paramount installed a large orchestra and a second troupe of Tiller Girls.[59] J. C. Graham was now the managing director of Paramount-Film Service Ltd., Plaza Theatre Company Ltd., Carlton Theatre Company Ltd., and Olympic Kinematograph Laboratories Ltd.[60] He would soon add many more European subsidiaries and companies.

In May 1930 Adolph Zukor arrived in England "in connection with a scheme for this organisation to acquire and build cinemas in most of the key towns in this country."[61] Only three years removed from the Birmingham mess, Paramount constructed the first shop window cinema outside of London in Manchester, England. The British exhibition industry, now replete with its own large chains (Gaumont-British, Granada Theatres, Provincial Cinematograph Theatres, etc.), was no longer as threatened by a single shop window cinema owned by an American film company. British cinemas and British cinema companies, operating dozens of deluxe cinemas throughout the country, could now hold their own. Paramount's shop window cinemas would instead provide a guaranteed first-run outlet for company films in major British cities and a model for local exploitation and showmanship, but they no longer presented an existential threat to the British film industry. Earl St. John, who had managed both the Plaza and Carlton Theatres in London was placed in charge of the growing Paramount British circuit.[62]

The Paramount Manchester was every bit as opulent as London's Plaza, seating three thousand patrons and designed, once more, by Frank Verity (and S. Beverley).[63] The Paramount Manchester, highlighting its stage and musical links with the London flagship cinema, employed nearly two hundred, making it a key job creator in the city and thus a predominately British one.[64] These sorts of economic benefits of American cinema expansion were highly promoted, especially amidst the global Depression.

In late 1930 Paramount also filed articles of association for a new company, Paramount-Astoria-Theatres Ltd., in order to acquire the four Astoria Theatres that had been built in and around London in Finsbury Park, Brixton, Streatham, and South Bermondsey.[65] By 1931 Paramount was now operating roughly fifty cinemas around the world, including new additions in Melbourne (Capitol), Havana (Encanto), Rio de Janeiro (Capitólio and Imperio), as well as newly completed leases or builds in Scotland, Ireland, Denmark, Panama, Costa Rica, Cuba, and Jamaica, all through local subsidiaries.[66]

Paramount added to its growing British circuit by opening new deluxe cinemas in Newcastle-on-Tyne and Leeds and aimed to have sixteen "key houses" in England by 1932.[67] Once again Paramount promoted the fact that, at its Newcastle cinema, "British materials and labour have been used throughout."[68] Another new Paramount Theatre in Leeds, which opened on February 22, 1932, attracted 1.2 million visitors in its first year alone.[69] The cinema was "a source of employment for a great many Leeds men," and, according to its opening program, was "built entirely with British materials and labour."[70]

By 1934 Paramount operated twelve cinemas in England and Ireland alone: in London, the Plaza, Carlton, and the four Astorias; the Paramount in Manchester, the Paramount in Newcastle, the Paramount in Leeds, the Capitol in Dublin, and two new striking additions: the Futurist in Birmingham (the source of so much consternation back in 1927) and the Capitol in Cardiff. Paramount was also still operating five cinemas in France—Le Paramount in Paris, Broglie in Strassbourg, Familia in Lille, Opera in Reims, and Le Paramount in Toulouse. Even after the company's bankruptcy reorganization in 1933, additional Paramount-operated cinemas remained in Brussels (Coliseum), Barcelona (Coliseum), São Paulo (Paramount), Melbourne (Capitol), and three cinemas in Sweden: the Palladium and Drott in Malmö and the China Theatre in Stockholm. Paramount also retained a "stock interest" and thus influence over bookings in three Kingston, Jamaica, cinemas: Palace, Movies, and Gaiety, as well as a "franchise interest" in the Prince Edward Theatre in Sydney, Australia.[71]

By the end of the year, on December 31, 1934, Paramount opened its latest palace in Glasgow, Scotland. Historian Bruce Peter notes that the Paramount had "the most extensive display of neon lighting on any building in Scotland . . . Glasgow had never seen a piece of architecture quite like it."[72] As always, the Paramount Glasgow was a "cultural embassy," selling American ideas, culture, and attractions. Setting foot inside was akin to walking on American soil and into an American movie house.

Paramount was not looking to expand its European holdings further by then, however, even as its European chain expanded. As early as September 1933, with the company filing for bankruptcy reorganization, Paramount's John Hicks was already trying to sell the European chain to "get the worry off of its mind."[73] Hicks managed to jettison Paramount's cinemas in Denmark, Japan, and much of the Caribbean, but the bulk of their foreign chain—especially their holdings in Europe—remained.[74] With no takers, Paramount moved ahead with its exhibition expansion in England, opening its *sixth* London cinema, the 2,600-seat Paramount at Tottenham Court Road, another Verity and Beverley commission, on February 13, 1936.[75]

The revenue generated by all of the new British Paramounts made up for the company's exhibition losses in Spain, where Paramount lost control of the Cine Coliseum during the Spanish Civil War.[76] The loss of the Coliseum was a foreshadowing of geopolitical troubles to come.

Budapest, Ufa, and MGM, and War Clouds Forming

While Paramount grew its holdings in England and France, Loew's/MGM had had little success in either market outside London's Empire Theatre. Six years after the 1929 dissolution of the Loew-Metro-Goldwyn and Gaumont-Metro-Goldwyn agreements—in which Loew's sold off its interest in thirteen Gaumont cinemas for roughly 14 million francs[77]—MGM attempted to regain control of the now combined Gaumont-Franco-Film Aubert, then in bankruptcy, by purchasing its assets. Those efforts, however, were "squelched" in February 1935 by the film subcommittee of the finance committee of the Chamber of Deputies and French finance minister, Germain Martin.[78]

Additional MGM shop window cinemas would have to be found, then, in other markets. By 1936 MGM had spread its wings even wider than Paramount, as it maintained positive cashflow throughout the Depression and had far less debt. MGM now had Metro Theatres or Cine Metros in Brisbane, Melbourne, Sydney, Rio de Janeiro, Santiago, Calcutta, Lima, Manila, Johannesburg, Cape Town, Durban, and Montevideo. In Europe, Loew's International operated the Empire in London, the Olympia in Paris, the Capitol in Madrid, the Cameo and Queens Hall in Brussels, the Majestic in Ghent, and Le Forum in Liège. As an example of how MGM marketed these cinemas and sewed them into the social and cultural fabric of each host country, MGM installed a medallion of the late King Albert in each of its Belgian cinemas.[79]

There was another key MGM venue as well: the Metro-Scala in Budapest, Hungary. In 1933 MGM had leased and begun operating the Radius Theatre as its Budapest shop window. That August the Kamara Theatre in Budapest, which had a "largely Jewish patronage," dropped Ufa films in response to the rise of virulent antisemitism in Germany. The Kamara then became another venue for MGM films, though not exclusively.[80]

With official and unofficial boycotts spreading across Europe—and in concert with Joseph Goebbels's desire to spread Nazi ideology to sympathetic audiences across the continent—the *Jewish Daily Bulletin* summarized a (British) *Cinema Magazine* report that claimed that "the National Socialist movement in Germany [wa]s prepared to spend millions of dollars for the purchase of cinema theatres outside Germany to facilitate the spread of Nazi propaganda." Reviewing the *Cinema* reportage, the *Jewish Daily Bulletin* noted that "Nazi advance agents have been visiting the leading European capitals intending to purchase chains of movie houses in important towns, preferably industrial centers," with "the Nazi Film Bureau being prepared to pay up to five million pounds for a specific number of moving picture houses." *Cinema* also reported that Nazi officials had already obtained the Aubert Palace through their investment in the Gaumont Franco-Aubert chain. Elsewhere, the *Bulletin* added, "The purchase of moving picture theatres outside Germany is regarded as an essential preliminary to the exhibition on an international scale of Nazi propaganda films, the production of which has been proceeding at a feverish pace."[81]

Despite these goals, Ufa's distribution and exhibition expansion in Europe was met with increasing opposition as Hitler's ideology and desire for global domination came into sharper focus by those outside Germany. In Hungary, by March 1934, Ufa's three Budapest theaters had already "slipped considerably" since the Nazi regime had taken over, the cinema's programming reflecting the company's new "Hitlerite tendencies." The "increasing popularity of American pictures," *Variety* reported, "also has to do with Ufa's losing ground."[82] In June 1934 MGM dropped its lease of the Radius due to the "too high rent" and was interested in taking over the Ufa-Urania, one of Ufa's three theaters now struggling amid the political blowback and increased competition from Hollywood films. Ufa agreed to lease the cinema to MGM only if it would be renamed the Metro-Ufa. MGM refused.[83] With American films rising in popularity and anti-Nazi sentiments affecting Ufa's Hungarian business, the German film company sold its two other cinemas, the Scala and the Corvin, to MGM and United Artists, respectively. The Corvin was a rare shop window for UA in Europe. MGM, meanwhile, made its American link conspicuous by renaming the cinema as Metro-Scala.[84] It was one of only a handful of the "important first-run picture theatres" in Budapest not owned by Stephen Gerö and his expansive Gerö circuit.[85]

Amsterdamned

Hungary was open to U.S. investment, but the Netherlands proved otherwise. As Loew's discovered—and as would be demonstrated time and again in other protectionist markets—local exhibitors were often successful in blocking these U.S. shop windows by threatening larger boycotts of Hollywood films and exacting other measures of industrial pressure. Trade unions and unified messaging were essential in keeping American film exhibitors out of these markets.

Loew's had co-owned a cinema in The Hague during the 1920s but was devoid of a Dutch shop window by the mid-1930s.[86] Loew's International head Arthur Loew visited the country in December 1934, meeting with MGM manager F. L. D. "Fritz" Strengholt as well as the country's most famous exhibitor, Abraham Tuschinski.[87] (Strengholt had previously served as head of MGM in Germany but was moved to the Netherlands in compliance with Nazi orders to remove Jewish officials from Germany's executive ranks.[88] Strengholt wasn't Jewish, but his wife was.) Tuschinski (also Jewish) had emigrated from Poland in 1903, became a prolific exhibitor in Rotterdam, and later opened the elaborate Tuschinski Theater in Amsterdam in 1921 and operated other important cinemas such as the city's Roxy Theater.[89] Tuschinki's cinemas had been reliable venues for MGM and other American films over the previous decade.

In January 1937 Loew visited Amsterdam again and purchased a plot of land on de Weteringschans near the Leidseplein in central Amsterdam. Arthur Loew told a local newspaper that a new Metro Theatre would soon be built there, and plans for its design and construction were already completed. The "design of the theater," he added, would "follow the latest American ideas" and be built "without balconies."[90] There was a significant problem with Loew's plan, however. In 1935 the Dutch Motion Picture Federation (Nederlandschen Bioscoop-Bond, or NBB) announced that any new cinemas in Amsterdam would require the federation's permission in order to "halt the serious competitive situation which had arisen within the industry."[91] While many distributors balked at the NBB's antigrowth pronouncement, the majority of its members were exhibitors (who had made up the previous Bond van Exploitanten van Nederlandsche Bioscooptheaters, or Union of Dutch Cinema Owners) and they were only too happy to ratify an edict that would prevent further competition—especially from Hollywood.[92] Loew's had not requested—and was even less likely to now receive—permission from the federation to build.[93]

In June the NBB formally rejected MGM's plan to build "a new, large and very modern movie theater" in Amsterdam and questioned whether the company "wish[ed] to behave according to the conventions of the Netherlands film industry and the regulatory provisions of the Nederlandschen Bioscoop-Bond."[94] The NBB journal added the following month that Strengholt was now provoking the organization and warned him not to "abuse his position" and the organization's "hospitality," especially as a foreign company operating among indigenous distributors and exhibitors who increasingly felt "threatened."[95] MGM then attempted to circumvent the anti-American feelings within the NBB by forming a new company, N. V. Niger Co., and claimed that the new company and cinema venture had "nothing to do with the [American] film company."[96] That statement rang hollow when it was easily revealed that the director of N. V. Niger was Strengholt, and its auditor was the head of MGM in Paris.[97]

By August 1937 tensions escalated further with a "possible boycott against M-G-M" throughout the country. Another Battle of Birmingham was brewing.[98] Loew's was in a more advantageous position in the Netherlands than Paramount had been in England, though. The company already had a "financial interest" in a new exhibition company that had taken over the Alhambra, Royal, and Corso cinemas in Amsterdam from the Royal cinema chain as well as the Capitol and City cinemas in Rotterdam. MGM films were also booked into the city's most heralded venue, the Tuschinski Theatre.[99] By December *Film Daily* reported that MGM's leases for the Royal, Corso, and Alhambra cinemas in Amsterdam had now been secured for a decade.[100] MGM's efforts to build another theater at the Frederiksplein, meanwhile, had also stalled.[101]

Like the example of Paramount in Birmingham, boycott threats from local (exhibitor) trade organizations were one of the only effective measures against American exhibition encroachment overseas. And by 1939 the NBB had grown even more protectionist. In addition to the ongoing denial of MGM's proposed cinema in Amsterdam, the federation also rejected a United Artists request to open a branch office and announced that MGM's "Metrotone News" had also been "banned because of existing competition in the newsreel field." Despite this, MGM and other American distributors/exhibitors were also card-carrying members of the NBB.[102] One additional reason Loew's may not have wanted to challenge the NBB is that the company's future in other markets like Germany was already in question. The possible closure of another territory would have hurt MGM's foreign revenues at a difficult time. (Spanish revenues, for example, had already plummeted during the recent civil war.)

The backlash against Loew's/MGM is noteworthy, though, because the company was not the only foreign entity operating cinemas in the Netherlands. By 1939 Ufa was operating its own cinemas in Amsterdam, Rotterdam, and The Hague while Ufa and Tobis were releasing up to sixty German films per year throughout the Netherlands.[103] In the end, like Paramount, in the face of local boycotts or opposition, the profits from foreign distribution still far outweighed foreign exhibition. For many countries and trade organizations, boycotting Hollywood films was their only leverage against those persistent American dreams of global cinema expansion. MGM never built a shop window in Amsterdam or any other Dutch city.

Warner Bros. Enters European Exhibition

For all of its protectionism, it was still England that remained the most hospitable and fertile ground for U.S. exhibitors. By the late 1930s Paramount was still operating more than a dozen cinemas throughout the United Kingdom, Fox was still benefiting from its investment in Gaumont-British, and Loew's was welcoming tens of thousands each week at the Empire and the adjacent Ritz (which it had reopened in December 1937) in London. (The 430-seat Ritz, previously a newsreel theater, served as a second-run, move-over house for MGM.[104]) RKO (Radio-Keith-Orpheum) and United Artists had also finally secured first-run outlets in London through leases.

It was Warner Bros., then, that remained without a single foreign shop window. In July 1937, confirming months of rumors, Warner Bros. announced it would finally build its "First 'Show Window' in Europe." The company planned to acquire Daly's Theater in Leicester Square—just a stone's throw from the Empire Theatre—and build a new $1.25 million cinema in its place. Early reports from *Film Daily* noted that "Warners were also interested in the French theater field with a view to 'Show window' extension" but no Paris or other Warner cinema was ever built.[105] Sam Morris, Warner Bros. International vice president, told *Film Daily* the following month that even though the company planned to build in London, "Warners are without plans for establishment of a British circuit and at present do not contemplate further acquisitions in Britain." The Warner Theatre, then, would be a true shop window cinema, not a stepping-stone to further real estate ventures. Devoid of a Parisian or another European cinema, *Film Daily* reported that the new Warner would be "the first W-B theater in foreign territory and will serve as a British-European show-window for U.S. Warner and First National product as well as the output of Warners' Teddington British studios."[106]

Warner Bros. completed its purchase of Daly's Theater in September 1937 from the Schlesingers, an internationally powerful pair of brothers (Isidore and M. A.) whose vaudeville and motion picture distribution and exhibition companies stretched from New York to London to Johannesburg (see part V).[107] Daly's Theater held its final curtain drop on September 25, 1937, and the 1,775-seat Warner Theatre, designed "of quiet architectural design," opened more or less on schedule one year later on October 12, 1938, with the Duke and Duchess of Kent on hand for the charity benefit premiere of *The Adventures of Robin Hood*.[108] The cinema was designed by E. A. Stone, who had been the principal architect of all four of Paramount's Astoria cinemas. Stone worked "closely" with Herman Maier, chief of theater construction for Warner Bros. Like many other British cinemas, the Warner Theatre was outfitted with both a café and a tearoom.[109] The last of the American shop windows to be built in Leicester Square, it would remain owned by, and the home of, Warner Bros. films for the next six decades. The Warner Bros. announcement briefly spurred Twentieth Century-Fox into considering its own new "show window" cinema, kicking off discussions with Gaumont-British for the sale of its eponymous Gaumont in Haymarket to Fox.[110] Amid the rumors, Sam Morris was careful to "spike" reports of a larger expansion in Europe beyond the construction of the Warner in London and a new agreement with the Apollo Theatre in Paris to become Warner's "show window" there.[111]

Paramount Recedes from Europe and Global Exhibition

One year earlier, in 1937, Oscar Deutsch's rapidly growing British Odeon Cinemas chain announced plans to build new deluxe cinemas in Leeds, Newcastle, and Manchester that would compete directly with Paramount's own cinemas. Allen Eyles writes that "this clearly prompted dialogue between David E. Rose, the British head of Paramount, and Deutsch over the possible sale or lease of Paramount's provincial cinemas to Odeon."[112] Two years later, on November 23,

1939, Paramount signed a lease agreement for seven of its cinemas—the Paramounts in Leeds, Newcastle, and Manchester, and all four Astorias—to Odeon for thirty-five years.[113] Deutsch picked up another valuable Paramount asset the following month when Earl St. John left the company to join Odeon in the management of its seven former Paramount cinemas.[114] In 1940 the three former Paramount cinemas were all renamed Odeon. The "stage staff, orchestras, bands and other acts" at all seven former Paramounts were fired in order to stay lean during the war years. Out of the ashes of the seven lease agreements came a much more important arrangement for Paramount: exclusive bookings of Paramount films in Odeon Cinemas—now the third-largest circuit in England—throughout the country beginning in September 1941.[115] Paramount retained its three other London cinemas as well as the Paramounts in Birmingham, Glasgow, and Liverpool for now.

Paramount's bookings at Odeon Cinemas, and Loew's and Fox's continued tie-ups with Gaumont-British, left Warner Bros. with few avenues for large chain distribution outside of ABC Cinemas and Granada Theatres.[116] The latter was run by producer-exhibitor Sidney Bernstein and in little need of American investment or takeover. ABC Cinemas, however, was ripe. In October 1940 John Maxwell, majority owner of ABC, died, leaving control of the cinema chain to his wife, Catherine. Warner Bros. sensed an opportunity. In August 1941, after months of negotiations, Warner purchased 50 percent of Maxwell's 4,014,000 ordinary shares in the Associated British Picture Corp. Ltd.[117] This provided Maxwell and Warner Bros. Pictures Ltd. equal representation on the ABPC board of directors.[118] Warner Bros.' British representative, Max Milder, now became joint managing director of Associated British Picture Corp. Ltd. as well as its Associated British Cinemas Ltd. subsidiary for a renewable period of ten years.[119] Warner Bros. now enjoyed joint management of ABC Cinemas, even though a Warner Bros. representative was only one of its seven board members.[120] The acquisition, though, was ill-timed. Warner's increased investment in foreign exhibition would now have to be largely redirected outside of Europe as the war expanded throughout Europe, Asia, and beyond. Besides the acquisition of the Park Theatre in Stockholm in July 1943, all of Warner's acquisitions and land purchases during this period were outside the immediate war zone in Auckland, Adelaide, Brisbane, Sydney, Tel Aviv, Cairo, Alexandria, Lima, and Mexico City.[121]

CHAPTER 3

A NEW BATTLEGROUND

U.S. Exhibitors Under Nazi Occupation, 1941–1945

Outside of England, nearly all Paramount and MGM European cinemas were systematically lost as the Nazis marched across these borders. In Belgium, for example, Belgian forces were quickly overrun by the Nazi invasion, and King Leopold III ordered the nation's surrender in May 1940.[1] Rene Poelmans, who joined MGM in 1931 and had been the manager of publicity for MGM's Belgian theaters since 1935, was called to the front by the Belgian army to fend off the invasion. He was captured in the disastrous Battle of the Lys in late May 1940 and became a German prisoner of war for the next five years.[2]

By late August the occupied, collaborationist Belgian government ordered MGM to cease distributing its films throughout the country. MGM's cinemas continued on, for a time, by playing non-U.S. films. MGM staff in Belgium— those who had not been killed or captured during the invasion—began leaving their posts.[3] American Consulate reports from Brussels on October 9, 1940, based on a response from Metro-Goldwyn-Mayer, S.A. director G. Trussart, noted that MGM had not shown any of its own films in its owned and operated cinemas since August 23 and that the Nazis had already seized twelve film prints. The rest of the company's film stock—minus five films unreturned from Belgian cinemas—had been placed under seal by German authorities. Most of MGM employees had now been laid off "except those absolutely necessary for operations and management of three theatres (Cameo, Queen's Hall and Forum) which are still working." MGM's cinemas were still operating under the safety of the U.S. Embassy, which had issued official protection certificates to Trussart on May 15, 1940, that covered all MGM property at its sales offices at 4–6 Rue des Plantes in Brussels, at the Cameo and Queen's Hall theaters in Brussels, and at Le Forum in Liège, Paramount Films, S.A. had done the same, and its films had also been banned since August 23 and placed under seal. All Paramount Belgium employees had been laid off except for Alfred Polis, chief accountant and commissaire of the Société Belge. Paramount's lone Belgian cinema, the Coliseum, was rented out to local concerns to alleviate its impossible circumstances.[4]

The Netherlands, too, fell almost immediately in May 1940, and with it Hollywood's influence in the market. German companies Ufa and Tobis immediately filled the vacuum. *Motion Picture Herald* observed a curious exception: while MGM, Paramount, and the other U.S. majors were squashed in the Netherlands, the RKO distribution office was able to operate almost unimpeded. RKO was reportedly acquiescent to whatever the Nazis desired in the Netherlands, since "all competition to RKO from other American film companies had been eliminated."[5] By January 1941, despite the Dutch film industry being "entirely reorganized since the Nazi occupation of Holland," RKO feature and short films were still being distributed throughout the country.[6]

The Nazi-occupied Dutch government also made no immediate effort to remove Fritz Strengholt—who had previously worked in Germany[7]—from the NBB where he served on the managing board, despite MGM's forced closure. "Ufa and Tobis, the German companies, now dominate this market," Philip de Schaap wrote. "They are the only companies releasing new product."[8] De Schaap later reported that "Holland's film trade was one of the first to be controlled by the arbitrary order of the invaders" with the NBB replaced by the Nazi-managed "Filmgilde," which prohibited the exhibition of all non-German films. The Filmgilde executed laws forbidding Jewish entry to cinemas and barred all Jewish distributors and exhibitors (like Tuschinski) from operating. Ufa and Tobis then carved up the Dutch market along with Nazi Odeon-Film, which distributed Czech, Hungarian, and Finnish films, and Centra-Film, which distributed children's and 16 mm films. Dutch studios were now commandeered for pro-German filmmaking.[9]

The Nazi invasion of France also took place in May 1940, and the brief battle was over by June. German films were foisted upon French exhibitors, although American films without controversial subject matter could still be found. Jan Letsch, a Dutch film representative working in France, later noted that films screened under the occupation were frequently met with "boos and cat-calls of Parisian audiences," which "forced managers to turn on the house lights."[10] The French underground also attempted to sabotage film premieres in Paris during the occupation. *Motion Picture Herald*, citing a report from singer-actress Lily Pons, reported that "whenever a new motion picture, play or opera was to make its debut top ranking officials would buyout [sic] the tickets. The underground would then print and sell thousands of additional tickets. When the time for the premiere arrived 10,000 Germans would be milling around the lobby of a theatre which could seat 1,500." A leader of the French underground remarked that "this would cause much bitterness and bad feeling among the Nazis."[11] Paramount was the last of the major American film companies still operating in Germany when it received orders from Nazi officials to vacate by September 12, 1940, and leave other occupied areas by October 1.[12] In April 1941 the Nazis formally seized the Paris offices of Paramount and other U.S. film companies despite protests by U.S. diplomats. Offices, company records, furniture, films, and other materials were all confiscated by the Nazis.[13] For France, Belgium, the Netherlands, and other European countries under occupation, Hollywood became a memory. Hollywood and its foreign cinemas were now on a bitter and long hiatus.

Le Paramount et La Résistance

There is enough material for many other books about U.S. film companies and their employees living, working, fighting, and dying overseas during World War II. American branch managers in Asia were interned in Japanese prison camps, Hollywood executives died in torpedo attacks visiting their foreign markets, European exhibition staff and partners ended up in concentration camps, and innumerable distribution, marketing, and exhibition personnel were conscripted into the war and died on the battlefield or the home front.

Much of this book deals with exhibitors, cinemas, executives, businesses, and their corresponding industrial and cultural transactions. In many cases, though, there is still scant information known about the key players who operated on the ground. While later chapters examine the importance of the Turnbulls in Australia and the Moodabes in New Zealand, information about Hollywood's early European surrogates is often difficult to discern. This is not true for some of Paramount's key exhibition staff in France before, during, and after World War II, however. In a story that reflected the travail of foreign sales and exhibition managers who found themselves under Japanese or German occupation during World War II, the experience of Paramount's theatrical staff in France began in the cinemas, extended to the front lines, and then back again, where its executives and its cinemas became part of the French Resistance.

The following history—a rather extraordinary case study of Hollywood's overseas staff under Nazi occupation—is based on numerous articles and photographs published during and after the war, by records held at Memorial de la Shoah, and by a trove of Ernest Bechet's medals which were photographed, certified, and auctioned in 2006 and then reauctioned in 2016.[14] Still, a complete narrative remains elusive. A fuller description of this history *was* sent to

Paramount International News in December 1944, but it was only excerpted at the time because it contained "confidential material" and was "so long that it could only be published serially."[15]

Some background is needed. In 1928 Andre Ullmann was appointed house manager of Le Paramount, the company's new Parisian shop window cinema.[16] Ullmann traveled to the United States in 1930 for a Paramount-Publix global sales convention, which cemented his relationship with Paramount's foreign office, then located in New York.[17] Later that year Ullmann was named general manager of Paramount's French and Belgian exhibition operations, in charge of all of Paramount's ten cinemas in France—one in each of the major cities—as well as others in Belgium, including the Colosseum Theatre in Brussels.[18] During the reorganization, Rene Lebreton, a French journalist who had visited Paramount's Hollywood studios while covering Maurice Chevalier's visit to Los Angeles in 1929, was appointed to be Ullmann's successor as the new manager of Le Paramount in Paris under Ullmann's overall direction.[19]

In 1935 Paramount merged its distributing and exhibiting operations into a new, $2 million French company, Films Paramount, that was "the largest subsidiary of any American film company on the continent."[20] The combination merged Société Immobilière du Vaudeville, which owned Le Paramount (which had been built inside the former Théâtre du Vaudeville), the distribution company Société Anonyme Française des Films Paramount, and Société des Grands Cinémas Français, which owned and operated Paramount's five additional cinemas remaining in France. All Paramount operations in France would now be under Films Paramount and under the direction of Fred W. Lange. Henri Klarsfeld continued to head distribution while Andre Ullmann continued to manage all of Paramount's French cinemas. Paramount's foreign head, John Hicks, still reflective of the domestic concerns over American cultural and industrial encroachment, told *Variety* that despite Paramount's venerable French exhibition chain, "We are not theatre owners here because we want to be exhibitors. Our theatres are intended to help distribution, to show our films and get publicity for them."[21]

In 1938, while still serving as general manager of Paramount's cinemas in France and Belgium, Ullmann's importance to the company grew when he was also appointed director of Paramount's French studio in Joinville.[22] As always, he remained intimately involved in the day-to-day operations of Le Paramount.[23] Rene Lebreton, while still managing Le Paramount, where he won several Quigley awards for showmanship, was promoted to assistant general manager of Paramount's French subsidiary under Ullmann in May 1939.[24] There was a critical reason to appoint such a successor; Ullmann was readying for possible war across the border, and Paramount needed a French heir apparent in case Ullmann was captured or killed. Ullmann, who had served in World War I for France and then helped sell Liberty Bonds throughout the United States, served on the Maginot Line for two months in 1938.[25] Two years later, on May 10, 1940, Germany invaded France. The campaign was quick, and the presiding French government fled Paris one month later. By June 14 the Nazis officially occupied Paris.

New American films were immediately blocked from importation to occupied France, but old Paramount and other Hollywood films that were free of anti-Axis content were still being shuttled to occupied and Vichy-controlled cinemas.[26] Wartime moviegoing in France was affected daily by nighttime curfews that cut short an evening's entertainment, and all exhibitors, distributors, and producers were required to have a license from the occupied Ministry of Information that could be revoked at any time for any reason.[27]

The human toll was far more dramatic. Jewish exhibitors, distributors, directors, producers, writers, actors, and others involved in film, radio, and the press were forced to leave their respective industries, stations, theaters, and studios in France.[28] Soon many would be rounded up and killed. Leon Siritzky, who was a key partner with Paramount on some of its French cinemas and owned one of the largest theater circuits in France, with seventy-five theaters, fled with his sons to the United States as the Nazis confiscated his business and installed pro-Nazi exhibitors who would show likeminded films.[29] In Holland, Abraham Tuschinski was sent to the Westerbork transit camp and then to Auschwitz, where he and nearly all of his relatives died. His business was confiscated by the Nazi-allied Filmgilde, and his eponymous theater renamed the Tivoli, wiping away its ethnic origins.[30] (Tuschinski's stunning 1921 cinema remains a tribute to his work as an exhibitor and is still one of Amsterdam's most famous attractions.)

Andre Ullmann left his post at Paramount in May 1940 and headed to the northern front. Like many others, he was captured by the German army and became a prisoner of war. Unlike his compatriots, though, he had a powerful ally working on his behalf behind the lines—Paramount—which still had contacts within the German government. *Variety* reported in November 1940, five months after Ullmann was imprisoned, that Paramount had finally learned of his whereabouts and began "using all its resources in an effort to secure [his] release" from a German prisoner-of-war camp.[31] While interned, Ullmann later told *Paramount International News*, he had "the opportunity to favorably influence 1,500 fellow officers by delivering a series of 10 lectures on the United States" that were based on his work for the film company and his many travels to the States over the past decade and a half. "The lectures were favorably received," he later told *Paramount International News*, "especially my details on American life, particularly that of Broadway and film and theatre activity." Due to Paramount's connections and their effort to free him, Ullmann was brought before the prison camp commandant to ensure he was in good health and provide a report back to Paramount International staff in New York.[32]

From June 1940 onward, Paramount's executive offices and its cinemas in France remained under Paramount control (albeit under Nazi-occupied regulations and careful observation). Finally, on April 16, 1941, Nazi soldiers forcibly occupied Paramount's production and distribution offices—and those of the other remaining American film companies—and told the French staff to leave.[33] The occupied government also placed a block on the French bank accounts of U.S. companies and planned to use American-owned studios, labs, offices, and cinemas in France for the "distribution of [Nazi] propaganda films."[34] Theater staff at Le Paramount and other company cinemas in France now worked under the yoke of the Nazis who requisitioned the cinema, divorcing the company's executives and its box office from Hollywood. While the cinema's name remained the same throughout the war, Le Paramount was no longer an American shop window but an occupied one—at least in outward appearance.[35]

Vive La Résistance

Andre Ullmann was released from a German prison camp in August 1941 "when the Germans gave what was supposed to be liberty to all World War I veterans" and the now former Paramount exec headed back to France.[36] He returned to Paris where he began organizing a cell of the French Resistance that involved every staff member of the cinema.[37] Ernest Bechet, who had been in charge of projection at Le Paramount and all Paramount cinemas in France and Belgium since 1927, later noted that the theater became "a center of the resistance movement" under Ullmann.[38]

From all appearances to the Nazis and the occupied government, Le Paramount was a loyal wartime movie house, dutifully carrying the Nazi flag.[39] But, Paul Perez later reported in *Boxoffice* magazine, Le Paramount was actually "a secret transmission center of the wartime underground movement." Here I quote Perez at length:

> Members of the staff, defying watchful German troops and the Gestapo, daily risked their lives as active resistance personnel.... Allied airmen who had parachuted to safety were brought to Paris secretly by the underground and given refuge in the theatre. There the concealed flyers ate and slept, and even watched movies, while uniformed Nazis seated within spitting range also viewed the French programs. The theatre was a storage place for resistance arms and explosives. Rene Lebreton, managing the house under German scrutiny, purposely overlooked all underground activity. Resistance mail cleared through the theatre. Intelligence was reported there and typed up by an underground operative working in the theatre as an usherette. Another usherette made frequent trips to Normandy, delivering and collecting underground documents. Throughout the occupation a uniformed German non-com was assigned to watch the theatre—but he never realized what was going on.[40]

Le Paramount, *Paramount International News* later reported, also became "a clearing house for mail and information."

> Two of the ushershettes [sic]—Gisele Willocq and Gisele Mondini—were the collectors and distributors of mail, documents, [and] orders.... Another Paramount usherette, Madame Woittequand, safely hid 20 Allied airmen in her apartment; and [projectionist Ernest] Bechet's office in Le Paramount was also a safety hatch for 4 U.S., 2 Australian and one Canadian airmen. Madame Mondini... gave refuge to five U.S. airmen.... Then, too, there was... Suzy Dabadie, theatre department secretary since 1925. She was Paris liaison for Mr. Ullmann, and rendered tremendous service.[41]

International Projectionist magazine later remarked that "mention of Le Paramount in Paris evokes memories of World War II when this theatre served as a 'drop' for escaped Allied fliers on their way to the Spanish border. Entrance was effected over the roofs of adjoining buildings into the projection room, on the door of which appeared the peremptory notice in French to the English equivalent of 'Extreme Danger—Explosive. Positively No Admittance.'"[42]

Like Ullmann, Bechet had also been sent to the front in 1940, serving in the French Third Army, and had been captured at Lorraine and held in a German prisoner-of-war camp for more than two years.[43] In October 1942, while interned, Bechet learned that the Nazi government planned to release all members of the French Navy incarcerated in Germany.[44] He destroyed his army documents and obtained forged papers that claimed he had served with an antiaircraft unit on a torpedo boat. A month later, "Bechet was back in France as an active member of the underground."[45] Working once again at Le Paramount, Bechet was put in charge of wireless and other communications at the theater. Code named "Rebelle," Perez writes that Bechet became "chief operative in charge of northwestern France" for the Marco Polo Resistance unit where "intelligence was passed to American OSS men in the Dordogne region, a radio communication system sent... data in code; mail went back and forth between London and the Continent by plane, and British aircraft also brought money for use in bribery and for sustenance."[46]

Bechet and Le Paramount's Resistance operations went undetected for almost two years until June 1944, when the local Gestapo arrested a member of the Marco Polo cell in Nice. Their prisoner was tortured and subsequently revealed information about a member of the Resistance in Paris who he believed to be the manager of Le Paramount. Andre Ullmann was in southwestern France at the time, performing intelligence work, when his secretary, Suzy Dabadie, sent word that three cars full of Gestapo had arrived at the theater on the evening of June 23, 1944, to arrest the manager of Le Paramount. Inside, Bechet watched helplessly as the Nazis hauled manager Rene Lebreton and another employee out of the cinema and brought them to Gestapo headquarters in Paris. Neither Lebreton nor the other employee fit the description of the suspect, however. The Gestapo, realizing this, subsequently returned to Le Paramount, saw Bechet, and took him in. Bechet subsequently "plead[ed] for the release of Lebreton"[47] and was then "tortured and beaten" over a five-day period.[48] Lebreton was eventually released and sent back to Le Paramount.[49]

Bechet, however, was not so lucky. Over the next two months, he was beaten and tortured eighteen times in an effort to extract information about the resistance unit. He was also thrice led out from his cell to (supposedly) be shot in an attempt to frighten him into talking. He never wavered. On August 15, 1944, just days before Paris was liberated, Bechet was herded into the last Nazi train deportation from the Pantin station and sent to the Buchenwald concentration camp. The hellish, five-day train ride without food or water was only the beginning of their 850-kilometer journey.[50] Bechet would remain in Buchenwald for nearly a year.[51]

HEROIC PARAMOUNTEERS. Madame Gisèle Willocq (left), Ernest Bechet, and Madame Gisèle Mondini. All are mentioned on this page. All of them wear La Croix de Guerre, Bechet's bearing the highest distinction - the Army palm.

FIGURE 3.1 The two Gisèles and Ernest Bechet featured in *Paramount International News*.

Bechet and Buchenwald

Four days after Bechet was sent to Buchenwald, the French Resistance led a citywide revolt against the Nazi occupation in Paris on August 19, and the city was finally liberated by American and French troops on August 25. A new French government was organized the following day. Rene Lebreton remained at the cinema during this period while Andre Ullmann shifted his work from Resistance fighter in Paris to military commander in the French southwest, part of the French Forces of the Interior.[52] The liberation of Paris, and soon all of France, reopened the lines of communication with Paramount executives in New York that had been completely severed for years. *Paramount International News* gleefully wrote to its global colleagues that many of its key executives and theater employees had survived the war and Nazi occupation.[53] By September Paramount's Paris sales office was reopened.[54]

With the Nazis finally gone, Le Paramount also became part of the Paramount film company once again. The cinema, which had served as "the secret key center of the resistance movement" was now, according to Paul Perez, the "first French theatre to illustrate its front after [the] departure of the Nazis."[55] Ernest Bechet, for the rest of 1944 and well into 1945, remained imprisoned in Buchenwald.

The U.S. Third Army finally entered Buchenwald on April 11, 1945.[56] Traveling alongside the Army unit were cameramen from various newsreel companies and services during a unique period of U.S. government news censorship and footage-sharing. Among those who entered Buchenwald that day was Gaston Madru, the French cameraman for MGM's *News of the Day* whose technique of hiding a camera among empty bottles in his bicycle basket enabled him to take images of occupied France.[57] Madru provided Ernest Bechet with a new set of clothes and organized his release from the camp and his travel back to Paris in a jeep.[58] Madru, who knew Bechet from their time together at Paramount, captured his drawn appearance in a photograph only days after being liberated.[59]

Before leaving for the front again with American general George S. Patton, Madru asked Bechet to bring his camera negatives and prints to his wife in France for safekeeping. Bechet returned to Paris where he learned that Madru had just been shot and killed in Leipzig by a Nazi sniper, his body identified by Paramount's newsreel cameraman, John Dored.[60] Madru's death was mourned by the entire newsreel community and was a featured part of the April 24, 1945, edition of MGM-Hearst's *News of the Day*.[61] Eight decades later, Madru's newsreel footage from Buchenwald continues to be screened as a vital source of visible evidence and was a constituent part of a 1945 compilation film, *German Concentration Camps Factual Survey*, that was, for a wide range of political reasons, released to the public only in 2014. The film was overseen by

FIGURE 3.2 Ernest Bechet (left) upon release from Buchenwald. (*Paramount International News*)

producer and (Granada Theatres exhibitor) Sidney Bernstein with assistance from Bernstein's frequent filmmaking partner, Alfred Hitchcock.[62]

Liberation

Ernest Bechet, saved from the ashes of Buchenwald, slowly returned to his position at Le Paramount in May 1945, needing six additional months to physically recover from his ordeal.[63] He was one of the lucky ones.

France celebrated V-E Day on May 8, 1945. The front of Le Paramount, Paul Perez wrote, "proudly bore a V two-stories high, and that night it was the first picture house in liberated France to blossom forth in a dazzling blaze of 'premiere' lights—a theatre at peace, its brilliant war record unique in theatrical history." In June Gen. Charles de Gaulle awarded Andre Ullmann's regiment its "flag" and a parade of "liberating troops" swept by Le Paramount in salute.[64] French general Jean de Lattre de Tassigny—who had led the French First Army in the allied landing in Southern France in 1944, commanded allied forces in their push across France and into Germany and Austria, and was the French representative at Berlin for the German surrender on May 8—later visited Le Paramount in March 1946 to "convey the French Army Command's profound thanks to the Paramounteers who played so noble and heroic a part in France's liberation."[65] In the ensuing years, Ernest Bechet was awarded the "Legion of Honour, Croix de Guerre, Medaille Militaire, Voluntary Combatants cross, Resistance Voluntary Combatants cross, French Resistance medal, 1939–45 French war medal, French Resistance medal for those deported, Voluntary service medal for Free French, medal for escaped Prisoners of War, French combatants cross, French medal for the Rhineland and Ministry of Work and Social Security medal."[66] He was also given a George VI Kings Medal for Courage and an award plaque from Paramount Europe, among many other commendations. The Croix de Guerre and the French Resistance Medal, both bestowed in 1946, were among "the foremost decorations in France for 'resistance' and 'underground' work."[67] Ullmann was similarly honored after the war. In addition, of the sixteen Le Paramount usherettes who had worked against the Nazis during the war, Gisèle Willocq and Gisèle Mondini were chosen to receive the Croix de Guerre for their service.[68] Paramount's U.S. executives also sent telegrams of commendation and awards, and Adolph Zukor visited the cinema to congratulate and be photographed with its staff. Paramount president Barney Balaban, Paramount International president George Weltner, and Paramount European head Robert Schless wired Andre Ullmann in August 1945 that the company was "MUCH ENRICHED DURING DARK DAYS BY LOYALTY OF FRENCH PARAMOUNTEERS WHO IN ARMY AND UNDERGROUND FOUGHT AND STRUGGLED WITH US AGAINST

FORCES OF DARKNESS. ALTHOUGH THERE ALWAYS LASTED CLOSE RELATIONSHIP, WE FEEL THAT THOSE BONDS ARE NOW STRONGER THAN EVER."[69]

Après La Guerre

With the war now over, the company and the global film industry slowly resumed its prewar manifestations. Weltner told *Variety* that Paramount would now, once again, "go in for foreign theatre building" as soon as "conditions permit."[70] The company had eleven cinemas in the region before the war but had only three operating cinemas in France and one bombed-out cinema in Brussels.[71] During his trips to Paris in late 1945 to meet with Schless, Weltner was "amazed at the fine condition of the Paramount theatre in Paris despite the war ravages. It's still a showplace in the French capital," he told *Variety*.[72] Paramount was the only U.S. film company operating cinemas in postwar Paris and remained, according to *Variety*, "the pace-setter for local exhibs."[73]

Ullmann left Paramount in June 1946 for an uncertain future. Rene Lebreton once more took over the reins.[74] Ernest Bechet's tenure, by contrast, was far longer. After continuing to head projection for all of Paramount's French and Belgian cinemas, he became assistant technical manager in France from 1948 to 1954 and served as Paramount's chief technical manager there from 1955 to 1961.[75] The theater remained a source of immense pride for the studio in the ensuing years, with *Paramount International News* writing in 1949 that it hoped "a permanent souvenir of this gallant work will someday be on display in Le Paramount in order that generations to come may know of the part that the theatre played." Paramount's internal magazine also printed another honor, this one a citation from General Eisenhower, for Ernest Bechet: "a man who put his God, his country and his people before all other things in life—including his own."[76]

Le Paramount had opened in 1927 as an American cultural embassy and an outpost of Hollywood in the very capital of France. After the war the cinema shifted from a venue solely associated with Hollywood to one associated as well with the French Resistance. As the decades drifted on, however, Le Paramount's historical importance was forgotten even as it remained the Parisian home of Paramount films. That legacy was still evident six decades later as the cinema, multiplexed now as the Paramount-Opera, remains a key Parisian film venue. French moviegoers still patronize the cinema today, nearly a century after it opened. Evidence of its continued prominence is seen in a May 2020 *Deadline* article about the reopening of French cinemas amid the COVID-19 pandemic that prominently featured a glistening nighttime photo of one cinema—the Gaumont Opera, né Le Paramount—a still emblematic Parisian house for Hollywood films.[77]

CHAPTER 4

POSTWAR EUROPE AND THE LEGACY OF HOLLYWOOD CINEMAS, 1945–1993

At Le Paramount and other postwar shop windows in Europe, American sensationalism and panache continued to be paired with local employees and aesthetics for a hybridized experience that celebrated a renewed sense of nationalism and yet a global desire for the glitz and glam sold by Hollywood in the postwar period. Le Paramount and other cinemas like the Empire in London served as a launching pad for the postwar expansion of American-owned circuits around the world. Victory over the Nazis had made the world safe again for Hollywood films and its global cinemas. That war was over. The next battles were just beginning.

In Amsterdam, *Motion Picture Herald* journalist Philip de Schaap emerged from his hiding spot in "an ancient cellar room" after fleeing there with his wife after his mother and brother and his wife's parents were all captured by the notorious Green Police that rounded up Jews and other targets of the Nazis and their Dutch collaborators. From September 10, 1942, until the end of the war, de Schaap and his wife crouched and slept in a small space that was "well concealed" inside a home built in 1630. "I could not stand upright," he reported after the war, "and we got fresh air through a very small window. We spoke only in whispers. In that cellar we passed our lives until the conclusion of the war. We should never have believed that it could happen to us. That we survived it is as a dream for us. Now we start all over again."[1] Like many, de Schaap returned to his work life, but his personal life was permanently altered. Exhibitor Abraham Tuschinski did not return. He had been hauled off to Westerbork during the war and then murdered in Auschwitz.

The NBB quickly reconstituted its power and, the *Motion Picture Herald* observed in March 1946, the organization was once again among the "theatre combines which have the effect of monopolies."[2] Fritz Strengholt had divorced his Jewish wife under Nazi occupation in Holland (she was later sent to a concentration camp[3]), and now, after departing MGM, he owned the "most important first run theatres in Dutch key cities" at war's end. During the occupation and subsequent liberation, Strengholt had managed to become the manager of two important distributing companies, Nova-Film and Nerderla Film, importing British and French films into the Dutch market. "Mr. Strengholt," de Schaap noted, "is expected to play an important role in the future development of the Dutch industry . . . [as] a member of the managing board of the Dutch Motion Picture Federation."[4] Strengholt would not continue as MGM's manager. He was now an important independent player that the Americans would have to negotiate with.

Belgium and Switzerland: A Study in Postwar Contrasts

Belgium had been a key focus of Loew's/MGM foreign exhibition before the war, and the company reacquired their Belgian cinemas shortly after the conflict ended. Rene Poelmans, MGM's former publicity director for its Cameo and Queen's Hall theaters, returned from the German prisoner-of-war camp where he had been held since 1940 and resumed his previous position, overseeing marketing for both of MGM's theaters, in July 1945.[5] MGM also expanded its Belgian circuit, adding to the Cameo and Queen's Hall by acquiring both the 2,500-seat Scala in Antwerp and Le Forum in Liège.[6] In France MGM added the Plaza in Toulouse, increasing the number of its global cinemas to forty-two.[7] Liège's Forum and Toulouse's Plaza had both been MGM cinemas before World War II but had been confiscated by each country's wartime governments. MGM, "after the untangling of legalities," reacquired both. The Forum and Scala theaters had both been damaged during the war, forcing new renovations.[8] Le Forum reopened on March 22, 1947, while the Scala was "completely rebuilt and re-equipped" and renamed Metro, becoming MGM's "second showcase" cinema in Belgium when it reopened on April 11, 1947.[9] Arthur Loew, president of Loew's International, was on hand for the Metro's opening premiere with the film *Thrill of a Romance*.[10]

Belgium represented an open market for Hollywood after the war, and its investment in the country's cinematic infrastructure seemed welcomed by a shattered industry and nation. Switzerland, however, whose cinema chains and distribution companies were not hobbled by physical and psychic damage, responded to MGM's new encroachment with a backhand. In November 1946, MGM bought both the Rialto in Geneva and the Capitol in

Lausanne.[11] These seemingly innocuous purchases set off a firestorm that mimicked MGM's prewar battles in the Netherlands and Paramount's earlier issues in England. Much of the conflict centered on Loew's and MGM's repeated assertions that the two companies were separate entities and that the purchase of cinemas by Loew's International did not constitute a vertical integration with MGM. This explanation, thirteen years before the divorcement of Loew's and MGM, fell flat.

Officials from the Swiss Film Distributors Association—which represented thirty-seven Swiss film distributors including MGM—contacted the American minister at Bern. The association's chief concern was not only the American encroachment into Swiss exhibition but that these cinemas would be able to book MGM films without fair negotiations for competing exhibitors in each city. MGM's Swiss subsidiary replied on November 26: "(1) that it had acquired no theater and had no intention of doing so; (2) that Loew's International Corporation had purchased the theaters in question; and (3) that 'we wish to point out that Metro-Goldwyn-Mayer, S.A., has no intention to retain for itself any exclusive right for M-G-M films in the Rialto [and] the Capitole; these two houses will continue to give other distributors the possibility to place films.'"[12] This supposed bifurcation of divisions was undercut by the fact that Jack Guggenheim was both the manager of Metro-Goldwyn-Mayer and had also represented Loew's International Corp. during the purchase negotiations. Further undercutting the assertion of a wall between MGM and Loew's in their international markets was that Metro-Goldwyn-Mayer was "a wholly-owned subsidiary of Loew's International Corporation," according to U.S. State Department documents. The American minister in Bern reminded State Department officials that "each member [of the Swiss Film Distributors Association] is a signatory of the Association's Statutes, Article 2 of which forbids its members, under penalty of expulsion, 'to participate directly or indirectly in any enterprise seeking to combine cinematographic interests in Switzerland' and requires them to 'oppose all foreign economic penetration into the trade and distribution of films in Switzerland.'" The minister's report added, "The Loew interests are accused of seeking to combine their production and distribution activities with exhibition, thus completing a vertical trust in Switzerland."[13]

A vote by the general meeting of the association was taken on January 14, 1947, and Metro-Goldwyn-Mayer was found guilty of violating its Article 2 and "imposed a penalty of three months suspension, besides a fine of 5,000 Swiss francs"—the maximum penalty allowed. The threat of a longer suspension or even a possible expulsion remained. The American minister at Bern wrote in his missive to the U.S. State Department that

> Mr. Guggenheim has called at the Legation several times to discuss the matter and has stated that he and Arthur Loew were aware of the fact that purchase

of the theaters would expose the Swiss branch to expulsion from the Association; that, after consulting local counsel, Mr. Loew decided to proceed nevertheless, in order to expand the outlet for their films in Geneva and Lausanne; that Mr. Loew has instructed him (Mr. Guggenheim) to file an appeal against the Association's decision and engage the best lawyers in Switzerland.[14]

The Swiss government, despite American requests, ultimately sided with the Swiss Film Distributors Association, and the punishment was upheld.[15]

Over the next two years, Loew's International and Metro-Goldwyn-Mayer worked out an informal agreement whereby Loew's would divest the Rialto and the Capitole. In February the Swiss Film Distributors Association created a special committee to negotiate MGM's transfer of the cinemas with representatives of Loew's International Corp.[16] By March the American Legation at Bern wrote that Guggenheim had informed the legation that the final settlement called for Loew's International to divest its two Swiss cinemas.[17] Loew's ended up spending SF65,000 in fines and compensation and was suspended from all activities for three weeks beginning May 6, 1949. The dustup, negotiations, and funds transacted were important enough for Arthur Loew to fly to Zurich for the final agreements.[18] The entire affair was a reminder that purchasing cinemas in foreign countries, even after the war, could generate political, trade, and financial issues for American film companies. It was also a reminder, once again, that American film distributors were welcome to supply indigenous cinemas with product abroad. American film exhibitors, however, were often seen and treated as invaders.

British Foxes

England, by contrast to Switzerland, once again remained a comparatively open market for American film exhibitors after World War II. London shop window cinemas like the Plaza (Paramount), Empire (MGM), and Warner flourished during this period, and by the 1950s additional U.S. film companies sought to open their own shop window cinemas nearly three decades after the first had opened. There were new technological and corporate reasons for this expansion.

Twentieth Century-Fox had two primary purposes for such a move. First, the consent decree in the United States had caused U.S. film companies to split up, divorcing their exhibition chains from their production and distribution enterprises. This settlement only affected *domestic* exhibition. In the case of Loew's Inc., for example, Loew's Theatres became a North American exhibition company only while Metro-Goldwyn-Mayer retained and continued operating the company's overseas cinemas after their corporate detachment in

1959. For Twentieth Century-Fox, the U.S. company divested its own domestic cinemas, and the new company became known as National Theatres. Twentieth Century-Fox, like Paramount and Warner Bros., maintained its overseas exhibition empires and expanded its overseas cinema holdings in a bid to drive up international revenue in addition to its domestic and international distribution operations.

Fox had another reason for exhibition expansion by 1953: new cinemas meant new outlets for CinemaScope in the company's drive for worldwide technological adoption. The company told its shareholders that it expressly leased the 1,100-seat Carlton Theatre from Paramount and the Odeon Marble Arch from Odeon Cinemas "in order to have two strategically located extended first-run showcases for our CinemaScope pictures in London."[19] The following year Fox acquired the 1913-era Rialto Theatre and installed CinemaScope projectors and a corresponding twenty-eight-foot CinemaScope screen. The extensive renovation of the cinema, which required only a twelve-day closure, was carried out by an old name, Verity and Beverley, the architecture firm (and the two architects) responsible for the Plaza, Carlton, and other Paramount cinemas that had opened in the 1920s and 1930s in Birmingham, Glasgow, Leeds, Liverpool, Manchester, and Paris.[20]

In 1958 Twentieth Century-Fox added another key cinema in Plymouth, the Drake, its first new build in England. The cinema heralded its place in "the task of rebuilding Plymouth" and as the home of "CinemaScope pictures." Multiple pages of the Drake's opening program were dedicated to the "Pioneers of CinemaScope." Another corporate promotion was its inclusion of "British Movietone News in Every Programme."[21]

Months later, on February 4, 1959, Columbia Pictures opened its first shop window in London as well—the aptly named 734-seat Columbia Theatre— "the first new cinema to open in London's West End since before the War" and "the first cinema ever owned by our company," according to M. J. Frankovsch, managing director of Columbia Pictures Corp. Ltd.[22] As cinema historian Allen Eyles writes, "Although the cinema opened with the Columbia name, its first attraction, *Gigi*, came from another studio, MGM."[23]

MGM and Loew's International—still three years away from divorce—were similarly busy in the mid-1950s. The company announced plans in 1956 to build a "representative exhibition outlet in every key city of West Germany, under its theatre expansion program," beginning with the takeover of the Waterloo Theatre in Hamburg.[24] By the end of the year another "M-G-M Theatre"—the company's fifty-sixth abroad—opened in Berlin.[25] It was a stark reminder of how much had changed in (West) Germany in just over a decade.

Loew's also set its sights on opening cinemas in Italy. As early as 1947 *Motion Picture Herald* noted "rumors" about MGM opening "a big modern theatre in Via Nazionale" in Rome with four thousand seats.[26] This was never built. In 1956, just weeks before the opening of MGM's new cinema in Berlin, Loew's International reopened the Astra in Milan, Italy, on November 30, 1956, as the Metro-Astra.²⁷ The company also continued its global expansion of drive-ins with the new Rome Auto Cine, a joint venture of MGM and a local Italian firm, which opened in August 1957 with space for 750 cars and, rather unique to Europe, 250 scooters. American and Italian tastes were commingled at the concession stand, with American standards like popcorn, hot dogs, and Coca-Cola products for sale alongside proper coffee options like espressos and cappuccinos.²⁸

Shop Window Conversions

Back in England, just blocks from the Columbia Theatre, MGM also decided to revamp the Empire Theatre for the second half of the twentieth century and reopened the vastly renovated cinema on December 19, 1962.²⁹

The mid to late 1960s, by contrast, were a lean time for Hollywood and its overseas exhibition, especially as MGM faltered and other American film companies were hit by declining domestic and foreign revenues given the rollout of television across the world after 1960 and a slate of films that were increasingly out of touch or time. One of the increasingly rare new builds was in Amsterdam, where Twentieth Century-Fox, in a co-equal partnership with Nationale Bio-scooponderneming N.V. (NABIO)—avoiding problems with the NBB—opened the Rembrandtpleintheater in Amsterdam on August 31, 1966.³⁰ The Rembrandtpleintheater joined two Fox-owned and -operated cinemas already operating in Rotterdam and The Hague.³¹

Fox also added to its small UK circuit, operating four cinemas in London well into the 1970s.³² The company also attempted to expand into France in 1974 by acquiring a 50 percent interest in the Meric circuit, with fifty-two screens in twelve venues across the country.³³ The newly merged French subsidiary would be named Foxmeric and, the *Independent Film Journal* remarked, "constitutes a basis for future expansion of Fox's theatre activities in France and elsewhere in Europe."³⁴ The deal ultimately fell through in September 1974 over "final terms."³⁵ Instead, in mid-1975 Twentieth Century-Fox leased the Weinzeile Theatre in Vienna, Austria, and Streit's in Hamburg, Germany, while continuing to maintain a 50 percent interest in their Dutch chain.³⁶ While most companies were scaling back their foreign exhibition investments, Twentieth Century-Fox was still looking for new opportunities, primed for the unexpected windfall of *Star Wars* two years later.

Paramount's international division also made some noise in 1967 when it announced plans to, like MGM's renovation of the Empire, reconstruct the Plaza cinema after four decades of cinemagoing. Following the trendline of the era, the Plaza was split in two—a new 972-seat Paramount cinema downstairs, with the cinema finally boasting that name, and another 820-seat Plaza cinema upstairs in the former balcony.[37] At its temporary closure, Paramount brought back Bert Herbert, the Plaza's original stage manager; Charles Smart, its original organist; and Barbara Aitken, one of the theater's first Plaza Tiller Girls, for a nostalgic touch.[38] As with the renovation of the old Rialto, the firm of Verity & Beverley was hired to separate the cinema into a twin.[39] The Paramount + Plaza reopened on June 21, 1968.[40]

The Plaza upstairs was renamed in 1972 as "Universal" after Paramount and Universal merged their foreign distribution operations into the new Cinema International Corp. (CIC). Paramount's Canadian chain, Famous Players, briefly operated the theater for the now-dissolved Paramount global circuit. Meanwhile, the Paramount name—finally branded onto the Plaza—never really stuck, and the whole cinema was renamed again in 1975. "Start saying the PLAZA—again," an advertisement for the May 15, 1975, rebranding announced. "People have never stopped calling the Paramount and Universal in Lower Regent Street the Plaza. So we have renamed our two cinemas the Plaza 1 and 2. Now we'll all be using the right name."[41]

MGM, in the waning days of its own foreign exhibition business, also renovated its Ritz in Leicester Square, making it, according to *Kinematograph Weekly*, an "extremely attractive first-run theatre, with the latest technical equipment, new seating, and improved sightlines."[42] The four-hundred-seat Ritz reopened on May 21, 1970. The Warner West End, after a previous "£146,000 refurbishment scheme" in 1964, also received the Paramount + Plaza treatment in 1970 after an extreme renovation created "two new ultra-modern cinemas on the site of the old Warner Theatre" in November 1970.[43] Four years later the theater was split up again, creating the Warner West End 1, 2 and 3, which reopened on September 26, 1974.[44]

Corporate Hollywood and European Exhibition

This book examines the foreign exhibition operations of Hollywood film companies overseas. The 1970s and 1980s, by contrast to the previous half-century, were far more complex in terms of conglomeration and joint foreign operations between Hollywood "studios" and other investors and companies. CIC, United Cinemas International (UCI), and other U.S.-based exhibition conglomerates must be examined here but must also be placed in context. For the sake of clarity and consistency, I outline below the machinations of some of these companies, such as CIC and UCI, but focus more intently on Warner Bros. International Theatres (WBIT), which was a singularly owned and operated cinema chain in line with previous iterations of Hollywood's global exhibition empires.

By 1970 the global film industry was lagging. Domestic box office in the United States had cratered, causing great concern at studios like Paramount and MGM. To lower overhead, Paramount and Universal, now owned respectively by conglomerates Gulf & Western and MCA Inc., created Cinema International Corp. (CIC), a vast distribution company that would jointly distribute Paramount and Universal films overseas with branch exchanges around the world. This would, of course, reduce employee overhead, real estate leases, and operating expenses through "the consolidation of sales forces, backroom operations, shipping, billing, computerization, etc."[45] CIC merged and then thinned their combined two thousand worldwide executives, shippers, and other personnel. Further cost savings were derived by placing CIC headquarters in Amsterdam rather than in London to save on corporate taxes. Joint heads of the company, Henri Michaud from Paramount and Arthur Abeles from Universal, traveled back and forth from Amsterdam and London, but all missives and filings were "datelined" from Amsterdam.[46] CIC formally launched on July 20, 1970, with Gulf & Western's Charles Bluhdorn and MCA's Lew Wasserman rotating the role of CIC chairman each year.[47]

By 1973 CIC was successful enough to begin leasing film and television rights and distribute all content overseas for the beleaguered MGM studio in both "foreign theatrical and television markets" for the next ten years. CIC also purchased all of MGM's foreign physical assets for $17.5 million that included MGM's remaining thirty-seven foreign cinemas, half of which were in South Africa and jointly owned with Film Trust. (The circuit there was subsequently renamed CIC-Film Trust.) The other nineteen cinemas were wholly controlled by MGM, including four that were leased (including London's Empire and Ritz) and another fifteen that were owned by MGM and principally located in South America and Egypt.[48]

The purchase of MGM's cinemas was a turning point for CIC. The company had been principally a distribution outlet until then. In January 1974 *Variety* reported that CIC now had "ambitious plans for the theatres in both hemispheres" and planned to make these cinemas "substantially enhanced by conversion, where feasible, into multiple sites (twins, troikas, quartets) under the umbrella of major realestate [sic] development programs—office shopping—entertainment complexes that would tie in local business partners."[49] By September CIC named Victor Hoare, previously Columbia Pictures vice president of Europe and then head of CIC operations in South Africa, as vice president in charge of theater operations for all of CIC, then headquartered in Amsterdam. The circuit had already grown to forty-two cinemas exhibiting films now from Paramount, Universal, and MGM.[50] The *Independent Film*

Journal remarked upon Hoare's ascension that "theatre acquisitions have become an important part of CIC," with further expansion planned for South Africa and the Netherlands.[51] In 1976, after operating a cinema in Amsterdam, CIC bought the Condor cinema chain in Brazil and its eleven cinemas, bringing CIC's site count up to fifty-eight.[52] Through the combination of Paramount and MGM's exhibition sites in England, for example, CIC ended up owning and operating both MGM's former Empire and Paramount's Plaza, the two key cinemas that launched the shop window / foreign exhibition boom half a century earlier.

It is worth noting—while not dwelling upon—the innumerable exceptions to any notion of a unified CIC that approached all territories equally. These three Hollywood majors—Paramount, Universal, and MGM—each had different policies for distribution and exhibition in different markets. In France, for example, Paramount was still working with a very old, pre–World War II partner—the Siritzky family—in operating Paramount cinemas in France. Jo Siritzky was now the president of Parafrance, one of the country's top cinema chains that was increasingly building "multiples"—multiplexes—across the country. In 1976 alone, Parafrance added a dozen new "multiples" across the country and renovated the Triomphe cinema in the Champs-Elysées in 1977 by adding seven additional screens and dubbing the eight-screen multiplex "Paramount City." Despite Paramount's relationship with CIC and that company's exhibition of Paramount films as well, Parafrance was 50 percent owned by Paramount but did not book CIC (Paramount, Universal, and MGM) product. The Paramount–Siritzky circuit, then, was both a legacy of the Paramount–Siritzky relationship, a brand-building opportunity, and a fifty-year profit center for the American film company. As Jo Siritzky noted, with the expansion of Parafrance, the "Paramount name is now emblazoned all over France." Parafrance also differed in its programming from CIC's circuit in the mid to late 1970s as some of its screens were booked with Hollywood films while others booked softcore films such as the *Emmanuelle* series and other French, international, art, and adult films.[53] Paramount's history could also be seen in England in CIC's interest in booking one of the auditoriums in the company's old Plaza Theatre, now a fourplex known as "The Picture Palace" and booking classic Paramount films from its vaults. "The company wants to let the public see their favorite old movies in the way they're supposed to be seen," a CIC rep noted at the time.[54]

CIC grossed over $145 million in global revenues in its 1977–1978 fiscal year from global film and television distribution as well as through its global exhibition circuit.[55] The company generated $293 million in 1978–1979, $220 million in 1979–1980, and $235 million in 1980–1981, making CIC the largest film distributor in the world. The company now operated seventy screens around the world, twenty-nine in Africa, twenty-eight in Latin America, and eight in the United Kingdom and employing roughly 2,400 workers. Its distribution apparatus had also grown with joint CIC–Warner operations in various territories, joint operations with Columbia Pictures in East Africa, and distribution agreements for Warner Bros. films in Jamaica and Columbia films in Uruguay.[56] Later that year, CIC announced a larger merger with MGM and United Artists and the creation of an even larger conglomerate, United International Pictures, which distributed films from Paramount, Universal, MGM, and United Artists beginning on November 1, 1981.[57]

As one more example of how complicated the foreign market became, Cinema International Corp. did continue on as an exhibitor known as the CIC Theatre Group. By 1987, the CIC chain extended from Europe to South America to Australia.[58] In 1989, after selling its South African CIC-Metro circuit to New Center in 1987, CIC's UK holdings merged with United Artists Communication Inc.'s foreign exhibition ventures to form United Cinemas International (UCI), which would become one of the country's largest and most powerful exhibition companies. In 1989 the company commented that "CIC's comfortable and technically excellent cinemas in central London (The Empire, Leicester Square and The Plaza, Lower Regent Street) provided the basis for the Multiplex sites which will, over the next decade, become familiar landmarks in the UK."[59] (UCI was originally intended to be a joint venture with U.S.-based AMC Cinemas, but AMC sold its screens outright to UCI instead.) UCI's chief operating officer was Millard Ochs, later a key player in Warner Bros.' global exhibition expansion.[60] UCI soon expanded its holdings into Ireland and West Germany with additional purchases.[61] In the years to come, UCI—still equally owned by Paramount and Universal—would operate cinemas in Austria, Brazil, China, Germany, Ireland, Italy, Japan, Portugal, Spain, Taiwan, and the United Kingdom.

The purchase of MGM's foreign cinemas in 1973 provided CIC with a pathway to foreign exhibition. Asset liabilities of aging cinemas on MGM's balance sheet helped create one of the world's most successful exhibitors in the late twentieth century and the self-described "pioneers of the luxury multiplex concept."[62]

Warner Bros. Cinemas and the Reboot of Hollywood Exhibition

Paramount and Universal were not the only American film companies invested in global exhibition by the late 1980s. (Those two companies were also co-owners of the domestic Mann Theatres chain in the United States, while Paramount retained its ownership of the dominant Famous Players circuit in Canada.) By 1987 Warner Bros. also jumped back into global exhibition, inspired, it seems, by the growth of UCI and those cinemas' ability to expand foreign markets for Hollywood films in each location.

Warner Bros. still operated its Leicester Square shop window cinema by the late 1980s but had shed its other cinemas in Lima, Peru; Bogotá, Colombia; and Havana, Cuba, decades earlier. Warner Bros. reentered global exhibition in a serious manner in 1987, though, under the guidance of exhibition industry veteran Salah Hassanein. Hassanein was born in Egypt, graduated from the London School of Economics in Cairo, and then went to work for the National Bank of Egypt. In 1942 he became Twentieth Century-Fox's assistant divisional manager for the Middle East. In 1945 he moved to the United States, joined the U.S. armed forces for two years, and then began working for George Skouras, nephew of Twentieth Century-Fox president Spyros Skouras, at the independent Skouras Theatres chain as an usher. Hassanein rose from usher to theater manager to film buyer and, later, president of the company.[63] United Artists Theatres later purchased Skouras Theatres, and Hassenein became executive vice president and a member of the board of directors of United Artists Communications.[64] In the mid-1980s Hassanein convinced Warner Bros. that building new multiplexes abroad would have an enormous "effect, internationally, upon Warner's own demand as a producer-distributor," and they hired him as president of WBIT to transform underperforming markets through new exhibition venues. Like the first wave of foreign exhibition expansion in the 1920s, Hassanein believed that foreign grosses could only expand with better-performing markets through better-performing cinemas. The double-edged benefit would be to generate revenue as both a foreign exhibitor and not just a distributor.[65]

After opening a series of Warner Bros. multiplexes in the United Kingdom, the Warner West End, Warner's first shop window cinema, was redeveloped by WBIT once more, transforming the cinema into a nine-screen multiplex that was to herald "the first of a new generation of Warner cinemas."[66] Steve Weiner, managing director for Warner Brothers Theatres (United Kingdom), argued in September 1993 that the cinema's consistency of purpose as Warner's key cinema, its shop window, was that it would continue to be "our showplace for Europe" into the next century. "Without it we would have been the only major without a central London site." The £15 million renovation, which gave the cinema more of a "European look," began in 1991 and the cinema finally reopened on September 24, 1993, with Warner Bros. "Our primary business," Weiner added, "is to get more movies seen by more people."[67]

Salah Hassanein's model for Warner's subsequent expansion beyond England was to build new multiplexes with joint partners, thus allowing local investors to assuage indigenous concerns about Hollywood domination while allowing this local investment to help clear legal and other regulatory hurdles. This joint cooperation model also resulted in the same kinds of "glocal" architectural approaches once adopted by Loew's/MGM, with "significantly larger foyers" for its German cinemas, for example, to accommodate "patrons'

FIGURES 4.1–4.2 The renamed Warner West End, ca. 1991 (top), and reimagined again as Warner Village Cinemas, ca. 1996 (bottom). (Cinema Theatre Association)

'pre-cinema' drinking customs, a popular Germanic movie-going trait."[68] Under Hassanein's leadership from 1987 until 1994 and then under Millard Ochs, the former chief executive of UCI who took over as president in 1994, WBIT (jointly) operated seventy-four multiplexes with 654 screens by 1998, with twenty-eight multiplexes in Austria, eighteen in the United Kingdom, thirteen in Japan, five in Portugal, four in Germany, three in Italy, two in Spain, and one new multiplex in Taiwan.[69] These joint ventures included collaborations with Filmes Lusomundo in Portugal (Warner-Lusomundo), the Sogecable Corp. in Spain, Morgan Creek and Chargeurs for planned ventures in the Netherlands, Metronome for new Warner cinemas in Denmark, and Niichi and Mycal in Japan (Warner-Mycal Cinemas). Their most prominent partnership, though, was developed with Australia's Village Roadshow which, Philip Turner notes, formed "a unified international network of cinemas trading under the aegis of Warner-Village Cinemas." Warner Village would eventually operate WBIT and Village Roadshow's cinemas in the United Kingdom, Germany, Italy, and Australia.[70] In the end, despite all of its success, Warner Bros. began selling off pieces of WBIT in Europe by the early 2000s as the company's focus moved toward less mature and developed markets in Asia that promised expansive growth. In 2003 Ochs sold off the company's British circuit, Warner Village Cinemas, for example, for $400 million.[71]

National Amusements and MGM Cinemas

WBIT and other studio-linked exhibition chains had sought to expand the market share for all Hollywood films through the growth of higher-performing multiplexes and megaplexes. Other U.S. film companies like National Amusements, whose Viacom division had purchased Paramount Pictures in 1987, also roared back into global exhibition in the 1980s and 1990s as multiplexes and blockbuster film cycles increased attendance throughout the region. National Amusements was a medium-sized exhibition chain (and a large multimedia holding company) that operated cinemas under the Multiplex Cinemas and Showcase Cinemas banners in the United States. Commensurate with its purchase of Paramount—and thus its takeover of Canada's Famous Players chain—National Amusements began exploring expansion opportunities in England and quickly became one of the top three circuits in that country, operating more than two hundred screens by 2001. National Amusements built additional cinemas in Europe, Asia, and South America over the next two decades.[72] By the end of the 2010s National Amusement still operated 950 screens in the United States, United Kingdom, and Latin America under the names Showcase, Multiplex, Cinema de Lux, SuperLux, and UCI, the descendant chain of CIC, which had become part of National Amusement's vast holdings.

Another global circuit tangentially tied to a U.S. film studio in this transitional period, between the late twentieth and early twenty-first century, was MGM International Cinemas. This zombie brand was the product of Kirk Kerkorian's sale of the company's logo and global brand to Cannon-Pathé for $1.3 billion in 1990. The acquisition provided Cannon with a more recognizable brand name for the company, now renamed MGM-Pathé, and a new moniker for its global cinema circuit, Cannon Cinemas, which was rebranded MGM International Cinemas. By 1994 the exhibitor operated 529 screens in the United Kingdom, Denmark, and the Netherlands, and MGM Cinemas (United Kingdom) had one-quarter of the market share during this period and was the dominant chain in the United Kingdom. The circuit was wholly distinct from the fledgling MGM film company still producing and distributing film content but, thanks to its 1990 purchase, MGM Cinemas proudly hoisted the famous MGM name and logo on company cinemas. By 1994, however, MGM International Cinemas needed a greater inflow of cash to renovate and operate the circuit, and Credit Lyonnais was brought in to sell the company. MGM Cinemas (United Kingdom) was sold to Virgin Cinemas for $320 million, its Dutch group was sold to Chargeurs and incorporated into the Pathé circuit there, and the forty-four-screen MGM-Nordisk company was sold to Nordisk Film.[73] MGM's overseas exhibition legacy was still imbedded, however, in the evergreen operation of the Empire Theatre in London's Leicester Square, still a major draw under UCI management.

With Loews Cineplex operating global cinemas throughout the 1990s, owned and operated by Sony, the parent company of Columbia Pictures, and WBIT operating into the 2010s, Charles Acland reminds us what the connections between WB and WBIT; between Sony and Loews; between Paramount, Universal, and UCI; between Paramount and National Amusements; and between producer-distributors and exhibition companies entailed during the 1990s and into the 2000s: "Significantly, when we speak of the international dominance of U.S. motion pictures, we must bear in mind that globalization concerns not only the supply of films to existing domestic chains. It equally involves the construction of cinema spaces and the capitalization of theater building and reconstruction on the part of major entertainment corporations."[74] In the years that followed, U.S.-based companies would continue to dominate many global exhibition markets but these companies, such as AMC, Cinemark, and even United Artists Theatres, were untethered to U.S. producer-distributors. They were distinctly exhibition companies. Still, they secured more and more foreign markets for Hollywood films, a central concern of the shop window boom that had begun more than three-quarters of a century earlier. Hollywood no longer needed to take on the expense and risk of operating cinemas overseas to secure distribution and prominence. And with a decline in studio branding—in an era when a film's release by Warner

Bros. or Paramount or Universal meant little to global consumers—the brand names of their cinemas meant little as well. Gone were the days when a Metro film and a Metro cinema meant something concrete and exciting to cinemagoers. Vanished, too, were the industrial motivations to still make exhibition a Paramount ideology.

Europe is only one of six regions in which Hollywood operated cinemas in various periods from the 1920s to the 2000s. Africa, Asia, Australasia, Latin America and the Caribbean, and the Middle East were all targets. In the succeeding chapters, covering each of these five additional regions, this book documents how a mixture of shop window cinemas and circuit ownership and operation secured first-run distribution outlets for Hollywood in variously complicated, acquiescent, and heavily recalcitrant markets. These cinemas helped spread Hollywood's movies and its messaging and constituted distinct cultural embassies for the expansion of American soft power in an increasingly hard world.

PART II

AUSTRALASIA

Banking on Australasia (1930–1982)
Global Banks and U.S. Cinema Ownership in Australia and New Zealand

CHAPTER 5

FOX CHASES HOYTS

U.S. Cinema Ownership in Australia, 1930–1936

> *The motion picture has certainly established itself as an important part in the lives of our brothers in Australasia. Metro-Goldwyn-Mayer's per capita return from these two countries is 90 per cent of its per capita return from the United States.*
> —Arthur Loew, *New York Times*, 1928

U.S. film companies owned and operated cinemas around the world from the 1920s to the 2010s, but nowhere was that ownership more concentrated than in Australasia. Twentieth Century-Fox's ownership of leading cinema circuits; MGM and Paramount's shop window cinemas; and, later, Warner Bros.' exhibition partnership with Village Roadshow (Warner Village) worked alongside Hollywood's widescale distribution operations to secure the Australian market for Hollywood films. Fox, in particular, derived large-scale profits and power from its model of owning exhibition companies, such as Hoyts in Australia and Amalgamated Theatres in New Zealand.

As a result, U.S.-owned cinemas exerted a tremendous cultural and industrial influence in Australasia during the 1930s and 1940s. Fox's control of Hoyts secured one of the two major cinema chains in Australia for American films, while MGM used its own shop window cinemas to draw attention and bookings for their films. Hollywood's control of the distribution and consumption of its films occurred against the backdrop of both British political and cultural anxieties over the growing dominance of American culture and industry in Commonwealth nations and Australia's more local concerns about the diminution of its cultural sovereignty and indigenous film production. Hollywood addressed these concerns regarding its outsized influence by using local branding (Hoyts, Amalgamated) and by using local cinema employees and partners as cultural and industrial ambassadors.

Australian exhibition, and by extension Australian cinema, was strongly influenced in its early days by the role that Australian and American banks and bankers played in shaping the industry's development. In the 1920s and 1930s local circuits Hoyts Theatres and Greater Union Theatres were forced into troublesome shotgun marriages, foreign sales, and bankruptcy reorganizations, all at the behest of local Australian banks and facilitated by the expansionist dreams of U.S. investment banks and bankers. Large stakes in Hoyts Theatres and New Zealand's Amalgamated Theatres were both sold to Twentieth Century-Fox under U.S.-owned Chase National Bank's direction, moves that pushed Fox into a debt-laden acquisition spree that would ultimately expand the film company's international cinema holdings and secure Chase's own control over Fox and its exhibition companies and subsidiaries around the world. This foreign ownership came with cultural consequences; it would, for example, ultimately determine the direction of Australian exhibition, distribution, and production for the coming century, hindering the growth of Australian film production by restricting the ability of Australian filmmakers to find spaces for their work.

Part II of this book, "Australasia: Banking on Australasia," seeks to highlight the role of investment banks and private and institutional investors on Hollywood's global exhibition expansion during the 1930s and well beyond. It traces the complex financial and organizational structure of Hoyts and Greater Union in Australia—and Fox Film during this period—before turning to New Zealand and Twentieth Century-Fox's acquisition of Amalgamated. This journey through a half century of Hollywood control concludes with the way insurance companies and corporate raiders eventually picked through the carrion bones of both Twentieth Century-Fox and MGM in the 1970s and 1980s, respectively, and how their own debt-laden buyouts and corporate looting affected the control of these cinemas throughout Australasia and beyond.

This examination provides a slightly different analysis of Australian and New Zealand exhibition and film industry history by taking a regional rather than a national approach to their collective development. Most works on Australian and New Zealand film industry history focus solely (and purposely) on each individual nation and do not analyze these markets through a regional lens. That is by design. A regional approach, however, addresses the influence Australian executives and Australian subsidiaries had on the New Zealand market, the role New Zealand film executives and local revenue streams later played in Australia, and the way foreign banks like Chase sought control over film companies throughout the region. As in the case of Egypt and Palestine/Israel analyzed later in this book, Australia's and New Zealand's exhibition history between the 1930s and 1980s are inextricably linked, and they remain so today.

Before the Banks

Before turning to the development of U.S.-owned and -operated cinemas in the Australasia region, it is necessary to examine the pre-1930 history of Australian cinemas and cinema chains.

Australia's oldest circuit, Hoyt's/Hoyts, dates to 1909 when a dentist, Arthur Russell, leased a hall on Melbourne's Bourke Street and began projecting films on Saturday nights. Adding more locations for motion-picture exhibition, Russell formed Hoyt's Pictures, which operated cinemas in Melbourne, its surrounding suburbs, and Sydney by the time of Russell's death in 1915. A decade later, in 1926, three small chains—Hoyt's, Electric Theaters, and Associated Theaters—now owned by F. W. "Frank" Thring and George Tallis—all merged to form Hoyts Theatres.[1]

By then Hoyts' greatest competition came from Union Theatres (UT), which had been formed through two successive mergers. In 1905 Spencer Cosens began exhibiting films from the Lyceum Hall in Sydney and, later, the city's Palace Theatre.[2] Cosens then formed Spencer Pictures and merged his growing circuit with T. J. West's West's Pictures and the Melbourne-based Amalgamated Pictures (owned by brothers E. J. and John Tait) to create the General Film Company of Australasia. In 1913 General Film merged with the Greater J. D. Williams Amusement Company to form Union Theatres, an exhibition "combine" (company), and Australasian Films, a distribution company, with film agents booking product for the chain in London and New York.[3]

The Australian trade journal *Everyones* remarked that "friendly competition" between Union Theatres and Hoyts Theatres developed into a full-scale war between 1926 and 1927, "when both companies embarked upon a policy of expansion by the erection of modern cinemas in the capital cities." Hoyts had concentrated "almost entirely upon Melbourne" in previous years.[4] The company now set its sights on expanding into Adelaide, Brisbane, Hobart, Perth, and Sydney, all former UT towns. Union, conversely, expanded into Hoyts' dominion—Melbourne. This caused the construction of dozens of new cinemas and the accumulation of debt by both companies.

Other sharks were circling. Paramount, hoping to add to its growing slate of international cinemas in Tokyo, Paris, London, and other cities, began negotiating to buy a controlling interest in UT in 1927. For reasons unknown, though, the deal was stillborn.[5] Instead, Paramount carved out key cinemas through close booking associations with local theaters. Canberra's new Capitol Theatre, for example, opened on December 8, 1927, with an eighteen-month exclusive contract for Paramount films. As an example of the close association between the theater and the studio, Franklin Barrett, the Capitol's first manager, previously worked in Paramount's exploitation department.[6] The Capitol's opening night, attended by Prime Minister Stanley Bruce, was coordinated by Barrett with the onsite assistance of Paramount New South Wales manager Fred Gawler.[7] MGM also began exploring exhibition opportunities in Australia by leasing the Prince Edward Theatre in Sydney and the Capitol in Melbourne—later operated by Paramount—in mid-1927 as shop window cinemas for MGM.[8]

Meanwhile, Union Theatres and Hoyts escalated their continuing battle for exhibition supremacy, especially as American interest in Australian exhibition grew. In September 1928 *Variety* wrote that "Union Theatres and Hoyt's Theatres are grimly battling to gain the upper hand regarding pictures in this country." Put simply: "It's a trade war." Stuart Doyle of UT secured the 1929 and 1930 slate of Paramount, Fox, First National, Universal, Pathé, and Master Pictures, providing the chain with 1,500 films. Hoyts held the decided disadvantage, having secured only British & Dominion Films' fifty-two films, and would thus have to piece together a global program and work with currently unaffiliated distributors like United Artists.[9]

Union Theatres spared no expense in its battle with Hoyts, hiring, for example, prolific American architect John Eberson to design its new 3,500-seat Capitol Theatre in Sydney. Construction costs for the elaborate picture palace forced Union to raise capital by issuing two million dollars' worth of shares.[10] However, in public testimony seven years later, Doyle attributed the decision not to the need to compete with Hoyts but to the Americans: "American film distributors brought pressure to bear on Union Theatres Ltd., to induce it to raise extra capital and build theatres for the presentation of American pictures, under the threat that they themselves would build." Doyle noted that he was told that Hoyts Theatres Ltd. "was called upon to act similarly. As a result, the State and Regent theatres in Sydney and Melbourne were built, and the Capitol and Plaza in Sydney."[11] He added that this "pressure" was coming not from the Australian film industry but entirely from "American film producers, the principal being Famous-Lasky Film Service Ltd., proprietors of Paramount Pictures."[12]

> It will, therefore, be seen that the principal construction activities of Union Theatres were created at the request and virtually under threats from certain American distributors for the purpose of finding an outlet for their pictures,

which, in their opinion, would earn greater revenue for them in larger modern theatres and place them on a parity with similar cities in U.S.A.... As a result of all this pressure, Union Theatres and affiliated companies were compelled to raise their capital from £807.601 to £2,611,198.[13]

With the additional pressure from Hollywood making Hoyts' and Union's domestic trade war untenable, bankers at English, Scottish and Australian Bank (ES&A Bank) "called the combatants together and compelled the signing of an armistice" in December 1929.[14] It is worth noting that Doyle's account of this period and the causes of this overbuilding were later challenged by MGM attorney K. C. Abrahams, who asked in a 1934 hearing, "Can you produce anything, any letter, or any minute of a meeting, to show that this was forced upon you by American distributors?" Doyle responded that proof was not necessary since "the American distributors were too astute to put anything in writing."[15]

In 1930 Paramount restarted its efforts to secure a controlling interest in UT, by then the largest cinema circuit in Australia. Paramount's Ed. J. Wall arrived in Australia in late July under the pretense of selling Paramount films but, according to *Everyones*, he was there "really to investigate the U.T. circuit and report on the proposition."[16] Paramount offered UT £290,000—a paltry sum for Paramount—but their negotiations with Union took too long. While Wall was dickering, bankers from ES&A called executives from Union and Hoyts together to create a "buying pool" that would be able to reduce their rental fees for increasingly expensive Hollywood films by roughly 20 percent through their combined circuit power, creating a local duopoly that could save roughly £140,000 of the £700,000 that both circuits were paying annually to overseas distributors. The estimated savings emboldened Union's bargaining power and enabled it to deflect Paramount's proposed takeover. It is hard to underestimate how much capital Paramount might have generated over the next century from this relatively small outlay of pounds. This delay and the collapse of the deal was one of the worst mistakes any company would make in its foreign exhibition investments.

Union Theatres and Hoyts Theatres instead continued to dominate the country's largest and most profitable urban venues as well as grow their circuits' suburban reach. Rather than continue to compete for product and build competitive theaters that would increase both companies' substantial debt and operating expenses, Hoyts and Union, at the behest of their ES&A bankers, began hammering out "the final details" of the buying pool that would "cover the whole of Australia" and strengthen their position with foreign distributors. "When completed," *Everyones* wrote at the time, "the organisation will be the biggest of its nature in the world." The agreement between Hoyts and UT granted Stuart Doyle, managing director of Union Theatres Ltd., "full power to buy pictures for both [the] U.T. and Hoyts circuit."[17] U.S. film companies had been blocked... for the moment. The situation was now shaping up to be another obstacle to Hollywood's efforts to expand into a growing English-speaking market, a situation similar to that experienced by American film companies in South Africa with Isidore Schlesinger and his African Theatres Ltd.

During talks between Hoyts and UT that August, ES&A bankers—who were financing both exhibition companies during their financial troubles—became convinced that a formal merger, rather than a buying pool between Hoyts and Union, would be most advantageous. The bank's plans called for UT to operate the combined circuit's city cinemas while Hoyts would operate its suburban houses.[18] The new company would then control 180 cinemas, and profits would be divided, with 60 percent to Union Theatres and 40 percent to Hoyts. UT head, Stuart Doyle, would be named head of the new holding company, and Edwin Geach and Gordon Balcombe of UT and F. W. Thring and G. F. Griffith of Hoyts would be named directors. Meanwhile, an interesting detail, mentioned briefly and then dropped, appeared in *Everyones* in mid-August about "the sudden departure of a distribution executive from Australia; that he had been given an option over a big holding and had gone to America to offer it to his principals after laying a smoke screen behind him." The trade journal added ominously: "Anything can happen."[19]

Everyones' report turned out to be exactly what Fox's Stanley S. Crick had been up to in August when Fox's Australian distribution head had gone to the United States to meet with Harley Clarke, president of the newly reorganized and Chase-owned Fox Film, about a proposed sale by Hoyts of large stock holdings in their circuit. "If Fox did not exercise that option the [UT–Hoyts] combine would have been formed," *Everyones* later reported, "and one of the first steps would probably have been to wipe out the Hoyts organization, leaving everything in the control of Union Theatre men."[20] However, after Crick's successful meetings in New York in late August 1930, the Fox Corp. "cabled instructions to buy," and Charles Munro, of Fox Films Australia, and Clifford Minter, one of Fox's legal advisers in Australia, traveled to Melbourne, and on Monday morning, August 25, 1930, Fox formally acquired the Hoyts holdings of G. F. Griffith and the Tait-Williamson group. Fox, *Everyones* declared, now "possessed complete control" of Hoyts. This seemingly simple acquisition would alter Australia's film industry for the next half century.

The Union–Hoyts combine was now officially "killed" by Fox's purchase of Hoyts for just £280,000.[21] (The chain had more than one hundred cinemas already around Australia.[22]) "STOP PRESS!" *Everyones* announced on September 3, 1930, as George Tallis, F. W. Thring, and the Tait-Williamson interests all sold their corporate holdings in Hoyts and retained only their "personal parcels" of A and B preferred shares of Hoyts stock.[23] Thring announced that he would soon resign as managing director and turn to independent Australian sound film production instead, with his feature films to be reportedly distributed by Fox and then screened at Hoyts Theatres.[24] (The optimism inspired by his new company, Efftee Film Productions, soon turned to frustration as American control of Australian screens remained firmly in place.[25]) Fox's Charles Munro, who would become managing director of Hoyts Theatres, assured a weary industry that "the entire Hoyts staff would remain intact and that the direction of the company would be kept entirely in Australian hands."[26] To that end, Fox announced that it would not only distribute Fox films throughout the greater Australasian region but would also begin making Australian talkies there—using talent playing Hoyts' local Tivoli circuit—and also create a local newsreel (*Fox Movietone News*) for Australasian cinemas using their own sound truck and local cameramen. The Australian *Movietone* newsreel was to be supervised by Fox's Stanley Crick.[27]

Hoyts as an Australian-owned company, though, was finished. The Fox Film Corp. had bought the majority of Hoyts' ordinary and preferred stock, and *Everyones* noted that any idea of Australian (or even British Commonwealth control) was simply "pap for the public."[28] There would be, it soon turned out, no large-scale support or investment in domestic film production, despite assertions on the part of Fox and Hoyts executives and investors.[29]

Dale Turnbull, who worked for Fox and Hoyts variously between 1947 and 1974—including twenty-seven years at Hoyts as the company's managing director—argues that Hoyts wasn't a shop window operation for Twentieth Century-Fox but an investment asset that also booked Fox films. Fox distribution and Hoyts exhibition in Australia remained wholly independent of one another during all of those years as corporate but not necessarily kissing cousins.[30]

Fox, Global Investment Banks, and Australian Consolidation

Fox Film's acquisition of Hoyts was not conducted in a vacuum and must be seen within the context of the impact of investment banks on Fox's aggressive acquisitions of significant shares of both Loew's Inc. and Gaumont-British Picture Corp. the previous year. In April 1929 Fox had purchased four hundred thousand shares of Loew's for $50 million, giving the company a 42 percent interest in one of its largest rivals. Fox had already taken on excessive debt from its own domestic theater acquisitions and expansion. In need of cash and looking for liquidity, Fox borrowed $15 million from AT&T's Western Electric division, whose own sound-on-film technology was Fox Movietone's chief rival. Fox then added an additional $20 million debt burden through the acquisition of a 49 percent stake in Gaumont-British, which provided Fox with investments in British film production and an exhibition outlet for Fox films throughout the three hundred cinemas in the Gaumont-British chain. This investment was secured in part by the $6 million loan Fox's investment bankers, Halsey, Stuart & Co., arranged with British banks.[31] As Vanda Krefft notes, William Fox "kept buying more and more theaters, with still more money he didn't have."[32] These and other Fox Film acquisitions ratcheted the company's debt burden up to $150 million, of which $90 million was higher interest, short-term loans.

At the top of the global film industry in mid-1929, the Fox empire and William Fox quickly unraveled. Fox was injured in a July 1929 car accident and unable to properly oversee his business. On October 29 the stock market crashed. Loew's stock dropped from $85 to $32, and Fox Film B stock plummeted from $105 to $19. The dramatic drop both in equity and cash on hand made repaying those short- and long-term debts increasingly problematic as 1930 began. Halsey and other investment banks were unable to loan Fox additional funds, and AT&T refused to further loans as well. As Barrie Wigmore writes, "What had been coups in buying out a competitor and a major UK chain became millstones, as the value of the Loew's investment shrunk to a fraction of its cost and permanent financing became impossible. The Fox companies now appeared overextended, vulnerable to the economic downturn because of their luxury nature, and led by an eccentric rather than a genius."[33] Richard Brody adds that as William Fox's debts kept rising, "investment bankers were both setting conditions for Fox's loans and other financial instruments and then counselling (or warning) other potential investors and financiers to deny Fox new terms and to let Fox flounder in mounting debt."[34] Halsey and AT&T subsequently told William Fox that his company was now in default and that his control of the company "should be turned over to a voting trust" of Fox; Halsey, Stuart & Co.; and AT&T. On the advice of Charles Evans Hughes, who would soon become chief justice of the United States, Fox relented and the company was held in a trust. The reorganized Fox Film Corp. was subsequently sued by investors in early 1930, and William Fox was forced to sell what remained of his shares to Harley Clarke and his General Theatres Equipment Inc. (GTE) for $15 million. Funds for GTE's acquisition of William Fox's shares were loaned, once more, by Chase National Bank and AT&T, giving Chase even more control over the company.[35] "Tightly tied together," Krefft writes, "GTE was essentially a Chase company."[36] Both Upton Sinclair and William Fox concluded that "the financial system, and the entire system of legal intricacies that sustain it" were "a grand-scale fraud, both in its corrupt practices and even in its deceptive formalities." At the end of the whole saga, Sinclair wrote, "the treasure was gone, and nobody but the lawyers and the bankers had anything!"[37]

Fox and its various companies and subsidiaries were subsequently refinanced in April 1930 with the aid of GTE, who acquired hundreds of thousands of shares of the newly reorganized company. In addition to large investments from other banks, including Pynchon & Co., Chase lent GTE the $15 million it needed for Fox's shares in addition to other "loans related to the Fox takeover." Now, with Pynchon & Co. nearly filing its own bankruptcy in 1930 (before shuttering completely in 1931), Chase also took over the failing investment bank's GTE securities "in foreviness [sic] of the loans against them." Meanwhile, Wigmore adds, "Halsey, Stuart & Co. was simply refusing to pay on its Chase loans against GTE stock," giving Chase even more control.[38] Thus, Chase gained a controlling interest in the company and continued to load up Fox with debt. From 1930 to 1933, Chase chairman Albert Wiggin consistently threw good money after bad by continually financing Fox-GTE and sinking the whole company in additional debt.

This background is important in understanding how the Hoyts takeover was part of a larger debt strategy for Chase, GTE, and the reorganized Fox Film Corp. Thus, when the opportunity arose to buy Hoyts in 1930, Chase and Fox's other benefactors simply opened their credit lines once more for yet another acquisition. Their Australasian investment, by comparison to Fox's other mounting debts, was small. But, as Hoyts grew over the next half century, Fox and its corporate descendants reaped an enormous yield from this Depression-era fire sale.

The investment in Fox by Halsey, Stuart & Co. and especially by Chase National Bank reminds us that, by 1930, Hollywood's studios were no longer individually owned companies managed by Horatio Alger-esque immigrant moguls. They were instead enormously large multimedia and multinational companies controlled by investment banks, lawyers, financiers, and other businessmen steering their growth for large annual returns on invested capital. The sale of Hoyts, engineered by ES&A Bank in Australia, and its purchase by Fox, orchestrated by GTE, Halsey, AT&T, and Chase, was another sign of the changing nature of global capital and the global film industry. For Fox to grow as a company and remain competitive, this new logic dictated, it needed new markets, new capital streams, new investments, and new narratives for lenders and investors. After Fox Film's failure to dominate the domestic market with its short-lived 1929 Loew's acquisition—quickly broken up by President Herbert Hoover's Justice Department at the behest of Republican power broker Louis B. Mayer, who had helped secure Hoover's 1928 nomination for the presidency—Fox became a global conglomerate instead, especially following its later merger with Twentieth Century in 1935.[39]

Most of this complex background was, it would seem, unknown to the Australian press. Most countries—and their journalists—still approached the U.S.

film industry with an assumption that a purchase by Fox meant it had been generated by William Fox, Winfield Sheehan, Clayton Sheehan, or other Fox representatives. Instead, these global deals were often engineered by lawyers and investment bankers "on behalf" of the Fox company. In this case, Harley Clarke, Albert Wiggin, and others were the parties with which Hoyts executives met to sell the chain.[40]

Hoyts' sale to Fox was orchestrated by another set of bankers and financiers, this time Australian, and not by local film company executives; the move, *Everyones* reported, "relieves the financial burden under which Hoyts"—and, by proxy, ES&A Bank, which owned much of its debt—"have operated."[41] As *Variety* reported after the Fox purchase of Hoyts, "American capital looks like the salvation of the picture industry in Australia, where the business in all branches has been staggering under heavy taxation and business depression."[42]

Back in Australia, though, *Everyones* was stunned by the surprise ending to the local film exhibition and banking saga: "How the combine plans crashed; how two huge circuits battled themselves to a standstill; how the banks commenced to force them together ... and how last Monday changed the whole face of the business, all make the most amazing chapter in the history of the film industry in Australia."[43] Surprisingly, the journal still misread the local situation and its impact, arguing that a Hoyts–Union combine would have been even worse for independent Australian distributors.

In reality, Fox's investment in Hoyts boosted the company's operations and Fox's and Hoyts' subsequent growth. Bank financing would also boost UT and its own control over this market. Hoyts and Union's collective urban/suburban duopoly would come to dominate some of the nation's most lucrative theaters and constrain independent cinema growth and independent distributor's power while providing almost no support for indigenous filmmaking. The Fox–Hoyts deal was instead just another sign that Hollywood, with the help of investment banks and other powerful players, was truly global and that local exhibitors and distributors did indeed have much to fear in Fox's first, but not last, circuit buyout. While Paramount and MGM retained their ongoing shop window strategy, Fox would come to embrace this idea of circuit power in many anglophone markets.

Hoyts Under the Fox Thumb

Fox's control of Hoyts officially began on September 1, 1930, with Charles Munro managing Hoyts for Fox and Stanley Crick appointed chairman of the board that now included Munro, Crick, and Minter (representing Fox), F. W. Thring, G. F. Griffith, and John Tait.[44] *Everyone's* reported, "One aftermath of the [Hoyts] deal was the rush of offers by independent exhibitors to sell their theatres to Fox."[45] Within its first two months, Fox took over control of the Capitol Theatre in Perth, added five new cinemas in Sydney including the Empire Theatre, and secured a five-year agreement for control of W. J. Howe's four cinemas in the eastern suburbs, including the Olympic Theatre.[46] Howe, head of the NSW Exhibitors' Association, subsequently joined Hoyts as general manager of shows.[47] Thus, the intimidating power of a Hollywood player in the market was inspiring exhibitors to sell out instead of trying to compete. In November a Hoyts advertisement bellowed: "From East to West, from North to South, Hoyts palatial Theatres dominate every Capital City. Massive, luxurious, the ultimate in entertainment, service and construction, they form imposing links in the most powerful motion-picture circuit in the Southern Hemisphere.... 110 first-class houses give Hoyts Theatres Ltd. the biggest film buying power in Australia."[48]

Fox's desire to purchase Hoyts had also likely stemmed in part from Australia's restrictive prohibitions on repatriating local distribution revenues back to the United States. As many other countries learned during the twentieth century, disallowing Hollywood film companies from sending their distribution profits back to the United States only spurred more (exhibition) investment domestically. If Fox couldn't take most of its foreign profits out of a given country, the company would simply pour it back into domestic film distribution and exhibition versus investments in local production. In short, local protectionism and dollar repatriation restrictions only served to hurt Australian film production and local ownership over exhibition chains. For example, a letter to the undersecretary of New Zealand—which erroneously charged that Paramount and Fox had each taken over UT and Hoyts, respectively—argued that it was

> fair to add that the control of theatres in Australia by two American companies... came about because of the prohibition of the remittance of monies from Australia to U.S.A. The two firms concerned, apparently decided to use their Australian revenue in their business by getting control of a portion of the exhibition side. This is one of the unexpected results of attempting to control the flow of commercial money by legislation.[49]

The letter writer, W. A. Daumer, noted that even when money was funneled back into local production, it did so for American quota requirements, not Australian or British companies: "Several American companies have formed British branches, and are producing films which qualify as British, but the revenues derived therefrom are, in the main, at the disposal of the parent company in the United States."[50] The net result of Australian restrictions on distribution revenue repatriation and of ES&A's orchestration of Hoyts' sale to Fox was, in the end, to place key parts of the growing Australian film industry under U.S. corporate control. The story of Hollywood's global exhibition expansion was often one of unintended consequences of local policy and regulations.

Paramount and Other Rumors

A week after the Fox–Hoyts deal was confirmed, Paramount was still conducting a survey of the entire Union circuit.[51] *Variety* reported that Doyle and Union had spiked their asking price to $15 million for only a 40 percent control of UT. The deal ultimately faltered, the trade journal surmised, because Doyle wanted to retain "executive control" after the sale, something Paramount refused to do.[52] After three years of negotiating—beginning with "informal conversations" between UT director Gordon Balcombe and Paramount officials in 1927—the proposed sale to Paramount failed. Doyle instead requested a loan of £250,000 from Paramount, intended, he would later note, to "tide us over [the] difficulties that were entirely due to the excessive film hire we were paying Paramount." "It was never intended that Paramount should purchase [UT]," Doyle would later testify. "They were asked for a loan; in return they demanded control of our circuit and we turned the proposition down." Doyle added that he "didn't want Paramount or any other foreign company to be interested with us." And, with the proposed loan from Paramount equaling nearly a year's revenue in exchange for permanent control of UT, Doyle remarked that he "considered the proposal outrageous."[53]

Paramount settled instead for a single shop window cinema in Melbourne, the city's palatial 2,150-seat Capitol Theatre, which Paramount secured with a ten-year lease beginning December 27, 1930. The Capitol's present manager, J. L. Thornley, continued on as general manager, and the theater, which had booked primarily Paramount films for years, remained a long-run shop window cinema now exclusively for Paramount films.[54] The local in-house publication, *Paramount Punch*, remarked that "Paramount's Capitol now represents the Australian link in Paramount's worldwide chain of de luxe theatres throughout England, the United States, Canada, Europe and other countries."[55] *Film Daily* was blunt about the acquisition of the Capitol: "This deal reported to indicate that the Publix negotiations for an interest in the Union Theaters circuit have not been successful."[56]

Paramount's purchase of even one cinema still set off British alarm bells. A letter signed "TRUE BRITON" to the *Sydney Morning Herald*, for example, voiced grave concern that the acquisition might be "the forerunner of this American concern obtaining control of a circuit of theatres throughout

Australia.... This is a British country, and British productions, pictures as well as all other commodities, should be assured of equal chances in comparison with the products of other countries."[57]

The Capitol remained the only cinema in Australia under the direct control of Paramount International and became a (cultural) embassy for Paramount in Melbourne, advertising the company's films and stars for those attending its cinemas and others passing by on foot, by automobile, or rolling along in street cars.[58] At the Capitol, the cinema was demonstrably American by design, attracting moviegoers by its very "Americanness" and the growing allure for Hollywood. Fox's purchase of Hoyts, however, was precisely the opposite. By maintaining an Australian patina, Fox tried to camouflage the very corporate and financial operation of this American asset and distribution delivery system.

Union Theatres, Hoyts, General Theatres Corp., and the Film Wars of 1933–1934

By 1931 Union Theatres was still in a far more precarious state than Hoyts. Stuart Doyle, UT's head, would later argue that it was the U.S. film companies, not the Australian banks, that were driving it to the brink. After generating a profit of £100,000 in 1930, UT would lose almost the same £100,000 in 1931, causing ES&A Bank "to demand the company's reconstruction." To raise revenue outside of film exhibition, Doyle tried (and failed) to diversify the company through radio broadcasting and miniature golf courses.[59] Instead, Union Theatres Ltd. was forced into receivership, "owing to the depression and the continual demand by American distributors for higher prices than the circuit could pay," Doyle noted. When UT defaulted on its debt, ES&A financed the creation of a new company, Greater Union Theatres Ltd., to purchase the assets of UT.[60] Historians Graham Shirley and Brian Adams provide a slightly differing account that portrays Doyle, not ES&A, as the spark for this new company.[61] The truth is likely in the middle. After all, it would have been ES&A that provided the £400,000 for Doyle's acquisition. There is little doubt, amid UT's troubles and the Depression, that Doyle did not have access to that much liquidity on his own.[62]

Meanwhile, Paramount signed a circuit deal with Hoyt's—not UT—in November 1931. "Hoyts' Regent Theatres in Sydney, Melbourne, Adelaide and Perth, as well as the Capitol Theatre in the latter city, will henceforth be Paramount's first city release theatres," *Paramount Punch* announced. "All of Hoyts' 110 theatres, except the Regent in Brisbane, will play Paramount's current and next year's releases."[63] Paramount now began using its own Melbourne Capitol Theatre and the Sydney's Prince Edward Theatre.

With Greater Union Theaters still struggling financially, and no American buyout in the offing, *Everyones* reported that ES&A Bank "which was carrying the overdrafts for both Greater Union Theatres, Ltd., and Hoyts Theatres, Ltd., desired the two concerns to merge [once again], and thus was created General Theatres Corporation of Australasia, Ltd., [GTC] a management company."[64] (The founding of the GTC amalgamation occurred in mid-October 1932.[65]) Graham Shirley and Brian Adams note that GTC's creation was certainly "prompted by the E S & A Bank, who wanted to curb the rivalry, expenditure and losses of both chains" by pooling their exhibition resources to corner the market.[66] GTC cinemas now controlled vast amounts of the urban and suburban cinemas of Australia. "Various attempts were made by the various American distributors to break up General Theatres Corporation," *Everyones* reported, and all were unsuccessful.[67] Fox now owned one-half of an even more dominant, unbreakable combine.

By the end of 1932 Hollywood's renewed efforts to control the Australian market through tough film distribution contracts led to what the *Sydney Morning Herald* called yet another new "war" between "the American film distributing companies and Australian exhibitors" that might cause many Australian theaters to close. "The American agencies demand that their terms for the supply of films in 1933 shall be accepted in full," the newspaper wrote in late December 1932, and the "Australian theatre-owners have made a determined stand against these terms, and, in particular, against the system of 'block booking,'"[68] Despite this local opposition, Hollywood distributors—including Fox—continued to try to foist a block booking strategy on this market. By the end of 1932 the two sides—U.S. distributors and Australian exhibitors—had reached a stalemate with "American interests declar[ing] that they would prefer to close down, and thus stop all supply of American films, rather than yield" while "Australian interests maintain that, rather than give way, they will close down their theatres" as well.[69]

Fox's purchase of Hoyts three years earlier had placed the company in an enviable position in Australia, especially given the conflicts between GTC and other U.S. distributors. In addition to Fox short, feature, and news films, Fox's "big interest in the Gaumont-British organisation, and with two representatives on the board of directors—Sidney R. Kent and Dixon Boardman" enabled Fox to funnel films from additional investments to Hoyts and other Australian screens including not only *Fox Movietone News* but also the British Gaumont Graphic and Cinemagazine.[70] Fox was now distributing all Gaumont-British, Gainsborough, Gaumont-Ufa, and "associated product" in both Australia and New Zealand in addition to Fox films.[71] Fox and Hoyts executives noted that, with all of this product flowing into Hoyts, 1933 would be the year that the company would be "able to present shareholders with the most satisfactory balance-sheet" since the Fox purchase in 1930.[72]

Bernard Freeman and MGM's Shop Windows

The extensive 1932–1933 battle over block booking and rental terms had additional consequences for Hollywood's (exhibition) control in this market. The skirmish had, behind the scenes, pushed MGM executives to begin securing key cinemas for the first-run exhibition of its own films in Australia. Stewardship of MGM's Australian affairs rested with Sir Nathaniel Bernard Freeman. Born in Sydney in 1896 to Russian Jewish émigrés, the Freeman family moved to Melbourne in the early 1900s. At sixteen, Bernard Freeman began working for cider makers. He later became a clerk and then a sales representative for women's clothes before enlisting in active service during World War I. After the end of the conflict, Freeman returned to Australia, where he resumed selling women's clothing, this time door to door in the Melbourne suburbs. His career (and life) changed forever on a visit to New York with his friend Clive Waxman, who had traveled there to visit relatives. Waxman's uncle, Bert Levy, was a member of the Friar's Club alongside Paramount's Adolph Zukor. Levy told Zukor about his Australian visitors, and a meeting was arranged. Zukor referred Freeman to Paramount's vice president and general sales manager. Taken with Freeman, Paramount executives gave him the opportunity to enter either film production, distribution, or exhibition. Freeman accepted their invitation and chose Paramount film distribution, beginning work in the company's shipping department, lugging cans of film around New York City. Paramount later promoted him through its publicity and sales departments, and he was asked to open Paramount's new sales exchange in Albany, New York, in 1920. Four years later, after a series of sales positions at Paramount and, following the creation of MGM by Loew's, Freeman "showed up in [Arthur Loew's] New York office with a confident 'I'm the man you want in Australia'" and was hired away to oversee the new MGM subsidiary for both Australia and New Zealand located on Castlereagh Street in Sydney.[73] Freeman subsequently established MGM's distribution and sales operations throughout Australasia. Michael Moodabe, who dealt with Freeman alternatively as an exhibition foe and a distribution partner, recalled him as "a tough no-nonsense Jewish showman very loyal to MGM."[74]

MGM opened new £30,000 administrative offices in Sydney on Chalmers Street at the end of 1933.[75] The opening of the new offices, coupled with the simmering smoke from the ongoing dispute between Hollywood distributors and GTC, caused *Everyones* to note that "the air is still charged with rumors concerning Metro-Goldwyn-Mayer's entry into the exhibiting field."[76] Freeman announced that MGM would, in fact, now build new shop window cinemas in Sydney, Melbourne, and Brisbane.[77] Freeman noted, "In our own theatre we will be in a position to give individual attention to each production and are confident we shall gain a benefit thereby. The Prince Edward has been in a position to give individual handling and showmanship to the pictures it has shown, and we believe this circumstance, in part, explains why the Prince Edward in the whole period of its existence has never failed to pay a dividend of at least five per cent."[78] Thus, MGM, rather than buying out the Fuller's chain as many had whispered, decided to strike out on its own, having already optioned potential theater sites in each city.

MGM's announcement hardened GTC's opposition to U.S. expansion even more, with each side "hurling grenades that are exploding heavily in the daily newspapers." GTC partners Hoyts and Greater Union, hoping to counter MGM and any other U.S. film companies from expanding their exhibition holdings into New South Wales, approached NSW government officials "requesting that no further licenses be issued for any more city picture theatres for some years." That Hoyts was a U.S.-owned company asking for protection against U.S. interests reflects the chutzpah that Fox brought to its Australian operations. GTC, meanwhile, released the following statement: "By building theatres," MGM and other U.S. companies plan "to force Australian exhibitors to pay their terms or go out of business." GTC pledged to "fight to a finish to stop any attempts by foreign companies to interfere with the rights of [GTC's Australian] shareholders."[79]

Freeman was careful to note that MGM's shop window cinema policy in Australia was not a move to set up a competitive exhibition company: "We want to make it clear that we intend to build only one theatre in each city," he told *Everyones*, and "we are doing this to provide an outlet for our product." Freeman laid the blame for MGM's needs for screens directly on the feet of GTC: "This policy has been forced upon us by the operation of the local exhibiting combine, General Theatres Corporation," adding that MGM's new builds followed its exhibition experience and expansion in South Africa where "A similar policy was forced upon us ... by a similar combine [African Consolidated Theatres]." Freeman went on to say that the "combine is aiming at a corner of oil film-buying, with a view to obtaining virtual dictatorship of the industry" that was against the "interests of the companies distributing films, whether British, Australian, or American" and "would eventually lead to the elimination of the independent exhibitors."[80] C. F. Marden, superintending manager of GTC, pushed back against MGM's claims (and those of the others) by trying to divide native exhibitors along patriotic lines:

> There is no disguising the fact that Metro-Goldwyn-Mayer is a foreign company owned and controlled by Americans, and has in the past imposed onerous terms on the Australian exhibitor which allow very small margin of profit, while the American distributor has collected huge sums of money in Australia. By building theatres they intend to force Australian exhibitors to

pay their terms or go out of business.... Metro-Goldwyn-Mayer intend to open as a foreign company running theatres throughout Australia.[81]

Freeman, in response, addressed the large, neon-colored elephant in the room: "Mr. S. F. Doyle, of General Theatres Corporation has attempted to cloud the issues by labeling one side Australian and the other American, [but] attention should be drawn to the fact that Fox Film Corporation, an American distributing Company, holds a substantial interest in Hoyts Theatres, Limited." Freeman then quoted from one of many letters he had received from independent exhibitors, including one that noted of GTC and its buying pools that "to submit to General Theatres' demands would give them complete monopoly over the exhibiting side of the picture business in Australia. This contingency is alarming, and would establish them in a position of dictatorship that would be both intolerable and disastrous."[82]

Freeman argued that it was not Australia versus America but GTC versus all other Australian distributors and exhibitors. Local exhibitors were, in fact, petrified by GTC's expansive business and lobbying efforts. David N. Martin, manager of Liberty Theatres as well as Universal's NSW manager, noted that he "understood that certain interests were [now] attempting to persuade the State Government not to issue licences for any more city picture theatres for a period of years. This was causing grave concern to him and to those associated with him."[83] (Universal—which had only made minor inroads in foreign exhibition in the years prior—made a surprise announcement when Martin announced his takeover of the Rialto Theatre in Sydney, providing a "first-release house for some Universal product."[84]) Martin noted that GTC's expansion, and its attempts to stifle local competition through the suspension of new theater licenses, would not only hurt Australian exhibitors but Australian filmmaking as well. "When the General Theatres Corporation leased the King's Cross and Majestic Theatres recently they brought every theatre of importance in the city under their control.... Thus they blocked the 'first-release' outlet for all pictures except those of distributing companies affiliated with themselves unless the distributors were prepared to comply with their wishes. The producers of Australian films are in a state of anxiety."[85] Martin joined those who now sought a NSW governmental investigation of GTC for its monopoly power.

GTC's efforts to control this narrative foundered due to its inherently hypocritical stance against foreign intervention since GTC was, by all rights, half controlled by a U.S. parent company in Fox. MGM cleverly aligned itself with Australian independent distributors and exhibitors and thereby flipped the nationalist script. This was also one of the very rare instances in which a U.S. film company (Fox) sought to compete directly and in open hostility to other U.S. film firms.

There was yet a third front in the "film war," not between GTC and U.S. films distributors and exhibitors but between Australian film producers—chiefly F. W. Thring's Efftee Film Productions—and GTC, Greater Union, Hoyts, and Fox. As Shirley and Adams write, "The formation of the General Theatres Corporation now eliminated Thring's bargaining power and reduced his terms with Hoyts. Where he and other producers formerly had the choice of two outlets for exhibition, they now had only GTC."[86] Thring argued that

> while as an Imperialist, I am cordially in favour of giving a measure of preference to the British product over that of foreign countries, the fact must not be lost sight of that to-day one of the largest producing companies in England, and the one which sends the greatest proportion of English films to this territory, is in itself, and through its subsidiary companies, largely composed of American capital. I refer to the Gaumont-British Corporation, in which the Fox Film Corporation of New York has large financial holdings and considerable representation on its directorate. This concern, by the way, also very largely controls the principal theatre exhibiting circuits in Australia. It is thus quite possible that a very large measure of the British protection granted by our legislators is in effect going to help the foreign producers to retain their stranglehold on the industry. These are facts of which our legislators appear to be blissfully ignorant.[87]

The Chase-backed purchase of Hoyts by Fox, in Thring's estimation as well as many others, had put the fate of Australia's indigenous film production directly in U.S. hands.

The Investigation Begins

A NSW government inquiry into the local film industry formally began on Tuesday, January 2, 1934, when "several of the film chiefs and at least six of their legal advisers assembled before [NSW Commissioner F. W.] Marks." First to testify against the combine was David Martin, who "spoke not as NSW manager of Universal, but on behalf of the proposed Liberty Theatres Ltd." Martin attacked GTC as "one of the worst Combines that has ever existed in any part of the world" and told F. W. Marks that Liberty Theatres "was also endeavouring to secure the lease of the Civic Theatre, Newcastle, but although his tender was unquestionably better than that of the combine the Newcastle City Council accepted [GTC's offer]. No reason had been given for that," he told Marks "and an inquiry should be held into the matter." Martin added that GTC's ability to secure the Civic with even less money "shows the operations of the combine." "To-day," he added, "as a result of the combine, the public does not have an opportunity of seeing these pictures. The only persons who decide whether Australian pictures should be seen by the public are this combine. It is the duty of the Government to protect Australian [productions]." Martin added as well that GTC was trying to make it "impossible" for non-GTC cinemas to succeed and that "the Combine" sought to control the flow and costs of all films distributed in Australia. GTC, he added, "denied outlets to pictures distributed by other companies, and so forced the independent exhibitors to come to it for films. By their monopolistic efforts, the corporation is trying to make it impossible for the independent exhibitors to operate." Then, he added, ominously, "When they can no longer carry on they are bought out." "What is wrong with the picture business today," he explained, "is that men have been trying to get control of it at the expense of everyone else connected with it. We are denied freedom to trade."[88] Martin added that Liberty Theatres simply wanted approval to build new cinemas in the state.[89]

The NSW inquiry then turned to MGM, where a local MGM representative (Mr. McIntyre) also charged that GTC was constraining local film distribution and exhibition. McIntyre supported Martin's concerns over the Civic Theatre episode in Newcastle and told Marks that MGM "intends to build a theatre in Sydney seating 2,200 at a cost of £200.000," despite the "real opposition to these plans [which] comes from General Theatres Corporation." McIntyre was incensed that MGM needed to jump through both Sydney's building regulations and *then* opposition within the film trade itself. "If we were going to build a huge store that would give work to hundreds would we have to fight for a license to do so? Why should we now have to fight?" Hoyts' attorney, Mr. Minter, argued that "there is a precedent. Hotels. And hotels are not built by foreign capital." David Martin then cranked up the temperature: "I would like to add to the agenda that this enquiry should investigate General Theatres Corporation." Minter responded, "Yes, and Universal Pictures, too."[90] Bernard Freeman shot back that

> General Theatres Corporation or Hoyts has a grip on every city theatre of any consequence, except [MGM's] Prince Edward.... General Theatres Corporation has created a very dangerous position in the Industry. With our own theatre, which we can provide with our own product, the Corporation could not dictate to us in the legitimate conduct of our business, and we avoid a position in which we are forced to come to the Corporation as the only avenue for obtaining Sydney releases. Having our own theatre, we could provide for a continuity of release, commencing when our product was ready and not when the Corporation chose to complete a deal.[91]

In arguing for theater licenses for MGM's new cinema in Sydney, Freeman noted that, except for a few shop window cinemas in major Australian cities, "M-G-M had no intention of building or acquiring theatres in the suburbs or country." Freeman argued instead that MGM would help independent exhibitors throughout the country through film distribution and by drumming up business for these pictures through their publicity at MGM's city shop window cinemas.[92] Stuart Doyle, managing director of Greater Union, retorted that if MGM and other independent urban and suburban exhibitors began constructing new cinemas in an already crowded market, it would hurt GTC's combined circuits and "would mean the total loss of between £4,000,000 and £5,000,000 of Australian shareholders' money." Frederick James Smith, a GTC director, argued that Sydney was already "over-theatred' with picture houses," and that "the preservation of the General Theatres circuit was, in his opinion, a matter of national importance." It was also, of course, of paramount interest to ES&A, which had invested a large amount of capital in GUO and GTC. Doyle added that "no fresh licences should be issued for any theatres in New South Wales unless it could be shown that the theatres in existence were not sufficient... and licences should not be issued for any theatre except to a British subject, or a company substantially owned and controlled by British subjects." Doyle then cleverly employed a bit of emotional blackmail. Having attracted 4,430 investors in Greater Union Theatres Ltd., he argued that "the shares represented the life savings of persons who depended entirely upon returns from theatre investments for their existence. If new theatres were built, it would spell ruin to them. Greater Union Theatres, Ltd.," he added, "was completely Australian-owned and staffed," and "any foreign organisation would not be concerned with the sentiment of Australians. The directors and executives of Greater Union Theatres Ltd. had a purely Australian outlook, and it would be a sorry day for Australia if the public sentiment of the country, by virtue of the foreign moving pictures presented, was dictated by foreigners."[93]

Once more Fox's control of Hoyts was ignored. The company's position was both incisive and deeply cynical. Having secured their duopoly with Greater Union—with allowances for other strong independent exhibitors here and there—the company now sought to strengthen its own position by claiming that their "desire" for "the restriction of licenses" would simply "uphold the protection principle" along nationalist lines and supposed concern for the "loss to investors and the 1391 employees of Hoyts." "There is no combine, monopoly," Munro also argued "or association of theatre proprietors injurious to the Australian industry, or operating unfairly towards either exhibitors or distributors."[94] This was not at all true, of course. Doyle went even further, "urg[ing] the passage of legislation to empower the Chief Secretary to withhold the granting of licences, and the appointment of a permanent board to regulate the industry."[95]

Paramount's J. W. Shand was not amused by the show Munro and Doyle had performed for the inquiry. He pointedly asked Doyle, "Is there any other country in the world that prohibits the issue of theatre licenses to foreigners?" Doyle's response was sublime: "Yes, America. Under the NRA Code covering the film industry. It stipulates that distributors or producers must not build in opposition to existing exhibitors, and my interpretation is that the intention of this clause is to cause a complete cessation of theatre-building for the present by all interests—foreigners, as well." When Doyle continued that "both Germany and Italy have prohibited foreigners from taking over theatres." Shand exclaimed, "Ah yes! Hitler and Mussolini!"[96] ES&A representative F. J. Smith also spoke up at the inquiry, backing their investments in Hoyts and Greater Union and speaking out against a free market, telling the inquiry that "there should be some control to eliminate the speculator."[97] Smith argued that Australia's cities were overseated and "the already unsatisfactory position must become accentuated if M-G-M and other foreign producers are allowed to enter the exhibiting end of the industry by inducing speculative builders to erect theatres for their benefit." MGM's representative, Mr. Abrahams, was ready for Smith's claims and asked, "While you say Sydney is overseated, you are building a new theatre on the old Tivoli."[98] Abrahams was even more incensed by the nationalistic turn, remarking, "You know that every member of the M-G-M organisation in Australia is Australian. . . . What have you done with respect to American pictures that was done out of patriotism and not for money?"[99]

The animus of Australia's independent exhibitors was further on display as H. J. W. Gyles, a representative of the Independent Exhibitors' Association of Victoria, testified before the NSW Film Enquiry that "many independent exhibitors have been forced either to close their theatres or enter into an agreement with [the] Hoyts group in the suburbs of Melbourne because of their fear that they may be unable to obtain satisfactory supplies." Gyles, bucking any notion that GTC and Hoyts' laments were in the best interests of Australia or the Australian film industry, noted that "the organisation I represent is positively of the opinion that it is essential to the successful running of their businesses to have an open market."[100] The open testimony revealed one clarifying truth: that the power of Chase National Bank in the United States and the ES&A Bank in Australia had not led to the stimulus of free market investment across the Australian exhibition industry but instead to a consolidated duopoly now seeking governmental assistance in constraining both foreign investment *and* domestic exhibitors hoping to survive against the reinforced power of GTC's bank-financed restraint of trade actions.

Between January 2 and April 20, 1934, fifty-four "public sittings" were held for eight-four different witnesses. Four thousand pages of evidence was collected. Commissioner F. W. Marks's report was finally released in four parts between late June and early July. In it he sided with MGM, Universal, and Australia's independent theaters, stating the need for "no government restriction of theatre licences, and no interference in such sensitive areas as film hire rates, blind and block booking and rejection rights."[101] To protect against further American influence in distribution, though, Shirley and Adams note, "Marks did urge . . . the introduction of a five year quota for Australian films, beginning with a four per cent quota for exhibitors and five per cent for distributors."[102] This was a paltry sum that in the end mattered little to the overall composition of booking and theater schedules. The net result of the NSW inquiry, despite all of that argument, was a new set of rather ineffective quotas, the New South Wales Quota Act, which was intended to force exhibitors to book more Australian films, thereby encouraging more investment in indigenous production. The quota was certainly not an especially arduous entanglement since, by 1934–1935, the box office was booming again in Australia.[103]

The fortunes of Hoyts had so profoundly shifted from their Depression-era depths that, after the inquiry, the company announced an extensive remodeling of its existing circuit *and* an expansion of its Sydney and Melbourne chains. Greater Union followed with its own "modernization" of its Melbourne and Sydney suburban holdings.[104] In the end, the inquiry had been all sound and fury amounting to very little in terms of change, but it had laid bare the issues related to U.S. ownership of foreign cinemas and the debate even within Hollywood's own executives and sales offices abroad.

The biggest loser was F. W. Thring, who was still trying to make indigenous Australian film production a reality. At the inquiry, ES&A's F. J. Smith noted that he "would regard Mr. Thring as being, perhaps, the leading producer in Australia," but "my experience, however, has shown that Australian audiences don't want Australian productions."[105] Thring later claimed to have secured an option "on five American stars and two directors" during a trip to New York in 1936. He returned excitedly to Australia but soon learned that he was dying and passed away that year. "The Australian cinema had lost its most persuasive advocate of the quota system," Shirley and Adams write, "and one whose political and business abilities might have made it work." In the end, Thring "gambled a private fortune . . . producing nine feature films and around eighty shorts. *Film Weekly* estimated that in film production and live theatre, he had lost a total of £75000."[106]

Greater Union and Hoyts, meanwhile, financially safeguarded their investments and largely kept the other American film companies out of local film exhibition through the size and scale of their allied circuits, which were in no way broken up, interfered with, or limited by the inquiry. MGM would grow a small cinema chain in Australia, but the financially beleaguered Paramount reported once more in 1936 that beyond its Melbourne "show window," "no theatre expansion is planned by the company in Australia."[107] With the 1934 NSW inquiry receding quickly into the past, the newly merged Twentieth Century-Fox was in the catbird seat by the late 1930s. Control of Hoyts provided the company with a dominant, local exhibition chain that generated annual revenues *and* a national outlet for Twentieth Century-Fox, *Fox Movietone News*, and Gaumont-British films. Backed by a combination of Australian (ES&A) and American (Chase) banks, Hoyts and Greater Union would remain the two most powerful Australian circuits for the next century.

CHAPTER 6

THE FOX CHASE IN NEW ZEALAND AND AUSTRALIA, 1936–1946

New Zealand was a small, but growing, English-speaking market for American distributors, with financial returns paling in comparison to the country's much larger neighbor to the west. By 1917, 550,000 New Zealanders were attending movie theaters each week. The two leading chains in Auckland then were Haywards and Fullers. Haywards' Enterprises had been formed in 1908 and operated thirty cinemas throughout the country by 1912. Fullers Ltd. was also formed in 1908 as a chain of vaudeville theaters that quickly shifted to motion pictures. The two companies—Haywards' Pictures Ltd. and Fullers' Pictures Ltd.—merged to become the jointly owned NZ Picture Supplies in 1913, with forty cinemas nationwide. Later renamed the Fuller-Hayward Theatre Corp., the chain controlled over sixty cinemas throughout New Zealand by the late 1920s. The company began borrowing money to expand the circuit and install synchronous sound technology. The timing was poor. Attendance in New Zealand dropped 45 percent at the onset of the Depression, forcing the Fuller-Hayward Theatre Corp. to declare insolvency, and the company was taken over by its debtors. John Fuller became one of the two trustees for the new owners while Henry Hayward and Phil Hayward left to start a new firm, Auckland Cinemas Ltd.[1]

Meanwhile, three additional chains were formed in New Zealand. In 1920 Thomas O'Brien had left Fuller-Hayward to create his own chain, first by buying a cinema in the South Island city of Dunedin and then purchasing Everybodys Theatre in Auckland. By the end of the 1920s he commanded the third-largest chain in the country, Thomas O'Brien Theatres Ltd. J. C. Williamson, who already had a circuit of theaters in Australia, also began operating Regent cinemas in New Zealand in 1926 under the corporate name of J. C. Williamson (New Zealand) Films Ltd. Despite their collective prominence, Thomas O'Brien Theatres Ltd. and J. C. Williamson Ltd. both became insolvent by 1932. O'Brien went out of business completely while a new company, J. C. Williamson Picture Corp. Ltd., bought out the insolvent Williamson chain and began operating under that name.[2]

The third chain was a bit more unusual in its origins. Hippodrome Pictures Ltd. was incorporated in Auckland on October 3, 1924, and a formal certificate of incorporation was registered on November 6, 1924.[3] The company was formed through an equal partnership of 750 shares divided between Frederick John Rayner, a Canadian-émigré dentist who had bought the city's Globe Cinema, and a former men's outfitter employee-turned-cleaner/manager of the King George Theatre, M. J. (Michael Joseph) Moodabe.[4]

M. J.'s parents, Ferris and Elizabeth Moudabber, had emigrated, according to their grandson, Michael Moodabe, from "the olive groves of Lebanon near Tripoli for the imagined richer fields of Australia" in the mid-1880s and settled in Sydney. Ferris purchased a horse and cart and became an unsuccessful pushcart peddler. Peddling was not the life that Ferris—who had been a nearly forty-year-old "playboy" when he entered an arranged marriage with Elizabeth when she was just sixteen—had imagined for them all in Australia. Their first son, Michael Joseph Moudabber, was born in Sydney in 1895. Four years after they landed, the still penniless Moudabbers emigrated to Auckland, New Zealand. It was there that one of the senior members of the Lebanese community, Assid Abraham Corban, suggested an anglicized name change. The *Moodabes* were born. Their second son, Joseph Moodabe, was born in Auckland in 1899. The turn of the century may have brought renewed hope, but it was quickly washed away by the sudden death of Ferris Moodabe in 1901. Elizabeth, now a young single mother of two boys, moved into Auckland's "seedy" Greys Street and opened a small grocery store.[5]

The formation of Hippodrome Pictures Ltd. in 1924 required a £500 coequal investment between Rayner and Moodabe. M. J. certainly did not have that kind of money but, through her grocery business, Elizabeth Moodabe did. She agreed to stake M. J. in Hippodrome Pictures Ltd. and was provided with five hundred shares of the company split evenly between herself and her other son, Joe. Joe was a worker, Michael was a showman, and Elizabeth Moodabe was hardly a silent partner. "Elizabeth Moodabe's influence and interest remained an integral part of [the company] until her death in 1973," her grandson Michael would later recall. "She insisted on being appraised of every major decision and development." In the years to follow, "Her son saw to it that every overseas business associate or partner was chauffeured to her home in Pah

Road, Epsom." Elizabeth was "a true matriarch," Michael Moodabe writes, and no matter how large in stature M. J. and Joe became, she "would and did rebuke [M. J.] privately and in public."[6] She was the silent but powerful partner in a soon-to-be growing cinema chain.[7]

After M. J. became a partner in Hippodrome Pictures in 1924, he also received the title of manager and a weekly salary of less than seven pounds per week. Hippodrome's early reputation was damaged by Rayner's attempted bribery of Prime Minister Joseph Gordon Coates in the prime minister's office. With Coates's departure in December 1928 and, later, Rayner's death in September 1931, M. J.'s "relationships" with the "succeeding governments steadily improved."[8]

M. J. slowly integrated Joe Moodabe more fully into the business, and the two brothers became a highly recognizable duo.[9] In October 1928 the name of the company was changed from Hippodrome Pictures Ltd. to Amalgamated Theatres Ltd. because, according to company records, "the old name [was] not being descriptive of the increased extent of the operations of the Company."[10] Despite the name change, though, the Amalgamated name was based largely on aspiration; the company still owned and operated only one theater. Competition from Fuller-Hayward and Williamsons was stiff in the late 1920s, and those two companies cornered the Auckland market using a tried-and-true exhibition strategy: prevent distributors from playing their films with Amalgamated by threatening boycotts of anyone who worked with the Moodabes.

Nonetheless, by cobbling together films from a variety of other distributors and keeping their acquisitions and overhead low, Amalgamated had accumulated thirty-two cinemas by 1932.[11] Many of those cinemas were previously operated by Thomas O'Brien Theatres Ltd., followed by J. C. Williamson Films Ltd., both of which had been forced into receivership. Once again, it was banking that altered the local exhibition industry and enabled Amalgamated to scoop up the profitable rubble for the small but growing chain. Amalgamated thus began operating the opulent Civic Theatre—Auckland's greatest movie house[12]—and owned outright the Plaza, Rialto, Tivoli, Regent, Britannia, and Royal cinemas. By 1933 Amalgamated had grown into one of the nation's larger circuits, with over forty cinemas.[13] "MJ had a good and loyal team who would travel with him outside Auckland as he established his chain," Michael Moodabe writes. "They would drive from provincial city to provincial city. They would find a hall. They did not build new theatres. They couldn't afford to. But they would redecorate, turning a hall into a cinema. Where no hall was available, they rented, not always to the circuit's advantage."[14] In fact, former Amalgamated Theatres executive Eric Kearney notes, the company built only one cinema in the early days—the Crystal Palace in Mt. Eden. The leasing and conversion business was fine with M. J., Kearney observes, because in his opinion M. J. wasn't truly passionate about cinemas but about racehorses, and he owned a cinema chain in order to enjoy (and presumably bet on) his actual passion.[15]

Amalgamated's growing circuit power by 1933 enabled the company to secure new booking deals for more than 100 Fox, Gaumont-British, and Gainsborough features and 376 shorts. This was a gamechanger for Amalgamated; with the deal, its rivals could no longer block Amalgamated from a steady supply of Hollywood product. Having survived the Depression well and with plans to open new cinemas in Wellington, Palmerston, North Hamilton, and Gisborne by the end of 1933, Amalgamated Theatres now claimed to be the largest independent chain in the dominion.[16] Amalgamated was also benefiting, Kearney argues, from a growing and overwhelming zeal for cinema on the part of New Zealanders. Grocery stores closed at 5:30 P.M. and were shut completely on Saturday and Sunday. Other retail stores closed around the same time, and only one evening of shopping was available each week on Friday nights when stores stayed open until 9:00 P.M. Pubs closed at 6:00 P.M. and were closed on Sundays. Few restaurants existed outside major cities, and coffee houses didn't begin cropping up until 1946. For entertainment, New Zealanders could stay home with the radio or go to the movies. Saturday at the cinema was the biggest night of the week in early to mid-twentieth century New Zealand.[17] This made the country ripe for entertainment investment by both local and foreign players.

Fox Hunting in New Zealand

By the mid-1930s film exhibition had become a highly stable, mature business in New Zealand, with little room for expansion. In Auckland, for example, after the Embassy Theatre opened in 1935, no other movie house opened or closed in the "inner-city area" of Auckland for another quarter century.[18] Urban areas were already packed with cinemas and fully built out. There was, therefore, considerable challenges for Fox or any other American film company intent on entering the Auckland exhibition market. Acquiring cinemas or even a circuit made far more sense, especially given the relatively small cost to do so. Further, the possibility of building an American-owned circuit in the dominion was prohibitive due to recent legislation that forced exhibitors to prove that any new cinema was being constructed in an area not already served by existing theaters. Therefore, the odds that Fox could have been given a license—without a New Zealand partnership—in all but the most desolate areas seemed remote, especially amid ongoing concerns about U.S. cultural, financial, and industrial expansion in the British Commonwealth.[19]

In May 1936 rumors of "reported negotiations" between the Fox-controlled Hoyts circuit and Amalgamated appeared in the *New Zealand Motion Picture*

Exhibitors' Bulletin (*NZMPEB*), a trade journal published by the country's dominant exhibition association. The industry's mouthpiece reported the news in an article about the fear and loathing around "foreign control and film rents" and the effects, once more, of bank control of the film industry in Australasia: "The process of bleeding the major [New Zealand] exhibitors by the major [American] distributors need only be carried to a certain point, and the whole exhibiting circuits will be ready to fall into the hands of the American interests," the *NZMPEB* opined. It also honed in on the control by banks: "The reported negotiations between Hoyts (Australia) and Amalgamated Theatres (N.Z.) give point to those fears. In the published list of affiliations of the Chase Bank, New York (required by the U.S banking legislation of 1933) appears the whole of the Hoyt theatre enterprises in Australia. Control of a New Zealand exhibiting circuit by Hoyts of Australia, means in effect control by the Chase Bank of New York." The Prime Minister of New Zealand sounded the alarm, arguing, "We cannot afford to allow picture combinations or any other sort of combination to come to New Zealand for the purpose of controlling any service that New Zealand requires. We are not going to have it. This thing has been in an unsatisfactory position for some years and the time has come for the Government to take a hand. No outside interests will govern us. That is definite."[20] Anti-American sentiment could also be found elsewhere in the *NZMPEB*. J. W. Mitchell, an exhibitor who had been in the business since 1910, noted, "Generally, I find the distributors of New Zealand fair to deal with. The only complaint I have is that the New Zealand managers are under the thumb of Sydney, and Sydney's thumb appears to be under the heel of America. That is the whole reason of any dissatisfaction."[21]

By September 1936 the Fox/Hoyts/Amalgamated rumors popped up again in *Everyones*.[22] Michael Moodabe argues that it was M. J., not Fox, who, in order to "guarantee a film supply," was actively trying to persuade Fox "to buy a half interest in Amalgamated."[23] In October, Fox and Amalgamated jointly announced that Twentieth Century-Fox, along with Stanley Crick and Charles Munro, had purchased "a substantial interest" in the circuit, now operating sixty-five cinemas across New Zealand. They were careful to point out that—for the moment—the tripartite investment meant "there will be no foreign domination majority, control remaining in the hands of British subjects."[24] M. J. Moodabe would remain general manager and chairman of the board of directors; Joseph Moodabe and Charles Munro would be joint managing directors; and Stanley Crick would join the board. M. J. confirmed the importance of Crick's involvement by noting that he and Joseph "would never have set this deal with anyone else but Stanley Crick."[25] Twentieth Century-Fox International head W. J. Hutchinson added, "We have bought an interest but we have not bought the control. The control remains definitely in the hands of the Moodabes and Messrs. Crick and Munro. That makes it distinctly British."[26]

The *Motion Picture Herald* observed that, with the investment, Twentieth Century-Fox would "now have a guaranteed and unquestionably a 'preferential' outlet in the 65 theatres which have either been owned or controlled by Amalgamated. This makes a total of nearly 140 theatres in the two Dominions in which the Corporation's product presumably comes first." This, the trade journal concluded, made Fox's local position "practically unassailable."[27] Michael Moodabe admits that "once 20th Century Fox had established its credentials as part owners of Amalgamated Theatres, film supply from them and other companies was guaranteed."[28] The 50 percent sale of Amalgamated to Fox also busted up the fading duopoly that Fullers-Hayward and Williamsons had previously enjoyed. In the succeeding years, Amalgamated (Fox) and Kerridge(-Odeon) (England's Rank Organisation) would form a far more powerful and lasting duopoly in New Zealand exhibition, spurred in large part by U.S. and British investment, respectively. In the end, foreign capital (and banks) also dominated New Zealand's film industry with Fox a key player after 1936.

The relationship between Fox distribution personnel in New Zealand and the Moodabes, as Dale Turnbull noted about the relationship between Fox executives in Australia and those working for Hoyts, could be intermittently frosty or even hostile. The two operations were corporate cousins but not partners. M. J. Moodabe added that "Mr. Crick has told us to go ahead—to buy our films as in the past, and to play the game with everybody."[29] Michael Moodabe argues that "this hands-off policy, dictated from the Fox New York head office, in spite of the fact that they now held fifty per cent, continued from that day [forward] in 1936." He adds, "Even after Fox controlled a hundred per cent [in later years], they insisted that the Moodabes run the show. And we did, with a minimum of overseas influence."[30] M. J.'s strong relationship with Fox executives in New York, which later blossomed into a close personal friendship with Twentieth Century-Fox president Spyros Skouras, "did not deter the almost autonomous Sydney and New Zealand branches [of Fox] from attempting to interfere in what they rightly perceived as half their business. M. J. fiercely defended his direct pipeline to New York and would answer only to them. This strong-willed approach frustrated Fox's local managers and made the occasional enemy."[31] Fox New Zealand and Amalgamated Theatres were not always in the same business; Fox New Zealand was responsible for distributing Fox films in the territory while Amalgamated screened Fox *and* other films. Instead, they were two separate but profitable cash registers of Fox's global holdings.

Chase and Bank Controls

Amalgamated's new position came with new questions and critiques. The *New Zealand Motion Picture Exhibitors Bulletin* not only questioned how much

Amalgamated would remain truly "British" with Fox's new investment but also not so subtly attacked the Moodabes for not being British at all. Here one can clearly see the not-so-subtle anti-Lebanese orientation of the journal in two places: first with a series of exclamation points after noting that "control is to be in British hands—i.e., the Moodabes (!!) and Messrs Crick and Munro" and in a more direct reference "consider[ing] the extent to which anything under the control of the Moodabes may be said to be under British control."[32] (The Moodabes had, of course, been British subjects for decades and at least before 1924.[33]) These xenophobic comments against the Moodabes in New Zealand mirror the antisemitic attacks against the Levys in Birmingham, England, a decade earlier. Exhibitors from "other" backgrounds had not only their business practices questioned but their citizenship as well.

Beyond the xenophobia of the era, the kind the Moodabes had battled since their first arrival in New Zealand, was a more existential concern on the part of many about Fox's investment in Amalgamated: the same powerful forces that had pushed Fox, Hoyts, and General Union further into debt were now spurring U.S. investment in New Zealand's fastest-growing chain: the banks. Behind all of these seemingly personal decisions and relationships that prompted the sale of half of Amalgamated to Fox lay, once more, the critical role of (U.S.) banks, principally Chase, which, as previously mentioned, was still actively pushing Fox to invest in foreign cinema chains despite the company's precarious Depression-era position. As the *NZMPEB* noted in October 1936, even the suggestion that the Moodabes still retained a controlling interest was now in public doubt.[34]

Fox subsequently created a new subsidiary for the distribution and marketing of its films in New Zealand, Twentieth Century-Fox Film Corp. (N.Z.) Ltd., whose "Memorandum of Association" included the right to "purchase lease or otherwise acquire land ... to alter enlarge rebuild decorate or otherwise improve any theatres or other buildings." The broad latitude of the corporation provided flexibility for Fox to aid Amalgamated or, if needed, commence building activities for local cinemas on its own.[35]

In October 1937 Fox executed drastic changes to Amalgamated's board that had the effect of reducing the influence of its Australian representatives and shoring up Fox's corporate position. These moves were concurrent with a meeting between the Fuller-Hayward Theatre Corp., New Zealand Theatres Ltd., and Christchurch Cinemas Ltd. with New Zealand prime minister M. J. Savage in Wellington on November 5, 1937, to discuss concerns over Fox's investment in Amalgamated. Savage asked the group "what you want me to do" about the growing threat of American distributing and exhibiting power in New Zealand; rumors were also swirling that both Fox and MGM were eyeing the Williamson circuit for acquisition. J. H. Mason, president and chairman of the Motion Picture Distributors Association of Australasia, argued,

"The only means by which any foreign renter could acquire representation in this country was by leasing or buying an existing interest." Prime Minister Savage, alarmed by the possibility that Fox or MGM might control even more of the country's distribution and exhibition, told exhibitors, "I am not a little bit interested in having a material interest in the picture industry, but I am interested in protecting the public . . . in order to protect the picture interests against foreign control?" Benjamin Fuller responded that he did not "want American domination, although, of course, we do want to see their film."[36] Here, once more, was the endless conundrum for the local exhibitor in a globalized marketplace: how to acquire Hollywood films without fueling its control.

In New Zealand, Amalgamated (and Fox) found themselves at odds with exhibitors again when the country's Film Industry Board amended its earlier 1937 Cinematograph Films Licenses Regulations in early 1940. All decisions for allowing additional cinemas to be built and operated would now be "left to the Magistrate." The *NZMPEB* added that these regulations grew out of a dispute between Amalgamated and Auckland's Civic Theatre, which charged that Amalgamated's relationship with Fox and domination of the city's cinemas (and thus its relationship with all major distributors) had starved the Civic Theatre of "an adequate supply of first lease film."[37]

This ongoing dispute was set to go into arbitration with the Film Industry Board and other government bodies when Amalgamated suddenly announced in May 1940 that it had joined the country's Exhibitors' Association, putting them firmly inside the combative local industry and on a path toward national détente. The *NZMPEB* was ecstatic by the news, noting, "The accession of such a large circuit to our membership is an event of great importance."[38] With the move, Amalgamated silenced its largest critics and the publication they used to lobby against Amalgamated's (and Fox's) growing power. In October 1940, to further allay local fears about American/Australian control, Fox Film Corp. Pty. Ltd. transferred its 48,000 shares in Amalgamated to Fox's new New Zealand–based subsidiary, Twentieth Century-Fox Film Corp. (N.Z.).[39] Amalgamated was now jointly controlled by the new subsidiary, giving Twentieth Century-Fox's control over Amalgamated an outward, more *New Zealander* appearance.

Amalgamated would eventually employ roughly 2,500 New Zealanders with an annual cinema attendance of more than 5 million each year.[40] Fox had bought into Amalgamated in 1936 at a very opportune time.[41] Historian Tony Froude notes that Fox's half-ownership in Amalgamated not only charted the company's more profitable future but also exerted its influence over cinema architecture throughout the country. Amalgamated's association with Twentieth Century-Fox, he writes, "led to the introduction of Art Deco designs and the modern movement as seen in the USA" as the company "tended to lease theatres for 15 years at a time, and to outfit them in Art Deco design. I believe we owe much to this chain for the introduction and development of this style, with its curves, use of neon, modern materials, waterfall curtains, and impressive centre lighting and wall lights."[42] Froude noted that an American style of operation was also parroted outside the cinemas wherever Amalgamated cinemas proliferated.

MGM's Australian Shop Windows

The expiration of the five-year General Theatres Corp. of Australasia Ltd. agreement on December 31, 1937, prompted a paradigm shift in Australian exhibition. Hoyts and Greater Union—forced into a shotgun marriage by ES&A Bank nearly a decade earlier—became separate companies and competitors. New Greater Union Theatres chairman Norman B. Rydge took on a very nationalistic stance. "Greater Union Theatres," he told *Everyones*, "has always been proud of the fact that it is an all-Australian organisation, owned and controlled by Australians, and working in the interests of Australia. Our policy is merely a declaration of our local independence!" Rydge, objecting to foreign influence and concerns that Hollywood might try to hone in further, noted that "I am sure no Government will hesitate to introduce legislation to protect, if necessary, the jobs of our large army of men and women employees, and the interests of about 5000 Australian investors."[43]

Despite Rydge's rhetoric, MGM's Bernard Freeman kept his focus on securing shop window cinemas in Australia's key cities.[44] Freeman's public interest in buying or building local shop windows sparked rumors in November 1941 that MGM had bought the St. James Building in Sydney and its opulent St. James Theatre from John Fuller of Fuller's Theatres. Both Freeman and Fuller denied the rumors; Freeman suggested that the arrangement was nothing more than a long-term booking agreement while Fuller declared, "There's not enough money in all Sydney to buy [the St. James] from me!" *Smiths Weekly* reported that the St. James Theatre, which MGM was already leasing as its Sydney shop window, *was*, despite all of these denials, being purchased by MGM using frozen funds "ordinarily remitted to America" and now stuck in Australia. Once again, domestic currency policies and restrictions had simply amplified American investment overseas.[45] Just over a week after John Fuller denied these reports, *Smiths Weekly*'s headline blared "THERE WAS ENOUGH MONEY!" for the sale of the St. James Theatre.[46] *Variety* would later report a $2 million figure for the sale of the whole building to MGM.[47]

The St. James acquisition followed the construction or lease of numerous Metro Theatres across the country during the 1930s. In 1934 MGM had opened its first new build in Australia, the Metro Theatre in Melbourne, designed by

C. N. Hollinshead. Like many other Metros built during this period, its construction was overseen by Harry Moskowitz, head of Loew's engineering department in New York. In 1937 MGM's Brisbane Metro Theatre had opened with "the hallmarks of an American design," as noted by architectural historian Ross Thorne.[48] MGM also took over the lease of Perth's Regent Theatre, which was remodeled by architects Alfred Baxter Cox and William Leighton and reopened it in September 1938 as the Metro Theatre.[49] Thomas Lamb, Loew's frequent house architect for domestic and foreign cinemas, was commissioned to design yet another Metro for Adelaide in 1939.[50] All of these shop window cinemas enabled MGM to present its short and feature-length films across the country and advertise the company's methods for exploiting these films to smaller cinemas and markets. The growing MGM circuit reflected MGM's policy of building, buying, or leasing shop window cinemas in major cities and then partnering with local chains (in this case Greater Union) for larger cinema distribution, a policy it had conducted in South Africa, England, and many other markets.

Hoyts, meanwhile, continued to take over even more cinemas. In March 1941 the company acquired six new cinemas from Sinder-Dean, providing the Fox-controlled circuit with additional theaters in Sydney (two), Melbourne, Brisbane, Hobart, and Launceston. With the expiration of Paramount's lease of Melbourne's Capitol, Hoyts also took over that palatial cinema.[51]

Wartime Moviegoing and the British Invasion of New Zealand

Hollywood might have been seen as outsiders before the war, but the Allied effort, and the decline in the small amount of Australian film production during World War II, made American film companies and their local representatives key parts of the local cinematic war effort. The National Films Council, which included Bernard Freeman of MGM and Ernest Turnbull of Twentieth Century-Fox, were key members advising the Australian Commonwealth Department of Information, which directed the country's propaganda efforts and national news production. With newsreels providing much-needed visual references of the conflict both near and far away and feature films, shorts, and cartoons providing distraction, cinema attendance surged, especially after 1942 and the arrival of thousands of American servicemen.[52]

Admissions to Australian cinemas reached a peak of 151 million per year in 1944–1945, compared with the later peacetime figure of 133 million in 1947–1948. In an industry speech, the head of Hoyts Theatres flippantly remarked that his company and Greater Union should erect a statue in honor of Hitler for what he had done to boost their business. Hoyts' Ernest Turnbull always felt that the war had indeed generated enormous returns for Hoyts. The boom in profits finally enabled Fox to pay off its debts to local banks. Those profits also enabled Hoyts to purchase Western Suburb Cinemas and their twenty-eight venues, strengthening their suburban cinema holdings around Sydney and beyond.[53]

Local conflicts did not abate during wartime in New Zealand, however. Four years after joining the Film Industry Board, Amalgamated was still haggling over its virtual control of the Auckland cinema scene. The independent Capitol Theatre on Auckland's Dominion Road, for instance, still alleged that Amalgamated (and Fox) were engaged in a "film monopoly, causing what was virtually a boycott of the Capitol" in the city. The *Independent Exhibitor* magazine noted that these kinds of disputes were "not capable of being adjudicated on by the Film Industry Board" because Amalgamated was now on the board.[54] Amalgamated and Fox had, therefore, outmaneuvered their vocal critics through their placement on the board of the *NZMPEB*, stifling previous critiques. That concentration of power was even more evident when two nominees from the New Zealand Motion Picture Exhibitors Association and two nominees from the Independent Cinemas Association were installed on New Zealand's Film Industry Board.

As the war came to an end in 1945, New Zealand hoped to chart a course away from American cultural influence and, through postwar Commonwealth patriotism, reestablish British—not American—dominion and culture.[55] The problem regarding cinemagoing was the dearth of British films in the pipeline after the war. The number was so low, in fact, that New Zealand had to waive its requirement that at least 20 percent of the feature films shown in each cinema were British.[56] Hollywood, once again, filled the void.

In March 1946 Rank made their interest in New Zealand exhibition even more prominent, announcing that they had purchased a 50 percent interest in Kerridge Theatres.[57] Robert Kerridge remained a director of the new company while J. Arthur Rank and his top executive, John Davis, became joint directors.[58] Wayne Brittenden contradicts contemporary press accounts, however, by noting that "Rank was refused a seat on the Board and never pressed for one. Kerridge returned to New Zealand in triumph, having become not only the exhibitor of the increasingly popular Rank films, but also its distributor and business partner."[59] Unlike the Americans' overseas operations, no Rank employees were sent to New Zealand. The New Zealand company, from all appearances, remained strictly New Zealander. Kerridge also cloaked the sale of half the company as patronage to Commonwealth and King: "The object of the partnership is to give the British film industry the opportunity it deserves, both from the patriotic and merit points of view.... The partnership also means that there will no longer be delay in British films reaching New Zealand."[60] Overnight, the two largest exhibition chains had sidled up to their outside benefactors: Amalgamated with Fox in the United States, and Kerridge with Rank in the United Kingdom. New Zealand's two largest cinema chains were now loaded up with outside financing.

Kerridge's sudden union with Rank was characterized in the press as postwar adulation for the British empire and their connected cultural *and* biological lineages. "Having had an opportunity of discussion with Mr. Rank and with other industrialists in England I have returned with complete faith in our race and in our nation," Kerridge told the *NZMPEB*.[61]

> The arrangements recently concluded by me with the Rank interests completes a nation-wide tie-up and to-day we have powerful organisations in England, South Africa, Canada, Ireland, Australia, New Zealand and certain foreign countries, all co-operating to ensure the establishment of this great industry for Great Britain. . . . I am convinced that Mr. Rank's activity is not actuated by a desire for personal profit, but only as a source of profit to our Motherland and to the establishment of world solidity and understanding.[62]

A new company, Odeon Holdings (New Zealand) Ltd., was established to control the "Dominion" interests of Rank—including its new half interest in Kerridge—in Auckland. In a complicated corporate structure, the capital investment in the company was divided into 800,000 £1 shares, with all but two held by Overseas Cinematograph Theatres Ltd., Rank's own foreign exhibition company based out of London. Two of the directors of Odeon Holdings were J. Arthur Rank and his right-hand man, John H. Davis.[63] The *NZMPEB* noted the following month that Rank's investment in Kerridge and its subsequent purchase of the J. C. Williamson Picture Corp. Ltd.—the circuit MGM and Fox had been circling—meant that "substantially all of the major locations throughout New Zealand, with the exception of those controlled by Amalgamated Theatres Ltd., are now controlled by the Rank-Kerridge organisation."[64] An internal memorandum from the New Zealand Board of Trade to the minister of Internal Affairs observed that the collusive nature of international capital was even more stunning for the restrictive flow of films throughout the dominion. Rank, the memo noted, already had "a contract with the 20th Century [Fox] Corporation of America under which the Corporation distribute all the Organisation's films in New Zealand."[65] Of course, Fox was the 50–50 owner of Amalgamated, suggesting a stunningly collusive relationship in New Zealand between Odeon, Rank, Gaumont-British, Twentieth Century-Fox, and Amalgamated Theatres.

With the purchase of Williamson by the newly renamed Kerridge-Odeon circuit, the two main circuits (Kerridge-Odeon and Amalgamated Theatres) now controlled more than 150 cinemas in New Zealand, with Kerridge-Odeon controlling 114 and Amalgamated, 44. (There were roughly 386 independent cinemas in the country, but Kerridge-Odeon and Amalgamated had an outsized investment in the largest and most important urban cinemas.) Over the years, Kerridge and the Moodabes continually attempted to "outfox" one another. Michael Moodabe cited children's clubs as one example. When Kerridge-Odeon created the Young New Zealanders' Club for child-oriented matinee performances in 1946, Amalgamated heard the news and preempted it with their own Chums Club.[66] In another instance, Wayne Brittenden notes, "Hearing that Kerridge-Odeon would be screening the first 3D feature, *House of Wax*, in 1953, Amalgamated undermined the event by hastily scheduling some inferior 3D productions."[67]

Despite their competitive battles, though, the two companies would turn to one another for support whenever threatened. "In the early 1950s," Brittenden writes, "when MGM's Australian office was believed to be moving towards establishing drive-in theatres in New Zealand, Amalgamated and Kerridge-Odeon made representations to ensure the proposed venture would be blocked by the government." This was possible, in part because of Kerridge's dual support for both the National Party and his close friendship with Tom Skinner, leader of the Federation of Labour. Kerridge and the Moodabes would go on to block MGM's efforts and then jointly own and operate Skyline Cinemas (drive-ins); regarding independent exhibitors, "both chains were consistently ruthless" with independent exhibitors, "constantly blocking their access to attractive product through the pressure they were able to mount on distributors." The duopoly between Kerridge-Odeon and Amalgamated may have been competitive, but it was punctuated by collusive efforts to block any possible internal or external threat and to co-operate the nation's leading drive-ins. "It could take a couple of years or more for a lucrative film to be seen at every venue operated by one of the big chains," Brittenden notes. "Only then were the independents, unless operating outside a certain distance from the cities, allowed to screen the film—and often on less favourable terms than Amalgamated and Kerridge-Odeon enjoyed."[68] As in Australia, New Zealand's exhibition industry was heavily dictated by a local cinema chain controlled by Twentieth Century-Fox.

CHAPTER 7

HOLLYWOOD AND AUSTRALASIAN CINEMAS, 1946-1982

With the war over, Warner Bros. fully intended to exploit the land it had purchased over the past decade for theatrical expansion. Warner Bros., like Odeon, focused its own postwar plans on Australasia. In July 1946 the company was primed to make use of the Sydney property it had bought at the coveted corner of George and Bathurst streets years earlier. Warner Bros. applied for "provisional approval" to build a new 1,664-seat "show window" there, and plans were drawn up by John and Drew Eberson's U.S. firm, with G. N. Kenworthy serving as a local consultant on the project. "The cinema," *Film Daily* reported, hoped "to be the best in Australia and equal to anything in the world."[1] The Sydney shop window was intended to be the first in a chain of Warner cinemas across the country.[2] However, despite all of Warner Bros.'s planning and excitement about the project, the year came and went with no approval. In May 1947 Warner Bros.' Stanley Higginson wrote to Sydney's town clerk to seek the city's approval and ensure that the proposed cinema would not compete with or obstruct the city's "re-planning activities" in the area.[3]

The project was doomed by outside forces, however—namely, the country's Theatres and Films Commission, which seemed unwilling to grant Warner Bros., an American film company, a license to operate its own cinemas in Australia. The Theatres and Films Commission, which was composed of three members appointed by the Australian government and which operated under the control of the colonial secretary and later the chief secretary, had been consecrated in 1938 as part of the country's Theatres, Public Halls and

Cinemagraphs Films (Amendment) Act, of 1938 and then formalized in 1939. In addition to determining regulations over standard distribution contracts and American and British quotas, the commissioners also had the right to "conduct an inquiry into any matter, dispute or question relating to films or to any particular film, or to the production, distribution or exhibition of films."[4] The commission denied Warner Bros.' application to build a cinema in the city, citing the current "shortage of building materials and labor." Warner Bros. appealed the commission's decision, especially in light of MGM and Fox's large investments in local exhibition. In August 1947 District Court Judge Studdert upheld the commission's ruling, arguing that the cinema "would be against the public interest in light of the shortages," despite Studdert admitting that "Sydney had substantially less cinema seating capacity than the other capital cities and he was satisfied that the company had made out a substantial case for an additional building." In fact, the *Sydney Morning Herald* noted, "Had the application been granted it would not have resulted in undue competition or economic waste within the meaning of the Theatres and Public Halls Act." The newspaper observed that many of Warner Bros.' possible competitors (and, awkwardly, exhibitors with whom Warner Bros. currently contracted with) were all at the same hearing as respondents to the appeal, supporting the government's efforts to keep Warner Bros. out of the exhibition business in Australia. Exhibitors present included executives from Hoyts Theatres Ltd. and Greater Union Theatres Pty. Ltd.[5] The materials shortages were the only real charge Warner Bros.' competitors could make in opposition. And it worked.

Warner Bros. was still determined, however, moving ahead with its planning regardless of the ruling. As required for construction, the city of Sydney's architect and building surveyor's department launched a pro forma inquiry for the company's interim development application in September 1947 for the proposed theater and determined that there was "no apparent objection" to the development of the property into a shop window cinema for Warner Bros. First National Pictures Pty. Ltd.[6] A "Minute Paper" from the town clerk in late September 1947 determined that "the site is not affected by any of the Council's planning schemes" and, after a yearlong inquiry, the Joint Committee recommended the council approve.[7] In April 1948 Higginson finally received approval from the council (of the Interim Development Authority) for the construction of the cinema "subject to the plans" being approved by the city building surveyor.[8] But that approval was only from the city. The Theatres and Films Commission remained steadfast in its objections for the next *five* years. By August 1953, frustrated and eager to turn some sort of profit on the property amid rising Sydney real estate prices, Warner Bros. dumped their shop window dreams and sold the lot.[9]

The Theatres and Films Commission ruling, and Warner Bros.' subsequent failure to build in Sydney, demonstrated once more that domestic protectionism was one of the best ways to block Hollywood and other foreign investment in local film exhibition. However, with so much of the country still dominated by Fox's Hoyts, the block on Warner Bros. was a pyrrhic victory for the commission. After all, Australia was awash in films made in Hollywood, many shown in Hoyts movie houses owned by Twentieth Century-Fox. The irony is that Warner Bros. had little desire to become a major player in Australian film exhibition. The company had simply wanted a single shop window cinema in Sydney to showcase its films. Fox, owners of one-half of a national duopoly, helped foreclose that possibility through Hoyts' lobbying of the commission under the guise of native protectionism.

MGM, Australia, and the 1950s

MGM, perhaps learning from Warner Bros.' frustrating experience, pursued a postwar expansion strategy that instead prioritized taking over existing cinemas instead of building new ones. In 1948, for example, David Martin sold his Minerva Theatre, a legitimate theater venue, to MGM. In April 1950 the renovated Minerva debuted as a third Sydney show house for MGM, with films shown day and date with the company's other Sydney shop windows, the Liberty and St. James theaters.[10] (Martin's Liberty Theatre had already been sold to MGM thirteen years earlier in 1937.[11]) The Minerva's gala reopening was feted by "the Lord Mayor, the Lady Mayoress and other political dignitaries in attendance," with an opening address by the mayor of Sydney.[12] With the addition of the Minerva, the 1950 sale of the Century Theatre in Manly (Sydney) to MGM, as well as the new Embassy in Malvern (Melbourne), there were now ten Metro cinemas throughout Australia. To reinforce its place within the Metro Theatres circuit in Australia, the Minerva Theatre was renamed the Metro King's Cross in August 1952.[13]

Programming changes were also in store. Deprived of guaranteed exhibition outlets following the 1948 U.S. Consent Decree, the major U.S. studios began lowering their production output. Arthur Loew told the *Film Weekly* that the days of MGM double bills in Australia were coming to an end. The trend, he noted, was for "fewer and better ... with MGM making 35 to 40 per cent less pictures than in the past, but perhaps spending more on the lineup." "The single-feature bill provides better balanced entertainment," he told the journal while reinforcing the importance of the Australian market, which remained "third or fourth" in the international box office share for the vertically integrated Loew's/MGM, trailing only England, Italy, and France, in that order.[14]

The chain expanded yet again to twelve cinemas in December 1953 when MGM acquired the lease of the Sesqui in Sydney; renovated, reseated, and recarpeted the cinema; and renamed it the Metro Crows Nest. Once more, the newest Metro would screen films simultaneously with other MGM houses, including its key St. James Theatre.[15] MGM had more cinemas in Australia than any other country in the world besides the United States, a statistic that reinforces how important and fertile this market was and how aggressively Bernard Freeman pursued it. Without competition from television, which didn't begin to penetrate Australia until the end of the decade, the 1950s were still very much an urban and suburban boom time for Hoyts, Greater Union, MGM, and other Aussie exhibitors. "On a good night," the Metro Crows Nest manager remarked, "the cars are parked from the theatre to St. Leonard's station, and well down the side streets"—"a distance of three bus stops, which means a good long string of cars!"[16]

Amalgamated, Kerridge, and the Battle Over Cinemascope in New Zealand

Hoyts also upgraded throughout the postwar boom, installing Fox's new CinemaScope technology into as many of its cinemas as possible, at an expense of £20,000 per screen. The first Australian Hoyts to be converted for CinemaScope was the Sydney Regent in 1953, with the Melbourne Regent following soon after.[17]

It was New Zealand's Amalgamated Theatres chain, however, not Australia and Hoyts, that received the first CinemaScope lenses for installation at the circuit's flagship Civic Theatre in Auckland. Joe Moodabe later noted that the privilege of debuting CinemaScope in New Zealand, rather than in Australia, was due to his father's close relationship with Spyros Skouras, forged in part as a result of their shared Mediterranean heritages and cultural similarities.[18]

To ensure the technology's safety on its intercontinental journey from the United States, M. J. Moodabe personally carried the lenses on board several planes as he traveled from New York to Los Angeles to Honolulu and then on to Auckland with his precious anamorphic cargo.[19] *The Robe* opened in Auckland at the Civic Theatre on November 27, 1953, "before a distinguished first-night audience" that was, according to *Film Weekly*, "a tribute to the powerful publicity barrage which heralded the coming of both 'The Robe' and CinemaScope to Auckland." When the wide screen was unveiled from behind the curtain "instantaneous and appreciate [sic] applause followed this moment, and was repeated at the end of the memorable motion picture."[20]

The installation of CinemaScope would yield another advantage in New Zealand for Fox and Amalgamated, unknown to both at the time. According to Michael Moodabe, Bernard Freeman pleaded with Robert Kerridge to install CinemaScope throughout the Kerridge-Odeon chain in order to screen MGM's upcoming slate of widescreen films, but Kerridge was uninterested.[21] Freeman told Kerridge that without CinemaScope, he would have to give MGM's new widescreen films to his rival, Amalgamated, for exhibition at the Civic in order for them to be properly screened in Auckland. Kerridge was so incensed by the threat that he told MGM executives if they did that, he would cease playing their films altogether. MGM called Kerridge's bluff and Amalgamated (and Fox) became the new exhibition partner for MGM films throughout New Zealand. Kerridge-Odeon later installed VistaVision lenses, but it was too late and Kerridge thus lost out on MGM's films in the process.[22] "We held [those rights] until the studio gradually faded away," Michael Moodabe notes.[23]

In Australia, *Film Weekly* gushed over the later December debut of CinemaScope and exalted Spyros Skouras for bringing the technology to its shores.[24] The journal produced fawning headlines such as "Spyros! You've DONE It, Spyros!"[25] CinemaScope's arrival in Australia was as tectonic a change as it was in New Zealand. According to Dale Turnbull, all 180 Hoyts cinemas were converted to CinemaScope within six months of the first *Robe* screening in December 1953, including Hoyts' burgeoning chain of drive-ins.[26] The rollout delighted the trade, but Fox's Murray Silverstone sounded a cautionary note: "If television," which had not yet begun in Australia, "comes here and the movie industry in Australia does not prepare for its coming, then God help them!"[27] However, by the time television arrived years later in Australia, widescreen was old hat and unable to keep anyone from staying home. While North American film historiography often catalogs CinemaScope and other widescreen processes as "the studios'" response to television, for many countries the rollout of television came years later, even a decade or more. CinemaScope and other widescreen films and processes did nothing to alter the impact of television abroad.

Australian Drive-Ins

Australia's postwar suburbanization—before the arrival of television—led to new opportunities for Hollywood- and locally owned exhibition companies through the construction of outdoor cinemas. The origin of drive-ins in Australia began not with Hoyts, however, but with its former southern division manager, George Griffith Jr., who left the company to open the 654-car Melbourne Skyline drive-in cinema in February 1954 in the Melbourne suburb of Burwood.[28] Not surprisingly, it was Griffith's visit to the United States that inspired him to build. The first of his Auto Theatres Pty. Ltd.'s drive-ins opened for a preview screening on February 18, 1954. Hoyts quickly bought the cinema from George Griffith and his partners and then built new drive-ins in Adelaide, Geelong, Perth, and other locations in the months that followed. The original Burwood would eventually be renamed the Burwood Skyline and then the Hoyts Drive-In where it remained the flagship drive-in of the circuit.[29] True to form, inroads made by major independents or by foreign entities simply encouraged the duopoly. In the years that followed, Hoyts and Greater Union cornered the early drive-in market and, harkening back to their association two decades earlier with General Theatres Equipment Inc., jointly formed a new company, Consolidated Drive-Ins, to build "ozoners" throughout Australia.[30]

Loew's International followed suit by opening its first drive-in in the country—and the first twin drive-in anywhere in the country—in Chullora, a suburb of Sydney, in October 1956 with the Metro Twin Drive-In. The expansive venue held 1,400 cars and brought the number of Loew's global venues to fifty-four.[31] The Metro drive-in was not only a prime spot for movies but also for food, with its Metro Dine-Inn restaurant on the premises.[32] The following year, another Metro Twin Drive-In opened in Clayton for 1,474 cars. A former patron recalled that "the snack bar was the size of [a] supermarket! I remember the donut area alone consumed more floor space than many entire drive-in snack bars." "More so than any other Melbourne drive-in," the patron added, "this is perhaps the most fondly remembered for many of my generation. An excellent location at the intersection of two major roads, screens that could be seen for miles around and unlike Hoyts drive-ins, access to Disney films every holiday period."[33] By the 1950s the MGM circuit had grown to become a truly national circuit—MGM's only expansive national chain outside the United States—as Freeman "acquired, renovated or built seventeen theatres, including drive-ins in all capital cities, those in Sydney and in Melbourne being the largest in the Southern Hemisphere."[34] Over the next two decades MGM staff in Australia—both in film distribution and exhibition—would grow to one thousand employees. MGM, therefore, was not just a national source of entertainment but of employment.

Television Comes, Segregation Goes

The growth of MGM as a force in Australian film exhibition raised considerable concern in New Zealand. As mentioned in chapter 6, Kerridge and Amalgamated pushed back against any effort by Freeman and MGM to expand into the New Zealand drive-in business by establishing their own jointly operated company, Skyline, and then, according to Michael Moodabe, "lobbying the National Government strongly not to grant such licenses to protect existing hard tops, and employees.... Eventually a sympathetic Minister of Internal Affairs, good friend Alan Highet, announced the government declined to even hear applications on the grounds that payment for the importation of necessary equipment would seriously deplete overseas funds."[35] This was one way that companies like Twentieth Century-Fox benefited from their local-global investments in local exhibition companies. Had Skouras gone to the New Zealand government directly and lobbied against MGM, he might have been laughed out of the building. But the Moodabes (and Kerridges) were New Zealanders, and they argued for their protectionism from a nationalistic, local perspective.

In the late 1950s, Amalgamated was not only doing well in Auckland and other cities, the company also operated "at least nine" suburban cinemas. "They were so popular that on a Saturday night a seat in the circle [mezzanine] was almost unobtainable," Michael Moodabe remembers. "It remained reserved for 'regulars' week after week. Suburban theatres were almost like a club."[36] With Fox's dominance in cities and suburbs secure, MGM closed its New Zealand offices in January 1959 and entrusted its film output entirely to Eric Rutledge and the Fox staff. This arrangement no doubt also solidified its exhibition outlets with Amalgamated.[37]

Television came to New Zealand in 1959 when an experimental broadcasting station was established in Auckland. Traditional programming did not begin until 1960 when two and a half hours were broadcast every weeknight beginning in November. By August 1961 four hours of programming monopolized home viewing for Auckland TV owners. The impact was small at first, with only 12,000 sets in New Zealand homes in 1961. By the end of the decade that number had risen to 250,000 homes, concentrated within Auckland, Amalgamated Theatres' corporate and cinematic base of operations.[38] The "impact on cinema attendances was catastrophic," according to Bruce Hayward and Selwyn Hayward. "The number of admissions in the Auckland area more than halved, from nine million per year in 1961 to four million in 1969. Before the introduction of television, there were 61 cinemas in Auckland, but during the 1960s and early 1970s cinemas closed at a steady rate so that by 1974 there were only 30 still open." Suburban cinemas were far worse off than the city center cinemas, they note: "During the first 15 years after the introduction of television, over half the original 47 Auckland suburban cinemas closed."[39] Amalgamated Theatres executives Herbie Freeman and Joe Moodabe have both cited television as the central cause for the decimation of the company's suburban inventory.[40] And there were other factors. Tony Froude writes that city cinemas in Wellington and Auckland also had an impact as urbanization and better infrastructure into these cities led to changes in transportation and thus moviegoing habits.[41] Michael Moodabe, however, challenges the overall impact of television. It was not until "a second channel and colour arrived," he notes, that "the cinema industry was rocked and Auckland suburban theatres began to close monthly."[42] Whatever the cause, the habitual moviegoing habit in New Zealand was permanently altered during this period.

A decade earlier in Australia, in 1962, *Film Weekly* began reporting that the rise in television viewership was already affecting cinema admissions and, thus, Hoyts' overall profits.[43] Dale Turnbull notes that there were 180 cinemas in 1962 before a steep decline over the following year. The only profitable cinemas, according to Turnbull, were the eight in the South Australian and New South Wales countryside, where television had not yet made an impact. From 180 cinemas in 1962, Hoyts would wind up with only 80 in a few short years; its 4,500 employees—some of whom had been with Hoyt's for thirty to forty years—were cut by two-thirds to just 1,500.[44]

Some employees left of their own volition for new business opportunities. Hoyts executive John Glass, for example, landed a position with Australian newspaper mogul, Rupert Murdoch, who then lured two of Hoyts' top accountants and another supervisor to join him, gutting Hoyts of key leadership roles at a tenuous moment. (Turnbull adds that one of those key Hoyts accountants was Mervin Rich, who brought his knowledge of American accounting methods to Murdoch's global businesses—one of the reasons for Murdoch's financial success and his ability to, ironically, buy out Twentieth Century-Fox two decades later.) Hoyts tried to offset its admissions decline by investing in television licenses, but it was barred from controlling television stations because it was a foreign-owned media company. (Murdoch would later get around this same thorny issue in the United States by becoming a U.S. citizen.) Hoyts was able to invest in these licenses (but not in stations) through a group headed by Frank Packer and consisting of Turnbull, representing Hoyts, and other investors including the NSW Trades and Labour Council and both the Catholic and Anglican church organizations.[45]

The steep decline in Australian admissions relieved one of Hoyts' most problematic social issues: the racial segregation (or exclusion) of Indigenous moviegoers at many of its cinemas as Australia maintained racial segregation (of Indigenous Australians) in the countryside well into the 1960s. In places like Moree, site of the 1965 Freedom Ride protesting the discrimination against Indigenous Australians entering swimming pools, movie theaters, and other public spaces, Hoyts operated segregated cinemas, all under the knowing ownership of Twentieth Century-Fox. There was no national Australian law enforcing such practices, but, just as Fox had done earlier in colonial Zimbabwe, the company allowed local executives and managers in the country cinemas to set racial policies out of fear of disturbing or incurring the wrath of its more racist patronage. Indigenous moviegoers were instead charged a lower rate and forced to sit in a cheaper, segregated front section, a flip of the racial orientation of segregated American cinemas. The rise of television and the steep decline in admissions gutted Hoyts' rural inventory and thus relieved the company of its thorny racial problem as many country cinemas closed in the mid to late 1960s as racially divisive Hoyts cinemas in Moree, Tamworth, Wagga, Young, and, later, Armidale, were shut down and, with them, the cinemas that most often practiced racial discrimination through either exclusion or separation.[46]

Generational Changes in Australia and New Zealand

In New Zealand, Joseph Moodabe sold his remaining 25 percent stake in Amalgamated to Twentieth Century-Fox, which later purchased the remaining 25 percent from M. J. as well, giving Fox complete control over Amalgamated.[47] The sale by the elder Moodabe men, Michael Moodabe notes, was wholly encouraged by M. J.'s sons, Michael, Joe, and Royce.[48]

More changes were on the way as Twentieth Century-Fox teetered on the financial edge in the early to mid-1960s and television wreaked havoc on Fox's Australasian business in both distribution and exhibition. Michael Moodabe writes that Dick Zanuck, just twenty-seven years old, who he dubbed "Little Napoleon," was appointed head of the studio under his father, Darryl, and subsequently "fire[d] everybody and close[d] [Fox] for seven months."[49] The Zanucks were keen to get rid of any of Skouras's old allies and prominent members of the previous regime. "Anyone in the U.S., or in the world for that matter, who was deemed to be a 'Spyro person' was suspect. Zanuck Snr dispatched a New York office 'hatchet' man, Seymour Poe, around the world to the Fox theatre circuits, including Hoyts Australia and Amalgamated New Zealand."[50] M. J. was decidedly a "Spyro person," having been a longtime associate and friend of Spyros and his wife, Siroula. Poe was determined to commit regicide in Australasia, deposing the fathers in favor of the sons. "MJ would never have retired gracefully," Michael Moodabe writes, "Lawsuits were threatened, but Poe's trump card was to offer long-term contracts to MJ's sons, something he could not ignore. The senior Moodabes retired the very same day."[51] The younger Moodabes, trained in part by their service to Skouras and Fox, had a more tempered, corporate mentality, a generational difference among many in the increasingly challenging global film business.

Meanwhile, a strikingly familiar story was playing out across the water in Australia. Ernest Turnbull had also been a close associate of Skouras. With Skouras pushed aside and Poe ascendant, Ernest's head was now on the chopping block. Poe arrived in Australia on May 30, 1963, and summarily fired Australia Fox distribution head Arthur Hill, local Fox publicity chief Stuart Coad, and Hoyt's Theatres head Ernest Turnbull, who was replaced by his son Dale. These corporate patricides enabled Fox to employ junior executives at lower salaries but with familiar and familial loyalties to Fox. Dale Turnbull had been groomed for this role. A decade earlier, in 1953, the Skouras brothers—Charles and Spyros, representing two sides of the Fox business—had approached Ernest Turnbull with a proposition for Dale to move to New York and apprentice under their wing. One day Ernest would retire, and he could reliably turn over the Australia Fox business to Dale. Skouras likely never imagined that that day would come without him at the helm. Dale took the job in 1963 with eyes wide open.[52] Dale Turnbull and the Moodabe sons managed Fox and Hoyts in Australia and Amalgamated and Fox in New Zealand in the years that followed.

MGM and Twentieth Century-Fox as Withering Overseas Giants

By the end of the 1960s MGM was in even worse condition than Twentieth Century-Fox. Amid the studio's decline in both production and profits, Bernard Freeman retired as managing director at the end of 1966, and after Kirk Kerkorian became the company's primary shareholder, the venerable film company began focusing more on real estate than movies.[53] This focus could be seen not only in the forthcoming redevelopment of MGM's backlots in Culver City for condominiums and other ventures but also in its overseas holdings. The company's Australian subsidiary, Metro Goldwyn Mayer Pty. Ltd., for example, began redeveloping some of its own Australian real estate (and aging movie palaces). In April 1969 Metro Goldwyn Mayer Pty. Ltd. applied for a proposed redevelopment of the eleven-story St. James building in Sydney that housed retail and office space as well as the company's St. James Theatre in order to demolish it and erect a new AU$5 million twenty-three-story office building.[54] The city's Interim Development Authority granted approval for MGM's application in August 1969 with various modifications needed in order to secure final approval.[55] MGM's plans for the new complex included twin subterranean cinemas with seven hundred and nine hundred seats, respectively.[56] In March 1970 MGM applied for another "Application for Development Permission" and began working with the local firm of Alexander Kann, Finch & Partners to develop plans for the new building.[57]

The complexities of securing council approval is one reason why MGM may have found it easier to later sell the building and its other local holdings. Redeveloping the St. James would have forced the cash-strapped company to invest millions. It was simply easier to sell the theater and the building outright in 1970.[58] In April 1971 MGM, rather than holding on to its local cinemas (something it did in South Africa and other markets where they transitioned into being part of the larger CIC conglomerate), sold twelve of its remaining fourteen Metro cinemas in Australia to Greater Union for $6.4 million. The deal provided MGM with a joint distribution agreement for its films through a new company—British Empire Films—jointly owned with Greater Union, with MGM foreign sales chief Andre Pieterse serving as chairman of British Empire Films.[59] Greater Union's Sixteen Millimetre Australia Pty. Ltd. also gained distribution rights over MGM films in that format.[60]

Hoyts, in keeping with Twentieth Century-Fox's own real estate divestment in the United States—most notably the sale of a large portion of its backlot to create Century City—also began shedding leases and other properties in Australia.[61] One of the only positive signs of growth for Hoyts was in the construction of the seven-screen Hoyts Centre in Sydney in December 1976.[62] Across the water, Fox's New Zealand holdings were also coming under pressure. By 1975 Twentieth Century-Fox Film Corp. (N.Z.) Ltd. announced that it was experiencing "a downturn in our business" due to New Zealand's ongoing "economic depression," and—perhaps even worse—the introduction of color television with the proliferation of these new sets in New Zealand homes and a new second channel of television programming. In addition, "the number of unemployed for the first time in many years became a significant figure, all of which meant more people were staying at home which in turn meant less people were attending the movies."[63] No one at Fox could yet imagine the box office boom of *Star Wars* or the way that it would boost foreign revenues between 1977 and 1978 (and in the years to come). Wayne Brittenden writes that Amalgamated did catch a break in the mid-1970s when Robert Kerridge, again either out of pride or frustration, told CIC representatives—distributing MGM, Paramount, and Universal films—that he would not allow a 50–50 split of their films with Amalgamated cinemas. "When Sir Robert responded testily, 'Take them all to Amalgamated,' that is just what they did. . . . In one inexplicably rash moment Kerridge had seriously undermined his cinema empire."[64] Fox was the beneficiary of another rash decision.

Twentieth Century-Fox remained intimately involved in Amalgamated's ongoing affairs during this period and also demonstrated the inextricable links between Fox, Hoyts, and Amalgamated that continued throughout the 1970s. Amalgamated was in contact with Hoyts, for example, about purchasing new and used projection equipment for its cinemas in 1979, and that same year Fox sought to transfer four hundred pinball machines from Hoyts in Australia to Amalgamated in New Zealand because they were "surplus to their Australian requirements."[65] (Three pinball machines were installed at Amalgamated's Civic Theatre in Auckland and additional installations were made at the company's Cinerama and Century theaters.) New Zealand official A. R. Dickinson wrote, "I did express my surprise that the Australian co. would donate these machines to Amalgamated, however it is apparently regarded as a transfer of assets within the Twentieth Century Fox organisation."[66] Further removing any lingering doubt about Fox's control over Amalgamated or Hoyts, when the New Zealand cinema chain sought to purchase land on Auckland's Hobson Street, the agreement included a telling proviso: "This agreement is entirely conditional upon the purchase being approved by the Twentieth Century Fox Corporation, U.S.A."[67]

"Into the '80s with Optimism"

In Australia, the future looked brighter for Fox and Hoyts by the start of the decade. In May 1980 Hoyts' managing director, Terry Jackman, announced the redevelopment of the old Regent Theatre in Brisbane into the opening of another new multimillion dollar, four-screen Hoyts Entertainment Centre. In addition to movies, the multiplex would also house two candy bars, a coffee shop, and "the largest McDonald's Family Restaurant in Australia, seating 400." The cinema planned to benefit from its lineup of films including *The Empire Strikes Back*. Hoyts hoped to duplicate the success of the revamped Hoyts Complex in Sydney, which had lured in two million visitors in one year.[68]

Twentieth Century-Fox's ownership of Hoyts and its association with the *Star Wars* franchise was highlighted at the opening of the new Hoyts Regent Entertainment Centre when Fox flew *The Empire Strikes Back* actors Billy Dee Williams and Carrie Fisher and producer Gary Kurtz to Brisbane for the opening of the Hoyts multiplex on August 1, 1980, and the film's Australasian premiere that night.[69] After the Brisbane premiere, an after party, demonstrating the local government's continued support of Hoyts, was held "Hollywood style" at City Hall, where "champagne flowed" and the 4QR Big Band and Johnny Farnham entertained the crowd.[70] Lord Mayor Joh Bjeike-Petersen noted that the Regent project "marked great faith in Queensland and in the film industry." Despite all of the excitement, though, Bjeike-Petersen admitted that Hoyts was "the only major cinema company actually building new theatres."[71]

Under the headline, "FORWARD INTO THE '80S WITH OPTIMISM," Jackman wrote in *Australasian Cinema* that Hoyts also hoped to rely on the burgeoning success of its new Hoyts distribution unit, which had launched in late 1978.[72] Hoyts touted other developments, including a new twin cinema at the Warringah Mall in the Sydney suburb of Brookvale and another under construction in Newcastle. Hoyts now operated seventy-three cinemas across Australia, with more planned to open in the suburbs.[73] The importance of the Australian market, and Fox's investments in Hoyts exhibition and distribution, was evident when Fox's chairman of the board, chief executive, and president, Dennis C. Stanfill, traveled to Sydney for a series of meetings with local

Fox executives. Royce Moodabe flew in from Auckland.[74] A few weeks later, Hoyts opened the AU$1 million Newcastle Twin "against a gala backdrop of famous names, plush surroundings and top-class entertainment."[75] The premiere was broadcast live and included a parade of local government leaders.

The Fox-Hoyts-Amalgamated corporate relationship became evermore entwined when Royce Moodabe, who had been appointed to the Hoyts Theatres Ltd. board in 1976 and named vice president of International Theatres of Australasia by Fox Films in 1978, was elected co-chairman of the board of Hoyts Theatres in 1981. With Royce's departure for Sydney and Hoyts, Joe Moodabe became managing director of Amalgamated Theatres Ltd. in Auckland.[76] The move consecrated the obvious: Hoyts and Amalgamated had become conjoined.[77] Appointing Royce Moodabe to Hoyts and uniting Amalgamated at long last with Hoyts may have been as much about consolidating a territory as it was about shoring up a corporate asset for sale. In the same issue of *Australasian Cinema* announcing Moodabe's appointment came this small but striking note:

> The Aetna Insurance Coy of Hartford, Connecticut, USA, is reported to have made a deal for fifty per cent of Twentieth Century Fox's interests. Such arrangements are to be confirmed concurrent with Fox's stockholders' meeting on June 8, 1981. Fox's subsidiaries so involved are: (i) Pebble Beach resort (ii) Aspen ski resort Colorado (iii) Coca Cola Bottlers (US) (iv) Hoyts Theatres Australia (which includes Amalgamated Theatres N.Z.).[78]

Whereas ES&A and Chase banks dominated so much of the early moves between Fox, Hoyts, and Amalgamated half a century earlier, it was now an insurance company and other institutions that had sway over the future of exhibition in Australasia.

Jackman sounded a typically optimistic note at the end of 1981, noting that "it was a busy year" for Hoyts with numerous theater openings and reopenings, yet he made no mention of the previous sale of Twentieth Century-Fox to Marvin Davis; the subsequent sale of Hoyts (and Amalgamated) to an Aetna-controlled subsidiary, Urban Diversified Properties; or of the larger possibility that Hoyts might be shipped off to another buyer entirely.[79] In February 1982 Jackman finally "confirmed" the "possible sale of Hoyts Theatre," acknowledging that the company was still in flux.[80] Five months later the Liberman Family Group, through their Stardawn Investments company, acquired Hoyts Theatres Ltd., citing Hoyts' rising "real estate values and box-office cash flow" as deciding factors.[81] The sale price was rumored to be AU$40 million.[82] Jackman and the rest of Hoyts' executives were kept on after the sale.[83] Hoyts' twenty-one drive-ins were sold off as Stardawn provided Greater Union (Organisation Pty. Ltd.) with an opportunity to purchase the other half ownership stake in their jointly owned drive-ins, which was quickly approved by Australia's Foreign Investment Review Board.[84]

In New Zealand Twentieth Century-Fox chairman and chief executive Dennis Stanfill resigned in June 1982 after an argument with Davis, and Amalgamated managing director Royce Moodabe was forced to acknowledge that Amalgamated was "'a going concern,' subject to 'the right price.'"[85] On August 6, 1982, under direction of Royce Moodabe, who was still a director of Twentieth Century-Fox Film Corp. (N.Z.), Amalgamated formally changed its name to Amalgamated Theatres Holdings Ltd. in order to "indicate more accurately the Company's present activities."[86] Less than two weeks later, Amalgamated, still operating thirty cinemas around New Zealand, was sold to the Chase Group of Companies of N.Z. (The New Zealand–based Chase Group bore no relationship to the still powerful U.S.-based Chase Manhattan Bank.) Royce Moodabe, sounding like a carbon copy of Jackman, noted, "We are delighted that Amalgamated has once again become 100% N.Z. owned and operated."[87] Royce Moodabe continued on as chief executive, Joe Moodabe remained as managing director, and Michael Moodabe was retained as director of marketing.[88] One major alteration lay ahead: Alan Flyger, Fox's representative on Amalgamated's board, resigned, and Chase placed two new officers in his place.[89] Hoyts and Amalgamated were now fully domestic Australasian companies once again. Independence, though, was brief. The Chase Corp. collapsed not long after the sale, and Amalgamated was subsequently acquired by Aetna Insurance. It was then sold back to Hoyts in two 50 percent chunks, reuniting Fox's two former Australasian cinema chains but without the U.S. parent control. Now fully owned by Hoyts, the Amalgamated name was jettisoned, ending six decades of New Zealand identification, and all the cinemas were rebranded as Hoyts.[90]

In a fitting end to a transformational year, Bernard Freeman died on November 26, 1982. The era of U.S. domination of Australasian exhibition was, after more than half a century, finished.[91] This mattered little, though, to Hollywood's control of the market. Decades after the dissolution of the British Empire, Australasian audiences and exhibitors cared less and less about resisting America's cultural influence. They wanted Hollywood films. That sentiment has not changed, even amid the rise of local filmmaking and global acclaim for Australasian films.

Coda, 1985–2019

Two other names from the past highlighted the changing nature of Hollywood's relationship to Australasia in 1985. First, Joseph Patrick Moodabe, the former business partner of M. J. Moodabe and co-owner of Amalgamated

Theatres, died on February 16, 1985, in Auckland.[92] Less than two months later, Rupert Murdoch, the Australian media tycoon who had poached a number of Fox's Hoyts executive two decades earlier, purchased a 50 percent interest in Twentieth Century-Fox Films Corp. for $250 million through his company, News Corp.[93] He would soon gain a controlling interest. Up until its sale to the Walt Disney Company in 2018, Twentieth Century-Fox remained one of the most dominant film companies in Australasia. With News Corp.'s purchase in 1985, an Australian, assisted by former Hoyts personnel, had taken over one of the most entrenched purveyors of global Hollywood in the region.

Hoyts, meanwhile, also reversed its own narrative. Instead of being owned by a U.S. company, the exhibitor expanded globally during the 1980s and began operating cinemas in the United States along with additional locations in the United Kingdom and Poland. When Hoyts finally exited the U.S. market in 2003, Hoyts America was sold to National Amusements, a U.S.-based exhibition company owned by Rupert Murdoch's rival and former exhibitor Sumner Redstone. Hoyts remained an Australian exhibition company through 2015 until the Chinese Dalian Wanda Group acquired the cinema chain as part of its global expansion. Once more, just as it was under Fox, Hoyts was now owned by the largest exhibition group in the world.

Warner Bros., which had been shut out of Australian exhibition in mid-century, finally found its way in toward the end of the twentieth century. The company created a close, enduring distribution partnership with Village Roadshow in the 1970s, and in the 1990s, as Warner Bros. International Theatres expanded, the two companies became both exhibiting *and* producing partners. It was Warner Bros.—not Fox and MGM—that was the last Hollywood film company to (co-)operate a large cinema chain in Australia.[94] That relationship finally ended in 2020.[95]

As for the Moodabe sons, they stayed on in the New Zealand exhibition scene. Joe Moodabe, journalist Tom Dillane would later argue, "was responsible for choosing about 70 per cent of the films playing on screens across New Zealand" from the 1970s to the 1990s.[96] He remained with Hoyts until 1997, when he was hired as managing director of New Zealand's Village Force Cinemas, retiring two decades later in 2006 from SkyCity Cinemas.[97] Royce Moodabe, by contrast, remained loyal to Fox, retiring in 2006 as well from Twentieth Century-Fox (N.Z.) after fifty-seven years with the company.[98]

Despite all the changes in the global film exhibition industry, familial legacies could still be seen around the world as (mostly) fathers passed down to their sons a network of contacts by which they could enter film distribution and exhibition. Twentieth Century-Fox's ownership of Hoyts and Amalgamated lasted a half century. In that time, the adoption of Hollywood films throughout Australasia had become utterly ubiquitous. The cinema chains and cinemas operated by Fox, MGM, Paramount, and Warner Bros. in this region were the veins and arteries by which American culture, ideology, consumer products, and industrial practices flowed into the body politic. The exchange of dollars and debts in the 1930s through both American and Australian banks fundamentally altered how and what Australians and New Zealanders have watched ever since. Under Fox ownership, Hoyts and Amalgamated were both local and foreign, familiar and exotic, offering a local, curated experience of Hollywood. These chains did not skip a beat in their transition to U.S. ownership in the 1930s, and their transition back to local sovereignty made just as little a mark. After all, the content on the screen remained largely the same before, during, after.

PART III

LATIN AMERICA AND THE CARIBBEAN

Hollywood in Cinelandia (1927–1973)
U.S. Cinemas and Local Politics in Latin America and the Caribbean

CHAPTER 8

CINE METROS Y CINE PARAMOUNTS, 1926–1941

MGM and Paramount's Latin American Shop Window Cinemas

In the summer of 2014, immediately upon my arrival in Rio de Janeiro to conduct research for this book, Brazilian film scholar João Luiz Vieira took me to a sumptuous party in a gorgeous Copacabana penthouse apartment overlooking the water. The city's cinema elite were there—producers, filmmakers, and film executives as well as film critics and film scholars—and the nighttime view from the balcony brought forth the sounds of the ocean mixing harmoniously with the sound of famed bossa nova singer Carlos Lyra (Carlos Eduardo Lyra Barbosa) performing a few feet away in the next room. This was Hollywood-level, scene-setting, memory-making magic. The only thing missing, however, was the nightcap I could only dream of: a walk down to the Metro-Copacabana, MGM's shop window cinema, which had been demolished in the 1970s. It had vanished by then, but Hollywood's legacy in this market (and its market share) lingers, as does the memory of the many MGM, Warner Bros., Paramount, Fox, and United Artists cinemas that once dotted the major cities of Latin America and the Caribbean.

The importance—or at least the promise—of the Brazilian market could be seen almost from the outset of Hollywood's interest in global film exhibition. Both Paramount and MGM operated shop window cinemas here by the end of the 1920s in São Paulo and Rio de Janeiro, with MGM creating their first international "chain" of cinemas in Brazil in 1926. The painful lesson MGM learned in Brazil, to prioritize total control of its cinemas rather than partnerships with local exhibitors, would define its exhibition strategies in Latin America for the next half century and, in fact, would cement the company's global strategy to own or operate shop window cinemas versus the ownership or management of local cinema chains.

Throughout Latin America and the Caribbean, internal and external politics played an outsized role in the success and failure of these U.S.-owned and -operated cinemas. U.S. foreign policy—from its "Good Neighbor" relations and anti-Nazi efforts in South America to its involvement in Puerto Rico and Cuba as well as British colonial dominion over Jamaica and Trinidad—set linguistic, industrial, political, social, and cultural policies for many of these cinemas. Owning real estate and managing leases and employees all required careful calibration with the shifting politics of countries where revolution, resistance, and recriminations as well as global warfare played an important backdrop for U.S. and, by proxy, Hollywood investment and ideological exportation. U.S.-owned cinemas served once more as essential cultural embassies for both Hollywood and the U.S. State Department, which sought through them to express the tenets of "democracy" and free market capitalism to nations and colonial territories debating socialism, militarism, communism, fascism, Nazism, and outright revolution.

Focusing primarily on Brazil, Colombia, and Peru in South America and Jamaica, Cuba, Trinidad, and Puerto Rico in the Caribbean, "Hollywood in Cinelandia" examines the ways in which U.S. film companies expanded their exhibition holdings in highly fraught and increasingly lucrative markets throughout these regions. Military dictatorships, repressive colonial and postcolonial regimes, labor crises, protests, massacres, and bombings all played a background role as Loew's/MGM, Twentieth Century-Fox, Warner Bros., Paramount, and even United Artists attempted to secure distribution of their films through lease, purchase, construction, and operation of local cinemas in the half century between the 1920s and the 1970s.

Paramount, mimicking its other global efforts, invested heavily in the late 1920s and early 1930s in Latin America and the Caribbean—with cinemas in Brazil, Cuba, Guatemala, Jamaica, and Mexico—but this brief moment of expansion, like those others, fizzled out as the company's economic troubles mounted and Paramount was forced to retrench after its bankruptcy reorganization in 1933. Paramount's postwar Cine Tacna in Lima, Peru—which was supposed to be a joint project with Twentieth Century-Fox—was an exception to this policy of retrenchment. Twentieth Century-Fox largely stayed out of Latin American and Caribbean film exhibition until the 1940s, when the company began operating cinemas in Brazil, Chile, Colombia, Mexico, and Peru (and tried to do so as well in Cuba). Warner Bros. also made successful forays into this region—operating shop window cinemas in Colombia, Cuba, and Peru—but, keeping with its corporate strategy, mostly avoided large investments in global exhibition and competing with local exhibitors. It was Loew's/MGM, more than any other U.S. film company in the region, that made Latin America a chief focus of its global exhibition expansion beginning in the 1920s. MGM remained heavily invested in Latin American exhibition for the next five decades, before and after its split from Loew's Inc. in 1959.

This section of the book begins with an examination of the rise of moviegoing in Argentina and Brazil and of Hollywood's interest in building cinemas throughout Latin America before turning to the Caribbean, where U.S. film company strategies to expand its distribution and exhibition networks ran up against local politics that reveal much about the industrial and political structures of these regions and the United States' political and cultural engagements therein.

Brazil in the 1920s

Argentina was the preeminent market in silent-era Latin America, but the size and scale of Brazil captured and recaptured the imagination of U.S. film distributors, as it has ever since. The end of World War I brought with it the end of European (particularly French and Italian) dominance over many Latin American screens, especially in Brazil. The postwar world, *Moving Picture World* opined, would be influenced less by political and territorial colonialism and more by the soft power of mass culture. In the case of Brazil, American films and, by extension, culture would wield enormous cultural, industrial, and political influence over the next century. John L. Day, South American representative for Famous Players-Lasky, returned from the region after five months and told *Moving Picture World* in February 1920 that

> motion pictures from this country are serving a highly important purpose as propaganda for American merchandise as well as for American films. Thanks to the movies, South Americans are becoming better acquainted with the people of the United States. The visualization of American scenery, fashions, business conditions and standards of living is the object of the keenest interest on the part of the men and women of South America. Our pictures are shown today in practically every high class theatre in South America and the demand for these films is increasing enormously. Leading exhibitors have told me that it will be impossible for European film exporters to supplant American pictures in the estimation of the public.[1]

Many Latin American film screens—even before U.S. film companies began operating cinemas there—were key advertising vehicles for the products and policies of an ascendant United States.

Paramount, the United States' largest foreign film distributor in 1920, reaped the earliest profits of this new paradigm and had already secured a first-run outlet, the Cinema Avenida in Rio de Janeiro, which was now doubling its seating capacity during an extensive remodel.[2] Paramount also opened distribution and sales offices throughout the region including in Rio, where its subsidiary, Peliculas D'Luxe Da America Do Sul, represented the company.[3] Over the next two years, Fox Films also opened distribution offices in Rio de Janeiro and São Paulo as well as in Buenos Aires, Montevideo, Havana, and Rosario.[4]

Like Paramount, Loew's International executives set their sights on Brazil, where the Portuguese-speaking country seemed ripe for investment. The successful launch of MGM's distribution operations in Brazil (Metro-Goldwyn-Mayer do Brasil, Ltda.)—and the company's slate of top-drawer attractions—gave MGM a quick burst of both power and brand recognition in both Rio and São Paulo. By 1926 MGM was already involved in an exclusive booking strategy in which MGM required cinemas exhibiting their films to show MGM—and only MGM—films.[5] Having seen that control of both local distribution *and* exhibition was a profitable strategy in the company's arrangement with Gaumont in France, MGM sought to provide its new distribution operations in Brazil with the kind of guaranteed profits only a cinema circuit booking its films could offer.

To that end, Loew's International organized a new, MGM-affiliated circuit, Empresas Reunidas Metro-Goldwyn-Mayer, Ltda., composed of independent film exhibitors in Rio, São Paulo, and Santos. MGM did not own these cinemas, just the exhibition holding company, but the cinemas were all collated as part of a booking agreement. The Rio-based segment of the "chain" was formed from Empresas Cinematográficas Reunidas, Ltda., which itself had been formed from a merger of Companhia Cinematográfica Brasileira with Sociedade Cinematográfica Paulista and D'Errico, Bruno, Lopes and Figueiredo.[6] In Rio, most of these cinemas were owned by Luiz Severiano Ribeiro and included aging but popular cinemas such as the Teatro Casino and the Theatro Rialto. In São Paulo, many of the twenty-two associated cinemas in that city were operated by influential exhibitor Francisco Serrador and led by MGM's key cinema, the Theatro Santa Heleña. An additional eight cinemas were added in Santos. J. D. "Jack" Elms, Harry Bernstein, and Louis Brock were all sent by Loew's in New York to help oversee the forty-four Brazilian cinemas contracted to play MGM films.[7] Like many Loew's personnel sent abroad over the next half century, Elms had previously managed a domestic Loew's theater—Loew's Astoria in Queens, New York. More unusually, Elms had also worked internationally, having previously run Loew's' small Canadian chain in Montreal and Toronto, experience that made him a perfect choice for general manager of the new Brazilian circuit.[8] The contracts for the formation of Empresas Reunidas MGM were signed in September 1926, but the new company did not begin operating as a chain under U.S. general manager Louis Brock until January 2, 1927.[9]

Jack Elms pledged great innovations throughout the new MGM circuit but, Luciana Corrêa de Araujo explains, much of this effort became a "disappointment." "Before they arrived in São Paulo," the theatrical columnist for *Diário da Noite* wrote, Empresas Reunidas MGM "said they were going to do some fantastic things. They promised new worlds of wonders and initiatives. But it was all the same" as what Francisco Serrador and other exhibitors had already been doing. Some of this criticism, Corrêa de Araujo writes, could be attributed to an ongoing "anti-American stance" among local critics, competitors, and tastemakers. This sentiment was not without cause. One of MGM's most tone-deaf sins was to exhibit *The Big Parade* in Empresas Reunidas MGM cinemas using Portuguese-language prints meant for the European market rather than those translated and inflected with *Brazilian* Portuguese for local distribution.[10] Loew's had wanted to exploit the growing Brazilian market but also wanted to do so with largely American—not Brazilian—management, making mistakes such as this all too likely.

The Theatro Santa Heleña in São Paolo was the main focus of MGM's attempts at "upgrading" Brazilian exhibition by making the cinema a first-run, shop window venue for MGM films. The cinema, which reopened on March 15, 1927, hired Luiz de Barros to oversee the upgrade and its management.[11] Phil Fabello, who had been a conductor of Loew's theater orchestras in the United States, was sent to São Paulo to arrange music for the Santa Heleña's live performances (and remaining silent films) and to conduct its orchestra.[12] Corrêa de Araujo notes that Fabello was hired not to replicate a Broadway picture palace policy but instead introduce a more intimate neighborhood aesthetic with a jazz orchestra just as he had previously done at the Loew's 7th Avenue in Harlem, New York. Despite its claim to be "the only South American cinema capable of rivaling, in luxury and elegance, the greatest of New York," Corrêa de Araujo notes that in its emphasis on live stage shows, the Santa Heleña was "similar not to the movie palaces [of Broadway], but the neighborhood houses" in Manhattan and throughout the other boroughs and outlying areas of New York City.[13] In other words, the experience Barros and Fabello brought to Brazil was more Bowery than Broadway.

With rising complaints from local critics about the quality of MGM's films and intense competition from other local cinemas, Empresas Reunidas MGM's attempts to differentiate itself through elaborate stage shows at the Theatro Santa Heleña became, Corrêa de Araujo notes, "less elaborate and attractive until they disappeared from the program" entirely.[14] Prices dropped along with it, and the whole foundering chain was summarily dissolved in December 1927.[15] Fabello returned to the Loew's 7th Avenue in New York, and most of the São Paulo cinemas returned to Serrador's control.[16] In the end, Loew's maintained control over only two shop window cinemas: the Alhambra in São Paulo and the Theatro Rialto in Rio.[17]

The failure to fully upgrade the Empresas Reunidas MGM circuit—and not just the Rialto and Santa Heleña—was a learning experience for MGM. When the company began its concerted expansion throughout the region a decade later, it made sure that its cinemas—whether bought, renovated, or built— were among the best, if not *the* best, in each city. Loew's failure in Brazil—and the quick fade of its Gaumont-Loew-Metro circuit in France—may be one reason why the company rarely operated more than one cinema in each foreign city in the decades to follow. (This policy also followed Loew's own North American system of *usually* operating only one key cinema in locations outside of New York City.) Loew's adoption of its own global shop window model rather than its weak circuit plans of the 1920s—exampled by the successful launch of the Empire in London (1928) and the first Metro Theatre in Johannesburg (1932)—ensured that the failure of the Empresas Reunidas MGM plan would never be repeated. Even when MGM operated three cinemas in Rio over a decade later, which MGM never marketed as a chain, the company heaped lavish attention and dollars on each neighborhood house to ensure that the MGM brand name it cultivated through film production would be properly matched with cinemas of equal quality and opulence.

In the years that followed, Leo the Lion and MGM's lavish films would more than rebuild any reputational damage done to the nascent brand name so soon after its launch. By the time MGM began to build new, opulent cinemas throughout Brazil and the rest of South America a decade later, the company's name was robust; the quality of these new theaters and the experience they provided local audiences would ensure that MGM's brand went from strength to strength.

Cine-Theatro Paramount, São Paulo

By 1927 Paramount had already developed its own global "shop window" strategy whereby it would construct, buy, or rent a key first-run house for its films. Following the operation of key cinemas in cities like London, Paris, and Tokyo, the company's next target was São Paulo. In 1929 Paramount debuted its shop window for the growing city and the first cinema in the country to be outfitted for sound films: the Cine-Theatro Paramount.[18]

Paramount's investment followed a series of distribution changes effected by the company. As João Miguel Valencise notes, during the 1920s long-term contracts between distributors and exhibitors were increasingly replaced by block-booking agreements in which exhibitors were forced to accept all of

FIGURE 8.1 Cine-Theatro Paramount, prior to opening in 1929. (*Mensajero Paramount*, New York Public Library for the Performing Arts)

Paramount's lesser films in order to receive its star-studded "A" pictures. By the end of the 1920s those contracts were extended beyond just a two-month window and now into annual block-booking agreements.[19] The opening of the Cine-Theatro Paramount provided the company with a shop window not subject to contract negotiations with local exhibitors but, as always, a reliable first-run outlet owned and operated by the company.

The 1,859 seat Cine-Theatro Paramount was the ideal place to see a Paramount film in part due to its opulence and sound technology (it possessed both Vitaphone and Movietone capability) and in part because Paramount (and other U.S. distributors) routinely imported only *three* prints of any given film into the country due to the high charges of importation from Brazilian customs officials. Thus, after playing the Cine-Theatro Paramount and Paramount's other showcase cinemas in Rio and beyond, these prints began to take on additional scratches, dirt, and other damage as they traveled to neighborhood houses, smaller cities, and much smaller cinemas. Seeing a Paramount film at Cine-Theatro Paramount, therefore, was to see the film in its most pristine sound and image quality and, of course, surrounded by an air of luxury.[20] This was one more advantage of Hollywood's shop window cinemas—in a nondigital age, access to a first-run deluxe screening meant first-class projection with a minimum of optical and audio defects.

This sense of technological perfection was undermined, however, by the actual logistics of the moment. The Cine-Theatro Paramount, located on Avenida Brigadeiro Luís Antônio, reflected the extravagance of a global movie palace but only when it was operational; the neighborhood where it was built suffered numerous problems with its electrical infrastructure, a reminder that all of this technology, money, and press was subject to the vagaries of urban development and municipal investments. Problems with the theater's functionality were, in fact, ongoing from its outset. The first test of the new Western Electric sound system on April 8 was postponed to April 10 so that Paramount officials could conform the cinema to the city's technical requirements.[21]

When it did finally open three days later with *The Patriot*, Cine-Theatro Paramount and local Paramount distribution staff argued that the company had now "taken the leadership with the presentation of the [country's] first sound picture."[22] Paramount also installed sound equipment into other Latin America cinemas. Synchronous sound technology was installed in Paramount's Fausto theater in Havana, Cuba, that year, and the Paramount-operated Cine Olimpia reopened in Mexico City with synchronous sound to "record breaking results." In Guatemala City, Paramount's Capitol Theatre featured new sound equipment by June 1929. (The Capitol in Guatemala City and another Paramount cinema in Panama City—both inherited in the purchase of the New Orleans–based Saenger Amusements—were the only two "Hollywood"-owned cinemas in Central America during this period. Both vanished from U.S. inventories by the 1930s.)[23]

Los Cine Metros, 1935–1940

The U.S. film company that most actively invested in Latin American exhibition during the 1930s was Loew's/MGM. In March 1935 Arthur Loew told the Loew's board of directors that in order to fight the exhibition "Consorcio" in Argentina, and in every other market, the international division planned to open cinemas in "every city in the world where there is a booking combination." "There is no limit," he added, "to the number of theatres we will build."[24] Loew added that the company would also build cinemas wherever "they are convinced that M-G-M productions cannot be presented in theatres representative of M-G-M's standards." "New theatres," he added, "usually attract to themselves thousands of local residents who are not picture-goers. Once their attendance is obtained, they go again and again and become rabid fans, attending not only the new theatre but all the others. The motion picture habit once contracted is a hard one to break."[25] Loew's International announced a new "worldwide theatre building campaign" that year with plans for several Latin American cinemas already under way. The Loew's board of directors, sensing the earning potential in foreign exhibition and its lack of competition in a number of rising markets, gave Arthur Loew and his international team access to unlimited funds. This confidence—not insignificant given the ongoing Depression—grew out of the company's recent successes in opening Metro Theatres in South Africa and Australia as well as ongoing exhibition operations in Europe.

Harry Moskowitz, head of the Loew's construction department, quickly began work on Loew's International's newest Metro cinemas—los Cine Metros—in Santiago, Chile, and in Lima, Peru. Both South American cinemas were slated to house 1,500 patrons and cost $250,000 to build.[26] Additional shop windows were also announced for Montevideo, Uruguay, and Rio de Janeiro, Brazil, representing an equally divided outlay of $1 million for four new South American Metros. Moskowitz traveled to all four of these cities over the next year to oversee their construction.[27]

Moskowitz and Loew's Theatres Construction Department worked on the blueprints for these overseas cinemas and then hired and supervised local architects, engineers, and builders in the design and construction of each Cine Metro/Metro Theatre abroad.[28] The company often employed "native architectural talent" to design and build these cinemas under Moskowitz's supervision. Over time, this "glocal" approach created an effective mélange of local aesthetics blended to match larger U.S. cinema trends. "These theatres are not only the last word in construction, equipment and appointments, according to our American standards," Arthur Loew noted at the time, "but added to Broadway's conception of the perfect cinema are those subtle refinements of taste and comfort arising from the native culture in each locality." Reinforcing Hollywood's (and the U.S. State Department's) belief that cinemas were soft power catalysts for U.S. companies, culture, consumer goods, ideology, foreign policy, and, of course, films, Loew argued that "a well-built, comfortable house, showing good pictures, is as great an aid in making new fans abroad."[29]

For his first two Cine Metros, Moskowitz spent six months in Lima and Santiago working with architects Jose Calderon and Guillermo Payet in Lima and with local architects Jorge Isaza and Sergio Garcia-Moreno in Santiago.[30] In Lima, Moskowitz and architect Calderon created a synthetic glocal mashup by mixing a neocolonial exterior that maintained a streetscape uniformity along with a striking Art Deco interior design.[31] The cinema was built across from the Plaza San Martín, one of the most visible public landmarks in the city, which was constructed in 1921 to celebrate the country's one-hundredth anniversary of independence. Without an Art Deco façade or another modern style to attract passersby, the Cine Metro erected a rooftop sign and a striking marquee, turning a historic plaza celebrating Peru's independence into a modern advertising space selling Hollywood's cultural colonialism. The marquee of the Cine Metro boasted MGM's lineup of short and feature films that was more in keeping with Times Square than postcolonial Lima.

The opening of the Cine Metro in Lima on May 2, 1936, was attended by Peruvian president Óscar Benavides, members of his cabinet, and the local U.S. diplomatic corps.[32] Peruvian representatives later presented the Cine Metro with a certificate for "outstanding civic enterprise."[33] MGM celebrated the opening of this Cine Metro with its own political goodwill as James Fitzpatrick and his famous *Traveltalks* series for MGM offered glowing coverage of Peru as a safe space for global capital. *Glimpses of Peru*, a *Traveltalks* short, announced that the city could now be called "a modern and up to date metropolis" in part because it had a U.S. movie theater—MGM's own Cine Metro—which just happened to be advertising the same *Traveltalks* series on its marquee. In a subsequent *Traveltalks* on nearby Chile, Fitzpatrick once again focused on Santiago's Cine Metro, enabling another corporate plug as Chile, according to Fitzpatrick, had joined the community of nations by having its own MGM cinema as well.[34]

MGM also considered Brazil to be ripe for development again.[35] A new Cine Metro in Rio's entertainment center, Cinelandia, would guarantee the company long-term control over all its first-run releases in Rio. Loew's contracted with local architect Robert Prentice for Rio de Janeiro's first Cine Metro, and he responded with a striking, modern exterior and a more traditional interior, a reversal of Lima's Metro.[36] A Brazilian journalist would later note that the Metro was "the first to take advantage of the bold lines of American architecture on its façade."[37] Unlike the Plaza San Martín in Lima or the traditional streets of Santiago, Rio's Cinelandia was a modern dreamscape in design and function, echoing the vertical style of New York. João Luiz Vieira and Margarete Pereira argue that the Cine Metro auditorium's "historicist references provide[d] a counterpoint to the exterior," which was, like Cinelandia, "bold, modernist."[38]

The interior provided one local innovation. In 1936 Rio had eleven first-run cinemas, and ten of those contained balconies—all but the new Cine Metro built by MGM. U.S. architects like Drew Eberson and Ben Schlanger began focusing on smaller auditorium sizes during the 1930s in order to increase a sense of intimacy and community rather than the phantasmagorical impact of movie palace scale and mass. These smaller cinemas eschewed balconies that separated patrons, instead keeping all moviegoers in the eyeline of one another.[39] Moskowitz and Prentice designed Rio's Cine Metro with mezzanines instead, facilitating a large communal space that united Cariocas under the MGM banner and metaphorically removed class boundaries. Once more the hybrid glocal mix of a "modern ornamental style" in the auditorium contrasted harmoniously with other areas of the cinema that were decked out in

"Colonial Brazilian," enabling audiences to vacillate between the exotic and the familiar within the same structure.⁴⁰ Hollywood films, dubbed into Brazilian Portuguese, further situated MGM films in an MGM cinema as an exotic but still local experience.

The Rio Metro's opening was the ultimate gala affair and, like a Hollywood premiere, was broadcast across the country on a "national hookup."⁴¹ William Melniker, who had begun his career at Loew's/MGM in Brazil and had just been promoted from head of MGM in South America to head of all foreign theater activities for Loew's International/MGM under Arthur Loew, returned to Rio from New York for the opening.⁴² Attendees included the daughter of the president (and current dictator) of Brazil, Getúlio Vargas; William Melniker and his wife; and the local heads of most of the major U.S. film companies: A. Judel from MGM, Al Selzer from Universal, Nat Libeskind from RKO, J. Carlo Bavetta and A. Rosenvald from Twentieth Century-Fox, L. Price from Warner Bros., E. Baez from United Artists, and S. Goldstein from Columbia. Conspicuously present was another name—Ugo Sorrentino—the local head of Ufa's Brazilian office.⁴³ The invitation to Ufa—an industrial and political competitor in Brazil—may say much about the need for diplomacy during Latin America's uneasy relationship with Nazi Germany and Brazil's own seesaw relationship with Nazi Germany and the United States. It may also have helped keep MGM's business in Germany in good stead, at least for the time being.

Although quotidian racial and class separations still kept Brazilians socially fragmented, paying customers at the Cine Metro were treated to the American showmanship model of in-theater class unity that matched the rags-to-riches tales up on the screen, where class mobility was part of the American dream. Vieira and Pereira note, "At all levels, the Metro sought to define to the public a specific way to consume movies, identified with its own brand." Rio's Cine Metro, they add, "like other Metro cinemas built in Brazil . . . reproduced the same visual [style] that, in the sphere of film productions, Cedric Gibbons, chief art director for . . . [MGM,] had already defined and characterized as the look of [MGM films]: rich, velvety, of dreams." "Far from being neutral surfaces," they note, these subjective spaces were intended to create a "dominant cinema." "After the Metro" they conclude, "exhibitors were forced to carry out urgent reforms in [their] auditoria in order to cope with the 'standard Metro' view."⁴⁴ Alice Gonzaga writes that moviegoing could be "divided into two periods [in Rio]: before and after the Metro."⁴⁵ The Metro quickly ingratiated itself into the upper echelons of Rio's social life by becoming a place for local debutantes and their escorts to meet on Saturday afternoons, a meet-up that became "the high point of elegance."⁴⁶

In addition to the new Metro in Rio, MGM opened another new Cine Metro shop window in Montevideo, Uruguay, in October 1936, the first air-conditioned cinema in the country.⁴⁷ Like other MGM showcases, the Cine

Metro was not intended to establish control of the local exhibition market but rather to provide a first-run outlet in the tightly controlled market of Montevideo.[48] Uruguay, in the mid-1930s, was still dominated by Don Bernardo Glücksmann, whose United Cinema chain operated nineteen cinemas in Montevideo alone and twelve others throughout the country.[49] Like his brother Max in Argentina during the silent era, Glücksmann had been the sole distributor for MGM, Paramount, Universal, and RKO before each agency opened their own distribution offices in Uruguay.[50] The Montevideo Metro, therefore, was a shop window only, an effort by Loew's to secure a first-run outlet for its films in a very closed market. Operating as a real competitor would have irked Glücksmann and cut MGM off its distribution business that was far more lucrative for the company than the operation of a single shop window.

Back in Brazil, Loew's International began construction on another new shop window cinema, this time in São Paulo, in the Centro district, in mid-1937.[51] MGM do Brasil worked with the Rio-based Companhia Constructora Nacional to request a permit from the city for a new five-story building that would include offices for MGM's exhibition, sales, and distribution employees as well as safety features for secure nitrate film vaults in compliance with local safety regulations.[52] The new "luxuoso cinema" opened less than a year later in March 1938.[53] Brazilian trade journal *Cine-Mundial* later noted that its "style and decoration" was certainly "analogous to that of the great theaters of the United States."[54] The cinema was designed once more by Rio-based architect Robert Prentice and built by a local contractor, all under the supervision of the Loew's construction department. Western Electric provided the sound equipment, Simplex the projectors, and Carrier the air-conditioning system that would lure in a city. Beyond its sumptuous surroundings, challenging those of Paramount's own shop window and the growing number of indigenous movie palaces, the Cine Metro announced that the cinema would debut MGM films sixty days before they were screened in any other cinema across the city. William Melniker traveled to São Paulo for the gala March 15, 1938, opening.[55]

The São Paulo Metro became another U.S. cultural embassy, screening MGM short and feature-length films, including a foreign version of the company's famous U.S. newsreel, *News of the Day*, narrated into Brazilian Portuguese.[56] Moviegoers were treated to *Tom & Jerry* cartoons, *Traveltalks* shorts, and a direct infusion of the Hearst-MGM newsreel's pro-U.S., anti-fascist ideology. Elsewhere in Brazil, MGM also took over the Cine Central in Rio de Janeiro, renaming it the Astoria and adding it to the company's South American holdings, which also included the new Teatro San Jorge in Bogotá, Columbia, opened in December 1938.[57] Over the next decade, Loew's would open additional shop window cinemas throughout South America, giving Loew's

International/MGM key first-run, deluxe venues throughout major cities in Argentina, Brazil, Chile, Colombia, Peru, Uruguay, and Venezuela.[58]

United Artists (UA) was not normally interested in overseas exhibition, but MGM's success in the Latin American market and the corresponding interest of Paramount and Warner Bros. persuaded the U.S. film company to scout for cinemas in the region. (It is important to note that this exploration was being conducted by United Artists and not by the separately organized United Artists Theatre Corp.) By October 1939 Walter Gould, head of United Artists' Latin American division, was in Brazil to coordinate a small chain of four São Paulo cinemas for United Artists films. These cinemas, like Empresas Reunidas MGM, were operated in cooperation with "local interests." The sub-run Astoria-UA and Opera-UA cinemas in central São Paulo, the 3,500-seat Roxy-UA in the suburb of Braz, and another unnamed UA house, were all part of a new expansion program for United Artists, which had "similar deals" planned for "the future where improvement of UA's position is regarded as essential and feasible."[59]

UA did not have a controlling interest in these cinemas, but the company did have an exclusive deal with local exhibitors who had been boxed out from other content since Francisco Serrador's chain had "sewed up" São Paulo with its own twenty-eight cinemas.[60] In addition to the four UA-affiliated cinemas mentioned above, *Film Daily* reported that "several other houses in the São Paulo territory are [also] becoming identified with UA."[61] Two years later, UA was still pecking at the edges of São Paulo exhibition, with Walter Gould planning to fly to Brazil in September 1941 in order to "lay the foundation for the acquisition . . . of three or more theaters in São Paulo."[62] The expansion of a small United Artists circuit in Brazil is further evidence of the openness and allure of the Brazilian market for many U.S. film companies, including those to follow.

CHAPTER 9

PROP(AGANDA) WINDOW CINEMAS, 1933–1945

Ufa, Hollywood, and the Battle for Hearts and Minds Through South American Cinemas During World War II

MGM, Paramount, and United Artists were not the only foreign companies operating cinemas in Brazil in the 1930s. The German film company Universum-Film Aktiengesellschaft (Ufa), under the control of the Nazi government beginning in 1933, was also anxious to gain a foothold in South America, especially in countries where neutrality (or even a tilt toward the Axis) was evident. Few countries were more reluctant to back the United States and its allies than Chile and Argentina, in part due to the large German and Italian populations in both countries and the successful inroads the Nazis had made in spreading their ideology abroad. Brazil, by contrast, despite its own large German émigré population, was more hesitant to back either side. Brazil's openness to both U.S. and German (film) propaganda and the need by both sides to try and win the ideological war there made the country, Luiz Nazario writes, "one of the main targets for Nazi propaganda strategies in South America." The Nazi's Brazilian propaganda was aimed at the "numerous German immigrants established in colonies in the Southern States (800000 to a million, to which should be added 80000 to 100000 resident Reich citizens)." Film, Nazario adds, was one of the most "insidious means of ideological dissemination used by the Nazis in Latin America."[1]

Nazi propaganda had been transmitted through film in Brazil beginning in 1934, when Hans Henning von Cossel, head of the National Socialists in Brazil (NSDAP), began working to spread Nazi ideology. Nazario writes that "the swastika decorated [the NSDAP's] meeting places, where they toasted

Hitler's health and criticised Brazil's politics" and dubbed Brazil, with its large mixed-race population, "a 'land of monkeys' that did not appreciate German orderliness."[2] Another party, the Brazilian Integrationist Action Movement (AIB) also advocated for the separation of the heavily German Brazilian south from the rest of the mixed-race nation. Naturally, antisemitism became central for NSDAP and AIB members, with sympathetic journalist Oswaldo Gouvêa singling out Hollywood, its films, its foreign cinemas in Brazil, and its foreign and domestic cinema employees for a range of anti-Jewish conspiracy theories and derision. In his 1935 publication "The Jews of the Cinema," Gouvêa blamed U.S. companies and their Jewish employees for causing a moral decline in Brazil and for destroying the possibility of a national cinema. Another publication, "The Mysteries of the National Cinema," argued that "Brazilian movie house owners are tied down to the hands of the Jews from Metro, Fox, Universal, United Artists and Warner Bros. As soon as the release of a new film is announced, Jewish persecution goes into action."[3] These sorts of attacks were coincident with the sudden distribution of German newsreels dubbed into Portuguese, all of which made Nazi-related ideology quotidian and normalized. Brazilian trade journals also followed President Getúlio Vargas's adoration of Nazi efficiency; in 1935 *Cinearte* published six articles "praising the policies adopted by the Third Reich cinema [and] recommend[ing] the application of the same methods."[4] Ufa newsreels exhibited in Brazil also contained the messaging, ideology, and footage emanating from Fascist Italy.

Nazario chronicles the many links between the Vargas government and the Nazis, including "a cooperation agreement between the Brazilian Police Force and the Gestapo to combat communism" which led to "Jews of both sexes" being "cruelly tortured and deported to Germany."[5] By 1937, Nazario notes, "President Vargas referred to Hitler as 'a great friend' and wished to 'tighten even further their good friendly relationship.'"[6] Vargas even plotted a fake coup d'état in order to justify further attacks against the Jewish citizens of the country, including some working at Hollywood's offices in Brazil.

With Brazil's increasingly hand-in-glove relationship with Nazis in Germany and the growing amount of antisemitic and pro-Nazi propaganda filling the nation's newspapers, radio shows, and cinema screens, the ground had been softened up for German embassies in Brazil to begin financing German-oriented cinemas. In 1936 in São Paulo, Francisco Serrador partnered with the German film company Ufa to open a new German shop window, the Cine Ufa-Palácio.[7] The opulent cinema was designed, ironically, by influential Jewish Brazilian architect Rino Levi.[8] It became, Nazario argues, "the principal Ufa movie theatre in Brazil . . . dedicated exclusively to the exhibition of German productions," and the site of "the prestigious premiere of *Olympia* (1938) by Leni Riefenstahl."[9] In Rio's Cinelandia, German agents also rented the

Cine-Teatro Broadway—an ironic name for such an anti-U.S. cinema—to exhibit German films exclusively.[10]

In São Paulo, the Cine Paramount and the Cine Metro—as well as the United Artists cinemas in that city—all played a part in the ideological war now being waged in and around the city in part through the short and feature films and newsreels that were projected nightly in these cultural embassies.[11] Thus, these American shop window cinemas were performing key work for the local U.S. embassy and the U.S. State Department. Before the war began, German, U.S., and Brazilian cinemas were all on the front lines of Brazil's internal conflicts.

After the start of the war, however, *Motion Picture Herald* detected a decided shift in programming with German films receding and "American films retain[ing] their lead in popularity."[12] Despite all of the German government's efforts, the political tide turned against them in Brazil, despite Vargas' affection for the Nazi party and Adolf Hitler. Money, trade, and geographical proximity all made the United States a far more natural and easier ally.[13] By January 1941, J. Carlo Bavetta, Twentieth Century-Fox's managing director in Brazil, reported that business was "good, theater building and modernization [were] going ahead steadily" and "German films have virtually disappeared from the screens."[14] By the end of 1941, after the Japanese attack on Pearl Harbor, Brazil was forced, Nazario writes, "to break diplomatic and economic relations with Japan, Germany and Italy."[15] U.S. soldiers arrived in Recife on December 23, 1941, to bolster the Allies' global positioning, and the Nazis, recognizing that Brazil was turning toward the United States, began attacking merchants ship sailing into and out of Brazil. Axis films were thereafter banned from Brazilian cinemas. U.S. film companies stepped up their efforts to rally Brazilians to the allied cause by advertising their films with a new transnational slogan: America Livre e Unida (America Free and United). *Motion Picture Herald* commented nearly a year later, in October 1942, "The domination of the market by American films is [now] unquestioned."[16] After Brazil's dalliance with pro-Nazi ideology and friendship, the country would end up becoming the only Latin American country to militarily fight against the Nazi regime.[17]

By contrast, five cinemas in Buenos Aires, Argentina, were "known" to be Nazi "outlets" in the city alongside "numerous minor outlets throughout the country." "Sooner or later," the *Christian Science Monitor* reported in June 1941, "UFA Films de la Argentina will have a string of theaters in which to show their pictures."[18] Ufa also "lined up numerous theaters" in Chile for pro-Nazi films.[19] One of those cinemas was the Nacional in Santiago. Nazis had used a local "straw man" to lease the cinema, with reports that the real money came from the local Nazi consul. Overnight, American films like *Out*

West and *Lady Hamilton* were cancelled, and the first title up was the global Nazi propaganda offering, *Sieg im Westen* (*Victory in the West*). The local Nazi apparatus in Santiago then "invited the Chilean army garrison to see 'Sieg' for free."[20]

MGM Expansion in Brazil During World War II

With Brazil's turn toward the United States after the start of the war in 1939—and Argentina and Chile proving more complex markets for the United States—MGM had announced the construction of two new cinemas in Rio for 1941. Loew's sent Samuel Burger, MGM's new foreign representative, to Rio in late 1940 to supervise the construction and opening of the two new Cine Metros in the Tijuca and Copacabana neighborhoods of the city.[21] MGM's initiative was highly unusual for Loew's. In no other city outside the United States—not in London, Paris, or Johannesburg—had Loew's *built* three Metro Theatres/Cine Metros for different sections of the same city. Loew's was so bullish on the possibilities of theatrical expansion in Rio, based in part on

 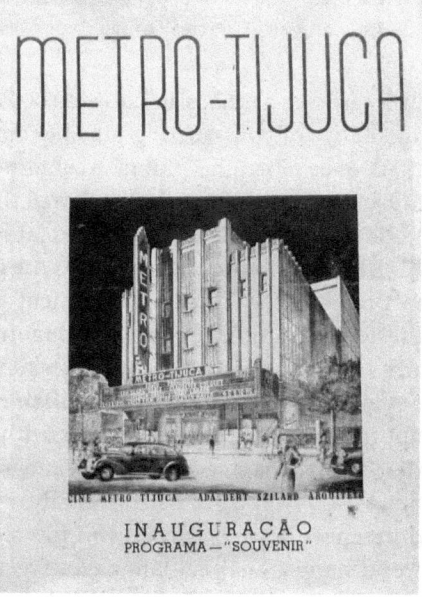

FIGURES 9.1–9.2 Inaugural programs for the Metro Copacabana (left) and Metro-Tijuca (right) in Rio de Janeiro. (Courtesy of Ivo Raposo)

FIGURE 9.3 The mobile, pervasive marketing of MGM's cinemas and films in Rio de Janeiro, ca. 1948. (Courtesy of Ivo Raposo)

their grosses at the original Metro(-Passeio), that they even announced the possibility of constructing cinemas in "five other suburbs" in Rio."[22] Loew's cited, once more, the "failure to obtain [a] satisfactory product deal" as a main cause for their sudden rise in "Brazil theatre-building."[23]

There were a variety of additional factors that led MGM to invest more in Brazilian exhibition. The first was the growing popularity of Hollywood films in Brazil as the Vargas government grew closer to the United States amid President Franklin Roosevelt's ongoing "Good Neighbor" policies and Brazil's turn away from Germany. The second reason, *Variety* noted in September 1941, was a boom in the Brazilian economy whose "principal cause for the upturn" was the "close workings with the U.S." As a result of these growing ties, "Brazil has become more and more Yank-minded and is demanding more Hollywood [films]."[24] Finally, and perhaps most concretely, linguistic differences between Brazil and the rest of Latin America played into Hollywood hands. Spanish-language Argentinian films were no less an obstacle to many Brazilians than English-language films from Hollywood or London. Thus, any concern over Argentina cutting into the U.S. market share in Brazil was neutralized because "the cost of sub-titling is so great that few

Prop(aganda) Window Cinemas   165

FIGURE 9.4   MGM continues its appeal to children around the world with *Tom & Jerry* and this "Festival Tom & Jerry" at "Nos 3 Cines Metros" (Our 3 Cine Metros), ca. 1962. (Courtesy of Ivo Raposo)

[Argentinian or Mexican] picts can make the nut [overhead]."[25] U.S. films were so ascendant during World War II that new cinemas built by Luis Severino Ribeiro and ex-MGM employee turned local exhibitor, Benjamin Fineberg, were "U.S. films only" venues.

With pro-U.S. sentiment increasing by late 1941—just weeks before the attack on Pearl Harbor—the opening of MGM's Metro-Tijuca on October 10, 1941, and Metro-Copacabana on November 5, 1941, were treated as grand affairs by Loew's/MGM with elaborate premieres.[26] On the streets, on street cars, in local store windows, and on its three Cine Metro marquees, with the newly renamed Metro-Passeio, Metro-Tijuca, and Metro-Copacabana, MGM and its films became omnipresent through advertisements for its films and cinemas throughout Rio, cementing its brand identity and consecrating MGM films and MGM cinemas as a local, integral part of the city but also as an alluring foreign, exotic import from "Hollywood." Stepping into MGM's Cine Metros across Rio, these highly visible cultural embassies transmitted their messaging of mass consumption, fantasy, and leisure, aided and abetted by sumptuous upholstery, air-conditioning, and the lights and sounds of the exported American movie palace experience. UA records demonstrate that the three Cine Metros typically out-grossed any other cinemas across the city, demonstrating scant allegiance to cinemas operated by local chains.[27] Each new Metro was also a new ideological battalion against any simmering pro-Nazi sentiment in Rio and São Paulo.

Shop Window Cinemas in Wartime Latin America

The Tijuca and Copacabana were the last Cine Metros built before the U.S. entrance into World War II and the accompanying materials shortages and restrictions on construction across the Americas. MGM had been "considering construction of four cinemas in the Argentine" in 1939, but no cinemas were under construction there by 1941.[28] Instead, Loew's added to its Chilean holdings by buying land in Valparaiso in 1941, approving building plans for a two-thousand-seat Cine Metro with municipal authorities that November, and opening a Cine Metro there in April 1942.[29]

Warner Bros. also expanded exhibition operations during World War II. The Teatro Central had opened in Lima, Peru, in May 1942 and was designed by architect Guillermo Payet, who had previously worked on Lima's Cine Metro.[30] Less than a year after opening, Warner Bros. signed a five-year lease of the Central on January 1, 1943, in order to create its own "shop window" cinema in Lima.[31] The following month, Warner Bros. purchased real estate across from the Hotel Reforma in Mexico City in order to build another shop window cinema there.[32] All of these moves were meant to expand the company's holdings and investments into one of the few regions that were not under imminent threat of an Axis invasion and ensuing confiscation of U.S. holdings.

Twentieth Century-Fox followed Warner Bros. almost move for move. Noting their own sense (in contrast to other studios) that Mexico was part of the North American market, Fox sent their domestic, not foreign, theater executives (from the company's National Theaters subsidiary) Charles Skouras and Dan Michalove down to Mexico City "to inspect a group of theaters" for purchase.[33] The following year Fox nabbed its own Lima shop window cinema by leasing the Cine Excelsior while securing another shop window in Bogotá.[34] The takeover of these Lima and Bogotá cinemas followed Fox's additional lease of the Cine Palácio—no longer a Nazi-oriented Ufa cinema—as Twentieth Century-Fox's new Rio de Janeiro "show window" in Brazil.[35] (In São Paulo, Fox films were still being screened "at the best house of the city," the three-thousand-seat Ipiranga.[36]) In his coverage of Fox's move into local exhibition in Brazil, Lou Pelegrine noted that the lease was directly related to Fox's (and Hollywood's) belief that "the heavy contribution that the United States is making toward the development of Brazil . . . will open vast new opportunities to the American film business in that South American land." Pelegrine noted that Twentieth Century-Fox "intends to extend the [shop window] policy to other cities of Brazil" and "help promote good-will for American enterprise."[37] The reopening of the Cine Palácio was feted by Fox executives at a premiere featuring local "celebrities" and city officials.[38]

Hollywood's wartime investment in South America spread further with United Artists' acquisition of the nine-hundred-seat Teatro Astral in Bogotá. The operation of the Bogotá UA, Fox, and MGM cinemas were all part of the U.S. film companies' efforts to circumvent local control by Jorge Isaza's Cine Colombia chain, which operated 142 cinemas in 96 cities in what was almost a virtual monopoly.[39] Argentina UA executive Len Daly was sent from Buenos Aires to the Astral to implement UA exploitation strategies.[40] UA Latin American supervisor Sam Seidelman noted that UA "had no post-war plans for Argentina because 'the country is a big question mark.'"[41]

By 1944 Nazi-era films had finally begun to vanish from those South American screens that had welcomed them during the first five years of the conflict. And yet, *Motion Picture Daily* reported, some German-controlled movie houses in South America still remained open to pro-Nazi filmmaking until the very end of the war.[42] Argentina, for example, only lifted its ban on anti-Nazi films in April 1945—not much of a profile in courage since the war against Germany was just weeks away from ending.[43]

CHAPTER 10

HOLLYWOOD CINEMA EXPANSION IN POSTWAR SOUTH AMERICA, 1945–1973

Warner Bros. began planning to operate new cinemas in Rio de Janeiro, São Paulo, and other cities in Brazil as the war came to an end.[1] With so much interest among U.S. film companies in expanding operations in Brazil and throughout South America, and with Warner Bros.' plan to join Fox, United Artists, Paramount, and MGM in operating local cinemas in Brazil, the Brazilian Administrative Department of the Public Service successfully lobbied the president of Brazil to appoint a special committee "to study, revise and consolidate the laws regulating the protection of the national motion picture industry."[2] These protectionist impulses were further galvanized when RKO's Latin American supervisor, Jack Osserman, noted in June 1945 that it would be wise for MGM and other American film companies to "build in every one of the 12 key cities of the country."[3] Wolfe Cohen, Warner International vice president, echoed RKO's intentions, telling *Motion Picture Daily* that Warner Bros. hoped "within the next couple of years to acquire an interest in theatres in every important capital of South America."[4] Meanwhile, Twentieth Century-Fox moved further into Latin American exhibition through its close association with the sixty-cinema Rodriguez circuit of Mexico and Fox's ongoing operation of the Palácio in Rio de Janeiro, the Excelsior in Lima, and a new shop window cinema, the Colon, in Cali, Colombia.[5]

MGM also expanded its reach as World War II came to an end with Arthur Loew dubbing Loew's International's new postwar plans as "the greatest international building project attempted by a film company." No longer subject to wartime building restrictions, MGM rapidly debuted three new Cine Metros in Colombia: a new Cine Metro in Cali, a remodeled Cine Metro in Barranquilla, and a new Cine Metro through acquisition in Medellin. Elsewhere, another Cine Metro was under construction in Valparaiso, Chile, alongside new office building/theater projects scheduled for postwar Buenos Aires and Havana. "All stops," *Film Bulletin* reported, were now "pulled for that South American market."[6] This increase in overseas construction was directly attributable to the decline in other world markets.[7] By the end of 1945, MGM's foreign rep, Sam Burger, added another Brazilian city—Bahia—to his list of target cities for MGM shop windows.[8] Warner Bros.' Wolfe Cohen remarked that he too hoped to have "theatres in all major cities, some 15 situations" with most "either purchased or rented rather than built." All cinemas, he claimed, would "operate with native partners" but the company would "maintain operational control."[9]

Fox, MGM, and Warner Bros. hoped to enter Mexican exhibition after the war as well. Twentieth Century-Fox had already sent its *domestic* executives to work on expanding the company's exhibition holdings to the south. Loew's, however, envisioned Mexico as outside of the Canada–United States North American relationship; this might be due to linguistics or to cultural prejudice. (As noted in chapter 11, Puerto Rico—an American colony turned commonwealth—was also handled by Loew's International rather than MGM even though it *was* part of the United States.)

In late 1945 Loew's hoped to follow Twentieth Century-Fox's 50–50 partnership with Rodriguez's Monterey Theatres circuit with its own move into large-scale exhibition in Mexico through a partnership with William Oscar Jenkins's eighty-cinema Puebla chain.[10] Unlike MGM's South American shop window model, reports at the time suggested that Jenkins, an American sugar tycoon operating cinemas in Mexico, would partner with MGM to "form a syndicate for the construction or acquisition of 60 theatres for the exclusive exhibition of Mexican films."[11] Meanwhile, Twentieth Century-Fox, building upon its partnership with Rodriguez, also hoped to expand by building, through its domestic National Theatres subsidiary, "a string of pre-fabricated houses in Mexico."[12] These plans were ultimately scrapped due to a "disagreement" between Twentieth Century-Fox and the Mexican government. When MGM's partnership with Jenkins also collapsed, National Theatres stepped in to purchase a 50 percent interest in Jenkins's chain, thereby providing Fox with two circuits in Mexico while MGM remained shut out.

Warner Bros. was similarly unsuccessful in its ambitions. Despite a tour of Mexico and Central America by Karl Macdonald, vice president of Warner International, and property purchased by the company in Mexico City, reports that Warner Bros. was building a "showcase" cinema in Mexico City never came to fruition.[13] Instead, Warner Bros. trained its focus back to South

America (and later the Caribbean) where it joined MGM, Fox, and United Artists by acquiring its own shop window cinema in Bogotá, the Teatro San Jorge, in September 1946. The cinema was renovated and reopened under Warner Bros.' direction on January 1, 1947.[14]

MGM's Postwar Expansion

MGM continued its focus on South America as well by investing in Colombia, buying two cinemas in Bogotá: the Teusaquillo, which was reopened as the Metro-Teusaquillo, and the Teatro Astral, reopened on April 1, 1947, as yet another Cine Metro. The two Bogotá Metros were now on a day-and-date policy of simultaneous film release.[15] The newest Cine Metros operated almost exactly as Loew's theaters did in the United States. For the (very late) debut of the *Thrill of a Romance* (1945), for example, MGM Colombia head Carl Flint and theater publicist Luis Ucko created a "walkie talkie man-in-the-street promotion" that was picked up by a local radio station and rebroadcast by Nueva Granada. Two fifteen-minute trailers were employed, four-column newspaper advertisements were coordinated with the local agency for Max Factor (another Hollywood import), and these same ads appeared in color on the backs of leading Bogotá magazines. Five thousand postcards of both Esther Williams and Van Johnson were handed out, and two thousand Max Factor/*Thrill of a Romance* souvenir envelopes were distributed in local drug stores. Finally, as was often the case, Flint and Ucko worked with the J. Glottmann department store on a window display promoting the film.[16] All of these exploitation techniques could be found at Loew's theaters throughout North America and at MGM cinemas around the world.

Arthur Loew would argue in 1949 that, through the company's efforts in film distribution and exhibition, "We are selling America and American democracy overseas, not consciously, for we are producing for entertainment, but indirectly."[17] A new MGM cinema was an effort, once more, to ingratiate the company and its films into the upper echelons of local politics, creating meaningful connections and opportunities for engagement between U.S. consular and local Latin American officials. The opening of the Cine Metro in Barranquilla, for instance, was attended, by "government officials and local dignitaries" including newly elected Colombian president Mariano Ospina Pérez.[18] This government presence was one of many reasons why U.S. State Department officials in Washington received briefings on these kinds of openings. And given the importance of motion pictures as a major export of the United States, these gala events provided ample opportunity for industrial and political connections to be forged into personal relationships that paid off in many official and unofficial ways. For local officials, the postwar investment of foreign capital was also heralded as evidence of the strength of their political leadership and a conferral of status as a global media capital. The architectural design and aesthetics of these shop window cinemas simply reiterated this fact, providing a visual reminder of local "progress." As a cultural embassy, the Barranquilla Metro's aesthetic of opulence intended to convey the power of the United States' wealth, industry, and technology.[19]

The Barranquilla Metro was MGM's fourth showcase cinema in Colombia; a fifth venue in Cali, Colombia, was already under construction.[20] In contrast, Argentina lacked almost any "Hollywood" investments in terms of film exhibition. MGM *had* purchased a new site in Rosario for a 1,500-seat Cine Metro and another property in Buenos Aires for a 2,600-seat showcase, but neither was yet in operation.[21] *Variety* noted that the construction of new Cine Metros would push "Native exhibs" to upgrade their cinemas, a key motivation for the shop window. The trade journal cited MGM's purchase of real estate in Buenos Aires as just one example in which a "native circuit immediately announced plans for actual construction" as a result.[22] MGM continued purchasing property in Latin America over the next few years, drawing up plans for a Cine Metro in Recife, Brazil, as well. All of these cinemas were veiled warnings to local exhibitors to either play MGM films or new competitive cinemas, backed by U.S. capital, would be built down the street.[23]

One of the driving forces behind MGM's sudden exhibition expansion—coming a decade after the first wave of Cine Metros were built—was the ever-rising grosses of "all-Spanish" dubbed versions of MGM films now being distributed throughout Latin America. These dubbed versions, naturally, made illiterate and visually impaired moviegoers able to enjoy Hollywood films (although they likely damaged prospects among the deaf and hard of hearing). In at least two locations, MGM reported a 300 percent rise in grosses using dubbed rather than subtitled prints.[24] Another reason for MGM's expansion was the same counterproductive, protectionist measures imposed throughout the world: blocking Hollywood profits from repatriation.[25] Once more, efforts to thwart U.S. film companies from transferring their distribution and exhibition revenues only served to further encourage U.S. film companies to buy and build more cinemas.

Paramount, Race, and the Cine Tacna

Paramount also hoped to mobilize local revenues (and blocked funds) to reboot its global exhibition footprint after World War II. This was a major policy change for the company, which had all but abandoned global film exhibition after its bankruptcy reorganization in 1933. The possibilities in Latin America, however, were too tempting to ignore.[26] Paramount International

Theaters Corp. announced that the first new cinema for the division would be the Paramount Tacna theater, slated to open inside a new ten-story complex in Lima, Peru.[27] The Paramount Tacna was named for its location on Avenida Tacna, one of the city's main boulevards, and was a joint venture with Inmobiliaria San Martín, S.A., the local real estate investment company that had developed the new office/retail/residential complex. The U.S. architecture firm Schlanger, Hoffberg, Reisner and Urbahn designed and engineered the cinema, which was constructed by the local firm Florez & Costa. Ben Schlanger, one of the most prominent U.S. theater designers of the 1930s and 1940s, was the lead architect. The 1,945-seat Cine Tacna was built to hold 883 seats on the main floor, 405 "deluxe" chairs on the mezzanine, and 657 additional seats in the balcony.[28]

Outside of its Rodriguez Theatres investments in Mexico, Twentieth Century-Fox still had only three Latin American shop window cinemas: the Palácio in Rio, the Colon in Cali, and the Cine Excelsior in Lima.[29] In 1947 the company announced its operational takeover of the Windsor cinema in Concepción, Chile. This was a perfect moment for Fox to make an investment in Chile; the U.S. government had just extended a new loan to Chile under President Gabriel González Videla, a prudent move with roughly $50 million worth of American goods languishing in Valparaiso docks awaiting political negotiations.[30]

Fox hoped to expand further in the region by moving away from simply leasing cinemas in Latin America like the Windsor and toward (joint) ownership. The Tacna project had been that first effort, originally a joint ownership venture between Paramount and Twentieth Century-Fox. Here, the consent decree, which had no jurisdictions over U.S. film company's foreign exhibition investments, did present an issue for Paramount and Fox—the only documented time in which Hollywood's drawn out settlement with the U.S. Department of Justice constrained U.S. film companies' exhibition efforts overseas. While the decree did not require U.S. film companies to divest their foreign holdings, Paramount and Fox executives broke off their partnership in the Tacna out of fear that their *joint* ownership of a foreign cinema might be seen to be a violation of the decree and a conferral of their oligopoly. That same fear also led Fox to pull out of another joint agreement with Paramount to organize, and thereby challenge MGM's Latin American supremacy with, 16 mm distribution operations throughout the region. "In each instance," *Variety* argued, "it was fear on the part of 20th that the Government would use the joint operations as added evidence of domestic collaboration among the majors."[31]

Now a sole Paramount project, the Tacna became eminently more complex to construct. An unspecified "export situation" required that "countless items had to be shipped pre-assembled," *Architectural Record* reported. "This included glass, mirrors, neon tubes pre-bent, stainless steel work, even millwork such as candy counters. Glass mosaic, liberally used in lobbies, was pasted in 2-ft.

squares, and skillfully assembled by native workmen who never had handled glass mosaic before."[32] Display cases, attraction boxes, and furniture also had to be shipped to Lima prefabricated from the United States. All of the seating and acoustical materials as well as the air-conditioning, sound, and projection equipment were shipped from the United States—a very large expense.[33]

To manage these and other complexities—especially since the Cine Tacna was supposed to reanimate Paramount's long dormant foreign exhibition unit—Abe Platt, chief assistant to Paramount International Theatres head, Clement Crystal, flew to Lima in February 1948 to "supervise" the Cine Tacna's final details and its opening.[34] Crystal followed shortly thereafter, and George Weltner, Paramount International president, and A. L. Pratchett, Paramount's division manager for Latin America, all arrived in late March 1948.[35] Former Philadelphia-based manager Gene Goodman, who completed his training for the position by Paramount in the United States, was sent to Lima to manage the new cinema.[36] All of these executives were on hand when Paramount International Theatres Corp. formally opened the Cine Tacna (now without the Paramount imprimatur) on April 1, 1948, with an elaborate marquee covered with white and gold mosaics, neon tubing, and a planter box, blending once more the local with the (Hollywood) exotic, a marriage of Peruvian horticulture with U.S. exhibition culture.[37] The Tacna opened with Paramount's *The Big Clock*, whose star, Ray Milland, was flown by Paramount to Lima on March 27 to be the guest of honor at its debut.[38] No opening night attendee was more important to Paramount, though, than Peru's president, José Bustamante y Rivero, whose favor Paramount (and other U.S. film companies) hoped to curry as protectionist sentiments grew against the local domination of cinemas by U.S. films.[39]

With Paramount's successful opening of the Cine Tacna, the city of Lima—perhaps more than any other in the world—had become the most vivid example of Hollywood's shop window strategy. MGM's Cine Metro, Warner Bros.' Teatro Central, Fox's Cine Excelsior, and now Paramount's Tacna all served as cultural embassies for U.S. culture, movies, and moviegoing. As a comparison, London would not have all four companies operating their own cinemas there for another six years.[40] Peru's interest in outside capital investments reflected the security that the country's oligarchical ruling class and military control provided for American and other foreign investment. The country had also managed to avoid the depths of the Great Depression, so Peruvian elites during the postwar period could certainly afford the leisure time and expense of a trip to the cinema. The country's repressive politics and rule had also squelched popular, leftist rebellion against the state, further making it a stable place for foreign investments and U.S. interests.[41]

The Tacna laid bare other troubling postwar realities. Clement Crystal and Paramount hoped to attract and unify all Peruvians inside the Cine Tacna, despite the country's stratified racial and class hierarchies. Ayumi Takenaka notes that Peru's infamous anti-Japanese riot of 1940 reflected "the salience of race in organizing Peruvian society," with labels such as "mestizo," "Indian," "white," "Negro," or "Asian" appearing on official government documents and reflecting the surface and hidden schisms in Lima's social structure.[42] These racial distinctions, of course, also intersected with class difference. Thus, Crystal's (hypocritical) plan was to "Americanize" the moviegoing experience at the Cine Tacna and, by doing so, encourage other exhibitors to attract all of Lima's potential ticket buyers—no matter their background—to boost profits in Peru. As Crystal told a meeting of the Society of Motion Picture Engineers in 1948:

> It is customary in Peru that balcony patrons must enter the theater from a different entrance than those who patronize the auditorium and mezzanine floor.... However, we feel that low-price patrons shall be considered just as important as the others, and we have equipped the balcony with fully upholstered seats, given the balcony a lounge, nicely furnished, carpeted the floor and aisles, to the balcony, and given them beautifully tiled, modern rest rooms. Major American companies all feel the same way and we are striving to bring to the people of the world the better things in life which we have all been fortunate enough to give to all classes of people in America. In America we are not allowed to have class distinction, but in many places throughout the world, and especially in Latin America, there is class distinction and the local theater owners and operators look down upon the low-admission people. American companies feel that they are the backbone of our business and that success can only come to us through continuous patronage of the theater by the middle and lower classes, and that a theater built to attract only the better classes can never be a successful venture.[43]

Crystal's remarks—in which he makes no mention of race or segregation in the United States—are missing one key aspect, of course: Paramount, through its many subsidiaries throughout the United States, especially in the South and Texas, operated innumerable segregated cinemas in small and big cities in 1948. The segregated balcony at the Paramount Theater in Marshall, Texas, for example, so angered a young James Farmer—after he suffered the "humiliation of climbing that buzzard's roost"—that he would use it as inspiration to cofound the seminal U.S. civil rights organization, CORE, the Congress of Racial Equality.[44] While Clement Crystal sought to desegregate Peruvian cinemas and those in other countries, he spoke from a nation and its industry that did not officially desegregate its own cinemas until 1964. Crystal's sleight of hand is to note the segregation of class in Peru only, as if this distinction was not embedded there, as elsewhere, in racial difference and skin privilege.

The Tacna's policies and Crystal's speech would later be echoed by Spyros Skouras's own contradictory remarks about desegregating cinemas in colonial Zimbabwe and the United States. Any effort to sell the United States as a postracial society and Hollywood films and cinemas as venues without consideration to race, class, and other forms of social difference all played into the U.S. Department of State's ongoing postwar plan to defeat the spread of communism through the salesmanship of democracy and capitalism as open and fair systems without discrimination.

Postwar Optimism Fades

Racial division was not the only problem plaguing Lima and Peru. Neither Paramount nor Bustamante y Rivero could have known it, but the opening of the Cine Tacna was the calm before a political storm as Gen. Manuel A. Odría led the first of a series of military coups just a few months after the opening of the Tacna on October 27, 1948. A series of military dictatorships, puppet regimes, and democratic governments would dominate Peru for the next three decades. Political turmoil in Latin America, the Middle East, and other postwar regions was just one of many reasons why Paramount balked at further exhibition expansion.

By July 1949—as Paramount was fulfilling its divestment of its domestic theater operations (which would be spun off into United Paramount Theatres on November 15, 1949, under Leonard Goldenson)—both Clement Crystal and Abe Platt had already resigned from Paramount's international theater operations (which were retained by the producer-distributor corporation not by the domestic exhibition company). Paramount's international cinemas were now managed instead by Lou Lazar, who had to deal with "crippling currency restrictions, [the] impossibly high cost of construction and uncertain economic conditions" that "have combined to axe all plans for overseas theatre expansion." Referring to the Tacna, *Variety* noted that the "defunct nature of Par's ambitious theatre-building plans overseas" meant that the Tacna was "the last to be built as part of the company's post-war blueprints for a flagship in every capital in the world."[45] Paramount wasn't alone. Hollywood's cinema construction in South America by the end of the 1940s had mostly ground to a halt.

In the mid-1950s, more than half a decade later, MGM International—still under the aegis of Loew's Inc. until their much-delayed divestiture—began opening more overseas cinemas, including a deluxe cinema in Buenos Aires.[46] The announcement of the Argentina project toward the end of 1955 may have been spurred by the end of Juan Peron's rule and subsequent exile and the (supposed) stabilization of the nation. Stability in that country and throughout the region, however, often remained elusive over the next thirty years, despite and due to both military and foreign (often U.S.) political intervention. Arthur Loew, still at the helm, continued to speak about "theater expansion in many areas overseas."[47] Loew's would once again begin to "spend 'many millions' in building and purchasing additional cinemas outside the United States."[48] Amid intense political instability, the opulent Cine Metro finally opened in Buenos Aires in October 4, 1956, one day after Loew had announced his retirement as president of Loew's Inc.[49] The man who had built, alongside William Melniker, the vast Loew's International chain, was gone. The U.S. film industry was foundering, MGM was declining, and Loew's Theatres were increasingly a collection of white elephants. The international business was no easier with so much ongoing political unrest. "Loew frankly admitted the pressures and problems were too much for him," *Film Bulletin* noted. "His health was beginning to suffer."[50]

Twentieth Century-Fox president Spyros Skouras and Fox International head Murray Silverstone were the rare U.S. executives then still looking to expand their exhibition holdings during this period. In 1959, through a newly organized company composed of Luiz Severiano Ribeiro Jr., Lucidio Ceravolo, and Fox's local subsidiary, Fox Filmes do Brasil, Fox began operating the Cine Marrocos in São Paulo as another shop window cinema alongside its longtime Palácio in Rio.[51]

Although this book mostly focuses on Hollywood's overseas exhibition empires, there were many other companies involved in foreign exhibition during the twentieth century who navigated the political, legal, financial, and logistical difficulties of foreign cinema ownership and operation. Gaumont, Ufa, African Consolidated Theatres, and Rank are just some of those involved. Another is Toho. Organized as the Tokyo-Takarazuka Theater Company in 1932, Toho was riding a wave of success in the 1950s largely on the back of their enormously successful Gojira franchise. Brazil (and São Paulo, in particular) was home to the largest Japanese population outside of Japan. Joining four other Japanese movie houses in São Paulo operating in the Japanese-Brazilian Liberdade neighborhood—including the Cine Niteroi, which opened in 1953— Toho leased the Cine-Theatro Paramount and reopened it on August 26, 1960, as the Toho Paramount, claiming the opulent cinema as its new "exclusive launcher" for Toho films.[52] The opening program featured filmed greetings by Hajime Sakai, chief executive of Toho Filmes América do Sul Ltda.; F. L. de Almeida Saltes, president of the São Paulo Cinematheque and *O Estado de São Paulo* critic; and Kiyashi Yamamôta, president of the São Paulo Society of Japanese Culture. In addition to the importance of Toho's need to secure a shop window or "launcher" in São Paulo, the Toho lease was an indication of how far Paramount had moved away from its own need to operate shop windows at all as part of its global distribution strategies during the 1950s and 1960s.[53] The Toho Paramount was not the only cinema the company operated outside of

Japan. In a foreshadowing reversal, Toho cinemas would also open in cities such as Los Angeles in 1961 and in New York in 1963.[54]

A Boa Vista of the Future

By the mid-1960s, with the rise of television in Brazil, cinema attendance finally began to decline and cinemas began closing in large numbers, becoming ice cream stores, laundromats, churches, and other spaces. MGM closed and demolished its original Metro-Passeio in Rio in the mid-1960s in order to replace it with a modern cinema in hopes of attracting moviegoers for its new widescreen spectacles. On January 23, 1969, the fading MGM company debuted its last cinema in South America, the Metro-Boavista, on the site of the original Metro. The midcentury cinema was outfitted with the latest widescreen technology, the short-lived but expansive Dimension 150 process, as well as six-channel stereo sound. The Metro-Boavista was designed in the modern, international style that rendered it short on embellishment but long (or wide) on sound and vision.[55] However, with so few MGM films being produced by 1969, MGM films might have been an initial focus, but they were certainly not enough to fill the Metro's screens year-round, except with long engagements.

The Metro-Boavista was not the last Metro cinema to open in Latin America. Despite its rapid decline, MGM's international division opened another venue in Panama City two months later in March 1969, the company's first and only Central American cinema. (Fox also had its own Panama City shop window, the Cine Bella Vista.[56]) The nine-hundred-seat Teatro Metro was the company's forty-eighth global cinema and was constructed in that most postwar of venues, a shopping center along the city's fashionable Avenida Balboa. Like the Boavista, the Teatro Metro's expansive seventy-eight-foot screen—not its exotic Hollywood opulence—was its main attraction, as was its six-track stereo sound. The Metro opened with *The Fisherman*, grossing $14,902 in its first week, the "largest initial-week take ever in Central America."[57] *Variety* did not account for why MGM had waited nearly thirty-five years since their Latin American expansion in the 1930s—and at a time when the company's finances were in far more brittle shape—to open their first cinema in Central America. Panama's ongoing political crises were certainly no less turbulent between 1968 and 1970.[58]

The Metro-Boavista in Rio and the Teatro Metro in Panama City—like all of the other remaining Cine Metros in Argentina, Brazil, Chile, Colombia, Peru, Uruguay, and Venezuela—became part of the new Cinema International Corp. chain on December 1, 1973.[59] CIC, managed globally by Victor Hoare and locally by the president of Brazilian operations, Paulo Fucs—who also oversaw CIC film production in Brazil; CIC's distribution of Paramount,

Universal, and MGM films there; CIC-TV (video sales); and the CIC cinema chain in Brazil[60]—expanded CIC's Brazilian exhibition operations by buying the local Condor Theatre chain. After shedding other Cine Metros around South America, the Condor purchase provided CIC with eighteen cinemas in Brazil by 1976 alongside twenty-two additional CIC cinemas in South Africa, four in England, the Metro Theatres in Cairo and Alexandria, Egypt, and one MGM house still remaining in Amsterdam. (CIC also had an exclusive booking agreement with Brazil's Art-Palacio circuit.)[61]

Once more, however, politics roiled best-laid plans. The edicts of the current Brazilian military government, led by President Ernesto Geisel, made the country an increasingly tough film market. Luiz Severiano Ribeiro Jr., who still operated 102 cinemas (with 35 in metro Rio alone), began closing more and more cinemas because of the low ticket prices set by the government that were impossible for exhibitors to maintain, given the rising prices for commercial rent, due in part to Rio's exponential population growth. Just as in the United States and other global markets, the return on selling real estate had become much higher than the measly margins of a movie house.[62] Eventually, the seesaw mismatch between real estate values and low ticket prices wiped away many of Rio's best cinemas, including the Metro-Tijuca and Metro-Copacabana.[63] Both cinemas closed on January 27, 1977, and remain vestigial memories.[64] Between 1968 and 1978 half of Rio's cinemas were closed.[65]

The Metro-Boavista was a survivor amid a steep decline in the number of "street cinemas," which faded away in favor of shopping mall multiplexes that offered security, newer seats and technology, and more screens. In 1997 the local offshoot of CIC, now owned by the Kenya-based British Capital Ltd., finally decided to sell this cinema as well.[66] It soon closed altogether. The Boavista's closure in the late 1990s—where it remained mummified in gutted disuse until 2015—was, not surprisingly, caused by the next wave of U.S. (and other) exhibition investment. Six multiplex operators—Paramount and Universal's United Cinemas International; U.S. operators Cinemark and AMC; Australia's Hoyts (formerly owned by Twentieth Century-Fox) and Greater Union; and Canada's Cineplex Odeon—all planned to open cinemas in Rio, São Paulo, and other Brazilian cities.[67]

Lasting Legacies

Before turning to Hollywood's exhibition operations throughout the Caribbean—which existed concurrently but separately in Hollywood's estimation and organization—it is important to consider the cultural legacy of U.S. film exhibition expansion in South America. On the one hand, resentment of U.S. cultural imperialism was omnipresent, especially with political insurgencies in countries such as Colombia and Venezuela. On the other hand, the decades-long presence of these U.S.-operated shop window cinemas cultivated a deep love and appreciation for Hollywood films and the American culture and products they celebrated.

The first example is in Colombia, where MGM operated four Cine Metros in Barranquilla, Bogotá, Cali, and Medellin from the 1930s until the mid-1970s, when they were sold off by CIC.[68] Amid an endless period of political violence—in which the communist-led FARC (Fuerzas Armadas Revolucionarias de Colombia) began a physical insurrection for the next half century against the government of Colombia (and its political and institutional enablers) in 1964, all four Cine Metros—none of which were still operated by MGM or CIC—were attacked by leftist forces in December 1975. Local police speculated that "since the theaters all carry 'Metro' in their names, the perpetrators mistakenly may have thought the theaters belong to Metro-Goldwyn-Mayer" and thus were prime targets as "Yanqui" investments.[69] Years after their divestment, these cinemas maintained their deep connections to nearly four decades of MGM and Hollywood marketing the United States.

A countervailing example can be found in Brazil. Although Rio's Metro-Passeio was torn down in the 1960s and the Metro-Tijuca and Metro-Copacabana were closed and demolished in the 1970s, in the small town of Conservatória, Brazil, in northern Rio state, projectionist-turned-lawyer Ivo Raposo, along with his weekend house manager Luiz Carlos de Jesus, built a

FIGURE 10.1 Metro-Tijuca, ca. 1973, in its waning CIC days before closure and demolition. (Courtesy of Ivo Raposo)

FIGURE 10.2 Ivo Raposo's stunning Metro-Tijuca in Conservatória, three hours north of Rio. (Ross Melnick)

"perfect, small-scale replica of the *Metro-Tijuca*" in 2005.[70] Using some of the Metro-Tijuca's original seats, chandeliers, projectors, and numerous other original elements, Raposo brought a picture-perfect two-story, sixty-seat version of this cinema back to life in a visceral experience one must see to believe. (I was fortunate, thanks to Raposo and João Luiz Vieira, to have visited this stunning location in 2014 to conduct research on site and examine Raposo's archive of MGM ledgers, programs, photographs, and other ephemera.) Raposo's backyard Metro on his estate demonstrates not only the way in which these shop window cinemas influenced South American cinemagoing but the way in which MGM films and MGM's cinemas established their centrality in the hearts and minds of moviegoers in Brazil and around the world. Raposo's "Cine Centimetro" represents, then, the social, industrial, and cultural impact these cinemas had and still have on those who remember them and the ideological influence they helped foster for the dissemination of U.S. films and exhibition standards in South America and in numerous other markets around the world. They also demonstrate—as does Raposo's "Cowboy" western cabin and other ephemera on his property—the enduring exportation of American mythology and cultural affinity. As Talitha Ferraz writes, visiting Raposo's Cine Centimetro "leads to the invigoration of affective, sensory,

FIGURE 10.3 Ivo Raposo inspecting a 35 mm film clip in one of three cinemas on his Conservatória estate. (Ross Melnick)

cinematic and architectural markers which were once inscribed into people's lives and the urban space in Rio de Janeiro, in which *Metro-Tijuca* had played an important role." Ferraz writes that MGM's nostalgic hold on older Cariocas can still be seen in their ongoing pilgrimages to Raposo's Conservatória tourist attraction with "the sight of spectators with tears in their eyes . . . especially the older ones who remember personal events connected to past cinemagoing practices and the *Metro-Tijuca*."[71] Raposo and his onsite cinema(s) are emblematic of the profound success of those shop window cinemas. Visiting his Cine Centimetro in Conservatória was one of the most important sites of inquiry—perhaps the most personally profound of any—in researching and writing this book.

MGM's employment of Metro Cub Clubs, *Tom & Jerry* cartoons, MGM short and feature films, and the implementation of luxury throughout these shop window cinemas were intended to inspire wonder—for MGM, Hollywood, and the United States. Cultural embassies like the Metro-Tijuca spread the United States' ideology of consumerism and democracy as well as the mythology of the United States as a nirvana where anyone could arrive with a few pesos or réis and convert them, like magic beans, into tall-tale dreams.

CHAPTER 11

CARIBBEAN DREAMS, 1929–1973

*Hollywood Cinemas in Cuba, Jamaica,
Puerto Rico, and Trinidad*

Hollywood's exhibition operations in the Caribbean were a jumble of region-specific decisions on the part of Paramount, Warner Bros., and MGM. These strategies differed from island to island and decade to decade, but all shared the intention of securing key venues for U.S. films in these colonial and postcolonial territories. To understand how the Caribbean became saturated with Hollywood's films (and cinemas)—crowding out Mexican, Argentinian, British, Indian, indigenous, and other competition—it is essential to apply a regional lens to these developments, as corporate dictates for this expansion and diffusion were made by Hollywood's Caribbean managers working on a geographically *regional* as well as a corporately organized territorial level composed of *local* branches and branch managers. Wherever Hollywood executives operated in foreign markets, they typically "colonized" and organized entire regions to facilitate labor and distribution efficiencies and profits with little to no regard or distinction for local borders. Like more traditional "colonists," Hollywood routinely ignored linguistic, cultural, political, and national differences in organizing the world for its businesses. Companies like Paramount, for example, established its *regional* dominion here with little regard for the stark differences between these varying colonial and postcolonial territories, nations, and peoples. The vast linguistic, political, and cultural differences between Cuba and Jamaica, for instance, were a cumbersome obstacle for Hollywood executives charged with managing the whole of "the Caribbean." Their regional jobs were, in effect, to overcome these differences by converting all these disparate territories and moviegoers into a mass market and a mass audience, unifying all into a regional, rather than territorial or national, audience for the U.S. film companies they worked for. This was accomplished through the creation of branch offices, distribution networks, and marketing efficiencies and promotions as well as by the operation of local cinemas.

Beginning in the 1920s Paramount's investment in and subsequent purchase of the Saenger Amusement company, which operated cinemas throughout the southern United States and the Caribbean, reflected the regional and transcontinental industrial, racial, and cultural sinews that existed between cities like New Orleans, Louisiana, and Kingston, Jamaica. From the 1920s to the 1940s, Paramount operated cinemas throughout Cuba and Jamaica, created tight distributor-exhibitor relationships in Puerto Rico, and outmaneuvered colonial and postcolonial protectionist policies targeting U.S. cinema ownership. Loew's/MGM also attempted to establish shop window cinemas in the Caribbean capitals of Port of Spain (Trinidad), Havana (Cuba), and San Juan (Puerto Rico). MGM's efforts in Port of Spain were blocked, however, by Trinidad's British colonial attorney general, while its Havana shop window cinema and high-rise project vanished amid the rising political and labor conflicts of prerevolutionary Cuba. MGM did manage to build and open El Teatro Metro in San Juan, Puerto Rico, which, despite being on U.S. soil, came under the direction of Loew's International division—instead of its domestic Loew's Theatres staff—exposing the complex racial and colonial politics of precommonwealth Puerto Rico. Warner Bros., too, made a significant play for Cuba, operating two shop window cinemas in Havana before labor strife, political conflict, and complex legal arrangements with its local partner led it to abandon its Cuban cinemas well before the revolution.

Hollywood's ignorance of local politics and regional strife—from the strength of British colonial pushback against U.S. influence in Trinidad and Jamaica to rising anti-U.S. (mainland) sentiment in both Cuba and Puerto Rico—all made the Caribbean more of a bust than a boom for Hollywood cinema expansion. The failure of Hollywood's Caribbean dreams demonstrates the importance of examining its interests through a regional as well as a territorial lens, understanding the strategic, political, cultural, and geographical distances and differences as well as the industrial linkages between all four islands for Hollywood and local distributors and exhibitors.

Early Investments in the Spanish-Speaking Caribbean: Puerto Rico and Cuba

In the late 1910s Paramount forged an agreement with the aptly named Caribbean Film Co. (CFC) to distribute its motion pictures in Cuba, Puerto Rico, "all the other islands of the West Indies" as well as nearby Venezuela, and "a large part of Central America." CFC also controlled sixty-five cinemas in Puerto Rico as well three hundred additional cinemas in Cuba, making it an ideal distribution and exhibition partner.[1] The chain provided Paramount with direct access to territories subject to varying degrees of U.S. influence as a result of the Spanish-American War.

Puerto Rico had become a U.S. colonial possession in 1898 and would only become a self-governing commonwealth in 1952. Cuba, which became a U.S. protectorate in the immediate aftermath of the Spanish-American War, had formally announced its independence from the United States a half century earlier in 1902. The newly independent Cuba still remained under the watchful, meddling eye of its northern neighbor, however, as the United States maintained its rights to intervene in Cuba's domestic and foreign affairs even under the new independent Cuban constitution. Over the next half century, the island became a fertile ground for U.S. investment, with growth focused in tourism, agriculture, entertainment, and all manner of organized crime. Until the 1959 revolution U.S. film companies enjoyed wide distribution in Cuba, as they did in Puerto Rico, both reliable cash cows for Hollywood.

As *Motion Picture World* observed, the Paramount–CFC deal offered "direct evidence of the influence of Americanization in the West Indies and Central America."[2] It also enabled Paramount to craft a system of runs, zones, and clearances for its films "in the same manner as they are booked in [the United States]."[3] Paramount maintained its standing as a key distribution partner for the CFC circuit throughout the 1920s while expanding its own reach in the southern United States and the Caribbean through its partnership with Saenger Theaters, which owned or operated more than 150 cinemas in the southern United States as well as cinemas in Jamaica, Panama, Cuba, "and many important Central American cities."[4] In 1929 Paramount purchased Saenger outright, thereby securing its status as it became a key exhibition player in the Caribbean.[5]

Saenger's holdings in Cuba included two showcase cinemas in Havana: the Fausto and the Encanto, the latter dubbed by *Variety* as "one of the most modern houses" in the country.[6] Saenger's focus on implementing a U.S. exhibition aesthetic—including air-conditioning by Carrier Engineering Corp., theater seats from American Seating Inc., lighting from the Major Electric Equipment Company of Chicago, and a large screen from the American Silversheet Company of St. Louis—had produced a cinema described by *Cine-Mundial* as a "masterpiece of comfort, luxury and art," able to rival "los 'Roxys' y los 'Paramounts'" in Manhattan.[7] The Fausto had been equipped for sound even before Paramount's acquisition, becoming, *Exhibitors Herald-World* noted, "one of the first of the Latin American theatres" to do so.[8]

Paramount, like Saenger, sought to ensure that the Encanto and Fausto operated just like the company's cinemas to the north. Leonard Grossman, who had managed several cinemas in the United States, became the new managing director of the Teatro Fausto in late 1929. The following year Paramount shifted him to the Encanto, where, he noted, he had continued the same practices for Cuban audiences.[9]

Warner Bros. reflected Hollywood's growing interest in Cuba when it completed its own plans in 1930 for a three-thousand-seat shop window cinema to be built in Havana. For reasons unknown, however, this Warner palace was never built, although the company would maintain a focused interest in building cinemas there for the next two decades.[10] Columbia Pictures—which would operate very few cinemas overseas—did manage to secure a friendly cinema in Havana as the head of their Cuban branch, Ernesto P. Smith, began operating the Campoamor cinema.[11] (Smith, it would turn out, would rise to become an important local player in 1930s and 1940s Cuban exhibition.) The focus on Puerto Rico was diverted for the moment, but it would return, as noted later in this chapter, when MGM identified the territory as a suitable place for another Cine Metro.

Jamaica and Saenger Amusements

Paramount's expansion into the Caribbean instead included investments in Jamaica, an example of how regional executives had to nimbly operate local branches and cinemas in vastly different territories. As a British colony (Jamaica would not achieve full independence from Britain until 1962), the island was subject to British control that resisted the spread of "Hollywood" films and American culture via its screens. U.S. distributors had two aces up their sleeves, though: first, U.S. films were incredibly popular in Jamaica and, second, U.S. film distributors were willing to rent their films to Jamaican exhibitors whereas British distributors insisted on selling them outright at higher rates (and with more risk) to local exhibitors. The growing popularity of American films, to the detriment of British films, led Jamaican colonial officials to author a 1928 bill that would "compel" cinemas to include British and Jamaican films at *every* screening. Local exhibitors, knowing they would have to buy these films from British distributors rather than rent more popular ones from U.S. distributors, rebelled at the bill's introduction.[12]

Statistics of the period, drawn from *Film Daily Year Books* and trade articles, confirm Keith Q. Warner's estimation that "the majority of the films shown in the pre-independence period—and after it, as it turns out—were American." Warner adds that, for both white and black audiences, movies in the sound era were seen over and over again, especially since travel off the island was prohibitively expensive. "Over and over," he writes, "we see instances where Caribbean young men made an almost instant connection and association with the world of the cinema—in speech, in dress, in every action."[13] These observations suggest that the 1928 Jamaican legislation was motivated not only by economic but also cultural concerns about the spread of U.S. films and culture. In England, Australia, Canada, and other outposts of the British Empire, American films were beginning to "colonize" local hearts and minds and thus posed a direct threat to the perceived superiority and importance of British culture.

Clearly among those who would have opposed the 1928 legislation would have been Jamaica's largest theater, the 2,033-seat Gaiety in Kingston, operated by Saenger Amusements' local subsidiary, the American-owned Palace Wilcox Saenger Company Ltd. The Gaiety, like Saenger's other exhibition venues in both Cuba and Panama, became a Paramount shop window cinema through the company's 1929 acquisition and would not have screened many British films without such political influence by local authorities.[14]

Saenger's Howard McCoy, who continued overseeing the Jamaican market for Paramount, brushed aside local concerns regarding the company's dominion over the key houses of both the Spanish-speaking and anglophone Caribbean by telling the *Daily Gleaner* newspaper, located in Kingston, that it was "not a question of monopoly" for Paramount to acquire the Saenger company and Jamaica's largest cinema "but of bigger opportunities for development." Saenger's holdings included another opulent (and even larger cinema) already under construction—the Palace in Kingston.[15] Soon Paramount's local subsidiary also opened the Movies Theatre in St. Andrews, giving the company three owned and operated cinemas in the colony.

McCoy hired local exhibitor Audley Morais to oversee all of the Saenger (now Paramount-owned) properties. McCoy, visiting Jamaica in April 1930 to supervise the installation of sound in all of Paramount's local cinemas, noted that he and Morais were there to shift Jamaican moviegoers from a desire for silent films toward a new passion for synchronous sound.[16] Morais had previously noted the advantage of sound films for a small market like Kingston, telling the *Gleaner* "that for the first time in the history of the business of the company, the Movies Theatre in St. Andrew is going to present exactly the same programme that the biggest de luxe theatre in England or America" could afford. "Such a thing has never been possible before," Morais added, because they "could not afford [live] orchestras" like those at larger, better-funded cinemas.[17]

Despite all of this Jamaican expansion, Paramount's exhibition holdings were once again decimated by its ongoing bankruptcy reorganization in 1933. All three of its Jamaican cinemas were no longer listed as Paramount venues by the end of that year, although the company still held a "stock interest" in the Gaiety, Palace, and Movies cinemas. Nonetheless, Paramount's early hold on distribution and exhibition through its three local shop window cinemas had performed to full effect. Two years after the reorganization, British United Film Producers argued that Paramount's lock on the island's key cinemas was still too difficult to penetrate, making the island a haven for Hollywood, not British, cinema.[18] Paramount's exhibition operations in the Caribbean—in both Jamaica and Cuba—was over for now, but its distribution apparatus in the region and its relationship with local exhibitors remained in full force.

MGM in Trinidad and British Colonial Pushback

Further south, American film companies had been involved in Trinidadian exhibition from an early stage. In 1916 American George Rosenthal leased St. Ann's Hall in Port of Spain and reopened it as the City Cinema. After abandoning the City, Rosenthal opened an outdoor venue, the Tent Cinema, before building the 1,200-seat Empire Theatre on adjacent property and opening it on September 25, 1920. Rosenthal later merged his holdings with British Guiana-based exhibitor William Pettigrew Humphrey in 1931, and together they formed the Colonial Film Exchange Company Ltd., which, Primnath Gooptar writes, "became the largest distribution company in the Caribbean." Humphrey later bought out Rosenthal, adding "British" to the company name and making the British Colonial Film Exchange Company Ltd. (BCFEC) a truly British entity.[19]

Gooptar adds that "the growing popularity of American films in Trinidad, during the late 1920s and early 1930s, forced American film companies to compete among themselves and with British and European companies to establish film distribution contracts in the Trinidad cinema circuit."[20] With U.S. film companies struggling to find acceptable venues (and rental terms) in Port of Spain, Loew's International began an effort to secure a shop window cinema in Port of Spain. Trinidad, untouched by Paramount/Saenger's claws, looked like a profitable bet for investment by Loew's, which did not share Paramount's extensive financial issues in the 1930s. MGM's own finances—given its much smaller debt and its profitable studio—all gave the company a sizable global advantage during this period.

In April 1932 MGM attempted to lease the Auditorium (concert hall) in the city-owned Prince's Building in Port of Spain from the residing City Council for £25 per month (roughly $120).[21] "The idea," MGM explained to the *Daily Gleaner*, was "to run motion picture shows as they do in many other parts of the world and to see how the people in Trinidad will receive them, so that they may acquire a spot in the City for erecting a cinema."[22] The impetus for leasing this temporary (and comparatively shabby) shop window space was also due to a dispute with William Humphrey's cinemas and BCFEC over rental terms. Humphrey then attempted to block MGM from doing so by lobbying the city. The Port of Spain City Council overruled Humphrey's and BCFEC's objection to the MGM Auditorium lease.[23]

This was only the opening salvo. In late April 1932 local exhibitors Lionel Belasco and N. M. "Meah" Gokool traveled to New York to complete a deal to operate the Auditorium in the Prince's Building—which would be remodeled into a one-thousand-seat venue due to open on June 1, 1932—and operate a new two-thousand-seat MGM shop window that would be built and completed by the end of 1932.[24] MGM also opened a new sales, marketing, distribution, and exhibition office in Trinidad—Metro-Goldwyn-Mayer of the West Indies—serving Trinidad, Barbados, and colonial British Guiana.[25] Charles Goldsmith, who had been with MGM in São Paulo, was sent to Trinidad to supervise the territory. MGM's Sam Burger also traveled to the West Indies to oversee the two new Trinidad cinemas and arrange for the opening of additional MGM-contracted cinemas in San Fernando and Port of Spain, Trinidad, and in Georgetown, British Guiana, operated "by local interests, all of which will have exclusive Metro playing contracts."[26] Demonstrating its deference to local colonial authorities, MGM confirmed its "strong, pro-British attitude" by showing "100 per cent British news-reels, and a large number of the best British pictures."[27]

MGM's efforts to curry British colonial favor did not prevent it from being blindsided by William Humphrey, though, who lobbied the Trinidad attorney general for a writ against the mayor, aldermen, and the citizens of Port of Spain seeking an injunction against the MGM lease of the Auditorium. This was "the first time in the history of lawsuits in Trinidad," the *Daily Gleaner* reported, "that an Attorney General has signed a writ in a lawsuit between private parties."[28] The case was litigated in the Trinidad Supreme Court in July 1932, and the presiding judge ruled that the City Council had exceeded its powers in granting the lease.[29] MGM lost its chance at the Auditorium and, after paying to renovate the venue, received only some of its construction costs back.[30]

MGM's two-prong strategy of leasing the Auditorium and building a new cinema meant that the absence of an aging shop window there was only a brief setback. MGM's investment in Meah Gokool's new $150,000 Metro Cinema gave the company a proper (if short-lived) shop window cinema in Port of Spain and the largest movie house in the city, with 1,800 seats. Gooptar writes that MGM soon ran into another problem:

> Not long after its opening there was a dispute between Gokool and the American MGM company as Gokool held that he reserved the right to decide what

films other than MGM's were shown at his cinema.... Gokool broke off relations with MGM and went on his own. A Globe sign replaced MGM's lion, signifying the new name of the cinema, The Globe Theatre.... He became an independent cinema operator and thus was able to show the first Indian movie screened in Trinidad.[31]

MGM, likely wary of trying again to invest in local Trinidad exhibition after both of these misadventures—having been burned by both local partners and the island's legal system—finally made a pact with BCFEC in 1935 to distribute its films throughout the company's circuit. "Through this new distribution deal MGM gained access to all of Humphrey's cinemas locally and internationally," Gooptar notes. "This was probably a better deal for MGM because instead of the single cinema deal with Gokool and the Metro cinema, they now had a chain of cinemas in which to release their movies not only in Trinidad but also in the Caribbean."[32]

The schism between Gokool and MGM was not without other consequences. Having lost MGM's films and needing additional outlets, the Indian-born Gokool imported more and more Indian films to his cinemas where, by 1941, Indian movies now covered roughly one-quarter of all of Trinidad's screens.[33] (Gokool was himself a very controversial figure in Trinidad, having tried and been convicted for attempting to burn down Humphrey's showcase cinema, the Empire, in 1937.) One last note from MGM's Trinidad adventures: in addition to the attorney general's successful effort to block MGM from leasing the Auditorium at the (symbolically rich) *Prince's* Building, the colonial power structure constrained the U.S. film industry's power once more in 1936, when quotas were instituted requiring the exhibition of British films throughout the island.[34] British colonial rule would last for another quarter century.

MGM, Massacres, and the Movies in Puerto Rico

Growth opportunities for U.S. film companies in the Caribbean were far more assured in islands the United States had secured, even if only briefly, by the Spanish-American War rather than in those colonized by England (Jamaica and Trinidad). Despite Puerto Rico's status as an American colony and unincorporated organized territory—in 1917 U.S. citizenship had been granted to anyone born on the island after April 25, 1898—Loew's still treated Porto Rico/Puerto Rico as a foreign territory rather than as a part of the United States and the North American distribution and exhibition ecosystem.[35] This was despite the fact that, unlike Cuba, where Argentinian, Mexican, and other Latin American films were growing in popularity, U.S. films captured 95 percent of the screen time in Puerto Rico's 125 cinemas by the end of the 1920s.[36]

Naida Garcia-Crespo argues that "Puerto Rico's position as a stateless nation allows for a fresh understanding of national cinema based on perceptions of productive cultural contributions rather than on citizenship or state structures." She argues that the 1898–1952 period—"the transition from a Spanish Colony to a U.S. commonwealth"—"was marked by highly pronounced political ambiguity for Puerto Rico's status as a nation, which encouraged the creation of a collective identity that paradoxically both appropriated and rejected attributes from both [historical] colonizers [Spain and the United States]."[37] "Separated by an ocean, a language, and four hundred years of Spanish history," Nelson Denis writes, "Puerto Rico and the United States existed on the same planet but in two different worlds."[38]

Puerto Rico's paradoxical situation as a colony and, later, commonwealth can be seen in the way in which the U.S. territory was split off from the jurisdiction of continental U.S. film distribution. Loew's theaters in Toronto and Montreal, Canada, by comparison, were not under the aegis of Loew's International but were instead managed by domestic Loew's exhibition and MGM distribution executives. Explanations for this discrepancy were not stated in the press at the time, and linguistics do not fully supply the answer. After all, Montreal was part of a province (Quebec) that was still heavily reliant on French and French culture. When MGM later opened El Teatro Metro in San Juan, it exhibited films in English for much of its existence and actually witnessed a severe drop in revenue when dubbed Spanish versions of MGM films were introduced.[39] Puerto Rico, however, before and after achieving U.S. commonwealth status in 1952, was treated like a foreign territory by Loew's/MGM. This sense of Puerto Rico as *other* was consistent with the U.S. government's own treatment of Puerto Rico as a reactionary and rebellious colony. Indeed, the resistance of Puerto Rico's ascendant Partido Nacionalista de Puerto Rico (Nationalist Party of Puerto Rico) to U.S. colonialization and military, political, cultural, and economic dominance made the island far less like a forty-ninth state and much more like a fractious, occupied territory.

Before Loew's built El Teatro Metro in San Juan, El Teatro Paramount had already opened in Puerto Rico, but its lineage and connection to Paramount is far more tangential. Originally opened in 1922 as Teatro Olimpo, the cinema was badly damaged by one of the many hurricanes—including San Felipe in 1928 and San Ciprián in 1932—that have torn apart the island over the past century. Following the devastation, Teatro Olimpo was subsequently remodeled in the Art Deco style in the early 1930s and renamed El Teatro Paramount. The name change was (reportedly) a legal provision for a renovation loan granted by Paramount to the Olimpo's owner, Rafael Ramos Cobián, managing director of United Theaters in San Juan and a key player in the region whose importance to the Cuban market is discussed later in this chapter.[40] El Teatro Paramount was not a shop window cinema for Paramount, though, and was never claimed as such. Paramount, United Artists, and other U.S. distributors all played their product at Cobiân's newly renamed Teatro Paramount and in his many other Puerto Rican *teatros* in the 1930s.[41]

Cobiân was a key player in Puerto Rico and throughout the Caribbean. He established his first exhibition company, Empresas Ramos Cobiân, in Puerto Rico in 1929. Six years later, in March 1935, Garcia-Crespo notes, "United Theaters Inc. had become so large that Ramos Cobiân had to fend off accusations of monopolizing film exhibition venues."[42] Cobiân's dominance on the island made him the key exhibition player there and a tough negotiator for film rental terms.[43] Cobiân's control of Puerto Rican screens created a power imbalance, one of the rare instances in which a local exhibitor could dictate terms to Hollywood.

Local politics were also a challenge. The combined damage from the global depression that began in 1929 and the two hurricanes that ravaged Puerto Rico in 1928 and 1932 hurt the island's sugar, coffee, citrus, and tobacco industries, among the other agricultural yields that were its main export to the continental United States and beyond. Unrest over Washington's appointed government in Puerto Rico—and its repressive labor, economic, and legal policies—also began bubbling over into a cohesive political movement, Partido Nacionalista de Puerto Rico, the Nationalists. Nelson Denis describes why one of its members marched alongside them:

> Julio Feliciano Colón... joined because he was tired of cutting cane sixty hours a week for a salary of $4 and because four Yankee companies owned most of the farmland in Puerto Rico. He joined because he was trapped like a caged animal. He joined because a man who gets up at 4 a.m. every morning, climbs a mountain in rain or fog or killing heat, and sweats all day with mosquitoes in his mouth does not need an empire telling him how to live, which flag to wave, what language to speak, and what heroes to worship.[44]

In the early to mid-1930s, Franklin Roosevelt sent equal measures of aid and forceful governance to Puerto Rico, replacing one ineffective Anglo governor (Robert Hayes Gore) with another in Blanton Winship, a former U.S. Army general who governed more as a military than political ruler. He was there in part to pacify and reduce the growing resistance of the local Nationalist movement led by Pedro Albizu Campos. He was "not sent to Puerto Rico to negotiate," Denis writes. "He was sent to crush labor strikes, subdue Nationalists, and kill them if necessary. It didn't take long before he did just that."[45] Winship also appointed the very non–Puerto Rican duo of Elisha Francis Riggs and Robert A. Cooper as chief of police and U.S. District Court justice, respectively. "All three," José Ché Paralitici writes, "were directly linked to the U.S. armed forces." The troika, led by Winship and under FDR's direction, began jailing

Nationalists in 1936 following a series of political and physical confrontations in 1935, including the Río Piedras massacre in which four Nationalists were killed by police. (Nationalists subsequently vowed revenge.)[46]

In February 1936 two Nationalists assassinated Elisha Riggs; they were subsequently captured and killed in police headquarters in San Juan. A large number of key Nationalist members—including Campos—were arrested in the subsequent days and accused of conspiracy to overthrow the U.S. government's rule over the island. This incendiary background culminated in one of the bloodiest massacres in Puerto Rico's history on March 21, 1937, when seventeen protesters were killed by San Juan police and hundreds of others were injured on Palm Sunday in the heavily Catholic island. The dead included the elderly, women, and children, and the violence sealed Winship's fate as another in a long line of despised Washington-appointed rulers. The police officers firing their guns did so under the direction of Police Chief Enrique de Orbeta with Winship's full support. In the succeeding months, the Nationalists were accused of trying to murder Justice Cooper, and ten more party members were subsequently arrested.[47] Winship's brutal policies were intended to pacify any resistance to foreign investment/control over Puerto Rican land and resources and reassert the dominion of the U.S. government over its Caribbean territory.

Loew's International brushed off all of this ongoing political unrest and in July 1937—just months after the Ponce massacre—announced its intentions to open a new shop window cinema in Puerto Rico, acquiring a site in the Santurce section of San Juan to build a new El Teatro Metro.[48] David Gould, MGM's Puerto Rico branch manager, made no mention of the political conflict in U.S.-based trade papers nor were these issues mentioned in newspaper accounts related to the cinema's construction. With Loew's International's investment secured by the government's crackdown, Loew's executive Sam Burger traveled to Puerto Rico in August 1938 to review the theater's progress with Gould.[49] Their visit followed that of William Melniker, who had also visited the ongoing El Teatro Metro project in February 1938.[50]

Five months after Melniker's visit, with the Metro's construction well under way, Nationalist Angel Esteban Antongiorgi attempted to gun down Governor Winship in retaliation for the Ponce massacre. His bullets went astray, however, killing only Puerto Rican colonel Luis Irizarry. Police instantly shot and killed Antongiorgi.[51] None of this slowed down Loew's International's investment. As El Teatro Metro neared completion, Loew's moved Harold Winston, the assistant manager of the company's Loew's Poli in Worcester, Massachusetts, to the Metro in San Juan.[52]

When completed, the pared-down $250,000 shop window held 1,200 seats—500 fewer than planned—and was outfitted with all of the usual American technologies: Carrier air-conditioning, Simplex projectors, and

ERPI-compliant sound systems.[53] As described by *El Mundo*, the theater was "equipped with all the advances and the great comforts of the screen" including "polished mirrors, modernist tapestries, wall lamps" as well as "a harmonious combination of colors." El Teatro Metro opened on January 18, 1939, to typically laudatory coverage in the mainstream local press.[54] Editions of *El Mundo* published before and during the opening were splattered with advertisements for the cinema and articles about its debut, raising questions about the newspaper's journalistic integrity amid all of MGM's ad spending. A January 7, 1939, advertisement placed in *El Mundo* noted that El Teatro Metro's highly trained staff could be "compared to that of any theater in the United States."[55] These offhand observations reflect Loew's International's sense of the Puerto Rican audience as a foreign constituency rather than U.S. citizens. The opening of El Teatro Metro, meanwhile, like the construction of other Hollywood shop windows, spurred an exhibition arms race on the island, with T. Llamas's Teatros Modernos circuit planning to open six new cinemas to compete.[56]

The gala premiere of the new Metro came at a very delicate moment in the history of Puerto Rico. U.S. corporate investment was reliant on a suppression of the Nationalist protests that had continued growing strength throughout the 1930s. Loew's executives—whatever their politics—needed this crackdown in order to stabilize the social and business climate for their investment. So it was no surprise, then, that David Gould invited Governor Winship to be on hand for the El Teatro Metro premiere, despite the problematic optics less than two years since the Ponce massacre and amid its ongoing investigations and arrests. For a *teatro* attempting to attract all Puerto Ricans under one roof, the invitation to Winship may have created local (leftist) hostility toward MGM, something the company had tried not to do in other politically fractious markets. And yet there was little chance MGM could avoid inviting the Roosevelt appointee and current governor of the territory that had granted them building permits, materials, labor, and ongoing police protection.

Harold Winston was sent back to the United States in June 1940 and was succeeded by Puerto Rican actor/singer Raul Barrera, who had been hired as assistant manager of El Teatro Metro in August 1939 and trained under Winston for nearly a year before replacing him.[57] Meanwhile, Governor Winship had also returned to the continental United States, recalled by FDR, who could no longer cover for nor countenance the scandal-plagued governor amid the ongoing uproar in Washington over the Ponce massacre. Winship followed a familiar path trod by other disgraced politicians: he became a lobbyist for U.S. corporations doing business in Puerto Rico and lobbied against the application of the Fair Labor Standards Act for a minimum wage throughout the territory.[58]

Cobián, Cuba, and the Return of Paramount

By 1941 El Teatro Metro had become a symbolic threat to Cobián's domination in San Juan, especially since Loew's International had just opened two new cinemas in Rio de Janeiro and there were concerns that the company would keep expanding its holdings throughout Latin America. Harold Winston was hired away by Cobián in February 1941—just one month after the opening of the new Cine Metros in Copacabana and Tijuca in Rio—to become the head of advertising and publicity for the twenty cinemas Cobián operated in Puerto Rico. The *Film Daily* concluded its announcement of Winston's return and his new role with an understated line: "Circuit is Loew's opposition in Porto Rico."[59]

Over the next decade, Cobián expanded his exhibition dominance in Puerto Rico, continuing to build new cinemas on the island, with four more under way in San Juan in competition with Teatros Modernos's ten Puerto Rican cinemas and MGM's sole El Teatro Metro.[60] Cobián bolstered his operations against both competitors by inking a two-year distribution deal with Twentieth Century-Fox, as well as with United Artists, Goldwyn, and other independent companies, against Llamas's Paramount and Universal product deals. (Cobián refused to bid for MGM films due to Loew's International's operation of El Teatro Metro.) Cobián filled his cinemas' remaining schedules with Spanish-language films, a reminder to Hollywood that space was always available to local distributors from Mexico, Argentina, and the Dominican Republic. "Although [Cobián] did not make films during the 1940s and 1950s," Garcia-Crespo writes, "he continued to influence local audiences' tastes and desires by controlling what films were played (and for how long) in Puerto Rico's biggest theater chain, United Theaters." She adds that "Ramos Cobián's story showcases the potential power of exhibitors to mold audiences' desires and expectations and thus to some degree to decide who portrays the nation and how."[61]

As for MGM, the company switched its own exhibition policies at El Teatro Metro in 1946 due to a steep decline in revenue, replacing Spanish-dubbed MGM prints with original versions featuring Spanish subtitles.[62] According to Cobián, the dubbed versions had been unwanted by Puerto Rico's bilingual American citizens, noting that "nearly all Puerto Ricans" spoke English, and "films offer a distinct opportunity to practice the language." "Loew's," he added, had "experienced a drop of almost 75 per cent in business at this house with dubbed versions."[63] It was therefore Cobián who understood his audience best.

Cobián's power in Puerto Rico also enabled him to seek out control of other Caribbean markets. None were as expansive or as lucrative as Cuba. A decade earlier, Paramount had shed both the Fausto and the Encanto in Havana by the end of the 1930s, their bankruptcy reorganization depriving them of even a single shop window cinema for company films and leverage against the largest exhibitors on the island: former Columbia Pictures manager Ernesto P. Smith and Jose Valcarce, who co-operated their two cinema chains together in late 1941 to form Smith-Valcarce. The combined circuit boasted five first-run cinemas and seven sub-run houses in Havana. Paramount, Universal, and Columbia all signed distribution deals with Smith for their films. MGM, Fox, Warner Bros., and United Artists, however, refused Smith-Valcarce's increasingly difficult rental terms. Their decision backfired quickly, however; with a product shortfall, Smith-Valcarce began booking Spanish-language films into Havana's America Theatre.[64] Hollywood feared the rise of the Mexican and Argentinian film industries in Latin America and their potential to draw away audiences. The U.S. film companies' hardline tactics were now providing an opening for more and more Latin American films to be screened.

Local exhibitors, meanwhile, kept U.S. film companies out of Cuban cinema operation by collectively refusing to sell their cinemas. Cuban officials tag-teamed those efforts by blocking U.S. film companies from building their own cinemas during the early 1940s by citing a wartime lack of building materials.[65] All of this meant that MGM, Fox, Warner Bros., and United Artists were forced to come to terms with Smith-Valcarce, to book their films into lesser independent cinemas, or to miss out on this growing market entirely. Fox, Warner Bros., and MGM buckled by March 1942, agreeing to new distribution contracts with Smith-Valcarce.[66] Hollywood's weakness against this powerful Cuban chain only reinforced the collective need for each U.S. film company to have its own cinema or cinemas on the island in order to better negotiate terms or secure its own first-run releases. Without a key cinema to demonstrate playability and create competition, all the U.S. film companies—as they were in South Africa (Schlesinger), Puerto Rico (Cobiân), and other dominated markets—were subject to the whims of locally powerful film moguls.

It was little surprise to anyone, therefore, that by September 1942 *Variety* was hearing "much talk about an American producing and distributing company contemplating building of a theatre." Smith-Valcarce's détente with U.S. distributors was short-lived. The trade journal reported that month, "The Nacional, now playing American pictures, may switch to Spanish films again" and the "Smith-Valcarce circuit plans to run stage shows only at the America during the month of November, and perhaps continue that policy should it not get together with local film distributors on terms."[67] The seriousness of the Cuban situation could be seen in the constant trips U.S. film executives made to the island, with both Stanley Chase of Paramount and Harry Bryman of MGM moving their offices to Cuba to battle it out with Smith and Valcarce. Twentieth Century-Fox was the first to announce its need to have its own

"Havana 'Show Window'" because of "its refusal to close new contracts with the [Smith-Valcarce] combine."[68] Fox identified the independent Nacional—whose lease expired in 1943—as a suitable "show-window for its product." To scrape the cinema away from Smith-Valcarce, Fox offered up far more profitable terms on the lease. The interest by Fox (and others) in obtaining cinemas now created a seller's market for exhibitors in which Fox and others were suddenly fielding offers from a number of local cinemas looking to hook a U.S. film company as either a tenant or buyer.

By 1943 Twentieth Century-Fox had, once again, refused to renew their contract with Smith-Valcarce over terms. The *Film Daily* was convinced, in mid-March, that Fox was about to pry away the Nacional from the local National Theaters chain and was "reported to be invading the exhibition business in partnership with another distributor—name not specified."[69] Spyros Skouras, acting international head Irving Maas, and Fox Caribbean head Joseph Mullen were all in Havana in March 1943 negotiating the deal. Less than two weeks later, however, Fox announced that renovations to the Nacional would take too long, and they pulled out. Plans for a newly built Fox "show window" were also kyboshed due to a "shortage of building materials" on the island, yet another block by Cuban authorities.[70] Fox turned back to Smith and Valcarce instead and, once again, booked their films into the chain's first-run cinemas. MGM, Paramount, RKO, and United Artists renewed their boycott of the chain. This prompted news that MGM would construct its own shop window cinema in Havana, an accusation that MGM executives then called "ridiculous."[71]

No new cinemas were constructed during World War II in Cuba, and no American film company was able to pry any cinemas away from Smith, Valcarce, Manuel Ramon Fernandez, or any other local cinema chains. In September 1944, however, Rafael Ramos Cobián, who now operated twenty-two cinemas in Puerto Rico, maneuvered his way around the Cuban opposition to selling cinemas to outsiders by leasing the newly independent Smith circuit's eight cinemas in Havana and the Manuel Ramon Fernandez circuit's four cinemas in Camaguey. Peter Colli, Warner Bros.' Cuban manager, became the treasurer of the new Cobián circuit in Cuba.[72] Warner Bros. and Twentieth Century-Fox tried to negotiate with Cobián to purchase a share of his company, but, despite Colli's relationship with both Warner and Cobián, the negotiations failed and Warner Bros., for the second time, was left without a cinema or cinemas in Cuba (and without a booking deal with Cobián).[73]

The end of the Cobián-Warner negotiations left an opening for Paramount to not only distribute their films to Cobián's Cuban cinemas but to also become equal partners in Circuito Cobián of Cuba, S.A. with a capitalization of $1 million. The Paramount–Cobián contract signed by John W. Hicks Jr., president of Paramount International Films Inc., and by Cobián, president of the new Cuban corporation operating the circuit, outlined an agreement whereby the partners would "participate equally" in the operation of the chain's eleven cinemas in Havana and Camaguey and of a new venue under construction.[74] Paramount and Cobiân now operated, among others, the first-run Encanto, Fausto, and Alcazar; the second-run Florencia, Favorito, Strand, and Universal cinemas in Havana; and additional cinemas in Camaguey.[75] After more than a decade, Paramount had regained control over the Encanto and Fausto again. MGM found a distribution partner in the now independent Valcarce circuit that now happily booked MGM's full lineup of films.[76]

Warner Bros.' Postwar Cuban Cinemas and the Struggle for Ownership in Havana

Throughout the 1940s and 1950s, despite this seemingly tidy relationship between U.S. businesses and Cuban institutions, labor issues plagued the transnational relationship between U.S. distribution and exhibition managers in New York and Havana and their Cuban labor force. The local labor union and Cuba's Labor Ministry were increasingly persistent about wage increases, employment practices, hirings and rehirings, and other issues—especially since U.S. wages for Cuban cinema workers were still "below general average comparable work [in] any other American industry," a letter to Motion Picture Association of America foreign managers noted, whether they toiled in "sugar, railroad, beer, bus, banks, restaurants and many other Cuban industries."[77] These issues, and the political turmoil roiling the island in the 1940s, would ultimately undo Hollywood's investments.

In 1943, however, those obstacles still seemed surmountable to Hollywood and to Warner Bros., which, despite the Cobiân sell out to Paramount, was not deterred from further attempts to build or lease cinemas in Cuba. As previously mentioned, the company had already leased the Teatro Central in Lima, Peru, in 1943 and would, a short time later, lease the Teatro San Jorge in Bogotá, Colombia, in 1946.[78] Clearly, its strategy of staying out of competition with local exhibitors had come to an end. In June 1945 Joseph Bernhard, vice president of Warner Bros. and its theater subsidiary president, and Karl Macdonald, vice president of Warner Bros. International, traveled to Havana to secure a "Cuban 'show window'" for the company's films and begin generating more exhibition revenue in the postwar era, "in line," *Film Daily* reported, "with the [company's] post-war overseas expansion program which has been mapped during the past 18 months."[79]

Warner Bros. Pictures Inc. board of directors met on July 27, 1945, and approved an agreement with Radio Centro that called for Goar and Abel Mestre and their Radio Centro, S.A. to purchase a lot at 23rd Street and "L" in the

Vedado borough of Havana and build a 1,600–1,700-seat cinema that Warner Bros. would lease and operate. The Warner Theatre became the company's first Cuban "show window" and was to be built by August 1, 1947, according to plans and specifications approved by both Warner Bros. Pictures Inc. and Warner Bros. First National South Films Inc. The cinema was part of the Radio City / Rockefeller Center-inspired "Radio Centro" radio-film-entertainment complex that housed the offices and studios for the CMQ network. Warner Bros. agreed to pay Radio Centro, S.A. a minimum rental of $30,000 per year against 15 percent of the gross receipts, the company purchased $75,000 of preferred stock from Radio Centro, S.A., and then deposited these shares as security for the eventual payment of the lease.[80]

Loew's International, after denying an interest in Cuban film exhibition, also sought to build a shop window cinema there as part of a planned $9,000,000 overseas "theatre building and remodeling program" in Latin America after the end of World War II. By January 1946 Loew's had purchased property in Havana and begun work on a ten-story air-conditioned office building that would house all of the U.S. film exchanges, a 1,500-seat Cine/El Teatro Metro, and another smaller 400-seat cinema at an estimated cost of $1.25 million.[81]

Paramount International followed the postwar boom by acquiring all of Ramos Cobián's stock holdings in their joint Cuban cinema circuit in late 1945 and then reorganized and renamed it Circuito Teatral Paramount.[82] Paramount now wholly controlled some of Cuba's most popular and influential cinemas and planned to expand further by building "a new deluxer for its firstruns." In addition to Paramount, Warner Bros., and Loew's, in 1946 Twentieth Century-Fox also announced the purchase of Havana real estate for its own, long-delayed shop window cinema. All told, *Variety* noted, "Four major U.S. companies, which previously played their pix through local exhibs, are planning construction of first-run showcases."[83]

Still, for all of the apparent promise of operating cinemas in Cuba, the investment of time and money was set against an increasingly complicated political backdrop. Cuban labor policies during President Ramón Grau San Martín's tenure (1944–1948) had already reset some of Fulgencio Batista's more capital-friendly policies. Grau's Partido Auténtico party, with its "Cuba para los Cubanos" ("Cuba for the Cubans") mantra, set a firmer tone for his administration's relationship with local and foreign management operating in Cuba, but this did little to quell the strife between the nation's film exhibitors and their workers.

In 1946 a Cuban Supreme Court ruling that seemed to favor workers—forcing exhibitors to rehire employees who had been recently laid off—sparked new tensions among Payret Theatre employees in Havana who had just replaced laid off workers and now refused to quit. In June hundreds of Havana cinema employees walked off their jobs in solidarity with labor leaders who had been arrested for organizing an "illegal strike" against the Payret Theatre, keeping it closed for several weeks.[84] Cuban labor leaders, outraged at low wages and cozy U.S.–Cuban business and political relationships, protested further against both Cuban and U.S. film exhibitors as well as the Cuban government. And when labor leaders weren't fighting exhibitors, the local Moving Picture Union's communist and noncommunist members were fighting each other. Clashes among the larger Cuban Confederation of Workers, of which the Moving Picture Union was a member, left four dead and more wounded. Due to the violence, general strikes and the possibility of martial law remained, further straining the reliability of exhibition workers and cinemas to stay open.[85]

In 1947 Cuban cinema screens were still dominated by Hollywood films distributed by Paramount Films of Cuba Inc.; Fox Films de Cuba; Metro-Goldwyn-Mayer; RKO-Radio Pictures of Cuba, S.A.; Warner Bros. First National South Films Inc.; and other local U.S. subsidiaries. According to a report by the Motion Picture Association of America, of Cuba's 484 cinemas (with a total seating capacity of over 308,000), over 95 percent were exhibiting U.S. product "in full or in part." These U.S. companies controlled some of the most important cinemas in Havana as well as the content on their screens. In Havana alone, Paramount operated the Alkazar (1,700 seats), the Encanto (1,150 seats), the Fausto (1,609 seats), the Favorito (1,528 seats), the Florencia (1,163 seats), the Strand (1,000 seats), and the Universal (1,048 seats).[86] These seven cinemas alone contained almost 9,200 seats or 10 percent of Havana's total seating capacity. Paramount's installation of air-conditioning in two of the chain's larger theaters was reportedly greeted with "jubilation" and "box-office records."[87]

U.S. control over Havana's key exhibition outlets only increased with the construction of the Warner Theatre at L and 23rd Street.[88] This was not a hands-off partnership for Warner Bros. with the Mestre brothers, though. Warner Theatres president and general manager Harry M. Kalmine and Warner Theatres construction department head Herman R. Maier traveled to Havana with Wolfe Cohen, vice president of Warner Bros. International, in November 1946 to review the theater's progress. Cohen was in the middle of a two-month review of the Caribbean, a detail that likely meant a review of Puerto Rico for possible exhibition sites there as well. (The trio also reviewed Warner Bros.' newly opened Mexico City cinema during their whirlwind tour.)[89] Other Warner executives visiting over the next year included Herbert Copelan, who had recently been named head of Warner Bros.' Latin American cinemas in Havana, Mexico City, and Lima.[90] Copelan added another Cuban cinema when Kalmine announced the lease of the eight-hundred-seat Plaza Theatre in Havana from Enrique Gaston in September 1947. Warner Bros. then renovated the Plaza, installing new seats and a new air-cooling system.[91] Charles J. Bachman, Warner Bros. sound supervisor, also traveled to Cuba in late October 1947 to oversee the installation of new sound equipment in both the Warner Theatre and the newly renovated Plaza.[92]

Warner Bros.' new flagship Havana shop window, the eponymous Warner Theatre, opened on December 23, 1947, with Goar Mestre, Harry Kalmine, Herbert Copelan, and Wolfe Cohen welcoming a bevy of local importance including Cuban president Ramón Grau San Martín.[93] Like the opening of El Teatro Metro in Santurce, the appearance of the Cuban head of state was a mark of the cinema's union of industry, politics, and culture and the gala debut of these shop windows was a conferral of Cuba's relationship with the United States and with one of its most prominent global industries. Each nation that hosted a U.S. shop window and sent its political leadership to the gala premiere was advertising itself as "open" for foreign (i.e., U.S.) business and capital investment.

The Warner Theatre showcased Warner Bros.' films as well as local and international performers (Cab Calloway was an early visitor), but a formal lease agreement between Warner Bros. and Radio Centro, S.A. was not actually signed until January 7, 1948.[94] The twenty-year agreement contracted Warner Bros. to pay Radio Centro, S.A. $20,000 per year in rent.[95] Two months later, the full complex, Radio Centro, described by its founders as "a miniature Radio City," opened on March 12, 1948, at a cost of $3 million.[96] That spring Warner Bros. sent Pat Notaro, manager of its Stanley Warner Bromley Theater in Philadelphia, to become the manager for both Warner Bros. cinemas in Havana. Notaro reported directly to Herbert Copelan, zone manager for Warner Bros.'s Latin American Theaters, which now included the Plaza and Warner in Cuba, the Teatro Central in Lima, the San Jorge Teatro in Bogotá, and the new cinema in Mexico City.[97]

Labor Troubles Begin in Havana

Cuban government intervention began almost immediately after Warner Bros. took over the Plaza Theatre as the Labor minister ordered Warner Bros. to retain the cinema's checkers so there would be no worker displacement. Warner executives were extremely frustrated by the government edict but eventually relented, worried that this restriction might soon be placed on the Warner Theatre as well (which had no previous employees and thus skirted this requirement).[98] As Cuban labor unions and labor ministers forced local employees and salary increases on U.S.-operated cinemas—and similar laws were also passed with respect to Cubans working for U.S. film distributors—rifts grew between these foreign film companies and their local Cuban workers. Megan Feeney writes that U.S. film companies were convinced that Cuban cinema checkers were misreporting grosses at Cuban-operated cinemas—depriving U.S. film distributors of their full revenue—while "Hollywood companies with new cinemas, like Paramount and Warner Brothers, complained that such local biases also led cinema doormen to let friends in without tickets, depriving them of their rightful earnings."[99] During this period there were numerous cases adjudicated before the Ministry of Labor that impacted Warner Bros.' ability to hire and fire employees and impose their will regarding wages and bonuses amid numerous other regulations. Cuban labor laws, for instance, made it impossible to fire an employee without filing for and receiving an "expediente" from the Ministry of Labor. Despite meeting with and appealing to the undersecretary of Labor for the ability to lay off some of the Plaza's staff and disregard the 30 percent raise required by a new law that had been enacted in May 1948, Warner Bros. was forced to keep all of its current Plaza employees on the payroll and to pay the 30 percent raise. Warner Bros. executive Pat Notaro was unsuccessful in removing even one employee: the sign painter, Julio Ponce, who was implicated by Warner Bros. in a robbery at the cinema. Following the company's failed attempts to fire him and the ensuing lawsuit, Ponce filed a new petition with the Ministry of Labor to keep his job (and receive the back pay owed).[100]

Faced with successive losses—and more legal hassles to come—U.S. companies attempted to reduce these labor problems by funneling money to Assistant Minister of Justice Jorge Casuso as well as "inside informants within the Cuban justice system," Megan Feeney writes, in order "to advise them on decisions before they were announced, thus allowing them time to offer minimal settlement offers" instead of waiting for a more financially deleterious ruling.[101] The brother of Warner Bros.' Cuban attorney, Dr. Francisco Espino, was reportedly close to the Supreme Court justices in Cuba and could therefore learn the results of their decisions in advance of the public, thus enabling the company to settle financial matters before the court rendered a verdict.[102] Rather than settling with its employees for less, Warner Bros. executives in New York routinely chose to try to procure privileged information for these kinds of cases instead. And, storing up future trouble, Feeney adds, Warner Bros.' New York management still "tended to deny all raises not regulated by the Cuban state, ignoring the recommendations of their local managers." The Americans, the Cuban *Cinema* magazine wrote, "practic[ed] the policy of good neighbour with only their own house in mind." Feeney argues that Warner Bros. and others shortsightedly "undermined their Havana representatives, who had to ask permission of 'papa' like children every time they want[ed] to solve a problem."[103] Further enraging the local union and Cuban cinema employees, United Artists also decided to discontinue Christmas bonuses for its distribution employees in Havana, while Warner Bros. cut all raises for its distribution and exhibition workers throughout Cuba. While the America, Radio Cine, Campoamor, Marti, and Paramount's Fausto and Encanto cinemas gave their stage electricians a raise, Warner Bros. refused the local union's request. Warner was the only exhibitor unwilling to support the union's pay hike, relenting only after numerous union delegates appealed to the company to avoid *complications* by paying up.[104]

By June 1950, two and a half years after its debut, the Warner Theatre in Havana had grossed over $1 million, while the Plaza had grossed less than $300,000 since the lease had begun at the start of 1948.[105] Whatever Warner Bros.' net profits might have been in Havana, they were being actively curtailed by the rising cost of labor, legal fees, concerns over admissions irregularities, and distrust of its local workers. Warner Bros. renewed their Warner Theatre lease anyway in February 1950 with Radio Centro, S.A., agreeing to an auditing system whereby Warner Bros. produced a statement of account for all income generated by the cinema (and then shared it with Radio Centro) and an agreement that granted Radio Centro the right to examine the cinema's and the company's ledgers and vouchers whenever it wanted to verify reported statistics. This was, of course, of great interest to Radio Centro as it pertained to their revenue sharing agreements.[106]

International labor relations, though, remained a constant source of tension. In February 1951 Warner Bros.' troubled Christmas bonus policy caused new conflicts between the company, its employees, and the unions. The General Syndicate of Movie Workers launched another protest with the company after Warner Bros. paid a bonus to some of its distribution workers but not to others. (RKO, MGM, Columbia, and other Hollywood companies all paid a bonus to their workers.) Warner Bros.' policy, the union reminded the company, was punishable by Cuban Law. The syndicate chastised Warner Bros. as a company that preached democracy but instead practiced "totalitarian" acts.[107] The labor situation—and the laws set up to protect workers from foreign *and* indigenous exploitation—may have been one of the reasons MGM, which had opened cinemas throughout Latin America, balked at their chance. Loew's retained its Cine Metro shop windows in more than half a dozen other Latin American countries but never ventured into Cuba. The large office building and cinema complex became a lost project for Loew's International.

As 1951 drew to a close Warner Bros. abruptly abandoned the Warner Theatre, and the Mestre brothers prepared a series of closing documents for the transfer of the Warner Theatre lease. The agreement forbade Circuito Teatral Radiocentro, S.A. from using the Warner or Warner Bros. name or the W or WB symbols. The circuit was also forced to remove the Warner neon sign from the façade. Radiocentro now assumed all obligations and future liabilities, while Warner Bros. transferred all of its previous agreements for the cinema to the circuit.[108] The timing was fortuitous. Less than two months later, on

FIGURE 11.1 Warner Theatre in Havana, Cuba, ca. 1949. (University of Miami. Library. Cuban Heritage Collection, Cuban Photograph Collection, Collection No. CHC0329, Digital ID chc03290015540001001)

March 10, 1952, Fulgencio Batista organized a military-backed coup, deposing current president Carlos Prío Socarrás and cancelling the country's upcoming elections. The coup rattled the country and especially Havana, immediately affecting cinemas and all other public amusements and venues. Warner's Plaza Theatre felt the impact of the coup immediately since it was close to the Presidential Palace, now occupied by the military.[109] Amid the country's ongoing political turmoil, Warner Bros. tried to offload the Plaza. In 1954 Nena Bénites, music critic for the *Diario de la Harina* newspaper, hoped to use the venue to present musical concerts featuring the Philharmonic Orchestra. This plan also fell through.[110]

Hollywood Exits Its Caribbean Cinemas

Warner Bros.' legal entanglements and the devolving political situation in Cuba did not scare off all U.S. film exhibition investment. After Warner Bros.'

divestment of its U.S. theater chain, Warner's now separated domestic exhibition company, the Stanley-Warner Corp. (SWC), was left without the direct counsel of its once corporate cousin and waded directly into Cuba's growing political and social unrest.[111] After removing Cinerama equipment from its own Warner Theatre in Oklahoma City in early 1957 (SWC had invested in Cinerama in 1953 and gained a controlling interest in 1958[112]), SWC sent the three-projector system to its latest Cinerama venue, the former Warner Theatre in Havana, now known as Teatro Radio Centro. Cinerama's Cuban debut on February 24, 1958, was greeted with both fanfare and phosphorous bombs thrown into the cinema by a "rebel group," ending the premiere abruptly.[113] The attack took place less than nine months after another bomb had exploded in the balcony of the Radio Centro, injuring nearby moviegoers. The attacks on Radio Centro were one of several by the 26th of July Movement, led by Fidel Castro, against prominent symbols of the economic, cultural, legal, and political relationships between U.S. cultural and material products and businesses and Batista's military dictatorship and sympathetic business leaders.[114]

In January 1959 Batista fled Cuba after years of repression and corruption, all of which helped usher in support for Fidel Castro and the Cuban Revolution that nationalized private businesses. By 1960 the nation's cinemas and its film industry were under the control of the Instituto Cubano del Arte e Industria Cinematográficos (Cuban Institute of Cinematographic Art and Industry). All Warner Bros. operations ceased in Cuba, and Herb Copelan and Pat Notaro exited the country, as did all other Hollywood executives. Goar Mestre also left after the Cuban government commandeered his $25 million broadcasting business, and he fled to Argentina where he established new television businesses there as well as in Venezuela and in Peru.[115]

Cuba represented one of the first nations to nationalize its cinemas in ways that would prove deleterious to foreign investment. Warner Bros.' experience in Cuban exhibition represents one of the more fraught examples of Hollywood's attempt to manage the political complexities of local and national laws alongside its overseas exhibition practices. Cuba was a stark reminder of the difficulties of investing in foreign real estate ventures where legal and political systems were either in flux or increasingly hostile to unfettered U.S. investment and control. In advantageous moments, U.S.-operated cinemas abroad could generate tremendous revenues and brand awareness and engagement for Hollywood films and companies. In more politically, financially, and legally problematic periods, though, these cinemas' embodiment of "Hollywood" and American political ideology roundly reversed this appeal and became, instead, a target of local resentment.

During the 1940s and 1950s Warner Bros. sought to expand its burgeoning international exhibition operations in the fraught Cuban market where labor issues and growing political and economic turmoil coincided with rising anti-U.S. sentiment. The Warner and Plaza Theatres (and Paramount's cinema chain) represented the latest manifestations of U.S. political, cultural, and economic expansion. While moviegoers from across Havana were attracted to these cinemas because of their Hollywood-branded name and film offerings, the cinemas also attracted the negative attention of local labor leaders and others opposed to foreign control of Cuban labor and capital.

As for Puerto Rico, Fox took over the old Paramount cinema in San Juan in the 1960s—part of its aggressive global expansion strategy—and MGM operated its own El Teatro Metro in Santurce into the 1970s.[116] One longtime moviegoer wrote nostalgically that the Metro, which was purchased from MGM by the aptly named Caribbean Cinemas, is the "only surviving movie theater of the once thriving (fifteen-theater) Santurce downtown district. It is still the place where most elegant movie premieres take place."[117] Today the now-triplexed Metro Cinemas, still operated by Caribbean Cinemas, remains a premiere venue for Hollywood films.[118]

***

With the former Warner Theatre in Havana now renamed the Cine Yara and with Paramount, MGM, and other logos long detached from the cinemas of this region, there is little trace of this tumultuous period when the Caribbean became a battleground for internal and external politics and a place where Hollywood's expansionist dreams often crashed against the dexterity and tenacity of local exhibitors, politicians, and revolutionaries opposed to their island becoming another outpost for U.S. films, cinemas, politics, and real estate investments. Few regions were as fraught as the Caribbean for buying, building, leasing, or operating these kinds of Hollywood-branded cinemas. What remains for historians to analyze, therefore, is the distinct reactions of the Caribbean's many island nations to this kind of U.S. film company expansion.

MGM's growing cinema chain throughout South America extended the company's "Good Neighbor"–era outreach during the 1930s and Hollywood's and the U.S. State Department's ideological battle against Ufa and the Nazi global propaganda machine during wartime. In the 1960s and early 1970s the company stood by, hand-in-glove, as some of the nations that hosted these Cine Metros turned to repressive dictatorships. Outside the doors of MGM's Cine Metros, as military dictatorships swept over Brazil in 1964, Argentina in 1966, and Peru in 1968, the world outside these American cultural embassies was certainly no Hollywood fairytale. During these later, waning years, before MGM sold off the chain to CIC and other exhibitors, MGM's cinemas in these countries became both sites of escapist entertainment and architectural symbols of the U.S. government's own support of these repressive dictatorships and of the growing hypocrisy of Hollywood's cinematic messaging, preaching the values of individual and political "freedom" even as the films were increasingly showcased in deeply "undemocratic" nations. (Three decades earlier, in the United States' own commonwealth, Puerto Rico, MGM's invitation to Gov. Blanton Winship to help open the El Teatro Metro in Santurce only months after the Ponce massacre had already demonstrated Hollywood's hypocrisy to leftist Puerto Ricans there.) Across the water in Cuba, Fidel Castro had already barred Hollywood's cinemas and its films from the island, demonstrating that repressive regimes were not relegated to anticommunist, right-wing dictators.

Research on Hollywood's cinemas in Latin America and the Caribbean reminds us that we are just beginning to scratch the surface of the political, cultural, industrial, and technological impact of U.S. film exhibition operations in these regions. As Ivo Raposo's glorious Centimetro, his mini Metro-Tijuca, demonstrates, the impact of Hollywood's cinemas has lasted far longer than their physical presence. These shop windows sold more than just Hollywood films; they sold an idea, a feeling, a sentiment, and a lifestyle. Through the marketing of stars, narratives, and style, these cinemas transcended the quotidian realities of their continental divide. Like the very metaphor of a shop window, Hollywood's Latin American and Caribbean cinemas sold American movies, American industrial practices, American values, and the American way of life. They were, to quote Conrad Hilton, "Little Americas," physical structures of mass entertainment and consumption that served as cultural embassies for the U.S. film industry *and* the U.S. government.[119] Like every other region covered in this book, they were both celebrated and demonized for that very duality.

PART IV

MIDDLE EAST

Hollywood's Muddle East (1925–1982)
Political Change in Egypt and Israel and the Consequences for Hollywood's Middle Eastern Cinemas

CHAPTER 12

BUILDINGS, BALLYHOO, AND BOYCOTTS IN EGYPT, 1925–1947

Alternating Realities at Hollywood's Egyptian Cinemas

Ask Egyptian director Mohamed Khan about the eighty-year-old Cinema Metro on Cairo's Tal'at Harb Street and a nostalgic vision of midcentury moviegoing, complete with tuxedoed ushers and sumptuous surroundings, is evoked.[1] But Ahmad Husayn, founder of the radical Young Egypt movement, or actor-producer Youssef Wahbi, would no doubt present a very different picture of Cairo's cinema culture during the 1940s and 1950s, when cinemas like MGM's Cinema Metro and Fox's Cairo Palace epitomized the pro-Western acquiescence they felt threatened to destroy Egypt's film industry and its culture. Situated on Cairo's main streets, Fox's and MGM's glittering movie palaces attracted both avid moviegoers and angry protesters who stormed the box office and its doors, smashing both during a tumultuous period between 1945 and 1952.

"Hollywood's Muddle East" examines how politically inspired attacks on U.S.-owned cinemas in Egypt, along with the concurrent efforts of Twentieth Century-Fox and other U.S. film companies to invest in the new State of Israel, had a profound impact on Hollywood's Middle Eastern expansion during this period. Beginning with the political boycotts of the Misr al-Fatat movement in Egypt in the 1930s, this section of the book follows Youssef Wahbi's anti-Zionist campaign against Fox and MGM in the 1940s through to the political upheaval in the 1950s that resulted in violent protests against Hollywood's local cinemas. In tracing this trajectory, this history reveals how ill-informed decisions on the part of Fox and MGM executives created deep divisions between Hollywood's Egyptian cinemas and their local audiences.

Meanwhile, Fox's efforts to jumpstart Israeli exhibition, as it had done in numerous other countries, stumbled amid the nation's cultural and economic growing pains. After the conclusion of the Arab-Israeli War in 1948, MGM and Twentieth Century-Fox identified Israel as a premiere opportunity for Hollywood to build new production, distribution, and exhibition facilities in the new politically fractious State of Israel. Fox's Spyros Skouras led the way, outlining new Fox cinemas in Israel as a way to bolster the nation's economy and cinematic infrastructure while making a Cold War play to push the nation away from both socialism and communism and toward "democracy" and an embrace of both American cinema and culture.

Hollywood's fractious attempts at exhibition expansion in Egypt and Israel in the 1940s and 1950s demonstrated both the rich opportunities and the high stakes risks for U.S. corporations (and the U.S. government) in expanding their cultural industries and political philosophies abroad through cinema and cinema theaters. Like the *regional* approach taken for Australia and New Zealand, in which Hollywood's actions in one nation often affected and interrelated with the other, the approach needed to examine Fox's investment in Israel, for example, must consider the impact on its industrial and political relations in Egypt. While both Egyptian and Israeli national cinema are highly independent of one another, they must be analyzed in the midcentury together when it comes to Hollywood's engagement in each country.

U.S. Films and Exhibitors in Egypt, 1925–1933

Although Loew's Inc., parent company of Metro-Goldwyn-Mayer, would later build its own cinemas in Egypt, its first foray into Egyptian exhibition was as a manager for Gaumont, assuming operational supervision of Gaumont cinemas in France, Belgium, and Switzerland as well as Tunisia, Egypt, Syria, and Palestine in May 1925. In Egypt the newly formed exhibition company Gaumont-Loew-Metro operated cinemas in both Cairo (Gaumont Palace) and Alexandria (Mohamed Aly).[2] Paramount also controlled cinemas during the mid-1920s, first the Cinema Triomphe, an open-air cinema in Cairo, and then the city's Empire Cinema.[3]

When the Gaumont-Loew-Metro deal expired in 1929, MGM—like Fox, Warner Bros., RKO, and Paramount—booked their films into Egypt's leading cinemas. U.S. appraisal of many of these local venues, especially outside of Cairo, had not been complimentary. Roy Chandler noted in December 1927, for instance, that Egyptian theaters were "mostly of the type that ours were fifteen years ago," adding that while Cairo's cinemas were increasingly comparable to European and American theaters, the "fair sized houses in Alexandria and Port Said . . . were still projecting their pictures on white-washed walls."[4]

These cinemas showed films from the United States, England, France, Germany, and other countries but were supported by the wealth of product generated by the growing Egyptian film industry. However, the U.S. Commerce Department observed that by 1934 Hollywood's profits were finally improving, due to the popularity of American sound films (Egypt had produced very few talkies), better marketing, improved coordination with local exhibitors and censors, and newly renovated cinemas. More Egyptian students were also learning English, supplying Hollywood with "regular cinema patrons." (Their taste, according to *Variety*, was not for British films and their "lack of action" but instead for those of MGM and the other Hollywood studios.)[5]

U.S. films did have to compete, at least somewhat, with French and German films for screen time, even despite the local Jewish community's Nazi-era boycott of German films in Egypt.[6] In order to circumvent the boycott, Ufa distributed its films at "cut rate prices" to cinemas willing to play their films, and in Alexandria Ufa officials rented a five-hundred-seat "second class picture house" and charged only "five and seven pennies" instead of "one and two shillings for admission," hoping to draw in audiences for its films. This would not only serve to keep the Egyptian market open for German films and profits but enable the new Nazi regime to export its films and cultural and political messaging in the future.[7] Some of those cinemas running Nazi-era Ufa films were the Ramses and Fouad. Another was the three-thousand-seat Wahbi Cinema in Cairo, owned by Egyptian actor-director-producer, Youssef Wahbi.[8]

This expansion of U.S. market share in Egypt, and Nazi film efforts to infiltrate this market, came at an increasingly fractious time. Only days after the U.S. Commerce Department report was submitted, the Misr al-Fatat (Young Egypt) movement, headed by Ahmad Husayn, called for a boycott against foreign-owned and operated cinemas—often by Greek and French exhibitors—in Cairo, Alexandria, and Port Said that often showed American, British, and French films. A nationalist, youth-oriented, anti-Wafdist, and anti-Western paramilitary organization and political movement—signified by and known as the "Green Shirts"—Misr al-Fatat sought to limit the power of moneyed Egyptians citizens (represented in the Parliament by the majority Wafd party), and British and other Western businesses and businessmen, by promoting the need for land reforms, for Egyptians to patronize only Egyptian businesses, and for "traditional Islamic values" as bulwarks against the proliferation of Western cultural influences: alcohol, gambling, and, of course, Anglo-American films and cinemas. (Among the group's early members were two future presidents of Egypt, Gamal Abdel Nasser and Anwar Sadat.)[9] The Green Shirts took their inspiration from both the Nazi Sturmabteilung's Braunhemden ("Brownshirts") and the Squadristi Camicie Nere ("Blackshirts") in Fascist Italy under Mussolini.[10]

In January 1934 Misr al-Fatat distributed leaflets throughout Cairo urging the "YOUTH OF EGYPT" to "BOYCOTT FOREIGN MOTION PICTURE THEATRES." The group reminded all Egyptians that "the employees of these establishments have been and still are always foreigners," "that until quite recently they separated you from the foreigners in these establishments," and that, in these cinemas, "the foreigner is always given preference." The leaflet added that foreigners "deliberately ridicule and distort our reputation abroad and provide us with poisons and drugs, as well as with alcoholic drinks, to destroy our minds and bodies."[11] "In ensuing years," historian Robert Vitalis writes, "cultural conservatives and authenticists of all stripes—from the Muslim Brothers to the Wafd's Vanguard—would blame Hollywood for the sexual obsessions of the young and the rising crime rate in the city streets."[12] To combat the American cinematic influence on Egypt, Misr al-Fatat laid out "The Ten Commandments" to Egyptian youths that "enable you to be a soldier" for the party. These included: "Speak only Arabic.... Enter no shop which has not its name written in Arabic" and "Buy only from an Egyptian. Wear only clothes manufactured in Egypt and eat only Egyptian foods." The group also commanded its followers to "Despise all that is foreign with all your might and be fanatical to the point of folly for your nationalism.... Your aim is that Egypt, a country proud to be composed of Egypt and the Sudan, allied with Arab countries and conducting the Islamic Movement, should dominate the world."[13] The boycott was aimed squarely at Egypt's foreign-run cinemas, with their English-language movies and Western names, as Misr al-Fatat asked its followers to pledge an "Oath for Boycotting Picture Theatres" and "henceforth not to frequent the foreign motion picture establishments and to spread this boycott among my friends, relatives and colleagues. This is my oath, and my conscience is the sole witness to its fulfillment."[14] It is notable that the movement did not call for the banning of foreign films but for the dissolution of cinemas owned by "foreigners," a pointed and charged term after the installation of the Egyptian Nationality Law of 1929.

In contrast to future Egyptian boycotts and protests against foreign cinemas, Misr al-Fatat initially "sought to unite all Egyptians, regardless of religion" and found recruits from across the country's multiethnic population. "Go to the mosque on Friday if you are Moslem, to church on Sunday if you are Christian, and to the synagogue on Saturday if you are Jew," the leaflet added. The Green Shirts ultimately demanded "Liberation" from foreign cultures, influences, and businesses: "We are disgusted with it and we are in revolt. We are going to begin by boycotting the foreign motion picture theatres."[15] Historian Mohannad Ghawanmeh notes that moviegoers attending foreign-owned cinemas were now being confronted by Young Egypt members pressing audiences to patronize Egyptian-owned movie houses instead. Egyptian police confiscated numerous pamphlets during these protests and even arrested two students who were protesting against the Levantine-owned Royal Cinema in Cairo directly from its balcony. When that failed, Young Egypt members threw stink bombs into the Royal to flush out moviegoers.[16]

The pointed attack on foreign businesses (especially cinemas) was a subject of growing concern within the U.S. embassy in Cairo and at the Department of State in Washington, as it threatened to curtail the screening of U.S. films in Egypt's largest cities and cinemas. U.S. ambassador to Egypt Bert Fish wrote to the U.S. Secretary of State that the Young Egypt campaign was "significant principally because of its brazen attempt to foment anti-foreign sentiment in general" through "an intense chauvinism which may do much harm among the ignorant masses."[17]

In the months that followed the distribution of the Misr al-Fatat leaflet, the Green Shirts began searching for a place to train new members of its growing nationalist movement. Their leader, Ahmad Husayn, finally made a formal agreement with Youssef Wahbi to use his Ramses City arts and entertainment complex to train new members. Soon after they settled, however, the Cairo police warned Wahbi against affiliating with the group, and he subsequently canceled their agreement; Ramses City never became a home to the Green Shirts.[18] Since Wahbi would later play a prominent role against U.S. involvement in Egyptian cinemas fourteen years later, this previous association with Husayn is worthy of attention.

Despite the concern raised by these protests, Misr al-Fatat's boycott had little to no impact on Egypt's foreign-owned cinemas and the proliferation of Hollywood films. Even the founding of the new, state-of-the-art Studio Misr did not slow Hollywood's expansion onto local screens.[19] With more Hollywood, European, and Egyptian films available by the early to mid-1930s, a new wave of theater construction swept through Cairo and Alexandria, part of a boom in urban construction that, according to the *Washington Post*, had "wrought a marvelous transformation in Cairo," especially "in the new modernistic type of architecture, the 'Art Moderne.'" These "new creations," the *Post* commented, "rise almost beneath the shadow of the Pyramids as if to challenge the ancient structures by their modernity."[20] In addition to pristine new cinemas managed by local exhibitors such as the Miami Theatre, numerous open-air theaters were now part of Cairo's increasingly modern streetscape. Changing social mores, including the growing freedom enjoyed by Egyptian women, also favored robust box office attendance. "Today," the *Christian Science Monitor* noted, "Miss Egypt attends dances, cinemas, theaters, and clubs."[21] Many of those attending these new cinemas, however, were watching Arabic-dubbed American films, which, according to *Variety*, dominated 78 percent of the Egyptian exhibition business despite an Egyptian government subsidy that hoped to spur local production.[22]

Cairo's Cinema Metro and MGM, 1940–1945

With conflict brewing in Europe, by the late 1930s Loew's had shifted its focus to African and South American territories that were ripe for exhibition expansion and seemingly further from military strife. In June 1938, despite the outbreak of anti-Zionist demonstrations, Loew's named Cairo as one of three international cities selected to open a new Cinema Metro, the twenty-sixth in the company's global chain.[23] Thomas Lamb, who had designed cinemas for Loew's since the 1910s, was chosen as principal architect, while the Loew's New York office oversaw land acquisition, financing, and physical construction with Loew's engineer Salo Rosenberger traveling to Cairo to supervise the project.[24] Located on what was then the fashionable Soliman Pasha Street, the Cinema Metro cost $300,000 to build and seated nearly 1,700 patrons.[25]

In advance of its grand opening on February 2, 1940, its promotional advertising was laden with superlatives: the Cinema Metro was "Egypt's most comfortable and beautiful cinema," "The Most Beautiful Cinema of the Orient," and "Cairo's Only Air-Conditioned Theatre" whose purpose was to "glorify Motion Pictures."[26] The American trade journal *Showmen's Trade Review* noted that the theatre hewed to the typical Loew's/Metro strategy that married a dazzling modern (American) aesthetic on the outside to a more locally inflected interior: "In its architecture and its decoration the theatre accomplishes a remarkable suggestion of a blending of the Egyptian ideas and those of American showmanship."[27]

On opening night, guests were treated to the MGM film *Out West with the Hardys* (1938) starring Mickey Rooney; a 1938 MGM *Traveltalk*, "Jaipur: 'The Pink City'"; an MGM cartoon, *Art Gallery* (1939); and an "Address of Welcome," a specially filmed greeting for the Cinema Metro's opening night starring Lewis Stone, one of the stars of *Out West with the Hardys*.[28] In a direct address to the audience, Stone lauded "this veritable temple of the talking picture" where "Metro-Goldwyn-Mayer has spared neither effort nor money in supplying Cairo with a cinema worthy of the splendid city. Its most comfortable chairs, perfect projection, unexcelled sound, air conditioning properly controlled, which is so important in the sub-tropical climate of the city, all combined in one magnificent edifice, which cannot fail to be a source of great civic pride." Stone, speaking on behalf of Loew's and MGM, added:

> It is often said that Egypt contains more historical wonders than any other land, that Cairo more charm than any other city in the world. Pyramids, sphinx, treasure houses filled with antiquities, continue to arouse the admiration and wonder of all who visit this fascinating capital. But modern Cairo is justly proud as well of its universities, hospitals, scientific institutes which

compare so favorably to those in other progressive cities the world over. And we're very proud tonight to add to the attractions of Cairo this veritable temple of the talking picture.... And I assure you that all of the efforts of the Metro-Goldwyn-Mayer studios will be directed in supplying the Metro Theatre in Cairo with the best entertainment that can be produced.[29]

The English-language *Egyptian Gazette*, with much upper-class dismissiveness, remarked that "one is surprised that such lavishness of equipment should be considered economically justified in a building which is to be filled three times daily by crowds of people a good many of whom are not over-particular in their treatment of other peoples' property."[30]

The *Hardys* soon gave way to Wallace Beery in *Thunder Afloat* on February 8 at the Metro, coupled with additional cartoons and shorts including MGM's soft-power offering of the *Metro-Journal*, the company's French-language newsreel.[31] Typical programs at the Metro lasted two hours and twenty minutes and included a feature film along with cartoons, newsreels, and travelogues. The Metro also provided a ten-minute intermission and generally offered three shows daily at 3:15, 6:30, and 9:30 P.M., except on Fridays and Sundays when a fourth show was added.[32] The theater also added special

FIGURE 12.1 Lewis Stone, filmed in Hollywood, with a special message for the Cinema Metro's opening night audience in Cairo. (Screen capture, TCM)

morning shows that week on Friday through Sunday at 10:30 A.M. for the "Moslem's New Year feast."[33] To maintain the theater's air of exclusivity and excitement, films shown at the Metro were not shown anywhere else in the country for six weeks.[34] (In Alexandria, before a Cinema Metro was built by Loew's International and opened there in 1948, MGM films were booked into the city's Royal and Mohamed Aly cinemas.[35])

More than half a century later, Samir Raafat noted in the *Cairo Times* that the cinema's sumptuous upholstery and surroundings, coupled with its air-conditioning—a first in an Egyptian cinema—made its afternoon screenings "the preferred summertime rendezvous for Cairo's white collar professionals."[36] The Metro's air-conditioning was not only a marketing advantage but also a programmatic one. All of Cairo's hard-top theaters closed during the summer heat when open-air cinemas drew audiences. Because of air-conditioning, the Metro was the only indoor theater in the country open all year round.

"The upmarket 'loge' and balcony had upholstered chairs which reclined backwards, inducing the more tired moviegoer into deep slumber," according to Raafat. "Despite the comfortable seats—and before he became obese—King Farouk would have a special armchair brought in whenever he attended a gala or charity event at the Metro."[37] It was the "only deluxe theatre in Egypt," according to *Variety*, with Al Lowe, United Artists' South African manager, remarking, "All the others have wood or straw seats, [are] dirty, [have] bad sound, and are badly managed."[38] The Metro's luxury was reflected in its ticket prices, which, at twelve piastres, were significantly higher than the average. Raafat notes that the Metro, which "sported the words 'pride of the Orient' under its roaring lion logo," was part of a hybrid and "thriving three-story, self-sustaining enterprise" containing leased offices, retail stores, a restaurant, and a Ford car dealership.[39]

The Metro's American (Hollywood) films were yet another draw, of course. *Variety*'s Will Saphir noted that while Egyptian films attracted local audiences to Egyptian-run movie houses, the new Cinema Metro and other cinemas that showcased Hollywood films were far more popular with "Europeans residing in Egypt" who "would not think of going to an Egyptian film." "The higher-class Egyptians," he added, "do likewise because they desire a more sophisticated story to their films and further technical achievement." The multinational attraction to American films sustained this mix of both Egyptian and Western audiences during the Cinema Metro's opening months. There was, perhaps, another reason MGM and other films attracted Egyptian and non-Egyptian audiences: Egyptian censors had long stipulated that "love making could only be portrayed," Saphir noted, "if there were no accompaniment of kisses."[40] Curiously, this requirement was only enforced for films made in Egypt, not for those imported from Europe or the United States, thus Ahmad Husayn's critique a few years earlier about the foreign (film) influence on Egyptian culture.

American films, even during the Production Code, contained a certain measure of titillation that did not exist in locally-produced Egyptian films.

Unlike other territories such as South Africa, where racial divisions remained, there were no "color bars" or other restrictions in Egyptian moviegoing. As Al Lowe noted in 1944, "All races mix freely in all parts of all theatres."[41] The cosmopolitan audience at the Metro also meant that films had to be shown "quadralingually" with an English soundtrack, French subtitles, and separate and corresponding slides with Greek and Arabic translations projected onto miniature silver sheets on either side of the proscenium. "Half the entertainment in seeing a picture here," *Variety*'s George Lait observed, "is to watch how the translators have wrestled with, and ultimately mangled, some nifty which took the Marx Bros. months to sweat . . . over."[42]

The Cinema Metro and the Metro Cub Club

The excitement around the new Cinema Metro remained for the next three decades.[43] The *Palestine Post*—published in Jerusalem some 250 miles and a border away—reported in June 1944, for example, that Cairo's Metro was "well known to people in this part of the world."[44] Mohamed Khan recalled,

> As a schoolboy, I remember very well how Thursday nights were allocated to "cinema-going" with my friends, and Fridays for going with my dad. He would usually take us to the 3:15 P.M. show at the famous Metro Cinema. Having had lunch at the Excelsior next door . . . we would always choose seats in row 'W' situated in the stall, which happened to be inches higher than the rest. We would then watch a Metro Goldwyn Mayer (MGM) movie while my dad dozed off.[45]

Khan added, "Occasionally, MGM [and later] Fox would kindly screen new Egyptian films at their respective cinema, but only after obtaining authorization from their Hollywood headquarters. This usually happened for limited runs, usually during holiday seasons."[46] Egyptian filmmaker Ibrahim al-Batout still fondly recalls the Metro's "magnificent marble staircase with its red carpet" as well as "the weekly Tom and Jerry cartoon screening that he regularly attended as a child. 'It was a combination of magic and splendour,'" he recalled in 2011, "adding that standing by the decorated glass doors, an usher in a long red coat and a black cap offered every child a free ice cream or a free bottle of Coca Cola."[47] Clément Dassa, whose father, Maurice Dassa, started his career with MGM as an assistant shipper in Alexandria in 1936 and eventually became general manager of MGM Egypt from 1952 to 1955, recalled that the Cinema Metro was a second home: "MGM was part of my family not

FIGURE 12.2 The global allure of *Tom & Jerry* is clearly marked in this program for the Cinema Metro in Cairo. The cartoon is still used today to sell Choquik to children. (Author's collection)

my Dad's job. Why? Because it was a culture of going to the movies 3–4 times a week.... Theaters were a way of life in those days. And from the poorest of the poor to the richest who could afford the best seats in the balcony of Metro-Goldwyn-Mayer [everyone went]."[48]

The Cinema Metro focused on cultivating a multigenerational attraction to MGM cinemas and films through its Metro Cub Club and its focused attention on Egyptian children. "Every Sunday, rain or shine especially in winter, we would go to children's cartoon sessions on Sunday morning." Dassa recalls that "people were given free coca cola [at] intermission and there was also a scheme where Metro-Goldwyn-Mayer would invite all the kids whose birthday was that same week and they would have a big cake on stage. And being the son of Mr. Dassa I was always given cake after birthdays in the office of the 'directeur.' Metro-Goldwyn-Mayer was a part of me."[49] Mohamed Khan adds that at the Cinema Metro, "There were no mid-film intermissions where you would go and buy popcorn.... Instead, we had ice-cream sticks and chocolate bars, which we devoured over the introductory *Tom and Jerry, Donald Duck* or *Woody Woodpecker* cartoons."[50] Another moviegoer at MGM's Cinema Metro in Alexandria, recalling the importance of American cinemas abroad for inculcating a close bond between foreign audiences and American films and consumer products, recalled that

> Sunday morning was the big day for kids. With just two piasters, you could go to the Metro. I think it was about two hours of cartoons and movie shorts. No assigned seating, like the regular performances, it was a free for all. All kids all the time. Cartoons and strange little cowboy and comic serials. At the Metro it was *Tom and Jerry* cartoons. My brother and I were there every Sunday. Intermission was the crowning point, pandemonium, a free Coke and a package of cookies from Arabisco, the equivalent [sic] of Nabisco. Ah, the joy of advertising. At [Twentieth Century-Fox's] Amir, you would get Pepsi and a chocolate.[51]

Along with its first-run allure for adults and its matinees for Cairo's children, the Metro's appeal to Cairo's growing middle class further boosted its revenues. In July 1942, for example, the *American Israelite* reported that "when the military situation in Egypt was at its darkest, the people of Cairo found relief and relaxation at the Metro Theatre..."[52] "Since the war," Al Lowe wrote to UA executives, "thousands of natives who never could visit the cinema before, are becoming regular customers."[53] In addition to the steady supply of civilians of all backgrounds, Lowe estimated that 60 percent of the audiences for Hollywood were now British troops. Tourists and locals made up the rest. (American troops in Egypt, serviced by the U.S. Army's Overseas Motion Picture Service, typically patronized their own theaters.) Even Egyptian royalty maintained the cinema habit; when *Fantasia* opened in Cairo at the Misr Theatre, the Queen and Princess Fayza were scheduled to be on hand.[54] "If there is one business in Africa which has not suffered by the war, show business is it," George Lait wrote in *Variety*. Local cinemas "can't find room for the patrons who crowd the lobbies for tickets beginning at 9 a.m.... Now, to fill the demand, more [cinemas] are running five daily."[55]

Still, education and language were major hindrances to Hollywood dominance in Egypt. An internal United Artists report estimated that the country's illiteracy rate was still at 60 percent by June 1944—making subtitled films impossible for non–English speaking Egyptian audiences—and "millions of these people have never had the price of a cinema, and have never seen one, excepting through or over the fence of some outdoor cinema." Thus, he argued, "It might be more correct to say that Cairo and Alexandria are the only two really important cities as far as our business is concerned."[56] Regardless, the boom in wartime attendance in Cairo spurred interest in U.S. cinema expansion in Egypt, with Warner Bros. purchasing the Opera Theatre in Cairo, the second largest in Egypt, in July 1943.[57] Warner Bros. also looked north to Alexandria and purchased property there to build a new theater and sales office after the war.[58]

Egypt, the Cairo Palace, and Political Unrest

Twentieth Century-Fox opened its own shop window cinema, the two-thousand-seat, air-conditioned Cairo Palace, in May 1945. Fox International head Murray Silverstone traveled to Cairo to oversee the opening of the cinema, which was managed by Twentieth Century-Fox in financial and operational partnership with the Egyptian Gaafar brothers, Moustafa and Mohammed.[59] There Fox films were projected in English with French subtitles along with accompanying slides in Arabic on top and Greek on the bottom.[60] The theater was opened not to secure Fox's position in Cairo but to highlight it and to use the Cairo Palace to advertise Fox films throughout the country and region. "Our pictures dominate the market [in] Egypt," Murray Silverstone commented with great confidence.[61] Despite rising anti-British demonstrations that had led to attacks on Jewish stores, on a local synagogue, and on individuals in Harat al-Yahud (the Jewish Quarter), Silverstone remarked naïvely, "We have no occasion for worry there."[62]

The Cairo Palace opened at an increasingly delicate moment in the relationship between the Egyptian government and foreign cinema owners. The spread of Hollywood films and U.S.-owned cinemas was beginning to alarm Egyptian government officials, who had failed to influence theater operators to include more indigenous productions. In contradistinction to the more aggressive announcement of Misr al-Fatat a decade earlier, in late March 1945 the Egyptian Minister of Social Affairs told the local press, "If cinema proprietors reject my proposition to show Arabic films for at least four weeks a year, I shall issue a military order forcing then to do so. The duty of the Government is to encourage all national industries and give them a chance to develop." U.S. embassy officials were concerned that the protectionist, nationalist sentiment would become a wider issue and dictated that this quote "must be paraphrased before being communicated to anyone other than a Government Agency." If not, "such an order if issued would curtail playing time [for] American films and force foreign owned theaters to buy second and third rate local productions."[63]

Joseph Rosthal, secretary and general counsel of Loew's International, wrote to Carl E. Milliken, executive secretary of the Motion Picture Producers and Distributors of America, that this announcement by the Ministry of Social Affairs followed the complaints of "several independent Egyptian producers" about the "lack of outlets," and he asked Milliken if he could "have this matter taken up with the State Department."[64] Milliken then contacted George R. Canty, assistant chief of the Telecommunications Division at the Department of State, and told Joseph Rosthal to "indicate" to the Egyptians "the interest of our government in protecting the American industry."[65]

Loew's International executive Morton Spring, writing from New York, telegrammed Cinema Metro manager George Chasanas on April 18, 1945, that the company still objected to the Ministry's demands "on principle" but ultimately agreed to the demands of the "Committee on the Projection of Arabic Film in High Class Motion Picture Houses" and agreed to screen one Arabic film each year. The committee formed "to distribute Arabic films to the theaters" consisted of local Egyptian "theater owners and representatives of the Ministry of Social Affairs" working to place the "first grade pictures" of Studio Misr, Mohamed Abdel Wahab, Om Kelsoum (Umm Kulthum), Farid El Atrash, Leila Mourad, Anwar Wagdi, and, of course, Youssef Wahbi.[66] The agreement to show one Arabic (read: Egyptian) film per year at MGM's Cinema Metro and at the new Cairo Palace co-owned by Twentieth Century-Fox was not the only demand from the Egyptian government. A new declaration required that all foreign films imported to the country after August 8, 1945, had to have Arabic—not French—subtitles.[67] U.S. companies were unable to dissuade officials from forcing them to adhere to the new law, winning only a concession that the practice would begin in 1946 instead.[68]

Politics and Violence at Cairo's U.S.-Owned Cinemas

Pressure on the Cinema Metro and the Cairo Palace was not solely based on economic or cultural protectionism. Some of the new, more aggressive stands against Hollywood films and cinemas were due to the ongoing Arab–Jewish conflict in British-controlled Palestine and the growing anticolonial sentiment toward the British in Egypt, which had already begun to inflame tensions between Egypt's Jewish and Muslim communities and between Egyptians and local, Western-owned businesses. In early November 1945 a wave of anti-Jewish rioting erupted in Cairo, Alexandria, Port Said, and other Egyptian cities, part of a days-long demonstration organized by the Muslim Brotherhood against the anniversary of the Balfour Declaration and the growth of Zionism in Palestine. During the melee, ten people were killed and another four hundred were injured. Rioters smashed the windows of Jewish-owned shops and then looted their stores.[69] In Cairo, "Zionism" became a rallying cry for students while protesters broke most of the shop windows along Soliman Pasha Street and directly targeted the Cinema Metro, which was full of moviegoers at the time, leaving five glass entrance doors shattered.[70] What had always enticed patrons to the Cinema Metro—namely, its very Western edifice and its Hollywood brand and logo—now made it a prime target.[71] "In Alexandria's shopping center," one report observed, "not one pane of glass remained intact. Communications were at a standstill, cafes closed and theatres not operating."[72] Many Arabic-language editorials condemned the attacks, and the Egyptian government vowed to reimburse cinemas that had been damaged.[73] The eruption of violence, however, was only a foreshadowing of more troubling times ahead, the first of three devastating moments for Cairo cinemas.

The growing anti-British sentiment in Egypt—part reaction to decades of colonialism and part reaction to British support for a Jewish state in Palestine, led to further problems for British films. Robert Vitalis writes, "During the student strikes in February and March 1946, exhibitors were pressured to stop showing English-language films and newsreels" altogether.[74] In March 1946, Georg Georgoussky, director general of RKO for the Middle East, wrote to RKO executives that "CERTAIN EXHIBITORS" had been "NOTIFIED IN WRITING AND VERBALLY" that "ALL PICTURES CONTAINING ENGLISH PROPAGANDA" would be barred.[75] This was in large part due to political pressure from the new National Committee of Workers and Students, which protested against Egypt's 1936 Treaty with the British and in support of the Arab population in Palestine. The National Committee of Workers and Students authorized all theaters in Alexandria showing Egyptian films to remain open while demanding that all others close down.

Disregarding the fervor on the street, the Miami Theatre (directly across the street from the Cinema Metro) continued to exhibit British films for the moment. During a screening of Eagle-Lion's British film *A Place of One's Own* (1945), a hand grenade exploded inside the cinema, killing two moviegoers and injuring forty others. "It was as if a bomb exploded in every theatre in the land," Jacques Pascal wrote in *Motion Picture Daily*. "Box office returns dropped overnight, in some cases as much as 80 per cent."[76] Monogram sales representative Ed Simmel reported, "Rising tides of nationalism ... are seriously dampening America's prospects of doing business in the Middle East." "Hatred and violence against white foreigners," he added, "together with deepening political turmoil, are throwing up barriers to products with a 'made in U.S.A.' label, whether it is films or soap." Britain, Simmel pointed out, "is the main target of the nationalist agitation but America has become confused with her in the popular understanding."[77]

Anti-British sentiment continued to grow in Egypt throughout 1946. *Variety* reported that numerous bomb threats had been made to theaters showing British films and, as a result, "British pictures [we]re no longer being shown in Egyptian theatres."[78] Georgoussky added that, in addition to concerns about Jewish–Arab violence in Palestine, this growing tide of "anti-British sentiment" was also "causing theatres to close an average of two days every week."[79] Due to the growing unrest, J. Arthur Rank's plans to build a new Rivoli Theatre in Cairo were "postponed," and distribution contracts with Egyptian exhibitors summarily canceled. This ultimately rendered Rank's cinema largely useless for its own films. (One of the principal reasons Rank's Overseas Cinematograph Theatres Ltd. had formed Odeon (Cairo) Ltd. and the company's motivation behind "financing the acquisition and building of the Rivoli cinema, was to exhibit British films, whether or not other films were available."[80]) By December 1946, *Variety* reiterated that "British pictures are no longer being shown in Egyptian theatres due to threats of mobs to bomb any house showing them." The trade journal blamed the "political situation" less on a singular anti-British sentiment and more on the "rivalry existing between Arabs and Jews in Palestine. It's the first real instance where political rivalry has crippled an entire section of the motion picture industry in a whole country."[81] By 1947, U.S. films were still being exhibited in Cairo, Alexandria, and Port Said cinemas, but Hollywood and other foreign films had all but vanished from "provincial theatres" in Egypt due to the "growing tide of nationalism."[82]

The anger in the streets did not abate. On May 5, 1947, a time bomb was planted underneath the balcony of the Cinema Metro while 1,500 moviegoers watched Wallace Beery in *Bad Bascomb* (1946).[83] Five people were killed and thirty-one were wounded, including two patrons whose legs were blown off. The bomb was powerful enough to collapse the roof of the theater. The attack was part of a protest against celebrations for the "eleventh anniversary of King Farouk's succession to the throne of Egypt."[84] Blame was placed in every direction. Some felt "it was the work of Palestine terrorists who sought to embarrass Farouk," while Cairo police were quick to blame Zionists for the bombing.[85] Eventually, an escaped German prisoner of war confessed to participating in the bombing along with members of the Muslim Brotherhood.[86] Samir Raafat, noted that "the theatre was closed for several months and it was some time before Fred Astaire, Esther Williams, and Tarzan lured Cairo's movie addicts back to the pictures."[87]

While political unrest ultimately canceled Paramount's and Warner Bros.' plans to build new shop window cinemas in Cairo and Alexandria, Rank was finally able to open its long-delayed Rivoli Cinema the following year on February 14, 1948, but only by showing Egyptian, not British, films.[88] To buttress any criticism regarding the cinema's origins, the opening program noted that the Rivoli was "a practical example of Anglo-Egyptian co-operation," with J. Arthur Rank's name placed alongside his Egyptian partners, Moustafa and Mohammed Gaafar, who had also partnered with Twentieth Century-Fox on the Cairo Palace. The Rivoli's opening program for the 2,100-seat cinema featured the Egyptian National Anthem, "Bilady, Bilady, Bilady," "News in Arabic," and an Egyptian feature film, *Saga Al-Layl* (*The Fall of the Night*, 1948). Much like its American-owned competition, Rank's Cairo theater incorporated signature elements of the chain's flagship, in this case the Odeon Leicester Square in London. Like that London cinema, the Rivoli contained a theater organ with an illuminated console that could be lowered and raised electrically—"the first of its kind in the Middle East." The Rivoli also boasted other very Western touches, such as a 170-seat restaurant, a cocktail bar, a dance floor, a dais for the orchestra, and, of course, air-conditioning.[89] The venue—Rank's Egyptian shop window—was "carefully designed to harmonise with the present-day trend of Egyptian architecture," *Ideal Kinema* wrote, and "a motif of an Egyptian hunter with cheetah."[90] With its Egyptian co-ownership, Arabic programming, and other local touches, the Rivoli had escaped the ire of the moment.

But only for a moment.

CHAPTER 13

NO MEETING IN THE MIDDLE, 1947–1956

Hollywood Cinemas, Egyptian Revolution, and Israeli Independence

Egypt had certainly been the most lucrative Middle Eastern market for Hollywood, but expectations for Palestine had been rising steadily since the mid- to late 1930s. American films benefited, by then, from the growing absence of German films in the Palestine market as the rise of Adolf Hitler and the Nazi takeover of the German film industry led to anti-Nazi boycotts by Palestine's rapidly growing Jewish population as a fervor for Zionism and the existential threat of Nazism in Europe pushed more and more Jews to emigrate there. For all denominations of moviegoers— Christian and Muslim Arabs, Mizrahi and Ashkenazi Jews, British colonial bureaucrats and businessmen and women as well as myriad other nationalities, ethnic groups, and religions coexisting (or not) in British Mandate Palestine—the number of cinemas were still few and far between, with Tel Aviv, Haifa, and Jerusalem presenting the three most important cities for Hollywood and its films. The largely Jewish city of Tel Aviv, for example, just north of Arab-dominant Jaffa, had only five first-run cinemas by 1937, while Haifa and Jerusalem—with large Arab and Jewish populations—had even fewer.[1] As strife between Jews and Arabs under British control of Mandate Palestine grew—and a wave of massacres occurred between 1937 and 1939—hopes for a growing box office declined steadily, as did Palestine's political and commercial stability.[2]

Five years later, in 1943, when Twentieth Century-Fox president Spyros Skouras hired Murray Silverstone away from UA and appointed him vice president in charge of foreign distribution at Twentieth Century-Fox, the Middle

East became a central focus of the company's overseas expansion.³ In 1945 Silverstone announced plans to open Fox branch offices throughout the Middle East in Beirut, Baghdad, and Tehran and was "especially enthusiastic" about plans for a new Palestine branch that would have a wholly separate operation and manager.⁴ "The influx of [British] troops into Palestine," Silverstone noted, "plus the fact that at a later date the [European] refugees would be potential customers indicated a great market for American films."⁵ Warner Bros. also made an exclusive booking deal with the Orion Theatre in Tel Aviv during the war, while England's Rank Organisation planned to build three new Odeon cinemas in Tel Aviv, Haifa and Jerusalem.⁶

Palestine Pressures on U.S. Exhibitors in Egypt

The bloodletting in Palestine reached across the border as the Egyptian government and much of its population protested the ongoing British occupation of Palestine as well as the British government's support for a Jewish homeland within post-Mandate Palestine. Less than a year after the May 1947 bombing of the Cinema Metro in Cairo, MGM and Fox both received a letter from the "High Committee of the Nile Valley for the Liberation of Palestine" in February 1948 demanding U.S. film exhibitors to "collect funds for the liberation" during the first week of March as part of its "Palestine Week" campaign in Cairo. "Considering that the cinemas constitute one of the best resources," the letter noted, "we rely on your cooperation . . . for the distribution of a P. 2 stamp to be sold with every ticket during the week in question. We hope that this desire which is simultaneously a duty, will receive your kind consideration, to the end that the will of the people be concentrated on the liberation and safeguarding of Palestine by all means."⁷ According to the U.S. Embassy, "The High Committee is being recognized by the Egyptian Government as the only organization authorized to collect funds for the liberation of Palestine."⁸

Mohamed Aly Allouba Pasha, president of the committee and a former minister of the Egyptian government and senator, was one of the key signatures in the letter.⁹ Three years earlier, in 1944, while serving as president of the executive committee of the International Arab Parliamentary Union Conference, Pasha had cowritten a letter with the Arab Union Society to U.S. president Franklin D. Roosevelt that argued that the bitterness between Jews and Arabs over Palestine "has naturally led to feuds and feelings which have left no hope of reconciliation or mutual understanding." The letter warned Roosevelt that "Democratic America" should not support the Jewish effort in Palestine because it was backed by "a race which is widely scattered in the world, and which only relies on the power of money for the realization of its designs."¹⁰

Faced with the full support of Pasha and other members of the High Committee, the U.S. Embassy wrote to the U.S. State Department in Washington that American film exhibitors in Cairo had little choice but to acquiesce to these demands. The embassy memorandum noted that "Fox and MGM have the only two American-owned theaters in Cairo," and "they fear that refusal to do so would lead to possible violence on the part of irresponsible persons and their fear is heightened by the fact that the MGM theater, the Metro, had already been bombed on May 6, 1947." Local representatives of both Fox and MGM sought the embassy's official backing to not sell the stamps for the committee, but a U.S. embassy official reminded them that "American companies were not supposed to take part in any religious or political activities outside the United States."[11] Before long, however, U.S. Embassy and MGM and Fox personnel in Cairo realized that "all other theaters were going to accede to the 'request' and that they, therefore, had decided that they also would fall in line." To ensure their compliance, before the Cinema Metro and Cairo Palace opened their box office on March 1, 1948, High Committee officials affixed "large posters depicting a Jewish hand being forced by an Egyptian hand to drop a bloody knife." The Metro subsequently posted signs notifying moviegoers that they had to "purchase a 2 [piastre] stamp with each ticket of admission" to support the "liberation," and the committee promptly took the posters down.[12]

The demand that U.S. exhibitors in Egypt raise money for the Arab cause in Palestine was likely a direct response to the efforts of U.S. film companies and executives to raise funds for the emigration of Jewish refugees and for the creation of a Jewish state. Paramount head Barney Balaban, for example, served as the national chairman of the United Jewish Appeal (UJA), which helped finance the migration of post-Holocaust European Jewish refugees to Palestine. RKO production chief Dore Schary also served as campaign chairman for the UJA's Motion Picture Division, while Fox president Spyros Skouras, a Greek Orthodox Christian, was named "non-sectarian chairman for the industry."[13] At a UJA luncheon for refugees in July 1947 Skouras, who was joined by Balaban and South African exhibitor (and Fox exhibition partner) Norman Lourie, joked with the other "circuit heads" that "corporate contributions to the United Jewish Appeal had better be much larger than last year's—or they wouldn't get any Fox product."[14]

Skouras's support for the UJA was recognized by the New York chapter of Hadassah, the Women's Zionist Organization of America, which made him the guest of honor for their first annual dinner in December 1947. Dorothy Silverstone, wife of Fox International head Murray Silverstone, served as the chairman of the dinner committee.[15] In addition, the "Amusement Division" of the 1948 UJA campaign was led by an advisory committee that included

Murray Silverstone and Skouras, who was solely in charge of a one-man committee for corporate gifts.[16]

The State of Israel and the Egyptian Response

On May 14, 1948, hours before the British relinquished control of Mandatory Palestine and withdrew its forces, David Ben-Gurion declared Israel's independence, prompting an invasion the following day by Egypt, Jordan, Iraq, and Syria. Youssef Wahbi quickly summoned the Egyptian film industry to support the war against Israel (and an economic boycott against Israel's Western benefactors). As head of the Egyptian Syndicate for Motion Picture Studio Workers, Actors, and Technicians, Wahbi implored the Egyptian film industry and its patrons to boycott all U.S. films and their locally owned and operated cinemas.[17]

Since 1934, when Wahbi starred in and produced the first all-Egyptian talking picture, he had become known throughout the Middle East, including in pre-war Palestine where the *Palestine Post* hailed him as "the most gifted Arabic film star."[18] By 1948 Wahbi had become a powerful figure within Egyptian film, political, and cultural circles, a stature reflected in his leadership of the Egyptian Syndicate.[19] Wahbi also had a financial interest in the newly opened Nahas Studio, "the most modern studio of the eight in Egypt," according to a U.S. Embassy report, and was a "large investor in domestic production."[20] As characterized by the historian Robert Vitalis, Wahbi was "artful in his weaving together of self and national interest story lines in his rallying cry" against the U.S. film industry.[21] To bolster the Egyptian market for Egyptian productions, Wahbi began actively "aiding the opposition" against Hollywood's efforts to dub their films (which would have made them accessible to illiterate moviegoers) and argued before the Egyptian government that opening up rural markets to Hollywood would constitute "the first nail in the coffin of the Egyptian film industry."[22] He wrote to the Egyptian Ministry of Social Affairs: "Allowing foreign companies to release Arabic-dubbed versions of their films threatens dangerously the existence of the Egyptian motion picture industry."[23] In late February 1948 he led a strike in the nation's studios to protest an Arabic-dubbed release of *Thief of Baghdad* (1940), which was "drawing record numbers" to the Misr Theatre in Cairo while Egyptian films were struggling to turn a profit. According to Vitalis, "in the case of the local investors represented by Wahbi, Hollywood was apparently a scapegoat to be used to rescue him and his comrades."[24]

Wahbi was successful in suppressing the number of Arabic-dubbed films marketed in Egypt to only three per year, despite lobbying efforts by U.S. Embassy staff and U.S. film distributors who met "at length" with the Egyptian minister of social affairs and his advisors. Despite what seemed to be a principled, nationalist stance, Wahbi had let local American distributors know that his opposition to their dubbing plans was up for sale and made "an indirect offer to withdraw his opposition for a consideration amounting to about $25,000," as reported by embassy staff. The U.S. Embassy offered the following summary of their concerns:

> It is quite possible that this line of attack, which principally has a reference to dubbing, pressages [sic] a renewed campaign to compel the Ministry of Social Affairs to discriminate against American motion pictures either through positive regulations or harassing censorship and other indirect action. Such a plan, if pursued by Wahby [sic], could, because of the considerable influence already displayed by him, have a serious effect on American motion picture interests in Egypt.[25]

While nationalist sentiments and actions urged the boycott of U.S. films and cinemas, placards were also being placed throughout Alexandria (and other cities) "calling on the population not to work for Jews and to boycott Jewish shops."[26] U.S. film companies were, of course, known to employ both Jewish and non-Jewish executives in both the United States and Egypt, many of whom supported the new Jewish state. It was a perfect storm. On May 26, 1948, eleven days after the Arab-Israeli War began, Wahbi published a call to arms in the Egyptian magazine *Dounia al-Fan* titled "The Zionist Peril in Our Country." He called on all "Arabs!" to "BOYCOTT AMERICAN FILMS!" "We give them money," he wrote, "and they turn it into bullets." His first line of attack was pointedly against Twentieth Century-Fox and the fundraising work of Skouras and Silverstone: "FOX IS A ZIONIST COMPANY," Wahbi wrote, "DO NOT ATTEND ITS FILMS. American companies have important positions in the Arab countries, but their real purpose is to help the so called Zionist cause." Wahbi added that he had previously "warned my compatriots against the danger of attending American films, and now my statement is confirmed: 'Every piastre paid for American films goes straight to the Jews.' . . . Let us now all cooperate to the destruction of Zionists and accellerate [sic] the Arab victory to our heroic soldiers who fight for God and the Nation!" He added:

> All members of the American [film] companies are Zionist, all their capitals Zionist, and their only aims are to serve the Zionist cause. America is a Jewish colony headed by a man whose only ideal is to obtain a certain number of votes for his election and his recognition of the Jewish Nation twelve minutes after its creation is unparalleled in history of meanness and treachery.[27]

In concert with Wahbi's attacks, Egyptian government officials blocked all "dollar exports" from U.S. films and cinemas from leaving the country and banned motion pictures starring Danny Kaye and Mickey Rooney because they "collect[ed] funds for Zionists."[28] The conflict also created new censorship practices that banned Hollywood films with "sympathetic reference to the Jewish question."[29] In August the *Jewish Telegraphic Agency Daily News Bulletin* began reporting on "pogroms, mob violence, mass looting and terrorism which is now taking place throughout Egypt against the Jewish population," much of it based on a French observer's first-hand accounts. "The most violent of these attacks," he observed, "occurred near the Odeon and Rivoli Theatres, in the center of Cairo, on July 17."[30] The choice of location may have been intentional, reflecting these theatres' symbolic value and foreign identities.

Israel and Hollywood

The situation for U.S. investment in the new State of Israel was quite different. Unlike in Egypt, individual cinema operators owned nearly all of Israel's movie houses, making distribution more complex and necessitating local representatives for each of the Hollywood studios. Profits were far less robust, with the average ticket price at thirty-five cents and American films composing only 55 percent of screen time (20 percent went to Russian films, reflecting the many Russian, Eastern European, and Communist émigrés to the country, and the remainder largely coming from French, Italian, British, and Egyptian films).[31] Hollywood's meager profits from the Israeli market were also hurt, historian David Shalit writes, because profits from distribution and exhibition were not paid in dollars but in Israeli shekels, and much of that money was frozen in Israel and unable to be repatriated to the United States. Thus, he adds, one of the options presented to U.S. distributors was to reinvest their frozen funds into the construction of local cinemas.[32]

Spyros Skouras and Murray Silverstone, along with Twentieth Century-Fox's European director Robert Harley, traveled to Israel in July 1949 "to study the possibilities for the corporation in this country," as "Israel's need for newer and better theatres is great," Murray Silverstone remarked at the time. Skouras also noted his desire to promote the new state, "hop[ing] that one day the company will make a film telling the world the story of Israel and its army." Their visit was feted with a special reception hosted by I. Klinov, head of the Ministry of the Interior's "film and cinema department," and with a special dinner hosted by Moshe Sharett, Israel's foreign minister.[33] Skouras and the Fox delegation also met with Israel's finance minister, Eliezer Kaplan, and David Horowitz, director general of the Finance Ministry. Skouras laid the groundwork for a new two-thousand-seat cinema to be built and, according to Shalit, telegrammed a dozen "influential businessmen and industrialists in the [United States] and encouraged them to invest and donate in Israel."[34]

Skouras's support for Israel was not confined to cinema bartering alone. David Shalit writes that Skouras, who had growing ties to Greece and the Greek government in the 1940s and beyond, was asked by the Israeli government to petition the Greeks to release two Israeli Air Force planes that had been "confiscated" when they illegally traversed Greek air space.[35] Skouras's deep connections with both Jewish and Greek Orthodox Christian figures in Israel could also be seen in a meeting between future Israeli prime minister Moshe Sharett; Jerusalem Archbishop Iakovos, "Primate of the Greek Orthodox Church in North and South America" and a leader of the World Council of Churches; and Spyros Skouras, described by the *Jerusalem Post* as "one of the leaders of the Greek community in the U.S."[36] During his visit to Israel, Skouras was also able to meet Pope Paul VI and Archbishop Iakovos, a testament to his growing geopolitical power and the connections he was able to make between Jewish and Christian leaders—and Israel's relationships to other powers—around the world.[37]

Skouras's support for Israel continued upon his return to the United States. It was certainly public knowledge that many studio heads backed the Jewish cause in Palestine. At a November 1949 UJA fundraiser that followed his latest visit to Israel, Skouras placed Fox's plans within the social and industrial context of the nation's development, especially the construction of offices for medical personnel throughout the country. Skouras declared the need to invest in new cinemas for Fox, and through these efforts the country's infrastructure would also grow.[38] In late 1949 Twentieth Century-Fox bought a 2,700 square meter site in Tel Aviv with U.S. dollars and then deposited "a large sum of Swedish francs" with the Israeli treasury in order to "build a theatre in Tel Aviv as an 'approved foreign investment,'" a designation that qualified for tax reductions, no duty imposed on imported equipment, "and other financial considerations."[39] After Tel Aviv, Skouras planned to build additional cinemas in Haifa, Jerusalem, and Natanya, with each "provid[ing] office space for doctors, dentists, etc., which," he noted, was "desperately needed at this time."[40] Fox's interest in building cinemas in Israel was also matched by MGM, which was now "joining the race for theatre construction in Israel," according to *Variety*, by planning to build three new cinemas in Tel Aviv, Haifa, and Jerusalem in the coming years.[41]

Fox and MGM were just two of several companies (and individuals) looking to develop cinemas, distribution offices, and studios in Israel as a means of industrial and political investment. As early as 1946 Paramount International head, Clement Crystal, had traveled to Palestine to investigate the possibilities of building new cinemas in Jerusalem, Haifa, and Tel Aviv.[42] In fact, the *Palestine Post* reported in May 1946, "In the past few weeks the Foreign Department bosses of all American film concerns have visited this country."[43]

Another key figure in Israeli exhibition was Norman Lourie, who had attended the UJA luncheon in July 1947 with Skouras. In December 1930

Norman Lourie and his wife, Nadia, had founded the Habonim movement in South Africa "to attract youngsters to the Zionist Idea."[44] The Louries were not just early supporters for a Jewish state in Palestine but also business partners of Fox in South Africa, co-owning the 2,100-seat 20th Century Theatre in Johannesburg, and another shop window cinema in Cape Town.[45] In 1944 Al Lowe had reported to UA management that the Louries, "who have built several theatres for us in South Africa" and were "ardent supporters of Zionism, and Palestine," were "interested in building a circuit . . . in Tel-Aviv, Jerusalem, Haifa, and Jaffa."[46] Lourie also made documentaries during World War II, including one released by United Artists and another by Fox.[47] (This may account for Youssef Wahbi's attack on Fox that the company had "put into production films encouraging the creation of a National Home for Jews in Palestine."[48]) While Lourie remained committed to producing documentaries—his first three in Palestine were produced for the UJA—he noted that the "greatest need in the Holy Land now" was "more modern 'A' cinemas"—a need he planned to fill "as soon as conditions permit."[49] Lourie's exhibition and real estate company, Cinemas Investment Corp., subsequently purchased land for a 1,750-seat cinema that would become "the most modern in the country" and additional "property for an 1,100-seat house in Haifa."[50] His ambitious plans for film production, distribution, and exhibition in Israel were aided by his growing industrial and political connections. In May 1948 Lourie's brother, Arthur, was named consul general in New York for the Provisional Government of Israel, while Arthur's wife, Jeanette Leibel Lourie, became the executive secretary of Hadassah, the Zionist women's group that had honored Skouras in December 1947.[51]

Film Production in the New State

The ongoing associations between Fox, UA, and the Louries in South Africa, and between Skouras, Silverstone, and Lourie through their fundraising efforts for Israel, may have played a key role in Fox's decision to distribute Lourie's documentary, *Israel Reborn*, for free throughout the United States.[52] Skouras and Silverstone's handling of the film, the *Chicago Sentinel* wrote, enabled it to be "shown in motion picture cinemas throughout the world, and will bring to audiences everywhere a first-hand account of the creation of the Jewish state."[53] Lourie's connections with United Artists also led to a subsequent commercial deal with that company for worldwide distribution of Palestine Film's ongoing *Israel Today* news series, which was negotiated during a 1948 trip to the United States under a permit from the Israeli army.[54]

Lourie's Palestine Films Inc. was only one of many companies, like Carmel Films, that hastily produced material about Israel in the immediate months and years after the formation of the country. While Murray Silverstone toured the region to build new cinemas for Fox, his wife, Dorothy, joined forces with philanthropist Martha Sharp to create Children to Palestine, a "Christian-sponsored group" working on behalf of "homeless Jewish refugee children."[55] In 1949 Sharp and Silverstone traveled to Israel with cameraman Fred Csaznik to film *The Magnetic Tide*, a short film about newly immigrated Jewish orphans and local Arab children living together in Israel that was distributed to cinemas and Protestant Sunday schools in the United States.[56] Silverstone invited her old friend Mary Pickford, with whom Murray had worked at United Artists before leaving for Twentieth Century-Fox in 1941, to attend an early screening at her home.[57] The completed film, *Variety* commented in November 1950, "is one of the better produced documentary shorts on Israel. Some of the mose [sic] eloquent shots are those in a hospital nursery where closeups of tots reveal the horrors that some of them underwent before they were given a haven. These few moments provided enough reason for the country. Producer-director Dorothy Silverstone (wife of 20th-Fox's foreign chief, Murray Silverstone) doesn't stir up any controversies; political and religious angles are brushed aside."[58] Skouras distributed *The Magnetic Tide* for free through Twentieth Century-Fox, with all proceeds for Children to Palestine's efforts to create multicultural programming in Israel for both Arabs and Jews.[59] Like Lourie's film, Silverstone's short was also booked into Fox's premiere showcase, the Roxy Theatre in New York, then managed by Barney Balaban's brother, A. J., who hosted a cocktail party to celebrate the film's release with Dorothy Silverstone, Arthur Lourie, and Israel's foreign minister, finance minister, and its ambassador to the United States.[60] In 1950 Arthur Krim and Norman Lourie planned to extend this kind of filmmaking, beginning negotiations with Robert Flaherty for a new ethnographic film about Israel and its inhabitants. Hoping to capture a *Louisiana Story* in the Holy Land, the proposed film would be directed by a *Flaherty* and not a *Silverstone* and would, in Krim's view, help buttress the documentary from charges of bias and ethnic privilege.[61]

New Cinemas for the New Country

Besides filmmaking, Norman Lourie was even more "optimistic" about the "distribution-exhibition side" of the market. With more Jewish refugees moving to Palestine/Israel in 1948, he told *Variety*, "For each $4 the American industry got out of the [region], it was formerly figured that $2 came from Egypt, $1 from Palestine and $1 from Syria, Transjordan, Iraq and Lebanon combined. Balance now is about $1.50 from Egypt and the same from Palestine."[62]

In September 1949 an agreement signed that year between the Israel Ministry of Finance and the Motion Picture Association of America granted that only $80,000 of *combined* annual "out-of-pocket" expenses could be transferred by U.S. companies out of the country.[63] Cinema investment, therefore, would enable Fox to spend what it had earned in local distribution by using those blocked funds to build cinemas.[64] The company now planned to build new cinemas in Tel Aviv, Haifa, Jerusalem, and Natanya. "We will be the first ones," Skouras told *Variety*, "to create the commercial interest of every American industry in Israel."[65]

With most of their funds still frozen, Spyros Skouras arrived in Tel Aviv in December 1949 to build "big Cinemas in Tel-Aviv and provincial towns." Plans for the Tel Aviv cinema were, according to Israeli newspaper *Al Hamishmar*, expected to be built in "the American Style."[66] Fox Israel manager Simcha Greenvald's successful negotiations with Tel Aviv city authorities, including Mayor Israel Rokach, resulted in Fox's purchase of a large lot on Pinsker Street in Tel Aviv's city center. By the end of 1949 Fox had purchased another site in Haifa and had begun scouting locations in Jerusalem.[67]

In December 1949 the Tel Aviv Cities Construction Committee approved Fox's application for "a cinema building" at the junction of Pinsker, Beilinson, and Glikson Streets with two thousand seats and, perhaps most importantly for the city, six floors of office space.[68] George M. Koigen, associate architect for the Fox Tel Aviv cinema project, wrote to the Cities Construction Committee that the office space would be for the use of Fox and leased out "only to doctors, lawyers and architects."[69] Architects John and Drew Eberson and associate architect Koigen completed plans for their new "Municipal Building and Cinema for Twentieth Century-Fox Import Corp." in Jerusalem in January 1951.[70] Meanwhile, plans for a "Cinema and Medical Arts Building for Twentieth Century Fox" in Tel Aviv were completed by the Ebersons in August 1951, and plans for a "Cinema and Office Building for Twentieth Century Fox" in Haifa were completed by the Ebersons in February 1952.[71]

In March 1950 Murray Silverstone and Simha Greenvald met with West Jerusalem Mayor Daniel Austrer to discuss the construction of two theater and cinema buildings there; they also spoke with other officials regarding cinemas in Tel Aviv and Haifa.[72] Trouble followed each of Twentieth Century-Fox's new projects. Fox's Jerusalem cinema, which was to be built on a large lot on King George Street, was blocked in April 1951 by the city's Financial Committee, which chose to build an office building there instead.[73] In Tel Aviv a soda kiosk vendor submitted a "forceful application" to the Cities Construction Committee of the Tel Aviv Municipality to deny any construction plans by "an American company, 'Fox-Film'" to build on the lot then occupied in part by his kiosk.[74] The vendor would ultimately lose, but another delay was triggered.

Hollywood Expansion and Expulsion in Egypt, 1949–1957

Quotidian exhibition (and marketing) in Egypt finally returned to a semblance of normalcy by 1949, following the Cinema Metro bombing in Cairo in 1947, the Arab-Israeli War, the battle over foreign film dubbing, and the forced fundraising in Cairo's Hollywood cinemas. The relative calm of the moment spurred Loew's to build a new Cinema Metro in Alexandria. The company had originally announced their plan in mid-May 1948, just days before the start of the Arab-Israeli War, "but the greenlight was held up," according to *Variety*.[75] A year later, on May 1, 1949, Loew's officially announced the construction of a new "showcase" house in Alexandria that would seat 2,000 patrons.[76] Like its Cairo shop window, which had been designed by Thomas Lamb, this new Alexandria Cinema Metro was designed by an American architect, John McNamara.[77] The new MGM cinema opened on August 30, 1950, and was immediately promoted as the most opulent in the city.[78] The Alexandria shop window allowed MGM to open its films in Egypt's two largest cities day-and-date in company-owned venues, attracting large audiences and persuading provincial cinema owners to book MGM films on subsequent runs.[79] These simultaneous releases enabled MGM's twin premieres to be almost national (urban) events.

Still, the problems related to Israel, a growing anti-Jewish sentiment in Egypt, and the potential boycott of Hollywood films and Hollywood-owned cinemas remained. The departure of roughly twelve thousand Jews between 1949 and 1950 after the end of the Arab-Israeli War and the rise of antisemitism in Egypt reflected the growing unease. Meanwhile, depictions of Jews in Egyptian films also changed dramatically during this period. As Viola Shafik writes, "they turned into rather unpleasant, mostly greedy and cunning foreigners."[80] In January 1951 moviegoers to the day-and-date release of Paramount's *Samson and Delilah* at the Mohamed Aly and Royal cinemas in Alexandria and the Diana in Cairo discovered that the film's distribution had been "indefinitely postponed" by Egyptian censors even after "cutting out parts of the introductory speech considered pro-Jewish."[81] (MGM's *Ivanhoe* attracted similar negative attention in some Arab countries because of its "favorable characterization of the Jews."[82])

Animus toward foreign cinemas was not restricted to those owned by Hollywood, with its supposed Jewish ownership and pro-Israel leanings. (The complexities of publicly traded companies, investment banks, corporate bonds, non-Jewish executives like Skouras and Zanuck, and other details did little to dissuade local anti-Jewish campaigns and campaigners that the industry was not an ethnic or industrial monolith.) In the early 1950s, the only group perhaps even more detested in Egypt than its Jews were the British. The hostility toward British soldiers, expats, tourists, and especially local business owners and managers created an opportunity for the Gaafar brothers, who co-owned the Rivoli Theatre with Rank's Overseas Cinematograph Theatres Ltd. The agreement between Rank and the Gaafars stipulated that "the Manager of the Rivoli cinema should continue to be exclusively appointed by the Board of directors"—which was majority-run by Rank and consisted of three members from the Rank company, and the other two were the Gaafar brothers.[83] Rank, which owned a 51 percent stake in the Rivoli Theatre, controlled the cinema's operation and accepted the Gaafars' input more as advice rather from an equal partner.

On January 3, 1952, the British manager of the Rivoli (Mr. Smeeden) was ordered to "present himself" and his passport within twenty-four hours to the Cairo police. This was interpreted by British consular staff in Cairo "to mean that Mr. Smeeden would be asked to leave the country, probably at short notice." According to a British Foreign Office (BFO) report, "Messrs. Rank were most concerned by this development, since they would be involved in heavy financial loss if they had to forego the profits from the theatre after the expulsion of the British Manager." The BFO was shocked by the summons because the Rivoli "had been most carefully run as an Egyptian and not primarily as a British theatre, and the policy had been to cater for Arab tastes [and to] give encouragement to Arab ideas."[84] Rank executives in England approached the Egyptian charge d'affaires in London who "telegraphed to the Ministry of Foreign Affairs in Cairo urging them not to expel Mr. Smeeden."[85] Also aiding Smeeden, the BFO noted, was that he was "a man of considerable influence in Egyptian circles."[86] A stay of (temporary) execution was granted.

The attack on Smeeden was not wholly unexpected. Five years earlier, Rank's Odeon (Cairo) Ltd. firm had signed an agreement to operate another cinema, the Capitol, with their Egyptian partners, Moustafa and Mohammed Gaafar, who were due £50,000 when it was completed. In November 1948, however, the cinema's roof collapsed during construction, and the Capitol was never completed or opened due, a BFO report concluded, "to the financial difficulties of the Gaafars over the last years." On June 23, 1951, the Gaafars, who were equal partners with Rank on the Rivoli Cinema, sued Rank's Odeon (Cairo) Ltd. for £E285,000 for unpaid "rent, cost of furnishings, loss of profit, etc." stemming from the aborted Capitol project. "Since the summer of 1950," the BFO reported, "there has been constant friction with the Gaafars over the management of the Rivoli Cinema owned by Odeon (Cairo) Ltd." In early

July 1951 meetings were held in London between J. Arthur Rank and John Davis (of Rank) and Moustafa Gaafar in which the Gaafars "renounce[d] their rights" and "sign[ed] a point by point renunciation of the allegations contained therein," in exchange for a payment of £35,000 to settle the Capitol disagreement over the Rivoli.[87] However, the BFO reported,

> As soon as the present political difficulties in Egypt commenced [in January 1952] the Gaafars again began to cause trouble. Articles appeared in the Egyptian Press attacking the British management of and interest in the Rivoli cinema. Demonstrations also took place in and outside the cinema. There is sufficient circumstantial evidence to point to the hand of the Gaafars behind all these troubles. In order to inform the Egyptian public of the true position, i.e. that the Gaafars had a 49% interest in the cinema, a banner was put up outside the cinema to bring out the fact of Egyptian participation without actually mentioning the Gaafars. Grave exception to this was taken by them and at their request it was removed.[88]

Smeeden's legal difficulties immediately followed these tit-for-tat disagreements. Arthur N. Cumberbatch, UK commercial minister for Egypt, wrote to Sir Roger Allen, head of the African Department of the UK Foreign Office, saying, "It seems quite clear that the whole affair was engineered by Messrs. Rank's Egyptian partners, who have for long being trying to obtain control of the business here, and that they had suborned a minor official in the Ministry of Interior" to deport or threaten to deport Smeeden.[89]

Smeeden's annual work permit was due for renewal on February 10, with no guarantee of approval by Egyptian authorities. In addition, angered further by Smeeden's ability to counteract their efforts to remove him, the Gaafar brothers "threatened to take action, either legal or otherwise, with effect from 31st January, unless some arrangement for sale of the cinema to Gaafar or letting [the Rivoli] with complete control in Gaafar's hands is arrived at."[90] Rank began to see little chance of a positive outcome, with the many political winds blowing against them and the BFO increasingly impotent in hostile territory.

By January 8, 1952, Rank had officially opened negotiations in London with the Gaafars' representative, Mr. Nabi, who was backed by Prince Talal bin Abdulaziz Al Saud of Saudi Arabia, who was financing the Gaafars' acquisition of Rank's majority ownership in the Rivoli Theatre.[91] Rank had offered to sell their holdings for £E280,000 while the Gaafars offered £E275,000 and "intimate[d] that if this offer is not accepted by 1st February, they will take legal action to expropriate Messrs. Rank." While Rank was under no legal obligation to sell their positions to the Gaafars, the BFO reported that "Messrs. Rank are most reluctant to give way any further."[92] Allen wrote to Cumberbatch that he was "somewhat puzzled that Messrs. Rank should make such a fuss about so small a sum as £5,000, and wonder whether there may not be more in this story than they have cared to tell us. Our main interest would seem to lie in the danger that this may prove to be the first clear case of victimisation of a British interest in Egypt."[93] Something far more ominous was brewing that month. Rank should have sold when it still had the chance.

Cairo Fire, January 1952

That same month, in January 1952, Ahmad Husayn, whose Misr al-Fatat movement had transformed over the past two decades into Egypt's Socialist Party, warned the Egyptian government that if its acceptance of Western cultural and political influence and its own disinterest in social equality did not change, the situation on the ground certainly would. "Will you continue, O you ministers ... to live in scandal, wealth, joy, and illuminations? Will our theaters and cinemas and our cabarets stay open?" he asked. "The anger that stirs up now the people has neither started nor ended. It looks for an exit to express itself."[94] On January 24, 1952, Husayn announced that the government's disregard of the people's anger toward British control of the Suez Canal and the continued prominence of foreigners in Egyptian commerce and society was untenable; he would soon "unleash the crowds" against the state, and "terrifying crimes" would ensue. As Anne-Claire Kerboeuf writes, "Two days later the 'crowds' were indeed unleashed."[95]

Following months of skirmishes, British troops stationed in the Suez Canal Zone killed fifty Egyptian police officers in Ismailia on January 25, 1952. The following day, Cairo was rocked by demonstrations and riots that targeted French, British, American, and Egyptian Jewish property, especially bars, gambling halls, foreign clubs, and, of course, foreign-owned and -operated cinemas.[96] This became known as Black Saturday and the Cairo Fire.

Rank's Rivoli Theatre was the first foreign structure to be deliberately burned; British officials reported that the cinema was "completely gutted," with "only the shell" of the building still standing.[97] Three witnesses later testified that Ahmad Husayn's driver was seen "coming from the direction" of the burning Rivoli, which was still under legal threat from the Gaafars at the time of the attack.[98] At the Cinema Metro, demonstrators "smashed all the windows," burned the cinema, and threw the "charred seats ... into the street."[99] The Metro's American manager, Robert Schmitt, "barely escaped through the back door when the crowd set it ablaze," and he "took refuge in the U.S. embassy."[100] Schmitt's second-in-command, Maurice Dassa, escaped through the roof. His family waited all day to hear news about whether he had been killed. His son, Clément Dassa, notes that the "Metro was an obvious target. It was an American theater."[101] The Miami Theatre across the street was scorched next, while

Fox's Cairo Palace was also burned and damaged in the melee.[102] "The afternoon and night of horror saw gangs quickly speeding from one establishment to another with benzine, burning cinema houses, department stores and business houses including both British-owned and American establishments and others in several parts of the city," a United Press report noted at the time. Protesters, the UP added, "began in the morning by setting fire to two movie houses in the heart of Cairo. They spread from there to nearby Shepherd's Hotel, the 'monument to British Imperialism,' and turned it into a sheet of flames.... The Cairo fire brigade was unable to cope with the fires—and with the arsonists who sometimes obstructed them—and by evening most of the city's leading movie theatres and restaurants were damaged." The U.S. Embassy sent an official protest to the Egyptian government about the destruction of U.S. property, including the Cinema Metro, and the rioting which had "endangered American lives."[103]

With anti-British sentiment at a fever pitch, the Rivoli Theatre charred, and numerous other British businesses also sacked, Rank executive Kenneth Winckles wrote to the British government asking whether it was finally time "to get out."[104] "The centre of Cairo," the British Embassy in Cairo wrote to the Foreign Office in London, "looks as though it has suffered from an incendiary air-raid or an artillery bombardment. Ruins and blackened shells are all that remain here," along with "the charred remains of offices, shops, cinemas, bars and depot.... As I have already reported, British interests—which were one of the main, though by no means the only, target—suffered severely.... Practically every one of these was a total loss." The British Embassy questioned the entire future of British investment in Egypt "and whether it is not better to work entirely through a local Egyptian agent under terms which will place upon him the entire (or at least a large part of the) risk of loss through such occurrences."[105]

The Cairo Fire was the subject of an extensive internal BFO "Committee of Enquiry into Riots in Cairo" that highlighted the indifference shown by the Cairo police. "When the Radio Cinema was first attacked," the report noted, "one or two policeman [sic] nearby made no attempt to prevent the crowd throwing bricks, and a lorry load of police passed through the mob without stopping." Meanwhile, "In the square opposite the Rivoli Cinema ... a large number of regular police were in the square but they took no action." Another witness observed Imam Bey, "the Assistant Commandant of the Cairo Police watching the first and the pillage of the rioters." A man asked a police officer watching the scene whether he intended to stop the crowd he replied, "Let the boys have their fun." Only the arrival of tear gas eventually dispersed the rioters. The same situation was reported at the Cairo Palace. After it was attacked, "a guard of one officer and four policemen did not impede the fire-raisers."[106]

The safety of certain nationalities was also privileged. A European member of the Rivoli Cinema staff arrived to search for the Rivoli's manager and his secretary but was "stopped by the mob." "The ring-leader asked whether they were Moslems and he replied that they were. This lie enabled him to continue his search." Other reports were even more troubling to the committee. "When an eye-witness of an incident asked the Police nearby why they were not taking action they replied they were angry with the British in the Canal Zone, that it was a 'good thing,' and there would soon be no British left in Egypt." One witness even reported that a policeman "was seen to give 6-inch sticks of what appeared to be gelignite to rioters."[107]

Meanwhile, following the rioting and looting, "considerable quantities of loot have already been found, much of which, it is stated confidentially, had been stolen by the Police."[108] The Army was also implicated by the committee. One journalist reported that the violence only "began to die down" after "jeeps loaded with soldiers patrolled the street with bayonets ready and cordoned off certain areas." Ahmad Husayn, Hollywood's nemesis since the 1930s and a prime suspect in the Rivoli Theatre attack, was immediately arrested by the Egyptian government and charged with "top responsibility" for the rioting.[109] A. H. King, of the BFO, pointed his finger elsewhere, though, based on "all reports, signed or anonymous, written or verbal," which convinced him that, instead of the socialists, "the Moslem Brothers were the perpetrators of the riots" who "acted with the connivance of the police and possibly also of the troops."[110]

Whoever was responsible was less material than the effects of the Cairo Fire, which were devastating to businesses across the city. Amany Aly Shawky writes that the riots "burned more than 300 shops down to the ground, and, after rebuilding, many boutiques never regained their former glamour."[111] Loew's had to decide, for the third time in less than eight years, if it would reopen the Cinema Metro. By early February, a Loew's spokesperson told *Daily Variety* that the cinema would indeed be repaired once more when "things cool down." The Metro's interior was covered by insurance, and Loew's hoped to recoup whatever was not protected by filing monetary damage claims against the Egyptian government.[112]

Maurice Dassa and the Company Law of 1947

In response to the growing tide of nationalism after the Cairo Fire, MGM reassigned their local general manager, Robert Schmitt, to Austria and placed Egyptian Maurice Dassa in charge of their enterprises as well as the lawsuit and renovations needed to reopen the cinema.[113] King Farouk's teetering government had far more serious issues to worry about than a few lawsuits by

American film exhibitors. In July 1952 the Free Officers movement, led by Gamal Abdel Nasser and Muhammed Naguib, overthrew Farouk in a coup d'état. Naguib subsequently became the first prime minister of Egypt, with Nasser taking a smaller role, for now, as minister of the interior.

In response, many American companies replaced their foreign employees with local Egyptians like Dassa. However, like many Egyptian Jews, Dassa was no longer regarded as an Egyptian citizen. Prior to 1947 the resident status of the Jewish employees in Hollywood's Egyptian offices had not posed much of a problem for MGM, Fox, and other foreign exhibitors and distributors, despite their second-class status. Two decades earlier, in 1929, Egypt's Jewish community (of roughly 75,000–80,000) had fallen under the government's new Nationality Law that categorized only indigenous Egyptian Jews as citizens. According to Joel Beinin, this automatically excluded the 30,000 Jews who had obtained foreign citizenship prior to this new law—often dating back to the Ottoman Empire's rule—and rendered an additional 40,000 Jews in Egypt stateless residents of a country that no longer considered them Egyptian. While many Jews applied for citizenship during the 1930s and 1940s, Beinin writes, "despite the nominally liberal language of the law, their applications were often subjected to bureaucratic delay and rejection."[114]

In 1947 the situation grew more dire as the country's growing nationalism spurred the creation of the new Company Law that required businesses operating in Egypt "to employ fixed quotas of Egyptians."[115] The law, Beinin writes,

> required 75 percent of all salaried employees, 90 percent of all workers, and 51 percent of the paid-up capital of joint stock companies be Egyptian. To monitor compliance, firms were required to submit lists of their employees stating their nationalities and salaries. They were thus forced to answer the question: "Who is an Egyptian?" There can be no unequivocal, transhistorical answer to such a question. Both the question and its answer are historically and socially constructed cultural categories.[116]

The effect of the law immediately constrained the number of Jews that could be employed by companies like MGM, and until the creation of this new law, "those who did not travel abroad had no need for a certificate of citizenship and rarely bothered to obtain it"—especially given the difficulty of having it approved or even reviewed by officials.[117] As a result of the Company Law's implementation, though, numerous Jews lost their jobs. After the creation of the State of Israel the following year, Egyptian Jews were also subject to the "occasional sequestration" of their property.[118] For those who remained employed as stateless Jewish residents of Egypt, not citizens, their ability to work was even more constrained.

The law also had an impact on Maurice Dassa, as he was unable to travel outside of Egypt to fulfill his position managing all of MGM's Middle Eastern territory (besides Israel) due to the lack of a passport, which was unobtainable due to his lack of citizenship. His son, Clément, notes that MGM then paid one of Egypt's "top lawyers" to sue the Egyptian government. Dassa notes that by the late 1940s, his family had been in Egypt for six to eight generations but was still denied the right to be deemed "Egyptian." The case went before a judge who "had studied in England" and "was very modern." According to Dassa, the judge scolded the government's lawyers saying, "can you prove for 200 years that you are here and Mr. Dassa has just shown us pictures of his ancestors buried in Cairo and Alexandria." That is how, Dassa notes, his father "got his citizenship thanks to Metro-Goldwyn-Mayer. Otherwise he could not have gotten it. I became an Egyptian citizen this way otherwise most Jews were stateless."[119]

Following the lawsuit, Dassa oversaw MGM sales and marketing in Iran, Iraq, Lebanon, Syria, Egypt, Sudan, Ethiopia, and many other African countries. Dassa also traveled to Turkey and Cyprus on behalf of MGM and to global MGM sales conventions. In Egypt he oversaw the company's operations throughout the country, from distribution to marketing and to the operation

FIGURE 13.1 Maurice Dassa (left), head of MGM Egypt, and Minister of State Anwar Sadat (seated, right), decades before Sadat became president of Egypt. (Courtesy of Clément Dassa)

of MGM's shop window cinemas in Cairo and Alexandria. He also worked with Egypt's official censorship office in the 1950s, sitting with censors negotiating cuts to MGM movies. Dassa always "order[ed] kebab and whiskey and coca cola to feed [them] in the private theater in the office." Dassa's plan was to make censorship officials distracted by all the food and drink and thus let more of the film remain intact.[120]

Out of the (Cairo) Fire

Twentieth Century-Fox also continued to operate in Egypt after the Cairo Fire and, despite the tremendous political upheaval in the country, managed to open a new cinema, the 1,250-seat Amir, in Alexandria in July 1952. *The 1952 Theatre Catalog* observed that the Amir "mark[ed] a new high in theatre luxury" and continued the Hollywood shop window model of architectural, cultural, and stylistic hybridity, blending American technology and opulence with local aesthetics. Abiding by a law that required that all advertising in a foreign language be duplicated in Arabic in "comparable size and elevation," the Amir's soaring vertical sign was emblazoned with the words "Amir" in both Arabic and English.[121] (The growing anti-Western sentiment in Egypt is likely the reason why the cinema was renamed from its original British/American-sounding Alex Cinema (for Alexandria)—as it appeared in John and Drew Eberson's original architectural plans completed in August 1950—to the Amir Cinema as it opened in 1952.[122]) The cosmopolitan nature of the Amir's façade was reflected, quite literally, in its composition of German granite, Belgian marble side units, and an Italian artificial stone centerpiece. Sure to offend Ahmad Husayn, the Amir featured four lavishly appointed lounges, including a main lounge that served gallons of booze as a "swank cafe complete with cocktail bar, tables, and booths." For the Amir's younger patrons, the Amir offered a selection of candy and soda.[123]

Back in Cairo, the Cinema Metro finally reopened on December 3 after a $300,000 renovation with a well-publicized ribbon cutting by Prime Minister Naguib at the Egyptian premiere of *Quo Vadis?* The renovated Metro now seated 1,600 patrons and featured all new air-conditioning, sound, and projection equipment. Maurice Dassa oversaw the reconstruction of the Cinema Metro alongside theater manager Gustave Zelnick.[124] Rather than appropriating the look of Loew's cinemas in the U.S. with an added Egyptian patina, the theater was redesigned with "samples of African masks and shields with some wild animals in the background," according to Samir Raafat. "The re-opening was staged so that a feeling of everything was business as usual even though the monarchy had been displaced by the Free Officers Movement. . . . It was therefore a smiling Naguib and a retinue of officers who showed up at the

Metro's re-launch."[125] Their appearance was symbolic of a continued cooperation between the new Egyptian government and American businesses and a signal that the theater was, for now, safe for audiences to reenter.[126] Annabel Wharton notes that the new Egyptian government was anxious to return to business as usual and "desperate to attract hard currency." These western edifices, she writes, "monumentalized Egypt's ambition to acquire international political status through modernization." The American-managed Nile Hilton, like the reborn Cinema Metro, "not only displayed modernity to the public, but also presented itself as a stage for the display of local and international elites to one another."[127] The diplomatic two-step of Cairo's Nile Hilton and Cine Metro converged in 1955 as Robert Taylor and Eleanor Parker were both flown to Cairo for the premiere of *Valley of the Kings* at the Metro, which Samir Raafat writes, "coincided with the festive events that followed the groundbreaking ceremony of the Nile Hilton Hotel on Tahrir Square. It was on that occasion that Samia Gamal dragged Robert Taylor onto center stage where the American superstar, wearing a tarboush and belted the traditional way, danced with Egypt's foremost belly dancer before an enthralled audience."[128] Donald A. Robb, who had worked as a unit manager on *Samson and Delilah*, wrote to Cecil B. DeMille that Prime Minister Naguib and his government were, like the former King Farouk, highly supportive of foreign investment in Egypt and, specifically, American dollars.[129]

The outward appearance may have been hospitable for foreign investment, but the ongoing conflict with Israel made life for Egypt's Jewish actors, producers, exhibitors, and everyday residents/citizens increasingly difficult. Togo Mizrahi, one of Egypt's most prominent film producers and a Jew, fled to Rome where he remained for the rest of his life.[130]

More Egyptian Cinemas for Hollywood

Despite the ongoing internal conflicts in Egypt, Twentieth Century-Fox planned to open two more cinemas in Cairo and Alexandria to add to its portfolio alongside its Cairo Palace and Amir Cinema.[131] Loew's also began exploring opportunities to build new drive-in cinemas in Egypt, as the country remained stable for now and, once again, open for foreign investment.[132] Egypt's decision to remove itself from the Arab League's "Boycotting Bureau Against Israel" initiative in 1954—which conducted a study of MGM, Columbia, Universal, and Paramount to "establish the number of Jews employed" by each company as well as whether their "principles" were "Christian or Jewish"—may have further assuaged American concerns over making additional investments in Egypt. Officials from Lebanon, Syria, and Jordan, by contrast, sent "letters and questionnaires" to U.S. film companies to fill out.

"Clear implication," *Variety* commented, "is that, if any of the distribs are found objectionable in any respect to the Arab League, their pix will be boycotted."[133]

These kinds of expansion plans were put on hiatus once again in October 1956 after British, French, and Israeli forces jointly attacked Egypt in an effort to gain control over the Suez Canal and overthrow President Nasser. Fighting between Egypt and the British and French lasted only a few weeks, but Israel maintained control of the Sinai for almost a year. "The war, which led to a surge of arrests, internments, and deportations," Robert Vitalis writes, "also licensed the stepped-up stereotypes of Jewish control of the film industry."[134] As a result, Egyptian customs officials blocked shipments of Paramount films until the company was free from "Jewish Associations," while MGM was also asked to declare that the company was "free" from "Jewish connections."[135] "Jewish film company personnel in Egypt," *Variety* reported "have been forced to leave as part of the general Egyptian crackdown."[136] (Dassa was no longer running MGM by then, having died tragically in July 1955 at the age of forty.[137]) *Variety* also noted that after banning British and French films, "the Cairo government" was "actively checking on the 'racial' background of performers appearing in Hollywood pictures," while "American firms also are supposed to be submitting affidavits on whether they have directors of Jewish ancestry on their boards."[138] Meanwhile, numerous Jewish-owned (as well as French- and British-owned) businesses were confiscated by the state. The Red Cross helped six thousand Jews emigrate from Egypt using funds raised by the UJA, one of many charities Fox's Spyros Skouras had long backed.[139]

In Cairo both the Jewish manager and assistant manager of the Cinema Metro, who had Tunisian and Spanish passports, respectively, approached the U.S. Embassy in Cairo about the possibility that they would be deported because of their religion. Because of the precariousness of their work and of the American enterprise in Egypt altogether, the Cinema Metro management "REQUESTED PERMISSION [to] DEPOSIT WITH EMBASSY COPIES [of] ACCOUNTING RECORDS," which the embassy agreed to hold for MGM "PROVIDED NO RESPONSIBILITY INVOLVED."[140] U.S. Embassy staff alerted the U.S. State Department in December 1956 to the local "DISCRIMINATION AGAINST JEWISH REPRESENTATIVES" in the film industry. The situation grew grave enough that "some of the local representatives are consulting with their home offices about closing out the Cairo offices as area distributors and making them into local distribution agencies only. At least three are said to have such plans afoot, placing the principal office in Beirut or elsewhere."[141] The measures were accompanied by Nasser's larger efforts to force the Egyptian Jewish community to leave en masse. "Being brought up within the Jewish community in 1936," when he lived among the Jews of the old Jewish alley (Harat El-Yahud), "didn't stop him from forcing the Jews out of [the] country from 1956 to 1967, on a 'Never to return' agreement," Youssef Darwish and Jack Husan write.[142] An Egyptian citizen, Hagg Assad, recalled that "Abdel Nasser forced the Jews of the alley out of the country, allowing each family 20 Egyptian pounds only at the time, while leaving their assets and businesses behind."[143] Within the next decade, Farah Montasser writes in *Al Ahram*, "most Jewish schools and synagogues were forcefully shut down and their private businesses were nationalised."[144]

With these conditions in mind, Skouras changed the ethnic and religious composition of Fox's Cairo office. U.S. Embassy staff wrote to the State Department that Fox's "Distribution and cinema interests in Egypt [would now] be turned over to an Egyptian (Moslem) national"—Fathi Ibrahim—"who the company believes is qualified to manage the local activity."[145] Walter Wanger would later write of Ibrahim, who would play a crucial role for Fox throughout the next decade: "Colorful and influential, Fathi speaks perfect English and handles himself like a character actor in a play. He is smooth, understanding, and able to get things done in a quiet way—but it must be his way. He is also very good on social contacts."[146] Fox had $1.5 million in assets in Egypt by 1956, including "$300,000 in remittances not approved, the Amir Cinema building constructed at a cost of $600,000, leasehold ground rental for 37 more years on the Amir Cinema property due at about $5,000 per year, cinema rental for the Cairo Palace about 13–14 years on a guaranteed minimum, and stocks of undistributed film, [worth] about $300,000."[147] Ibrahim's first charge was to secure all of these assets and then keep both the office and the lines of communication with the Egyptian government open and functioning.

The Egyptian government had another conflict with U.S. and British firms. After the 1956 Suez crisis, the U.S. and British governments had frozen all Egyptian assets in their respective countries. In response, the Egyptian government had refused to grant any import licenses for Fox, MGM, or any other U.S. film company, thus choking the supply for the Cinema Metro and the Cairo Palace at the border. Fox's new film man, Fathi Ibrahim, successfully persuaded Egyptian authorities to let Hollywood films reenter the country. From then on, Ibrahim served as the principal point person for Hollywood and the Motion Picture Association of America's relationship with the Egyptian government. The global import license for Fox and other U.S. film companies were all signed in his name due to his relationship with local gatekeepers.[148]

In addition, despite all of the troubles for Hollywood executives in Egypt due to their so-called Jewish associations, the anti-British and anti-French sentiments of the moment tipped the scales in favor of Hollywood, not British or French films, regardless of their ethnic origin. According to a U.S. State Department report, no French films were screened in Egypt between 1954 and 1956, almost no Australian pictures were being shown, and only about ten

British films were receiving distribution there per year.[149] As Samir Raafat writes, "The 1950s were good times for Cairo film audiences," with "popular Friday and Sunday matinees and Xmas day cartoon shows sponsored by the Progres Egyptien when door prizes were given out and when costumed Tom and Jerry look-alikes greeted wide eyed preteens and toddlers as they walked in clinging to an assortment of multilingual nannies." Gamal Abdel Nasser was once again among the many loyal patrons of the Cinema Metro. According to Raafat, Nasser "had a preference for Marilyn Monroe" and Kazan's *Viva Zapata*, reportedly watching it "over and over again."[150] Of Fox's Amir in Alexandria, one moviegoer recalled a sumptuous setting that ignored the tumult of the era: "For two piasters again, you could sit, in the first row, in the far right side and watch a Cinemascope movie, wonderfully distorted," a former patron recalled half a century later.

> The movies were subtitled in Arabic and French. We saw Sinbad with the skeletons there. I will never forget their size and the distortion from our seats. I think 14 piaster seats were the most expensive. You would get a newsreel, a short and a cartoon. Intermission with candy sellers in the aisles and then the movie. Each movie before it started had some kind of Egyptian government declaration. I remember the key number was the weight, the number of kilos the movie weighed. That told you the length. I remember Lawrence of Arabia, when the kilos were declared, there were gasps in the theater in unison. Fourteen piasters and all those kilos of movies.[151]

Hollywood's films and its cinemas were also—quite ironically—boosted by the Nasser Revolutionary government's decision to place the Egyptian film industry under the Ministry of National Guidance in 1957, the first step in the industry's eventual nationalization.[152] This ultimately depressed foreign and domestic investment in Egyptian production and encouraged audience fidelity to the consistency of the more well-funded Hollywood films.

CHAPTER 14

AFTER THE REVOLUTION, 1957–1982

Twentieth Century-Fox, Egypt, and Israel

While the attacks and instability in Egypt had the effect of spurring Hollywood's continued interest in Israel, developing its exhibition presence there posed challenges of its own. In mid-1952, as just one example, nearly all cinema construction had ceased as "building materials and labor costs skyrocketed."[1] The sudden economic inflation in Israel spooked Fox executives, who immediately suspended their construction plans on the company's first shop window cinema in Tel Aviv. At the same time, the Israeli Treasury's decision to raise the import and income taxes paid by U.S. film companies prompted Fox and other U.S. distributors to stop their films from clearing Israeli Customs. By early February 1953 almost one hundred American films had already piled up at the Haifa port, and U.S. distributors threatened to send all of their fallow prints back to the United States—permanently. Finally, David Shalit writes, a U.S. representative flew to Israel, where the Israeli Treasury agreed to lower some of the increased taxes, thereby ending the stand-off.[2] The turmoil had a very negative impact on cinema construction, with Twentieth Century-Fox's local representative, Simcha Greenvald, forced to petition the Tel Aviv Municipality Construction Department to extend Fox's construction permit for yet another year.[3]

These frustrations did little to dampen Spyros Skouras's overall enthusiasm for the country, however. Over the next few years, he continued his active involvement in supporting the growth of the state by serving, along with Barney Balaban, Harry Warner, and Walter White (president of the National Association for the Advancement of Colored People), as national co-chairs of the "Bonds of Israel" campaign.⁴ In 1953 Skouras also served as "honorary chairman of the dinner concert" at the Waldorf-Astoria, with proceeds donated to the American Fund for Israel Institutions.⁵ Skouras was honored again at a United Jewish Appeal luncheon in 1954 and was the guest of honor at the 1955 annual American Fund dinner "in recognition of his work in behalf of cultural institutions."⁶ Skouras told the crowd that he hoped to lobby the U.S. government to promote a permanent peace between Arabs and Jews in the Middle East and to secure the country's politics toward democracy and away from communism.⁷

Skouras, like many of the heads of the U.S. film industry, was an ardent anticommunist, and he saw the expansion of U.S.-operated cinemas in the new socialist nation of Israel as part of a larger struggle against the Soviet Union's geopolitical (out)reach. For the U.S. State Department, the hearts and minds of the Israeli public were up for grabs, especially given the sizable number of communists who had immigrated there before and after 1948. These Cold War tensions played out in Israel's cinemas, which communist activists frequently targeted as sites of political protest.⁸ In 1950, for instance, twenty "Red agitators" broke up a screening of the United States Information Service documentary *The UN Aids Korea* at the Orion Theatre in Tel Aviv by rushing the screen, shouting at the audience, and throwing anti-UN leaflets denouncing Israel's cooperation in the Korean War.⁹ A week later, "communist sympathizers" tore up the screen of the Mograbi Theatre in Tel Aviv to protest the exhibition of U.S. newsreels.¹⁰ At the time 20 percent of all films playing in Israel were Russian-language productions for the large Russian-speaking population.¹¹ Israeli authorities were also reluctant to approve anticommunist films for public screenings, banning the 1949 MGM releases of *Conspirator* and *The Red Danube*.¹²

Skouras spoke often about Israel serving as a key Middle Eastern beachhead for U.S. cinema and ideology. "From this standpoint," he told *Variety* in 1953,

> it is a Twentieth Century-Fox solemn responsibility . . . to increase motion picture outlets throughout the free world because . . . no medium can play a greater part than the motion picture in indoctrinating people into the free way of life and instilling in them a compelling desire for freedom and hope for a brighter future. Therefore, we as an industry can play an infinitely important part in the worldwide ideological struggle for the minds of men and confound the Communist propagandists.¹³

The following year, Murray Silverstone told *Variety* that his company considered the Middle East "the turning point of civilization" and "intended to back it heavily." Fox planned to build or acquire a total of ten cinemas in the region.[14] (In the years to come, especially as the relationship between the Egyptian government and the Soviet Union grew closer, Egypt also became an ideological battleground waged in part through cinema and cinema theaters with Soviet officials, like Ufa two decades earlier, approaching cinemas like the Miami Theatre in Cairo and the Royal Cinema in Alexandria with offers to purchase or lease them exclusively for Soviet films.[15] This followed a decade in which the Soviets had been dubbing their films into Arabic to attract local audiences.[16])

Exhibition in Israel in the 1950s was often just as complicated as it was in Egypt's largest cinemas. Skouras's "personal intervention" was required, for example, in order to encourage the Israeli censors to drop their objections to its first CinemaScope film, *The Robe* (1953), which had been stymied by "a small but vocal Orthodox group in Israel which objected to the CinemaScope pic on religious grounds."[17] With the recent influx of what Herb Golden wrote in *Variety* was a "less-educated class from Europe, North Africa and semi-Oriental countries," the need for multiple subtitles had also grown. "There isn't just one set of subtitles translating the dialog but as many as five."[18] Hollywood films also had strong competition for Israeli audiences due to ongoing and considerable influx of European refugees and thousands of others now fleeing Middle Eastern and North African countries as a result of the Arab-Israeli conflict and the subsequent rise in antisemitism throughout both regions. "European product is giving the Hollywood imports a run for their money in Israeli theatres," Norman Lourie reported to *Variety*.[19] Egyptian films also found very willing audiences in Israel from Egyptian and other Arabic-speaking Jews who had recently arrived there. With linguistic, religious, cultural, and economic challenges, Israel was not the easy setting for foreign investment that many in Hollywood had hoped for during the late 1940s and early 1950s, for film production, distribution, or exhibition.

As part of the global expansion plans announced in 1954, Twentieth Century-Fox recommitted to building cinemas in Israel. Fox planned once again to build or acquire a total of ten cinemas in the region, including new "showcases for Tel-Aviv, Jerusalem and Haifa."[20] Once again, there were new stumbling blocks. In February 1955 Teddy Kollek, director general of the Prime Minister's Office, had to write to Pinchas Sapir, minister of trade and labor, demanding that the Israeli government keep the promises that David Horowitz had made to Simcha Greenvald "on the basis of the generous loan which Fox gave to the [Israeli] Treasury." Kollek, David Shalit writes, also "emphasized the help and the special attitude which Fox reached out to Israel."[21] Five months later, in July 1955, six years after Fox's Pinsker Street land purchase and four years after the Ebersons and George Koigen first drew up plans for Fox's Tel Aviv cinema, Skouras and Silverstone finally received approval from the director of the Ministry of Finance to begin building the cinema under the

1950 Law for Encouragement of Capital Investments. Fox also received approval for the right to repatriate foreign currency that had been stuck in Israel for the past six years and approval to import supplies that had stalled construction.[22]

Building the Cinema Tel Aviv

By September 1955 there were eleven new cinemas either under construction or in the planning stage in Israel. "Leading the field," the *Jerusalem Post* noted, was "the 2,000-seat luxury house that 20th-century [sic] Fox recently started building." The *Post* noted that, like other Fox houses overseas, the cinema would be "fitted with all the latest American installations, including a giant 20-metre wide screen" that was, *Motion Picture Herald* noted, "especially designed for CinemaScope films."[23] The construction firm of Walberg and Udassim estimated that the theater would take eighteen months to complete.[24] (Two years later it would still be under construction.) In April 1956 a cornerstone was laid for the Fox cinema in a ceremony attended by Murray Silverstone, numerous Fox international executives, Tel Aviv's mayor, and an U.S. government attaché.[25] In January 1957 advertisements for office space in the "Fox Theatre Building" began appearing in local newspapers luring potential lessees with "modern conveniences" and a "Swiss elevator." Fulfilling the desires for medical offices in the country, the Fox Theatre Building ads—emblazoned with the Twentieth Century-Fox logo—noted that "interior walls can be adapted to individual requirements" and were "also suitable for physicians."[26]

By then, the continued growth of the Israeli exhibition market had boosted local profits, with fourteen cinemas under construction in Israel that year, including Twentieth Century-Fox's new cinema. "The new Fox theatre has been causing a tremendous amount of excitement and comment in Israeli theatre circles," Nadia Lourie wrote on behalf of the Israel Film Bureau, noting that the elaborate cinema would soon be the largest, "most luxurious," "most artistic and elaborate theatre ever built in Israel."[27] (The theater had also received a large advertising campaign in the coverage of its construction, David Shalit writes, through "document[ing] the process of the Tel-Aviv cinema building" for local newsreels.[28]) The cinema eschewed the wood chairs and bare floors found in other Israeli cinemas, installing two thousand upholstered seats and plush carpeting throughout. It also boasted a deluxe lounge, uniformed ushers, the largest CinemaScope screen in Israel, stereophonic sound with twenty-eight amplifiers, public telephone booths, dressing rooms for wardrobe and makeup, and, like other shop window cinemas, the nation's first air-conditioned movie house. A Fox spokesman told Lourie that with all of these modern luxuries, even "primitive" people would "behave properly in pleasant surroundings if given the opportunity."[29]

To ensure the cinema provided top-notch projection and sound and that its aesthetic qualities mirrored that of other Fox cinemas of the period, Silverstone sent Fox's head building engineer to Tel Aviv.[30] David Idzal, who had until recently managed the five-thousand-seat Fox Theatre in Detroit, was also sent to Tel Aviv more than three months before the opening of the theater to oversee its final construction and to introduce "American theatre management methods in Israel." These included the installation of those two thousand American Seating Company chairs and "all the American comforts in the new theater—including hand-driers which [were] hitherto unknown here." Idzal also began "training a staff in American ways of ushering," a job complicated by the oversight of Histadrut, the Israel Federation of Labor, which controlled the hiring and firing of staff and insisted that all of Idzal's employees be between thirty-five and forty years old, escalating their labor costs and diminishing the cinema's overall profitability.[31]

A more significant change had come to Fox's Tel Aviv cinema. As early as January 1950, *Maariv* had noted that all of the Israeli Fox cinemas would be named after the company and called "20th Century Fox'" (or perhaps like its Johannesburg shop window, "20th Century").[32] Seven years later, however, with the Arab League boycott of Israel ongoing and Fox's growing concerns about its larger business in the Middle East, *Maariv* reported on "the boycott fear" now worrying Skouras and Silverstone. The newspaper reported that Fox "tried to do everything in order to hide" the fact that the cinema was built and belonged to the American company, including changing the cinema's name from Fox to the Cinema Tel Aviv. "The American movie company hinted that the cinema building in Israel may lead to boycott on their movies by the Arab countries," the newspaper wrote in October 1957. "Therefore, it was declared officially that [the] 'P.B.G' Company, a private American building and investments company, is the one which built the most magnificent and modern cinema in the middle east. After an investigation, the 'secret' of these initials was discovered. Their meaning is simple almost as the 'Columbus Egg'—Pinsker, Beilinson, Gikson, the names of the 3 Tel-Aviv streets [at] the location of 'Tel-Aviv' cinema."[33] The *Jerusalem Post*, whose English-language readership extended well beyond the country's borders, however, was happy to aid and abet the American company's charade, reporting that "the 2,000-seat theatre was built by an American firm called B.P.G. Inc.," which had "invested IL2.5m. [2.5 million shekels] in the enterprise."[34]

The fear of boycott was certainly valid. Curt Strand, former president of Hilton International, recalls that the company's hotels in Tel Aviv and Jerusalem came under immense pressure. "We were threatened by governments of various Arab countries, including Egypt, that we would lose our agreements with these hotels and we must abide by the Arab contract." Conrad Hilton appealed directly to the Arab Boycott Committee that their demand that Hilton pull out of Israel was "absolutely counter to the principles we live by.... As Americans, we consider Arabs and Jews our friends and hope ultimately we can all live in peace with one another." He would later remind the committee that "there was no threat from Israel when we opened our hotel in Cairo."[35]

The gala premiere of the Cinema Tel Aviv—now officially stripped of its Fox imprimatur—took place on October 26, 1957. The opening was a benefit screening for the Israel Infantile Paralysis Fund and featured a blend of entertainment and nationalism with the Israeli anthem performed by the Zodikoff Choir of the Tel Aviv Labour Council, a dedication by the mayor, appearances by visiting stars, and a U.S.-made film titled *Ten Years of Achievements* "Depicting Important Milestones in the History of the State of Israel."[36] The inaugural program noted that films would come direct "from the studios of Twentieth Century-Fox" and "this great organization's world-acclaimed motion pictures."[37] To the "people of Tel-Aviv," the program added, "I am your new cinema; my existence will be dedicated to your pleasure. I will project movies to you on new dimensions—CinemaScope—and I will play exceptional and sophisticated sounds of High Fidelity for you to hear."[38] The "elegantly dressed audience" at the premiere included members of the Israeli diplomatic corps, the Israeli attorney general, and other notable figures.

FIGURE 14.1 Postcard of the Cinema Tel Aviv, stripped of its Fox moniker. (Author's collection)

The presentation of *Ten Years of Achievement* and the evening had been dramatically choreographed for maximum effect: "When everyone had taken his plush seat in the magnificent auditorium," the *Jerusalem Post* reported, "the curtain rose slowly and out of a purple glow a voice welled up to promise that the cinema would be devoted only to good films. The audience [then] rose to its feet to sing Hatikva," the Israeli national anthem.[39]

An advertisement for the Cinema Tel Aviv in the *Jerusalem Post* noted that its opening had forged "A New Era in Motion Picture Entertainment" that was "'Made to Measure' For Your Pleasure" with "Perfect Vision," "Cushioned Seats" and "Modern Refreshment Bars."[40] Audiences watched *An Affair to Remember* on the cinema's sixty-five- by twenty-five-foot lenticular Cinema-Scope screen and heard Cary Grant and Deborah Kerr romance each other through twenty-eight loudspeakers installed in the auditorium.[41] The *Post* review of the cinema's premiere week, alluding to the technical issues of other local cinemas of the era, noted "how agreeable it is to go to a cinema where every word spoken can be clearly heard and even the long-legged can sit in comfort!"[42] The *New York Times* dubbed the Cinema Tel Aviv the "largest, most resplendent movie house in the Middle East, which returning travelers contend makes Radio City Music Hall look old-fashioned."[43] It was, journalist Uri Klein recalled,

> Broadway on Pinsker [Street]. . . . People flocked to the Tel Aviv cinema just to see the movie house. They wanted to feel the carpet beneath their feet and to see the pleated curtain, which as it rose to expose the large screen, changed colors, thanks to what at the time were sophisticated lighting effects. The cinema's exterior was also impressive, decorated with colorful mosaics, with the title of the current movie encased in a frame of shining bulbs. We felt as though Pinsker was indeed Broadway.[44]

The cinema "gave the people in Tel-Aviv (then not such an Americanized modern city as it is today) the feeling that this theatre was an actual part of America," a former moviegoer recalls of the cinema's role as an American cultural embassy. "During it's [sic] glory days it showed famous Fox movies such as 'Cleopatra,' 'The Sound of Music,' [and] 'Hello Dolly.' . . . In 1977 it was also the place where 'Star Wars' opened in Israel."[45] "It was the biggest in the city with the best sound and the biggest screen," city engineer Yisrael Godowicz recalled decades later.[46]

Fox manager David Idzal stayed on after the opening to oversee the staff and "to arrange for the exclusive use of Twentieth Century-Fox films." Idzal's placement in Tel Aviv was also to oversee the construction of additional cinemas in Israel for Fox, a task that demonstrated that the company was still dedicated to opening cinemas in Haifa, Jerusalem, and other cities. Journalist

Philip Slomovitz noted, "It may take another five years before Israel will have television" and, thus, "the movie theater therefore is the major attraction for entertainment-hungry people."[47]

Still, despite the optimism surrounding the opening of the Cinema Tel Aviv, labor and tax issues remained evergreen problems. Even before the cinema opened, its management had to contend with the need for cuts to feature films as the nation's ushers' union began demanding double pay for every minute past two hours in which their members worked.[48] And only half a year after the opening of Fox's newest shop window, the owners of Israel's 190 cinemas closed all of the country's cinemas in protest of the exorbitant taxation rate that was estimated to be 129 percent of the original ticket price. This, the *Jewish Telegraphic Agency* wrote, "drastically trimmed movie attendance" and "left Israelis bereft of their most popular form of entertainment." Exhibitors asserted that the socialist government's national and local taxes were robbing them of patrons. To protest, exhibitors promised that all cinemas would remain closed "until there was a 'considerable reduction' in taxes."[49] Fox had waited almost a decade to open a cinema in Israel. In less than a year, the lights were already out on Pinsker Street.

TV and Personal Contracts Aiding Theater Development in Egypt

Egypt, with its multiple American-owned cinemas, thus remained an easier place for real estate investment. There were other opportunities there as well. In May 1960, at the same time that Skouras and Fathi Ibrahim were negotiating to secure television sets for the United Arab Republic (UAR)—the new political union between Egypt and Syria—Fox became the distributor for all television programming in the UAR.[50] Ibrahim told Skouras that this would have a key benefit in that it would improve Fox Television's international standing with other Middle Eastern television stations, who were desperate for content, and would improve the sale of local and foreign films (including Fox TV and films) to the region's burgeoning television stations. Following the deal, Ibrahim conducted meetings with TV executives from Lebanon, Iran, and Iraq in Cairo (during their visit to see Minister Hatem) to cement relationships with television stations in those countries as well.[51] Fox was now earning a 30 percent commission for the licensing of French and German product to UAR TV, for example. Once licensed for UAR TV (with broadcasting in Egypt, Sudan, and Syria), the same material was easily licensed again to TV stations in Lebanon and Iraq with plans to expand its distribution to countries not yet set up for national broadcasting.[52] By the end of 1960, business in the UAR was important enough to the international film department, headed by Silverstone, that Skouras asked Ibrahim to send weekly reports on television activities as he had been doing on their local film distribution and exhibition businesses.[53]

Why did Twentieth Century-Fox get such favorable positions in the Egyptian film and TV market despite the growing anti-Western sentiment of Nasser and his increasingly cozy relationship with the Soviet Union? According to U.S. State Department memoranda, Skouras was now quietly working on behalf of the UAR government to secure enormous loans from the U.S. government and private banks as well as the flow of Egyptian exports to the United States.[54] Skouras cultivated this relationship with Nasser during the 1960s through gifts and letters of praise for his leadership.[55] Then, in 1961, Nasser fully nationalized the Egyptian film industry. Egyptian director Yousef Shaheen would later argue that Nasser "wrecked the industry" by putting "soldiers in charge of the studios as managers" who "didn't know anything."[56] The nationalization turned out to be a boon to the Hollywood cinemas and distributors operating in Egypt who were exempt from nationalization and allowed to operate unfettered. With the quality and ideological variety diminishing in Egyptian cinema, American films became even more popular.[57]

Due to their increasingly close ties to the Egyptian government, in 1961, Fox executives plotted an expansion of their film business in Egypt. Skouras and Silverstone planned to open a new drive-in theater in the outskirts of Cairo that would include space for 1,400 cars as well as a restaurant, bar, playground, and swimming pool. The company received a sweetheart deal from the Egyptian government in which it would buy the land at cost and then build a new drive-in. The Egyptian government also planned to build, at its own expense, five hard-top theaters in Cairo and Alexandria, including three with an adjoining open-air theater, all of which would be co-owned by Twentieth Century-Fox and the Gaafar brothers. Like its previous deals with the Gaafars, Fox would have control over management and operations at all five cinemas. Two of those cinemas would have been quite large for the era—2,250 seats for a new Cairo cinema and 1,500 seats for a new Alexandria house. These cinemas were to be constructed by the Egyptian government and then leased to Fox for the next fifty years.[58]

The first open-air cinema under the agreement was sited in the center of Cairo, seated 1,600 patrons, and exclusively showed either Fox-produced films or films distributed by Twentieth Century-Fox. The films were either in their second run after premiering at the Cairo Palace or were second-rate films that would never play Fox's Cairo shop window. After meeting with Skouras in Egypt, the minister of municipality, Abou Nosseir, also turned over exhibition of the one-thousand-seat open-air Semiramis theater in Alexandria to Fox, and it reopened under Fox management in early August 1961. Ibrahim and Nosseir also signed an agreement for Fox to operate a three-thousand-seat cinema in the city of Suez.[59] Nosseir also began negotiations to have Fox operate cinemas in Tanta, Luxor, Damanhour, Zagazig, and Asswan. Like the others, the agreements required no investment from Fox or any upfront monthly costs. They were completely rent-free. Fox was thus given control over management, programming, and marketing of these theaters while the Fox films shown therein earned Fox 50 percent of the box office revenues as well as a 5 percent management fee.[60] Nosseir's offer was heartily approved by the Twentieth Century-Fox board in New York.[61] Egypt's nationalization was now becoming something of a golden opportunity for American film companies—especially Fox.

Adding to their growing number of cinemas in Egypt, Ibrahim also negotiated a deal with the Gaafar brothers whereby Twentieth Century-Fox would take over an existing air-conditioned cinema and an open-air cinema in Heliopolis that the Gaafars had been operating.[62] This deal was predicated on the Gaafars repaying a £50 thousand loan they owed Fox and with the guarantee that the cinema would play at least 50 percent Fox films.[63] Thus, in Egypt, Fox was constructing more complex arrangements for theatrical expansion that did not include sole or joint ownership or even lease agreements but joint investments that were predicated on other financial arrangements. Either way, they guaranteed increased distribution of Fox films and increased revenue from their further investment in Egyptian exhibition.[64]

Ibrahim also renewed Fox's lease of an unnamed roofless cinema (open air) for eight years.[65] With all of these new contracts inked in 1961, Ibrahim wrote to Skouras assuring him that the nationalization of the Egyptian film industry had had no negative impact on their cinemas or distribution operations in Egypt.[66] Meanwhile, Robert Vitalis adds,

> The nationalization of the production and exhibition segments of the Egyptian film industry in the early 1960s was by all accounts (save by those who looted this particular cash cow for a while) a mega-disaster. In the hands of bureaucrats, the studios racked up new enormous losses and production ground virtually to a standstill. Despite the rapid growth in population, the number of movie theaters in Egypt actually declined. This was clearly *not* the outcome that Yusuf Wahbi and the other studio owners had in mind when they began to lobby for government subsidies and protection in the late 1940s and more insistently after the July 1952 revolution.[67]

Rather than bolstering Egypt's proud national cinema industry and culture, Nasser constrained the growth of the Egyptian film industry through nationalization at the same time that he began handing Twentieth Century-Fox new cinemas and opportunities on a silver platter.

With the number of Egyptian Fox-operated and Fox-affiliated houses growing, Ibrahim looked east for even more opportunities. In 1961 he created exclusive booking arrangements with a first-run cinema in Lebanon, two cinemas in Syria, and another house in Iraq for all Fox releases. Although not owned, operated, or leased by Twentieth Century-Fox, these cinemas would become known in each city as the home of Twentieth Century-Fox films.[68]

Cleopatra, Elizabeth Taylor, and Twentieth Century-Fox

In addition to the benefits to Fox's distribution and exhibition operations in Egypt as well as its burgeoning television businesses there, Skouras and Ibrahim hoped their increasingly close relationship with Nasser and other Egyptian political figures would further the company's interests in shooting films in the UAR in the early 1960s.

None of those films were more important than *Cleopatra*, which, given its Egyptian subject matter, was already a delicate matter. More controversial, of course, was the decision to cast Elizabeth Taylor, now a convert to Judaism, as the Egyptian queen.[69] Taylor's films had been banned in Egypt due to her new religion, her visits to Israel, and her prodigious fundraising—she had personally bought $100,000 of Israel bonds in 1959, which "made waves in the Arab world"—forcing Skouras to appeal directly to Nasser in July 1960 in hopes of being able to shoot scenes in Egypt with Taylor.[70] "Skouras is incredible," *Cleopatra* producer Walter Wanger wrote, and "one of the most charming men in the world—when he wants to be. He seems to know everyone in the Egyptian government, and they love and respect him." From Wanger's perspective, this was in part because of what he promised to bring to Egypt. At a luncheon with Egyptian leaders, he announced that Fox would make five films in Egypt. "He made it sound as though—thanks to him—Egypt would soon rival Rome as a world film center."[71]

Still, Skouras was unable to secure approval for Taylor to shoot the film in Egypt, despite his relationship with Nasser and other Egyptian ministers due to the hatred—and fear of public backlash—for Elizabeth Taylor, who had made large contributions to (Jewish) Israeli charities. While Skouras could be forgiven by Nasser's circle for his own support of Israel, Taylor offered no entrée to the U.S. State Department or the global banking industry. She also infuriated Skouras (and Egyptian officials) when she told *Look* magazine that in filming *Cleopatra*, "It will be fun to be the first Jewish Queen of Egypt." Wanger noted, "The statement was annoying to the Egyptian government, which had promised us co-operation."[72] Reporter Lloyd Shearer noted in 1961 that, in an effort to placate Nasser, "who wasn't about to let Liz Taylor into Egypt because she's Jewish, Fox's Spyros Skouras ordered to Egypt at great expense most of the actresses under contract to the studio, including Julie Newmar, Barbara Eden, and Barbara Steel, to appear at the Sound Light Festival. (Marilyn

Monroe, who had also converted to Judaism in 1956 and had just divorced playwright Arthur Miller, did not respond to Skouras' request.)"[73] Egyptian reservations regarding Taylor continued unabated.

Negotiations for shooting any part of *Cleopatra* in Egypt remained intense, and Wanger complained in July 1962, two years into the film's beleaguered production, that there was "still no firm stand on Egypt. One day we are going to shoot there, commitments are made, schedules planned. The next day Egypt is called off and we are to shoot the battle sequences in Spain and/or the United States."[74] When the possibility of filming in Israel came up, Skouras, according to biographer Carlo Curti, responded, "The Egyptian army will declare war on already located Twentieth Century-Fox if the studio does any filming in Israel." Conti added, "The Egyptian government would not have given Skouras permission to film [in Egypt] if Israel had been a choice. Besides that, the Israelites were sensitive about having a film about Egypt shot in their land."[75] Approval to film parts of *Cleopatra* in Egypt was finally given in early July 1962, and the Egyptian government even offered to supply five thousand Egyptian army soldiers for the production. Taylor hoped to join the production in Egypt, but production manager Doc Merman, who spoke with local production personnel in Egypt, persuaded Wanger and Skouras to keep her away. Merman, Wanger writes, "was told that if she goes to Egypt there is a good chance she will be killed or there will be riots. . . . Merman is convinced it would be dangerous for her."[76] Gen. Essam Elmasri, head of the Cairo bureau of the Israel Boycott Office, also insisted that she would not be allowed to travel there in "accordance with the Arab League's ban on all persons aiding Israel" and specifically because she "supports Israeli causes."[77]

Skouras's failure to gain entry for Taylor did not reflect a lack of effort or a break with his Egyptian counterparts. Taylor was simply verboten due to her support for Israel. With this in mind, Robert C. Strong, director of the Office of Near Eastern Affairs, expressed to Assistant Secretary of State James P. Grant his amazement at Skouras's position with the Egyptian government and how active he was in Egyptian affairs despite having been "an advocate of the Israel cause." More impressive, and surprising for Strong, was Skouras's efforts in 1962 to secure a reported $250 million loan for the UAR through a "consortium of United States investment banks," with the U.S. State Department serving as guarantor. Skouras felt confident enough in his contacts with the U.S government and U.S. banks to have discussed the loan with UAR Economic Minister Kaissouni during the minister's May 1962 visit to the United States. Strong wrote to Grant:

> We can only speculate on the possible motivations for Mr. Skouras' involvement in this matter.
> They include the following:

(1) For boycott reasons, the UAR has denied Elizabeth Taylor and the Cleopatra crew permission to enter Egypt for thirty days of additional background shooting in order to complete the motion picture. Mr. Skouras may seek to have this prohibition set aside.

(2) Skouras is financially involved in a motion picture distribution organization in the UAR whose earnings are blocked from transfers outside of Egypt. He may seek to have these funds released. While transfers of motion picture earnings are arranged from time to time the terms and conditions are difficult.

(3) Skouras' son owns and operates a shipping line touching Mediterranean ports. Skouras may seek some advantage for his son's shipping interest.[78]

Strong told Grant that the U.S. government had now "authorized our Embassy in Cairo to open negotiations for an investment guaranty agreement."[79] As is evident through his work in Egypt, Israel, South Africa, and in many other countries during the mid-twentieth century, Spyros Skouras was not just a powerful mogul but an increasingly international political player, able to broker deals with and for governments and not just for studios and cinemas. It is not an understatement to suggest that his importance to the history of Hollywood has not been properly calculated.

By 1963, with the Egyptian economy faltering and its film industry waning even further, *Variety* reported that "Egypt, which once banned Jewish actors and refused to play certain American films, no longer is anti-Semitic." The Egyptian government, George Nader told the trade journal, was now "eager to attract American coproduction[s]," as there was no longer any "objection with regard to race, creed, color or religion for filming by American companies in Egypt." The change in Egyptian attitude was not cultural or political but entirely logistical: the local government, Nader noted, was "vitally interested in furthering the industry there." According to *Variety*, the only films still banned were those that were vehemently "anti-United Arab Republic."[80] The proclamation was too late to benefit Fox and the filming of *Cleopatra*. With one more troublesome stipulation seemingly retired, Skouras and Ibrahim began planning to open another Fox drive-in cinema in Egypt.[81]

Fox in Israel: A Last Stab at Expansion

In Israel, the early 1960s had also produced a bevy of activity for the company. Fox had not yet given up on the idea of building additional cinemas there. Despite the company's precarious finances and *Cleopatra*'s ballooning production costs, Skouras and Silverstone were still hellbent on theatrical expansion, disregarding the heady costs of building, operating, and maintaining another cinema like the Cinema Tel Aviv. And with their favorable deals with the Egyptian government in mind, Skouras and Silverstone were anxious to operate new cinemas without additional overhead.

Enter investors Charles Clore and Isaac Wolfson. Wolfson was a Scottish Jew who had risen from relative poverty in Glasgow to become the chairman of Great Universal Stores, the leading mail-order clothing firm in England which, in 1955, grew powerful enough to purchase the vaunted Burberry company (in time for its brand expansion and prominence during London's swinging sixties).[82] In 1956 Wolfson founded G.U.S.-Rassco and began investing in Israeli businesses and donating funds to Israeli social, cultural, and academic institutions. "The aim of this company," the *Jerusalem Post* reported, "is to invest in [local] industry, and thus help the industrial growth of Israel."[83] In 1960 Wolfson was working to spur economic development in Israel's chaotic system for foreign investment that had stymied Fox's interest in greater development there. Without capital of its own to invest in further cinema expansion in Israel—and perhaps weary of raising the ire of the Egyptian film industry and the growing film distribution center in nearby Beirut that actively boycotted Israel—Murray Silverstone began working with Wolfson to build cinemas for Twentieth Century-Fox in Haifa, Jerusalem, Natanya, and Beersheba. (The Wolfson family was no stranger to film exhibition. Isaac Wolfson's wife, Edith Specterman, was the daughter of British film exhibitor Ralph Specterman who had built cinemas around England.[84])

With Wolfson's finances, Fox could finally profit from its earlier land purchase in Haifa that had laid fallow for years and develop its plans for cinemas in Haifa, Jerusalem, Natanya, and Beersheba. Skouras and Wolfson crafted an agreement whereby Wolfson would purchase Fox's Haifa cinema site and build a cinema there as well as others for Fox in the aforementioned cities. Fox would then pay Wolfson an annual rent equal to 6 percent of the cost of the land and 10 percent of the cost of the building, thus reducing the need for Fox to outlay the full costs of these cinemas upfront during these lean times. The cinemas would be fully equipped, designed, and furnished by Wolfson, with Fox supplying only projection and sound equipment.[85] Wolfson, working with his G.U.S.-Rassco associate director Mordechai Stern, agreed in principle to the Fox proposal—though rental terms were deemed too low for Wolfson—with Haifa chosen to be the first location.[86]

Still, all of these moves in Egypt, Israel, and other countries were not enough to save Skouras's precarious position due to the huge cost overruns on the production of *Cleopatra* and other missteps. Darryl Zanuck was forced to accept early resignations and retirements of key executives as part of Fox's new "streamlining" project that followed an independent audit of its harrowing finances and multimillion-dollar losses. One of those retirements was Murray

Silverstone who, though scheduled to retire in December 1962, took an early exit that August.[87] The key figure behind Fox's international theater expansion was out. Skouras soon followed.[88] Zanuck and a bevy of executives like Seymour Poe took over Fox's international operations, but none of them had the Rolodex or the political clout of Spyros Skouras. The next twenty years were often about winding down Fox's foreign exhibition operations, not continuing to build it up.

During the mid-1960s, with the delayed rollout of television in Israel, moviegoing had flourished without interruption. Carl Alpert, writing in the *Southern Israelite*, claimed that, in 1967, "every adult Israeli over the age of 15 went to see a motion picture no less than 30 times during the year."[89] However, Alpert added, competition from television was finally sinking in with "a gradual but obvious fall off in attendance at picture shows. On nights when Israel, even in its limited format, offers a particularly good [television] program, the movie houses are almost empty. The people are staying home in droves."[90]

There was another reason for this decline. James Feron's *New York Times* article, "Bombs—a Hazard of Moviegoing," observed that Israel's cinemas were increasingly becoming "a favorite target of terrorists." Fatah's decision to target civilians after the 1967 Six-Day War included a time bomb under a seat in a Jerusalem cinema and another in a Tel Aviv cinema a few months later. Another was found outside a Jerusalem movie house during the summer of 1968.[91] Cinema bombings by the Palestine Liberation Organization continued through the 1970s. In December 1974, for example, a grenade attack at Tel Aviv's Chen cinema—not far from Fox's Cinema Tel Aviv—killed three patrons, including a British engineer, and injured sixty others. The attacker had purchased a ticket for another cinema, and when he went inside and found that the audience was too small, he left for Dizengoff Square where the Chen, Esther, and Cinema Tel Aviv were located. He bought another ticket for the Chen and, once inside, detonated several grenades.[92]

Terrorism was only one of the problems at the Cinema Tel Aviv. By 1975, after Fox and Warner Bros. had joined forces in distributing their films in the Israeli market and begun jointly managing the cinema, labor issues became disruptive enough in June 1975 that Fox considered selling the cinema outright. Tel Aviv's eight ushers demanded an immediate salary increase—what they dubbed a "violence bonus"—not from terrorists but from Israeli moviegoers who they claimed were "unruly patrons" that put them all in "constant danger of violence." Ephraim Gilad, general manager of Warner-Fox, "refused to negotiate" with the ushers, however, reminding them that any salary negotiations would have to be conducted with the Histadrut, the national labor organization that had negotiated their collective agreements, and remarked that they were now "in defiance" of their contracts. The ushers' protests escalated into threats against the cinema's chief projectionist, forcing Gilad to call the police to remove the ushers and close the cinema on its busiest night. All of this, the *Jerusalem Post* added, raised "the possibility that the owners, 20th Century Fox, may sell the property."[93]

The labor conflict and Cinema Tel Aviv manager David Zakkai's insistence that the theater would "not reopen unless the strikers return to work" presented an opportunity for Fox to contemplate unloading this increasingly problematic venue less than twenty years after it opened.[94] Gilad was also forced to deny "reports" that Fox was "using the strike as an excuse to get rid of its Israeli property in order to accommodate the Arab boycott."[95] The cinema eventually reopened, and Warner-Fox remained as operators before the two companies severed their Israeli partnership in December 1976.[96] Twentieth Century-Fox sold the Cinema Tel Aviv two years later in January 1979 for $1.7 million to a group of investors headed by Inkay Film Distributors.[97] It was one of the last cinemas Twentieth Century-Fox still operated outside of Australia and New Zealand.

Hollywood in Egypt from the 1960s to the 1980s

For all of Fox's prominence in Egypt, Samir Raafat writes that, for Egyptian audiences, MGM and the Cinema Metro had always "dominated the Cairo cinema scene." While recalling "Fox's Cairo Palace and Société Orientale du Cinema which ran 40 cinema theaters in Egypt as well as the firm of Gaafar Brothers which managed the handsome Opera, Radio, Kasr al-Nil and Rivoli (ex-RKO) cinema theaters," he writes, "None were as innovative or as attention getting as Cinema Metro." By the late 1960s, he adds, and despite cultural mores, "Cinema Metro had enough clout to make yet another first when it projected the uncensored version of Antonioni's pop culture parable 'Blow-up' in which Vanessa Redgrave [was] featured wearing tight Levi's and a naked torso. Even with her arms crossed over her breasts (most of the time) it was considered quite risque at the time."[98] By then, MGM's shop window cinema, with few MGM films being produced, began expanding its programming amid the rise of global art films, changing tastes at the genesis of the New Hollywood, and new political sensibilities in Europe and around the world. Egyptian government censors had also become increasingly liberal with their ban on pro-Israel actors. In 1968, five years after Egypt, the USSR, and East Germany refused its exhibition, *Cleopatra* was finally shown in Egypt and booked into 125 theaters in the UAR. Egyptian censor Mustafa Darweesh remarked that the decision to show the film was based on its value as "good propaganda for Egypt."[99] A private screening was held for President Nasser.

MGM began ending its exhibition operations abroad in the early 1970s, and, along with the rest of its circuit, the company transferred its remaining twenty-seven cinemas—plus fourteen more under construction—to Cinema International Corp. (CIC) on December 1, 1973. For the first time since their construction, the Cinema Metro in Cairo and Alexandria were no longer booking MGM films as a priority.[100] "The last hurrah of the Cinema Metro came in 1978," Raafat writes, "when England's Princess Alexandra of Kent attended a special screening of Agatha Christie's 'Death On The Nile.' But by this time, the Metro was in headlong decline. Even Metro's signature number from John Philip Sousa's march of Sounds and Stripes Forever was no more."[101]

Like their Israeli counterparts, terrorism had also begun affecting Egyptian cinemas and cinemagoing, including Fox's remaining cinemas in Egypt. In August 1976, for example, the U.S. Embassy in Cairo alerted the U.S. State Department to a "SPATE OF RECENT BOMBINGS IN CAIRO, ALEXANDRIA AND ELSEWHERE," all of which it blamed on Libya, which "HAVE CAUSED GROWING SENSE OF APPREHENSION AND FEAR AMONG EGYPTIAN PUBLIC." The embassy highlighted the fear of additional violence after several attacks including a report of a woman killed by a sniper in a Heliopolis open-air cinema on August 18th—"ALL OF WHICH BLAMED ON LIBYANS." The result has been a "THINNING OUT OF CROWDS IN CAIRO AND ALEXANDRIA CINEMAS AND A RELUCTANCE ON PART OF MANY TO GO TO ANY PUBLIC PLACE."[102]

Throughout the economic, political, and social tumult, CIC continued operating the Cinema Metro in Cairo as a premiere outlet for Universal, Paramount, and MGM films. The Cairo Palace, still majority-owned by Fox, was screening Fox as well as UA and Disney films. More than four decades after the Cinema Metro's opening in Cairo, the Cinema Metro and Fox's Cairo Palace, along with the Cinema Metro and Fox's Amir in Alexandria, were still showcase houses for MGM and Fox films, respectively. The Cairo Palace and the Cinema Metro also became premiere venues for the new Cairo International Film Festival.[103]

However, with the rising costs of subtitled prints and advertising, coupled with the unexpected and intense competition from private video clubs that projected films from videocassette recorders "sometimes before some pics open in Cairo cinemas," Hollywood had grown especially weary of investing any more money in Egypt. *Variety* quoted one executive in March 1982 who commented that "Egypt is a losing proposition. We are here only to keep the flag flying and to feed the families." As for new Fox or CIC cinemas, "Reluctance to build is based both on the precarious Middle Eastern situation and on the spiraled cost of real estate."[104]

Two years later, with the situation deteriorating and videocassettes proliferating in both homes and private video clubs, director Salah Abou Saif noted that the days when "the film used to change every week . . . and opening night really was a gala occasion" were long gone. Once, he added, "everyone wore tuxedos and gowns and the papers reported the next morning who had sat in what box and who had worn what. A fine era it was."[105] By then, David Lamb observed condescendingly in the *Los Angeles Times*, these now "filthy theaters attract[ed] crowds of noisy peasants but hardly anyone else." By mid-decade, only 150 theaters remained open throughout Egypt, with 65 percent of these cinemas owned by the Egyptian government. "The seats are broken, the air conditioners don't work, [and] the aisles are littered with trash," Lamb added, and "the audiences are made up almost exclusively of young men who hoot and holler at the sight of a woman on the screen."[106] "The audiences that used to support the first-class theaters just doesn't exist any more," actor Salah Zoufoukal commented. Videotapes, run-down theaters, a 50 percent tax on tickets, and no parking all contributed to the death of middle class moviegoing. Producer Shawky Abu Ali added, "As far as our theaters go, well, they're the worst cinemas you'll find anywhere in the world."[107] Raafat described the Cinema Metro at the end of the twentieth century as a "smelly auditorium with stray cats meandering about and a broken acoustic system which struggled to compete with sounds of an undisciplined public eating and spitting [peanuts]. And with censorship becoming ridiculously austere, going to the movies had become more of a headache than a pleasure."[108]

The Cinema Metro has since been renovated to become a three-screen cinema and refurbished for (mostly) Egyptian films. The Cairo Palace has also remained open as a single-screen movie house restored to look as it first did when it opened seven decades ago. As for the Metro, one patron noted that although the Metro no longer showed MGM (or mainly Hollywood) films, the cinema was still known for its "weekly cartoon screenings [that] make it an ideal place to take the kids."[109] Those looking for Hollywood films in Cairo can still find them at cinemas like the Vodafone IMAX and Plaza Cinemas at the Americana Mall or the Hilton Ramses Cinema at the Hilton Ramses hotel. The Miami, Metro, Diana, Cairo Palace, Radio, and other older cinemas from Cairo's cinema heyday largely exhibit Egyptian and other Arabic-language films now, obscuring their pasts as showcase cinemas for Hollywood, reinvented for Egypt's complex future.

***

In 2010 Uri Klein wrote of Fox's old shop window cinema, the Cinema Tel Aviv, "The building still stands there today, big as ever, but shuttered, dilapidated and filthy. One can still see the mosaic that decorated it, and the spot from which its name could be seen from afar, in big lights."[110] Four years later, and less than fifty years after it opened, the triplexed cinema was demolished as part of the city's constant real estate redevelopment amid incessant growth and price escalation. Despite being "a well-known city landmark," and a featured property in the Israeli version of the Monopoly board game, the Cinema

Tel Aviv was torn down with little objection or fanfare.[111] Few today remember the building as it once was: an American cultural outpost and embassy, a symbol of Hollywood's early support for the State of Israel, and the most luxurious cinema in the country.

Prospects for cinema-building in Israel encouraged great optimism for Hollywood after 1948, but the new country ultimately presented unique political, cultural, and industrial challenges that stifled U.S. expansion. The Cinema Tel Aviv was, in the end, Fox and Hollywood's only owned and operated cinema in all of Israel.

Twentieth Century-Fox's experiences in Egypt and Israel represent one of the more intriguing chapters in Hollywood's efforts to rescreen the world in its own image. After all, bringing Hollywood films and U.S.-owned cinemas to Egypt and Israel was only one part of Skouras's vision for the Middle East's political, cultural, and industrial future. He, along with the Silverstones, worked to influence Israel's entertainment industry in an effort to thwart the growth of communism in the Middle East and increase Hollywood (and U.S.) prominence in the new socialist state. In addition to their precarious Egyptian cinemas and distribution operations, the highly visible, and highly Americanized, Cinema Tel Aviv was the capstone to Skouras and Silverstone's eight-year passion project—the physical embodiment of their cultural, political, and industrial support of Israel and their desire to create a new market there for Hollywood films and cinemas and for U.S. cultural and political ideology.

Cinemas have long since lost the kind of psychological and metaphorical power they held during the 1950s, but more than half a century ago, Cairo, Alexandria, and Tel Aviv's cinemas were key battlegrounds in which political movements as well as Hollywood (and the U.S. State Department) fought for linguistic, cultural, political, and industrial power.

PART V

AFRICA

An "Unhappy Image of the United States Before an African Population" (1932–1975)
Race, Industry, and Rebellion at Hollywood's African Cinemas

CHAPTER 15

MGM AND THE "UNCROWNED KING OF SOUTH AFRICA," 1932–1937

Hollywood Shop Window Cinemas in a Bitterly Protected Market

As mentioned in this book's introduction, the opening night of Twentieth Century-Fox's Royal Cinema in Salisbury, Southern Rhodesia, strictly forbade all "non-Europeans" from entering. In doing so, Fox's local executives undercut the theme of the film they were premiering—*South Pacific*—and directly opposed the Southern Rhodesian government's stated policy of "multiracial partnership" that would have allowed all races if Fox had accommodated integration.[1] (The film's interracial romance between a U.S. marine and a South Pacific island woman is framed through torrid close-ups and supported by the song "You've Got to Be Carefully Taught," by Oscar Hammerstein II and Richard Rodgers, which observes, "You've got to be taught to hate and fear . . . people whose skin is a different shade.") Over the next two years, Fox executives in Southern Rhodesia, South Africa, and in the United States as well as local U.S. diplomats struggled to contain the public relations crisis that erupted following this racially segregated premiere, which exposed deep rifts between colonial Zimbabwe's nonwhite population, American officials, and U.S. multinational film companies that operated cinemas throughout Africa during the British Colonial death rattle of the late 1950s and early 1960s. Part V of this book examines MGM and Twentieth Century-Fox's decades-long operation of (segregated) cinemas in South Africa, colonial Zimbabwe, and Kenya in order to understand how Hollywood's global exhibition expansion in this region led to complicated and controversial decisions about race, class, and industrial practices, and about the role U.S. and local politics and politicians played in their development.

After 1945, and certainly during the 1950s, the U.S. government used its foreign embassies, diplomats, and businesses to promote capitalism and democracy in a Cold War–bid to counteract the spread of communism. Hollywood was a critical part of that weaponry, and the Motion Picture Association of America worked closely with the U.S. State Department to open and keep open foreign markets for American films that could deliver the images and rhetoric of gender, racial, and social equality. When those films traveled to segregated cinemas in sub-Saharan Africa before 1956, American film companies could typically wash their hands of the travails "non-European" moviegoers endured to gain access to these films. Even if their local movie house served up segregation, Hollywood was typically immune to indigenous scorn since U.S. film companies provided the content on the screen—and not the screen itself. However, as the major American film companies began eyeing new markets to buy, build, or lease cinemas after World War II, they entered several markets with highly fractious political and social problems. This was especially true in sub-Saharan Africa, where local governments were still implementing a wide range of racial policies for its Black, "Coloured," Asian, and European populations, from apartheid in South Africa to "partnership" in Southern Rhodesia.

This is the backdrop for Twentieth Century-Fox's acquisition of African Consolidated Theatres (ACT) in 1956, the largest pan-African cinema circuit on the continent, with roughly 150 cinemas in South Africa, Kenya, and colonial Zimbabwe (Southern Rhodesia). While the U.S. State Department hoped to continue selling its mythology of a post-racial America, where Black and white citizens lived in harmony without fear or injustice, Fox's operation of the largest segregated cinemas in Southern Rhodesia fostered a growing animosity among nonwhite audiences toward the United States, its corporations, and its diplomats, whom they correctly perceived as powerless to force an American movie company to sell them a ticket to Hollywood's locally operated dream houses.

Using diplomatic records from the U.S. State Department, trade and newspaper articles, and correspondence in the Spyros P. Skouras and United Artists papers, this part examines Hollywood's influence on film exhibition in colonial South Africa, Zimbabwe, and Kenya, and the cultural, legal, industrial, and political institutions at play on each side of their borders. Its aim is to extend this analysis well beyond Twentieth Century-Fox's influence on the South African film industry and focus instead on the way in which the Royal Cinema in Salisbury exemplified the complications of a U.S. company operating a pan-African cinema chain in the 1950s and 1960s that cut across national, ideological, and political borders and was directly affected by shifting racial and economic policies and debates. This research also addresses the stakes for Fox and the U.S. government in South Africa, colonial Zimbabwe, and colonial and postcolonial Kenya as well as other nations where Hollywood hoped to extend its vast network across the African continent. It also demonstrates that Fox and MGM were not bystanders to the racial segregation and politics operating across the continent but important facilitators and profiteers, especially after 1956.

Scholarship on Hollywood's overseas cinema circuits in more than two dozen countries remains scant, but South Africa is one of a handful of nations in which film historians have excavated key aspects of this complex relationship. In 1946 Thelma Gutsche completed *The History and Social Significance of Motion Pictures in South Africa, 1895–1940*, a thesis later published in 1972, which provides a detailed overview of MGM and Fox's influence on motion picture distribution and exhibition (and audiences) in South Africa from 1931 to 1940.[2] Neil Parsons argues that since Gutsche was an employee of African Films Trust, part of Isidore Schlesinger's massive media empire, during the writing of her dissertation, "it would be surprising if she had not picked up some of Schlesinger's own prejudices—regardless of the fact that she never formally interviewed her employer."[3] The sweep of her work (1931–1940), however, predates the postwar U.S. expansion in Africa and the period from 1956 to 1969, when Twentieth Century-Fox became the dominant player in South African film exhibition.

Keyan Tomaselli's dissertation "Ideology and Cultural Production in South African Cinema" "draw[s] on much of the historical detail provided by Gutsche" and the "cooperation" between Hollywood and South African distributors and exhibitors that "lubricate[d] Hollywood imperialism." For Tomaselli, the South African film industry was tied in to the mechanization of global capital—in this case, MGM and Fox's need for international expansion and the local political establishment's lax antimonopoly statutes—which enabled the establishment of Schlesinger's exhibition empire before 1956, built largely upon the revenues his cinemas earned from Hollywood films, and then its subsequent takeover by U.S. interests.[4] Since then, however, few scholars have conducted extensive appraisals of Hollywood's intervention in sub-Saharan Africa between 1925 and 1969 and the foreign operation of what was then the country's most dominant, vertically integrated film company.[5]

Further north, there is also an absence of research on the distribution and exhibition operations by U.S. film companies (and local operators) in colonial Zimbabwe.[6] James Burns's book *Cinema and Society in the British Empire, 1895–1940* explores this relationship but, like Gutsche's timeline, ends just as Twentieth Century-Fox was beginning to have its largest impact on colonial Zimbabwe and the rest of the continent.[7] Charles Ambler adds that

> scholars have largely ignored the complicated interplay between African audiences and popular films. Researchers have focused instead on the

post-independence emergence of local filmmakers and indigenous cinemas and on the representation of Africa in films, but the important body of work they have produced does not, for the most part, touch on the impact of Hollywood films, or other forms of popular media, in African communities or other societies shaped by colonialism.[8]

A broader pan-African film *industry* history remains elusive, James Brennan notes, as "there is [still] no adequate business history of film distribution and exhibition in sub-Saharan Africa, excepting Gutsche."[9] This part aims to fill in a small but integral part of that lacuna.

"The Uncrowned King of South Africa"

To understand the formation of the South African film industry, it is necessary to first examine the most important player in its development—Isidore William Schlesinger—who, alongside his family, maintained control over this market (and several other sub-Saharan African film markets) from the 1910s to the 1950s. Schlesinger was not South African himself. Born in New York City's Bowery in 1871 to Hungarian Jewish immigrants like Paramount's Adolph Zukor and like William Fox, he grew up a stone's throw from Marcus Loew, who was born in New York's Lower East Side only one year prior to Schlesinger.[10] Loew's parents were destitute; Schlesinger's family, by contrast, traded up as their father shifted from his initial work in New York City cigar making to becoming a banker, loaning money to new immigrants like Zukor and Fox.

In 1894, a decade before Loew would start his own theatrical business, Isadore Schlesinger sailed for the "goldfields of South Africa" to make his fortune in a far less developed country.[11] When he arrived, he pawned his watch for a train ticket to Johannesburg.[12] His stationary, Neil Parsons writes, was always headed "I. W. Schlesinger, American citizen," and he never relinquished his American citizenship despite his lifelong residency in South Africa. Once settled, Schlesinger "moved from selling American novelty products, such as chewing-gum, to managing an agency for the U.S.-owned Equitable Insurance Company. Within two years, he had risen 'from abject poverty to affluence' by tirelessly travelling to sell insurance, from Swaziland in the east to German territory in the west, earning up to a thousand pounds a month in commission." Equitable sent him to Southern Ireland but, Parson notes, "the business opportunities in postwar South Africa were too good to be missed, and he returned to Johannesburg to run his own real estate firm." From insurance, real estate, and banking, he turned to agriculture, launching Zebediela Citrus Estate, growing, packing, and selling fruit. He later added "merino sheep ranching, American-style drugstores, hotels and catering, bus lines, and shipping."[13] He entered the local entertainment business in April 1913, buying Cape Town's Empire Theatre for £60,000. In June he acquired the independent Palladium, the African Amalgamated Theatres (AAT) chain—which included Johannesburg's "ritziest" vaudeville and movie house, the Orpheum, and its Springbok Film Company—forming a new combined concern, African Theatres Trust, which became known as the "octopus," as the company gobbled up theaters across the country.

Seemingly overnight, Schlesinger had become the dominating figure in South African vaudeville, cinema, and cinemas. AAT also included the country's largest newsreel, *The African Mirror*, which provided Schlesinger with power over the nation's moving image news and thus its ability to craft narratives and policy positions on race, culture, history, and politics for internal and external consumption, as AAT was linked and shared footage with *Pathé Gazette* in London.[14] *The African Mirror* would become the "world's longest running cinema newsreel."[15] Its footage was later "used by all the other large film news companies in the world."[16] Schlesinger also controlled one of South Africa's most popular entertainment magazines, *Stage and Cinema*, making AAT and Schlesinger a profoundly powerful player as the desire for entertainment grew in South Africa by the white population who were allowed to participate.[17]

AAT's power by 1915 was profound, as the company owned one-third of the 150 cinemas operating between Cape Town in South Africa to the colonial Belgian Congo city of Elizabethville (now Lubumbashi). As European film exports dropped during the war and American film rentals increased in price, Schlesinger boosted his production operations by forming African Film Productions (AFP) as a separate company to fill in the gaps created by a decline in European imports and as a position of leverage in negotiations with American firms. If Schlesinger's distribution company, African Film Trust, could book its own AFP films into AAT cinemas, it could, like the other vertically integrated film companies to come, negotiate from a position of strength instead of weakness. AFP subsequently built the twenty-six-acre Killarney Film Studios just north of Johannesburg and hired away two American film directors to produce films for the growing cinema chain.[18] AFP produced fifteen films in 1916, including the landmark production of *De Voortrekkers*, directed by Harold Shaw. Along with his trusted employee A. H. "Harry" Stodel, by the end of the 1910s, Arnold Shepperson and Keyan Tomaselli write, Schlesinger "controlled most sectors of the entertainment industry."[19] In the coming years he would add radio stations, newspapers, and circuses to his vast portfolio.[20]

By 1921 Isidore Schlesinger's African Theatres Ltd. chain, which totaled 163 cinemas, extended from South Africa to Kenya.[21] His other businesses—insurance, finance, real estate, hotels, lumber, mining, advertising, farming, and citrus—fueled the expansive growth of his film exhibition, distribution, and production empire.[22] There was one Achilles' heel, however, and it would haunt his dominance: despite the burst of filmmaking in 1916 from AFP, the company made only twenty-two films over the next six years. "South African production declined rapidly after 1922," Shepperson and Tomaselli write, "as the country was unable to compete with the United States, was too far away from world markets, and lacked the financial power to muscle in on global distribution."[23] Despite all of African Theatres' power, it needed product, and by the 1920s much of its audience wanted Hollywood films. ATL would concentrate its power for a while, then, not by making and distributing its own films but by controlling distribution of Hollywood's output in South Africa during the 1920s. The *Times* (London) remarked that while there were up to three hundred independent cinemas in the Union, by the end of the decade "they all hire their films from African Theatres Limited," no matter if made in South Africa, England, or Hollywood.[24]

By mid-1927 Kinemas, S.A. sought to chip away at African Theatres' dominance by opening its own film exchange in Johannesburg "backed by British capital."[25] A few months later, Kinemas, S.A. merged with other independent companies to form the larger Kinemas Ltd. to begin buying, building, and leasing cinemas throughout South Africa in direct competition with African Theatres Ltd.[26] Schlesinger announced his own £1,000,000 spending spree for deluxe cinemas to be built in the major cities of Cape Town, Durban, East London, Johannesburg, Port Elizabeth, Pietermaritzburg, and Bloemfontein. The new cinemas were intended to thwart any new competition from the growing Kinemas firm. Schlesinger then sailed to Europe and the United States to gain inspiration for the design and operation of his new cinemas.[27]

Schlesinger's media power began growing in other ways. His African Theatres Ltd. was granted a license for radio broadcasting in May 1927 and consolidated even more when the company purchased radio stations in Cape Town, Durban, and Johannesburg, forming the new African Broadcasting Company.[28] Like cinemas in the United States and England, Schlesinger then relayed the live entertainment being provided by his cinemas over the air to help fill the schedules of his growing network and promote his cinemas using radio broadcasting.[29]

Schlesinger's power grew from year to year, according to U.S. diplomat C. J. North, controlling "300 out of 400 theaters in South Africa and Rhodesia" where his company "constitutes the most complete film monopoly in the world." Schlesinger, through his brother M. A. Schlesinger's New York office, dictated the terms of film rental to any Hollywood film company hoping to enter the increasingly lucrative but largely closed market. "American firms have for sometime [sic] been at swords points with the Schlessinger's [sic] over what they consider the unwarrantable low prices offered for American films," North wrote in April 1927, "but of course, they cannot get into the South African market any other way though at least on two occasions they have tried."[30]

Schlesinger's power grew even more by purchasing the source of Kinemas' film supply in Johannesburg, which complemented his pipeline of British films through his position on the British International Pictures board of directors, a key part of his large investment in the British entertainment industry that included both his International Variety and Theatrical Agency and his ownership of ten variety and film theaters in London.[31] Schlesinger boosted his presence in England in 1929 by purchasing London's famous Daly's Theatre, a premiere site for musical comedy in the city, and made other investments in British businesses.[32]

Back in South Africa, Kinemas Ltd. reacted to African Theatres Ltd.'s various moves by allying the chain with Ufa, Film Booking Office, and Pro Patria for their entire slate of films in 1929—constituting thirty-five films alone from Ufa—and by booking twelve releases from Gaumont-British, ten from the Gainsborough Company, ten from British International Films, six from British & Dominion Films, and five from Archibald Nettlefold Productions.[33] By 1929 the affiliated Kinemas chain had grown to eighty cinemas, twenty-four of which were owned outright by Kinemas Ltd. while the others were "hooked or operated by it." *Variety* reported in November 1929 that, through these distribution deals, the company had finally "broken through the stone wall of showdom erected in South Africa by the Schlessingers [sic] during the past 20 years." Kinemas' executive Sidney Hayden proudly noted in November 1929 that the company had "no intention of selling out to the Schlessingers [sic], that instead it would prefer to buy the Schlesinger [sic] houses."[34] Still, despite Hayden's bluster, Schlesinger controlled much of the South African market, as the *Times* (London) observed in March 1929:

> The South African film industry differs from that in other Dominions in that it is a practical monopoly. Mr. I. W. Schlesinger, the "Uncrowned King of South Africa" as he has been called, on account of the size and multitude of his enterprises in the Union and its neighbouring countries, controls all entertainments in the Union. African Theatres Limited, of which he is chairman and in which he has the controlling interest, owns almost all theatres and music-halls, the chief cinema houses, the broadcasting stations, and numerous cafes and cabarets. It will thus be seen that South Africa's film industry is part of a great entertainment monopoly ... [as] Mr. Schlesinger's grip on the industry is fairly complete.[35]

The Lion's Meow

As cinema ticket sales grew in South Africa—and competition between Kinemas and African Theatres heated up—the revenue generated by American film companies should have increased exponentially. However, with African Theatres Ltd. still crowding out competition from most other cinemas, American film distributors had little leverage for their rental terms. U.S. film companies also had to compete for space with British and German distributors as well as with domestically produced Afrikaans- and English-language productions.

MGM's establishment of its own sales exchange in South Africa in 1929, with Carl Sonin serving as managing director, did not change this. Sonin failed to significantly boost MGM's sales revenue, and the company's weak position with Schlesinger led to a rather lopsided distribution deal in 1931, with a new entity known as Union Theatres, a new and thinly disguised cinema chain owned by Isidore Schlesinger. Union Theatres (Pty.) Ltd. was expressly created to "screen M-G-M product at certain cinemas 'taken over' by Union Theatres."[36] The deal provided MGM with distribution throughout the country but not at terms Arthur Loew was happy with.

In April 1931, in concert with the Loew's corporation's global desire for first-run outlets for MGM films and its desire to boost local revenues in this still tightly controlled market, Loew's International purchased a Johannesburg site for a new first-run MGM theater that was slated to become the "first of a chain throughout the Union of South Africa."[37] The move by the U.S. major, and supposed Union/Schlesinger partner, spooked the market. By the end of the year, on December 2, 1931, owing in part to Metro's expansion, Kinemas and African Theatres agreed to merge—despite Hayden's earlier pronouncements—creating African Consolidated Theatres, which had a virtual monopoly on South African film exhibition and distribution that would prove almost impossible to break.[38] Arnold Shepperson and Keyan Tomaselli also place the Kinemas/African Theatres merger, "one of the biggest business deals ever transacted in South Africa," on a broader set of concerns. "The combined effects of the Depression, overcapitalization, uneven audience attendance, particularly in the smaller towns (affecting Kinemas more than African Theaters), and the sustained competition for the same audience," they write, "created the conditions whereby only an amalgamation could safely ensure the future of the industry."[39]

The merger exacerbated MGM's concerns and further demonstrated the need for a first-run release house in Johannesburg that was not susceptible to the whims and power of Isidore Schlesinger and his ever-expanding empire. The forthcoming Metro Theatre in Johannesburg would have to attract South African moviegoers by the coolness of its Carrier air-conditioning system, the sumptuousness and modernity of its design, and the desirability of its feature films.[40] Air-conditioning, always a key draw for a Metro Theatre, was singularly important at a time when, *Variety* noted, "the very ancient cinemas run by African Consolidated Theatres are in a bad way to cope with the summer heat, with poor equipment to cool the atmosphere."[41]

The Metro Theatre opened on November 4, 1932, to "the biggest crowd waiting to get admission ever seen in South Africa," *Variety* noted.[42] The premiere of MGM's 2,800-seat Metro Theatre "created a considerable sensation in Johannesburg," historian Thelma Gutsche later recalled. "In this insidious manner the cinema ingratiated itself into the affection of the public with as much effect as through the films it showed."[43] The cinema's opulent surroundings, well-groomed ushers, and multiclass admissions policies were intended to blend harmoniously with the rags-to-riches tales flickering on the screens above. But not everyone was entitled to experience this dreamscape. The formation of the Union of South Africa in 1910 had strengthened white-majority rule; socially, politically, and culturally, segregation in the Union routinely meant "Europeans only." Apartheid was not yet codified in the legal structure of the Union, but it was unspoken law, even for foreign cinema operators.[44] The new Metro Theatre—MGM's first to be given this moniker—was a picture palace for whites only and a South African beachhead for the film company in the enemy territory of Isidore Schlesinger's African Consolidated Theatres.

Charles Raymond, formerly the manager of the Loew's Theatre in Rochester, New York, was sent to Johannesburg to open the new shop window cinema, while American organist Archie Parkhouse was hired away to play at Metro's new South African cinema.[45] An American—not South African—produced newsreel, the *Metro News Gazette*, was projected at each screening.[46] Arthur Loew's plan to visit the new Metro Theatre shortly after opening was delayed by his plane crash that emphasized, once more, the inherent danger in Hollywood's expansion abroad. On November 17, while flying from Victoria Falls in colonial Zimbabwe to Johannesburg, Loew's plane—which belonged to Hal Roach, who had declined the trip at the last minute—hit a tree and crashed to the ground, immediately killing the pilot. Loew survived.[47]

The excitement over the new Metro Theatre was visceral, but it made little difference in terms of power. MGM had secured a first-run, opulent, shop window cinema for its films but little else. It still had to negotiate with ACT for playdates nearly everywhere else. ACT was also right behind MGM in attracting South African moviegoers to new picture palaces by building the Colosseum Theatre in Johannesburg, soon to be ACT's corporate headquarters, and the new Plaza Cinema (formerly a Kinemas Ltd. project before the merger) in Cape Town.[48] There was, in fact, barely any room for additional cinemas unless they were of the quality and size of the Metro. *Variety* observed in March 1933 that there were already "too many cinemas" in Cape Town, Johannesburg, and Durban, and the "newly erected show theatres represent a seating capacity that is a strain on the population, even to fill the houses at least twice a week."⁴⁹ The Metro's brief advantage in size and scale was wiped out in less than a year. Meanwhile, H. W. Leasin of RKO and Henry Kahn of Fox Film Corp. also traveled to South Africa that year "to look over the field" for possible exhibition sites, but neither decided to build or buy. H. Hanson argued that, despite complaints about ACT's monopoly and the fact that local moviegoers had been "forced to be content with a very mediocre class of entertainment," its domination of the market made it a "case of 'take it or leave it.'" American distributors were so cowed by Schlesinger's position that they were even "hesitant to discuss the South African situation." After all, Hanson added, "if terms laid down by the Schlesinger monopoly were not acceptable . . . the Schlesingers went elsewhere for their product—chiefly to minor independents both in this country and in England."⁵⁰

In April 1935 *Variety* reported that Arthur Loew planned to try to increase the company's control of the market by "develop[ing] M-G-M interests over here" and building "several cinemas in the principal towns."⁵¹ A legal battle between MGM and Union Theatres then began in February 1936 in which MGM sued to break a five-year option on their contract. MGM claimed that the five-year option "had been wrongfully obtained by Schlesingers" and, according to Loew, Carl Sonin, MGM's local manager, "had never been authorized to sign the option for Metro and had acted on his own."⁵² (Sonin was not available for the trial, having previously committed suicide.⁵³) The suit concluded with a settlement victory for MGM just before going to trial.

Loew subsequently purchased property in Cape Town and Durban for two new cinemas and began negotiating with local builders.⁵⁴ Prospects for both cinemas, and for MGM, were rising, as *Film Daily* noted that the number of film patrons in South Africa had doubled in the previous five years, enabling the once oversaturated market to easily absorb two new glistening MGM shop windows outside of Johannesburg.⁵⁵ By August 1937 the first opened in Durban.⁵⁶ The real battle between Hollywood and Schlesinger was yet to come.

CHAPTER 16

FOX HUNTING ON THE AFRICAN CONTINENT, 1937–1956

Twentieth Century-Fox and the Struggle for Control of African Cinemas

Despite South Africa being a growing market with many English speakers, the kind Twentieth Century-Fox had focused on for global exhibition expansion throughout the 1930s, the company had been remarkably quiet until this point. Fox had already purchased a large stake in England's Gaumont-British (and its cinemas) in the late 1920s, a controlling interest in Australia's Hoyts Theatres in 1930, and a 50 percent interest in New Zealand's Amalgamated Theatres in 1936. In August 1937—the same month in which MGM opened its Durban shop window as a challenge to African Consolidated Theatres' supremacy—Fox opened its first sales exchange in Johannesburg.[1] Fox executives had long been "dissatisfied" with grosses from South Africa,[2] and the move was precipitated by Fox's inability to sell its entire slate to either Schlesinger's African Consolidated Films distribution arm or Loew's' MGM.[3] After relying on either for national distribution, Twentieth Century-Fox had, like MGM, now decided to go on its own.

In March 1938 Fox's Otto Bolle consecrated a distribution pact for Fox films to be exhibited in cinemas owned and operated by Independent Picture Palaces Ltd.—which included thirty-six cinemas in Bloemfontein, Cape Town, Durban, East London, Johannesburg, Maritzburg, Port Elizabeth, Pretoria[4]—and began setting up "distribution centers in all important South African cities."[5] Fox would also boost the company's foreign revenues by securing its own distribution networks in Kenya, Mozambique, Tanzania, and the Rhodesias, depriving Schlesinger of almost exclusive domain over commercial cinema in each country.[6] Independent Picture Palaces subsequently constructed a new

$500,000 cinema in Durban, following MGM's lead, to be named Twentieth Century after its new distribution partner.[7] Fox also invested its own money—approximately $200,000—into another cinema in Johannesburg, the 20th Century Theatre, that would be co-owned and co-operated with local film exhibitor (and diamond merchant) Harry Lourie of Lourie & Katz. (Harry was the father of future Palestine Films' founder Norman Lourie).[8] Fox then announced that it would begin "sponsoring" the construction of other cinemas by granting fifteen-year franchises of Fox films for each new cinema built by independent exhibitors in the affiliated circuit.[9] Independent Picture Palaces subsequently announced the construction of a new $500,000 cinema in Durban, also to be named the 20th Century Theatre, reflecting its distribution partner.[10]

Fox International head W. J. Hutchinson told *Film Daily* in June 1938 that the purpose of Fox's new Johannesburg shop window cinema was "to have a 'show window' for our product.... We believe that when independent exhibitors see major companies with a permanent stake in South Africa they will be encouraged to build more houses. Thus, our market will be enlarged and business in general will benefit."[11] *Variety* remarked that with another Cape Town shop window set to open the following year for Fox as well, "all indications are that 20th-Fox is planning considerable building activity."[12] With its move into distribution, shop window cinema operation, and the affiliation of a growing exhibition circuit, it would be Twentieth Century-Fox, rather than MGM, that turned out to be Schlesinger's "chief competitor."[13] While Paramount, RKO, and Warner Bros. remained "definitely committed against such a policy" of independence, United Artists followed Twentieth Century-Fox's aggressive moves by cancelling its distribution agreement with ACT and began distributing its films through the Fox-affiliated circuit and the new 20th Century Theatre shop window set to open in Johannesburg.[14] UA and Fox signed no formal agreements, maintained separate distribution offices, and kept up the appearance of being uncoordinated companies to avoid violating local monopoly laws. The unofficial agreement granted Fox 60 percent of playing time in its affiliated circuit with the remaining 40 percent secured, at least initially, for UA-distributed films.[15] By the end of 1938 Fox's circuit and its various agreements with UA had helped the company organize fifty-three affiliated cinemas to exhibit UA and Fox films outside of the Schlesinger stranglehold, with ten more cinemas soon to be added to the circuit.[16] Local capital for existing and forthcoming cinemas was organized by Twentieth Century-Fox through Cinema Theater Investments (Pty.) Ltd.[17]

By 1939, at a time when Hollywood's future in Europe and Asia looked perilous at best, Loew's International exhibition head William Melniker declared that MGM's cinemas in South Africa were "as safe as the gold dollar," while South Africa now had "the highest cinema per capita ratio in the world" for *white* moviegoers.[18] Many of the nation's most lucrative cinemas were either being remodeled by Schlesinger's ACT or built new due to the fifteen-year franchises Fox had handed out.[19] Fox upped its investment in the new 20th Century Theatre to $250,000 in April, and the remaining costs ($1.5 million) were pooled by a group composed of Lourie (Harry and son Norman Lourie) & Katz who, in partnership with William Boxer and S. R. Potter, already operated eleven additional cinemas through the Associated Cinemas of South Africa chain.[20]

The new 20th Century Theatre opened in March 1940 at a cost of $2 million.[21] It was operated by South African and American executives through the Twentieth Century Co. and was chiefly "operated under Twentieth Century-Fox supervision."[22] At a time when Fox's European manager, Ben Miggins, argued that there was "no hope for revenue from [Europe] for a long time to come," Otto Bolle told *Motion Picture Herald* that "South Africa is a market in which business is so good that there has been no reason to restrict the export of currency and in which building of theatres is proceeding at an unprecedented pace—approximately 30 having been built at a cost of $3,500,000 in the past two and one-half years." The "building boom," Bolle noted, was directly tied to Fox's (and UA's) support for the nation's non-ACT affiliated cinemas and its own chain and cinemas.[23]

In on the ACT

ACT wasn't cowed by Fox's increasing interventions. The company built 10 new cinemas in 1941 alone, totaling 155 in the chain. Historian Thelma Gutsche writes that "competitive building activity" between Fox and ACT "reached almost ludicrous proportions" during the late 1930s and early 1940s with many of their cinemas within "a stone's throw from each other."[24] $4 million was also spent on fifteen new Fox and UA-affiliated cinemas, growing their combined chain to roughly 85 in opposition to ACT by 1941.[25]

Competition between these rivals was anything but friendly. A letter from UA vice president Arthur Kelly to South African territory manager Al Lowe sheds light on the boiling temperature of the film war in South Africa. In October 1939, after receiving a report from Lowe that he had been meeting with local executives including those from Schlesinger's ACT and ACF, Kelly dressed down his subordinate in much the same way a CIA director would ream a field officer. The following letter highlights not only the unparalleled fear UA and other executives felt toward Isidore Schlesinger and his minions but the way in which he was, quite uniquely, seen as a formidable foe who could actually beat the Americans at their own game:

> You state you have met I.W. Schlesinger several times and that the meetings have been very pleasant.... You were fully warned before you went away that [he] is a very capable individual and one who will try and gain his ends, legally or otherwise.... Consequently you have to be on the alert and be careful you don't fall into a lot of traps.... [They] always try to work the social angle, until a friendship is built up. Then, through friendship and familiarity, they try to find out the long suits and short-comings of either the man or his wife. When they feel they have gained sufficient knowledge on this point, they start to lay the foundation for their next move. For instance, if your weakness were gambling, ways and means would be found that would tempt you to gamble, and get you in a knot ... If your troubles were over money matters, that is to say, if you conveyed the thought you weren't earning sufficient to give you the luxuries of life, you might very easily be cut in on some kind of deal whereby you have to borrow money.... If you do not become involved along these lines, similar tactics would be tried on the weaker sex. You may think all this is tommyrot or schoolboy talk, and feel that you know how to take care of yourself.... You ought to worry more about the employees you engage and see that they are not also on his payroll and that the janitor of the building is not paid to take out letters from your files at night time to have them copied.[26]

Kelly then reminded Lowe that, "[Max] Schlesinger once told me in New York that at one time they had a paid employee in every film office in America.... Bullock and Schlesinger and others in that company are past masters in the art of mosaicry (to coin a word) so the little bits that you drop in the presence of these people is recorded and finally pieced together and from it they make their deductions and moves. I. W. Schlesinger," he noted, "carries on a policy of fear."[27]

UA and Fox, undeterred by Schlesinger's tactics, jointly announced the construction of a new 20th Century Theatre for Cape Town, in association with Norman Lourie. The $1.25 million cinema was designed to seat 1,800 and included a restaurant and a dance hall.[28] Several other 20th Century Theatres opened during this period, not financed by Twentieth Century-Fox but instead part of the affiliated circuit created through Fox-UA franchise agreements. These included the 20th Century in Pretoria, which opened on June 5, 1941, and another 20th Century in Maritzburg.[29]

Growing tensions between Norman Lourie and William Boxer, partners in the UA/Fox-affiliated Cinema Theater Investments circuit, and Isidore Schlesinger and ACT finally came to a head in April 1942 when Lourie and Boxer were "arrested in connection with the disappearance of film stock held by African Consolidated." The two men were found guilty of theft and sentenced in 1943 to four months of hard labor.[30] This may present one additional reason why Lourie would leave shortly thereafter to restart his life and business in Palestine.

Out-Ranked

By the end of 1945 Fox and United Artists were distributing their films to 165 independent theaters in a "territory that formerly was monopolized by the Schlesinger circuit."[31] The continued success of ACT and the rise of so many independent cinemas able to book a steady stream of Hollywood films had catered to stationed allied soldiers and others during wartime, all of which had led to an "overseated" nation, according to UA executive Al Lowe, seemingly unable to absorb any more cinemas for white audiences.[32] (There were a growing number of cinemas built and operated for nonwhite audiences in nonwhite areas, but they were separate and deeply unequal in terms of programming, opulence, and attention.) White attendance was so voluminous, in fact, and the need for content so great, that Columbia, Paramount, Universal, and Warner Bros. all began exploring the ability to end their contracts with Schlesinger and open their own exchanges.[33] Hollywood films now occupied 85 percent of South African screen time, with British films filling in the small remainder.[34] Efforts to boost South African film production, especially for the limited amount of Afrikaans filmmaking, was largely ignored by the wartime government.[35]

Rank's films were also picked up by Twentieth Century-Fox in 1945 for distribution throughout its affiliated circuit and its own shop windows. The British firm made no secret of its own plans to build cinemas in South Africa for its films.[36] British media mogul J. Arthur Rank preferred to avoid a conflict with Schlesinger and his "policy of fear" in South Africa. Instead of building, following the merger of Universal Pictures with Rank's UK-based United World Pictures and International Pictures in 1946, creating Universal-International (U-I), Rank purchased a significant stake in ACT in 1947 in exchange for distribution of both Universal and Rank films through ACF.[37] The U-I deal with ACT "hit 20th-Fox hard," *Variety* reported, since Fox had been negotiating with Rank and Universal for a similar deal. Schlesinger couldn't have known it, but his turn to U-I instead of Fox would have far-reaching consequences.[38]

While the focus of this book is primarily on Hollywood's expansion overseas, it is important to highlight the vast reach of Rank's global exhibition empire. By 1946 Rank's global cinema holdings were, in fact, larger than almost any other film company in the world, with 1,280 cinemas, including 340 Gaumont-British, 338 Odeon, and 42 other British cinemas; 50 percent investments in the Kerridge-Odeon (New Zealand) and Norman Rydge circuits in Australia; a growing chain of cinemas in Ireland; and a new partnership with

Universal and its own exhibition holdings. Rank's control over the British and British Commonwealth market was so dominant, in fact, that Rank had to promise the British Board of Trade that he would acquire no more British cinemas during the ongoing postwar materials shortage.[39]

Expansion for Rank, then, had to be found overseas in other English-speaking markets through a new jointly owned Rank cinema (the Rivoli) in Cairo and the highly lucrative investment in Schlesinger's ACT. "Rank and U-I," *Variety* noted, "by buying into Schlesinger's theatre and distribution interests, will now have virtual control and preferential playing time in Africa."[40] The infusion of U-I capital was equally important for ACT as the company planned a new round of building "luxury theatres" throughout the "chief urban centers of the Union."[41] By then, U-I's investment included ACT's current holdings of 128 cinemas, in addition to 21 "tea-rooms showing pictures," as well as its vast control over distribution, booking an additional 244 cinemas throughout South Africa.[42] The U-I investment in ACT was finally settled in 1948, with U-I paying £619,822 for 250 shares of ACT.[43]

Universal and Rank's deal with ACT rippled throughout the local industry, with MGM and Warner Bros. joining Fox and UA in "contemplating building programs in this country" in order to secure distribution.[44] Loew's International, in order to "offset" the U-I deal with ACT and reassert its own position, was forced to abandon its policy of signing short-term deals with ACT and instead sign a long-range "sweeping" ten-year contract with Schlesinger.[45] The new deal, negotiated by Arthur Loew and Isidore Schlesinger, "guarantee[d] Metro films at least as much playing time as they received under the old deal and, since it pre-dates the Rank pact, it is not subject to the Rank 'favored-picture' policy."[46] This agreement encouraged Goldwyn to sign his own with MGM to funnel his films into ACT cinemas that were unencumbered by the U-I/ACT agreement. The MGM/ACT deal also guaranteed distribution of MGM and Goldwyn films through ACT cinemas, *Motion Picture Herald* reported, in "British Southwest Africa [colonial Namibia], Rhodesia [colonial Zambia and Zimbabwe] and Tanganyika [colonial Tanzania] and Kenya [then under British rule], covering not only present Schlesinger theatres but also any that may be built during the circuit's long-range building program."[47]

Twentieth Century-Fox was equally interested in the rest of sub-Saharan Africa. The company had opened its own branch offices in Nairobi, Kenya, in 1946 and extended its circuit there with twenty-four new affiliated cinemas.[48] The desire for expansion northward was certainly to further solidify Fox's position throughout the continent but also because cinema expansion in South Africa was almost entirely frozen due to materials and skilled labor shortages as the government prioritized building new housing over new cinemas after the war.[49] Still, Norman Lourie, unnerved by the increased power of ACT after the Rank/U-I and MGM deals, announced that his own eleven-cinema chain, Associated Theatres of South Africa Ltd., also planned to build an additional thirty-five cinemas "to compete with the powerful African Consolidated Theatres."[50]

Fox and UA had other problems to overcome, as they discovered that Schlesinger had clandestinely acquired some of their circuit's cinemas, and he was now refusing to renew distribution agreements with both companies at these theaters. "Thus," one UA executive wrote, "the operation was deprived of playing time and consequently ran into an operational loss."[51] The decline in revenue was so severe that United Artists was unable to pay its producing partners for the exhibition of their films in South Africa.

Outfoxing Schlesinger

In 1948 the Afrikaner-dominated National Party defeated the more liberal United Party in South Africa, and apartheid was consecrated through a new system of laws.[52] John S. Saul and Stephen Gelb note that this "logic of racial capitalism" benefited the party's power base—"the Afrikaner petty bourgeoisie, agrarian capital, [and] the white working class"—through a color bar in employment and every other facet of South African society.[53] Nicoli Nattrass adds that economic development "was profoundly structured" by these kinds of "racial labour policies, moulded by ideology and a violent racially repressive socio-political environment."[54] Two laws in particular—the Population Registration Act (1950), which categorized all South Africans by race and thereby limited social, cultural, and political access for Blacks, "Coloureds," and "Asians"; and the Reservation of Separate Amenities Act (1953), which made it legal to segregate or exclude nonwhites from public services and venues, including hardtop and drive-in movie theaters—served as two central pillars of South African apartheid.[55]

Following its victory in 1948, the National Party had also blocked Fox from taking out of the country money generated by its distribution and exhibition activities; in response, Fox used those blocked funds to buy or build theaters. In the ensuing years, the government's new policy only encouraged Fox to build or acquire more cinemas, which had the unintended consequence of bolstering foreign influence on South Africa's cinema industry.[56]

ACT's grip on sub-Saharan Africa also began to slip on March 10, 1949, when Isidore Schlesinger died, leaving control of the company to his son John and his brother Max.[57] John and Max would have to oversee a new kind of Schlesinger Organisation and a new kind of African Consolidated Theatres that could adapt to various technological, cultural, and political shifts. They began, for example, working with J. Arthur Rank to bring television broadcasting to the country. In March 1950 the South African Broadcasting

Corp.—in "co-operation" with ACT—launched a demonstration of television through the offices of J. Arthur Rank.[58] Four months later, in July 1950, ACT formally inaugurated "big screen television" in South Africa with a large-scale demonstration of live TV at the Rand Agricultural show in Johannesburg.[59]

Max Schlesinger died in 1953, and control of the £50 million Schlesinger Organisation's real estate, insurance, citrus, entertainment, restaurant and catering, hotel, and newspaper as well as its many other highly successful divisions fell singularly to John.[60] Like his father, John Schlesinger had also retained his U.S. citizenship and identity, having been educated at Harvard University and served as a bombardier in the U.S. Air Force.[61] Now, with the elder Schlesingers gone, John became chairman of ACT and its chief decision maker. One of his first moves was to buy United Artists' 50 percent interest in Rank's Odeon Cinema Holdings Ltd., which did not give Schlesinger control over the management of the global Odeon cinema chain but, according to the *Sydney Sunday Herald*, made him "an important partner" in global film exhibition, "film-making, photographic equipment, television and radio." Schlesinger dubbed the purchase "a nice golden jubilee present for my firm" on its fiftieth anniversary.[62] The acquisition put the Schlesinger Organisation further into the television market years before TV broadcasting was formally launched in South Africa. The new media landscape was changing, but so was the old film business. John Schlesinger had ascended to the throne at a very tumultuous moment for ACT.

Fox's fifteen-year franchise agreements with all of its affiliated cinemas ended that same year, and with Fox's future position in South African increasingly uncertain, the company began acquiring more and more cinemas. Fox picked up the Royal and the 20th Century cinemas in Durban, adding to its eponymous collection, and another lot in the city for a future cinema. By 1953, as its agreements came to an end, the company sought additional outlets, including acquisitions of the Ritz in Bloemfontein, the Van Riebeck in Cape Town from ACT, the previously independent 20th Century in Pietermaritzburg, the Embassy in Port Elizabeth, all joining the company's existing Royal and 20th Century cinemas in Durban as well as the 20th Century cinema in Johannesburg (still co-owned with the Louries, who held a majority 56.25 percent stake).[63] Yet another 20th Century was already under construction in Port Elizabeth, with additional cinemas planned for Durban, a new 20th Century in Germiston, and another Fox-owned and -operated cinema on Kirk Street in Johannesburg for 1,100 patrons. The company noted in its annual report that the burgeoning circuit of 20th Century Fox cinemas "assure[d] ideal representation for our product in Africa" and, with the exception of the co-owned 20th Century Theatre in Johannesburg, all of these new cinemas were "wholly-owned" by Twentieth Century-Fox.[64] Over the next two years, Fox kept opening new cinemas to bring "CinemaScope to every principal city in southern and eastern Africa."[65] Expansion after 1953, then, was not just about asserting control over the territory for Fox films but, once again, about securing a new market for the company's CinemaScope technology as it fought for market share against other widescreen processes. This was especially important because by November 1953 all of MGM's South African cinemas and the "principal" ACT cinemas had already been equipped for widescreen cinema.[66]

By 1954 ACT had other problems besides Fox's expansion. Arthur Loew was displeased at the presentation of MGM films within the circuit, and although MGM would still distribute its films to ACT cinemas, it refused to renew "contracts giving certain Schlesinger keys the full run of Metro product." MGM also announced plans to build three new cinemas in Cape Town in May 1954 and build or acquire additional cinemas throughout South Africa and Rhodesia. Perhaps most alarming to ACT, MGM planned to create, as Fox had, its own affiliated circuit by securing "franchise arrangements with progressive local showmen." This, *Variety* reported, "was more than a subtle hint" as MGM began "breaking its arrangements with the powerful Schlesinger circuit."[67]

Fox's small chain of cinemas had grown to fifteen by 1955, and the company augmented its distribution pipeline and the offerings at its owned and operated cinemas by acquiring local distribution rights from Republic Pictures as well, prying away the small studio's output from ACF exchanges and ACT cinemas. As Fox and MGM's power and independence grew, ACF and ACT became increasingly alarmed by the possibilities of a mutiny by its Hollywood distribution "partners." As U.S. diplomat Charles Reed wrote in a missive to the U.S. Department of State, "Though African Theatres still has short term (1 to 2 year) contracts with several American film companies, it is faced with the possibility of Twentieth Century-Fox acquiring the distribution rights from those companies in the near future due to its large number of outlets."[68]

OutFoxed: Fox Purchases ACT

As the fifteen-year agreement Fox had signed with its affiliated cinemas expired in 1953, Murray Silverstone, president of Twentieth Century-Fox International, flew to South Africa "with the intention of breaking the distribution agreements" that ACT held with numerous other film companies. The pressure placed on ACT resulted in a new two-year agreement between Fox and Schlesinger "whereby African Theatres would construct theatres in South Africa for Twentieth Century-Fox to be leased on a twenty-year basis." Two years later no new cinemas had ever been built. "Apparently," Charles Reed wrote to the State Department, "African Theatres realised shortly after entering into the agreements that the construction of theatres for 20th Century Fox would not only necessitate a capital outlay of some £3,000,000, but with the twenty-year lease would be equivalent to Twentieth Century Fox having erected its own theatres."[69] Fox's representative in South Africa, Eddie Lomba, recognized ACT's double cross and pressed Skouras to purchase ACT (and ACF) outright. Loew's, *Variety* reported, was also suddenly interested in purchasing the companies from John Schlesinger, who wanted to leave South Africa and move to London.[70] Fox raced forward, urging Schlesinger to fly to New York and meet with Spyros Skouras and other Fox executives.[71] By mid-June, Twentieth Century-Fox treasurer Donald Henderson, Hoyt's Theatres head Ernest Turnbull, and a Fox company attorney were all in South Africa negotiating with Schlesinger.[72] Spyros Skouras arrived in late June.[73]

Days later—and after years of battling the Schlesingers—Twentieth Century-Fox had landed their South African whale.[74] Officially, the purchase of ACT and ACF was accomplished by Fox Theatres South Africa Proprietary, acquiring ACT and ACF after the 100 percent approval of both the shareholders and board of African Consolidated Investments Corp. (ACIC).[75] Fox Theatres South Africa Proprietary had in fact bought far more than just ACT and

FIGURE 16.1 Twentieth Century-Fox's Spyros Skouras (left) and Al Lichtman (right). (Author's collection)

ACF; the transaction with the Schlesingers gave Fox a "holding interest" in African Consolidated Theatres United, African Theatres United, African Films United, African Consolidated Films, Rhodesian Theatres Ltd., and many more companies in South Africa, colonial Zimbabwe, and Kenya.[76]

The Schlesingers' sale of ACT, ACF, and these other entertainment-related companies, John Schlesinger told ACIC shareholders, was triggered by the "ever increasing burdens of administration of African theatres, the growing difficulties of film exhibition, with its complex and changing developments, the reduction in film production, the rising costs of films, and especially the impact of television." Fox's purchase of African Theatres also included a provision whereby John, Julian, and M. A. Schlesinger as well as A. E. Hamel would not participate in a "business in competition with African Theatres and Fox in Africa south of the Equator for a period of 20 years" without compensation to Fox.[77] Skouras remarked that the acquisition would fill a key revenue gap created by the loss of Fox's domestic theaters due to the consent decree with the U.S. Justice Department. Noting his "immense confidence in South Africa's future," Skouras "regarded the Schlesinger deal as a first rate investment" and planned to operate ACT "on precisely the same lines as is the large Hoyt's circuit in Australia, which is controlled by 20th-Fox, namely, it will have complete autonomy with an exclusively South African board of directors, except for one American member."[78] This claim of South African autonomy would be challenged in the court of public opinion less than five years later.

The acquisition of ACT and ACF was a good deal for both parties and more than doubled Fox's global holdings from a base of Australian, New Zealand, and other scattered cinemas. After completing the deal, Charles Reed recounted the rather staggering reach of ACT:

> Twentieth Century-Fox will control 607 movie theatres, which is all but 15 of the total European and non-European movie theatres located south of the Sahara. This includes approximately 150 theatres which will be owned outright by, or which will be under lease to 20th Century, with the remainder controlled through exhibitor contracts, and comprises 461 in South Africa, 67 in British East Africa (Tanganyika, Uganda, Kenya, Zanzibar), 29 in Southern Rhodesia, 11 in Northern Rhodesia, 19 in Portuguese East Africa, 13 in South West Africa and 7 in the Protectorates of Bechuanaland, Basutoland and Swaziland. Also included in the transaction are some of the leading office buildings in South Africa and the Rhodesias in which movie theatres are located, as well as Wembley Stadium in Johannesburg, Boswell's Circus and subsidiary organisations for the production and distribution of films.[79]

Fox saw the acquisition as a chance to expand its foreign revenues through film distribution and exhibition, whereas the State Department—which tended not to be directly involved in such matters—envisioned a golden opportunity to extend its Cold War outreach to Africa. As Reed wrote, "The new organisation will give Twentieth Century Fox control over one of the most important information media in Southern Africa and should provide an opportunity for greater presentation through news reels and information films of American interests and viewpoints."[80]

During the negotiations, Skouras met with the U.S. ambassador and consul general and with South African prime minister Johannes Strijdom, pledging to "produce some films in the Afrikaans language" and "encourage a greater exchange through the film media of information concerning America and South Africa."[81] Further, *Motion Picture Daily* reported, Fox gave "public assurances" that it would "play the product of other companies, in addition to native African features," produce "CinemaScope features here [in South Africa]," "continue the operation of Schlesinger's legitimate stage theatres," and "establish a Fox Movietone base" in the country.[82] Twentieth Century-Fox was careful to keep ACT's day-to-day operations almost entirely in South African hands to avoid any charges of foreign influence. Eddie Lomba, an American citizen and the managing director of Twentieth Century-Fox Films (S.A.) (Pty.) Ltd. in Johannesburg, became managing director of ACT and one of the very few Americans working for the circuit.[83] This was a critical component of Fox's insulation strategy—whenever questions of film content or racial policies came to the fore, the company simply insisted that local ACT managers in Johannesburg had jurisdiction over such matters. In addition, Fox avoided trouble with the local projectionist's union because, although the company had repeatedly refused to sign an agreement with the local union, ACT had recently signed a five-year agreement that Fox was forced to honor.[84]

To allay any additional South African fears that American ownership would change the company's philosophical orientation—especially its racial policies—Skouras arranged personal meetings with Prime Minister Strijdom, one of the architects of the government's apartheid strategy, and members of his National Party. Strijdom reiterated the "need for South African pictures from the standpoint of world appreciation of this country" and the production of "pictures for home consumption in the Afrikaans language."[85] Skouras told Strijdom "that both of these ideas were already included in his planning."[86] Fox also pledged to distribute the South African company's newsreel content internationally, giving it a global distribution platform that would expand the country's political and cultural visibility.[87] Skouras described his meeting with Strijdom as "highly satisfactory." "In fact," U.S. diplomat Edward Wailes added, "I have rarely seen an American businessman as enthusiastic over a twenty to thirty minute talk." "From the American point of view I feel that the consummation of this deal will be helpful," Wailes wrote. "As the Embassy has indicated in the past we would benefit by more direct information from the

United States in this country. Twentieth Century-Fox is, I believe, in a position to furnish at least some of this information through its newsreels whereas to date the press has not been entirely to our liking."[88] From all accounts, the U.S. government viewed Fox's purchase of ACT as a boon to American media expansion that would benefit its global outreach during the Cold War.[89]

Getting in on the ACT

By June 1956, Fox had formally completed the stock purchase of ACT and directly owned and operated 128 cinemas in South Africa, 8 in Southern Rhodesia, and 4 in Kenya, with more under construction.[90] The acquisition was part of a wave of U.S. investment in South Africa where 55 percent of all of U.S. investment in the African continent was now focused.[91] South Africa was a mature market with major cities and white neighborhoods already flush with cinemas. Growth opportunities instead included cinemas for nonwhite audiences; for Southern Rhodesia, where ACT built new 1,200- and 1,000-seat hardtop cinemas and purchased a drive-in to compete with independents already operating in the country; and for Kenya, where Skouras announced the construction of three new cinemas in Nairobi, including the flagship 20th Century Theatre and the new Fox Drive-In, for white patrons only.[92] Fox also planned to construct eleven new drive-ins in South Africa, with more to follow in Northern and Southern Rhodesia as well as in Kenya.[93] (During this period, MGM also began opening drive-ins in South Africa and in Southern Rhodesia such as the 870-car MGM Drive-In in Salisbury.[94]) In 1956 alone, Fox Theatres South Africa (Pty.) Ltd. "purchased fifty-five different properties," the "bulk" of which were cinemas that were subsequently leased directly to ACT. Thus, Fox's South African subsidiary was, in fact, directly involved with the expansion of ACT, and, by leasing its property to the exhibition company, used ACT as an immediate income source for Fox's South African real estate investments and then profited again by the cinema's box office receipts.[95] It did not, however, measurably increase attention on moviegoing venues for nonwhite audiences.

Fox's acquisition demonstrably altered film exhibition in South Africa after 1955. There were then only four major distribution companies operating in the country—two owned by Fox—that controlled the distribution of films as well as in the Central African Federation, South West Africa, and Portuguese East Africa. Fox's ACT distributed Columbia, United Artists, Paramount, Warner Bros., Universal, Allied Artists, Rank, and British Lion films, and its existing Twentieth Century-Fox sales office in Johannesburg distributed its own films and those of Republic, RKO, and Disney. Of all the Hollywood majors, only MGM distributed its own films. Another company, Empire Films, distributed

British and "Continental" releases.[96] With roughly 150 theaters in operation or under construction from Cape Town to Nairobi and with a vast distribution network through hundreds of independent cinemas, exhibitors in much of sub-Saharan Africa were forced to work with—or reckon with—Fox. Coupled with 180 Hoyts cinemas in Australia and another 50 Amalgamated cinemas in New Zealand, Skouras noted that "these three circuits are very important to us in developing maximum film rentals" with "combined gross receipts of these foreign theatre circuits" at roughly 37 million dollars.[97]

Unsurprisingly, local acceptance of ACT's new masters was not uniformly positive. One man, credited as "Man in the Street," noted in a South African newspaper that under Fox's management he felt "sure that if I. W. Schlesinger could walk into one of his former theatres he would get the shock of his life. Shorn of all dignity, the foyers, overcrowded with popcorn, sweet and soft drink kiosks, showcases with men's clothes and rubbish bins, now have the appearance of a sideshow at Coney Island."[98]

The early years of Fox's ownership of ACT were a period of growth. By 1957 ACT was now operating 140 cinemas in South Africa, 8 in Southern Rhodesia, 4 in Kenya, with more under construction or planned.[99] In addition to new hardtop cinemas, the Fox-owned ACT also opened new drive-ins in South Africa and points north. In mid-1958, for example, ACT debuted the nation's largest ozoner with space for 1,000 cars at Brakpan, Transvaal, near "adjoining mine dumps." The drive-in was the first to feature an "especially designed American cafeteria."[100]

The following year Fox also created a new subsidiary, South African Screen Productions (Pty.) Ltd., set up to purchase Schlesinger's African Film Productions and its studio at Killarney.[101] It was the threat of competition that led Schlesinger to jettison this remaining film asset of the organization. As African Film Productions Ltd. secretary J. Rosen told shareholders, "A failure to approve the transaction might result in FOX establishing its own laboratories and commencing the production of films in this country, which would not be in the interests of the Company." Purchase of AFP now provided Fox Theatres South Africa (Pty.) Ltd., the holding company for Twentieth Century-Fox's ACT (and other) cinemas in South Africa, with twelve additional lots of land in Killarney as well as farmland.[102]

After two decades of battling the Schlesingers in South Africa, Twentieth Century-Fox was now in total control of the South African film market and the tentacles of both distribution and exhibition of Hollywood films throughout the increasingly lucrative African continent, stretching from Kenya to the north to colonial Zimbabwe and down to South Africa.

CHAPTER 17

A "ROYAL" MESS

Racial Strife in Colonial Zimbabwe, the Struggle for Independence in Postcolonial Kenya, and the End of Hollywood's Control of South African Cinemas, 1959–1975

Apartheid and the South African government's positions on race were not relegated only to the audience composition and social structures of cinema houses. In South Africa, censorship of films—often related to issues of race and race-mixing—was also strictly enforced before any films could reach ACT screens for both white and nonwhite audiences.

An example of the government's disdain for sympathetic narratives (and film companies) can be seen in the aborted 1952 adaptation of Stuart Cloete's 1937 novel *The Turning Wheels*, a global sensation banned by South Africa's minister of the interior because of its depiction of an interracial love affair (importation of the book was illegal until 1974).[1] In 1952 Rank sold its rights to *The Turning Wheels* to MGM, and producer Sam Zimbalist planned to follow the filming of *Mogambo* (1953) in Nairobi with an adaptation of Cloete's novel, which he planned to shoot in "Dutch East Africa."[2] ACT's Jack Stodel (Harry Stodel's son) received an urgent phone call that Eric Louw, the government's minister of economic affairs, demanded a meeting with ACT. When Stodel arrived, Louw accosted him over the production, objecting specifically to the depiction of a relationship "between an Afrikaner Boer and a Cape Coloured woman." Stodel told Louw to contact MGM's representative in South Africa, Morris Davis. When Stodel phoned Davis, he replied "that the Government can go and jump in the river as far as Metro Goldwyn Mayer are concerned and that they will never allow themselves to be intimidated by the Minister's attitude." In person, Louw told Davis point blank: "If MGM produce[s] *Turning Wheels*, I say irrevocably that not another MGM film will ever be allowed to come into South Africa." Davis, according to Stodel, "didn't say another word and MGM cancelled the production of the film."[3] (When Twentieth Century-Fox optioned the film rights to and "bankrolled" the writing of another Cloete novel five years later, *Variety* was careful to note that there were "no 'race' angles" in this new property.[4])

In other cases, films featuring mixed-race relationships and other objectionable material were banned outright in South African cinemas whereas others, with a great deal of effort, could enter the distribution pipeline only after excessive cuts. Spyros Skouras would later remark that to get *South Pacific* played there—with its interracial themes and romance—he had to ask Eddie Lomba to "sweet-talk the South African Board of Censors." Skouras remarked that the company's Johannesburg staff had become "expert at cutting whole sequences out of films with colored people in them . . . 'almost so you wouldn't know the difference.' In editing [*South Pacific*] down a half-hour," he added, "filmgoers were shown that the lieutenant merely had an *idea* about a love affair with the island girl."[5] With nonwhites absent from "Europeans only" cinemas—or visible only as employees—and with narratives cut to conform to segregationist mores, moviegoers in Fox's ACT cinemas could easily forget, at least for two hours, that the great majority of the population was absent. Cinema and cinemas in South Africa, no matter the company of origin, were meant to reflect this illusion.

In areas north, such as in colonial Zambia (Northern Rhodesia), multiracial partnership was the ruling racial policy, and the screening of films like *South Pacific*, with its progressive racial ideology, revealed the stark differences in moviegoing across the continent. Frederic Fox noted that when *South Pacific* came to Kitwe-Nkana, he had gone to see the film "with a party of eighteen black African students":

> The whites in the theatre outnumbered my group thirty-three to one—just the reverse of the ratio that exists outside. Any Negro who could afford the $1 ticket—about an average day's pay—would normally have been given a seat in the front row, right under the wide-angle screen. But we were lucky. We got a nice English lady to go to the box office on our behalf and book us farther back. She was able to buy all the seats in one row so that no white person would have to sit beside us. THESE circumstances added a special zest to the Rodgers and Hammerstein show, which, of course, is concerned in part with mixed marriages. . . . For us the hit song was the one on race relations including the line, "You've got to be taught to hate and fear."[6]

Other films such as *Carmen Jones* (1954), starring African American actress Dorothy Dandridge, also became controversial subjects for others operating in regions covered either by ACT exhibition or by ACF distribution. Dave S. Klein, owner of the Astra theater in Kitwe-Nkana, noted, "We expected trouble with this film, since the racial feeling in this southern part of Africa is bad. We have many Afrikanders [sic] here who suffer from inferiority complex. They cannot bear to see a black man who might be better than they are." Klein noted, however, that "if the nationalistic minded South African government not only saw the film fit enough for European [white] screenings in South Africa, but also highly recommended it, then it was good enough for screening in our country, which is supposed to be British." "Prejudice or no prejudice," he added, local audiences flooded the Astra to see Dandridge, as "they came along in droves to give us outstanding houses, something even Fox in Johannesburg was in doubt about."[7]

"That Incident in Salisbury": Race and Exhibition in Colonial Zimbabwe

While the South African government had turned to racial isolation as its social and political policy, the Central African Federation, comprising Northern and Southern Rhodesia and Nyasaland, had based its newest racial policies, Allison Shutt and Tony King remark, on a supposed "multiracial partnership" footing that was "distinct from South African-style apartheid." Southern Rhodesian officials actively cultivated an elite African middle class that they hoped could be turned away from revolution and instead toward loyalty to the colonial state. Thus, Southern Rhodesian officials used economic barriers, instead of sole reliance on race, as a means of separating its citizens.[8] This was the stated policy, but it had proved complicated (and often hollow) in ordinary social and cultural settings—especially if American, British, and South African companies refused to embrace racial "partnership" in their local business activities.

Even before "that incident in Salisbury," as a State Department would later call Fox's disastrous premiere of *South Pacific* in a letter to Eric Johnston of the Motion Picture Association of America (MPAA), the racial policies of American exhibitors were already causing problems for the U.S. State Department and its public relations campaigns in sub-Saharan Africa.[9] On June 22, 1959, an uncredited *African Daily News* article reported that "American efforts" were "being undermined in the Federation of Rhodesia and Nyasaland" by U.S. firms "involved recently in discrimination controversies." The writer cited, as an example, a Bulawayo cinema where four university students "were refused admission because of colour." The theater involved was operated by a Fox-owned subsidiary. "Many Africans who admire America are having second thoughts since some of these incidents took place in the Federation," the article noted. "That is not just because of the two recent incidents. These have just added force to previously held convictions." The article concluded that "every single word of self-praise uttered in America provides Africans here with the opportunity to decry American 'Big-Business' in this country."[10]

The *Daily News* article set off a flurry of concerned letters between Joseph Palmer II, the American consul general in Salisbury, Southern Rhodesia, and Joseph C. Satterthwaite, the assistant secretary of state for African affairs in Washington. Palmer identified the unlisted author as Masotha Mike Hove, former editor of the *Bantu Mirror* and a parliamentary member of the Central African Federation, and began looking for a way to counteract growing resentment within the country.[11] Palmer wrote Satterthwaite about the possibility of "encourag[ing] some non-governmental organization to sponsor a conference of American businessmen interested in Africa in an effort to make them see the importance of conforming in their foreign operations to the image which we are trying to project abroad of the United States. . . . Even from a purely commercial point of view, this seems to me to be good business practice since the great area for expansion here is the African market." "Incidentally," Palmer added,

> the theatre mentioned in the attached article is controlled . . . by Twentieth Century-Fox. It debars Africans from its theatres as a matter of policy. While this practice also reflects certain realities in municipal ordinances, such as requirement for separate toilet facilities, it would help at least to some extent if the firm showed some disposition to press the municipalities to overcome such obstacles. In view of its monopolistic position, it is apparent that if African Consolidated does not carry the ball on this, no one else will. I wonder whether it would not be possible for someone in the Department to have a quiet word with Twentieth Century Fox along this line.[12]

Satterthwaite wrote back to Palmer that "Eric Johnston [of the MPAA] was especially interested in the discussion in your letter" and "will discuss the specific incident reported in the article from the *African Daily News* with Twentieth Century Fox." Satterthwaite, who was invited to speak at a meeting of the African Affairs Society of America, pledged to use "some of the material in your letter in the hope that it may have a useful effect on some of the businessmen present."[13]

Roughly a week after Satterthwaite's letter to Palmer—during the first week of September 1959—preparations were under way for the opening of the new Royal Cinema in Salisbury. ACT had two choices in constructing the new movie house: build one set of restrooms and exclude anyone but "Europeans" or build a separate set of restrooms so that nonwhites could also attend. ACT chose the first option, thus removing any possibilities that university students or any other nonwhite patrons would attempt to procure a ticket. While Black ushers guided patrons through the aisles of the new theater, only "Europeans" would be allowed to sit.[14] Integrationists saw the Royal—and its exclusion of nonwhites—as emblematic of the government's empty lip service to racial partnership and indicative of their growing sense of American hypocrisy.

Integrationist upset turned to anger, though, when it was revealed that the opening night premiere of Twentieth Century-Fox's *South Pacific* for "Europeans only" would be a benefit for the Red Cross—an organization for all races—and that it would be attended by government officials, including the acting governor of Southern Rhodesia, Sir John Murray. The Capricorn Africa Society—a leading multiracial organization founded in 1949 by David Stirling that sought to stave off a growing African nationalist movement through the avocation of a pluralistic, racially coexistent society—was particularly incensed at the local government. Although the Southern Rhodesian government also promoted "multiracial partnership," its rhetoric was not always supported by its deeds, as evidenced by the Royal Cinema incident.[15] Capricorn's then-leader Gaston Thornicroft and former Southern Rhodesia prime minister Garfield Todd and his Central Africa Party both "protested loudly and publicly against the exclusion of non-Europeans from the Royal—and indeed from other cinemas in the ACT group."[16]

A meeting of "Asians and Coloureds" was held in Salisbury before the premiere to urge the Red Cross to "withdraw its name," arguing that the exclusion of non-Europeans was "not in keeping" with the organization's mission. One Red Cross official responded that while "the organisation was sympathetic . . . both these communities would suffer if the Red Cross dissociated itself from the performances, as much of the proceeds would eventually be used for their benefit."[17] A sympathetic "European" attendee suggested that perhaps "the best way to end discrimination based on colour and race alone in the cinemas would be to nationalise all the establishments"—a development that would have shattered Fox's recent investment.[18] (The comment foreshadowed movements to come in other nations.)

Thornicroft, of course, found it outrageous not only that Asian, Black, and "Coloured" patrons were barred from entering but also that "Chinese are allowed to enter public places while 'Asians' [Indians] and Africans are barred. That also applies to the Japanese, who are readily accepted as guests in hotels," Thornicroft added. "People who do not even belong to the Commonwealth are allowed privileges withheld from those who belong to it." He ended with the following assessment: "The whole concept of color in Rhodesia appears to be that the visitor is a better person than the citizen paying taxes."[19] (By way of contrast, moviegoers in Northern Rhodesia could watch *South Pacific* in segregated but commingled cinemas.[20]) The meeting ended with a resolution calling on the government to "withdraw from and/or decline the invitation to attend the function."[21] That request was ignored.

Racial integration in Southern Rhodesia was simply not a priority for ACT's South African executives or their Fox bosses in New York. Royal Cinema management also declined responsibility for the racial exclusion, arguing that "the 'Europeans only' edict had come from the Johannesburg headquarters."[22] The chorus of protests that greeted the Red Cross, ACT, Fox, and Southern Rhodesian officials only grew louder after the premiere was over, especially as the Royal Cinema staff maintained their policy of racial exclusion. Following the premiere, "a delegation of Asians and Coloureds" organized a meeting with the Southern Rhodesia minister of justice, Reginald Knight, who claimed legal impotence to change the Royal Cinema's policies (or that of any other movie house in the country), although he promised to discuss the matter directly with "a representative of African Consolidated Theatres." The Capricorn Africa Society also released a statement proclaiming that it was

> deeply concerned that the Government should have sanctioned the presence of the Acting-Governor of Southern Rhodesia at the opening of the Royal Cinema, under circumstances that were a flagrant violation of the principle of partnership, upon which the Federation is based, and on which its future depends.... It is regrettable that any place of public entertainment should exclude a large section of the public, but it is even worse that the Government should condone an action so contrary to its declared principles, in however good a cause.[23]

The *African Daily News* piled on, noting that it "agree[d] with the Coloured community that Her Majesty's representative should not be allowed to take part in functions which discriminate against sections of Her Majesty's loyal subjects.... Those who put profit before the interest of the country and the racial harmony of its citizens should have strong pressure brought to bear against them."[24] The Central Africa Party added that the minister's "refusal to take action" was "evidence that the Government's professed policy of partnership was 'nothing but a sham.'" A local African leader, Stanlake Samkange, argued that ACT's color bar at the Royal Cinema "was the most outrageous attack on the policy of partnership since the Federation was created."[25] Thornicroft and others subsequently pleaded with white Southern Rhodesians to boycott the cinema.

The Royal Cinema incident, coming on the heels of other events in Southern Rhodesia in 1959, contributed to the sense of despair many felt over the failure of the government, led by Southern Rhodesia's prime minister, Edgar Whitehead, and by Federation of Rhodesia and Nyasaland's prime minister,

Roy Welensky, to adhere to its purported policies "promoting racial partnership." The *New York Times* cited three examples of that failure: the government's failure to pay nonwhite rail employees a livable wage, the government's inability to desegregate hotels in Salisbury, and "the imposition of the color bar at the benefit opening of a new motion picture theatre here." The *Times* made sure to note that the Royal was "owned by African Consolidated Theatres, Ltd., which is controlled by Twentieth Century-Fox Film Corporation, headed by Spyros Skouras."[26] In the *Rhodesia Herald*, Alexandra Rema wondered whether local politicians and moviegoers had "lulled their consciences with the thought that, as the cinema is Union-controlled, they were at the mercy of foreign laws, rules, and regulations, and that their presence at the glamorous first night did not therefore condone a policy of apartheid?"[27]

Thus, the problematic nature of foreign theater ownership was laid bare in Southern Rhodesia. Ownership of foreign theaters meant grappling with internal politics and policy debates that often satisfied no one. Twentieth Century-Fox was intimately involved in the business operations of ACT throughout Africa but had purposely left matters of social and racial policy to its South African employees, whose position on race clashed with Edgar Whitehead's United Federal Party and its supposed "'liberal' policy of partnership" that had promised increased—not decreased—"opportunity for a black middle-class and a relaxation of racial discrimination."[28] As racial policies and social norms continued to shift in Kenya and Southern Rhodesia, Skouras hoped to insulate Fox from having to answer for these decisions by placing them at the discretion of ACT's Eddie Lomba and Harry Stodel in Johannesburg. This strategy did not work.

An "Unhappy Image of the United States Before an African Population"

As the public and press condemnations piled up in Southern Rhodesia, and as the international coverage of the incident grew, American diplomats tried their best to contain the damage. On September 10, three days after the Royal Cinema premiere, Satterthwaite reminded an African Affairs Society of America meeting in New York—"a Who's Who of banks, shipping lines, mineral producers, exporters, importers and traders having business interests in the African continent"—that "many Africans form their judgment of the U.S. by the way they are treated as employees or customers of firms bearing American names." The *Central African Examiner* later noted that "the decision to release [these] remarks—originally made off-the-record at a businessmen's luncheon—is perhaps Washington's answer to the Royal Cinema incident."[29] The response was meager and accomplished nothing.

Palmer and Satterthwaite, who had made no impact on Fox during the summer of 1959, were emphatic about the need to confront Skouras directly. Palmer was particularly incensed about the program handed out at the premiere, which featured a "picture of Spyros Skouras and a message from him for the occasion in which he hailed the work being done by the Red Cross 'which knows no boundaries of race.' Considering the controversial nature of the occasion," Palmer wrote, "his words seemed somewhat hollow to those denied an opportunity to see this great film and the disparity was not lost on the local press." Palmer also wholly discounted Skouras's attempt to shift the blame for the Royal's discriminatory practices to ACT and its South African staff. First, Palmer noted, South African law had no jurisdiction over Southern Rhodesian practices, and second, ACT could easily lead the way in breaking racial barriers because it had virtually no domestic competition. "With only two minor exceptions," Palmer wrote, ACT "owns all the cinema houses in the Federation lock, stock and barrel. Since we seem currently more vulnerable on the question of theaters than on any other aspect of commercial discrimination here, I hope that this latest incident can also be brought to the attention of both Mr. [Eric] Johnston and Mr. Skouras. The time is very ripe for some action in this field."[30]

Over the following few months, attention remained fervently on "that incident in Salisbury" as a symbol of the fight for social equality. The premiere had also highlighted American business involvement in Southern Rhodesia—and its indifference to racial segregation—generating, the *Central African Examiner* wrote, an "unhappy image of the United States before an African population."[31] The Royal Cinema incident was highly counterproductive to President Dwight Eisenhower's economic, cultural, and political mission in Africa. As Andrew DeRoche explains, "Eisenhower had praised the potential of cultural relations instead of military ties," but with the Royal Cinema incident reverberating throughout Southern Rhodesia and beyond, "events in the Federation in the fall of 1959, however, demonstrated that cultural relations could in reality be problematic in their own right." As the State Department failed to sway Skouras and Fox, the powerlessness of the American government became evident. "This inability exemplified the potential dangers of private investment in foreign countries" as "the American-owned theaters in Southern Rhodesia clearly showed that cultural relations could do more harm than good."[32]

Fall of Diplomacy

Throughout October 1959 Palmer worked to assuage local feelings by meeting with representatives from the "Asian and Coloured" communities and promising to press their concerns directly with Skouras.[33] Satterthwaite, meanwhile, also kept up his contacts with Skouras and the MPAA. On October 16, 1959, he held a lengthy phone call with MPAA vice president Kenneth Clark, who told Satterthwaite that Eric Johnston had already spoken with Skouras, whose response to the controversy was that ACT "does not have a policy to exclude negroes or any other race. However, they are bound by their Public Building Certificates issued by local authorities which in some instances bear an inscription that the public building is restricted to Europeans only." Skouras argued that, rather than pushing for more segregation, the company had been "working quietly with the local authorities to remove this restriction but they do not want to make a public issue of it." Skouras added that Fox needed to be "extremely cautious in handling a racial question and [did] not think it wise to do anything to embarrass the local government. As a consequence," he told Johnston, "they are being blamed for the state of affairs by local integrationists." Skouras added that he knew desegregation was inevitable but chose to "be patient and let this come about through a more tolerant policy of the government."[34]

Satterthwaite shared the conversation with Clarence Randall, chair of Eisenhower's Council on Foreign Economic Policy, who then wrote to Johnston with supreme irritation: "Those of us who deal with foreign economic policy have been deeply distressed at that incident in Salisbury. This incident, in my opinion, has greatly damaged the image which Africans have of our country, and the effect is far wider than that on the local public in Southern Rhodesia." Randall also dismissed Skouras's argument regarding the building certificate, arguing:

> [First,] they could have foregone the benefit with its attendant publicity. There could hardly have been a choice of sponsor more calculated to create embarrassment than that of the Red Cross, which is dedicated to the service of mankind without respect to creed or color. Secondly, it seems to me the onus might well have been left with the municipal authorities, and not placed on our flag, by a public request to the authorities to waive the limitations for that opening night.[35]

ACT management, of course, had done neither.

By late October Satterthwaite, Palmer, and Randall were still struggling to fix the situation. Skouras had not yet been approached directly by anyone in the Eisenhower administration—Johnston had instead worked as an intermediary—and Satterthwaite told Palmer that more direct and forceful contact was needed. By then, Senator John F. Kennedy had also reportedly "written [Skouras] a letter urging a change in the admission policy of his Rhodesian theaters."[36]

Skouras and Randall finally exchanged letters in late October and early November, with Skouras writing Randall again on November 6, 1959, to concede that, "while we might have handled the matter more skillfully than we did[,] . . . we were in no position to criticise the local government and its policy without creating an awkward incident from the standpoint of the American government."[37] Skouras assured Randall that "our greatest hope is that the restrictions will be relaxed."[38] Randall then sent Skouras's November 6 letter to Joseph Palmer for review. Palmer's own exasperation is burned into a letter he sent to Satterthwaite:

> I don't know what local government policy Mr. Skouras is talking about. As you know, the local government policy is one of "partnership," and there is certainly nothing inconsistent with this and the admission of non-European races to local theatres. The only requirement is that there must be separate toilet facilities. Thus, according to assurances given me by the Mayor of Salisbury and reported in our Despatch No. 191, African Consolidated Theatres, Limited, has the very simple—if not completely satisfactory—remedy of providing such separate facilities. In other words, it would appear quite clear that the obstacle to multiracial use of cinemas is not the policy of the local government but of African Consolidated Theatres. It appears equally clear that whatever Mr. Lomba may say on the question of relaxing restrictions (to paraphrase Mr. Skouras' words), the ball is clearly in the court of African Consolidated Theatres, Limited, an American-controlled company and widely known by all races here as such.[39]

While Randall, Palmer, and Satterthwaite struggled to find a solution that would satisfy the "Asian" and "Coloured" communities (no one seemed concerned about "African" audiences), the fervor suddenly died down. "For some reason which we are unable to fathom," Palmer wrote Satterthwaite, "the leaders of the Asian and Colored communities have not followed up on their original intention to send through us a memorandum to Mr. Skouras. . . . This may simply be a question of ineptness or inertia." Thornicroft's responses to American consular inquiries were also suddenly dispassionate. Palmer began to detect that an unreported solution may have been found in "circumventing the ban." An Asian citizen told Palmer that he could now "gain admission to the balcony of certain theatres controlled by the group by sending one of his employees with a chit for tickets well in advance of the performance. With tickets in hand, he says, he can usually secure admittance without difficulty. If, however, he draws attention to himself by joining the ticket queue just before the performance, he is usually refused admittance." Palmer wondered whether this new workaround had become more desirable than protest, as many had become "apprehensive about becoming involved in the wider issue of the admission of Africans."[40]

Satterthwaite and Palmer continued to try to persuade executives at Fox and ACT to change their policies over the next year. Skouras knew there was a solution—separate restrooms—"but he evidently is not going to break with local custom," Satterthwaite wrote to Palmer. "However, shortsighted it may be, he has apparently decided to go along with his local manager's recommendations." Satterthwaite reiterated that the Eisenhower administration was powerless to change the policies of an American corporation operating outside the United States. Instead, he urged the start of a public relations campaign to "(1) point out to the Asian and Coloreds that the U.S. Government has no control over the American parent firm, and (2) assure that the parent company is made aware of the implications of its subsidiary's policies."[41]

In February 1960 Palmer learned that Skouras planned to travel to Salisbury, prompting Satterthwaite to ask Randall to reach out to Skouras to plan "a chat" during his visit.[42] Skouras wrote back that his plans had suddenly changed and the trip was indefinitely postponed.[43] Skouras may have shrewdly concluded that with the 1960 U.S. presidential election under way, Palmer and other Eisenhower appointees were lame ducks who would likely be replaced in the coming year. Thornicroft and others may have made the same calculations. Instead, Eric Johnston traveled to Southern Rhodesia in September 1960 to discuss the issue with Edgar Whitehead, who assured Johnston that "multiracial cinemas would be established in October of that year."[44] Whitehead, who served as prime minister and minister of native affairs in Southern Rhodesia from 1958 to 1962 (succeeding Garfield Todd), believed in a two-pronged approach to domestic unrest. On the one hand, he declared a state of emergency in 1959 to suppress both "nationalist unrest and intimidation" and the African National Congress by introducing the Law and Order Maintenance Act and the Emergency Powers Act, which gave the Southern Rhodesian government sweeping powers to crush insurrection and maintain white political and social order. But on the other hand, Whitehead's sticks were served up with carrots, as he oversaw the desegregation of trade unions, hotels, and public swimming pools to create a white-ruled "orderly multiracial society."[45] Despite Whitehead's assurances, though, the desegregation of movie houses was suddenly "delayed indefinitely" due to "political disturbances at that time."[46]

Following the election of John F. Kennedy and his administration's interest in African affairs (and African American civil rights at home), E. H. (Hugh) Ashton, chair of the Bulawayo Race Harmony Committee, began a new campaign to integrate Southern Rhodesian cinemas. In March 1961, two months before the founding of the Republic of South Africa, Ashton wrote to Harry

Stodel at ACT "to enlist his support in trying to modify and ultimately remove discrimination that is widely practiced in cinemas he controls."[47] Ashton conceded that "some Europeans" might stop going to ACT cinemas, but he urged Stodel to examine the industry's "experience in Kenya and Northern Rhodesia," where integration had had a positive effect on attendance with little racial conflict. "We hope that the adverse financial effects will, in fact, not be very great, and that you will not be deterred from making the enormous contribution you can to saner and more healthy race relations in this country."[48] Stodel did not respond to Ashton's letter, and a local representative of ACT asked him not to pursue the matter "at the present stage."[49]

Ashton also wrote to the new American consul general in Southern Rhodesia, John K. Emmerson, to see if he would contact Skouras directly.[50] Emmerson's letter to Skouras asked whether he "would be good enough again to review this issue which has caused the United States a significant loss of goodwill among a sizable portion of the African, Asian, and Colored communities of Southern Rhodesia." Emmerson also refuted the local contention that "multi-racial cinemas would reduce an already dwindling patronage which has been seriously affected by the inauguration of TV":

> I believe this argument can be refuted by experience in other African countries where multi-racial cinemas have resulted in an increase in business. I am told, for instance, that in Nairobi where multi-racial cinemas have been established for some time a form of economic segregation meets the criticisms of those white Europeans (many of whom are steady movie-going customers) who object to association with members of other races at theaters and other public gathering places. I believe that a similar pattern would occur in the movie theaters of Southern Rhodesia which, at present prices, could only be patronized by well-to-do Africans, Colored, and Asians, who, obviously, would cause no offense.... The trend in all of Africa, and it is being felt in Southern Rhodesia, is towards elimination of all restrictions based on color. I think that a business with sizable American interests should be in the forefront of encouraging such elimination of barriers ... before the press of events may force such a step.[51]

After Skouras's dismissive response to this letter, Emmerson wrote to Olcott Deming, director of the Office of Eastern and South African Affairs in the State Department's newly formed Bureau of African Affairs, saying he should remind Skouras that

> (1) The Southern Rhodesia Prime Minister, the former Mayor of Salisbury and other government officials have assured officers of the Consulate General that there is no legal bar to multi-racial cinemas, although there are certain

requirements, e.g., separate toilet facilities, which would have to be met; and (2) The Twentieth Century Fox connection with African Consolidated Theatres is well known to prominent Africans, Coloreds, and Asians in Southern Rhodesia, who resent the link of 'color bar theatre' with a distinguished American business.[52]

Emmerson noted that live theater had already been desegregated there and there were positive results in desegregated cinemas in Northern Rhodesia, Kenya, and Nyasaland. Emmerson also felt sure that a new form of "economic segregation" would still keep out lower-class moviegoers and placate the "Europeans."[53] In the months that followed, Skouras remained undeterred.

Fox Chases Rabbit Ears

There may yet be another reason Twentieth Century-Fox was unwilling to press the race issue with the South African, Southern Rhodesian, and Kenyan governments between 1959 and 1961. Months before "that incident in Salisbury," Fox was in talks with all three governments about investing in broadcasting companies and other licenses to bring television to these countries. Eddie Lomba's initial discussions with South African officials were fraught with roadblocks. Among the problems were opposition by the Dutch Reformed Church, the belief among many Afrikaners that TV would negatively affect home life, the inability to prevent "Native" South Africans from watching television, and the lack of infrastructure to reach both urban and rural areas due to related start-up costs.[54] Fox remained persistent and partnered with Television International Enterprises Ltd. (TIE) in the summer of 1959 to establish television operations in and programming for southern and central Africa. TIE and Fox understood that any deal there would require the support of each country's political, cultural, and industrial leaders.[55] On the day of the Royal Cinema opening in Salisbury, TIE chair David Stirling—the founder of the Capricorn Africa Society who had resigned from the group in 1958—wrote to Fox's Donald Henderson to set up a meeting with Spyros Skouras to discuss their TV plans for South Africa and other central and western African nations.[56] While current Capricorn members like Gaston Thornicroft were busy lobbying ACT to break the color bar in Salisbury, Twentieth Century-Fox (and TIE) were far more concerned with upsetting these governments by not following their written *and unwritten* racial laws. By the end of 1959 Fox's agreement with TIE called for a 15 percent interest in a proposed television network in South Africa and a 50 percent interest in a jointly owned company that would provide programming and advertisements.[57] TIE and Fox also signed an agreement to work together on a proposed Southern Rhodesian TV network.[58] The TIE–Fox agreement—secured through Fox's Rhodesian Theatres Ltd.—called for the establishment of a commercial network throughout the Central African Federation. The TIE–Fox agreement for Southern Rhodesia was signed less than two weeks before the ill-fated premiere of *South Pacific* at the Royal and all of its accompanying troubles.[59]

TIE was not the only film-related entity interested in Southern Rhodesian television. *Rhodesia Property & Finance* wrote in September 1959 that the Schlesinger Organisation, despite having sold its entertainment businesses to Twentieth Century-Fox, might seek entry to Southern Rhodesia's potential television market given its ownership of Afamal, "the largest group of advertising agencies in Southern and East Africa" at that time. J. Arthur Rank, meanwhile, was already involved in local television concerns as one of the principal investors in the Central African Television company "through one of the three British TV concerns which has formed that company."[60] (Britain's ATV and ABC were principal investors.[61]) The journal added that Rank and Schlesinger were indeed still "very closely associated" and British TV manufacturer Bush was, in fact, a constituent part of the Rank Organisation. "Thus," the journal concluded, "an eventual Rank Schlesinger tie-up [for television] is not impossible." Fox's ACT, through their TIE investment, was similarly interested in gaining the television license for the territory, the journal claimed, because box office in Southern Rhodesia had "dropped off in the past year or two, and the Rhodes (Salisbury), the largest indoor cinema in the Federation[,] has had to introduce advertising stunts in its lobby, together with "talent" contests and similar promotions." "In theory," the *Rhodesian Property and Finance* report concluded, "the prospects to the African [television] market are enormous," especially "in view of illiteracy."[62]

By mid-September 1959 the *Daily Mail* (Johannesburg) reported that John Schlesinger might indeed be the "power name" behind the Central African Television application "in this struggle for the Federation's television service in which only millionaire interests could possibly compete."[63] Other applicants included Granada TV Network; Rhodesia TV Ltd., backed by Netherlands-based Philips Radio Ltd.; and a mysterious P. Holender, "who has a local wireless and electrical business" and might be, according to *Rhodesian Property and Finance* and the *Daily Mail*, a front man for a "mystery group" possibly backed by John Schlesinger and J. Arthur Rank.[64] All of this swirling investment and intrigue followed was reflected in a new U.S.I.A. report about a notable amount of "increased activity in Africa" regarding television.[65] For ACT, Rhodesia Theatres Ltd., TIE, and other Fox-related entities, there was a need to not only lobby and placate the Southern Rhodesian government for these licenses but do no harm with the South African government as well, especially those who saw in television a dangerous promotion of interracial contact and political messaging at odds with the country's strict apartheid rule.

Twentieth Century-Fox's need to maintain strong political relationships with the South African government was also due to an ongoing Board of Trade and Industries investigation into the company's possible violations of the Regulation of Monopolistic Conditions Act that began in March 1959.[66] The investigation stretched out over the following two years, during which time the Republic of South Africa was formed and strict apartheid laws were maintained. The board eventually ruled that while it "concedes that the size and scope of [Fox's] undertaking stand in direct relation to monopolistic power ... the above mentioned Act is concerned with the way in which such power is applied and is not aimed at the mere possession of monopolistic power." Fox's decision not to integrate Southern Rhodesian cinemas may have been part of its efforts to win approval from South Africa for "the way in which such [monopoly] power is applied."[67] Fox's concerns over antagonizing the South African and Southern Rhodesian governments at a delicate moment in their lobbying efforts for new television contracts and concerns over monopoly investigations in South Africa may have played a substantial role in the company's reluctance to challenge racial norms in Salisbury and Bulawayo cinemas. The company's disregard for nonwhite patrons may have been nothing more than a calculated business decision aimed at not upsetting ongoing discussions to launch TV businesses throughout the continent or not challenging exhibition practices while under scrutiny for monopoly.[68]

In the end, all of this behind-the-scenes maneuvering mattered little. By November 1959 the South African government postponed granting any licenses for television as the country was "taking no chances on video's voo doo influence on kids & natives" as "South Africa has decided that TV is unwelcome & unwanted in the land of the Boers."[69] Posts & Telegraphs Minister A. A. Hertzog further cautioned citizens about television's likely "destructive effects on children & the less developed races."[70] Any subsequent hopes of gaining a South African TV license were stunted by a May 1960 government announcement that television would be delayed in South African until a nationwide color TV system could be implemented. And, whatever the technology, commercial licenses would not be auctioned off, and television instead would be strictly controlled through the government's own South African Broadcasting Corp.[71]

Meanwhile, Fox struck out with Southern Rhodesia television as well, with the territory's commercial TV service awarded to Rhodesia Television Ltd., backed by media mogul Roy Thompson and the Dutch Philips company. Fox may have been the biggest loser of the sweepstakes. Not only had the company invested a great deal of time and money into these ventures but ACT's

Southern Rhodesian cinemas would soon suffer the immediate effects as commercial TV service began in Salisbury in 1960 and would extend to Bulawayo by 1961.[72] Skouras still pondered the efficacy and possibility of buying into Rhodesia Television Ltd., but Eddie Lomba cautioned against it, telling Skouras in August 1961 that the company would not be able to effect much change given its minority position.[73] Fox executive Donald Henderson wrote to Lomba that Skouras seemed fixated on buying, regardless of their advice.[74] Fox corporate left the door open to future television investments in their annual report to shareholders: "Through Twentieth Century Investment (Pty.) Limited (South Africa), we have acquired an interest in Television Kenya Ltd. and are exploring the opportunities of investing in other African countries where television will play an important role in their development."[75]

Royal Flush

By 1961, two years after the controversial premiere of the Royal Cinema in Salisbury, Fox and ACT had still not changed the theater's or their circuit's racial policies. Despite all the local protests, despite all the American political intervention, nothing could convince ACT and Fox to change their practices. Instead, change came from within as the Southern Rhodesian government amended the country's Entertainment Control and Censorship Act.[76] On October 4, 1961, "non-Europeans" were finally admitted to the Royal and other cinemas when local movie houses were officially desegregated.[77] Lomba hoped that more Asians than Blacks would attend, however, because, in his view, they had more money.[78] "At first the non-whites were shy and slow in joining the whites," *Variety* reported in January 1962, "but they are getting used to attending the big houses in spite of mixed feelings and demonstrations from both sides." The planned "economic segregation" also came to fruition, *Variety* observed, as "the prices of admission are above the means of most non-whites," but "the managers hope they will fill the gaps."[79]

Alan Cousins writes that this kind of desegregation in Southern Rhodesia was little more than window dressing. In the early 1960s, "as the government and their supporters attempted to show the outside world that progress was being made towards a greater African share in government and public life, it became of crucial importance for the government and press to assure white Rhodesians that in reality there would be only limited change." The *Rhodesia Herald* also assuaged white concerns over social integration by arguing that the "values, behavior, and attitudes" of those who could afford to attend Southern Rhodesia's newly desegregated public venues were "the same as those of the European community. This, after all," Cousins notes, "was what 'civilized' implied to the white community."[80]

David Gainer and Laura Fair note that by 1961, when Southern Rhodesia finally desegregated its theaters, South Africa was still firmly opposed to any such liberalization. Even at its drive-ins—with a reported seventy dotting Johannesburg alone—where moviegoers were already separated within the confines of their own vehicles, "mixed" audiences and nonwhites were supplied with only a "handful" of drive-ins that they could attend.[81] Correspondence in the Spyros Skouras Papers between Fox's South African employee, Leon Goldstein, and Spyros Skouras show a conflicted sentiment, with Goldstein vacillating between the company's business interests and his personal desires for limited racial progress, if only to improve the status of South Africa in the world's eyes.[82] Goldstein was not a champion of indigenous rights.[83] In addition to all of the motivations of Fox's South African executives—from concerns over investigations of monopolistic practices to the need to curry favor with local governments to try and gain TV licenses—another facet of the Royal Cinema affair and ACT's continental policies is reaffirmed: local executives were just as racist or accommodating to racism as most other businesses and businessmen and -women in and around South Africa. Fox and ACT were certainly not exceptions. They were just highly visible.

Even before the consecration of apartheid in South Africa, David Gainer notes, Cape Town's Bioscopes had already been highly segregated. Twenty-three of the city's forty-four cinemas were "exclusively for Europeans, 14 for Non-Europeans, and 7 theatres for mixed European and Non-European audiences." Still, racial exclusion was most pronounced in the Central Business District where audiences—white audiences—could find "the super-cinemas, or picture palaces, where the newest American films premiered to European-only audiences." In Cape Town, for example, the two main houses on St. Georges Street, the Colosseum and the Metro, were Fox's and MGM's showcase cinemas respectively and for whites only. These and other cinemas, Gainer notes, "were located where Capetonians lived, exposing them to the Americana of Hollywood films, their hoardings, bright neon signs, and elaborate advertising gimmicks ... And these cinemas in Cape Town were part of an elaborate South African system which provided and reprovided Hollywood's images of America to a South African [white and racially exclusionary] audience."[84]

Hollywood's facilitation of segregation in movie houses was evident both at home and abroad. In 1963, two years after Southern Rhodesian cinemas were officially desegregated in 1961, U.S. Attorney General Robert F. Kennedy summoned forty U.S. Southern exhibitors to the White House as he and President John F. Kennedy made desegregating U.S. movie theaters part of the upcoming Civil Rights Act of 1964.[85] In response, Spyros Skouras (now an ex-president of Twentieth Century-Fox) earnestly sent his congratulations to the attorney general, extolling the virtues of equality for all Americans.[86] This gesture, of course, only highlighted the paradox of Skouras's own pro-integration politics at home versus Fox's corporate positioning in Africa.

Big Trouble in Colonial Kenya

These kinds of racial divisions and segregation were just as dramatic in colonial Kenya. For example, British foreign officer J. L. Keith had written two decades earlier on June 30, 1941,

> From my experience in Africa, I gather that the real reason why Africans are excluded from the principal cinemas in Nairobi and elsewhere (e.g. Northern Rhodesia) is that Europeans object to their presence in places of amusement which the European community regard as their own. This is pure selfishness on the part of the European community, or profit mongering on the part of the cinema owners, who wish to maintain high prices and fear that the admission of Africans will mean decreased attendance in the more expensive seats.[87]

Keith, like American consular officers nearly two decades later, worried that these discriminatory practices would have reverberating effects on the views of West African soldiers stationed in Kenya regarding British colonial rule. Little had changed two decades later when Fox took over ACT's cinema circuit in Kenya in 1956, right in the middle of the Mau Mau Uprising (1952–1960) against oppressive British colonial rule. The rebellion, according to recent estimates, led to roughly 25,000 "Africans" killed and many more injured or incarcerated (32 "Europeans" were also killed during the long conflict).[88]

Fox's ownership and operation of segregated cinemas in the British colony was already well known in Kenya and abhorred by "non-Europeans." Further, by 1960, that the entire Fox-owned operation was based in South Africa was another mark against the U.S. film company to many Kenyans. One of the missions of the anticolonial, antiracist Pan-African Movement for East and Central Africa (PAMECA), founded in 1958, was to boycott any and all South African businesses operating in Kenya. This quite naturally presented a new problem for both Fox distribution and its ACT cinemas for white moviegoers aligned with the boycott. In mid-1960 Julius Nyerere, chairman of PAMECA, penned a statement published in the *Tanganyika Standard* calling for a potential boycott of films distributed in East Africa by companies based in South Africa. Fox's Kenyan manager, William B. Delaney, reached out directly to Nyerere to explain that the company paid taxes in Kenya and that none of its East African revenue was sent to South Africa, even though prints used in

Kenya, Tanganyika, and Zanzibar were shipped directly from Johannesburg. To allay any further confusion, Skouras and his Kenyan Fox representatives decided to form a separate East African subsidiary—Anglo-American Film Distributors Ltd.—owned itself by Fox's London-based subsidiary—to conduct all of Fox's regional business and avoid any taint of South Africa's politics of apartheid.[89] That British ownership did not outrage Kenyans as much as South African ownership demonstrated the intense animus toward South Africa by the end of the bloody Mau Mau Uprising.

Skouras sent off two letters in June 1960: one to Nyerere and the other to Eric Johnston of the MPA, explaining the formation of the new East African subsidiary and assuring Johnston that this new company would reduce racial tensions.[90] Johnston saw the pacification of Nyerere and PAMECA as essential to cultivating the region.[91]

COMACICO, SECMA, the MPEA, and West Africa

In addition to its ongoing operations in Kenya, Skouras also began meeting with the Ethiopian government in order to begin building cinemas there as well.[92] Skouras's trip to Ethiopia was part of Eric Johnston's (and the United States') increasing focus on spreading American commerce to East as well as West Africa. In late 1960 Johnston made his own extensive tour of the continent to compile information useful to the Motion Picture Export Association (the MPEA) and its Hollywood membership. Examining "French West and Equatorial African" countries, Johnston's report noted that film distribution to these regions originated in Paris and then went through the port city of Dakar, Senegal, where two cinema chains—COMACICO (Compagnie Marocaine Cinématographique et Commerciale), headed by Maurice Jacquin, and SECMA (Société d'Exploitation Cinématographique Africaine)—dominated the region.[93]

COMACICO had been the leading cinema circuit in colonial French West Africa since Jacquin, originally from France, set up operations there in 1926.[94] It was, in fact, Maurice Jacquin's open-air Rialto Theatre in Dakar that was one of the childhood cinemas of filmmaker Ousmane Sembene and a key source of his early film education. Jacquin's Rialto Theatre, unlike Dakar's Palace and Piazza theaters, was desegregated and a favorite of Sembene and his childhood friends. Samba Gadjigo writes that Jacquin had been a brutal cinema manager and describes how Sembene was "nearly 'killed' at the Rialto" one day when he was a child when he and his friends, who had "gatecrash[ed]" the open-air Rialto in order to enter the cinema without paying, were caught. Jacquin grabbed the young Sembene and violently held his head under water in a barrel. "This disciplinary measure," Gadjigo writes, "had a strong deterring effect on the more timorous ones, but Sembene was not the kind to be easily cowed by these scare tactics."[95] Boubacar Diop adds that at the Rialto, Sembene was often "caught and abused by ... Jacquin."[96] One can only wonder, of course, how this frequent interaction with Jacquin at the Rialto could have helped shape a lifetime of struggle against French colonial and postcolonial influence and French cinema's dominance in Senegal. After all, Gadjigo writes, it was at Jacquin's movie house that a young Sembene first saw Leni Riefenstahl's *Olympia* and "started to gain awareness of race as a concept and of racism as a social phenomenon."[97]

Maurice Jacquin's influence and power only grew in the succeeding years, even after he returned to France in 1960 following Senegal's independence to set up two new companies, the production company Copernie, and a distribution outlet with the same moniker as his African company, COMACICO. (Jacquin would go on to produce a wide range of films in France including Jean-Luc Godard's *Week-end*.)[98] Back in Senegal in the early 1960s, while the Fox-owned African Consolidated Theatres was expanding its own cinemas and exchanges in East and Southern Africa, COMACICO and SECMA were still the two largest distribution and exhibition companies across West Africa. Many of their combined 135 theaters were open-air cinemas like the Rialto, with films dubbed into French due to "low literacy[, which] inhibit[ed] the use of subtitles." The two companies' hold on exhibition maintained their ability to deny American film companies a foothold in West Africa, even though roughly 60 percent of the films screened in the region were from Hollywood. The remainder were primarily French or Indian films, the latter not dubbed into French but retaining their original dialogue and soundtrack.[99]

In 1962, aware of the great potential of the market, Twentieth Century-Fox once again eyed an expansion of its own fleet of cinemas westward. That year Spyros Skouras entered into negotiations with local exhibitor P. de Lesquen for a group of aging cinemas in West Africa before ultimately declining Lesquen's $3 million price tag.[100] It was Hollywood's MPEA, not Fox alone, that instead began narrowing in on a purchase of both COMACICO and SECMA in an effort to secure control of the West African market for its own member companies in Hollywood. The purchase price for both chains, which had now grown to 160 35 mm cinemas and roughly 90 16 mm cinemas, was $6–8 million, a price that would deliver the vast majority of the commercial cinemas throughout francophone West and North Africa, stretching from Morocco and Algeria to the north all the way south through Senegal, Mali, Niger, and the Ivory Coast. (A separate Hollywood-backed entity focused on Nigeria and other former British colonies.) Annual gross of the COMACICO and SECMA postcolonial cinemas was roughly $8 million, with a net profit of $2 million per year, meaning that the MPEA's investment could break even in less than four years. (At the time, distribution revenue only provided $300,000 per year to all of the MPEA member companies combined.) Yet another reason for the potential purchase was that the French government was itself trying to acquire a 50 percent interest in the two chains and would, it seems, attempt to place even more French cinema in the region to retain its cultural and linguistic influence over its former colonies and secure a reliable string of theatrical venues for French film productions. This would likely mean a diminution in the amount of Hollywood fare being screened in this market. A meeting to discuss the potential MPEA acquisition was held with representatives from member companies on August 23, 1962, where Eric Johnston promised to engage political leaders from each of the countries where COMACICO and SECMA had cinemas in order to gauge their reaction to possible American ownership.[101]

The proposed purchase came at an opportune time for political engagement. Eric Johnston was informed in October 1962 that under the Kennedy administration, Secretary of State Dean Rusk had written to all American ambassadors abroad that part of their new mission was to help develop foreign business for American companies.[102] By November 1962 Johnston had also approached U.S. government officials about the proposal to buy the two chains and received a positive response. An official MPEA audit of COMACICO was commissioned in late October using Price Waterhouse, and another Parisian auditor began working on SECMA. Meanwhile, another group had been sent from Paris to examine each of the companies' individual cinemas for a formal report to be delivered to the MPEA in January 1963.[103]

By December 1962, however, for reasons unspecified, *Variety* reported that the MPEA had now "abandoned any idea of getting into exhibition itself in the[se] African territories."[104] Six months later, in June 1963, despite its declaration that it would remain only a distributor of Hollywood product, the MPEA hired former Universal executive vice president Alfred E. Daff "to represent member companies in dealings in Africa" and, once again, "to negotiate the purchase" of COMACICO and SECMA. "Assuming a deal goes through," *Variety* noted, "the properties would [now] be owned jointly by MPEA members so inclined to participate, in collaboration with the French government." *Variety* was careful to point out that the U.S. partnership with the French government would divert attention away from local resistance to American ownership since French postcolonial possession of local film companies across the region was far more normalized and quotidian and would lead to less charges against "outright ownership by foreign (American) interests" which "would be neither politically healthy nor wise." COMACICO's eighty-four and SECMA's fifty-eight 35 mm cinemas were offered again to the MPEA for $8 million and $5 million, respectively. For $13 million, then, Hollywood would gain 50 percent control, in partnership with the French government, over film distribution and exhibition throughout West Africa. "These

142 houses," *Variety* reiterated, "just about represent all of [the film] exhibition in the wide area. There are only 23 others, independently operated." The trade journal further reminded its readers that "the top exhibitors in the country also function as distributors, and so it is that the only way for the Yanks to lower the trade barriers is to buy their own exhibition outlets. Joint ownership of theatres would [then] set a precedent which likely would be adapted in other foreign locales."[105]

For reasons yet again unspecified, the MPEA did not purchase COMACICO or SECMA.[106] Instead, French industrial and cultural control over the francophone film industries in West Africa remained an enormously important tool in maintaining French cinematic influence throughout the region. This was no small thing. Gordon Kitchens remarked a decade later in 1972, that "finding distribution within Africa for African films remains a problem because all distribution and theater ownership are controlled by two French-based companies, Secma and Comacico."[107] For his part, Maurice Jacquin told *Journal Du Show Business* in 1970, without a hint of self-reflection, that the rising African nationalism of the postcolonial region actually fit the plans for COMACICO since "my policy has always been the promotion of African cinema."[108] Despite this canard, COMACICO and SECMA were able to swat away any indigenous or other efforts to control local screens or book any additional "Black Films" because, Kitchens noted, the two companies have "on several occasions . . . boycotted whole African nations that attempted to nationalize or control their [own] theatres."[109] Control of local cinemas meant control over cinema and culture.

Nigerian Dreams

Of all the countries that had been profiled in Eric Johnston's earlier 1960 MPEA report, it was Nigeria that suggested even greater possibilities for Hollywood. Johnston was unimpressed by the current duopoly dominating the country: West African Pictures Ltd. (WAP) and Farrah Ltd. WAP, like many other global chains, was related to banking interests, in this case owned and operated by the National Bank of Nigeria, whose chairman of the board, J. A. Doherty, was the head of both the bank and the film company. Only fifty-five cinemas were operating in the newly independent country, and only one was an indoor "hardtop" venue, the only one in the nation featuring Cinema-Scope.[110] WAP operated thirty of Nigeria's fifty-five cinemas, and all were open-air and functioned as parking lots during the day before giving way to one singular nighttime screening. Farah was foreign owned, in this case by a Lebanese company, which operated six cinemas and a distribution office. The remainder of Nigeria's cinemas were independently owned and operated.

With a growing population and economy and the first commercial TV station below the Sahara, Johnston correctly reasoned that Nigeria was ripe for American investment.

On November 2, 1962, MPEA vice president George Vietheer left New York for a "three-week look-see" of MPEA's new West African distribution company, American Motion Picture Export Co. (Africa) Inc. (AMPEC), which was based in Lagos, Nigeria, and distributed films to that country and others, such as Ghana.[111] Once again, *Variety* reported, the MPEA "abandoned any idea of getting into exhibition itself in the African territories," though "American capital for this purpose would be welcome and, in his estimation, it's a fertile field for investment."[112] MGM did commission the architecture firm of John McNamara, who built many cinemas across the United States, to design a one-thousand-seat domed cinema in Nigeria in 1964—presumably in Lagos—but there is no indication that this project ever moved beyond its blueprints.[113] (By the end of the 1960s, AFRAM Films Inc. [Afro-American Films Inc.] had been created by the MPEA to distribute Hollywood films in West Africa, directly competing with COMACICO and SECMA, but a wholesale investment in exhibition there was absent from this strategy.[114])

Kenya, Fox, TV, and Film

Fox and the MPEA did not expand their exhibition holdings to other countries in Africa in the early to mid-1960s, despite the MPEA's efforts and Fox's own tire-kicking in Ethiopia. In the end, as in many politically turbulent markets, distribution was a less physically obtrusive and obvious form of American soft power extension. As noted by the State Department's need to gauge the reaction of local governments to a proposed purchase of local cinemas, control over local exhibition *felt* like an intrusive foreign control. Local ownership of film distribution, by contrast, provided the semblance of local governance—even if legacy French colonial companies locked that control down with no interest in indigenous production or development.

With no ability to expand much further in West or East Africa, and with investment in Ethiopia more dream than reality, Skouras refocused Fox's regional desires in South Africa, Southern Rhodesia, and Kenya in the early 1960s and tried, once more, to gain a television license, this time for Kenya. South Africa and Southern Rhodesia had blocked Fox's efforts, but Kenya, still controlled then by the British Colonial Office, signaled it was open for business. Norman F. Harris, Kenya's minister for information and broadcasting, held meetings with interested parties for Kenya's first television station. Many were part of previous efforts, including the Granada TV Network and a combined "syndicate" that included Scottish TV, NBC, and Twentieth

Century-Fox.[115] Harris ultimately invited many of these suitors to join the new company known as Television Network (Kenya) Ltd., which would become a subsidiary of David Stirling's Television International Enterprises Ltd., with key investments and ownership stakes from NBC; Twentieth Century-Fox; Associated British Cinemas Ltd.; Associated Television Ltd.; Scottish Television and Northern Broadcasting Company of Toronto; Television Wales and West of England; East African Newspapers Ltd.; and Nakuru Press Ltd. Stirling's TIE and Nakuru Press had the highest levels of control over the company, with co-equal 20 percent stakes, while Scottish Television, Television Wales and West, and Twentieth Century-Fox all controlled 12 percent of the company.[116] Noting once more the infiltration of banks and former bank executives, R. G. Ridley, previously the East African general manager of the Standard Bank of South Africa, was named chairman of the Kenya Broadcasting Corp., the government entity overseeing television in the colony. Television Network Kenya Ltd. planned to debut its first station in Nairobi in mid-1962 to an estimated 56,000 television sets already in use.[117] The first station, and additional outlets set to be launched in Mombasa and Kisumu, would all be co-operated between Television Network Kenya and Kenya Broadcasting.[118] Despite the supposed firewall that Skouras noted between the South African branch of Fox and the Kenyan operation, ACT employee Eddie Lomba immediately began firing off letters to perspective parties about securing programming on the new network.[119] As evidenced by documentation in the Spyros Skouras Papers, it is clear that Fox's board appointee, Roger Berry, was in direct contact with Stirling regarding the Kenya broadcasting network.[120] The walls between South Africa's Fox subsidiary and Kenya's Fox subsidiary were so permeable that Skouras did not hesitate to put Berry on the board even though he was officially an employee of Fox Theatres South Africa Pty. Ltd.[121] As for Stirling, he seemed untroubled by the recent controversy in Salisbury at the Royal Cinema and, as the evidence suggests, worked hand in hand with Fox to administer Kenya's first television station in the waning days of Kenya's colonial occupation. Business was business.

Fox, Africa, and the 1960s

In December 1963 Kenya finally declared its independence, and, Gwen Thompkins writes, "the rest of Kenya came to sit under the stars" at the once-segregated Fox Drive-In, including "Arabs, Somalis, black people, and Kenyans of South Asian descent."[122] In Southern Rhodesia, the Royal Cinema, too, became a movie haven for all. But in South Africa, ACT employees simply dug in, backed year in and year out by the South African government and by Fox's unwillingness to challenge their host country's racial laws. With Skouras no longer part of Twentieth Century-Fox management, and now three years after

FIGURE 17.1 Twentieth Century-Fox's ACT not only enforced apartheid throughout its African cinemas, it also produced elaborate live shows, some in blackface, ca. 1965. (Author's collection)

the desegregation of Southern Rhodesia's cinemas, Seymour Poe felt confident enough to write to Fox shareholders that "Twentieth Century-Fox is a global organization" whose "many subsidiaries around the globe ... add luster to the Twentieth Century-Fox name here and abroad."[123] Fox's ownership of African cinemas grew even larger in the years that followed. On July 1, 1965, following the death of their former exhibition partner, William Boxer, Fox's ACT picked up an additional thirteen cinemas from Boxer's Empire Films in South Africa and Southern Rhodesia. Fox also expanded ACT's footprint by acquiring the "Cinerama franchise" in South Africa and planned the construction of new Cinerama cinemas in both Johannesburg and Durban.[124]

In a decade of ownership, investment, and expansion, Twentieth Century-Fox had become another Schlesinger Organisation in South Africa, involved in numerous industries far beyond its initial investment, mimicking the way American cinema circuits had begun diversifying in an age of conglomeration and diversification. Fox had also trimmed the underperforming fat of the ACT circuit, pursued a "rehabilitation program" for its fleet of cinemas, and now expanded beyond those initial three countries, with *Variety* reporting in April 1967 that ACT now operated 109 cinemas including 20 drive-ins in "Kenya, Rhodesia, Mozambique and South West Africa," reflecting the growing popularity of so-called alfrescos throughout the continent. When Fox/ACT wasn't dominating exhibition in specific markets, it was still dominating distribution, handling the film supply of Twentieth Century-Fox, Warner Bros., United Artists, Twentieth Century-Fox, Disney, Universal, and American International as well as four British companies, Rank, Anglo-Amalgamated, Lion International, and Associated British. Still, despite all the bravado, there was a whisper of trouble. *Variety* noted that Fox and ACT were beginning to "face some growing competition from the Republic's youngest combine, Ster Films" which was already distributing Paramount and Columbia films.[125]

Ster Films had been a small film distribution company in the South African market until 1962 when insurance company Sanlam, "with the explicit intention of providing cinema predominantly for Afrikaner patrons," David Wigston writes, acquired a major stake in the firm and began expanding its presence and possibilities. Sanlam quickly presented Ster Films as a growing challenge to Fox/ACT by building three cinema "complexes" in Durban, Johannesburg, and Pretoria.[126] In 1967 Ster acquired the Ocean City Icedrome in Durban, which included a Cinerama theater, the Art Theatre, and "a discotheque and restaurant." *Variety* reported that Ster had also purchased the Curzon in Cape Town, to become another Cinerama Theatre, and hatched a "similar plan" for Johannesburg. The arms race for drive-ins had already brought Ster and ACT nearly to a draw: Fox owned twenty alfrescos while Ster already operated seventeen.[127] For the first time since purchasing ACT, Fox had real competition in the South African market.

Film Production at Twentieth Century-Fox's Killarney Film Studios

The increasingly beleaguered Twentieth Century-Fox, needing revenue wherever in the world it could be found, redoubled its efforts to maximize the

African Consolidated Theatres profit machine. This included the increasing production of films at the Fox-owned Killarney Film Studios outside Johannesburg—often focused on South African–based "spaghetti westerns" that had been roundly assailed by U.S. film production unions not only for the company's support of apartheid but because the studio was a (runaway) threat to local film production back in Hollywood.[128] Fox had fulfilled its 1956 promise to Johannes Strijdom by churning out four Afrikaans features per year in addition to English and Afrikaans versions of the *African Mirror* newsreel, along with documentaries and advertising films. After being exhibited throughout Fox's ACT circuit, they were shipped off to theatrical and nontheatrical venues across the country, a process that could take up to four years throughout the whole of the republic.[129]

The growing allure of Killarney Film Studios and local production in South Africa was manifold for Fox. "Government subsidies are available, competent technicians plentiful, and the [local] industry has no trade unions," the *Los Angeles Times* later noted. "The weather is excellent for outdoor shooting and there are plenty of exciting locations."[130] These subsidies—which paid out more if the films were made in the Afrikaans language—helped employ more than six hundred South Africans in local filmmaking, with millions of dollars paid out to local productions. And since South African Screen Productions was a local company, Fox was able to make these films on the cheap and then exploit them in other markets and ancillary revenue streams. Pax Moren, managing director of Killarney, admitted later that filmmaking in South Africa is "like bounty killing in the Old West: You do it for the subsidy."[131] Here, once more, Hollywood won on both ends. To curry favor with the local government, Fox followed the racial politics of the moment, making films that treated Asian South Africans as exotic shopkeepers or servants and, worse still, as dangerous communists, race agitators, or spies. And for Black and "Coloured" South Africans, the forcibly vanished population was either missing almost entirely in these films or often depicted through subservience or depictions of ethnic ritual and dance. Meanwhile, Fox pocketed the government subsidies in its local corporation and used these films to sell tickets to its own cinemas throughout South Africa and then used these films again as filling fodder for global TV licensing packages and B-list theatrical distribution deals in the United States and other global markets.

In 1967, sensing a growing threat from the Afrikaner-owned Ster company's films and theaters, Fox met this growing nativist challenge by sending "long-time Fox director" Robert D. Webb to South Africa to remake at Killarney both Samuel Fuller's noir thriller, *Pickup on South Street*, as *Cape Town Affair*, and William Wellman's western, *Yellow Sky*, as *The Jackals*. Webb was not unfamiliar with the western genre, having directed Fox's *The Proud Ones* starring Robert Ryan and Virginia Mayo a decade earlier.[132] This may be one reason why *The Jackals*, featuring a rather jocular Vincent Price, is a more solid remake of *Yellow Sky* than the plodding *Cape Town Affair*, which had none of the crackling energy of Samuel Fuller's film. As one recent review noted, *Cape Town Affair* is a "horrendously unworthy remake of Fuller's classic."[133]

In both the framing story of *The Jackals*, in which Webb swaps the Apaches of the old West for the Tsonga-speaking people in South Africa's Transvaal, and in the header of the *African Mirror* newsreel, nineteenth-century Black South Africans are depicted in much the same manner as twentieth-century Black South Africans: in ritual dress and outside of mainstream white South African society. Fox's *The Jackals* and its *African Mirror* reinforced the National Party's framing of Black South Africans as an exotic spectacle. Not only did Fox enforce racial discrimination in its African movie houses but it also distributed fiction and nonfiction films throughout Africa and beyond that reinforced the republic's ideology of white racial superiority through the depictions of white urban modernity in these racially evacuated cities or rugged white rural individualism in contradistinction to the representation of Tsonga-speaking and other ethnic groups in South Africa that are strikingly, in *The Jackals*, cinematically aligned through editing with the region's wildlife. It is worth noting that *The Jackals*—and its historic depictions of the Shangaan people—was made precisely during the creation of the separate but deeply unequal Gazankulu area in the Northern Transvaal Province. This apartheid region or "Bantustan" would be granted self-governing status six years later, in 1973, and attests to Webb's transference of Native Americans with the Transvaal Shangaan, seeing Gazankulu as a kind of South African reservation.[134]

Of course, presenting caricatures of various ethnic groups did not make the republic and its local filmmaking by Twentieth Century-Fox unique. Hollywood, before *Little Big Man* and many other revisionist westerns, had made "cowboys and Indians" films global favorites, with films like *Stagecoach* and *They Died with Their Boots On*. Charles Ambler, for example, has described the adulation of these kinds of Hollywood films in Northern Rhodesia amid the formation of the so-called Copperbelt Cowboys. These were self-styled Black workers in the British colonial mines who identified not with the Indians fighting the colonization of their land by white settlers but instead with the white cowboys, often nicknaming themselves "Jack" or "Jeke" and appropriating their outfits and style, a surprising phenomenon that historian Laura Fair recounts in her own work on the influence of Hollywood films on colonial and postcolonial Tanzanians. It is a deep, lasting influence on the region that could also be seen in the Congo city of Kinshasa, where young men, similarly influenced by American westerns, modeled themselves after Hollywood cowboys, organizing into groups known as "Bills" or "Yankees." Here once again we can see that to fully understand Hollywood—as a medium and a mythology—requires examining the full power of Hollywood's global cultural and political influence.[135]

It was *Cape Town Affair*, however, even more than *The Jackals*, that clearly articulates South Africa's racial politics and Twentieth Century-Fox's acquiescence to those values in its local filmmaking. Here Webb transposed Fuller's original New York setting and its own anticommunist ideology to contemporary Cape Town and the policies and politics of apartheid, which were bound up in the specificity of midcentury South African anticommunism. Webb flew to Johannesburg in October 1966 and began scouting locations for the film just one month after the assassination of Hendrik Verwoerd, a key founder of the South African Nationalist movement and a fervent proponent of the apartheid regime. He was, therefore, a martyred figure for the nation's political elite. Throughout the *Cape Town Affair*, a framed photo of the slain Verwoerd can be seen throughout police headquarters, reinforcing his vision of racial superiority as a founding principle of the police and therefore the city's and state's "law and order." Although Webb mimics much of Fuller's direction, he doesn't follow him in framing the interrogation of James Brolin's character at police headquarters. In fact, by flipping their arrangement within the mise-en-scène from the original film, it allows the detective to be framed, mirrored, and reflected within the hallowed vision of Verwoerd, reinforcing the legal and racial authority of the police and the larger narrative that communists are dangerous subversives working to thwart white racial rule and authority. Joseph K. Heumann and Robin L. Murray write that since "white-only audiences in South Africa" were "paranoid about communist-led Black insurrections... they would not miss the values [Verwoerd] represents" as the film served as a reminder of South Africa's "law and order" versus the political unrest in nearby Angola, Mozambique, and colonial Zimbabwe, which served as an unspoken backdrop to the film.[136]

Since many of these Killarney-made films were produced for more rural Afrikaner audiences, these moviegoers would have been keenly attuned to portrayals of urban Cape Towners and other city dwellers as "dangerously" promoting racial equality, a small number of whom were communists. Communism in South Africa, rather than being an existential threat from the Soviet Union in *Pickup on South Street*, was an existential threat from within to the republic's racial hierarchies and the ongoing whites-only rule of the National Party. For another demonstration of the way that Fox's local films reproduced these kinds of narratives, Webb carefully lays out the communists' headquarters with African art, a telling adornment that South African audiences would easily recognize as denoting their interracial leanings through their valorization of local cultures and a threat to the spartan postwar modernity of the police station and other settings that were more distinctly "European." Webb also added an Asian henchman to the communist group, a striking bit of casting only one year after the famous declaration of Cape Town's District Six as a whites-only area under the Group Areas Act, a new law that led to the forced removal of upward of sixty thousand Asians and other nonwhites throughout the area.[137]

The aesthetic and thematic reinforcement of white rule in *Cape Town Affair* by the local police and the ongoing real-life suppression of the African National Congress and other antiapartheid, pro-independence groups was palpable in 1967 following the sweeping changes across Africa in Kenya, Angola, Mozambique, and beyond, including across the border in Southern Rhodesia. Killarney films like *The Jackals* and *Cape Town Affair* were also not simply internal domestic products. These films screened theatrically well beyond South Africa and made their way to global televisions, becoming key parts of Fox's return to feature film syndication.[138] In 1967 Twentieth Century-Fox Television sold these two films, along with nine others, to CBS stations around the United States, including in Atlanta and St. Louis, where racial tensions only a few years after the passage of the Civil Rights Act remained on semipermanent boil.[139]

The *Cape Town Affair* is therefore a reminder that Twentieth Century-Fox's ownership of ACT, ACF, and other entertainment companies, including *The African Mirror* and Killarney Film Studios, puts midcentury U.S.-ownership of South African producing, distributing, and exhibiting companies into much clearer focus. Fox, despite its objections during the Royal Cinema incident in Salisbury, was not at all a mere bystander in Africa's racial politics. Instead, Hollywood companies like Fox and MGM facilitated the racial politics of the South African apartheid regime, even beyond the republic's geographical borders, and, in terms of production and exhibition of motion pictures, one of its most important local enforcers and enablers.

Kenyan Nationalization

Kenya was an entirely different market and situation, however, after its 1963 independence. Edwin Ngure Nyutho writes that four years later, in 1967, "only a paltry 30% of Africans in Kenya and Tanzania were attending theatres to watch films," and all feature films exhibited in Kenya were "imported by the 8 main importer/distributors who were all unfortunately non-Africans. The films were then distributed to the 80 theatres (cinema houses) in East Africa which were owned by non-Africans, mostly Asians. The distributing companies were all owned by non-Africans. In a nutshell, the industry was totally controlled by non-African foreigners." Meanwhile, Nyutho adds, little of the social composition of Kenyan cinemas had changed as a result, as "the main cinema goers were [still] Asians and Europeans who comprised 70% of the market."[140] While Hollywood film companies—namely, Fox and to a much lesser extent MGM—dominated much of South African exhibition, Asian (Indian) exhibitors and films also had a substantial role here as they did in other African film markets like Tanzania.[141]

Nyutho argues that "film distribution in Africa from the USA was a monopoly of one Anglo-American company"—owned by Fox—"a South African company that had sole distribution rights throughout Africa and was the one spearheading curtailing the establishment of KFCp," the Kenyan government's nationalized film distribution company. Fox's Anglo-American Film Distributors Ltd. was not, in fact, a South African company but a British one.[142] So, despite Fox creating a separate East African subsidiary—Anglo-American Film Distributors Ltd., which was based out of the company's Kenya Theatre building in Nairobi and was owned by Fox's London-based subsidiary and not by its South African subsidiary—the Kenyan government either did not believe this was the case or had credible evidence that Fox was lying.[143] This does not appear to have been the case. And, of course, the whole of the corporation—however it was divided into subsidiaries—was controlled from the United States, now by Darryl Zanuck. Fox, like other American companies operating in Africa, toed the political line of colonial, apartheid governments and often—including here—pushed back against newly independent states run by (mostly) nonwhite Africans, especially those looking to wrest control of local film industries and film exhibition from Hollywood. Meanwhile, as Nyutho notes, permanent secretary of the Ministry of Commerce, Industry, and Cooperatives Kenneth Stanley Njindo Matiba regarded the money Fox and others took out of Kenya from film distribution and exhibition as "a huge loss of foreign exchange to a young government which was trying all ways of entrenching the Africans who had been kept out of formal business during the colonial era into the business culture through a Kenyanisation policy."[144]

One of the reasons why a regional, pan-African analysis is so important to understanding how Hollywood secured its global influence through exhibition is that a regional analysis removes any confusion about how companies like Twentieth Century-Fox operated during this period. In some ways Kenya before independence had been even more restrictive than apartheid South Africa. As Nyutho writes,

> the astounding thing to note is that films that were regularly shown to all audiences in Cape Town and Johannesburg were forbidden to African audiences in the Rhodesias. In Kenya where there were no theatres for Africans, it means the films could not be seen by locals because the mobile cinema vans which were the only option, were exhibiting propaganda and didactic cinema only created for that purpose to captive native viewers. Until the late 1950s, virtually the only films screened for Africans in these colonies were heavily edited American "western" genre films.[145]

Thus, between "Asian" ownership of cinemas with large Indian and other movies and "European" domination of movie houses with Hollywood and British films, Kenyan cinemas showed foreign films to "European" and "Asian" audiences with little to no control or representation of the politics and identity of a newly liberated and independent Black Kenyan audience.

To counter this foreign influence—both Indian and American—the government-owned Kenya Film Corp. Ltd. (KFC) was created on July 14, 1967, "wholly owned" by Kenya's Industrial and Commercial Development Corp. and, according to Nyutho, "given exclusive rights to import and distribute 35 MM theatrical films throughout Kenya." KFC demanded that it be allowed to distribute all films entering the country and take a 30 percent fee for the distribution of Fox, MGM, and all other nonindigenous film product. Most of the country's cinemas—both Indian- and American-owned—closed their cinemas out of protest, depriving KFC of essential revenue.[146] Fox immediately closed its Nairobi cinemas—two of which were the premiere venues in the country—and refused to distribute any KFC films in Kenya.[147] Nyutho, surprised about American corporate policy, notes that "one of the most incredible ironies on the issue is that the US cinema industry was openly doing business with the apartheid racist regime companies and they were unwilling to deal directly with a company set up by a democratically elected Kenya government."[148] Understanding Fox's African strategy makes this hardly surprising.

It would take over a year, until September 1968, for the MPEA, working on behalf of Fox and other U.S. distributors, to sign an agreement with KFC whereby the Kenyan government would receive only a 10 percent fee for each film distributed in the country, as KFC was forced to relinquish its attempted monopoly. The resumption of film distribution, on terms favorable to both sides, led to a reopening of Fox's 20th Century, Nairobi, and Thika Drive-In theaters.[149] The large number of Indian-owned cinemas that did not sign an agreement with KFC were subsequently requisitioned by the Kenyan government and sold off to exhibitors willing to work with the newly nationalized distribution system.[150] For the MPEA and its Hollywood cohort, the trade group signed this bartered agreement in an effort to dissuade regional impulses toward nationalization and film and cinema confiscation—as occurred in Algeria—in favor of private–public partnerships that ultimately benefited the constant flow of U.S films (and ideology).[151] Fox and other American films would continue to flow into Kenya for the next half century.

Out of Africa

Hollywood had solved one problem in Kenya, but it had much greater concerns back home. By the end of 1968 Fox, like other aging film companies, was hemorrhaging money. The ACT investment had remained Fox's most successful foreign exhibition holdings, surpassing its net revenues in Hoyts in Australia and other investments in New Zealand, England, and beyond.[152] In addition, *Variety* reported that "with the skyrocketing of land and real estate prices over the past decade" the value of ACT's assets had "multiplied in value tenfold since the 1956 sale."[153] The larger Twentieth Century-Fox company lost roughly $37 million in 1969 and more than double that figure by 1970.[154] A sale of profitable assets was seen as the best way to balance out its debt.

With this valuation in mind, and following the sale of a considerable part of the backlot in Los Angeles, Zanuck divested Twentieth Century-Fox's assets—including the Killarney Film Studios and the *African Mirror* newsreel—in South Africa and colonial Zimbabwe by selling these holdings back to John Schlesinger and the Schlesinger Organisation in 1969 (Kenya was not part of this sale as it was still separately held through the British subsidiary).[155] While Fox exited exhibition in both territories, the company continued operating its own distribution offices in South Africa. Fox did garner one very important concession in the deal with Schlesinger: a thirty-year agreement to exhibit Fox films in the newly renamed Kinekor chain.[155] With that agreement, Fox could reap the financial rewards of the South African market without bearing, for now, any of the additional global costs and controversy of its political affiliations with the South African government.

With Fox no longer controlling the former ACT chain, by January 1970 Sanlam (South African National Life Assurance Mutual) and the Schlesinger Organisation renamed African Consolidated Theatres the Kinekor Organisation, thereby removing Fox and ACT's historic legacy. M. K. Jordi, chief executive of Kinekor, remarked, "It is most appropriate that the Group should seek to change the name and image, so that it will be identified as a forward-looking South African organization."[157] Kinekor's 123 cinemas in South Africa and Rhodesia—before the company's updates—included 101 hardtop cinemas and 22 alfrescos. Sanlam was, of course, not only invested in Kinekor but also—through its Satbel (Suid Afrikaanse Teaterbelange Beperk—SA Theater Interests Ltd.) "shell" company, Ster Films—operated 44 more cinemas throughout the country, with 11 new cinemas added in 1969 alone.

Fox's ownership of Nairobi's two most important cinemas, coupled with favorable distribution terms supported by the local government, ultimately led Twentieth Century-Fox to exclude its Kenyan operations from the 1969 corporate asset sell off. There was one more reason to hang on: Twentieth Century-Fox's ongoing investment in Kenyan television and its value as a hedge against the declines in theatrical distribution and exhibition as television adoption spread throughout Nairobi and beyond.[158] Well into the mid-1970s, Fox maintained both film distribution and exhibition operations in Kenya as well as key investments in local television.[159] Twentieth Century-Fox, meanwhile, retained its Kenya cinemas as a publicly owned American company with the Fox Theatres (not African Consolidated Theatres) name, all under the aegis of Wim van Ewijk Jr. until the sale of the chain in 1975.[160] Fox Theatres, without Fox ownership, remained a recognized name in Kenyan film exhibition for the next four decades.

Hollywood Continues On

It was MGM then, not Twentieth Century-Fox, that remained a key player in South African film exhibition. As noted in chapter 1, by 1973 CIC was successful enough to lease film and television rights and distribute all content for the beleaguered MGM studio in both "foreign theatrical and television markets" for the next ten years. CIC also purchased outright all of MGM's foreign physical assets for $17.5 million. That purchase included MGM's remaining thirty-seven foreign cinemas, half of which were in South Africa and jointly owned with Film Trust. The circuit there was subsequently named CIC-Film Trust.

The purchase of MGM's cinemas was a turning point for CIC. The company had been principally a distribution outlet until then. By January 1974 *Variety* reported that CIC now had "ambitious plans for the theatres in both hemispheres" and planned to make these cinemas "substantially enhanced by conversion, where feasible, into multiple sites (twins, troikas, quartets) under the umbrella of major realestate [sic] development programs—office shopping—entertainment complexes that would tie in local business partners."[161] The circuit had already grown to forty-two cinemas exhibiting films now from Paramount, Universal, and MGM, with further expansion planned for South Africa and the Netherlands.[162] As for the CIC-Warner distribution company, Ster-Kinekor, in a repeat of Isidore Schlesinger's activities, attempted to control exhibition and distribution terms throughout the country by "freez[ing] out" all of the companies distributing through CIC-Warner in favor of its own distribution partners like Twentieth Century-Fox. This, *Variety* reported, forced CIC-Warner to "scrounge for playing time in the several hundred indie theatres, many of which are all-black [and] under official imposition of apartheid."[163]

Television was finally introduced to South Africa in 1976, and the box office declined dramatically. By 1979, though, cinema attendance had returned to pre-1976 levels, and with a newly stable industry, Satbel merged their Ster and Kinekor units into one company, Ster-Kinekor, which still had distribution agreements with Fox, Disney, Orion, Rank, Anglo-EMI, and AVCO-Embassy. Other overseas interests had once again realigned themselves into the CIC-Warner group for local distribution. The latter organization was half-owner, along with South African group, MGM Film Trust, of the Cintrust distribution network. Cintrust, in turn, had contracts with U.S. majors like MGM, Paramount, Warner Bros., and Universal.[164]

In terms of exhibition, CIC generated $293 million in 1978–1979, $220 million in 1979–1980, and $235 million in 1980–1981, making CIC the largest film distributor in the world. The company now operated seventy screens around the world, twenty-nine in Africa, twenty-eight in Latin America, and eight in the United Kingdom, employing roughly 2,400 workers.¹⁶⁵ In 1981 CIC announced a larger merger with MGM and United Artists and the creation of an even larger conglomerate, United International Pictures, which distributed films from Paramount, Universal, MGM, and United Artists beginning November 1, 1981.¹⁶⁶ As one more example of how complicated the foreign market became, CIC continued on as an exhibitor as the CIC Theatre Group. By 1987 CIC extended from Europe to South America to Australia.¹⁶⁷ The South African CIC-Metro circuit was not sold off to New Center until 1987.¹⁶⁸

The Long Arm of Apartheid

The sale of ACT to what became Ster-Kinekor and the conversion of MGM into CIC masked Hollywood's continued participation in South African apartheid. These were issues that concerned American corporations in terms of publicity but rarely ever in terms of their bottom lines. They did, however, present thorny issues for local consular staff and the U.S. Department of State. In 1976, for example, during the waning days of the Ford administration, Secretary of State Henry Kissinger wrote to the American embassy in Pretoria concerning an incident in which an African American Peace Corps volunteer, Janeth Rudolph, was denied entry to the Ster-Kinekor-owned Kine Center movie theater in Johannesburg on August 25 "because of her race," prompting Kissinger to direct the U.S. ambassador to South Africa to call the South African Foreign Minister Hilgard Muller or the ministry's head of Foreign Affairs, Bernardus Gerhardus Fourie. Kissinger also planned to "RAISE [the] MATTER" with Ambassador Pik Botha in Washington. As Kissinger telegrammed to staff in Pretoria, "THE INCIDENT WAS SERIOUS" and "PRESENTS US WITH A DOMESTIC POLITICAL PROBLEM" with "AN ESPECIALLY UNFORTUNATE IMPACT IN WASHINGTON."¹⁶⁹ The incident may have even been the impetus for a Senate Committee on Foreign Relations Subcommittee on African Affairs to request detailed information on U.S. corporate activities in South Africa.¹⁷⁰ By offloading formal distribution operations but keeping their long-term contract in place, Fox could argue that the company did not operate in South Africa even though it was making millions there each year.

It was not until a decade later, in 1986, when Warner Communications finally "divest[ed] some of its business operations in South Africa as a way to show its displeasure with apartheid." This followed a request from Rev. Jesse Jackson, who had run for U.S. president two years earlier. Warner spokesman

Jeffrey Holmes told the *Baltimore Afro-American*, "This is the only way we can voice our displeasure with the policies of the South African government."[171]

By the end of the 1990s (after the end of apartheid), Ster-Kinekor and Nu Metro (the former CIC-Warner circuit) had, according to Shepperson and Tomaselli, "strengthened its grip" on the country leading to "fewer independent cinemas."[172] Further, David Wigston wrote in 2004, "Despite the original intention of SATBEL to provide Afrikaans films as a counter to American culture, with the [1970s] merger Ster-Kinekor became the conduit for Hollywood into South Africa with control of 76 percent of all distribution. The remaining 24 percent being controlled by UIP-Warner."[173] "How could this happen?," Lucia Saks writes.

> The answer lies in the way South African distribution and exhibition circuits operate as an oligopoly of two companies, Ster-Kinekor (now part of the multinational conglomerate, Primedia Group) and Nu-Metro (formerly CIC Warner). The same companies who controlled the circuits under apartheid continue to control it today. They have restructured in response to government's affirmative-action objectives and taken black board members, but their close alliance to Hollywood's conglomerates is the same as always, as is their risk-aversive business model. They continue to pursue a rigid bottom-line mentality when it comes to local products, citing statistics that show that only 1 percent of South African movies shown each year are financially viable.... Both Ster-Kinekor and Nu-Metro remain wedded to prepackaged Hollywood films ready to go on the screen and into the commercials without any extra investment.[174]

With such broad representation over the entire desegregated South African market, there was now little incentive for U.S. film companies to wage a war against either company in this market by building, buying, leasing, or operating local cinemas. In Kenya, too, Nu Metro remained a key exhibitor well into the 2010s, as did Fox Theatres.[175] However, by 2018, John Kamau noted that much had changed during that decade. "Nairobi," he opined, "is now a cemetery of cinema halls—and those who walked this city from the '60s to '90s have nostalgic memories of Odeon Cinema, Globe Cinema, Shan Cinema, Embassy, Cameo Cinema, ABC, Kenya Cinema, Fox Drive-In, Bellevue, and 20th Century. Apart from 20th Century, which still has some presence in Nairobi, the rest are dead business—and all we have about them are memories."[176]

***

With the end of apartheid and global trade sanctions against South Africa, CIC-Warner was reorganized and renamed Nu Metro, bringing the heralded name of MGM's faded shop windows back into association with the remnants of its global distribution operations.[177] Three decades after the end of apartheid and five decades since the sale of ACT to Sanlam/Satbel/Schlesinger, Ster-Kinekor, the company now known as Ster-Kinekor Theatres, has remained the country's largest exhibitor. The company is still a division of Primedia Unlimited and a prime exhibitor of all of Hollywood films.[178]

More than half a century after Fox divested its African holdings, the residual memory of U.S. ownership of all of these African cinemas is fading faster than the now vanished Fox Drive-In's weatherworn sign in Nairobi.[179] What lingers instead are questions about the treatment of nonwhite moviegoers in many other countries throughout the Africa continent during this period. Twentieth Century-Fox's African operations reflected the U.S. film industry's split approach to race during the mid-twentieth century: on the one hand, it often challenged prejudice on screen through films like *South Pacific*; on the other, it engaged in or cooperated with discriminatory behavior in foreign cinemas under the cloak of respecting local traditions. For decades Hollywood producers and distributors exhibited their films in company-owned cinemas in deeply segregated nations (including the United States). This record reminds us that examining American film distribution abroad is only one half of a much more complex history. That history tells us not only about which films were distributed to specific markets and then cinemas but what the contexts of their exhibition meant for the contours of their reception. Indeed, studying the cultural embassies that Hollywood owned and operated throughout this market reveals a highly generative source of the animus already building against the United States in various regions and a growing sense that Hollywood films presented an idealized sense of reality that simply did not match its policies in the movie theaters it operated in South Africa, colonial Zimbabwe, or colonial Kenya. In other words, Hollywood's cinemas spoke a truth to its nonwhite patrons in Africa that its films did not.

PART VI

ASIA

Eastern Promises (1927–2013)
Hollywood's Cinemas in China, India, Japan, and the Philippines

CHAPTER 18

BENSHI AND BALLYHOO, 1927–1973

Hollywood's Shop Window Cinemas in Japan and the Philippines

The benshi at [Paramount's] Hogaku-Za was a conservative satirist: urbane, witty, a man of the Japanese world who saw its near-perfect order threatened by the alien civilizations beyond the sacred islands. With endless drafts of scorn and wit he worked to repel this invasion of foreign ideas and manners.

—Oswald Wynd, novelist and former Hogaku-Za cinemagoer, 1985

The quote above, from Scottish novelist Oswald Wynd, who had been a young bilingual cinemagoer in Tokyo during the late 1920s, reflects both the excitement and the danger of Hollywood's efforts to expand its exhibition empires into Asia for much of the next century, between the Japanese bookends of the opening of Paramount's Hogaku-Za in Tokyo in 1927 and Warner Bros.' sale of its Warner-Mycal Cinemas in Japan nine decades later, in 2013. In between, U.S. exhibitors—Paramount, Twentieth Century-Fox, Warner Bros., and MGM—encountered industrial, technological, political, and cultural resistance in Japan; destruction, internment, and death in the Philippines during World War II; alternating moments of anti- and philo-Americanism in India; and brief flowerings and abrupt closures in postwar and post–World Trade Organization China for MGM and Warner Bros., respectively.

More than any other region, Asia maintained a lasting hold over Hollywood's interest in exhibition expansion, despite enormous political, cultural, and industrial challenges. After Paramount leased the Hogaku-Za theater in Tokyo and created a chain of Japanese cinemas with the Shochiku company, MGM would secure its own shop window cinemas in the 1930s in colonial Bombay and Calcutta, Manila, and Shanghai. Seven decades later Warner Bros. would make the strongest exhibition commitment to the region in a daring land grab for new Chinese cinemas that boomed and then busted, leaving Chinese partner and exhibitor Dalian Wanda with the management, expertise, and infrastructure to foment its own plan for global expansion.

Hollywood's exhibition operations in Asia clearly reflect the political and cultural shifts of each nation in which they operated. Unlike their activities in Europe, South America, and Australasia, there was little comprehensive regional strategy; instead, companies like MGM, Fox, and Warner Bros. approached each nation and their domestic industries as individual territories despite having regional managers trying to manage these vast and disparate geographical areas. Asia held great promise for Hollywood—especially given the continent's enormous population and the possibilities of the market—but it proved to be a politically fraught region, with tremendous potential as well as tremendous potential for conflict. The U.S. government's passage of the Immigration Act of 1924 damaged relations between the United States and Imperial Japan as it barred Japanese citizens from emigration. This animus played a critical role in attacks on Paramount's cinemas in Japan by both journalists and fellow exhibitors. As noted above, Oswald Wynd detected an air of subterfuge in the heralded *benshi* (live narrators) who worked for Paramount at their Hogaku-Za, as they also began working against a growing sense of American cultural and technological imperialism with the advent of American sync-sound films that threatened to diminish the popularity of locally produced Japanese silent films and the very *benshi* themselves.[1]

Japan, Nationalism, and the Politics of Silent and Early Sound-Era Exhibition

A century ago, Japan, not China, was the most lucrative territory in Asia for Hollywood films. By 1922 Famous Players-Lasky had made distributing Paramount films in Japan a key priority. Tom D. Cochrane, who had been Universal's representative in Japan from 1919 to 1922, was named general manager of Paramount's new Japanese company, Famous-Lasky Paramount Films Ltd. With the opening of new distribution offices in Tokyo that August, Paramount had its first owned and operated film exchange in the Asian market.[2]

That foothold in Japan would receive a serious shock the following year, when the massive Tokyo-Yokohama earthquake or "Great Kanto Earthquake" struck on September 1, 1923. Cochrane, who had been staying at the Fujiya Hotel in Miyanoshita, described seeing "mountains sliding into valleys, roads obliterated and houses and buildings transformed into piles of débris in a few minutes."[3] He was injured during the earthquake and fled to Kobe.

Cinemas across the country were devastated, and print supplies destroyed. U.S. film companies began shipping prints to Japan almost immediately after the earthquake to replenish their stocks, and Universal announced that it would establish "temporary theatres throughout the country to provide much needed diversion for the sufferers."[4] Paramount and other U.S. film companies attempted to curry favor with Japanese audiences by raising funds for the national reconstruction effort and providing free screenings of American films. Robert McIntyre, head of Paramount's office in Kobe, Japan, told the *New York Times* that

> one of the first acts of the Japanese Government after the work of rescue had been well launched was to request the cooperation of the motion picture companies in providing entertainment for the homeless people.... Free motion-picture shows were given outdoors in many parts of the city each evening as a means of turning the minds of the people away from their sufferings and losses.... The patrons are content to sit on the ground. With the aid of the latest pictures from the United States they forget for a few hours their losses of last September.[5]

The earthquake damaged Hollywood's business in Japan. But in an instance of soft power in hard times, these temporary cinemas enabled the audience for American films to quickly grow.

All of the goodwill Paramount and other U.S. film companies had generated in 1923 was wiped out the following year.[6] The United States' Immigration Act of 1924, which was enacted on May 26, targeted Japanese migrants and was viewed in Japan as outrageously racist. As Yuko Itatsu notes, "The act was a huge slap in the face for the Japanese because it demoted Japan to the same level as China and the rest of the Asian nations, from which the US had banned immigration earlier.... It was also hurtful to her because the act was implemented at a time when the Japanese had such enthusiasm for American popular culture."[7] Reactions to the new law—a violation of the so-called Gentlemen's Agreement between the two nations—were swift. In one memorable incident at Tokyo's Imperial Hotel, "ruffians" attacked a dance party "attended by many members of the foreign community." Thirty *"ronin"* "took possession of the dance floor and made a number of bitter and profane anti-American speeches, which they punctuated by dances with naked swords drawn. Two American women fainted." The *New York Times* recounted the scene:

> The ronin distributed handbills urging a boycott of all American goods. Upbraiding the Japanese present, numbering about 150, the ronin accused them of "associating with foreigners in a frivolous amusement when their nation was insulted and in danger." While the speeches of ronin echoed the sentiments on the handbills, they were couched in the most vulgar and insulting language.... The handbills bore the signature, "Great Forward Association," and read:
>
> "This is not a time for discussion but a time for action. Now is the time for the young men of the Empire to rise.
>
> "We demand deportation of all Americans.
>
> "We demand boycott of all American motion pictures.
>
> "We demand boycott of all American goods.
>
> "We demand prohibition of the entrance of Americans into Japan and abrogating of all Japanese-American treaties.
>
> "We demand abolition of the evil of dancing, which is ruining our country."[8]

Throughout Tokyo, the *Times* reported, "gangs of ronin" forced cinemas showing American films to close and staged other protests with "the intention of evicting all Americans from the country." The anti-American boycott of films lasted for days, and Tom Cochrane left Kobe for Tokyo, where he announced his intention to close the local office.[9]

On June 8, members of the right-wing nationalist group Taikosha—the Great Forward Society—organized a formal shut-down action against cinemas exhibiting American films. Those who did not comply were served with death threats. Additional cinemas in Tokyo and Manchuria were also forced to close, Itatsu writes, while a cinema in Chiba was rendered inoperable after a protestor slashed its screen during the projection of an American film. Between June 11 and June 12, Universal's offices in Osaka were firebombed. The Chiyoda-kan and the Musashino-kan, independent cinemas operating outside the dominant circuits of Shochiku and Nikkatsu, were also threatened with arson and immediately stopped showing American films.[10]

The anti-American boycott extended far beyond cinemas and into a wide range of American cultural and material products. To align the nation further against the United States, Itatsu writes that "Nationalist Tokutomi Soho declared July 1 Kokujokubi or 'National Humiliation Day,'" and "right-wing nationalist organizations, women's organizations, and Christian groups organized protest rallies where thousands of people gathered, not just in Tokyo and Osaka, but in many other cities, especially in prefectures which had sent to America many of the immigrants." The reaction inside the local and American film industry was palpable: "Some benshis refused to narrate American films.... Hollywood stars such as Douglas Fairbanks, Mary Pickford, westerns star Tom Mix, and adventure film star Ruth Roland cancelled their trips to Japan. The Fairbanks, fearing they would be harassed for being Americans in Japan, reportedly made attempts to make use of their Swedish ancestry, and identify themselves as Swedish actors."[11] Tom Cochrane noted, "We are empathetic that the Japanese movie distributors are boycotting American films because of the anti-Japanese Immigration act. We are saddened by the turn of events but we are prepared to leave Japan, and close our offices here, although we feel there are ways to compromise."[12] All of the post-Kanto goodwill evaporated in just a few weeks.

Support, however, from Japanese fan magazines and many independent cinemas that were still showing American films, and even from many Japanese moviegoers who continued to flock to cinemas showing movies from the United States, meant that the anti-American film boycott led by the major Japanese film companies bloomed and died within a few months (boycotts of other American products lasted far longer).[13] Over the next two years, the tension remained between the Japanese film industry and American film distributors as well as between anti-American activists and American cultural products (and films). Itatsu notes that while "supporters of the boycott considered Hollywood movies a national product of the United States and justified their position as retaliation to the political decision made by the US government," others who

> opposed the boycott considered Hollywood movies as what may be called a "supranational" cultural product. In other words, they considered Hollywood movies a universal art form, which happened to be made in the US, and did not let their feelings of nationalistic humiliation influence their movie-going practices. They were able to separate the cultural allure of Hollywood films with the political hostility felt from the US government.[14]

This distance, between U.S. films and U.S. foreign policies, enabled American films to remain a constituent part of the Japanese exhibition ecosystem over the next decade. These kinds of tensions subsided, but anti-Americanism remained an undercurrent even as film companies like Paramount and Universal expanded their operations. The boycott of American films by the major Japanese exhibition chains highlighted an obvious problem for Paramount and one not unique to Japan: without a shop window cinema in Tokyo, for instance, there was no guarantee of a showcase cinema release in the city, especially with the ongoing political tensions at play.

A *Benshi* in the Box Office

The growing financial importance of the Japanese market for Paramount—after the end of the boycott—was signposted by the company's announcement in March 1927 that it had signed a lease for the 1,700-seat Hogaku-Za theater in Tokyo, formerly a live performance theater, for at least the next three years.[15] The theater, which *Film Daily* described as a new "shop window" cinema, "a presentation theater controlled by Paramount," reopened in April 1927.[16] Tickets for the Hogaku-Za were 40 percent more expensive than other local cinemas for films accompanied by stage performances and "foreign dance troupes." Class status was maintained through variously priced tickets that provided all with "a classy but affordable experience."[17] In keeping with Paramount's deluxe picture policy used for shop window cinemas in cities like London, the Hogaku-Za featured a mélange of live and filmed entertainment. "The exploitation and advertising conducted for the Hogakuza [sic]," *Motion Picture News* observed, "are as Western as the policy of operation. Lobby displays and outside posters are used to attract the attention of the public and arouse interest in the presentations at the house."[18]

The Hogaku-Za blended American-style management with local artists and entertainment. Paramount hired Kosaku Yamada, one of the foremost composers and conductors in Japan and a former organizer of the Japan Symphony Orchestra, to lead its orchestra in performing Western melodies such as Bizet's "L'Arle-Sienne" and accompanying ballet performances by local artists such as Kanzi Kunieda.[19] "Under Paramount," *Yomiuri Shimbun* opined, "the Hogaku-Za has not only movies but a wonderful lineup of music and dance." Yamada's conducting, the newspaper added, "truly makes the movie experience great. This week's music lineup contains five pieces from [Bizet's] *Carmen* and traditional Japanese pieces that call out for music lovers. The sight of so many amazing musicians on the stage itself is worth the ticket."[20]

While there may have been a Western cast to the music and ballet performances, it was in the exhibition of motion pictures that the silent-era Hogaku-Za truly reflected its cultural and industrial hybridity. Industrial practice in silent-era Japanese cinemas was, of course, to employ a *benshi* that performed alongside the film, interpreting, for example, the subtitles and cultural markers on screen for the audience. In 1927 the chief *benshi* at the Hogaku-Za were Ikoma Raiyu and Otsuji Shirou, both of whom, *Motion Picture News* noted, were "ranked among the most accomplished and popular artists specializing in this semi-dramatic profession" and were "the one purely Japanese feature included in the presentation."[21] *Yomiuri Shimbun* remarked that the work of the three rotating *benshi* "wakes up the sleeping Japanese movie industry."[22] Oswald Wynd, the aforementioned Scot who spent his childhood in Tokyo, provides a detailed account of the impact of the Hogaku-Za and the importance that Raiyu, who he dubbed "the Gielgud of the Tokyo picture houses," held in altering and subverting Paramount film narratives:

> The benshi at the Hogaku-Za was a presence from the moment the credits faded, even though the audience never actually saw him. . . . The voice began, totally assured, re-creating from this foreign import something comprehensible to the Oriental mind, clothing the nakedness of mere moving pictures with a richness of varied sound. . . . We didn't just see Douglas Fairbanks slitting sails but heard him do it, and heard also a Japanese comment on what a stupid way that was to try to stop a ship, plus the fact that a galleon was a pretty cumbersome product of Western marine design anyway, nothing as sensible as a junk. It was, of course, in the area of Western mores and social behavior that the benshi had his real field day. . . . The huge pictures presented an incomprehensible shambles that needed only a benshi's comment to make it seem totally repugnant.[23]

This blending of foreign cinema operation and local cultural practice made the Hogaku-Za popular by harmonizing the exotic (American) with the familiar (Japanese), a typical hallmark of Hollywood's foreign shop window cinemas.

Anti-Americanism and the Coming of Sound, 1928–1929

The successful launch of the Hogaku-Za in 1927 was, Donald Kirihara writes, part of Paramount's plans for a larger industrial presence in Japanese film exhibition. Between 1926 and the Hogaku-Za's reopening as a Paramount theater in April 1927, Kirihara notes that Paramount had already "began acquiring leases" and "controlled eleven major urban theaters in Japan." In addition, "Through booking arrangements made with other large theaters, Paramount was the largest foreign movie concern in Japan, controlling key showplaces and circulating the most films of any foreign producer in 1927 and 1928."[24]

The company's increasing prominence added to an already combustible situation. The anti-American tensions that had flared in 1924 had remained at a low boil. *Yomiuri Shimbun* had also become increasingly antagonistic in calling out the Hogaku-Za as culturally and socially harmful. In an August 11, 1928, article titled, "A Place for Sex, Hogaku-Za Is Glared Upon," the newspaper noted that the "foreign managed high end movie theater . . . has lately been providing obscene movies to the young men and women [and] to the wealthy sirs and madams." In addition, "the Paramount managed Hogaku-Za has become a place for delinquents to hang out. As erotic scenes are shown in movie theaters, an increasing number of these couples are seen heading off to 'hotels' after each screening. The police are answering these rumors by sending undercover detectives to screenings to crackdown on these problems." Tokyo police arrested two Hogaku-Za moviegoers, Fujita Keigo and Asada Mitsuon, for example, on "charges related to prostitution." Oswald Wynd, however, undermines local police accounts of the Hogaku-Za as some kind of 1920s porn theater. He recalls that "police censorship demanded" that any films shown at the Hogaku-Za had to have all "kissing be sliced from the film, this particular Western practice being considered likely to undermine national morals in spite of the fact that a considerable percentage of the sixteen-year-old males in the audiences were already steady brothelgoers."[25] The focus on the content and audiences at the Hogaku-Za and its supposed moral insurrection may have been due to a wider set of political and cultural factors.

American film companies were also the cause of additional upset and unrest in Tokyo a year later when technological developments (synchronous sound) began displacing Japanese film workers. In March 1929 Paramount announced that sound would be installed in the Hogaku-Za, one of two first-run cinemas the American company now operated in Tokyo (the other was the Shochiku-Za).[26] A demonstration screening of Fox *Movietone* films was projected there on May 9, 1929, and Paramount announced that it would install a Western Electric sound system by June, with an additional installation at the Shochiku-Za.[27] Wynd recalls that the first sound screening he attended "was packed to the doors by the curious."

> It may have been faulty wiring, but the sound track incorporated a steady roaring that sounded like trains passing each other on an elevated railway. And when Al [Jolson] started to sing "Mammy," it shattered the eardrums. The audience was stunned. If this was Western music, they didn't want it. Neither did I. I searched the shadows beneath a ten-foot face. The box was empty. Everyone was very upset.... [For the next film,] the management turned down the volume, and there was a voice again from the pulpit, the benshi back at work. But he was a shaken man. He knew his days were numbered.[28]

The excitement over sound—if there was any on the part of Japanese moviegoers acculturated to the *benshi*—was certainly offset by sentiments and experiences like Wynd's, by press reports about the human cost of automation, and by a growing outrage on the part of the nation's *benshi*.

Three Paramount cinemas, the Hogaku-Za, the Shochiku-Za, and the Musashinokan, had already converted to sound by mid-1929, although only the Hogaku-Za had announced the firing of their entire orchestra.[29] By July Yamada's Japan String Orchestra had left the Hogaku-Za for good, and

Shochiku Kinema Ltd., Japan's largest theater chain, announced that seven of its "principal" theaters had already wired for sound.[30] By August Paramount was now operating nine "wired" cinemas throughout Japan. *Benshis* were maintained, *Variety* reported, in order to "perform" over the hushed tones of Paramount's synchronous sound films.[31] Not only had *benshi* like Matsui Suisei not been fired, but he was even brought to Hollywood to "host" the Japanese-language version of *Paramount on Parade* for its release in Japan in 1930 as well as its premiere screening at the Hogaku-Za.[32]

Still, Suisei remained highly concerned about the long-term viability of his profession. Markus Nornes writes that in late 1929 Suisei had "predicted that the next year or two would be rough and decisive, and called for an all out struggle against the transition to sound. If the benshi failed to do so, he imagined they would only be working for foreign talkies."[33] With attendance in wired cinemas up at least 60 percent, the Hogaku-Za began experimenting with late-night screenings on Friday and Saturday nights without *benshi* "to target the intellectual fans and the linguistic researchers," with *Yomiuri Shimbun* drawing a distinction, as Paramount did, that the consumption of foreign films unaccompanied by *benshi* was for its most highbrow patrons.[34] Customers of prior performances with a *benshi* were even invited to stay for free, while third-class seats were offered at "a 30% discount to push for the education of linguistic students." This, the newspaper wrote, "is thought to be a precursor to the installation of the nationwide no benshi days."[35]

Hollywood in Japan Before the War

Silent Japanese-made films still dominated local screens in 1930, but when synchronous sound films were shown, American films accounted for over 90 percent of those playing in Japan. Even when more sync-sound films were being produced in Japan, including Kenji Mizoguchi's *Hometown* (1930), American films still accounted for over 60 percent of the sound-film market in Japan in 1931, and, further eliminating the need for *benshi*, Hollywood began superimposing titles on all of its films for the Japanese market.[36]

Paramount's growing position in Japanese film distribution and exhibition made it a key partner for the Japanese Shochiku company, and the two firms merged their exhibition chains on May 29, 1931, to create the Shochiku Paramount Company, the largest cinema circuit in the country, exhibiting both domestic Japanese and Hollywood films.[37] The Shochiku Paramount–operated Hogaku-Za was still the "pantheon for the true bourgeois movie fan" after the merger, *Yomiuri Shimbun* observed, and many patrons arrived as couples along with "western fashionistas" adorned with "mustaches" and "Dietrich faces."[38]

For the next two years, the Shochiku Paramount Company held a dominant position in key cities such as Osaka, where the Shochiku-Za was operated by the combined company showing Paramount films in addition to local cinemas such as Daini Sumiyoshi, Osaka-za, and the Kinema Palace.[39] According to *Variety*, the profitable chain had the "ace houses of Japan," and its booking power enabled it to bargain effectively with local distributors who were "glad to let material go cheaply" because the "prestige" of their films showing in a Shochiku Paramount cinema "more than made up the difference in the provinces in increased rentals."[40] Hoping for a similar success, MGM's Japanese subsidiary formed its own partnership with the rival Nikkatsu film company in 1932, and Fox contemplated joining that new film group to create a "large circuit in competition with the Shochiku-Paramount group."[41]

In May 1933 the operational agreement between Shochiku and Paramount expired, and in June Paramount, having fallen into receivership as the Depression wore on, relinquished control of its Japanese cinemas to the resurgent Shochiku in exchange for a one-year booking agreement for Paramount films.[42] It was hardly an equitable swap. Donald Kirihara writes, "The exchange strengthened Shochiku's exhibition position even more, while Paramount imports dropped in 1933 and 1934."[43] Shochiku subsequently formed a new company, Shochiku Youga Koukousya, to distribute and exhibit forty-three films from Paramount, fifteen from Columbia, and six from MGM.[44] Joining Shochiku in the top tier of Japanese exhibitors was Ichizo Kobayashi's Tokyo-Takarazuka Theater Company (later known as Toho), whose first-class cinemas in Tokyo battled with Shochiku for domination.[45] (Toho cinemas would later globalize in the 1960s, appearing in cities like New York, São Paulo, and Los Angeles.)

While Paramount had officially exited Japanese exhibition, MGM began operating cinemas in both China and Japan in 1932.[46] Three years later, in 1935, MGM announced plans to build new shop window cinemas in both Osaka and Tokyo, with Harry Moskowitz, head of Loew's construction department, overseeing the blueprints for both. Construction was set to begin on Metro's new 1,800-seat Tokyo cinema in February 1936, which, like other Metro theaters, would be a "combination theatre and office building" with a new feature for the city—"air cooling" in every office and retail store.[47] The Tokyo Metro was part of MGM's broader Asia strategy, which included plans for additional cinemas to open in Hong Kong, Singapore, and Ceylon (now Sri Lanka) to join MGM's existing venues in China, Japan, the Philippines and India.[48]

The Japanese occupation of China in 1937, the U.S. pushback over the attack on Nanjing and the occupation in general, and the subsequent Japanese attack on the USS *Panay* docked outside Nanjing in December 1937 all led to a drop in Japanese patronage of American movies. *Boxoffice* noted in May 1938 that distribution of American films in Germany, Japan, and China had now "practically ceased."⁴⁹ The situation in Spain and Japan was dire for American-owned cinemas, which were still open but "doing practically no business."⁵⁰ Soon, as war began between the United States and Japan in December 1941, MGM would no longer have a film exhibition or distribution apparatus in the country. It would be another half century before Hollywood invested in Japanese film exhibition again, with the formation of Warner-Mycal Cinemas in the 1990s.

MGM in Manila: The Philippines, World War II, and U.S. Exhibition in Asia

In September 1932 MGM expanded its network of shop window cinemas by securing a Filipino cinema through an agreement with the Roces family, owners of Manila's premiere but aging Cine Ideal. The new company, Metro-Goldwyn-Mayer Manila Co., was 51 percent owned by Loew's International with the remaining 49 percent stake held by the Roces. According to the terms of this partnership, MGM managed the Ideal for the Roces and booked the cinema with MGM films. The Roces family later sold their stake in the new company and made plans to replace the aging wood-frame Cine Ideal on fashionable Rizal Avenue with a new art deco, 1,200-seat Cine Ideal with air-conditioning and other "modern" aesthetics. Pablo Antonio designed the new cinema, which opened in 1933, and it quickly became one of the city's more iconic buildings. The larger Cine Ideal building also housed the offices of the Metro-Goldwyn-Mayer Manila Co.⁵¹ MGM also managed the newly leased cinema as its Manila shop window and booked it accordingly.⁵²

As World War II expanded to include the Pacific arena, the Philippines took a direct hit as Japan attempted an invasion of the former U.S. colony. Days after the attack on Pearl Harbor, *Motion Picture Herald* reported that international shipping routes for films throughout the hemisphere were cut and "theatre business in Manila has been completely halted." "Total blackouts," *Motion Picture Herald* reported, "have been imposed."⁵³ Isadore Cohen, general manager for MGM in the Philippines and stationed at the Cine Ideal, was captured in Manila and interned by the Japanese, along with Julian Berman, MGM's Far East managing director.⁵⁴ MGM abandoned its lease of the Cine Ideal, and management of the theater reverted to the Roces family during the war. Films showing at the Ideal were now Japanese only.⁵⁵ The loss of the Filipino and Japanese markets during the war decreased foreign revenues for the U.S. film companies as 90 percent of Philippines' screens and 75 percent of Japan's cinemas had been occupied with American product before 1942.⁵⁶

Business, of course, quickly became an afterthought for many of the Hollywood distributors in the Philippines as most were hoping just to escape the region with their lives. *Motion Picture Daily* noted that those currently or formerly working for Paramount and other companies were already being reported as war casualties. They included Australian John Groves, Paramount's manager in colonial Malaya in Singapore, who was killed with his son "defending that city against the Japanese invader."[57] James E. Perkins, Paramount's general manager for the Far East, had reportedly "remained at his desk until the Japanese entered" and was now "interned there." *Motion Picture Herald* reported in January 1942 that "Paramount's Chinese staff and manager in Hongkong [sic]" had also "not been heard from since the fall of that city."[58] Twentieth Century-Fox's manager and district supervisor for Manila had also gone missing after the Japanese attack, as had many other studio executives in the area. Paramount subsequently moved its wartime Asian offices to India, hoping to ride out the storm in relative safety.[59]

In October 1943 Perkins and Cohen became part of a prisoner exchange program with Japan in which 1,236 American citizens were traded for Japanese prisoners.[60] Cohen didn't make it back to the United States until December 1943.[61] Other foreign executives were interned even longer. Local Universal manager Larry DiPrida, United Artists manager Charles Core, and Warners Bros. Philippines manager Cliff Almy weren't liberated from Japanese prison camps in Manila until March 1945, spending nearly three years in captivity.[62] Even when Almy was finally released, the effects of the war still lingered for years afterward.[63]

The situation for the Roces was just as dire during the war. Under occupation, the Cine Ideal became a Japanese propaganda house for films like *Ano Hata O Ute* (*Tear Down the Stars and Stripes*), released in the Philippines and screened at the Ideal as *Liwayway ng Kalayaan* (*Dawn of Freedom*). The Cine Ideal, much like the Nazi-occupied Le Paramount in Paris half a world away, now lived its own double life under occupation. "Unknown to the Japanese," Isidra Reyes writes,

> until a Filipino double agent named Franco Vera Reyes infiltrated the group, clandestine meetings of the guerilla movement were held in a dark room at the Ideal Theater led by Roces scion, Rafael "Liling" Roces, Jr. Liling was later arrested on March 2, 1944 and executed by the Japanese Imperial Army along with fellow members of the guerilla movement . . . at the Manila North Cemetery in August 1944. Among the personal effects found in the massacre site was Liling's key to his office at the Ideal Theater.[64]

By the waning days of the war, both the Ideal and Manila were a mess. The Japanese military had ramped up their attacks on the city's infrastructure before departing the city, purposefully burning ten of the city's most opulent cinemas in the Escolta area as they cleared out that section.[65] The Cine Ideal's interior was badly damaged during the Battle of Manila but, Reyes notes, its "sturdy reinforced concrete structure remained standing."[66]

In the end only three of Manila's twenty cinemas survived the war and only one, the Times, was still operable. When the Americans swept into the city, the U.S. Office of War Information (OWI) made plans to open the Times as soon as power was restored to the area. The other two surviving cinemas, the Ideal and Lyric, required more extensive rehabilitation. The OWI was not only tasked to repair and reopen these cinemas but to restart the distribution of Hollywood films. Screenings at the Times, and later the Lyric and Ideal, were supplemented with the *United Newsreel*, the OWI-crafted newsreel using footage from Hollywood's various newsreel divisions. Robert Perkins, the former Universal representative in the Far East, was placed in charge of OWI film distribution and exhibition in the Philippines.[67]

MGM's former shop window cinema, the Cine Ideal, reopened in June 1945 with Universal's *Phantom of the Opera* as OWI hoped to get the city's cinemas back up and running.[68] By July forty-four cinemas were operating across the Philippines. Cliff Almy returned to the Philippines, restarting Warner Bros.' local business.[69] Isadore Cohen also returned to Manila for MGM in November.[70] Normalcy was beginning to return to the market. By August, six of Manila's "pre-war first-run theaters" were "running at top business, with a third to open as soon as cement becomes available to patch up shell-blasted walls and floors."[71] Admissions prices, film distribution, and other cinema-related matters were all overseen by the OWI.

After the Army's Psychological Warfare Division relinquished the city's cinemas back to private control in November 1945, the Cine Ideal resumed its position as MGM's shop window cinema.[72] In the decades that followed, it would serve as a first-run venue for MGM films as well as a setting for gala premieres, acting as a cultural embassy for Hollywood and its ideological output. As Regina Roces-Paterno, whose grandparents owned the Cine Ideal, recalls, "We watched (movies) almost every day . . . because it was the people's way of escaping the memories of war," and, for the family, the murder of Liling Roces.[73]

The Ideal continued to be a showcase house for MGM well into the 1960s. The cinema and the Filipino market were important enough in 1960, for example, for Seymour Mayer, vice president of Metro-Goldwyn-Mayer International, to fly to Manila for the June 8 premiere of *Ben-Hur*.[74] MGM's eventual departure from the venue coincided with its swan dive in the late 1960s as its feature film output declined and its foreign operations were heavily curtailed and then sold off to CIC. The Cine Ideal was destroyed by fire a decade later in 1978, ending its long theatrical run and any physical trace of MGM's shop window days in the Philippines and its connection to wartime memories under occupation.[75]

CHAPTER 19

JOINING THE GLOBAL METRO CUB CLUB, 1936–1973

MGM and Fox's Shop Window Cinemas in India

Hollywood's efforts to operate cinemas in India also engaged rapidly shifting local politics as MGM's Metro cinemas were built under the British colonial government and swayed in popularity and rebuke with the growing independence movement of the nation during the 1930s and 1940s. In the post-independence period MGM began an effort to inculcate a new generation of Indian moviegoers through "Metro Cub Clubs," which drew Indian children to the Metro cinemas in Bombay and Calcutta in an effort to suture American cosmopolitanism and consumerism on top of their growing national identity of political and economic independence.

The Filipino market, however important for MGM, was minute compared to the magnitude of the possibilities in India. Hollywood's efforts to build and operate cinemas in the nation was always confined to a few major cities and constrained by the cultural, aesthetic, political, and logistical headwinds it encountered. India, to put it bluntly, did not need Hollywood for its cinematic entertainment. From the earliest decade of the twentieth century, before and after British colonial rule, India's indigenous, multiethnic, and multilingual film industries have filled local screens. The nation's Hindi, Tamil, and Telugu films have booked up the thousands of cinemas operating throughout the country in urban and rural cinemas as well as the screens of the nation's once numerous *bioscopewalla*, itinerant film exhibitors who traveled from town to town screening films in areas without dedicated hardtop cinemas. In the 1920s Hollywood still imagined an India open for exploitation. It harbors no such illusions a century later.

To trace Hollywood's early interest in Indian exhibition—and its desire to secure distribution for U.S. films in cities such as Bombay—it is necessary to return to the colonial, silent era. In April 1927 *Bioscope* reported that an unnamed U.S. film company was interested in purchasing the ninety-one-cinema Madan Theatres circuit with venues in India, Burma (Myanmar), and Ceylon (Sri Lanka).[1] The unnamed circuit was likely Loew's, which, instead of buying the Madan chain, entered into a partnership instead. (The move coincided with other Loew's agreements such as with Gaumont in France and the formation of Empresas Reunidas MGM in Brazil.) Loew's executive George Mooser was sent to India in September 1927 to coordinate marketing and exhibition plans for MGM films throughout the Madan Theatres chain.[2]

Other companies were also circling British colonial India, including Universal, which, according to *Billboard*, "purchased the biggest movie house in Bombay, and is negotiating for the lease of eight other theaters here." Paramount, seeking to extend their Asian circuit beyond Japan, also "purchased a site in Calcutta to build a new theater at the beginning of a great chain thruout [sic] India." With Paramount, First National, Universal, and MGM opening branches in Bombay and reportedly operating cinemas, "Indian cinema interests are alarmed and are sending a deputation to the Indian government to demand steps to safeguard the Indian industry."[3]

Even RKO, which had not participated in the global shop window boom—or circuit buying like Fox—leased its own cinema in Calcutta, the RKO Elphinstone, to serve as a rare company shop window cinema.[4] J. Remi Crasto, RKO publicity and exploitation manager in India, spread RKO publicity throughout the city through his creative marketing campaigns and staging of the cinema.[5] Despite "municipal, police and governmental regulations" against print and public advertising, *Motion Picture Herald* reported, "RKO Radio window displays, planned by an artistic window dresser, are one of RKO Radio's most appreciated picture selling helps." Crasto partnered with many local retailers to make "Indian shopkeepers 'movie minded.'"[6]

MGM also had designs on a Calcutta shop window, and that same year the company began construction of a new 1,200-seat cinema there. It would be one of the first Metro Theatres / Cinema Metros built according to the 1932 Johannesburg model.[7] The Metro in Calcutta was designed by Thomas Lamb, Loew's de facto house architect since the 1910s, who had also designed the Empire in London and the Metro in Johannesburg. "Typical of the theatres being erected by Loew's-Metro in their worldwide theatre expansion program," *Motion Picture Herald* commented, it was designed "in the straight architectural lines of modernity."[8]

The Metro Cinema opened on December 6, 1935.[9] The excitement of its premiere, and a general growth in cinephilia, inspired the construction of two more cinemas in Calcutta. "Opening of the Metro theatre last November started the ball rolling," *Variety* reported, "exert[ing] a vast influence on other cinemas, who have gone in for redecorating and general refurbishing."[10] It was in Calcutta then, not Bombay, where MGM and RKO set up the country's first Hollywood shop window cinemas in India.

MGM Continues to Expand

MGM planned its next Indian shop window cinema for Bombay. Work on the new Metro Cinema there was slowed by delays in obtaining steel, which set its debut back to 1938.[11] (Western India Theatres' Central Theatre served as an exclusive venue for MGM during construction of the Metro.[12]) The Bombay Metro featured a sumptuous lobby, a ground floor for accumulating rental income from retail stores, and a four-story surrounding office building like all Loew's International real estate projects. Before one ticket had been sold, all of its rental spaces had been leased. To accommodate its size, Bombay city planners and engineers had reoriented troublesome streets to make travel to and from the cinema more efficient. The new roads were designed to highlight the cinema's striking Thomas Lamb–designed, very American exterior. Adding to the theater's evocation of Hollywood and the United States were its chairs and carpeting, imported directly from the States, along with the "the cinema's soda fountain, cocktail bar with lounge, smoking rooms, cosmetic rooms, drinking fountain, [and] lavatories."[13]

Before it opened, the president of the Motion Picture Society of India, Sir Phiroze Sethna, met with Home Minister Kanaiyalal Maneklal Munshi to protest the Metro. Speaking on behalf of the country's exhibitors, Sethna explained that the Bombay Metro would negatively "affect the progress of Indian talkies," and he found a sympathetic ear in Munshi, a supporter of Indian independence, who announced he "would do all he could, to help [the] Indian industry."[14] Loew's sent Calcutta Metro Theatre manager Al Buehrig to Bombay to handle the Metro's opening and this growing backlash against its construction and its opening on June 8, 1938.[15]

Like many other Metro Theatres around the world, the Bombay Metro was expressly designed to blend the exotic (American-style luxury, technology, and design) with the local. This was important to counter local hostility and to attract local moviegoers with both the opulence and exoticism of its *American* exterior while instilling a sense of local familiarity through its *Indian* interior. To achieve this result, MGM hired the director of the Bombay School of Art, Mr. Gerard, to oversee his students' installation of an interior design that, the *Times of India* noted, was "rich in decorative effects."[16] While its exterior design, management, technology, and films were all imported from the United States, the Metro's striking auditorium featured murals—up to forty feet high—depicting "Vedic jungle scenes echoing Hindu epic mythology."[17]

FIGURE 19.1 Metro Cinema in Calcutta, ca. 1930s. (Author's collection)

FIGURE 19.2 Metro Cinema in Bombay, ca. 1930s. (Author's collection)

The glitz of the opening night—in which the audience reportedly "frequently broke into applause"—did nothing to quell (and probably exacerbated) the local, simmering unhappiness about MGM's encroachment into Bombay's exhibition landscape.[18] *Variety* reported, for example, ongoing tensions between the Metro and local Indian cinemas, which now felt pressured "to modernize their houses."[19] This opposition may have played a role in the Bombay government's decision not to renew the Metro's license for a liquor bar—the first cinema in the city to face such a restriction. Despite efforts by the American consul to appeal the decision to the chief secretary to the Bombay government, the matter was "closed" by local officials, arguing "that it is merely a coincidence that the first refusal happened to affect an American theater."[20]

Filmindia's influential and charismatic editor, Baburao Patel, fanned this growing resentment, attacking MGM's new cinema in a screed titled, "METRO INSULTS THE NATION! The Home Member & The Police Commissioner Must Act."[21] *Filmindia* was an important voice, and, as Sidharth Bhatia notes, "Patel was the most feared journalist in the Indian film industry."[22] MGM's chief offense, according to Patel, was placing a very American notation on tickets stating, "Management reserves the right to refuse admission." This was "the pawn-ticket of self-respect that admits a patron as a suspect after paying for it," Patel wrote with his trademark snark. "Wouldn't it be better if they searched every one before admitting?"[23]

MGM and its Metro cinemas attempted to cultivate favor, box office, and popular support in India through the same kinds of activities their exhibitors had employed in the United States, Europe, and elsewhere. In March 1940, for example, the Metro Cinema in Bombay hosted a benefit screening and gala of *The Secret of Dr. Kildare* and *Angels of Mercy* for the Indian Red Cross and St. Dimstan's Fund.[24] Other benefit performances in 1940 included the premiere of *The Mortal Storm* for the benefit of Bombay's War Gifts Fund. On hand for the gala screening was the governor of Bombay. "Enjoy a great film," the *Times of India* wrote, "and also discharge your duty for the defence of Bombay by contributing to the War Gifts Fund."[25] These kinds of events helped cement the relationship between Bombay's governor, Sir Roger Lumley, and the Bombay Metro Theatre, which hosted Lumley for the world premiere of *Court Dancer*, "India's first film with English dialogue for the international market." The screening, the *New York Times* gushed, "included a brilliant cosmopolitan gathering including Indians, Englishmen and Americans."[26]

The Metro Cub Club or How the Lion Meowed

By 1946, as anti-British sentiments grew during the apex of the Indian independence movement—and the British government prepared to grant autonomy to India—Patel observed that nationalism was setting the tone at many of the nation's cinemas, including the Metro in Calcutta:

> On the eve of our country's freedom, as a people we are fast acquiring very bad manners. Admitting that politics take a lot of our mind these days, there is no earthly reason why our people, particularly our politically hypersensitive students, should take bad manners to our cinema theatres, where people go merely for entertainment and relaxation. Incidents have been reported from the Metro Cinema in Calcutta and other theatres in the principal cities of India, in which the rowdy elements in the audiences have either cheered or hooted at our public leaders appearing in news reels, according to their different political complexions.[27]

A month later he added, "The present political atmosphere in our country has affected rather sadly the friendly relations between our different communities," and he suggested that the nation's cinemas—like the soon-to-be-divided nations of India and Pakistan—might need to be separated along religious lines. Patel argued that "it is not right for these people to break our chairs, tear our screens and try to burn down our cinemas, just because in the field of politics some of them have become bitter through frustration." He added that these internal divisions only enabled the exploitation (and invasion) from Hollywood and "the menace of foreign competition."[28]

The rise of nationalism and anticolonialism in India—and the bitter divisions between Hindus and Muslims and between the local Indian and British communities in Calcutta and Bombay—no doubt contributed to MGM's concerted efforts to inculcate a new, unified, and loyal generation of pro-American, pro-Hollywood moviegoers. In June 1947 MGM became the first "major" American film company to plan a "large-scale children's show program overseas" to build and develop new audiences. David Blum, head of advertising and publicity for Loew's International, produced a twenty-page brochure titled "Special Children's Shows—Why and How" that provided a global manual for attracting and developing a new generation of MGM moviegoers. Blum wrote that there was a solid "dollars and sense" reason for the global program: exploiting fallow hours in the cinema not yet being used for screenings. He argued for the promotion of these child-oriented programs to local "PTA groups, politicians, business men," and "the very sections of the public that have attacked the cinema." The booklet urged theater managers to screen MGM product such as *Adventures of Huckleberry Finn*, *Tale of Two Cities*, and *The Yearling* alongside a program of newsreels, travelogues, cartoons, and other shorts dealing with "science, sports, music and history." The brochure added, "Admission prices should not be set too high for the kids." In addition, "Since most kid programs are offered on Saturdays, Sundays and holidays, the brochure call[ed] attention to the point that the exhibitor should make sure there is no objection by religious groups to Sabbath programs." Metro Cinema managers in India (and elsewhere) were advised to curate a "children's program" that took place on the stage of the theater and create an "amateur program" of fifteen minutes or less. Children's programs typically included birthday parties "with [a] local grocer providing cake free, in exchange for publicity" and a "Radio program to broadcast the [amateur] kid talent with a 'reputable merchant to sponsor it.'" Blum's plan included enticing local "Teachers to plug essay contests" and "Librarians to dovetail books with pix" as well as the creation of local "Merchant tie-ups" for specific films. Metro managers were also advised to stand in the lobby and greet every child who entered the cinema to create a personal connection to the Metro (and MGM). Metro cinema managers were also encouraged to create local Metro Cub Clubs, whose theme song was inspired by that of *The Wizard of Oz*. Proof of concept was noted by the Metro Cub Clubs created at the Cine Metros in Valparaiso and Santiago, Chile; Lima, Peru; and Montevideo, Uruguay in South America, by programs created by Hoyts and Greater Union in Australia, and by ABC and Odeon in the United Kingdom.[29]

One year later, with the successful introduction of the Metro Cub Club in India, Blum updated his kids club brochure with a new one: "Promoting Extra

Revenue Through Special Children's Shows." Blum specifically cited how children's programs and the Metro Cub Club were helping the "movie habit" to be "built among today's children—tomorrow's patrons." Blum's brochure highlighted the "practical experience of the Metro Theatre in Bombay, India, where despite unsettled political conditions and religious problems, children's shows were instituted and a 'Metro Cub Club' was organized with great success." *Boxoffice* highlighted Metro's success in "contacting and securing the cooperation of schools, the clergy and the press" as well as "the promotional success of club pledges, birthday gifts and records, as well as exploitation tieups."[30]

The success of the Bombay Metro Cub Club inspired new clubs to open at the Cine Metros in São Paolo, Brazil, and Medellin, Colombia, and directly influenced the development of the Metro Cub Club in the Calcutta Metro.[31] As *Boxoffice* noted, India's Metro Cub Clubs quickly became a "Model For Loew International Theatres" and many others. The journal observed how these clubs were created by "American theatremen, adopted by British showmen and have become popular with kids everywhere," and would soon have "special significance for youngsters in every foreign country where MGM is represented either by theatres or an exchange center."[32]

For India, and other nations turning toward independence, Metro Cub Clubs filled an important cultural role for children at a time of growing nationalism and political unrest. As *Boxoffice* reported, "the club encourages obedience, good attendance in school, diligent study, patriotism, opportunity to develop individual talent for dancing, singing, elocution and many other factors for proper child development." They also encouraged the further consumption of American films and consumer products. By the end of 1948 more than two thousand Bombay children had joined the club, with nearly one thousand each week attending its events.[33] The club was a weekly direct infusion of global culture—an attempt to suture Hollywood into a new generation of Indian moviegoers—precisely at a flowering moment of local nationalism.

These and other Cub Clubs hold a mythical, nostalgic status in the memories of Metro moviegoers around the world. Salman Rushdie, for example, who grew up in Bombay, recalls their effect in his classic work, *Midnight's Children* (1981): "The ten-thirty-in-the-morning show! It's Metro Cub Club day, Amma, pleeeese!" . . . There was air-conditioning, and Cub Club badges pinned to our clothes, and competitions, and birthday-announcements made by a compere with an inadequate moustache; and finally, the film."[34] Rushdie's former classmate, Anvar Alikhan, wrote that the Metro Cub Club was not only the place where the author encountered the Western world but was a seedbed for his budding imagination:

> Rushdie was a few years senior to me in Bombay's Cathedral School and one place I often remember seeing him as a kid was at the Metro cinema: we were

members of something called the Metro Cub Club, which screened film shows for kids on Saturday mornings. Many years later, reading Rushdie's interview in The Paris Review, I discovered that he believes the turning point in his life as a writer was watching The Wizard of Oz at the Metro as an 11-year-old: he went straight home and wrote his first story, "Over the Rainbow," about a little boy who's walking down a Bombay footpath when he suddenly finds the beginning of a rainbow, with steps cut into it, which takes him up into a fairy-tale world in the sky. By some freak chance I, too, saw The Wizard of Oz at the Metro Cub Club, which means I must have been sitting just a few seats away while one of the world's great literary epiphanies was being shaped.[35]

"When we were young," Rushdie recalls, "there used to be the Metro Cub Club for children to watch Sunday morning films. And you would sit there with your Vimto and potato chips and watch Seven Brides for Seven Brothers or King Arthur. I was very influenced by the fact that we were growing up in this golden age of international cinema. I feel I got a lot of my education [there]."[36]

Sanji Kripalni Mukherjee recalls the Cub Club's impact on Calcutta's children. First recalling the multicultural era of the moment, Mukherjee recalls the way that "Chinese, Sikh, Jewish, Muslim and Anglo-Indian children" spent time together in that "best of all possible worlds, a cosmopolitan one." She recalled "old Mr. Hafesjee" a "Bohra muslim" "who organized the Metro Cub Club to which we went every Saturday. He was affectionately called Uncle Leo after the well-known roaring lion in the Metro-Goldwyn-Mayer logo. Rushdie talks about a similar club in his beloved Bombay." Mukherjee notes that the Cub Club created a pacifying effect among the children in this group, as "there were as yet no major repercussions from the trauma of Partition. Sometimes one heard the odd politically incorrect reference to Muslims or Bengalis or Gujaratis, or Anglo-Indians but one barely noticed it."[37] Rushdie and Mukherjee's middle-class childhoods are depicted as mainstream and cosmopolitan, surrounded by friends and the leisures of their class: movies, movie theaters, and the American cinema clubs.

The Metro Cub Club was a cultural seduction, injecting Hollywood and American mythology into a generation of post-independence moviegoers as hell-bent on Indian nationalism as American cosmopolitanism and its cross-class capitalistic consumption of Coca-Cola. The exhibition of Hollywood's English-language films in India in the early to mid-twentieth century often required a caste, a cultural interaction, and an education that made American narratives and their linguistic and colloquial underpinnings accessible and even desirable. The Metro Cub Club appealed to a new generation of middle- and upper-class children in Bombay and Calcutta who were increasingly attuned to the growing sense of independent nationalism around them *and* the rise of post-independence consumerism, addressed here by American films,

American brands, and American capitalistic and consumerist values. In short, the Metro Cub Club was inculcating the same sensibilities in Indian children as in the United States. In this way, the Indian Metro cinemas were not just children's clubs but ambassadors and promoters of a very American brand of childhood filled with *Tom & Jerry*, Coca-Cola, and other American icons.

MGM in Independent/Nationalist India

With nationalist sentiment running high, MGM continued its efforts to instill American films and culture into Bombay and Calcutta during the earliest days of India's postcolonial independence. The Metro in Bombay attempted to address these trends by demonstrating a sense of local pride with screenings of films such as *Bapu Ki-Amar Kahani*, a one-reeler about the life of Mahatma Gandhi that was "highly appreciated by the spectators."[38] Still, questions remained, including one by Arain S. Sayvant of Bombay, who wrote to *filmindia* asking, "Why is the Metro Cinema not changed into an Indian picture house even with the achievement of independence?" Patel was blunt, as always: "Metro is not a citadel of British imperialism. It is an American counting house where silver rupees change into gold dollars."[39]

The fully branded experience of the Metro cinemas in Calcutta and Bombay did conflict with the nationalist spirit in other ways. The *Indian News Review* newsreel, which had been produced and distributed by the new Indian government, became less and less prominent by June 1949, enough so that *filmindia* began referring to them as the "vanishing newsreels of India!"[40] P. N. Sharma noted that the Calcutta Metro had not made room for the newsreel in its program, and only the Elite Cinema was screening the government-produced reels. "If exhibitors are not co-operating," Sharma wrote, "I think the Government should make it compulsory for all cinemas to show the 'Indian News Review.'"[41] Patel lambasted MGM's Bombay shop window as well for similar practices. "The Metro Cinema of Bombay still seems to imagine itself to be a part of America the way it shuns the newsreels produced by our Ministry of Information and Broadcasting," *filmindia* observed at the time. "Rather than show these newsreels, the Metro management thrusts on us three trailers.... And they say India is a free nation."[42]

Nationalism showed up in other ways at the Metro. Jews were a constituent part of the Indian film industry, as they had been in Egypt, where they were a small but culturally visible minority. Their relative foreignness is reflected in some of Patel's colorful and sometimes antisemitic *filmindia* commentary. He referred to Sabita Devi of Sagar Movietone, for instance, as "another Jew girl whom her producers have mentally placed on the supposed pedestal of stardom."[43] When he wrote about Chandulal Shah, the non-Jew head of Ranjit

Studios, for example, he noted that Shah was "producing rotten stuff nowadays.... Like the proverbial Jew, Chandulal seems to have become a junk merchant."[44] Patel also began seeing Jews wherever he looked. In two different articles in the same issue of *filmindia*, the journal managed to describe Charlie Chaplin as a "silver-haired Jewish comedian" and assert that the non-Jewish Darryl Zanuck's 1946 hopes to make films around the world, including in India and China, meant that "this influential Jew has India on his brain."[45] Patel also noted incorrectly that *The March of Time* would only depict Palestine in a way favorable to Jews because "Henry Luce, a Jew, owns the 'March of Time' documentaries. You can't expect a Jew to fall in love with Arabs."[46] Luce, of course, was the son of Presbyterian missionaries and, according to historian Robert E. Herzstein, was, along with his colleagues at *Time*, a promulgator of the era's virulent "social anti-Semitism." *Time*, Herzstein writes, even "went out of its way" in the 1930s "to identify Jews who were criminals, Communists, and reprobates."[47] Patel's *filmindia* also asked whether Ben Hecht was a "Dirty Jew" for declaring that there was a "'little holiday in his heart' every time a British soldier was killed in Palestine."[48] After the founding of Israel, which Patel viewed as a British colonial giveaway to the Jews, his comments became more pointed. In October 1948 Patel, who *filmindia* journalist (and later screenwriter) Kwaja Ahmed Abbas noted "hit hard (when necessary) and (not infrequently) when not necessary, and thus came to be a model of the 'sledge hammer' style of film journalism," remarked that one of the problems with Israel was that, to him, the Jew should remain a stateless cosmopolitan, a diasporic figure that provided an infusion of culture to the peoples of the world who were actually worthy of nationhood.[49]

Patel's most egregiously antisemitic attack, though, and his attack's relevance for the American film industry and its cinemas abroad, could be found in his writing, pseudonymously as "Judas," in the article, "Red Rag to the White Bulls," in which Patel attacked a group that he encountered at the Metro Cinema in Bombay, who he insisted were Jewish:

> We have always said that our National Flag should not be shown in cinema theatres where it is always respected the least by a motley crowd of filmgoers who primarily come to pay their respects to their favourite film stars and get some entertainment in the bargain.... But where it hurts the most is when we find in a cinema, like the Metro in Bombay, a crowd of Continental Jews walking out with lofty contempt at the sight of our National Flag.... It is a pity that in the intoxication of their newly created nationalism as free citizens of Israel, the Continental Jews in India should so quickly become ungrateful and bite the very hand that fed them at a time when they came to India after the Nemesis of their past had hounded them out of their homes. We still hope that the proverbial wisdom of the Jews will rescue them from this newly

acquired racial arrogance but in the meantime we would appeal to the government to stop displaying the national flag in the cinema theatres and not provide an opportunity to the foreigners to insult it.[50]

F. W. Pollack, the secretary of the Central Jewish Board of Bombay, was outraged by Patel's account and wrote back in a letter published in the next issue asking, "What proof has he got that the crowd he saw walk out of the Metro 'with lofty contempt' at the sight of the national flag consisted of Continental Jews, or even contained any Continental Jews at all?" Patel replied that the incident "was witnessed by me personally and the comments of 'Judas' were written under my personal instructions. The responsibility is therefore entirely mine." Judas was, after all, simply a nom de plume for Patel, who argued that he had long "studied the peculiar characteristics of many races and I have always thought that the Jews have more distinctive racial characteristics than others with the exception of the Negroid races." He added, "Instead of asking me for an explanation and thereby betraying a certain amount of aggressive inferiority-complex and some racial hyper-sensitiveness," Pollack "ought to have issued a general circular to your community and pointed out to its members, particularly to the foreign contingent, the virtue of respecting India's National Flag which, in common with others, belongs also to your community."[51]

The significance of this public debate lay in the Metro's complicated status as a foreign cinema in a time of nationalism and ethnic conflict, with growing discord between Muslims and Hindus and Indians and Anglos. The "foreigners" highlighted by Patel were not just an ordinary group of moviegoers filled with "racial arrogance." They were to him interlopers—not Indians but "Continental Jews"—out to enjoy American films in an American cinema, a group of "foreigners" at a foreign-owned theater viewing a foreign film. Whatever efforts the Metro cinemas made to blend into their community, each remained exceedingly "foreign." As always, Hollywood's shop windows were celebrated as foreign, exotic embassies of Hollywood in moments of philo-Americanism and then denigrated and hated as such during moments of pointed nationalism.

Loew's/MGM India After 1950

For those who attended and celebrated the two Metro cinemas in India, a trip to these American-owned cinemas meant an encounter with Hollywood and MGM's celebration of American exceptionalism, a specific brand of escapist fantasy that consecrated American movies and its movie theaters as cultural embassies for America's soft power argument of consumerism and liberal democracy against the Soviet Union's increasing interest in India and its own avocation of communism at the dawn of a newly independent nation grappling with its own postcolonial identity and political future and ideology. Thus, the bevy of klieg-light premieres at the Bombay Metro for new MGM films, the New Empire for Fox films, and the Eros Theatre for Warner Bros. films were not just Hollywood's efforts to promote itself but U.S. State Department–enabled publicity events for American culture and cultural products and for the promotion thereof.

The Bombay Metro's Indian premiere of *Quo Vadis?* in November 1952, for example, brought with it America's most effective ambassadors—"Celebrities from every walk of life" who "attended the premiere ... while thousands thronged the square outside the theatre." Photos of the event were splashed across national newspapers, promoting Bombay, MGM, and the Metro Theatre. The Indian Navy Band played outside as "searchlights made dazzling patterns criss-crossing the darkness of Dhobi Talao, packed by ten thousand sightseers, a continuous stream of cars unloaded celebrities from every walk of Bombay life and society at the Metro Theatre." The evening was attended by leading political figures including the chief justice of Bombay, industry figures such as Chandulal Shah of Ranjit Studios and Keki Modi, as well as "practically all the leading producers, directors and stars of the Indian motion picture industry."[52] The attraction of India's political and cultural elite was part of the one-two punch in Hollywood and the U.S. government's strategy to peel India away from its growing interest in communism and the Soviet Union, highlighted by Nikita Khrushchev's visit to India three years later.

MGM continued to lavish attention and dollars on its Bombay and Calcutta shop windows in the years to come, installing India's first "panoramic screens" (widescreen) in August 1953 at both Metros.[53] As always, one of the advantages of shop window ownership abroad was the showcase they provided for American technologies and the films that used them. By publicizing widescreen cinema at the Metros, MGM would begin to pressure local exhibitors to make similar installations and book American films using this technology. Thus, local films, which still retained a traditional aspect ratio and did not implement Technicolor, would begin to appear older and passé, providing the American film companies and their cinemas with yet another advantage. The lavish premiere of *Quo Vadis?*, then, was as much a booster for MGM and its cinemas (and specifically for their new, updated technology) as it was for American culture, technology, and consumerism.[54]

Fox in India

The Metro Theatres were fully American cinemas in style, management, and ownership. Twentieth Century-Fox pursued a different strategy in India, however, operating their own cinemas beginning in 1949 in an arrangement that obfuscated their national origins. Fox theaters appeared to the average moviegoer to be Indian cinemas showing American films, a situation intended to minimize any issues relating to American influence and cultural imperialism. Fox made a deal to lease three Indian cinemas—the New Empire Theatre in Bombay, the Plaza Cinema in New Delhi, and the Elite Cinema in Calcutta—as shop window cinemas for Twentieth Century-Fox films. Unlike other Fox-operated cinemas of the period, in which the company bought controlling interests in theater chains, Fox began operating these three at the end of 1949 by leasing them from exhibitor Keki Modi through his Western India Theatres Ltd.[55]

By 1959, one year after Warner Bros. followed the MGM model by taking over the 1,200-seat Eros Theatre in Bombay from Cambatta Bros., Twentieth Century-Fox sought to negotiate new ten-year leases for each of its three cinemas with Keki Modi and pursued new, fifteen-year leases for four more theaters—the Minerva, Elphinstone, Excelsior, and West End.[56] This was only an opening gambit. Skouras, as he had with previous companies in Australia, New Zealand, South Africa, Kenya, and colonial Zimbabwe, now sought to buy a controlling interest in Western India Theatres Ltd. and thereby gain access to its distribution contracts and its cinemas.[57]

Modi's terms appear to have been too high for Skouras—involving loans to Western India Theatres and joint ventures to buy additional Indian cinemas—and the deal languished.[58] Two years later, P. V. Prabhu, still managing director of Twentieth Century-Fox Corp. (India) Private Ltd., wrote to Murray Silverstone that Modi had left for London and then New York to meet with him and Skouras.[59] For reasons unknown, however, the deal was never consummated. Instead, Twentieth Century-Fox operated a collection of its own (leased) cinemas in New Delhi, Bombay, Calcutta, and Madras in the early 1960s.[60] By 1965 that list had been pared down to the Regal in Bombay and the Globe in Calcutta, mirroring MGM's own focus on just those two cities.[61]

The 1970s and the Complicated Sale of the Metros

By the dawn of the 1970s, as mentioned throughout this book, MGM was foundering and looking to dump foreign assets. In 1972 MGM sold its stakes in the Metro Theatre Bombay Ltd. and Metro Theatre Calcutta Ltd. to a Swedish company, Tramarsa, S.A., for $1 million. Tramarsa claimed no tax liabilities for the 1973–1974 fiscal year by claiming that the sale had protected the cinemas from assessment since it was transacted between two non-Indian firms, MGM and Tramarsa.[62] These statements soon came under question. By March 1973 the national government challenged Tramarsa's ability to transfer Metro cinemas funds abroad until what the minister of state for finance called a "shady and fraudulent" deal had been fully investigated. In the end, Tramarsa turned out to be a ruse. The company was registered in Geneva, but it was the Indian Gupta brothers—one living in Geneva, one in Brazil—who turned out to be the buyers.[63] The Tramarsa scandal generated calls for the nationalization of the Metro cinemas, although the minister of state for information and broadcasting, I. K. Gujral, "made it clear that the government's policy was not to nationalise cinema houses," despite previous government plans to "establish a chain of theatres to make up the big shortage in the number of cinema houses available."[64]

Yet another company, Golden Films & Finance Private Ltd. (GFFPL), caused an additional uproar when this "Indian-operated Swedish firm" acquired Metro-Goldwyn-Mayer Films of India outright and then tried to buy the two Metro cinemas from Tramarsa. The sale of MGM India to another shadow company with murky origins infuriated the government, and the Indian Reserve Bank roundly refused permission by GFFPL to buy the former MGM cinemas.[65] For reasons unknown, GFFPL was eventually able to buy the two cinemas anyway in 1974 for $1.3 million.[66] Three years later, in March 1977, the Metro in Calcutta became a fully nationalized cinema when Film Finance Corp. management began operating the former shop window.[67]

There are two important codas to this discussion of MGM's cinemas in India. One in the (now) Mumbai Metro's transformation into the key cinema for the BIG Cinemas chain and the other as a location of a devastating terrorist attack in 2008. In Lashkar-e-Taiba's deadly attack throughout the city of Mumbai, the U.S. House Homeland Security Subcommittee on Counterterrorism and Intelligence Hearing found that the terrorist organization selected, among its targets, the Chabad House "at the insistence of [Lashkar-e-Taiba] organizers seeking the global symbolism of a synagogue or Jewish cultural center; St. Xavier's College[, which] may have served a similar function for its Christian symbolism" and the Metro Cinema and Leopold Café, which may have been accidental or "at the behest of local facilitators," as reflective symbols of the West. A witness testified before the committee, "The Bombay attack had special meaning for me: I used to live in Bombay, just a few blocks from the site of most of the attacks. I used to buy American newspapers from the Taj bookshop, stop by the Leopold Cafe for a cold beer, watch a movie at the Metro Cinema, take trains from the terminal that locals still call by its colonial-era initials of 'VT.'"[68] The Mumbai Metro had dropped its American affiliation four decades earlier, but its identity was still bound up with MGM, *Tom & Jerry*, the Metro Cub Club, and the Western influence of the art deco aesthetic—all of which makes it a nostalgic and contested place for India's colonial and postcolonial memory. It also made it a target for the lingering resentment of American hard and soft power abroad. Only in recent years, as discussed in chapter 20, did the Metro shed its past and become synonymous with India's cinematic present and hopeful future.

CHAPTER 20

CHINA AS HOLLYWOOD'S FINAL FRONTIER, 1946–2013

Hollywood's Chinese Cinemas and the End of Hollywood's Exhibition Empires

In China, MGM sought to control its own shop window cinema in Shanghai before the onset of World War II and then began operating the MGM-Roxy there after the war had ended. Those efforts were also short-lived as the Chinese Communist Revolution dislodged Hollywood, its cinemas, and its executives for the next half century. At the beginning of the twenty-first century, Hollywood—namely, Warner Bros.—reengaged overseas exhibition in both Taiwan and China. Warner Bros. placed all its chips on China, selling off other circuits around the world in order to fund a risky post–World Trade Organization Chinese film exhibition expansion. Warner Bros.' gamble that it could overcome local political and industrial resistance to Hollywood's growth in this market led to its abrupt departure after only a few key cinemas had been built. All told, perhaps no other continent provided Hollywood with so much promise *and* so much heartburn. As part VI takes us from 1927 to 2013, when Warner Bros. sold off its last cinema chain in Japan, it is a fitting end to Hollywood's effort to rescreen the world in its own image. It is also a fitting end to this book since, nearly a decade later, Hollywood's major film studios have shown no desire to try, once more, to project their power through the ownership or operation of foreign cinemas.

Hollywood's fitful expansion in China bears little similarity to its work in Japan, the Philippines, or India. Until the twenty-first century, China was a vastly underscreened market, a situation that limited film revenues that could otherwise have boosted the indigenous film industry. Prior to World War I,

European films had dominated Chinese screens. Afterward, American films often dominated cinemas in Peking (Beijing) and Shanghai.

China's early cinematic infrastructure was troubled by piracy, underdevelopment, and foreign influence. The Ramos Amusement Company, a Spanish firm, operated two of Shanghai's key cinemas, the Victoria and Olympia Theaters, with a contract to exhibit all of Paramount's films. First National films also appeared in Chinese cinemas, with the Isis Theater in Shanghai, the China Theaters in Tientsin (Tianjin), and other cinemas operated by the British Hongkong Amusement Company "forming a syndicate for the purchase of pictures." Despite these licensed screenings, United Artists executive Alexander Krisel noted that First National films were still being shown throughout the country using "stolen or duped copies of pictures." Even "legitimate" exhibitors like the Ramos company used agents in Europe and the United States to procure stolen or duped copies for its Chinese cinemas.[1] Piracy has often been an issue in Asia (and elsewhere), as noted by Nitin Govil and Eric Hoyt's research on the unlicensed duplication and distribution of *The Thief of Baghdad* (1924) in India, one of many films that wended its way around the networks of Indian cinema distribution *outside* of United Artists' legal and industrial control.[2]

By the late 1920s, as Hollywood combated piracy by organizing and systematizing their distribution operations and contacts with exhibitors, Ting Wang notes that "Hollywood achieved de-facto monopoly over China's film distribution and exhibition sectors." Of the 250 cinemas operating in China by 1930, nearly two hundred specialized in American (and European) films, and U.S.-produced films now composed 75 percent of all motion pictures shown in China. In growing, cosmopolitan cities like Shanghai, Wang adds, that figure "could be as high as 90%."[3] In Shanghai, MGM films typically played at the Carlton Theatre, while Fox films were often booked into the Nanking.[4] The Nanking also projected American foreign policy and other ideological messaging as the Shanghai home for the company's *Fox Movietone News*.[5] As always, a physical foothold in a foreign nation meant far more than simply an industrial beachhead for American films. Local exhibitors already provided that. American sales offices, affiliated cinemas, bus and train advertising, promotional tie-ups, and key cinemas and shop windows all provided a foothold for transmitting U.S. intellectual property and consumer brands as well as political, social, cultural, and other ideology sold with both *stars* and stripes. Sales offices also served double duty, with ground-floor windows creating key spaces for street-side advertising for American films and military muscle. The *China Press* reported on one such MGM display in November 1930 that featured a machine gun lent to the company by the U.S. Marines.[6]

Shanghai had the largest number of cinemas of any city in China in the 1930s (roughly forty), and Hollywood films dominated the screens of those first-run, downtown houses where, historian Poshek Fu, writes, "the setting and amenities were as important a draw as the film itself." These cinemas, Fu adds, created "a virtual index of modern life in Chinese cities" in which "their architectural design, ambience, and amenities" contributed to the "glitter and dazzle of metropolitan Shanghai," seen more and more then as "Hollywood of the East."[7] The city's deluxe cinemas had yet another advantage in the quality of the prints exhibited. After premiering at these cinemas, Hollywood films—accumulating scratches, dirt, and other imperfections—would trickle down through the subsequent run market in second-, third-, and fourth-run venues while the quality of the projection and their ticket prices notched lower and lower with each rung. "This class-based exhibition system overlapped with a colonial structure of power relations," Fu argues. "As a spatial expression of semi-colonialism in Shanghai, the best theaters were all located at the heart of the foreign concessions, and most marginal houses were tucked away in the lower-class neighborhoods in the Chinese areas. Cinemas showing *xipian*, or Western films (predominately from Hollywood), whether first- or second-run, were grander and more prestigious than their counterparts devoted to Chinese pictures."[8] Shanghai's four most opulent movie palaces, the Grand, Nanking, Metropolis, and Cathay, were all in the most prosperous locations, tempting middle and upper-class Chinese and foreign patrons with their plush seats, top notch service, ornate décor, and air-conditioning.

Meanwhile, in British-controlled Hong Kong, Paramount expanded beyond distribution to exhibition, operating the city's King's Theatre as its shop window cinema. "America is not the only country having its dapper ushers," *Motion Picture Herald* noted alongside an image of the King's staff. "Here is the staff of the Paramount Publix theatre, the King's in Hong Kong, China. In all respects they compare with the Paramount [in Manhattan] at the crossroads of the world."[9]

The box office boom in Shanghai and elsewhere stalled, however, when the Chinese economy faltered in the mid-1930s, and Chinese audiences began to turn away from American films and toward indigenous product. American film receipts were down 40 percent, and the first-run cinemas that had lured American booking contracts were now almost entirely filled with foreign visitors. American patrons were estimated to compose 85 percent of these cinemas' local patronage. Chinese audiences, the bureau reported, increasingly wanted Chinese films.[10] Poshek Fu notes that the downtown palaces showing American films catered instead to "the upper echelon of foreign concession society—colonial officials, foreign taipans, Chinese businessmen and professionals" and "promoted a new moviegoing decorum and new viewing habits." By contrast to other entertainment venues, "which were markedly noisy, scruffy, and messy, movie palaces called for a new code of behavior shaped by the bourgeois values of self-restraint, orderliness, privacy, and respectability that befitted the urban modernity their sleek surroundings embodied." This new aesthetic, Fu writes, "became a marker of new taste and a modern culture; going to the Grand or the Cathay was a way of acquiring and displaying the 'symbolic capital' of being modern and cosmopolitan." The "Hollywood" style of moviegoing inflected every aspect of these downtown palaces. "Ushers in the four elite theaters treated patrons with impeccable manners, and managers checked during each show to make sure everything was in order," a stark contrast to "the ruffianly employees of the rundown houses [that] were always harassing and insulting moviegoers," Fu adds. "This complexly organized and class-based exhibition system, with its discursive association with the cultural meaning of modern life, contributed to making Shanghai the capital of pre-war Chinese cinema as well as of urban modernity in China."[11]

The Japanese invasion of China in 1937 closed Shanghai's cinemas—and stalled the national exhibition industry—but the city's cinemas reopened in September as Japanese troops retreated.[12] In June 1938, despite the economic downturn, Sam Burger, MGM's foreign manager, stated that the company hoped to build a new $500,000 shop window cinema in Shanghai.[13] The instability and violence delayed construction while restrictions on wartime building restrictions and materials caused further delays.[14]

MGM was the most aggressive in overseas expansion in the mid to late 1930s. The company's Depression-era war chest was the largest among the five majors, and it used those winnings to expand its distribution and exhibition networks. In China, MGM struck a new deal with the Asia Theater Group to exhibit all of MGM's films first-run in the new 1,500-seat Roxy Theatre in Shanghai when it opened in December 1939. (The Roxy name was thoroughly American, of course, named for U.S. exhibitor and broadcaster Samuel "Roxy" Rothafel and the eponymous 5,920-seat theater he opened in New York in March 1927.) The new Shanghai Roxy, Fu writes, was the "most-talked about new movie house" in the city, designed with a "modern Euro-American architectural style" and marketed as the "most up-to-date, best-equipped movie palace in the East." The cinema was outfitted with an American air-conditioning system and other technical details imported from the United States. "With an exclusive contract with M-G-M," Fu writes, "the Roxy became the epitome of the glamour, sophistication, and cosmopolitanism of modern urban life."[15] MGM films shown at the Roxy were not only an opportunity for Hollywood escapism but also a training ground in English for Shanghai's cosmopolitan moviegoers. Like the Hogaku-Za for Tokyo audiences, Hollywood films were screened at the Roxy without Chinese subtitles so that "Chinese anxious to learn English [could] blend education with their entertainment."[16]

World War II in China

Following the Japanese occupation of China and the United States' entrance into World War II, Hollywood lost access to much of this now Japanese-controlled market. In January 1943, this market closed completely when the Wang Jingwei government in Nanjing joined Japan in declaring war on the United States and its allies and banned Hollywood films from Chinese screens. "To demonstrate that Japan, not Great Britain or the United States, was now the master of Shanghai mass culture," Poshek Fu notes, "Zhonghua [China Film United] premiered Japanese films at the Roxy," striking directly at what had been an important American and Hollywood cultural embassy.[17] The Roxy's designation as an MGM showcase was over (for now). After the Zhonghua takeover installed a Japanese film-only policy, Fu notes that "only 'intellectuals curious about everyday Japanese culture or trying to learn the Japanese language' showed up at the theater."[18] Shanghai audiences had sought out Hollywood's more universal narratives despite their foreignness; wartime Japanese cinema may certainly have felt oppressive and forced under occupation. The Roxy was still a premiere cinema but, under Zhonghua, an emptier one.

American personnel serving in China faced a similar predicament as those in the Philippines. When the Japanese occupied Shanghai, Warner Bros. executive Harold Dunn was captured and interned.[19] Julian Berman, MGM manager for Japan and China, was also captured and not allowed to leave occupied China. By 1945 Loew's International had lost contact with him.[20] Others, now serving in the U.S. armed forces, weren't struggling to get out but fighting their way back in. As U.S. forces battled there in 1944, Sgt. Nat Rubin, who worked for Loew's Lyric Theatre in Bridgeport, Connecticut, and other members of the 14th Air Force set up a "civilian theatre" in a U.S. encampment in China named the "Loew's Rice Paddy."[21] "There will be many more Loew's Theatres in China to come," Rubin wrote to Loew's in-house magazine, *LO!* in October 1944. "Nowhere else in the world have I seen people crazier about the movies than the Chinese." *LO!* reported that their makeshift U.S. Army cinema—open to both American troops and locals—"plays to a full house all the time." Films for the "Loew's Rice Paddy"—like other American battle front cinemas—were supplied by the U.S. Army's Overseas Motion Picture Service.[22] This was certainly a very different kind of cultural embassy.

The War Ends, the War Begins

Imperial Japan announced its surrender on August 15, 1945, and the Chinese market officially reopened to American film companies as the defeated nation ceded China (largely) back to the Chinese. A bilateral business covenant was quickly signed between the U.S. and Chinese governments that enabled American products, including film, to flow back in. Ting Wang notes that the American film companies immediately reconstituted their businesses through the Film Board, a collusive amalgam that helped each company "enforce exhibition contracts," "schedul[e] among themselves," and "arbitrat[e] business disputes of various kinds."[23]

Still, profits were not easily repatriated back to the United States. The Chinese government had frozen 85 percent of foreign film rental in 1945, forcing most of those grosses to remain in China. Coupled with postwar "runaway inflation," the economic impact of these protectionist policies was to "forc[e] American companies to protect their capital by investing their idle coin in a safe medium—amusement real estate."[24] Amerigo Benefico, the Shaw Bros.' New York sales agent, noted that, just as other countries had discovered, blocking American firms from withdrawing their local film rental only boosted American exhibition interests in China.

MGM was first in line for investment. In January 1946 Tommy Farrell was sent to Shanghai to take over the territory as acting manager for MGM China.[25] MGM did not renew their relationship with the Roxy as a key cinema but inked a new contract instead with the Dahua Theater. Then, in August 1946, *Shen Bao* reported that MGM was now preparing to build one of the largest movie theaters in the region at the corner of Bubbling Well Road (now Jing'an Temple Road) and Myburgh Road that would be "better than the Grand Theater and Majestic Theater" and would even "surpass" the deluxe MGM cinemas in India. Shanghai mayor Wu approved MGM's new cinema, but construction was delayed due to lengthy negotiations with the Public Works Department over the need for a parking lot and safe exits for patrons.[26]

MGM finally received approval from the city to begin construction in mid-November, but the approval was too late.[27] Postwar labor and material shortages, complex logistics, and rising costs made the project increasingly unattractive to Loew's International.[28] In the end, the new MGM shop window was never built, and MGM began operating the air-conditioned Roxy—its former showcase in Shanghai—as its shop window cinema, rechristened the MGM-Roxy. Farrell was named its manager in addition to his position as head of MGM's China operations. The theater reopened as the MGM-Roxy on February 4, 1947, with *Ziegfeld Follies*.[29] Between August 1945 and May 1949 more than one thousand American feature films were released in Shanghai cinemas, crowding out local and other international product, and the MGM-Roxy benefited from the postwar Chinese and expat appetites for U.S. narratives and cinematic spectacles.[30]

Intermission

Politics and war intervened again to thwart American dominance in China. The commencement of the Chinese Civil War led to increasing restrictions against American films by mid-1949. The two Americans who had been on the Chinese government's censorship committee were quietly replaced by Chinese members who adhered to the new nationalist spirit.[31] By the end of February 1950 a resolution had been passed by Peking exhibitors—under direction by the Chinese authorities—that no more American or British films would be screened at all.[32] The Cinema and Theatre Workers Union of Shanghai City and the Cinema Distributors Branch Union subsequently issued a "threatening" letter to the Shanghai Foreign Distributors group in May 1950 saying, the British Consulate General in Shanghai wrote to the British Foreign office, that "may well be the prelude to action against the British and American film distribution in Shanghai on the lines of that already taken in Peking and Tientsin [Tianjin]."[33] In mid-July the minister of culture of the Central People's Government announced five new "temporary" regulations that, the *People's Daily News* noted, were implemented "to promote the native motion picture industry, boycott poisonous American films, protect and support [the] private movie industry," and "enforce the policy of caring for private and state enterprises alike." With these new regulations, the *Daily News* observed, the "poisonous American films and old Chinese films on the market could [now] be boycotted and replaced, and thus win complete supremacy on the market for progressive films."[34]

Enforcement of the ban was simple because all production companies, studios, distributors, and exhibitors had to apply for registration status from the Cinema Bureau of the Central People's Government, later known as the Central Cinema Bureau. No cinemas could exhibit films without censorship certificates, and, of course, none would be granted to Hollywood films, no matter how "progressive" they might have been. And if any theaters were caught exhibiting old American or British prints, the prints would be detained and "serious offenders" would have their exhibition registrations cancelled.[35] By October the MGM-Roxy had begun showing Chinese and Russian films for the first time.[36] Although British and American films managed to still find their way to some Shanghai and Canton (now Guangzhou) screens during the summer and early fall of 1950, they were officially banned by November, with Canton holding out the longest of any Chinese city. The MGM-Roxy was finally forced to drop its studio hyphen as the American cultural pipeline was severed to mainland China.[37]

China's borders were officially closed to American films, personnel, and certainly cinema ownership or operation by the end of 1950.[38] It would be nearly a half century before another successful effort was made to exploit this enormous market. The world's most populous nation could have greatly enriched Hollywood's pockets over the intervening five decades, but it remained shut. China represented an enormous untapped market for Hollywood throughout the remainder of the twentieth century, a sleeping giant whose film industry would awaken not only to stand on its own but, through Dalian Wanda, to become the site of the world's largest exhibition company that would come to own the descendant corporations of some of the most important legacy players in global film exhibition, including AMC, Loews, Hoyts, Odeon, and United Cinemas International.

Warner Bros. International Cinemas, China, and Twenty-First-Century Film Exhibition

In the early 1990s China had begun to embrace limited economic and cultural reforms that included boosting the national film industry through foreign investment in domestic film distribution, co-productions, new technology, and a wide-ranging campaign to build cinemas around the country. The China Film Corp. lowered its drawbridge for foreign investment by allowing Golden Harvest, based in pre-unification Hong Kong, to distribute films across China through a revenue-sharing deal that would become the blueprint and siren song for Hollywood.[39]

In September 1994, following in the wake of this landmark deal, Warner Bros. began discussions with Chinese government officials, becoming one of the first American media conglomerates to open such negotiations. As a result of the ensuing revenue-sharing agreement, Warner Bros.' *The Fugitive* was exhibited in fifty-seven cinemas in six Chinese cities and grossed over $3 million, a relatively modest but promising figure. "This historic deal between Warner Bros. and China Film was an epoch-making step not only in China's film reform, and in Sino-US film relations, but also in Hollywood's global expansion," Ting Wang writes. "It opened up the Chinese market once again to Hollywood after the latter's absence for 45 years, bringing the major Hollywood studios closer to realizing their long-awaited ambition of cracking the vast, largely untapped and potentially lucrative Chinese market, one of the few remaining distribution and exhibition gold mines in the world."[40]

After departing the Peruvian, Colombian, and Cuban exhibition markets in the 1950s, Warner Bros.' sole overseas cinema was its flagship Warner West End in London. Warner Bros. did not reenter global film exhibition (beyond London) until 1987, under the guidance of exhibition industry veteran Salah Hassanein, who convinced Warner Bros. that building new multiplexes abroad through a new company, Warner Bros. International Theatres (WBIT), would transform underperforming markets through new exhibition venues. WBIT's model for foreign expansion became the operation of local multiplexes with joint partners, thus allowing local investors to assuage indigenous concerns about U.S. domination while allowing local investors to help clear legal and other regulatory hurdles.[41]

Millard Ochs succeeded Hassanein in 1994, and by 1998 WBIT operated seventy-four multiplexes around the world with 654 screens, including thirteen multiplexes in Japan and a new venture in Taiwan.[42] These joint ventures included collaborations with Niichi and Mycal in Japan (Warner-Mycal Cinemas) and a prominent partnership, Warner Village Cinemas, with Australian exhibitor-distributor-producer Village Roadshow.[43] In January 1998 WBIT made its first foray into Asia with the new Warner Village Multiplex in the Hsin Yi district of Taipei, Taiwan—a seventeen-screen multiplex that was the first in the region to offer digital sound, stadium seating, and computerized ticketing (and auditing) systems. Michael Curtin writes that the new Taipei multiplex was "more than a theater complex," with "thirty shops, restaurants, and related entertainment activities."[44] The cinema's technological and architectural innovations, as Hassanein had predicted, did create a larger market for Hollywood films, with nine out of the eleven films booked in its seventeen screens.[45] In its first year alone, the new Warner Village in Taipei sold roughly three million tickets, consumed 25 percent of the local market, and accounted for 13 percent of the country's total ticket sales. Warner Village would later open five more multiplexes in Taiwan, grabbing more than half of all Taiwan's ticket sales in these six venues.[46]

The success of WBIT's international cinemas—and especially the opening of the Warner Village in Taipei—encouraged Warner Bros. and Ochs to try and expand into China with its untapped market of over a billion potential moviegoers. One key impediment to the growth of the Chinese film industry remained its woefully outdated exhibition sector. Between 1990 and 1994, ten thousand of the country's fourteen thousand "authorized" cinemas were closed due to age or lack of efficacy.[47] Even with some new multiplexes, China not only remained extremely underscreened but its cinemas failed to attract the country's growing middle class and those looking for an alternative to the widespread availability of pirated DVDs and VCDs and other forms of access to domestic and international films. Chinese officials, hoping to generate interest in building new venues for Chinese films, removed the prohibition against foreign investment in theatrical exhibition.

In 1997 the Hong Kong–based United Artists Cinema Circuit (UACC) built its first mainland multiplex in Wuhan. By 1999 UACC operated four multiplexes in China, including a new six-screen in Shanghai.[48] Against the background of UACC's Chinese expansion and the ongoing trade negotiations between the United States and Chinese governments, Time Warner chief executive Gerald Levin wrote a letter in March 1999 to Chinese premier Zhu Rongji laying out the company's plan for its "comprehensive cooperation" with China. These objectives included joint ventures for media coproductions, distribution operations, and ancillary revenue streams as well as "other movie-related businesses, such as movie theaters and theme parks."[49] On November 19, 1999, the United States and China announced a bilateral trade agreement followed by a similar accord between the European Union and China on May 19, 2000. By September the U.S. Congress had granted China permanent normal trading rights.[50] At the same time, China's State Administration of Radio, Film and Television (SARFT)—later known as the State Administration of Press, Publication, Radio, Film and Television (SAPPRFT)—and its Ministry of Foreign Trade and Economic Cooperation issued new regulations that encouraged foreign investment in multiplex construction and management. The new foreign-invested enterprise (FIE) regulations set out numerous legal stipulations for cinema construction based on foreign investments, including that (1) foreign-invested movie theatres could not be singly owned by foreign companies but had to be part of equity joint ventures or contractual joint ventures; (2) foreign-invested theatres could extend terms for no more than thirty years; and (3) Chinese partners had to retain at least a 51 percent share in an equity joint venture or the primary management rights in a contractual joint venture.[51] New multiplexes had to follow all FIE theater regulations for construction and approvals and agree to "profit allocation and timing for return on investment," James Zimmerman writes, "notwithstanding the requirement that the Chinese party or parties control the operation."[52]

Global exhibition companies like WBIT salivated at the opportunity to expand into a largely untapped market amid overbuilding in the United States and Western Europe, and at the impending bankruptcy reorganizations of North American exhibitors like Loews Cineplex, General Cinema, Regal Cinemas, Edwards Theatres, and others. The foreign exhibition market—in Asia and Latin America—was the leading growth opportunity for venture capital and expansion in exhibition during this period, with China among the most lucrative in terms of potential. (A 2014 report noted, for instance, that while "box office in developed markets remained relatively flat" with a 0.4% compound annual growth rate (CAGR) between 2010 and 2013, "overall industry growth was driven primarily by rapid growth in emerging markets, including Latin America (16.8%) and Asia Pacific (7.7%) with a total 11.3% CAGR for all emerging markets."[53]) A decade and a half earlier, as executives forecasted the next decade of global exhibition expansion, Peter Dobson of WBIT told a March 2000 audience at ShoWest—then the annual trade convention for motion picture exhibitors—that the lucrative Chinese market was "just sitting there waiting for the taking."[54] Warner Bros.'

development of Chinese exhibition was also a key part of its antipiracy strategy. "We're cooperating with the government to fight piracy by being inside," Ochs later noted, "not standing outside and talking about it."[55] On November 11, 2001, China officially joined the World Trade Organization and would now have to tackle piracy in a more meaningful way while also regulating new foreign investments in its domestic cinemas.[56]

Time Warner also created additional strategic alliances and business ventures between China Entertainment Television, Turner Broadcasting System Asia Pacific, and Warner Bros. International Television, while Warner Music Asia Pacific also created Warner Music China as a new Warner Music International affiliate under a license agreement with the official China National Production Importation and Exportation Corp. "and other state-owned distributors."[57] People's Republic of China president Jiang Zemin noted that China, following its entrance into the World Trade Organization, "welcome[d] more overseas investment, new investment projects in China, and long-term stable cooperation with us by business communities around the world."[58]

WBIT Begins Building in China

The first WBIT project in China, the Shanghai Paradise Warner Cinema City, was a nine-screen multiplex in Shanghai, announced in March 2002 as a joint venture between Shanghai Paradise Co. Ltd. and WBIT, operating as Shanghai Paradise Warner Cinema City Co., with financing also provided by Broadband Investment Ltd. of Hong Kong, a local restaurant and leisure operator.[59] (Shanghai Paradise's relationship with Warner Bros. stretched back to 1986, when the company had co-produced Steven Spielberg's *Empire of the Sun* (1987), portraying the Japanese invasion of China and the internment of American and other Western prisoners.[60]) At the time Shanghai Paradise was the region's top distributor-exhibitor, garnering roughly 80 percent of the city's total box office from domestic and foreign films, and it operated fifty-seven local cinemas with 126 screens, accounting for roughly 75 percent of all venues in Shanghai.[61] Following the creation of the FIE laws, the joint venture represented an investment of 28 million yuan (roughly $4.5 million in 2015 dollars), with Shanghai Paradise Co. owning 51 percent of the shares while WBIT controlled the remaining 49 percent.[62] Shanghai Paradise, not WBIT, applied to the Central People's Government in Beijing and the municipal government in Shanghai to approve the cinema's design, investment, and construction plans. Ochs noted that WBIT's key contribution was in assisting Shanghai Paradise from the early stages with the complex's design and technical specifications and management and employee training.[63]

The new cinema, located in one of Shanghai's largest shopping malls in the Xujiahui district, the Grand Gateway, offered up the decades-old, successful combination of both the exotic and the familiar through the hybridity of foreign and domestic cultural markers. The multiplex was "designed as a completely immersive Warner Bros. entertainment experience," a WBIT press release noted, "with numerous scenic and design elements featuring the stars of Warner Bros." and its "world-class library of movie and animation properties."[64] And yet it also featured a "large mural of the Bund (the historic Zhongshan Road) in which Chinese movie stars Jackie Chan and Gong Li stand shoulder-to-shoulder with the likes of legends Humphrey Bogart and Clark Gable." The union of Hollywood's past (Bogart and Gable) and China's present (Chan and Li) paid homage to Warner Bros.' legacy, its production and distribution history in Shanghai, and the WB-branded cinemas that would soon exhibit films starring global Hollywood and local Chinese stars. Shanghai Paradise received final approval from the Chinese government to open a nine-screen cinema on July 12, 2003, with the local launch of Warner Bros.' *The Matrix Reloaded* (2003).[65]

As the company's focus turned eastward, Warner Village Cinemas, Warner Bros.' and Village Roadshow's joint venture, found an opportunity to exit the increasingly crowded British market, and in May 2003 SBC International Cinemas had purchased Warner Village Cinemas for over $400 million. Ochs noted that leaving the British market "enables us to further our strategy of seeding new markets."[66] Warner Bros. confirmed its turn toward China by developing local production as well, financing its first Chinese language film, *Turn Left, Turn Right*, written and directed by Johnnie To and Wai Ka-fai, along with signing a new agreement between Warner Bros., the Chinese production company Century Heroes, and the Hong Kong–based Salon Films.[67]

A Gold Fish Called Wanda

Following the successful launch of the Shanghai Paradise Warner Cinema City, the Shanghai Cinema Group announced in October 2003 a new 200-million-yuan plan to build ten new joint WBIT cinemas throughout China, including a new multiplex in Nanjing and another in Wuhan. The new agreement had one significant change: SARFT had suddenly agreed to relax local laws in Beijing, Shanghai, Guangzhou, Chengdu, Xi'an, Nanjing, and Wuhan that would now allow Warner Bros. to control 51 percent of their new investments in these cities, rather than holding only a minority stake.[68] WBIT then announced a new venture with the Dalian Wanda Group to build and operate thirty Warner Wanda International Cinemas in 2003, with the first cinema to open in the Tianjin Municipality in January 2004. The agreement called for Wanda to invest in their construction "while Warner Bros. will provide overall technical, operational and management services." Over the next four years, Warner and Wanda planned to open twenty-nine more cinemas in Beijing, Shanghai, Harbin, Dalian, Shenyang, Wuhan, and Zhengzhou. "China's cinema market is young and full of opportunities," Ochs buoyantly observed. The law firm of O'Melveny & Myers LLP helped WBIC negotiate terms with the Dalian Wanda Group. Warner Bros.' Shanghai attorney and O'Melveny & Myers LLP partner Walker Wallace, along with attorney Yu Aihong, negotiated the "largest co-development deal for cinemas in China to date" and "the first of its kind between a Chinese property developer and a Hollywood studio."[69]

WBIT's optimism was further boosted by another new law, the Temporary Regulation on Foreign Enterprises' Investment in Chinese Cinemas law that now allowed foreign investors like Warner Bros. to hold a 75 percent stake in "joint venture cinemas in seven of China's largest cities" beginning January 1, 2004. Zhang Pimin, vice director of SARFT's Film Bureau, observed that the new more flexible law made China "a more attractive place for foreign cinema giants" and hoped that "the coming of Warner Bros. is just a prelude of the foreign inflow in China's movie market" which could help reverse China's "poor cinema conditions." At the time the country still had only 1,200 cinemas with roughly 2,000 screens—a profoundly minute average of one screen for every 650,000 citizens.[70] (By comparison, the United States had more than 6,000 cinemas with more than 36,000 screens in 2004).[71]

Warner Bros. applied for government approval for even more multiplexes in Wuhan and Nanjing as the majority partner in a joint venture with Shanghai United Circuit, and for an agreement with Guangzhou Performance Co. for a new Warner Bros. International Cinemas (WBIC; WBIT had now changed its corporate name from "Theatres" to "Cinemas") multiplex in Guangzhou.[72] WBIC became the first Western cinema investor to hold a majority interest in a Chinese multiplex through its new joint venture with Shanghai United Circuit in Nanjing that offered WBIC a 51 percent interest, following the new SARFT guidelines and those of China's Ministry of Commerce and Ministry of Culture. Millard Ochs noted at the time that the revised ownership rules and the approval given to Warner Bros. was "a great honor."[73]

By the end of 2005, the Paradise Warner Cinema City remained the country's most profitable cinema over the previous three years, while WBIC cinemas grossed over 120 million yuan (US$15.2 million) that year alone.[74] WBIC now planned to increase the number of screens it operated in Shanghai to 170 by the end of 2007.[75] With its UK circuit sold and its European holdings dwindling, WBIC announced plans to move its entire cinema design unit from London to Shanghai "as part of a continuing expansion into the Chinese market." From there, executives would handle all multiplex design work for the company's circuits in China, Japan, and Italy, and for future partnerships in India and Vietnam.[76] The cinema design employees would join the forty-six staffers already working in Warner Bros.' Shanghai offices.[77] The changes in foreign investment laws and Warner Bros.' early success, *Sina Finance* later reported, spurred "the eight major US film companies" to express "their desire to build their own cinemas in China, thereby expanding the proportion of their films."[78]

Too Fast, Too Furious

In 1950 new regulations of the Revolutionary government in China had ended Hollywood's ambitions of building cinemas in China. Fifty-five years later, Chinese government regulations would upend Hollywood's dreams once more.

In July 2005 SARFT released another new set of laws titled Several Opinions in Foreign Investment in Culture Industry, which retracted the ability of foreign companies to hold majority positions in Chinese exhibition ventures. Once more, reporter Zhang Rui noted, Chinese mainland investors had to "own at least fifty-one percent or play a leading role in their joint ventures with foreign investors."[79] After exploring its legal options for the law's repeal, and "after looking at all possible solutions for the past year," Warner Bros.' China publicist Gao Ming announced WBIC's immediate exit from the Chinese exhibition market in November 2006. "While we are disappointed that we must stop our investments in cinemas due to significant regulatory changes," Ming added, "Warner Bros. remains committed to its other businesses in China including local language film production, a home video joint venture, consumer products and studio stores all of which have different legal structures, business models and regulatory requirements."[80] (SARFT officials refused to comment on the reasons for the legal change.[81])

All of WBIC's Chinese partnerships quickly came to an end, and the company began selling its stake in operating and uncompleted cinemas.[82] The *Los Angeles Times* noted that the "about-face" highlighted "Hollywood's long-standing tensions with China" that had been papered over during Time Warner and WBIC's historic four-year expansion in the country. Yu Guoming, vice dean at Renmin University's School of Journalism and Communication, observed that WBIC may have tried to go too fast in its exhibition expansion: "For global media companies to enter China, you should have more patience to gradually penetrate into the market. Warner and many other foreign media giants want to make progress by leaps and hit some milestones.... This is against the rules of the game in China."[83]

The country remained heavily underscreened, but Warner Bros. was unwilling to risk the next regulatory or legal challenge. Once more, it was film exhibition—not production or distribution—that most challenged issues of nationalism and foreign investment. As Xing Yan, a public relations officer for Beijing's Hua Xing Cinema, noted in 2004, a "foreign capital influx into China's cinema market" would ultimately serve to "erode the interests of local cinemas" even if it boosted the country's box office.[84] Film production was transient, contingent, temporary, and did not create a sustainable industrial base. Film distribution remained largely invisible and still dependent on domestic exhibitors. It was foreign ownership and operation of local cinemas, though, that had long spelled trouble, as evidenced by the economic boycotts over the past century of American exhibitors in England to political violence against cinemas in Egypt, as noted throughout this book.

WBIC reasoned that without clear legal protections, its real estate investments and its exhibition operations in China would be conducted without control, assurance, or according to conventional Hollywood wisdom. David Wolf, a media consultant in Beijing, remarked that these new "hostile regulations and uncertainties of the future" forced foreign media companies to reconsider their business plans. "They're really beginning to question the assumptions of coming here in the first place."[85] Lulu Hansen, a director of international development at the Yunnan Film Group, noted that many American media investors in China do not understand the unwritten rules or how to avoid personal/political disputes that can quickly kill foreign investment: "With many things in China, contracts are seen as negotiable, sometimes even after execution. Or in some cases where it would be the norm to have a contract," Hansen noted, "there is none because a verbal or personal agreement is seen as more honorable. Sometimes, the best way to avoid/resolve legal disputes is to avoid/resolve personal or professional disputes." Hansen argues that while business affairs departments and attorneys are the foot soldiers for these kinds of conflicts, in China, "it can be easier to resolve a dispute through personal rather than legal means. And once mutual trust is lost, everything gets exponentially more difficult."[86]

WBIC's planned circuit of forty Chinese cinemas quickly vanished.[87] Between 2006 and 2008 WBIC sold all its remaining shares in these joint ventures to their partners. According to Chinese law, equity transfer agreements also had to be approved by the government.[88] The equity transfer agreement between Shanghai Film Group and WBIC was signed on February 12, 2007, with WBIC selling its 49 percent stake in the enormously popular Shanghai Paradise Warner Cinema City and its 51 percent stake in Nanjing SFG-Warner Cinema City.[89] Replacing the "WB" with a "WD" (for Wanda) quickly airbrushed the American imprimatur from WBIC cinemas around China.[90]

Warner Bros. International Cinemas was not the only company affected by SARFT's change in the investment laws. The Golden Harvest–Village Roadshow joint venture in China also came to an end amid the difficult environment for foreign investors and operators. "So multiplexing is here to stay, but the day of the foreign joint venture is over," Scott Rosenberg wrote (erroneously) in *Film Journal International*. "Multiplexing has gone indigenous," and "local investors now take all the risk and profit."[91]

Since 2007 Warner Bros. has actively maintained joint ventures in film, television, and other media enterprises in China but has strictly avoided theatrical exhibition. "China is developing methods for consumers to view movies outside the cinema in a legitimate fashion," Jim Wuthrich, president of International Home Video and Digital Distribution for Warner Bros. Home Entertainment Group, stated in 2011. Through new Blu-ray, DVD, and video-on-demand deals, he added, "millions of potential consumers will be able to view our films."[92] Gala openings for WBIC cinemas, though, were long gone from the cityscapes of Beijing and Shanghai, even if the company's films could still easily be found in private homes and public cinemas.

In the end, Warner Bros.' abrupt exit from operating cinemas in China caused the media conglomerate to miss out on a massive exhibition boom as millions visited "modern cinemas for the first time," David Pierson wrote in March 2011. "State-of-the-art theaters are replacing dilapidated movie houses not only in wealthy urban centers like Beijing and Shanghai but in outposts like Shengzhou ... which has grown into a bustling city of about 800,000." Two years later China became the world's second-largest exhibition market, surpassing the EU and Japan.[93] In 2014 alone, China added 1,015 cinemas and 5,397 screens, bringing the country's screen count up to 23,600. "On average," Zhang Hongsen, SAPPRFT's film bureau chief, noted, "15 more screens were added each day."[94] By 2017 China had remained the world's second-largest exhibition market and would have been the pillar of a booming WBIC.

The maximum 49 percent foreign investment, determined by the revised FIE laws, did not scare off all exhibitors/investors, though. Canada's IMAX Corp. opened hundreds of branded screens across China, while South Korean companies like Lotte, CJ CGV, and Megabox also built dozens of new cinemas across China.[95] WBIC was early to market and early to exit.

Contracts for international trade between media conglomerates like AT&T/Warner and Chinese firms and producers may continue to grow in the coming years, but movie theaters are no longer part of the U.S. media conglomerate playbook. Future deals, instead, may look something like the $50 million investment Time Warner made in June 2013 in China Media Capital to grow the company's interest in homegrown Chinese film and television content. "Increasing our global presence is one of Time Warner's strategic priorities," chairman and chief executive Jeff Bewkes commented at the time, "and China is one of the most attractive territories in which we operate."⁹⁶ Attractive, indeed, for other initiatives but not for the ownership of cinemas.

The End of Hollywood's Exhibition Empires and the Rise of Dalian Wanda

The Chinese debacle spelled the end of the Warner Bros. International Cinemas chain and the last Hollywood effort to expand into overseas theatrical exhibition through a single "studio." In December 2012 Warner Bros. announced that the Japanese AEON Group (formerly Mycal) would purchase Warner's remaining 50 percent stake from its partner in the Warner-Mycal chain. This purchase enabled AEON to merge its wholly owned exhibition chain with its Warner-Mycal properties to become that country's largest exhibitor.⁹⁷ At the close of negotiations, with its European cinemas long gone and even its flagship property in Leicester Square sold off, Warner Bros. effectively ended its three quarters of a century in international theatrical exhibition in all markets.

The erosion of Warner Bros.' Japanese chain was part of the overbuilding that plagued many mature markets—another reason why the opportunities for expansion in China had been so vast and attractive. Alongside the sale of Warner's last circuit in 2013, Millard Ochs announced his own retirement from WBIC. Asked to summarize the net effect of the company's foray into China and the legal barriers that stopped its progress, Ochs noted that the global scene had dramatically changed in less than a decade. "When the government changed rules we moved out of China, but we left them with that knowledge base and they've improved upon it," he told *Screen Daily* in June 2013. "Now China is the number one international box office territory outside the U.S. and by 2020 China will be the number one box office territory in the world."⁹⁸ Ochs was correct.

There is, however, an important footnote to this history. In mid-2019—while China was still battling variously with North America to become the world's largest theatrical market⁹⁹—the Chinese box office plateaued after years of meteoric growth and China's National Development and Reform Commission announced the removal of film exhibition from its "Negative List" of sectors that could be controlled by foreign investors. On June 30, 2019, amid the ongoing U.S.-China trade war under the Trump administration, the commission announced the stipulation that "the construction and operation of cinemas must be controlled by a Chinese party" had been removed from its official policy. With 64,000 screens now dotting China, the country was turning more and more into a (very) mature market. The official policy change was therefore not the siren call it had been two decades earlier. Lindsay Conner, a partner at Manatt, Phelps & Phillips, which brokers international deals for Chinese studios, noted in early July 2019, "You certainly can't say that companies going into theater construction in China now will be getting in on the ground floor." Nor was the Chinese box office growing, with box office revenues actually dipping in the first half of 2019.[100] Even Sina Finance, a Chinese media outlet, was forced to acknowledge that box office "earnings may become more and more difficult," even before the pandemic began and those sales figures, of course, fell off a cliff.

During the 2010s, domestic cinema companies like Dalian Wanda and SMI had also suffered high profile troubles within their corporate structures, with the latter grappling with "poor management and high debt." In all, three hundred Chinese cinemas had already closed across China by mid-2019, and further restructuring, closures, and consolidations were expected.[101] In addition to political and industrial body blows to dominant exhibitor Dalian Wanda over the previous few years and the growth of foreign companies such as South Korea's CGV and Canada's IMAX in China, Rance Pow, president of cinema consulting firm Artisan Gateway in Shanghai, added that it was indeed "significant that this announcement has come now, because what we see is that the Chinese industry is in transition."[102] Then, in January 2020, the public disclosure of the COVID-19 outbreak in Wuhan and the subsequent closure of all seventy-thousand Chinese cinemas, made the local exhibition business even more problematic, certainly far less profitable and stable.[103]

That's All Folks: Closing Arguments

In advantageous moments, Hollywood's overseas cinemas generated tremendous revenues, cultural goodwill, and brand awareness and engagement. In more politically, financially, and legally problematic periods, though, their embodiment of "Hollywood" and American cultural exportation reversed this appeal, making American-owned cinemas a target of local resentment.

Warner Bros.' experience in China reflects the increasingly complicated relationship between global investment, national identity, and the shifting nature of law as it sways with political and cultural winds. Warner Bros.' twenty-first-century Chinese cinemas attempted to lure moviegoers through the company's brand legacy, but their geographical location in city centers and the homogeneity between numerous multiplexes—whether they were WBIC, Wanda, or CJ CGV—made their corporate branding less important and more susceptible to changing politics and legal constraints. Media-related theme parks like Hong Kong Disneyland (and Shanghai Disneyland Park) may be more insulated from these fluctuations because local visitors go precisely because of their corporate identity and the branded experiences they offer inside. These parks and the brands and attractions they employ are not easily reproducible by local operators. (Dalian Wanda, Warner Bros.' former Chinese partner and the owner of U.S.-based AMC Cinemas, opened Wanda Movie Park in December 2014, "to compete with Disney, DreamWorks and Universal, which," *Hollywood Reporter* noted, "all have theme park ambitions in China."[104]) While media-related theme parks are routinely tied to branded characters and franchises and are specific to its conglomerate affiliation, these Warner co-owned movie theaters were far more agnostic, forced by their contemporary screen counts to show films from numerous companies. In the end, Warner Bros. films could be seen in numerous multiplexes around China. Cinemas without the Warner Bros. name are inherently viable; Disneyland without Disney is not.

As the media business—film, television, music, video games, publishing, and so on—grows more and more digital, the need for U.S.-based multinational media conglomerates to take on the expense and the (legal) risks of international exhibition has decreased, although the challenges of international trade law certainly remain with digital products. Warner Bros. has drawn up numerous agreements with international producers, distributors, and exhibitors over the past decade, but it has not reentered global film exhibition. Like other multinational media conglomerates, the company is still working steadily and successfully within the laws of the land without having to build any new cinemas upon it.

With the rise of the COVID-19 pandemic in late 2019, ownership of global cinemas became not just undesirable for American media conglomerates like AT&T (Warner Bros.), Comcast (Universal), Walt Disney Company (Disney, Fox), Viacom (Paramount), and Sony (Columbia) but an extraordinary liability on a balance sheet. In October 2020, with most American movie theaters shuttered and cinemas around the world in various states of closure and insolvency, Donna Langley, chairman of Universal Filmed Entertainment Group, and Ann Sarnoff, chair and chief executive of Warner Bros., were asked if their companies planned to reenter film exhibition and begin buying up distressed cinema chains. They both had the same response: laughter.[105]

EPILOGUE

*Global Exhibition Flows in Reverse Before
the Pandemic, 2013–2019*

Since the sale of Warner Bros.' last foreign chain and the closure of its international exhibition business in 2013, the other major Hollywood studios and their larger corporate conglomerates have almost entirely forsaken ownership of foreign cinemas and cinema chains.

The same has also been true in North America, where Viacom, for example, the parent company of Paramount Pictures, had already sold its stakes in both Canada's Famous Players in 2005 and Mann Theatres in the United States in 2011.[1] Sporadic efforts by U.S.-based producer-distributors to operate cinemas since then have instead primarily been in niche environments to enable premieres and exclusive showcases. During the late 2010s, for example, Netflix began operating two cinemas (the Paris Theater in New York under a lease agreement and the Netflix-owned Egyptian Theatre in Hollywood), much like Disney's own El Capitan Theatre on Hollywood Boulevard. All three venues were a new kind of domestic shop window cinema for the launch of company-owned films in a highly branded and curated environment. Other domestic efforts to unite distribution and exhibition included IFC (IFC Center in New York; exhibition) and IFC Films (distribution); Music Box Theatre (Chicago) and Music Box Films (distribution); and Alamo Drafthouse (exhibition) and Drafthouse Films/NEON (distribution), as well as Charles Cohen's ownership of the art house distributor Cohen Media Group and two of the most prominent art house cinema chains, Landmark Theatres in the United States and Curzon Cinemas in the United Kingdom.

Legacy Hollywood film companies, as they developed their own streaming platforms such as Disney+ (Disney/20th Century-Fox), HBO Max (Warner Bros.), Paramount+ (Paramount), and Peacock (Universal) and focused more and more on generating revenues from premium video on demand, subscription video on demand, and other streaming models, moved further and further away from global theatrical exhibition and from physical media distribution as well.[2] Rising costs of cinema operation, the declining financial importance of theatrical exhibition in relation to overall film revenues, and a growing number of overdeveloped markets all meant that the business of exhibition was largely dominated by companies like Wanda Cinema Line that focused primarily on this end of the film industry. These increasingly powerful exhibition chains forged a new wave of global expansion and corporate consolidation that created economies of scale as well as increasing power to control local markets and negotiate with Hollywood and other film distributors. Meanwhile, Hollywood's disinterest in theatrical exhibition continued even after the U.S. Justice Department's August 2020 dissolution of the 1948 consent decree that had upended stateside vertical integration over seven decades earlier and had itself spurred Hollywood's interest in global exhibition as a countervailing measure in search of replacement revenue.

Global exhibition expansion and consolidation in the twenty-first century was instead largely carried out by a new breed of "foreign" chains *not* based in the United States. No company or country was more influential than China's Dalian Wanda during this period, fomenting a wave of billion-dollar mergers and acquisitions that remapped the global exhibition landscape. During the period between 2008 and 2019—before the COVID-19 pandemic's devastating effect on theatrical exhibition—global exhibitors like Wanda, Cineworld, CJ CGV, and Cinépolis reversed Hollywood's historic transnational influence by not only dominating many important markets for Hollywood film distribution but also acquiring the two largest exhibitors in the United States, AMC (Wanda) and Regal (Cineworld). Understanding the rapid expansion of foreign companies into this arena and Hollywood's own disinterest underscores theatrical exhibition's declining importance for Hollywood and its legacy studios by the end of the 2010s.

Shanghai Surprise: Dalian Wanda Takes Over

A century earlier, during the mid-1920s, Loew's Inc. expanded its portfolio of cinemas around the world. Eight decades later, in 2006, Loews Cineplex Entertainment, the descendant company of Loew's Theatres, was purchased by rival U.S. exhibitor AMC Entertainment. In 2014, with the Chinese-owned Dalian

Wanda Group looking to expand its real estate and entertainment presence beyond its borders and into the United States, its exhibition subsidiary, Wanda Cinema Line, purchased AMC for $2.6 billion. The purchase made Dalian Wanda the world's largest exhibition company.[3] Three years later, Wanda-owned AMC purchased Hoyts Theatres, once the Australian beachhead for Twentieth Century-Fox, for $750 million. (Hoyts, in 2015, was still operating fifty locations—forty in Australia and ten in New Zealand—for a total of 450 screens.) J. Sperling Reich wrote that both purchases provided Wanda with economies of scale to negotiate with both content and technology providers. The move, he added, was also part of "Wanda's Strategic Soft-Power" initiatives in which the vertically integrated entertainment company could begin

> manufacturing, distributing and selling its own products, much like the Hollywood studios did before the Paramount Decree outlawed such practices in 1948. In other words, by operating a large number of theatres in three different countries, Wanda is insuring that cinemas will play the films its studios will be producing. There may be an initial cultural obstacle of getting English speaking audiences in North America and Australia to appreciate Chinese films, but owning the distribution channels gives Wanda the luxury of a little extra time to gain adoption of its content. . . . Before Wanda purchased the circuit, AMC rarely, if ever, booked Chinese films in its theatres. Now the chain is showing more than ten Chinese titles per year.

Reich added cryptically that exhibitors shouldn't "be surprised if you see [Wanda] show up in Europe to acquire a major circuit there too."[4] One year later, in November 2016, Wanda-owned AMC purchased UK-based Odeon and UCI Cinemas (the latter once co-owned by Universal and Paramount), with 244 cinemas totaling 2,251 screens in Europe, for $1.1 billion. The purchase provided Wanda with key cinemas in Ireland, Italy, Spain, and the United Kingdom as well as $1.14 billion in annual revenue.[5] Unlike the global expansion of Paramount and MGM cinemas nearly a century earlier, Dalian and AMC did not rebrand these venues to accentuate their foreign ownership. Instead, Odeon, UCI, Cinesa (Spain), and other Wanda-owned cinemas (including AMC) retained their legacy brands. Wanda stressed AMC's *American* influence over these and other chains it had purchased as AMC chief executive Adam Aron touted the exportation of American "plush powered recliners, enhanced food and beverages," Dolby and IMAX technologies, and a continuing trend toward "AMC premium experiences" abroad.[6] Wanda further expanded its hold on the U.S. market in 2016 as well as its global market share by announcing the purchase of U.S.-based Carmike Cinemas, then the fourth-largest exhibitor in the United States, for an additional $1.2 billion at the same time as it concluded the Odeon and UCI acquisition (the Carmike acquisition followed on the heels of two major American content buys for Wanda as well, for Legendary Entertainment for $3.5 billion and Dick Clark Productions for $1 billion).[7] The global acquisition spree by Dalian Wanda is only comparable in scope and scale to Twentieth Century-Fox's buyouts of Hoyts, Amalgamated, and African Consolidated Theatres. Those, however, took place over a quarter century, not in the span of just a few years.

Given this sudden rise in Dalian Wanda's global power and prominence, it was no surprise that arguments that once surfaced against American ownership of cinemas in England, Egypt, France, and innumerable other film markets arose once more, now regarding Dalian Wanda and its control of American exhibition, production, and distribution companies. The purchase of Legendary, coupled with the fast rise of other Chinese producers co-financing Hollywood and other films, fueled these concerns, as did Wang Jianlin, chairman of the Dalian Wanda Group, who reportedly told a Chinese interviewer before the Carmike acquisition that "(AMC's) boss is Chinese, so more Chinese films should be in their theaters where possible."[8] Producer and entertainment industry consultant Robert Cain had been suspicious of Wanda's stated reasons for buying AMC from the start. "The rationales offered by Wanda's billionaire chairman Wang Jianlin have so far been unconvincing," he wrote upon the Wanda-AMC deal, especially since "the opportunity costs for Wanda are huge. The $3.1 billion they're spending on AMC could instead have acquired or built thousands of Chinese and Asian cinemas." Cain offered one political theory, echoing Reich, that there was indeed a "soft power" importance to Dalian's global exhibition spread:

> I may be going out on a limb here, but the fact that Wanda will now have a major beachhead in the world's most important media market could greatly enhance Wang Jianlin's standing with the Communist Party. The party leadership has repeatedly emphasized the critical importance of soft power initiatives, especially in the west, and with AMC Wang will now have China's largest mouthpiece in the U.S. It's unlikely that AMC theaters will be running the Chinese national anthem before screenings of Communist Revolution-set propaganda dramas any time soon, but Wanda can now position itself as leading the charge in spreading Chinese values to the west.[9]

Wanda, perhaps worried about such appearances, maintained AMC's semblance of American ownership by keeping Leawood, Kansas, as its corporate headquarters and Adam Aron as chief executive and president. AMC even retained control over Wanda's European cinemas with a newly created position of head of AMC Europe.[10] Unlike the more striking Chinese ownership, American control of European cinemas was a familiar trend over the past century, most recently with the shuttered Warner Bros. International Cinemas and the still-operating Showcase Cinemas, the British cinema chain owned by Viacom parent company National Amusements. In Europe, Australia, and the United States, where Hollywood had always marketed its foreignness as an attraction, Dalian Wanda used its American subsidiary, AMC, to soften the increasingly problematic politics of Chinese ownership and control. In this sense, Hollywood's global exhibition history helped deescalate the foreignness of AMC's global expansion under Dalian Wanda's ultimate control.

The problematic nature of Chinese "soft power" abroad was on full display, however, just weeks after Wanda/AMC's purchase of Carmike, as the *Washington Post* reported on an organized protest outside the AMC Empire 25, AMC's flagship cinema in New York City, featuring "red signs proclaiming 'AMC = American Movie Communists' . . . targeting AMC's Chinese owner." "The message of the protest," Ana Swanson wrote, "was that any attempt to extend Beijing's control over American mass media must be stopped." This protest was hardly spontaneous, having been organized by Berman and Co., a Washington, D.C., lobbying firm, who had launched the "China Owns Us" campaign "nominally run by the Center for American Security, a registered trade name for a 501(c)4 nonprofit called the Enterprise Action Committee, according to D.C. government records." The "China Owns Us" campaign fanned out across the country, where signs labeling AMC "China's Red Puppet" were erected outside AMC's headquarters in Leawood, Kansas, and to the west on Sunset Boulevard in the heart of Hollywood. "Berman and his groups wrote opinion pieces, produced YouTube videos, appealed to think tanks and hired a lobbyist to reach out to Congress, Berman said, to warn people of China's insidious influence," Swanson reported. "Berman says he launched the campaign because he fears that Dalian Wanda could use its theater screens to subtly influence people's views about the United States and China. 'What I'm trying to do is stop somebody else from managing the culture here,' Berman says." While much of this appeared to be political pushback against a very politically connected Chinese company and its executives, many "industry experts" told the *Post* that Berman was, in fact, connected to Philip Anschutz, a conservative media mogul who owned a controlling interest in Regal Entertainment Group, AMC's chief rival in the United States, whose company would move from the largest chain in the United States down to second place after the AMC buyout of Carmike. "What matters is whether or not what I'm saying is right," Berman told the *Post* about his motivations. "And if it's right, it doesn't matter that somebody gave me the money to go out and say it." All of this followed on the heels of growing chatter about Hollywood's internal censorship with respect to China (and its growing market and political power) and changes to the way in which China was being depicted in Hollywood films such as *Red Dawn*, *Looper*, *World War Z*, and others. Comedian and talk show host Stephen Colbert profiled this growing reticence to criticize China and its human rights policy through a segment he dubbed "Pander Express." Wang Jianlin, defending the company's expansion overseas and its stated hands-off policy, remarked that Wanda's films and cinemas had "no political point of view." Despite Jianlin's comments, "Americans should consider the possibility that Dalian Wanda could one day use its massive distribution network to suppress a film that was critical of China. 'Would that happen? We can't be certain,'" media scholar Aynne Kokas told Ana Swanson, "'But the fact is that the possibility is significant, and given the nature of film distribution in China, it's not actually that far off.'"[11]

Sony's own earlier expansion into the United States in the 1980s and 1990s—and its acquisition of both Columbia Pictures and Loews Theatres—had exacerbated earlier fears of Japanese domination of U.S. real estate, technology, entertainment, and other industries. Now, with the global ascendancy of China in the 2010s, some in the United States, Australia, and Europe were concerned about the rise of Dalian Wanda and its ownership of many of the world's leading cinema circuits. This was one more example of how movie theaters, and not movies, can be the physical expression of a country's global economic and political power. However, the *lack* of concern among those in Hollywood about Dalian's purchase of AMC and other circuits is also striking as it reflects the relative disinterest in this sector of the film business by Hollywood by the end of the decade. Gao Jun, former deputy general manager of Beijing's New Film Association, told the *South China Morning Post* in 2012 that the power of movie theaters was now so diminished that "Wanda's acquisition was not thwarted by [U.S.] government departments, like those of some Chinese technology companies" because "the cultural nature of the deal is not very political." Chinese film critic Zhou Liming, echoing those same sentiments, told the *South China Morning Post* that "what consumers care about was the movie and the service, not who owns the cinema."[12] Ultimately, Gao expressed the obvious: while Robert Cain and "China Owns Us" may have worried about the impact of Chinese ownership of American cinemas in the years that followed, theatrical exhibition in the United States was still so heavily dominated by Hollywood films—and exhibition had fallen so far in the esteem and importance for the major conglomerates—that the Dalian Wanda buyouts of AMC and Carmike were treated as merely the reshuffling of deck chairs on the Titanic shortly before hitting streaming and COVID-19 icebergs.

The kind of boycotts that had greeted Hollywood in England, Egypt, and other markets in the previous century ultimately failed to materialize as Dalian Wanda continued its global dominance. By the end of the 2010s, however, Dalian Wanda had amassed its own financial and political troubles at home, making its control over global exhibition markets increasingly tenuous. The company had spent billions, debt was rising, and with the onset of the

COVID-19 pandemic those shuttered U.S. assets would become even more heavily distressed by mid-2020. By 2021, Dalian Wanda had retreated from the U.S. exhibition market altogether in a rather stunning pandemic-related sale of its remaining AMC investments.[13]

The New "Cultureplex": CJ CGV, South Korea, and a Global Exhibition Player

Chinese exhibitors were not the only ones that had expanded during this period. In 1996 South Korean conglomerate CheilJedang (CJ), Hong Kong's Golden Harvest, and Australia's Village Roadshow formed the CGV chain ("Cultural, Great and Vital") as a joint venture to expand throughout the growing South Korean exhibition market. CGV's first multiplex opened in 1998, and the venture was later taken over by CJ to become CJ CGV. CJ CGV, following the dissolution of WBIC's foray into China, opened its first multiplex in Shanghai in 2006. It has since become one of the largest exhibition companies in the Chinese market. This was accomplished by taking 49 percent ownership positions in some venues while using CGV's Hong Kong home base to adopt China's "Special Administrative Region's Closer Economic Partnership Arrangement" rules, which allowed the company to take 75 and 100 percent ownership stakes in the new venue, a stark contrast to the restrictions that had led to WBIC's withdrawal from the market. In addition to China, CGV also bought out Vietnam's Megastar circuit in 2011 and became a leading exhibitor there as well. In succeeding years CJ CGV became a prominent exhibitor as well in Malaysia, Myanmar, and Indonesia. CJ CGV's expansion, much like Hollywood's in an earlier moment, was, CGV executive vice president Yun Ik-jun noted, to "implant our philosophy, translate best practices, and"—perhaps most importantly—"increase our Korean content." Once more, it was film exhibition that could secure the foreign distribution and exhibition of content, not just film distribution. CGV also sought to bring its very Korean-ness to these cinemas by creating so called cultureplexes that, *Variety*'s Patrick Frater noted, were set up to "integrate [Korean] lifestyle and food into the mix. While similar claims are made by other chains worldwide, few can boast the amenities offered by CJ theaters, which include home shopping and offline communications in the mix." Charges of foreign control popped up once more here as well, especially among rival independent cinemas. Frater noted that CGV would encourage the booking of local, independent films by bringing forth its "Movie Collage" initiative (now CGV Arthouse) to bring in more art house fare, a program it dubbed "cultural therapy."[14] In 2017 CJ CGV chief executive Seo Jung added that its own expansion overseas in film production, distribution, and exhibition was about using

CJ CGV as a "platform for expanding Korean Wave culture."[15] In addition to expanding the market for Korean films abroad, CJ CGV also used its foreign cinemas to expand its technological developments from its panoramic ScreenX technologies—providing a wider vista than even CinemaScope and Cinerama—to its motion and other sensory 4DX seats. CGV cinemas abroad were intended to bring both Korean films and Korean technologies to a global marketplace and to global consumers.[16] This two-step mimicked Hollywood's own exportation of films and synchronous sound technologies in the 1920s through global exhibition expansion as well as its exportation of widescreen cinema in the 1950s using American-owned and operated cinemas.

In the years that followed CJ CGV expanded its presence throughout China, Vietnam, and Turkey and then, like Dalian Wanda, into the United States. The first CJ CGV cinema opened in June 2010 in Los Angeles' Koreatown. This was followed by CGV cinemas in Buena Park, California, in 2017 and in San Francisco in early 2020. The San Francisco cinema promoted all aspects of the CGV global expansion—Korean and other films and ScreenX and 4DX technologies—all within the cultureplex, which the company noted was "a culture playground where people can experience all different types of cultures including films, music, performances, games, sports, food, drinks and so on—beyond the multiplex." CJ CGV was now the fifth-largest global exhibitor, with 3,828 screens at 524 locations in seven countries around the world.[17]

BIG Ideas: Indian and Mexican Cinema Chains and Global Expansion

This global rise of Asian exhibitors could be seen as well in India, where Mumbai-based Reliance MediaWorks, then a key exhibitor in India, began expanding its own exhibition presence in the United States. After Indian exhibitor Pyramid Saimira bought the small Texas-based FunAsia cinema chain, which had featured Indian films for the growing Indian diasporic community, Phil Zacheretti, president and chief executive of Knoxville, Tennessee's Phoenix Big Cinemas Management, sold a half-interest in his U.S. chain to Reliance in 2008.[18] Reliance's Indian Adlabs cinema chain held its own footnote to Hollywood's earlier expansion. The flagship Adlabs cinema in Mumbai was none other than the former Metro Cinema that MGM had opened seven decades earlier. The revamped and renovated Metro BIG Cinemas had become once more a key venue for Mumbai cinemagoers but now under Indian, not American, management and featuring Indian films.

In the United States, the Phoenix-Reliance co-owned BIG Cinemas chain was now made up of cinemas featuring both Hollywood and Bollywood (and

FIGURE E.1 The revamped Metro BIG Cinema in Mumbai, former Metro Cinema, now part of an expansive Indian cinema chain. (Courtesy of Nicke.me/Wikimedia)

the Telegu-language Tollywood) as well as other Indian films. "Company's objective is not to force the pace of crossover by Bollywood movies but to play popular movies from a wider range of sources," Patrick Frater noted at the time. "Hollywood films will be the majority, but we could also show popular Chinese or Korean cinema," Reliance Capital senior vice president Anil Arjun told *Variety*. "Hindi-language Bollywood films are currently all that America sees of Indian films. We will play Tamil and Telegu too." Arjun, cognizant of the need to avoid domestic resistance to changes in the Phoenix chain, remarked that despite Zacheretti maintaining his management of the circuit, "It is important we are seen as an independent American chain, rather than an extension of an Indian company." BIG Cinemas had 250 screens at twenty-eight North American locations at the time, many of which were located in communities that were "close to centers of ex-pat Indian and Asian populations," including those in Atlanta, Chicago, Detroit, Los Angeles, New Jersey, New York City, San Jose, the state of Washington, and Washington, D.C. Somewhat akin to CJ CGV's own "Cultureplex" concept, BIG Cinemas featuring Indian films modified their concessions as well to include Indian culinary favorites.[19]

Like the expansion of Dalian Wanda and CJ CGV into the United States, Reliance's expansion into the United States reflected India's growing power on the world economic and political stage as well as the growing size of its diaspora. As Patrick Frater noted, the "move also underlines Indian companies' growing appetite for international properties and influence. Having conquered global steel, IT and auto sectors... Indian firms are now looking at entertainment."[20]

Over the next five years, *Film Journal International* noted, BIG Cinemas "helped make Hindi and other South Asian films recognized as a viable source of film revenue."[21] By 2012 Reliance and Dalian Wanda even announced their intention to codevelop cinemas in both India and the United States.[22] The Wanda–Reliance pact faded quickly, however, and Reliance closed all of its Indian cinemas in 2013 and exited the U.S. market altogether.[23] Still, Reliance's co-ownership of BIG Cinemas from 2008 to 2013 reflects, alongside the expansion of CGV and Wanda, the growing influence that Asian exhibitors were enacting on U.S. and global film exhibition.

Cinema chains in China, South Korea, and India were only a few of the companies and countries now expanding their holdings around the world. The Mexican cinema chains Cinépolis and Cinemex also created vast portfolios of global cinemas abroad. Cinépolis began earlier, expanding globally during the 2000s and opening its first U.S. cinema in San Diego in 2011.[24] Cinépolis, by contrast to Phoenix's more modest American cinemas for Indian films, focused on bringing luxury cinemas and a "global cinematic experience," according to Juan Llamas-Rodriguez, to international markets, primarily in outdoor shopping centers and other upscale locations.[25] Cinépolis also became the only foreign exhibitor to find large-scale success in India by marketing, alongside Indian companies like PVR (Priya Village Roadshow, originally a joint venture between India's Priya Cinemas and Australia's Village Roadshow), an upscale, elite venue that catered to the classes and not the masses. (Cinépolis was one of the only exhibitors in India that managed to actually add screens—twenty-six—in 2020.[26]) That same upscale marketing was employed in the United States where Cinépolis's accented name and brand was purposefully cosmopolitan. (Was it French? Spanish? Mexican?) By the end of the 2010s, Cinépolis was operating thirty luxury cinemas across the United States. Mexico-based Cinemex also built its own U.S. chain under the CMX banner and planned to expand its investments by purchasing the Star Cinema Grill chain, an acquisition that would make CMX/Cinemex the seventh-largest exhibitor in the United States.[27]

Operating both of these circuits in the United States was not intended to inculcate Mexican content to American screens; that, ironically, was far more likely at Moctesuma Esparza's Maya Cinemas, which were built in California and Nevada expressly "in underserved, family oriented, Latino-dominant communities."²⁸ For Cinépolis, the expansion into the United States and other markets did not come with the intention of booking more Mexican films, despite Cinépolis's own art house distribution company, Sala de Arte Distribución, and its more commercial distribution outlet, Cinépolis Distribución.²⁹ The lack of promotion of Mexican films abroad was part of a larger pattern for both Cinépolis's and Cinemex's Mexican cinemas in which Mexican film distributors had long complained about the lack of available screens for Mexican films *in Mexico*.³⁰

Instead, these global chains created perfectly upscale cinematic experiences for an increasingly homogenized global audience for both Hollywood and other films. By 2020 the success of Cinépolis around the world had made it the world's second-largest exhibition company, with 738 multiplexes and 5,848 screens serving more than 338 million cinemagoers in seventeen different countries, including 30 luxury Cinépolis cinemas across the United States.³¹ In May 2020 Cinépolis expanded its U.S. investments further by taking a minority 2.4 percent stake of rival exhibitor Cinemark, which itself had a large presence in Latin America.³²

Cineworld and European Expansion into the United States

Perhaps the most telling sign of Hollywood's disinterest in theatrical exhibition abroad, where AMC, UCI, WBIC, and other cinemas and cinema chains once proliferated, was the takeover of the U.S.-based Regal Entertainment Group by European exhibition giant Cineworld. The global exhibition company, after acquiring UGC (originally Union Générale Cinématographique) in the United Kingdom in 2004, Picturehouse in the United Kingdom in 2012, and Cinema City International in 2014 with cinemas around the world, gobbled up the second-largest U.S. cinema chain in buying Regal in 2018.³³ One year later, Cineworld, in an ongoing rivalry with Dalian Wanda and Cinépolis, announced its intention to lock up a significant chunk of North America with the purchase of the Cineplex chain in Canada that historian Paul Moore noted would cause the formation of "an overflowing, megasized network of megaplexes." He added of the prospect of losing Canadian ownership of Canadian cinemas to Cineworld, "Movie theatre chains, like cinema itself, were born on a global stage. The acquisition of Cineplex only reminds us that remains a familiar story."³⁴ Cineworld chief executive Mooky Greidinger, in arguing for the need to acquire Cineplex, told investors that "scale matters" "as it negotiates deals with Hollywood studios." David Friend, writing in *Canadian Press*, remarked that Greidinger's comments demonstrate that Cineworld and its chief executive are "interested in leveraging his company's strength to broker agreements for Marvel superhero movies and other huge blockbuster franchises that would play on Canadian screens, at its U.S. chain Regal and other brands it owns in Ireland, Israel and across Europe."[35] Once again, foreign ownership of Canadian cinemas kicked up concerns among local exhibitors about competition, lack of access for local films, and the overall effects on Canadian cinema and culture. Friend reported that

> a group of independent Quebec movie theatres lambasted the Cineplex acquisition in a statement that called on Canadian Heritage Minister Steven Guilbeault and provincial Culture Minister Nathalie Roy, to "vigorously" defend the country's cultural industries from outside influence. "We must take all available means to prevent foreign content from suffocating our domestic film production," said the group of signatories, which included Mario Fortin, who oversees three Montreal independent cinemas. "Going to the movies is the most important leisure activity for Quebecers and Canadians. Are we going to let a foreign multinational decide which films we are going to see? Are we going to leave it to Cineworld Group to decide the future of our cinema?"[36]

In the case of Cineworld and its European ownership, locals perceived the threat not from England, despite the company's British roots, but instead from Hollywood once more. Echoing the sentiments of local distributors, filmmakers, and exhibitors over the past century, Canadian filmmaker Warren Sulatycky remarked that "it's time federal leaders seriously consider imposing a screen quota system that could bolster the local film market against the perceived cultural threat of Hollywood. It's a concept that's been used in many countries, including France, South Korea and Spain, to ensure local stories are given space, though critics question the concept's success." Sulatycky remarked on the difficulties of getting his films onto Cineplex screens even before the Cineworld news: "It was so hard to get into theatres—to get any time—in Toronto, Vancouver, Calgary or Montreal. . . . And it's going to be harder now."[37]

Conclusion (Without One)

The preceding pages of this epilogue are, in fact, now prologue to the COVID-19 pandemic that upended the global exhibition business in the early 2020s.

In late 2019, word of the virus began shutting down cinemas, first in China, then Italy, and then around the world. As the pandemic spread, global cinemas closed down in fits and starts and, with it, many of the corporate dreams that had been hatched just months earlier. Cinemex's takeover of U.S.-based Star Cinema Grill was aborted and, in April 2020, CMX, the U.S. subsidiary of Cinemex, was forced to file for Chapter 11 bankruptcy reorganization.[38] Two months later Cineworld's own $2.1 billion purchase of Cineplex was cancelled, leading to a contentious lawsuit for breach of contract and damages related to the failed acquisition.[39] Dalian Wanda, meanwhile, saw its Chinese Wanda cinemas stay open far more than its AMC cinemas in the United States, which had teetered on the edge of bankruptcy before completing a remarkable share price turnaround based in part on the Reddit-fueled "meme stock" phenomenon that drove AMC's shares far beyond their price-to-earnings ratio, especially given the ongoing pandemic and concern over the future of moviegoing. This was the turbulent backdrop for another direct challenge to the survival of theatrical exhibition as Jason Kilar, chief executive of Warner Media, announced that all of Warner Bros. films in 2021 would be released day-and-date in cinemas and on its own streaming platform, HBO Max, just as other vertically and horizontally integrated companies like Walt Disney laid out their own aggressive streaming strategies through Disney+ in which Pixar films like *Luca* skipped a theatrical release altogether and others, like Disney's *Cruella*, were available for a premium day-and-date on Disney+ as well.[40] The October 2020 laughter of Donna Langley and Ann Sarnoff, when asked about buying cinemas again, now made more contextual sense.[41] They knew.

This epilogue was updated in July 2021, so you, dear reader, know far more about the ultimate fate of theatrical exhibition in this decade and beyond. As this book went to press, cinemas around the world continued opening and reclosing as new variants and new strategies harassed an already deeply stressed sector of the global film industry.[42] Meanwhile, streaming companies and legacy film studios remained more and more focused on pushing cinema further into the cloud, demonstrating the versatility and ability for Hollywood and its films to find audiences wherever they might be. With theatrical exhibition suffering its worst existential crisis since its inception, this conclusion is a rather ironic end to a book focused on the power that cinemas once had and might still in the years to come.

Former WBIC president Millard Ochs wrote at the end of 2020: "2021 is a time to refresh and 2022 is a return to normalcy."[43] You, more than I, know whether Ochs's predictions turned out to be correct or whether this book captures the end of a long era of global film exhibition and the cinema as a privileged space of contact between filmmaker, film exhibitor, and their global audiences. As W. Gavazzi King, general secretary of the British Cinematograph Exhibitors' Association, once told *Bioscope* in October 1925, "The cinemas are the fortresses of the industry, of which the studios are merely the munition factories."[44] It is now, more than ever before, a question of how and where those munitions will be sent and how they will or won't fire up future generations of moviegoers.

NOTES

Abbreviations Used in the Notes

ANZ-Auckland	Archives New Zealand, Auckland
ANZ-Wellington	Archives New Zealand, Wellington
CSA	City of Sydney Archives, Sydney, Australia
CTA	Cinema Theatre Association (UK) Archives, Margate, England
DCCSS	Desegregation of Cinemas Correspondence with Spyros Skouras, National Archives and Records Administration, College Park, Md., United States
MHL	Margaret Herrick Library, Academy of Motion Picture Arts and Sciences, Beverly Hills, Calif., United States
NA-UK	National Archives, Kew, England
NARA	National Archives and Records Administration, College Park, Md., United States
NARA-AAD	National Archives Access to Archival Databases, https://aad.archives.gov/aad/.
NFSA	National Film and Sound Archive of Australia, Canberra, Australia
NZNL	Alexander Turnbull Library, New Zealand National Library, Wellington, New Zealand
SPS	Spyros P. Skouras Papers, Stanford University Special Collections, Stanford, Calif., United States

UA-WHS	United Artists Corporation Records, 1918–1969, Wisconsin Historical Society, United States.
WB-USC	Warner Bros. Archive, University of Southern California, Los Angeles, Calif., United States
WITS	Historical Papers Research Archive, University of the Witwatersrand, Johannesburg, South Africa
Wolfsonian-FIU	John and Drew Eberson Architectural Records Archive, Wolfsonian-FIU, Miami Beach, Fla.

Introduction

1. Philip D. Turner, *MGM Cinemas: An Outline History* (St. Paul's Cray, UK: Brantwood, 1998), 1.
2. Charles Acland, *Screen Traffic: Movies, Multiplexes, and Global Culture* (Durham, N.C.: Duke University Press 2003), 135.
3. Maggie Valentine, *The Show Starts on the Sidewalk: An Architectural History of the Movie Theatre, Starring S. Charles Lee* (New Haven, Conn.: Yale University Press, 1994), 3, 12, 61.
4. I explore and theorize the larger meaning of an evening's entertainment through its "unitary text." Ross Melnick, *American Showman: Samuel "Roxy" Rothafel and the Birth of the Entertainment Industry, 1908–1935* (New York: Columbia University Press, 2012), 14–15.
5. Richard Maltby, "Introduction: 'The Americanisation of the World,'" in *Hollywood Abroad: Audiences and Cultural Exchange*, ed. Richard Maltby and Melvyn Stokes (London: BFI, 2004), 16.
6. Toby Miller, Freya Schiwy & Marta Hernández Salván, "Distribution, The Forgotten Element in Transnational Cinema," *Transnational Cinemas* 2, no. 2 (2012): 197.
7. "Metro's Overseas Empire," *Variety*, January 14, 1970, 3.
8. *United States v. Paramount Pictures Inc. et al.*, U.S. District Court, S.D. New York, 1948–1949 Trade Cases 162,377 (March 3, 1949), Department of Justice, https://www.justice.gov/atr/page/file/1084056/download.
9. Dale Turnbull, interviewed by Graham Shirley, 2001–2004: Oral History. Title No. 587140. National Film & Sound Archive of Australia (hereafter, NFSA).
10. "Loew Defines M.-G. Foreign Policy," *Motion Picture News*, July 4, 1925, 44.
11. Dale Turnbull interview, NFSA.
12. Michael Curtin, *Playing to the World's Biggest Audience: The Globalization of Chinese Film and TV* (Berkeley: University of California Press, 2007), 85, 101.
13. Annabel Jane Wharton, *Building the Cold War: Hilton International Hotels and Modern Architecture* (Chicago: University of Chicago Press, 2001), 1.
14. Wharton, *Building the Cold War*, 2.
15. Wharton, *Building the Cold War*, 6.
16. Wharton, *Building the Cold War*, 7.
17. Samir Raafat, "Cinema Metro"(unedited version), *Cairo Times*, Thursday, May 15, 1997, reprinted on EGY.com, http://www.egy.com/landmarks/97-05-15.shtml.
18. Quoted in Wharton, *Building the Cold War*, 198.
19. Wharton, *Building the Cold War*, 8.

20. "Loew, Dietz, Speak at MGM Convention," *Motion Picture Daily*, February 10, 1949, 6.
21. Spyros P. Skouras, "Skouras Sees Greater Global Markets for U.S. Films; Also as Potent Force vs. Communism," *Variety*, January 7, 1953, 15.
22. Wharton, *Building the Cold War*, 159.
23. Ai Lin Chua, "Singapore's 'Cinema-Age' of the 1930s: Hollywood and the Shaping of Singapore Modernity," *Inter-Asia Cultural Studies*, 13, no. 4 (2012): 592–604.
24. "What Is a U.S. Embassy?" National Museum of American Diplomacy, https://diplomacy.state.gov/diplomacy/what-is-a-u-s-embassy/.
25. Wharton, *Building the Cold War*, xiii.

1. Hollywood's British Invasion and the Battle of Birmingham, 1919–1929

1. Books covering Hollywood's overseas distribution apparatus include I. C. Jarvie, *Hollywood's Overseas Campaign: The North Atlantic Movie Trade, 1920–1950* (Cambridge: Cambridge University Press, 1992); Kristin Thompson, *Exporting Entertainment: America in the World Film Market, 1907–1934* (London: BFI, 1985); John Trumpbour, *Selling Hollywood to the World: U.S. And European Struggles for Mastery of the Global Film Industry, 1920–1950* (Cambridge: Cambridge University Press, 2002); and Kerry Segrave, *American Films Abroad: Hollywood's Domination of the World's Movie Screens from the 1890s to the Present* (Jefferson, N.C.: McFarland, 1997), among others.
2. Arthur Loew, "The Value of Theatres," *New York Times*, March 18, 1928, 125.
3. "Marcus Loew's World's Circuit," *Billboard*, May 23, 1914, 6.
4. Loew did not open new theaters in Europe, South America, and beyond during the 1910s, but the company did expand its North American circuit by opening a new deluxe Loew's Theatre in Montreal in November 1917 to match the company's existing twin Elgin and Winter Garden theaters in Toronto.
5. "Represented in 70 Foreign Lands," *Motion Picture Herald*, August 8, 1931, 94.
6. "News of the Week in Headlines," *Wid's Daily*, June 22, 1919, 1.
7. "Particulars Respecting Directors of Famous Players-Lasky British Producers Limited, Company No: 154144," May 3, 1919, BT 31/24514/154144, National Archives, Kew, England (hereafter, NA-UK).
8. "English Chain," *Wid's Daily*, June 21, 1919, 1.
9. "English Capital of Millions," *Variety*, July 11, 1919, 65.
10. "P.P. Ltd. Selling Stock," *Variety*, June 27, 1919, 4.
11. "Famous Players Buy," *New York Clipper*, July 23, 1919, 17.
12. "Explosion by British Marks American Invasion of London," *Variety*, June 27, 1919, 4.
13. "Explosion by British," 4.
14. Sir Sidney Low, "Behind the Screen," *Saturday Review*, August 30, 1919, 195, 196.
15. "British Not Opposed to Yankee Films," *Billboard*, August 2, 1919, 85.
16. "Anti-American Film Agitation in England Takes Serious Turn," *Exhibitors Herald and Motography*, August 16, 1919, 33.
17. "Anti-American Film Agitation," 33.
18. "Metro Will Make Further Expansion," *Exhibitors Herald and Motography*, August 16, 1919, 43.

19. "Capitulate," *Wid's Daily*, August 27, 1919, 1, 2.
20. "Building Ban Ends," *Wid's Daily*, April 18, 1921, 1, 2.
21. "Theater Need Great," *Wid's Daily*, March 16, 1921, 2.
22. "Building Ban Ends," 1, 2.
23. "Famous-Players in French Terrain," *Los Angeles Times*, August 31, 1921, III4.
24. "El Nuevo 'Cine' Coliseum," *De Barcelona Blanco y Negro* (Madrid), October 28, 1923, 20. Mexico City's Teatro Olimpia also became the key first run cinema for Paramount films in 1923. "Mexican Firm Contracts for Paramount Pictures," *Exhibitors Herald*, January 28, 1922, 73; and "New Paramount Manager in Mexico City," *Motion Picture News*, February 3, 1923, 555.
25. "Editorial," *Variety*, July 26, 1923, 11.
26. "Loew Leasing Palace, London," *Variety*, August 9, 1923, 2; The Tivoli, Strand (London) Grand Opening Programme, September 6, 1923, Tivoli Theatre (London) Files, Cinema Theatre Association (UK) Archives, Margate, England (hereafter, CTA); and "Loew Gets Tivoli," *Film Daily*, August 15, 1923, 1.
27. "Marcus Loew Is in Tivoli, London, with Metro Films," *Variety*, August 16, 1923, 2, 18.
28. The Tivoli, Strand (London) Grand Opening Programme.
29. "Hearst Opening Two Specials at Empire," *Variety*, June 7, 1923, 16; and "Empire Unaffected," *Variety*, June 21, 1923, 2.
30. "London Rentals," *Variety*, August 23, 1923, 2; "Opening of London Palace," *Motion Picture News*, September 22, 1923, 749; and "Two American-Made Pictures at Pavilion and Tivoli, London," *Variety*, September 13, 1923, 2.
31. "'U' Takes Empire," *Variety*, September 27, 1923, 3.
32. "'Covered Wagon' Makes Picadilly Circus Great White Way," *Exhibitors Trade Review*, October 27, 1923, 1008.
33. "British Salaries Skid," *Variety*, November 8, 1923, 17.
34. "Three Fine Films," *New York Times*, July 1, 1923, X2.
35. "Grauman Is Glad to Be Home Again," *Los Angeles Times*, October 25, 1924, 14.
36. Richard Maltby and Ruth Vasey, "Temporary American Citizens," in *"Film Europe" and "Film America": Cinema, Commerce and Cultural Exchange, 1920–1939*, ed. Andrew Higson and Richard Maltby (Exeter: University of Exeter Press, 1999), 44.
37. "Famous-Lasky's New Programme," *Bioscope*, May 28, 1925, 24.
38. Alderman Trounson, "The Exhibitor's Parliament," *Bioscope*, January 15, 1925, 50.
39. "Things That Matter," *Bioscope*, January 8, 1925, 56.
40. "Leeds Picture House Deal," *Bioscope*, June 18, 1925, 34.
41. "The Producer-Exhibitor 'Menace,'" *Bioscope*, October 22, 1925, 21.
42. "Carl Laemmle Entertained," *Bioscope*, October 1, 1925, 44.
43. "Loew Defines M.-G. Foreign Policy," *Motion Picture News*, July 4, 1925, 44.
44. "Loew Combines with British Film Men," *Billboard*, September 12, 1925, 8.
45. "Two American-Made Pictures at Pavilion and Tivoli, London," *Variety*, September 13, 1923, 2; and "Marcus Loew Announces Plans for Big Presentation Circuit," *Billboard*, July 10, 1926, 6.
46. "Future of the Empire Theatre," *Times* (London), August 26, 1925, 8.
47. Consulate, Leeds, England to Department of State, February 3, 1925, 841.4061/43, National Archives and Records Administration, College Park, Md. (hereafter, NARA).
48. "Plight of British Films," *South Wales News* (Cardiff, UK), February 25/26, 1925, 841.4061, NARA.
49. A. B. Cooke to Department of State, "Report No. 37: Motion Picture Films Propaganda Against the American Product," March 12, 1925, 841.4061/56, NARA.

1. Hollywood's British Invasion   397

50. "Film Monopoly Attacked," *Daily Express*, October 22, 1925, 2.
51. "American Film Men to Get London House," *New York Times*, December 3, 1925, 28.
52. "London Theatre Ends Forty Years' Career," *New York Times*, January 23, 1927, 21.
53. "The Tivoli News," *Tivoli Strand Program*, September 10, 1926, 5, British Library.
54. "Fear American Film Invasion," *Los Angeles Times*, February 15, 1926, 4.
55. "American Film Men to Get London House."
56. Red, "News Flashes from U.S.A.," *Bioscope*, December 31, 1925, 27.
57. "Famous Players Doing Well," *Wall Street Journal*, July 2, 1925, 1.
58. "The Plaza," *Kinematograph Weekly*, September 10, 1925, 60.
59. G. A. Atkinson, "London 'Shop-Window' For American Films," *Daily Express*, January 1, 1926, 11.
60. "The Plaza Plans: Big Paramount Super Kinema to Open Next Month," *Kine Weekly*, January 7, 1926, 56.
61. Jan Dalgliesh, "Paramount UK Style," *Console*, October 1978, n.p.
62. "Say Plaza," *The Times* (London), March 2, 1926, 17.
63. "The Plaza Plans," 56.
64. "London's Palatial Plaza," *Bioscope*, February 25, 1926, 38.
65. "The Plaza Plans," 56.
66. "Paramount's Shop Window," *Kinematograph Weekly*, February 25, 1926, 3, 4.
67. "London's Palatial Plaza," 38.
68. The Plaza Opening Programme, March 1, 1926, Plaza Theatre (London) Files, CTA.
69. "Plaza's Brilliant Opening," *Bioscope*, March 4, 1926.
70. H. F. Kessler-Howes, "Some Observations on the Plaza," *Kine Weekly*, March 11, 1926, 65.
71. "Cinema-*Variety* at the Plaza," *Bioscope*, October 28, 1926, 61.
72. "The Plaza Projection Room," *Bioscope*, March 4, 1926, iv; "Wurlitzer Organ at the Plaza," *Bioscope*, March 4, 1926, v; and "London's Palatial Plaza," 38.
73. "Cinema-*Variety* at the Plaza," 61.
74. "Starr 'Waiting to See,'" *Bioscope*, May 5, 1927, 30; and "United Artists and Theatre Control," *Bioscope*, October 27, 1927, 35.
75. "United Artists and Theatre Control," 35.
76. "The Battle of Birmingham," *Bioscope*, January 20, 1927, 41.
77. "Events of the Year," *Kinematograph Year Book*, 1928, 19–30; and Ernest W. Fredman, "British Alarmed," *Film Renter*, December 30, 1926, 1, 7.
78. "Paramount Secures Seven Year Lease on Two Theatres in Birmingham, England," *Motion Picture News*, January 7, 1927, 41.
79. "British Alarmed," *Film Renter*, December 30, 1926, 1, 7.
80. "British Exhibitors to Fight Famous Invasion," *Film Daily*, January 5, 1927, 1.
81. Homer Brett to Department of State, "Feeling Against American Films," January 18, 1927, 841.4061/64, NARA; and Clipping from *Nottingham Guardian*, January 19, 1927, Enclosure No. 1 from Homer Brett to Department of State, "Feeling Against American Films," January 18, 1927, 841.4061/64, NARA.
82. "The Film World," *Times* (London), January 19, 1927, 12.
83. Clipping from *Nottingham Guardian*.
84. "Backs Birmingham," *Film Daily*, February 7, 1927, 1, 2.
85. "British Exhibs in F. P. Boycott: Not Serious," *Variety*, February 16, 1927, 5.
86. "British Exhibitors Frown on Boycott," *Film Daily*, February 25, 1927, 1.
87. "The Boycott Blunder," *Bioscope*, February 17, 1927, 52.
88. "Is A Boycott Justified," *Bioscope*, March 3, 1927, 32.

89. "The Boycott Called Off," *Bioscope*, 17 March 1927, 26.
90. "British Boycott Off," *Film Daily*, March 16, 1927, 1.
91. "Futurist Theatre," *Birmingham Gazette*, March 21, 1927, Futurist Theatre (Birmingham) Files, CTA; and "Sol Levy to Control the Futurist," *Bioscope*, March 24, 1927, 37.
92. C. J. North to C. Grant Isaacs, "The Paramount Boycott," April 23, 1927, Bureau of Foreign and Domestic Commerce, Motion Pictures—United Kingdom, 1927, file no. 281, NARA.
93. Marc Zimmerman, *The History of Dublin Cinemas* (Dublin: Nonsuch, 2007), 112, 113.
94. "Paramount Busy Taking over British Theaters," *Film Daily*, January 30, 1928, 1, 4.
95. "London Theatre Ends Forty Years' Career," 21. The *London Times* also reported that the Empire would be "designed on the lines of [the] Capitol Theatre in New York." "Last Days of the Empire Theatre," *Times* (London), January 1, 1927, 8. Still, others have noted that in elevation and design it is more closely aligned with Lamb's Albee Theatre in Cincinnati, which had opened in 1927. "Empire," Theatres Trust website, https://database.theatrestrust.org.uk/resources/theatres/show/1073-empire-london.
96. "Harry Portman Appointed," *New York Times*, July 12, 1927, 29; and "Portman New Mgr. Loew European Circuit," *Motion Picture News*, July 22, 1927, 188.
97. "Jury-Metro-Goldwyn Moves," *Bioscope*, September 22, 1927, 24.
98. "Loew Loans Albert to London Opening," *Exhibitors Herald and Moving Picture World*, October 27, 1928, 44.
99. "Loew Attending London Premiere," *Billboard*, November 3, 1928, 25.
100. "The Opening of the Empire, Leicester Square," *Daily Film Renter*, November 9, 1928, reprinted in *Cinema Theatre Association Bulletin*, March 1967, n.p., Empire Theatre (London) Files, CTA.
101. "The New Empire a Reality Distinguished First Night Audience," *Bioscope*, November 7, 1928, 33.
102. J. B. Priestley, "Super-Super," *Saturday Review*, December 8, 1928, 757, 758.
103. Allen Eyles, *Granada Theatres* (London: BFI, 1999), 10–11.
104. "Significance of 1928," *Kinematograph Weekly*, January 3, 1929, 97.

2. Hollywood's European Adventure, 1925–1941

1. Georges Clarriere, "Latest from France," *Bioscope*, April 30, 1925, 27.
2. Georges Clarriere, "Latest from France," *Bioscope*, May 7, 1925, 46; and Red, "News Flashes from U.S.A.," *Bioscope*, May 7, 1925, 47.
3. Georges Clarriere, "Latest from France," *Bioscope*, May 28, 1925, 25.
4. Georges Clarriere, "Latest from France," *Bioscope*, June 11, 1925, 20.
5. John S. Spargo, "Schiller and Rubin Sail," *Exhibitors Herald*, June 20, 1925, 36.
6. Georges Clarriere, "Latest from France," *Bioscope*, July 23, 1925, 32; and Georges Clarriere, "Latest from France," *Bioscope*, September 17, 1925, 44.
7. Georges Clarriere, "Latest from France," *Bioscope*, December 24, 1925, 15.
8. "Dowd to Redecorate Paris House," *Film Daily*, August 15, 1926, 1; and "Dowd Joins M-G-M in Europe," *Film Daily*, September 20, 1927, 2.
9. "Gaumont Palace Redecorated," *Film Daily*, September 22, 1926, 14.
10. Serge Leslie, *The Seven Leagues of a Dancer* (London: C.W. Beaumont, 1958), 21–27.
11. "Major Bowes Returns from European Journey," *New York Times*, August 7, 1927, X3.
12. Martin Quigley, "Our American Letter," *Bioscope*, September 2, 1926, 38; and "Portman Gets French Honor," *Film Daily*, December 5, 1926, 27.

13. "Gaumonts Here," *Film Daily*, September 30, 1926, 1; and "Gaumont-M-G-M Building French Houses," *Film Daily*, December 31, 1926, 1.
14. "The Pictures," *Argus*, February 17, 1927, 16.
15. "Gaumont-M-G-M Building French Houses," 1.
16. "More American Exploitation," *Bioscope*, October 13, 1927, 34.
17. "Screen for Panorama Invented in France," *Film Daily*, March 21, 1927, 1.
18. "'Napoleon' Hits Record," *Film Daily*, July 24, 1927, 5.
19. William A. Johnston, "France," *Motion Picture News*, March 11, 1927, 845.
20. "M-G-M Active in Buying Theatres Abroad," *Motion Picture News*, January 21, 1927, 221.
21. "M-G-M Continues to Buy Theaters Abroad," *Film Daily*, January 12, 1927, 1; and "Newspaper Specials," *Wall Street Journal*, February 5, 1927, 7.
22. "Moscowitz Has Optimistic View of Loew's European Activities," *Billboard*, April 16, 1927, 12.
23. Red Kann, "Time to Be Merry," *Film Daily*, January 2, 1927, 4.
24. William A, Johnston, "Holland," *Motion Picture News*, March 25, 1927, 1033; and "Loew's Out of Belgium; Going into Holland," *Variety*, September 7, 1927, 14.
25. "Loew's Out of Belgium; Going into Holland," 14.
26. "Notables at Opening of Paris Paramount," *New York Times*, November 25, 1927, 25.
27. "The Finest Theatre in Paris," *The Showman / Motion Picture News*, June 1928, 1843, 1845–1846.
28. Morris Gilbert, "French Screen Notes," *New York Times*, November 10, 1929, X7.
29. "How the Trade Is Growing," *Bioscope*, March 15, 1928, 58.
30. Georges Clarriere, "American-Controlled French Cinemas," *Bioscope*, September 22, 1927, 26.
31. Pierre Kefer, "Revue Des Programmes," *Du Cinéma*, February 1928.
32. "American Film Men Make German Deal, *New York Times*, December 31, 1925, 10.
33. William A. Johnston, "England," *Motion Picture News*, March 18, 1927, 940–42; and Paul Rotha, *The Film till Now: A Survey of the Cinema* (New York: Jonathan Cape & Harrison Smith, 1930), 28.
34. "'U' Plans Acquisition German Theaters," *Film Daily*, March 16, 1927, 1, 7; "Jacoby Film Opens New 'U' House," *Film Daily*, March 20, 1927, 5; and Heinrich Fraenkel, "Europe's Biggest Movie Palace In Berlin," *Bioscope*, March 2, 1927, 31.
35. "'Michael Strogoff' At Berlin Mercedes Palast," *Motion Picture News*, October 9, 1926, 38; and "Germany," *Film Daily*, October 10, 1926, 10.
36. "Einstein Quits 'U,'" *Film Daily*, June 26, 1927, 11; and "Einstein Quits German Post," *Film Daily*, March 20, 1927.
37. Untitled clipping, *Universal Weekly*, October 23, 1926, 19; and "New Universal Theatre In Berlin Opened with 'Michael Strogoff,'" *Universal Weekly*, October 9, 1926, 20.
38. "Release of 'Michael Strogoff' Set for Jules Verne's Birthday," *Universal Weekly*, November 20, 1926, 10, 22.
39. "'U' Active in Europe," *Film Daily*, October 3, 1926, 1.
40. "German Theaters Expect Greater Patronage This Coming Season, Erne Rapee Says," *Film Daily*, August 31, 1926, 2.
41. Heinrich Fraenkel, "Latest from Germany," *Bioscope*, August 6, 1925, 49; Red, "News Flashes from U.S.A.," *Bioscope*, September 3, 1925, 35; and Red, "News Flashes from U.S.A.," *Bioscope*, September 24, 1925, 41.
42. "Berlin Movie Palace Like One on Broadway," *New York Times*, September 26, 1925, 17.

43. Erno Rapee, "What Price Music," *Variety*, June 8, 1927, 12.
44. Siefried Kracauer, "Cult of Distraction: On Berlin's Picture Palaces," Reprinted in *New German Critique* 40 (Winter 1987): 91–92.
45. "Boom German-Made Films," *New York Times*, October 29, 1925, 29.
46. "The Year Abroad," *Variety*, December 29, 1926, 6.
47. "Fox Gets 27 Houses in Foreign Lands Via Loew," *Film Daily*, March 15, 1929, 16–17.
48. "FOX Film Reorganization," *Times* (London), April 9, 1931, 19.
49. "The Americanization of Amusement," *Saturday Review*, April 11, 1931, 521–22.
50. "Around the World with Paramount," *Variety*, August 7, 1929, 66.
51. "Paramount Tar Hand Om China" (Paramount takes hand on China), *Svensk Filmtidning*, October 1928, n.p., transcribed article, Swedish Film Institute.
52. "China Theatre, Stockholm, Is Newest Paramount Film Palace," *Paramount Around the World*, November 1, 1928, 3; and "New China Theatre in Stockholm, Sweden, Is Tribute to Paramount Management," *Paramount Around the World*, November 1, 1928, 20.
53. "Infor Öppnandet Av China, Storbiografen Vid Berzelii Park" (Info re opening of China, business point at Berzelii Park), *Filmnyheter*, October 1928, n.p., transcribed article, Swedish Film Institute.
54. "Handy Index to Paramount's Theatres Around the World," *Paramount International News*, June 1, 1934, 10; and "Uppgift Till Taxeringsnämnden I Det Taxeringsdistrikt, Där Skattskyldig Skall Taxeras Till Statlig Inkomst-Och Förmögenhetsskatt, Om Taxering I Annat Distrikt" (The task of the taxation board in the taxation district, where taxpayers are to be taxed at state income and wealth tax, about taxation in another district), Rörelsens Konto (Operating Account), May 30, 1933, Swedish National Archive.
55. "New London Theatre," *Times* (London), April 23, 1927, 8.
56. Carlton Theatre Opening Programme, April 27, 1927, Carlton Theatre Files, CTA.
57. "The Film World," *Times* (London), March 21, 1928, 14.
58. *CTA Bulletin*, untitled clipping, March/April 1973, Carlton Theatre Files, CTA.
59. Jan Dalgliesh, "Paramount UK Style," *Console*, October 1978, n.p., Carlton Theatre Files, CTA.
60. "Particulars of Directors or Managers of Paramount-Astoria-Theatres Limited and of Any Changes Therein," December 4, 1930, 252413/5, NA-UK.
61. R. J. Whitley, "'City Lights' Ready," *Daily Mirror*, December 8, 1930, 21.
62. Whitley, "'City Lights' Ready."
63. "Manchester's Great New Cinema," *Manchester Evening News*, October 2, 1930, 4.
64. The Paramount Theatre Manchester Opening Souvenir, 1930, Paramount Theatre (Manchester) Files, CTA.
65. Memorandum of Association of Paramount—Astoria—Theatres Limited, December 2, 1930, 252413/5, NA-UK; and Whitley, "'City Lights' Ready."
66. The prominence of Loew's Capitol Theatre had led to naming duplications around the world. "Rapid Expansion in Foreign Office," *Motion Picture Herald*, August 8, 1931, 98.
67. "Paramount to Have 16 Key Houses in England by 1932," *Motion Picture Herald*, August 8, 1931, 98.
68. "Luxury and Magnificence: Paramount's New Newcastle House," *Cinema, Theatre & General Construction*, October 1931, 35.
69. "Odeon Leeds," Cinema Treasures website, http://cinematreasures.org/theaters/1717.
70. The Paramount Theatre Leeds Opening Souvenir, February 22, 1932, 8, 13, Paramount Theatre (Leeds) Files, CTA.
71. "Handy Index to Paramount's Theatres," 10.

2. Hollywood's European Adventure   401

72. Bruce Peter, *100 Years of Glasgow's Amazing Cinemas* (Edinburgh: Polygon, 1996), 46, 48, 50.
73. "Par Don't Want Theatres in Europe," *Variety*, September 5, 1933, 13.
74. The cinema was listed as a Paramount house in 1933 and vanished by 1934 along with others in Japan, Jamaica, and Cuba. "36 of Par's Foreign Theatres and Nearly All to Profitable Trade," *Variety*, February 7, 1933, 17; and "Paramount Theatre World Activities," *Paramount International News*, June 1, 1934, 10.
75. Jan Dalgliesh, "Paramount UK Style."
76. Harry C. Plummer, "Distributor Rights Respected in Spain," *Motion Picture Daily*, August 12, 1936, 2.
77. "Inside Stuff-Pictures," *Variety*, August 21, 1929, 15, 49.
78. "Metro's Q.T. Attempt to Buy Up French Gaumont Chain Defeated," *Variety*, February 12, 1935, 15; and "Anti-American Whisper Campaign in Paris; May Be Political Move," *Variety*, February 27, 1935, 21, 64.
79. "Melniker Made MGM Foreign Theatres Head," *Motion Picture Daily*, June 9, 1936, 7; and "Lawrence's Contest Honors Late Ruler," *Motion Picture Herald*, July 6, 1935, 97.
80. "Budapest Ousting Ufas, Other Imports Balance Shortage of Germans," *Variety*, September 5, 1933, 12.
81. "See Nazis Buying Up Movie Theatre Chains Throughout Europe," *Jewish Daily Bulletin*, September 3, 1933, 2.
82. "Ufa Can't Pull Nazi Weight in Budapest, *Variety*, March 1934, 15.
83. "Metro Drops Budapest House, May Take a Ufa," *Variety*, July 3, 1934, 25.
84. "Acquire Foreign Houses," *Film Daily*, November 16, 1934, 4.
85. "Ten Theatres Is a Trust in Test," *Variety*, July 1935, 11.
86. Johnston, "Holland," 1033.
87. "Arthur Loew te Amsterdam: Een gesprek met den vermaarden leider van Metro-Goldwyn-Mayer" (Arthur Loew in Amsterdam: A conversation with the celebrated director of Metro-Goldwyn-Mayer), *De Telegraaf*, December 13, 1934, Morning, 42.
88. "U.S. Film Units Yield to Nazis on Race Issue," *Variety*, May 9, 1933, 13.
89. "Arthur Loew te Amsterdam," 42.
90. "Weer een nieuw theater te Amsterdam?" (Another new theater in Amsterdam?), *De Graafschap-Bode*, January 27, 1937, 1; and "Loew's Planning Two More Foreign Houses," *Motion Picture Herald*, March 6, 1937, 79.
91. The EYE Amsterdam museum notes that during the 1930s the NBB "became the omnipotent ruler of the Dutch film world." "Nederlands(ch)e Bioscoopbond," EYE, n.d., https://www.eyefilm.nl/en/collection/film-history/article/nederlandsche-bioscoopbond.
92. "Nederlands(ch)e Bioscoopbond."
93. Philip de Schaap, "Dutch Federation in Conflict with Metro," *Motion Picture Daily*, August 23, 1937, 9; and Philip de Schaap, "Dutch Act to Prevent Cut Rate Admissions; Federation Discusses Forming Board to Protect Prices; Delays MGM Theatre Approval," *Motion Picture Herald*, August 7, 1937, 76.
94. "Reglementaire Bepalingen En Usances Behooren Te Worden Gerespecteerd" (Regulatory provisions and practices ought to be respected), *Officieel Orgaan Van Den Nederlandschen Bioscoop-Bond*, June 1, 1937, 5.
95. "Indrukken Van De Ledenvergadering" (Impressions from the meeting), *Officieel Orgaan Van Den Nederlandschen Bioscoop-Bond*, July 16, 1937, 1–3.
96. de Schaap, "Dutch Federation in Conflict with Metro," 9; and de Schaap, "Dutch Act to Prevent Cut Rate Admissions," 76.
97. Untitled, *Officieel Orgaan Van Den Nederlandschen Bioscoop-Bond*, July 16, 1937, 8.

98. de Schaap, "Dutch Federation in Conflict with Metro," 9; and de Schaap, "Dutch Act to Prevent Cut Rate Admissions," 76.
99. de Schaap, "Dutch Act to Prevent Cut Rate Admissions," *Motion Picture Herald*, August 7, 1937, 76.
100. "M-G-M Takes 10-Yr. Leases on 3 Amsterdam Pix Houses," *Film Daily*, December 11, 1937, 2.
101. "Dutch Finally Ok Metro's Amsterdam," *Variety*, November 16, 1938, 13.
102. Philip de Schaap, "Popularity of American Films Showing Wide Cain In Holland," *Motion Picture Herald*, August 26, 1939, 72.
103. Philip de Schaap, "Dutch Production Increases but U.S. Films Remain Most Popular," *Motion Picture Herald*, July 15, 1939, 52.
104. "Leicester Square's Latest," *Kinema*, December 2, 1937, Empire Theatre Files, CTA.
105. "Warners to Build $1,250,000 House as Its First 'Show Window' in Europe," *Film Daily*, July 2, 1937, 1, 4.
106. "Warners Planning No British Circuit," *Film Daily*, September 14, 1937, 1, 7.
107. "WB's Daly's, London," *Variety*, September 1937, 46.
108. "New Warner London House Opens Today," *Motion Picture Daily*, October 12, 1938, 737, 738; and "The Warner Theatre, Leicester Square, W.C.2," *Builder*, October 14, 1938, 1, 4.
109. "The New Warner Theatre," *Ideal Kinema*, November 4, 1937, 11.
110. "Report 20th-Fox May Take London Theater," *Film Daily*, December 31, 1937, 12.
111. "$3,500,000 Budget for WB Brit. Films . . . Plan No Theater Expansion," *Film Daily*, November 4, 1938, 7.
112. Allen Eyles, *Oscar Deutch Entertains Our Nation*, Odeon Cinemas, no. 1 (London: BFI, 2002), 221–23.
113. "Odeon Takes Over Seven Para. Houses," *Film Daily*, November 27, 1939, 1.
114. "St. John with Deutsch," *Film Daily*, December 21, 1939, 12.
115. Eyles, *Oscar Deutch Entertains Our Nation*, 221–23.
116. "Schenck Says Loew's Has $3,500,000 Invested in Gaumont British," *Wall Street Journal*, September 24, 1941, 13.
117. M. Milder to National Provincial Bank Ltd., August 8, 1941, Box 3093, Folder FO1191, Warner Bros. Archive, University of Southern California, Los Angeles (hereafter, WB-USC).
118. Mrs. Catherine Scott Maxwell and Warner Bros. Pictures Ltd. Agreement, August 8, 1941, Box 3093, Folder FO1191, WB-USC.
119. Eric G. M. Fletcher to Joseph H. Hazen, November 10, 1941, Box 3093, Folder FO1191, WB-USC.
120. W. G. Wallace, "Subjects Purchase by Warner Bros. Pictures Ltd. of 2,007,000 Ordinary Shares of Associated British Picture Corporation Ltd.," CA, August 1941, Box 3093, Folder FO3868, WB-USC; and Morris W. Klein to VAULT, June 20, 1942, WB-USC.
121. "W. B. Adds Theatres Around the World," *Motion Picture Daily*, July 19, 1943, 1; and "WB Acquires 4 More Foreign Outlets," *Motion Picture Daily*, May 17, 1944, 2.

3. A New Battleground

1. Cordell Hull to Krecke, Care of Loew's Incorporated, August 31, 1940, Belgium, 855.4061-Motion Pictures/22, NARA.
2. "Rene Poelmans in Charge for MGM in Brussels," *Motion Picture Herald*, November 30, 1946, 111.

3. A New Battleground   403

3. Cordell Hull to Krecke.
4. Memorandum for Mr. Dow, Subject Situation, of American Motion Picture Companies in Belgium, American Consulate, Brussels, October 9, 1940, Belgium, 855.4061-Motion Pictures/27, NARA.
5. Philip de Schaap, "Ufa and Tobis Take Control in Holland," *Motion Picture Herald*, October 19, 1940, 47.
6. Philip de Schaap, "Nazis Reorganize Trade in Holland," *Motion Picture Herald*, January 25, 1941, 67.
7. Ben Urwand, *The Collaboration: Hollywood's Pact with Hitler* (Cambridge, Mass.: Belknap Press of Harvard Unity Press, 2013), 107.
8. de Schaap, "Nazis Reorganize Trade in Holland," 67.
9. Philip de Schaap, "Dutch Industry Goes Back to Work Under Own Steam," *Motion Picture Herald*, July 21, 1945, 23.
10. "Paris Booed Nazi Films," *Showmen's Trade Review*, November 11, 1944, 9.
11. "Invitational Premieres," *Motion Picture Herald*, April 28, 1945, 9.
12. "Problems Abroad," *Motion Picture Herald*, August 31, 1940, 9.
13. "Theatres in 14 States Affected by U.S. Army 'War' Blackouts," *Motion Picture Herald*, April 26, 1941, 50.
14. "Historically Interesting Medal Grouping Awarded to French Resistance Fighter, Ernest Bechet, part of C & T Auctioneers," *The Saleroom*, lot 34, https://www.the-saleroom.com/en-gb/auction-catalogues/candt-auctioneers/catalogue-id-srct10024/lot-39cb115b-d2fe-4997-92e1-a59b00dbcdae; and "Orders, Decorations, Medals and Militaria," *Dix Noonan Webb*, lot 94, September 22, 2006, https://www.dnw.co.uk/auction-archive/lot-archive/lot.php?auction_id=94&lot_id=130475.
15. "Andre Ullman's War Adventures a Real Saga of Drama and Courage," *Paramount International News*, December 28, 1944, 3.
16. Ed G. Kendrew, "Chatter in Paris," *Variety*, August 8, 1928, 35.
17. "Times Square: Paris Chatter," *Variety*, May 21, 1930, 42; and "F-P Foreigners Here," *Variety*, May 21, 1930, 46.
18. "Great News in Three-Chaptered Cable," *Paramount International News*, October 1, 1934, 11.
19. "French Scribes Due Here Today for Studio Visit," *Los Angeles Times*, October 24, 1929, A16; "Osso Resigns as Paris Head," *Variety*, May 28, 1930, 7, 65; Theodore Wolfram, "PARIS," *Billboard*, July 12, 1930, 38; and "Film Expansion at Joinville," *Wall Street Journal*, May 8, 1931, 4.
20. "Par Merges Distrib and Theatre Cos. in France; New Taxation Law," *Variety*, December 4, 1935, 11.
21. "Par Merges Distrib and Theatre Cos. in France," 11.
22. By then, Joinville had diminished in utility for Paramount and had been leased to Pathé-Natan. "Ullman to Manage Joinville Studio," *Motion Picture Herald*, June 11, 1938, 27.
23. "Round Table in Pictures," *Motion Picture Herald*, May 21, 1938, 57.
24. Pierre Autre, "French Exhibitors Protest Plan for Government Rule of Receipts," *Motion Picture Herald*, February 4, 1939, 53; and "Lebreton Aide to Lange," *Film Daily*, March 9, 1939, 7.
25. "Par Trying to Get Andre Ullman Freed," *Variety*, November 13, 1940, 3.
26. "Out of Vichy," *Motion Picture Herald*, October 17, 1942, 9.
27. "Totalitarian Rule Governs French Films," *Motion Picture Daily*, December 10, 1940, 5.
28. "Law Forces Reorg. of French Industry," *Film Daily*, October 23, 1940, 1.

29. After World War II the Siritzky family wanted their cinema circuit returned after having it "taken away from us by the Germans at the point of a gun" in November 1940. Ownership, instead, transferred to the French government after the war, which eyed the cinemas as part of a new effort to nationalize the film industry. In January 1947, after a legal battle, Vice President Sam Siritzky traveled back to France to reclaim his family's cinemas from the French government. "France Seeking to Nationalize Film Industry," *Motion Picture Herald*, April 27, 1946, 38; and "Siritzky Sails for Paris to Recover French Houses," *Film Daily*, January 17, 1947, 2.
30. It was renamed "Theater Tuschinski" again after the war, and one of Abraham Tuschinski's only surviving relatives, nephew Max Gerschtanowitz, became its director. "Theater Tuschinski," EYE, n.d., https://www.eyefilm.nl/en/collection/film-history/article/theater-tuschinski.
31. "Par Trying to Get Andre Ullman Freed," 3.
32. "Andre Ullman's War Adventures," 3.
33. "U.S. Film Offices Seized: Nazis Take Over Distribution Facilities in Paris," *New York Times*, April 17, 1941, 2.
34. "Report Nazis Take Majors' Paris Offices," *Motion Picture Daily*, April 17, 1941, 1.
35. "U.S. Filmers Doubt Pix 'Bootlegging' in Paris," *Variety*, April 29, 1942, 5.
36. "André Ullmann Recounts Epic Story of Courage Under Bitterest Conditions," *Paramount International News*, March 22, 1946, 10, 11.
37. "Andre Ullman's War Adventures," 3.
38. Paul Perez, "Now It Can Be Told . . .," *Boxoffice*, August 17, 1946, 22, 23.
39. "André Ullmann Recounts Epic Story," 10, 11.
40. Perez, "Now It Can Be Told . . .," 22–23.
41. "André Ullmann Recounts Epic Story," 10, 11.
42. Jean Vive, "Serving Art Through Technique," *International Projectionist*, December 1959, 20.
43. Perez, "Now It Can Be Told . . .," 22–23.
44. This was one month before the Nazis attempted to capture all of the French Navy vessels at Toulon during Operation Lila, many of which were scuttled on November 27 by French admiral Jean de Laborde on behalf of the Free French Naval Forces. History.com Editors, "French Scuttle Their Fleet," History.com, November 5, 2009, https://web.archive.org/web/20190509212925/http://www.history.com/this-day-in-history/french-scuttle-their-fleet.
45. Perez, "Now It Can Be Told . . .," 22–23.
46. "The Ron Penhall Collection," Dix Noonan Webb Auctions, lot 94, September 22, 2006, https://www.dnw.co.uk/auction-archive/special-collections/lot.php?specialcollection_id=423&lot_uid=130475; and Perez, "Now It Can Be Told . . .," 22–23.
47. Perez, "Now It Can Be Told . . .," 22–23.
48. "André Ullmann Recounts Epic Story," 10, 11.
49. Perez, "Now It Can Be Told . . .," 22–23.
50. Perez, "Now It Can Be Told . . .," 22–23.
51. "André Ullmann Recounts Epic Story," 10, 11.
52. "André Ullmann Recounts Epic Story," 10, 11.
53. "Paramounteers In Paris Found to Be Ok," *Variety*, September 27, 1944, 23; and "André Ullmann Recounts Epic Story," 10, 11.
54. "Robert Schless Leaves for European Post," *Exhibitor*, April 18, 1945, 24.
55. Perez, "Now It Can Be Told . . .," 22–23.

56. April 11, 1945, is the official liberation date provided by La Fondation pour la Mémoire de la Déportation for Bechet. La Fondation pour la Mémoire de la Déportation, *Le Livre-Mémorial des déportés de France arrêtés par mesure de répression et dans certains cas par mesure de persécution: 1940–1945* (Paris: Ed. Tirésias, 2004), 54.
57. "It Happened in Paris," *Pathé Gazette Newsreel*, September 18, 1944, https://www.britishpathe.com/video/it-happened-in-paris/query/gaston+madru.
58. Perez, "Now It Can Be Told . . .," 22–23.
59. That photograph is now part of a collection owned by Jacques Rancy.
60. "The Ron Penhall Collection"; and Perez, "Now It Can Be Told . . .," 22–23.
61. "Gaston Madru, Newsreel Ace, Dies in Action!," *News of the Day* 16, no. 266 (April 24, 1945), UCLA Film and Television Archive.
62. *German Concentration Camps Factual Survey Film* (1945/2014), Imperial War Museum website, https://www.iwm.org.uk/partnerships/german-concentration-camps-factual-survey#text_with_media_24833.
63. "Orders, Decorations, Medals and Militaria"; and Perez, "Now It Can Be Told . . .," 22–23.
64. Perez, "Now It Can Be Told . . .," 22–23.
65. "Jean de Lattre de Tassigny," *Encyclopaedia Britannica*, July 20, 1988, https://www.britannica.com/biography/Jean-de-Lattre-de-Tassigny; and "André Ullmann Recounts Epic Story," 10, 11.
66. "Orders, Decorations, Medals and Militaria."
67. "Another Honor for Ernest Bechet," *Paramount International News*, July 12, 1946, 5.
68. Perez, "Now It Can Be Told . . .," 22–23.
69. "A Pair of Cables to Make You Glow," *Paramount International News*, August 31, 1945.
70. "Weltner Gabs Par's European Plans, Tells of Moves to Lam Svensk Curb," *Variety*, December 19, 1945, 9.
71. "Ullmann Quits Par," *Variety*, June 26, 1946, 18.
72. "Weltner Gabs Par's European Plans," 9, 20.
73. "Weltner to Set New Paris Theatre Policy," *Variety*, November 13, 1946, 13.
74. "Ullmann Quits Par," 18.
75. "Orders, Decorations, Medals and Militaria."
76. "Le Paramount's Ernest Bechet Is Given an American Citation," *Paramount International News*, January 21, 1949, 4.
77. Nancy Tartaglione, "French Cinemas Could Re-Open in Early July, Says Culture Minister," *Deadline*, May 15, 2020, https://deadline.com/2020/05/france-movie-theaters-re-opening-july-culture-minister-1202935727/.

4. Postwar Europe and the Legacy of Hollywood Cinemas, 1945–1993

1. "Herald Correspondent Evaded Nazi Gestapo in Ancient Cellar Room," *Motion Picture Herald*, July 21, 1945, 23.
2. "Eric Johnston Reports State of Film World," *Motion Picture Herald*, March 30, 1946, 12, 13.
3. Ben Urwand, *The Collaboration: Hollywood's Pact with Hitler* (Cambridge, Mass.: Belknap Press of Harvard University Press, 2013), 144, 287.

4. Philip de Schaap, "Says Dutch Now Willing to American Deal in Amsterdam," *Motion Picture Herald*, December 15, 1945, 30.
5. "Rene Poelmans in Charge for MGM in Brussels," *Motion Picture Herald*, November 30, 1946, 111.
6. "Loew's Int'l Adds 6 New Houses Abroad," *Film Daily*, February 11, 1947, 1, 5; and "Belgium Dates Set On 'Battleground,'" *Showman's Trade Review*, October 1, 1949, 16.
7. "Loew's Int'l Adds 6 New Houses Abroad," 1, 5.
8. "Loew International Gets 6 Runs Abroad," *Motion Picture Daily*, February 11, 1947, 1.
9. "MGM's Metro Theatre Opens in Belgium," *Motion Picture Herald*, April 26, 1947, 55; and "Antwerp House for Metro," *Motion Picture Herald*, April 5, 1947, 42.
10. "MGM's Metro Theatre Opens in Belgium," 55.
11. "Loew's Int'l Adds 6 New Houses Abroad," 1, 5.
12. "Suspension of Swiss Branch of Loew's International Corporation from Swiss Film Distributors Association," American Legation Bern, January 28, 1947, 854.4061 MP/1-2847, NARA.
13. "Suspension of Swiss Branch," NARA.
14. "Suspension of Swiss Branch," NARA.
15. Letter from Gerald R. Canty to Gerald M. Mayer, June 20, 1947, 854.4061/6-1147, NARA.
16. VINCENT, American Legation at Bern to Secretary of State, February 11, 1949, 854.4061 MP/2-1149, NARA.
17. VINCENT, American Legation at Bern to Secretary of State, March 10, 1949, 854.4061 MP/3-1049, NARA.
18. VINCENT, American Legation at Bern to Secretary of State, March 28, 1949, 854.4061 MP/3-2849, NARA.
19. Twentieth Century-Fox, "Review of Operations," *Twentieth Century-Fox 1953 Annual Report*, 11, New York Public Library for the Performing Arts.
20. "Rialto, Coventry Street: Redesigned for Cinemascope," *The Ideal Kinema Supplement to Kinematograph Weekly*, November 4, 1954, n.p., Rialto Theatre (London) Files, CTA.
21. Drake Plymouth Souvenir Programme Gala Opening, Drake, Plymouth, UK (1958): 2, 3, 6, 11–13, 16, Drake/Odeon (Plymouth) Files, CTA.
22. Allen Eyles with Keith Stone, *London's West End Cinemas* (Swindon, UK: English Heritage, 2014), 49; M. J. Frankovsch, "Columbia Cinema of the Future," *Supplement to Kinematograph Weekly*, February 12, 1959, and D; "Curzon Soho," Cinema Treasures website, http://cinematreasures.org/theaters/6244.
23. Eyles with Stone, *London's West End Cinemas*, 154.
24. "Loew Expands Exhibition in W. Germany," *Motion Picture Daily*, Friday, April 27, 1956, 1, 4.
25. "Loew's Opening New Berlin Theatre," *Motion Picture Daily*, December 6, 1956, 3.
26. Argeo Santucci, "U.S. Firms Accept Italian Program," *Motion Picture Herald*, March 15, 1947, 47.
27. "Loew Theatre Opens in Milan, Italy," *Motion Picture Herald*, December 1, 1956, 62; and "Loew's Opening 55th In Overseas Chain," *Motion Picture Daily*, November 29, 1956, 3.
28. Kerry Segrave, *Drive-in Theaters: A History from Their Inception in 1933* (Jefferson, N.C.: McFarland, 1992), 104; and Kurt Ernst, "A Night at the Drive-In—in Rome, Italy," *Hemmings Daily*, June 20, 2014, https://www.hemmings.com/blog/2014/06/20/a-night-at-the-drive-in-in-rome-italy/.

29. The New Empire Theatre, Leicester Square, Gala Opening Program, December 19, 1962, CTA.
30. "Rembrandtsplein Heeft Weer Een Bioscoop" (Rembrandtsplein has another cinema), *Algemeen Handelsblad Van Woensdag*, August 31, 1966, 4.
31. Seymour Poe, "Our World Inventory," *Twentieth Century-Fox 1965 Annual Report* (New York: Twentieth Century-Fox, 1966), 5–7.
32. "Raphel Brings over So. African Showmen for Fox Conclave," *Variety*, February 26, 1969, 3; and "Fox's 50% Buy of France's Meric," *Variety*, March 20, 1974, 5.
33. "Fox's 50% Buy of France's Meric," *Variety*, March 20, 1974, 5; and "20th-Fox Affiliate to Buy into French Theatre Chain," *Boxoffice*, March 25, 1974, W6.
34. "Fox Expanding Theatre Activities in France," *Independent Film Journal*, April 1, 1974, 11. See also "Rosenthal's Position," *Variety*, May 1, 1974, 27; and "New Posts," *Independent Film Journal*, May 15, 1974, 29.
35. "Fox, Meric Deal Off," *Variety*, September 25, 1974, 4.
36. "20th-Fox Names Oscar Lax Theatre Operations Head," *Boxoffice*, June 30, 1975, 10; "Fox in Hamburg; Has 121 Theatres Around the World," *Variety*, July 23, 1975, 7; "Twentieth Century-Fox Promotes Stephen Roberts to V-P," *Boxoffice*, May 20, 1974, 4; and "Stephen Roberts Heads Fox Foreign Theatres," *Boxoffice*, June 9, 1975, 8.
37. "Paramount Plus Plaza Fine Addition to Swingin' London," *Daily Cinema*, June 21, 1968, 3.
38. Robert F. Hawkins, "London Show Biz Takes Refreshing Pause to Salute Plaza and Wilcox," *Variety*, April 4, 1967, 2, 62.
39. "Bovis Build the Cinema with the Cinema Upstairs, Technical Details," Press Release, June 20, 1968, Plaza Lower Regent (London) Files, CTA.
40. "Paramount Plus Plaza Fine Addition," 3.
41. "Plaza 1 + 2 Advertisement," ca. May 1975, Plaza Lower Regent (London) Files, CTA; see also Eyles with Stone, *London's West End Cinemas*, 175; and "Vue Piccadilly," Cinema Treasures website, n.d., http://cinematreasures.org/theaters/2503.
42. "'Strawberry' Opens New-Look Leicester Square Riti of Luxurious Cinema-Going," *Kinematograph Weekly*, May 30, 1970, 11.
43. "Warner West End—Past, Present and Future," *What's On*, August 18, 1993, 32, Warner Theatre (London) Files, CTA; and "The Warner West End Makes," *Kinematograph Weekly*, November 7, 1970, 8.
44. "Three into One Will Go—the Warner Way," *CinemaTV Today*, September 14, 1974, 28.
45. "Fox O'seas Will Handle ABC," *Variety*, April 15, 1970, 3.
46. "Detail Sales Realignment in Par-U Foreign Combine," *Variety*, May 20, 1970, 6.
47. "Junket to Amsterdam," *Variety*, July 29, 1970, 3, 22.
48. "CIC Gets Distribution for MGM Overseas," *Boxoffice*, November 5, 1973, 3.
49. "Cinema Intl. Corp. Sanguine on Potential Earnings from Former Metro Global Theatres," *Variety*, January 16, 1974, 5.
50. "Cinema Intl. Corp. Sanguine," 5; and "CIC Names Hoare Theatre Op Veep," *Variety*, September 11, 1974, 5.
51. "CIC Appoints Hoare To Top Theatre Post," *Independent Film Journal*, September 1974, 12.
52. "CIC Buys Condor, 11-Site Brazil Chain," *Variety*, August 25, 1976, 35.
53. "Continued Growth of Multiples Vital, Says Parafrance's Siritzky," *Variety*, March 30, 1977, 33.
54. "CIC Revives Oldies in London Cinema," *Variety*, February 1, 1978, 44.

408   4. Postwar Europe and Hollywood Cinemas

55. "Cinema Intl. Corp. Sees $145,000,000 Fiscal Yr," *Variety*, February 15, 1978, 3.
56. Roger Watkins, "CIC Sights A $235-Mil Global Windfall," *Variety*, April 29, 1981, 3, 34.
57. "CIC Status Update," *Variety*, October 14, 1981, 5, 28; and "United Intl Staffing Up," *Variety*, October 21, 1981, 53.
58. "CIC FACT FILE," Cinema International Corporation Files, CTA.
59. "CIC FACT FILE—Case History," Cinema International Corporation Files, CTA.
60. Don Groves, "CIC/UACI Makes It Simple: Exhib Group Now Just UCI; Brit Loop Eyes German Sites," *Variety*, May 3–9, 1989, 18.
61. UCI Puts on a New Front," *Screen International*, June 3–9, 1989, 1.
62. "CIC FACT FILE," CTA.
63. Sophie Hanscombe, "On Target for 2043," *Moving Pictures UK*, September 23, 1993, CTA.
64. "Salah M. Hassanein," *Moving Pictures UK*, September 23, 1993, Warner Bros. International Theatres Files, CTA.
65. Philip Turner, *Warner Cinemas* (St. Paul's Cray, Kent, UK: Brantwood, 1997), 12, 16–17.
66. "No Expense Spared," *Moving Pictures UK*, September 23, 1993, Warner Bros. International Theatres Files, CTA.
67. "No Expense Spared."
68. Turner, *Warner Cinemas*, 12, 16, 17.
69. "Warner Bros. and Village Roadshow Open Their First Multiplex in Taiwan to Blockbuster Attendance," Time Warner Press Release, February 12, 1998.
70. Turner, *Warner Cinemas*, 8, 17.
71. Leon Forde, "UK's Warner Village Cinemas sold to SBC for $402m," *Screen International*, May 13, 2003, http://www.screendaily.com/uks-warner-village-cinemas-sold-to-sbc-for-402m/4013294.article.
72. Francesca Dinglesan, "A National Treasure," *Boxoffice*, March 2001. http://web.archive.org/web/20030101060107/http://www.boxoff.com/issues/mar01/na.html.
73. Turner, *Warner Cinemas*, 7–10, 30.
74. Charles Acland, *Screen Traffic: Movies, Multiplexes, and Global Culture* (Durham, N.C.: Duke University Press 2003), 141.

5. Fox Chases Hoyts

1. Albert Moran and Errol Veith, *Historical Dictionary of Australian and New Zealand Cinema* (Lanham, Md.: Scarecrow, 2005), 165–67.
2. Terry O'Brien, *The Greater Union Story, 1910–1985: 75 Years of Cinema in Australia* (Sydney: Greater Union Organisation, 1985), 9.
3. O'Brien, *The Greater Union Story*, 17–23, 32. In 1928, under general manager Stuart Frank Doyle, Union Theatres forged an additional association with Birch Carroll & Coyle, with cinemas in Queensland. Moran and Veith, *Historical Dictionary*, 147–49.
4. "Fox Buys Hoyts. Combine Killed!," *Everyones*, September 3, 1930, 6–8.
5. "Fox Buys Hoyts. Combine Killed!," 6–8.
6. "The Capital of Australia to See Paramount's 100% Program," *The Whole Show*, November 10, 1927, 1.

7. "Canberra Theatre Opens To-night with Paramount's 100% Program," *The Whole Show*, December 8, 1927, 2.
8. "'Ben Hur' in Australia," *Film Daily*, July 24, 1927, 5.
9. "Chain Battle Waxing Warm in Australia," *Variety*, September 5, 1928, 6.
10. "Talkies for Australia," *Motion Picture News*, October 27, 1928, 1272-C.
11. "Film Inquiry," *Sydney Morning Herald*, January 13, 1934, 15.
12. "Doyle Replies: Alleges Distributors Forced U.T. to Build Big Theatres. Opposes American Interests in Exhibiting Field," *Everyones*, January 17, 1934, 5.
13. "Doyle Replies," 5.
14. "Fox Buys Hoyts. Combine Killed!," 6–8.
15. "'Everyones' at the Film Enquiry: Doyle Under Fire for 9 Hours. Makes Sensational Charges. Cross-Examination," *Everyones*, January 17, 1934, 16, 17.
16. "Fox Buys Hoyts. Combine Killed!," 6–8.
17. "U.T. and Hoyts Forming Buying Pool. Rental Slashes," *Everyones*, August 6, 1930, 7.
18. "Is It A Merger?," *Everyones*, August 13, 1930, 6.
19. "Is It A Merger?," 6.
20. "Fox Buys Hoyts. Combine Killed!," 6–8.
21. "News in Headlines," *Everyones*, September 3, 1930, 4.
22. "Hoyts, Fox Merger On in Australia," *Variety*, September 3, 1930, 7.
23. "Stop Press! Munro Gives *Everyones* First Official Statement from Fox, MGM in Deal," *Everyones*, September 3, 1930, 4.
24. Graham Shirley and Brian Adams, *Australian Cinema: The First Eighty Years*, rev. ed. (Hong Kong: Currency Press, 1989), 109.
25. Shirley and Adams, *Australian Cinema*, 112, 113.
26. "Stop Press!" 4.
27. Eric H. Gorrick, "Australia," *Variety*, September 11, 1930, 28.
28. "Fox Buys Hoyts. Combine Killed!," 6–8.
29. "Big Movie Deal," *Mirror* (Perth, WA), September 6, 1930, 8.
30. Dale Turnbull: Interviewed by Graham Shirley, 2001–2004: Oral History. Title No. 587140, NFSA.
31. Barrie A. Wigmore, *The Crash and Its Aftermath: A History of Securities Markets in the United States, 1929–1933* (Westport, Conn.: Greenwood, 1985), 171–75.
32. Vanda Krefft, *The Man Who Made the Movies: The Meteoric Rise and Tragic Fall of William Fox* (New York: Harper, 2017), 520.
33. Wigmore, *The Crash and Its Aftermath*, 171–75.
34. Richard Brody, "The Hollywood Story of Upton Sinclair and William Fox," *New Yorker*, January 31, 2020, https://www.newyorker.com/culture/the-front-row/the-hollywood-story-of-upton-sinclair-and-william-fox.
35. Wigmore, *The Crash and Its Aftermath*, 171–75.
36. Vanda Krefft, *The Man Who Made the Movies*, 649.
37. Brody, "The Hollywood Story of Upton Sinclair and William Fox."
38. Wigmore, *The Crash and Its Aftermath*, 171–75.
39. Steven J. Ross, *Hollywood Left and Right: How Movie Stars Shaped American Politics* (New York: Oxford University Press, 2011), 52, 65; and "Fox Says He Was Forced to Quit," *Wall Street Journal*, November 24, 1933, 5.
40. Red Kann, "An Insider's Outlook," *Motion Picture News*, April 12, 1930, 20.
41. "What Will Happen Next?," *Everyones*, September 3, 1930, 4.
42. "Buys Abroad Boomerang," *Variety*, September 10, 1930, 7.

43. "What Will Happen Next?," 4.
44. "Fox in Charge," *Everyones*, September 10, 1930, 6; "News in Headlines," *Everyones*, October 29, 1930, 4; and "Thring, Griffith Resign as Managing Director of Hoyts," *Everyones*, October 1, 1930, 7.
45. "Fox in Charge," 6.
46. "Hoyts Take Over Perth Capitol Theatre," *Everyones*, October 15, 1930; "News in Headlines," *Everyones*, October 29, 1930, 4; and "Charles Munro Takes Charge of Hoyts for Fox," *Everyones*, October 29, 1930, 6.
47. "Charles Munro Takes Charge of Hoyts for Fox," 6.
48. Hoyts Theatres, Ltd. Advertisement, *Everyones*, November 5, 1930, 20.
49. W. A. Daumer to Undersecretary, June 21, 1932, Archives New Zealand, Auckland (hereafter, ANZ-Auckland).
50. Daumer to Undersecretary.
51. "Fox in Charge," 6; and "U.T. and Paramount Chiefs Deny Finality on Deal," *Everyones*, September 17, 1930, 7.
52. "Buys Abroad Boomerang," 7.
53. "'Everyones' at the Film Enquiry," 16, 17.
54. "Paramount Buys Melb. Capitol," *Paramount Punch*, December 24, 1930, n.p.; and "Proud Of Paramount!," *Paramount Around the World*, February 1931, 19.
55. "Welcome to Capitol Staff," *Paramount Punch*, January 28, 1931, n.p.
56. "Publix Gets Melbourne Capitol; Union Circuit Deal Reported Off," *Film Daily*, December 28, 1930, 1.
57. "British Films," *Sydney Morning Herald*, December 23, 1930, 6.
58. J. L. Thornley, "The Capitol in Melbourne, Conduct of Prominent Australian Paramount Deluxer Is Described; Operates on Reserved Seat Plan," *Motion Picture Herald*, October 19, 1935, 112.
59. O'Brien, *The Greater Union Story*, 64, 68, 75.
60. "Film Inquiry," 15.
61. Shirley and Adams, *Australian Cinema*, 110.
62. "Doyle Replies," 5.
63. "Paramount Pictures for Hoyts," *Paramount Punch*, November 4, 1931, 1; and Cliff Holt, "Union Circuit Gets Edge on Hoyt in Race for Films in Australia," *Motion Picture Herald*, January 9, 1932, 26.
64. "Film Inquiry," 15.
65. "Merger of Theatres," *Northern Advocate* (Whangarei, NZ), October 15, 1932, 7.
66. Shirley and Adams, *Australian Cinema*, 123.
67. "Film Inquiry," 15.
68. "Picture War," *Sydney Morning Herald*, December 31, 1932, 11.
69. "Picture War," 11.
70. "Consolidation of Fox," *Everyones*, August 16, 1933, 3.
71. "Fox-Gaumont Deal Finalised. Immediate Distribution," *Everyones*, July 19, 1933, 6.
72. "Deny London Reports of Fox Selling Out Hoyts Interest," *Everyones*, September 13, 1933, 5.
73. R. Brasch, *Australian Jews of Today and the Part They Have Played* (Stanmare: Cassell Australia, 1977), 41–45; and "Opening of M*G*M's New Syd. Building. Loew's Tribute," *Everyones*, December 20, 1933, 6.
74. Michael Moodabe, *Peanuts and Pictures: The Life and Times of MJ Moodabe* (New Zealand: Michael Moodabe, ca. 2000), 36, 37.
75. "Opening of M*G*M's New Syd. Building," 6.

76. "Combine Replies to Distribs, Loew Leaves for the East," *Everyones*, December 20, 1933, 7.
77. "N.S.W. Government Will Enquire into Film Business," *Everyones*, December 27, 1933, 6.
78. "'Everyones' at the Film Enquiry," *Everyones*, January 10, 1934, 7.
79. "N.S.W. Government Will Enquire into Film Business," 6.
80. "Film War Declared," *Sydney Morning Herald*, December 28, 1933, 7.
81. "Film War Declared," 7.
82. "Film War Declared," 7.
83. Shirley and Adams, *Australian Cinema*, 123.
84. "What Are Loew and M.G.M. Plans for Australian Theatres," *Everyones*, December 13, 1933, 8, 9.
85. "Film War Declared," 7.
86. Shirley and Adams, *Australian Cinema*, 123.
87. "The Future of Australian Films as seen by F. W. Thring," *Everyones*, December 13, 1933, 10.
88. "Enquiry Opens," *Everyones*, January 3, 1934, 5, 6.
89. "'Everyones' at the Film Enquiry," *Everyones*, January 10, 1934, 7.
90. "Enquiry Opens," 5, 6.
91. "'Everyones' at the Film Enquiry," January 10, 1934, 7.
92. "Freeman Denies New Theatre is Threat to Q.T.," *Everyones*, January 10, 1934, 8.
93. "Film Inquiry," 15.
94. "'Fox Never Tries to Fetter Hoyts Board,' Says Munro," *Everyones*, January 17, 1934, 7.
95. "Film Inquiry," 15.
96. "'Everyones' at the Film Enquiry," January 10, 1934, 7.
97. "How G.T.C. Chiefs Regard Australian Quota," *Everyones*, January 17, 1934, 7.
98. "New Theatres Mean End of Hoyts & G.U.T—Smith," *Everyones*, January 17, 1934, 12.
99. "'Everyones' at the Film Enquiry," *Everyones*, January 17, 1934, 16, 17.
100. "Melb. Independents See Safety in More City Theatres," *Everyones*, January 24, 1934, 6.
101. Shirley and Adams, *Australian Cinema*, 124.
102. Shirley and Adams, *Australian Cinema*, 124.
103. Shirley and Adams, *Australian Cinema*, 124, 139, 140.
104. Shirley and Adams, *Australian Cinema*, 139.
105. "How G.T.C. Chiefs Regard Australian Quota," 7.
106. Shirley and Adams, *Australian Cinema*, 124–26.
107. "Australian Quotas Expected to Spread Thursday," *Motion Picture Daily*, May 28, 1936, 9.

6. The Fox Chase in New Zealand and Australia, 1936–1946

1. Bruce W. Hayward and Selwyn P. Hayward, *Cinemas of Auckland, 1896–1979* (Auckland: Lodestar, 1979), n.p.
2. Like Fullers, Williamson sold its cinemas in 1946 to what was now Kerridge Odeon. Hayward and Hayward, *Cinemas of Auckland, 1896–1979*, n.p.
3. Hippodrome Pictures Limited Declaration, October 3, 1924; and Certificate of Incorporation, Amalgamated Theatres Limited, October 28, 1928, both Container Code C

155 036, Archives Reference No BBNZ A1607 21462, Box 36, Record Number 41744, Cinema Properties Limited (Amalgamated Theatres Limited), ANZ-Auckland.
4. "Memorandum of Association of Hippodrome Pictures Limited," September 30, 1924, Container Code C 155 036, Archives Reference No BBNZ A1607 21462, Box 36, Record Number 41744, Cinema Properties Limited (Amalgamated Theatres Limited), ANZ-Auckland; and Michael Moodabe, *Peanuts and Pictures: The Life and Times of MJ Moodabe* (New Zealand: Michael Moodabe, 2000), 16.
5. Moodabe, *Peanuts and Pictures*, 11, 12.
6. Moodabe, *Peanuts and Pictures*, 13, 16, 17.
7. "His devotion [to her] was supreme," Michael Moodabe writes, adding that M. J. would drive to his mother's home in Epsom everyday "to visit with her." Moodabe, *Peanuts and Pictures*, 17.
8. Moodabe, *Peanuts and Pictures*, 17, 24; and "Obituary," *Poverty Bay Herald*, October 1, 1931, 6.
9. Moodabe, *Peanuts and Pictures*, 46.
10. Joseph Moodabe to the Assistant Commissioner of Stamp Duties, March 26, 1929, Container Code C 155 036, Archives Reference No BBNZ A1607 21462, Box 36, Record Number 41744, Cinema Properties Limited (Amalgamated Theatres Limited), ANZ-Auckland; and Certificate of Incorporation, Amalgamated Theatres Limited, October 28, 1928, ANZ-Auckland; "Minutes of Special Resolutions of Hippodrome Pictures Ltd., August 6, 1928," Container Code C 155 036, Archives Reference No BBNZ A1607 21462, Box 36, Record Number 41744, Cinema Properties Limited (Amalgamated Theatres Limited), ANZ-Auckland. By November 14, 1929, Rayner owned 5,000 shares and Michael Moodabe owned 5,000. List of Members of Amalgamated Theatres Ltd., November 14, 1929, Container Code C 155 036, Archives Reference No BBNZ A1607 21462, Box 36, Record Number 41744, Amalgamated Theatres Limited), ANZ-Auckland.
11. Moodabe, *Peanuts and Pictures*, 24.
12. Wayne Brittenden, *The Celluloid Circus: The Heyday of the New Zealand Picture Theatre, 1925–1970* (Auckland, NZ: Godwit, 2008), 147, 157.
13. "N.Z. Amalgamated's 100p.c. Buy of Fox, Gau.-British," *Everyones*, November 1, 1933, 6.
14. Moodabe, *Peanuts and Pictures*, 21.
15. Anna Soutar, "Interview with Eric Kearney," October 24, 2000, Alexander Turnbull Library, OHInt-0546-05, New Zealand National Library.
16. "Amalgamated Plan Four New Theatres," *Everyones*, July 12, 1933, 21.
17. Soutar, "Interview with Eric Kearney."
18. Hayward and Hayward, *Cinemas of Auckland, 1896–1979*, n.p.
19. "Lull in the Building of Theatres in New Zealand," *Film Weekly*, October 15, 1936, 5.
20. "Foreign Control and Film Rents," *New Zealand Motion Picture Exhibitors' Bulletin* (hereafter, *NZMPEB*), May 2, 1936, 1.
21. "Outrages on the Industry," *NZMPEB*, July 25, 1936, 2.
22. "Munro Denies Deal on With Hoyts-Moodabe," *Everyones*, September 23, 1936, 18.
23. Moodabe, *Peanuts and Pictures*, 24.
24. "Twentieth Century-Fox, Crick, Munro Buy into Moodabe N.Z. Circuit," *Everyones*, October 7, 1936, 12.
25. "Twentieth Century-Fox, Crick, Munro," 12.
26. "Moodabes Sell an Interest in Amalgamated Theatres Ltd.," *Film Weekly*, October 8, 1936, 4.

27. Cliff Holt, "20th-Fox Widens Its Outlet in Australia: Company Is Handling Gratis Distribution in Commonwealth of Film Made Within Country," *Motion Picture Herald*, November 28, 1936, 96.
28. Moodabe, *Peanuts and Pictures*, 24, 25.
29. "Moodabes Sell an Interest," 4.
30. Moodabe, *Peanuts and Pictures*, 24, 25.
31. Moodabe, *Peanuts and Pictures*, 25.
32. "Whither Are We Tending? The New Amalgamation," *NZMPEB*, October 17, 1936, 1.
33. Statement "A," October 3, 1924, Container Code C 155 036, Archives Reference No BBNZ A1607 21462, Box 36, Record Number 41744, Cinema Properties Limited (Amalgamated Theatres Limited), ANZ-Auckland.
34. "Whither Are We Tending?," 1.
35. "Memorandum of Association," September 29, 1937, Container Code C 33 845; Archives Reference No BBNZ A1762 5181 Box 12134; Record Number 62777 (Amalgamated Theatres Holdings Ltd.), NZ-NA-Auckland.
36. "Proposals to Ensure New Zealand Control of Picture Theatre Business," November 8, 1937, IA 64/11, Archives New Zealand, Wellington (hereafter, ANZ-Wellington).
37. "Film Industry Board," *NZMPEB*, March 16, 1940, 1.
38. "Amalgamated Theatres Ltd," *NZMPEB*, May 25, 1940, 1.
39. Form of Annual Return of a Company Having a Share Capital, Amalgamated Theatres, June 5, 1941, Container Code C 87 870, Archives Reference No BADZ A32 5586 Box 130 Item Reference e, Record Number 1924/174 (Amalgamated Theatres Limited), ANZ-Auckland.
40. Moodabe, *Peanuts and Pictures*, 24, 25.
41. "New Zealand Motion Picture Exhibitors' Association Report of Dominion Executive. Presented to Annual Conference 21st January," *NZMPEB*, January 23, 1937, 1.
42. Tony Froude, *Where to Go on Saturday Night: Wellington Cinemas and Movie Halls 1896–2000* (Paraparaumu, NZ: T. Froude, 2000), 11–13.
43. Quoted in "Foreign Control in Australia: Will The Government Act?," *NZMPEB*, September 25, 1937, 1.
44. "Loew Circuit Adds 7,000 Seats Abroad," *Film Daily*, August 27, 1937, 1, 10.
45. "No Sale of St. James," *Smiths Weekly*, November 29, 1941, CP5/1, 16/271, Metro Goldwyn Mayer Pty. Ltd., NFSA.
46. "There Was Enough Money!," *Smiths Weekly*, December 6, 1941, CP5/1, 16/271, Metro Goldwyn Mayer Pty. Ltd., NFSA.
47. "GUO Takeover of MGM Chain Stirs Sydney Show Biz," *Variety*, April 21, 1971, 5.
48. Ross Thorne, *Cinemas of Australia via USA* (Sydney: Architecture Dept., University of Sydney, 1981), 80–87.
49. M. D. Bell, *Perth: A Cinema History* (Lewes, UK: Book Guild, 1986), 83–87.
50. Thorne, *Cinemas of Australia via USA*, 224–28.
51. "Hoyts Adds 6 Antip Cinemas," *Variety*, March 12, 1941, 13.
52. Andrew Pike and Ross Coon, *Australian Film, 1900–1977* (Melbourne: Oxford University Press in association with the Australian Film Institute, 1980), 188–89.
53. Dale Turnbull: Interviewed by Graham Shirley, 2001–2004 Oral History, Title No. 587140, Production Date March 12, 2004–March 12, 2004; Production Date: November 9, 2001, NFSA.
54. "Film Industry Board and Film Supply. Can The Board Adjudicate?," *Independent Exhibitor*, December 1, 1944, 1.
55. "British Films Only Plans of Theatre Circuit," *NZMPEB*, December 22, 1945, 6.

56. "British Films, Increased N.Z. Quota," *Evening Post*, March 9, 1946.
57. "British Film Industry," *Evening Star* (Dunedin), March 28, 1946; and "Visit of Mr. R. J. Kerridge to England," *NZMPEB*, April 13, 1946, 3.
58. "Films to Be Made in N.Z.? Plans of New Organisation," *Evening Post*, April 16, 1946, 7.
59. Brittenden, *The Celluloid Circus*, 282.
60. "Films to Be Made in N.Z.?," 7.
61. "Welcome Home to Mr R. J. Kerridge," *NZMPEB*, June 22, 1946, 2-4.
62. "Welcome Home to Mr R. J. Kerridge," 2-4.
63. "New Company Formed to Control Rank Film Interests in New Zealand," *NZMPEB*, July 20, 1946, 2.
64. "J. C. Williamson Picture Corp. Ltd. Now Under Rank-Kerridge Control," *NZMPEB*, August 31, 1946, 3.
65. "Cinematograph Films," Memorandum from the Board of Trade, September 27, 1946, NZ-NA-Wellington.
66. Moodabe, *Peanuts and Pictures*, 57.
67. Brittenden, *The Celluloid Circus*, 35.
68. Brittenden, *The Celluloid Circus*, 35.

7. Hollywood and Australasian Cinemas, 1946–1982

1. "WB to Build Australian 'Show Window' in Sydney," *Film Daily*, July 18, 1946, 5.
2. "WB's New Theatre Down Under Nixed," *Variety*, November 20, 1946, 28.
3. Stanley W. Higginson to The Town Clerk, May 22, 1947, Town Clerk's Department Correspondence Files, Municipal Council of Sydney / City of Sydney, City of Sydney Archives, Sydney, Australia (hereafter, CSA).
4. "Theatres and Films Commission, State Records Authority of New South Wales," Research Data Australia, https://researchdata.ands.org.au/theatres-and-films-commission/165541.
5. "Court Ban on Erection of Two Theatres" *Sydney Morning Herald*, August 12, 1947, 5.
6. "City Architect and Building Surveyor's Department," September 17, 1947, Development Application Files, Development and Building Collection [City of Sydney], CSA.
7. "Minute Paper," Proposed Theatre. 564 George Street And 80/88 Bathurst Street—Interim Development Application," April 8, 1948, Town Clerk's Department Correspondence Files, CSA.
8. E. W. Adams to The General Manager, Warner Bros. First National Pictures Pty. Ltd., April 22, 1948, Sydney Council Archive, CSA.
9. "WB to Sell Key Sydney Property," *Film Weekly*, August 20, 1953, 1.
10. "Minerva Going Over to Films Soon," *Sydney Morning Herald*, April 18, 1950, 4.
11. Martha Rutledge, "Martin, David Nathaniel (1898–1958)," *Australian Dictionary of Biography* (National Centre of Biography, Australian National University, 2000), http://adb.anu.edu.au/biography/martin-david-nathaniel-11069/text19703.
12. "Leo's Theatre Empire Grows," *Lion's Roar* (UK), May 26, 1950, 1.
13. Rebecca Gross, "The Minerva Theatre and Metro Kings Cross," *Dictionary of Sydney*, 2016, http://dictionaryofsydney.org/entry/the_minerva_theatre_and_metro_kings_cross.
14. "Public Wants Variety, Says Loew," *Film Weekly*, December 24, 1953, 1.
15. "MGM to Open Crows Nest This Month," *Film Weekly*, December 3, 1953, 1; and "Metro Crows Nest Opened," *Film Weekly*, December 31, 1953, 12.

16. "Patrons Are Proud of the New Metro," *Film Weekly*, February 25, 1954, 11.
17. "Hoyts To Spend £11/2m On C'scope £20,000 Per Theatre," *Film Weekly*, October 22, 1953, 1.
18. Interview with Joe Moodabe, February 13, 2001, Auckland Civic Theatre Year 2000 Oral Archive project (OHColl-0546), Alexander Turnbull Library, New Zealand National Library, Wellington, New Zealand (hereafter, NZNL).
19. Moodabe, *Peanuts and Pictures: The Life and Times of MJ Moodabe* ([New Zealand]: [Michael Moodabe?], [2000]), 32.
20. "'Robe' Hailed in Auckland," *Film Weekly*, December 10, 1953, 1.
21. Moodabe, *Peanuts and Pictures*, 36, 37.
22. Interview with Joe Moodabe, February 13, 2001, NZNL; and Moodabe, *Peanuts and Pictures*, 36, 37.
23. Moodabe, *Peanuts and Pictures*, 36, 37.
24. CinemaScope Advertisement, *Film Weekly*, December 10, 1953, 4.
25. "Spyros! You've DONE It, Spyros!" *Film Weekly*, December 10, 1953, 2.
26. Dale Turnbull: Interviewed by Graham Shirley, 2001–2004: Oral History, Title No. 587140, Production Date March 12, 2004–March 12, 2004; Production Date: November 9, 2001, NFSA.
27. "Theatre TV Next Step: Silverstone C'Scope 'Not the End,'" *Film Weekly*, January 14, 1954, 1, 6.
28. "Ins and Outs of Australia's First Big-Scale Drive-In Theatre," *Film Weekly*, February 25, 1954, 15; and "Burwood Skyline (Hoyts)," *Drive Ins Downunder*, April 3, 2019, http://drive-insdownunder.com.au/burwood/.
29. "Burwood Skyline (Hoyts)," *Drive Ins Downunder*.
30. Dale Turnbull interview, NFSA.
31. "Loew's Opens 1st Twin Drive-In in Australia," *Motion Picture Daily*, October 29, 1956, 1.
32. Margaret Simpson, "Remembering Australia's Drive-ins," Museum of Applied Arts & Sciences, February 9, 2016. https://maas.museum/inside-the-collection/2016/02/09/remembering-australias-drive-ins/.
33. "Clayton Metro Twin, Village Clayton," *Drive Ins Downunder*, May 13, 2019, http://drive-insdownunder.com.au/377-2/.
34. R. Brasch, *Australian Jews of Today and the Part They Have Played* (Stanmare: Cassell Australia, 1977), 44.
35. Moodabe, *Peanuts and Pictures*, 61.
36. Moodabe, *Peanuts and Pictures*, 43.
37. N. R. Ford to N. J. Clover, January 15, 1959, Folder 135, Kerridge Odeon Archive, Records, 1911–1987, Auckland War Museum, Auckland, New Zealand.
38. Bruce W. Hayward and Selwyn P. Hayward, *Cinemas of Auckland, 1896–1979* (Auckland: Lodestar, 1979), n.p.
39. Hayward and Hayward, *Cinemas of Auckland*, n.p.
40. Interview with Herbie Freeman, October 20, 2000, OHInt-0546-04, NZNL; and interview with Joe Moodabe, February 13, 2001, NZNL.
41. Tony Froude, *Where to Go on Saturday Night: Wellington Cinemas and Movie Halls 1896–2000* (Paraparaumu, NZ: T. Froude, 2000), 14, 15.
42. Moodabe, *Peanuts and Pictures*, 43.
43. "Hoyts Profit Affected by TV," *Film Weekly*, November 22, 1962, 3.
44. Dale Turnbull interview, NFSA.
45. Dale Turnbull interview, NFSA.

46. Dale Turnbull interview, NFSA.
47. "Big New Zealand Cinema Circuit in Hassle with RKO, Col on Terms," *Variety*, May 28, 1952, 10.
48. Moodabe, *Peanuts and Pictures*, 43.
49. Moodabe, *Peanuts and Pictures*, 44.
50. Moodabe, *Peanuts and Pictures*, 45.
51. Moodabe, *Peanuts and Pictures*, 15.
52. Dale Turnbull interview, NFSA.
53. "Sir Bernard Freeman, Dominant Figure in Film Dies at 86," *Australasian Cinema*, December 17, 1982, 10.
54. "Application for Development Permission," 107/111 Elizabeth Street [76/82 Castlereagh St.], Sydney, New building; theatres, shops and offices, Metro Goldwyn Mayer, April 30, 1969, Development Application Files, Development and Building Collection [City of Sydney], CSA; "City Building Surveyor's, Premises, Nos. 107/111 Elizabeth Street and Nos. 76/82 Castlereagh Street, Sydney—New Building—Interim Development Application," April 30, 1969, Development Application Files, Development and Building Collection [City of Sydney], CSA; and J. H. Luscombe to The Director, Metro Goldwyn Mayer Pty. Limited, August 1, 1969, Development Application Files, Development and Building Collection [City of Sydney], CSA.
55. "Application for Development Permission," 107/111 Elizabeth Street [76/82 Castlereagh St.], Sydney, New building; theatres, shops and offices, Metro Goldwyn Mayer, April 30, 1969, Development Application Files, Development and Building Collection [City of Sydney], SCA.
56. "Minute Paper 2043/69," Premises: Nos. 76/82 Castlereagh Street (West Side of Elizabeth Street Between King Street and Market Street)—New Building, Interim Development, June 26, 1969, Application, Development Application Files, Development and Building Collection [City of Sydney], CSA.
57. "Application for Development Permission," March 20, 1970, Development Application Files, Development and Building Collection [City of Sydney], CSA; and D. W. Baxter to The Town Clerk, The City Council, Town Hall, Sydney, March 20, 1970, Development Application Files, Development and Building Collection [City of Sydney], CSA.
58. "Fox, Like MGM, Unloading," *Variety*, July 8, 1970, 3.
59. "12 (of 14) Metro Australian Houses to Greater Union," *Variety*, April 7, 1971, 3, 22; Brittenden, *The Celluloid Circus*, 145–47.
60. "British Empire Films to Distrib MGM in Aussie," *Variety*, July 21, 1971, 20.
61. Dale Turnbull interview, NFSA.
62. Ross Thorne, *Australian Cinema Via USA* (Sydney: Architecture Dept., University of Sydney, 1981), 181–84.
63. "20th Century Fox Film Corporation (N.Z.) Limited Report of the Directors," December 15, 1975, Container Code C 33 845, Archives Reference No Bbnz A1762 5181 Box 12134, Record Number 62777, Amalgamated Theatres Holdings Ltd., ANZ-Auckland.
64. Brittenden, *The Celluloid Circus*, 38, 39.
65. R. E. Ferguson to R. A. Bullen, January 25, 1979, Container Code C 52 367, Archives Reference No Baja 5919, Box 22, Title Amalgamated Theatres Ltd., ANZ-Auckland; and "In Support of Application," ca. February 1979, Container Code C 52 367, Archives Reference No Baja 5919, Box 22, Title Amalgamated Theatres Ltd., ANZ-Auckland.

66. A. R. Dickinson, "Minute Sheet, Amalgamated Theatres Ltd. Appln. 29874," February 22, 1979, Container Code C 52 367, Archives Reference No Baja 5919, Box 22, Title Amalgamated Theatres Ltd., ANZ-Auckland.
67. "Agreement for Sale and Purchase of Urban Land, 103–107 Hobson Street, Auckland," September 2, 1980, Container Code C 155 036, Archives Reference No Bbnz A1607 21462, Box 36, Record Number 41744, Amalgamated Theatres Limited, ANZ-Auckland.
68. "Terry Jackman Sets Date for Brisbane Opening of Hoyts Entertainment Centre," *Australasian Cinema*, Friday, May 16, 1980, 2.
69. "Hollywood Stars for Bris. Hoyts Opening," *Australasian Cinema*, July 18, 1980, 3.
70. "Smash Hit Opening for Hoyts Entertainment Centre, Brisbane," *Australasian Cinema*, August 15, 1980, 3.
71. "Terry Jackman Pays Tribute," *Australasian Cinema*, August 15, 1980, 2.
72. "Forward Into the '80s With Optimism," *Australasian Cinema*, July 18, 1980, 3.
73. "Hoyts Distribution," *Australasian Cinema*, August 15, 1980, 4.
74. "Top Fox Execs Visit Aust.," *Australasian Cinema*, September 5, 1980, 1.
75. "Hoyts Open Newcastle Twin," *Australasian Cinema*, January 30, 1981, 5.
76. "Top Film Job to NZ Man," *NZ Herald*, May 7, 1981, n.p.; and "Hoyts Theatres, Aust.—Amalgamated Theatres, New Zealand, Merge; Royce Moodabe Co-Chairman of Hoyts Theatres," *Australasian Cinema*, Friday May 15, 1981, 1.
77. "June 8th Is D Day for Fox," *Australasian Cinema*, May 15, 1981, 1.
78. "June 8th Is D Day for Fox," 1.
79. "Xmas Messages from Industry Leaders: A Busy Year for Hoyts," *Australasian Cinema*, December 18, 1981, 3.
80. "Hoyts Up for Sale?," *Australasian Cinema*, February 5, 1982, 1.
81. "Stop Press | Hoyts Cinema Group Sold: Stardawn Investments of Melbourne Purchase Hoyts for $40 Million," *Australasian Cinema*, July 16, 1982, 8a.
82. "Xmas Messages from Industry Leaders: Terry Jackman: 1982: An Exciting Year for Hoyts," *Australasian Cinema*, December 17, 1982, 3.
83. "Stop Press," 8a.
84. "GUO Purchases Hoyts' Interest In 21 Drive-Ins," *Australasian Cinema*, August 6, 1982, 1.
85. Richard Fletcher, "Theatre Chain's Future Ownership in Doubt," *Business Review*, February 15, 1982.
86. "Declaration as to Change of Name," August 6, 1982, Container Code C 33 845, Archives Reference No Bbnz A1762 5181 Box 12134, Record Number 62777, Amalgamated Theatres Holdings Ltd., ANZ-Auckland.
87. Amalgamated Theatres Ltd. Press Release, August 18, 1982, Ngā Taonga Publicity Files, Jonathan Dennis Library, Ngā Taonga Sound & Vision (archives), Wellington, New Zealand.
88. "NZ Amalgamated Theatres May Grow," *Australasian Cinema*, November 12, 1982, 2.
89. Amalgamated Theatres Ltd. Press Release, August 18, 1982; and "Amalgamated Theatres N.Z. Now Owned by Chase Holdings Ltd.," *Australasian Cinema*, September 10, 1982, 1.
90. "Interview with Eric Kearney, Printed Transcript," OHA-3077, Auckland Civic Theatre Year 2000 Oral Archive project, 2001, New Zealand National Library.
91. "Sir Bernard Freeman, Dominant Figure in Film Dies at 86," 10.
92. "Theatre Man Dies," *Evening Post* (Wellington, NZ), February 16, 1985, 3.

418   7. Hollywood and Australasian Cinemas

93. "Rupert Murdoch Buys 50% of 20th Century Fox," *Australasian Cinema*, March 29–April 4, 1985, 1.
94. Claudia Eller, "Warner, Village Roadshow Plan 20-Movie Joint Venture," *Los Angeles Times*, December 10, 1997.
95. Patrick Frater, "Warner Bros. Cuts Village Roadshow Theatrical Ties in Australia, New Zealand," *Variety*, September 21, 2020, https://variety.com/2020/biz/asia/warner-ends-village-roadshow-theatrical-deal-australia-new-zealand-1234777255/.
96. Tom Dillane, "Pioneer of the NZ Cinema Industry Joe Moodabe, 'Mr Movie,' Dies 82," *New Zealand Herald*, December 14, 2019, https://www.nzherald.co.nz/nz/pioneer-of-the-nz-cinema-industry-joe-moodabe-mr-movie-dies-82/V434VXHEUXQHZRL76GLNS2EHWQ/.
97. John Drinnan, "'M' Is For Movies—And Joe Moodabe," *New Zealand Herald*, November 10, 2006, https://www.nzherald.co.nz/business/news/article.cfm?c_id=3&objectid=10410245.
98. Philip Wakefield, "SHORT END: Royce Rolls Off, Croft Clocks In," *OnFilm*, August 2006, https://web.archive.org/web/20110724191752/http://archivecentral.co.nz/?webid=ONF&articleid=22854.

8. Cine Metros y Cine Paramounts, 1926–1941

1. "Films Encourage Trade Relations Between the Americas, Says Day," *Moving Picture World*, February 7, 1920, 904.
2. "Films Encourage Trade Relations," 904; and "Cheap Films Face Hard Fight in So. America," *Motion Picture News*, January 29, 1921, 986. In addition to Brazil and the Cinema Avenida, Paramount had already secured a relationship with the American-owned 3,500-seat Olimpia in Mexico City by 1921. The theater was part of R. P. Jennings' American-owned circuit of roughly twenty cinemas. "Paramount Arranges for Its Film Distribution in Mexico," *Moving Picture World*, January 21, 1922, 299; and "After S. A. Trade," *Wid's Daily*, January 20, 1921, 5.
3. "Cheap Films Face Hard Fight in So. America," 986.
4. Fox Film Corporation Ad, *Cine-Mundial*, April 1923, 249.
5. Alice Gonzaga, *Palácios e Poeiras: 100 Anos de Cinemas no Rio de Janeiro* (Rio de Janeiro: Ed. Record, 1996), 138.
6. João Miguel Valencise, "A Chegada Do Som Nos Cinemas: De São Paulo Segundo A Folha Da Manhã (1928–1933)" (Ph.D. diss., São Carlos, Universidade Federal De São Carlos, 2012), 41.
7. Gonzaga, *Palácios e Poeiras*, 138; "M.-G.-M. to Operate 44 Houses in Brazil Through Owners Arrangement," *Motion Picture News*, December 11, 1926, 2229; "M-G-M Theatre Deal New Move: South American Arrangement Unique; Elms, Bernstein to Manage Houses," *Motion Picture News*, December 25, 1926, 2408; and "M.-G.-M. Assumes Operation of 44 Brazilian Theaters," *Billboard*, December 11, 1926, 54.
8. "J. D. Elms Made Gen. Manager of Loew Theaters in Brazil," *Billboard*, December 18, 1926, 16.
9. Luciana Corrêa de Araujo, "'Cinema as an Event': Stage Attractions and Screen at the Cineteatro Santa Helena in São Paulo (1927)," *Significação* 45, no. 49 (January–June 2018): 19–38.
10. Corrêa de Araujo, "'Cinema as an Event'," 24.

11. Valencise, "A Chegada Do Som Nos Cinemas," 78.
12. "Loew's Sell 18 Film Houses in Brazil," *Variety*, January 4, 1928, 12.
13. Corrêa de Araujo, "'Cinema as an Event'," 34–35.
14. Corrêa de Araujo, "'Cinema as an Event'," 28–29.
15. Valencise, "A Chegada Do Som Nos Cinemas," 41; and Isaac Franckel, "Cinema Rialto," *Metrogramma*, January 18, 1928.
16. "Loew's Sell 18 Film Houses in Brazil," 12; and Document, List of São Paulo Cinemas Under EMPREZAS REUNIDAS-METRO-GOLDWYN-MAYER, LTDA. November 3, 1927, Processo No. 45473, São Paulo Municipal Archive / Prefeitura Municipal de S. Paulo.
17. Valencise, "A Chegada Do Som Nos Cinemas," 41; and Franckel, "Cinema Rialto."
18. "São Paulo Hears Its First Sound Film," *New York Times*, April 14, 1929, 9.
19. Valencise, "A Chegada Do Som Nos Cinemas," 36.
20. Valencise, "A Chegada Do Som Nos Cinemas," 36.
21. Valencise, "A Chegada Do Som Nos Cinemas," 46.
22. E. E. Shauer, "Foreign Market Awake," *Exhibitors Herald-World*, June 15, 1929, 127.
23. Shauer, "Foreign Market Awake," 127.
24. "Loew Launching Theatre Program to Cover Globe," *Motion Picture Daily*, March 20, 1935, 1, 7.
25. "Loew-MGM Building Theatres Abroad to Insure Representation," *Motion Picture Herald*, June 27, 1936, 32.
26. "Loew Launching Theatre Program to Cover Globe," 1, 7.
27. "More Houses for MGM in Foreign Keys," *Motion Picture Daily*, November 22, 1935, 1, 6.
28. "World Drive for Theatres Set by Loew," *Motion Picture Daily*, March 20, 1935, 7; and "Loew-MGM Building Theatres Abroad to Insure Representation," 32.
29. "Loew-MGM Building Theatres Abroad to Insure Representation," 32. Loew's did not completely abandon the idea of building a chain like Empresas Reunidas-MGM. In Mexico City in 1936 the company organized ten local cinemas, including the Cine Iris, into a small network of MGM-related but not owned cinemas. That move was matched by RKO, which also reportedly organized fourteen cinemas, "operating as two separate circuits," *Film Daily* reported, "for the exclusive showing of its product in Mexico City." These cinemas were not owned by MGM, and thus lie outside the scope of this book, but represent efforts, once more, to find creative strategies for MGM distribution and control over the exhibition thereof in competitive markets. "10 Mexican Houses Lined Up by M-G-M," *Film Daily*, February 28, 1936, 1, 4.
30. "Moskowitz to Start House in Santiago," *Motion Picture Daily*, September 14, 1935, 3.
31. Ken Roe, "Cine Metro," Cinema Treasures, n.d., http://cinematreasures.org/theaters/25004.
32. "New Movie House in Lima: President Attends Opening of Metro-Goldwyn-Mayer Theatre," *New York Times*, May 3, 1936, 39.
33. "Cine Metro, New Rio Theatre, A Neo-Classic," *Boxoffice*, November 14, 1936, 45.
34. James Fitzpatrick, dir. *Glimpses of Peru* (documentary short, MGM, 1937); and James Fitzpatrick, *Chile: 'Land of Charm'* (documentary short, MGM, 1937).
35. "Brazil—Competitors & Competitive Grosses," 99AN/1F, Box 1, Folder 7, United Artists Corporation Records/Wisconsin Historical Society, (hereafter, UA-WHS).

36. João Luiz Vieira and Margarete C. S. Pereira, "Cinemas da Metro e a dominação ideológica" (Metro cinemas and the ideological domination), *Filme Cultura*, August 1986, 59–61.
37. "O fim do Çinema Carioca," Unknown. August 5, 1995, Cinédia Archive, Rio de Janeiro, Brazil.
38. Vieira and Pereira, "Cinemas da Metro e a dominação ideológica," 59–61.
39. As one internal United Artists report noted at the time of Rio's cinematic balconies, "hardly anyone goes there and the people dislike being forced into the balcony" during "a successful picture." "Brazil—General," UA-WHS, 99AN/1F, Box 1, Folder 5.
40. Photo caption, *Better Theatres*, September 19, 1936, 5.
41. A. Weissmann, "Metro Opens First Run in Rio Janeiro," *Motion Picture Daily*, October 26, 1936, 11.
42. "Melniker Made MGM Foreign Theatres Head," *Motion Picture Daily*, June 9, 1936, 1, 7; and "Alumni News," *Cornell Alumni News*, October 8, 1936, 17.
43. Weissmann, "Metro Opens First Run," 11.
44. Vieira and Pereira, "Cinemas da Metro e a dominação ideológica," 59–61.
45. Gonzaga, *Palácios e Poeiras*, 182.
46. "Building Fever in Rio, 13 on Way; Par, Metro Plan New S. A. Cinemas," *Variety*, August 11, 1937, 25.
47. "CHATTER—Montevideo," *Variety*, October 14, 1936, 68; Paul Bodo, "Uruguay, Film-Conscious, Turns to Launching Ten New Theatres," *Motion Picture Herald*, May 16, 1936, 64; and Paul Bodo, "New Company Starts First Uruguay Film," *Motion Picture Herald*, January 25, 1937, 11.
48. Loew's International executives filled any gaps in its schedule by securing a contract to exhibit eighteen Twentieth Century-Fox films as well. Bodo, "New Company Starts First Uruguay Film," 11.
49. Delmaur Ltd. also operated six cinemas in Montevideo. Bodo, "Uruguay, Film-Conscious," 64.
50. Paul Bodo, "Glucksmann in Uruguay Marks Forty Years," *Motion Picture Herald*, December 7, 1946, 65. MGM was not the only company making exhibition inroads in 1936; Gaumont-British also rented the seven-hundred-seat Teatro Urquiza in Montevideo as its own shop window, demonstrating the city's rising importance.
51. "Metro Adding 5 Houses to Int. Chain," *Variety*, May 19, 1937, 6.
52. E.R.M. (MGM Do Brasil) to Mayor of São Paulo, July 13, 1937, Cinema Metro, São Paulo, São Paulo Municipal Archive, São Paulo, Brazil; and "Memorandum for the Construction of a Building for Cinema and Offices," Cinema Metro, São Paulo, July 13, 1937, São Paulo Municipal Archive, São Paulo, Brazil.
53. "This Week in Pictures," *Motion Picture Herald*, May 14, 1938, 10.
54. "Hoy: El Metro De São Paulo, Brasil," *Cine-Mundial*, April 1940, 5A.
55. "Melniker Going to Brazil for Loew House Opening," *Film Daily*, February 4, 1938, 2.
56. Cine Metro, São Paulo Inaugural Souvenir Program, Cinemateca Brasileira, São Paulo, Brazil.
57. Jose Inacio de Melo Souza, *Salas De Cinema: E Historia Urbana São Paulo (1895–1930)* (São Paulo: Editora Senac São Paulo, 2016), 344.
58. "Loew Acquires 7 New Theatres in Latin America," *Motion Picture Herald*, November 9, 1946, 48.
59. "UA Entering Brazil Exhib'n Via 3 Houses," *Film Daily*, October 18, 1939, 1, 7.
60. "Latin America Eyed by Metro and UA for Theatre Expansion," *Variety*, August 9, 1939, 11.

61. "UA Entering Brazil Exhib'n Via 3 Houses," 1, 7.
62. "UA Will Invade Detroit, Chicago Theater Fields," *Film Daily*, September 10, 1941, 4.

9. Prop(aganda) Window Cinemas, 1933–1945

1. Luiz Nazario, "Nazi Film Politics in Brazil, 1933–42," in *Cinema and the Swastika: The International Expansion of Third Reich Cinema*, ed. Roel Vande Winkel and D. Welch (New York: Palgrave Macmillan, 2007), 85.
2. Nazario, "Nazi Film Politics in Brazil, 1933–42," 87.
3. Quoted in Nazario, "Nazi Film Politics in Brazil, 1933–42," 88.
4. Nazario, "Nazi Film Politics in Brazil, 1933–42," 91.
5. Nazario, "Nazi Film Politics in Brazil, 1933–42," 91.
6. Nazario, "Nazi Film Politics in Brazil, 1933–42," 91.
7. "Consolida-Se A Av. São João," *Diario de São Paulo*, May 9, 1954.
8. Debora Cordeiro Rosa, *Trauma, Memory and Identity in Five Jewish Novels from the Southern Cone* (Lanham, MD.: Rowman & Littlefield, 2014), 45.
9. Nazario, "Nazi Film Politics in Brazil, 1933–42," 88.
10. Nazario, "Nazi Film Politics in Brazil, 1933–42," 94.
11. Nazario, "Nazi Film Politics in Brazil, 1933–42," 88–95.
12. L. S. Marinho, "Exhibition in Brazil Feels War Effects," *Motion Picture Herald*, November 25, 1939, 33.
13. "Brazil's President Welcomes Mr. Kent," *New Dynamo*, June 3, 1939, 18A.
14. "Brazil Film Biz Good, 20th-Fox's Bavetta Reports," *Film Daily*, January 27, 1941, 2.
15. Nazario, "Nazi Film Politics in Brazil, 1933–42," 94.
16. Alfredo C. Machado, "Axis Sent 19 Films to Brazil in 1941," *Motion Picture Herald*, October 10, 1942, 48.
17. Nazario, "Nazi Film Politics in Brazil, 1933–42," 95–96.
18. Vincent De Pascal, "Nazi Grip Closes on Argentine Movie Industry," *Christian Science Monitor*, June 26, 1941, 11.
19. De Pascal, "Nazi Grip Closes," 11.
20. "Chile Nazis' Propaganda Cinema," *Variety*, October 22, 1941, 18.
21. "Burger to Open Two New Loew Houses in Brazil," *Film Daily*, November 26, 1940, 2.
22. "Metro Plans Erection of Brazilian Theaters, *Film Daily*, March 8, 1940, 2; and "Metro Adds More Theatres in Brazil," *Motion Picture Daily*, March 8, 1940, 1.
23. "New Nabe Sites in Rio Eyed for M-G Theatres," *Variety*, March 13, 1940, 14.
24. "Yanks Cue Brazil on Modernizing, Theatre Building," *Variety*, September 24, 1941, 16.
25. "Yanks Cue Brazil on Modernizing," 16.
26. Alice Gonzaga, *Palácios e Poeiras: 100 Anos de Cinemas no Rio de Janeiro* (Rio de Janeiro: Ed. Record, 1996), 306.
27. "Brazil–Competitors & Competitive Grosses," ca. August 1935; "Brazil-Competitive Grosses," ca. September 1942; both from 99AN/1F, Box 1, Folder 7, Black Books, Foreign Statistics: United Artists Corporation Records, Series 1F, circa 1935–circa 1950, UA-WHS; and "Brazil-Taxes," ca. July 1941, 99AN/1F, Box 1, Folder 6, Black Books, Foreign Statistics: United Artists Corporation Records, Series 1F, circa 1935-circa 1950, UA-WHS.
28. "Latin America Eyed by Metro and UA for Theatre Expansion," *Variety*, August 9, 1939, 11; and "Burger Finds M-G Biz Okay in Latin America," *Variety*, October 8, 1941, 16.

29. "Metro Will Construct Second Chilean House," *Film Daily*, Tuesday, November 18, 1941, 2; "M-G'S 8TH in S. A.," *Variety*, December 3, 1941, 15; "New M-G-M Theater Gets the Green Light," *Film Daily*, November 21, 1941, 5; and "Theatre Planned in Chile," *Motion Picture Herald*, November 22, 1941, 14.
30. Ken Roe, "Cine Central," Cinema Treasures, n.d., http://cinematreasures.org/theaters/25179.
31. "Warners Buy Lima House, Theater Site in Sydney," *Film Daily*, March 16, 1943, 2; "Modification of Lease," July 22, 1946, Lima, Peru-Central Theatre Folder, WB-USC; "Lease Digest Form," May 9, 1947, Lima, Peru-Central Theatre Folder, WB-USC; and D. W. Cherry to H. V. Linnekin, November 5, 1956, Box 1584A, Central Theatre Folder, WB-USC.
32. "Warners Buy Theater Site in Mexico City," *Film Daily*, February 11, 1943, 6; and "Warners Boosts Outlets in Australia, Palestine," *Film Daily*, May 17, 1944, 7.
33. "Warners Buy Theater Site in Mexico City," 6.
34. Lou Pelegrine, "Brazil Set for Post-War Boom; U.S. Firms Alert: 20th-Fox Leases Rio's Palacio as 'Show Window'; To Extend Franchise Policy," *Film Daily*, January 14, 1944, 1, 9; and Ray Josephs, "Increasing Threat of Mexican Pix Pointed Up by Latin-Amer. Survey," *Variety*, July 26, 1944, 19.
35. "A Reabertura do Cine Palácio," *Correio da Noite*, December 3, 1943; and Pelegrine, "Brazil Set for Post-War Boom," 1, 9.
36. Alfredo C. Machado, "Group in Brazil to Study Protection of Home Industry," *Motion Picture Herald*, October 28, 1944, 62.
37. Pelegrine, "Brazil Set for Post-War Boom," 1, 9.
38. "American Showcase in Rio," *Better Theatres*, March 4, 1944, 72.
39. Ray Josephs, "Increasing Threat of Mexican Pix Pointed Up by Latin-Amer. Survey," *Variety*, July 26, 1944, 19.
40. "Colombia House First UA Foreign Showcase," *Film Daily*, March 15, 1944, 1, 9.
41. "Films in Spanish Create New Audience," *Film Daily*, July 7, 1944, 3.
42. "Heavy Building in South and Central Americas, Says Daff," *Motion Picture Daily*, January 10, 1944, 1, 8.
43. "Argentina Lifts Ban on Anti-Nazi Movies," *Christian Science Monitor*, April 13, 1945, 2.

10. Hollywood Cinema Expansion in Postwar South America, 1945–1973

1. "Warners Considering Brazil 'Showcases,'" *Motion Picture Daily*, July 18, 1944, 1, 8.
2. Alfredo C. Machado, "Group in Brazil to Study Protection of Home Industry," *Motion Picture Herald*, October 28, 1944, 62.
3. "Osserman Says Majors Should Build in Brazil," *Motion Picture Herald*, June 9, 1945, 43.
4. "WB Is Third to Set Foreign Theatre Plans," *Motion Picture Daily*, June 21, 1945, 1, 7.
5. "20th Partner Policy Abroad Will Continue," *Motion Picture Daily*, July 6, 1945, 1, 6.
6. "Studio Size-Ups," *Film Bulletin*, September 17, 1945, 2.
7. "Business Up 37% In South America," *Motion Picture Daily*, December 18, 1945, 1, 12.
8. "Dubbing Boosts Latin Trade 50% in Year," *Motion Picture Daily*, December 21, 1945, 3.
9. "Business Up 37% In South America," 1, 12.

10. Andrew Paxman, *Jenkins of Mexico: How a Southern Farm Boy Became a Mexican Magnate* (Oxford: Oxford University Press, 2017), 271–73.
11. "M-G-M May Enter Mexican Exhibition," *Motion Picture Daily*, December 27, 1945, 1.
12. "F-WC's Pre-Fabs Hit Snag in Mex," *Variety*, September 11, 1946, 11; and "20th-Fox Buying into Jenkins Mex. Houses," *Film Daily*, October 26, 1946, 1, 3.
13. "Macdonald Reports Building in Mexico," *Motion Picture Daily*, April 25, 1946, 8; "Mex Boom of Theatre Bldg.," *Variety*, November 14, 1945, 13; and "Personal Mention," *Motion Picture Daily*, December 4, 1946, 2.
14. "WB's Colombia HQ Shifted to Bogotá," *Film Daily*, July 31, 1946, 1; "Warners Adding to Foreign Theatres," *Motion Picture Daily*, September 18, 1946, 2; "Bogotá Deluxe to WB," *Film Daily*, September 18, 1946, 1, 3; "Warners Acquire Theatre in Bogotá, Colombia," *Motion Picture Herald*, September 21, 1946, 37; and "Warners Buy Theatre," *Motion Picture Herald*, January 6, 1947, 2.
15. "M-G-M Opening 2nd In Bogotá, Col.," *Film Daily*, August 26, 1947, 1.
16. "Radio Plays Big Role in Bogotá," *Motion Picture Herald*, November 1, 1947, 44.
17. "Loew, Dietz, Speak at MGM Convention," *Motion Picture Daily*, February 10, 1949, 6.
18. "Burger to Columbia to Open Showcase," *Motion Picture Daily*, December 9, 1946, 2.
19. "Melniker Unveils S. A. House," *Film Daily*, December 13, 1946, 1, 4.
20. "Metro Will Have Four in Columbia," *Motion Picture Daily*, July 8, 1947, 3; and "New MGM House Opened in Bogotá, Colombia," *Motion Picture Herald*, August 30, 1947, 41.
21. "Loew Acquires 7 New Theatres in Latin America," *Motion Picture Herald*, November 9, 1946, 139; "Loew's to Open 4 New Theatres, 3 Remodeled Ones in Latin-America," *Variety*, November 6, 1946, 23; and "Loew's Sets Latin American Expansion," *Showmen's Trade Review*, November 9, 1946, 9.
22. "See Wave of New Theatres Abroad," *Variety*, November 6, 1946, 23.
23. "Loew Acquires 7 New Theatres," 140; "Loew's to Open 4 New Theatres," 23; and "Loew's Sets Latin American Expansion," 9.
24. "M-G's Upped Grosses in So. America Prove Dubbed Pix Top Titled Versions," *Variety*, June 12, 1946, 15.
25. "Loew to Have 42 Foreign Houses by End of 1947," *Motion Picture Herald*, February 15, 1947, 49.
26. "Crystal on Looksee for Latin-Amer. Showcases," *Variety*, September 4, 1946, 19.
27. "Para. Theatre in Peru," *Motion Picture Daily*, September 26, 1947, 4.
28. "Para. Int'l Previews Lima Theater Bow," *Film Daily*, October 3, 1947, 1, 7.
29. "20th Partner Policy Abroad Will Continue," 1, 6.
30. Ray Josephs, "Chile Postwar Show Biz Trend up but Dollar Exchange Lack Balks H'wood," *Variety*, November 12, 1947, 17.
31. "Anti-Trust Scare Even Cuts Par-20th Pool in Lima, Peru, Showcase," *Variety*, June 25, 1947, 9, 18.
32. "Projecting Paramount Pictures in Peru: Tacna Theater in Lima," *Architectural Record*, April 1949, 92–97.
33. "Tacna Theatre Lima, Peru," *Boxoffice*, November 20, 1948, 22.
34. "Coming and Going," *Film Daily*, February 10, 1948, 2.
35. "Weltner, Pratchett Off on Latin American Tour," *Film Daily*, March 8, 1948, 2.
36. "Ray Milland Helps Bally Par's New Lima Showcase," *Variety*, March 24, 1948, 15; and "Para. Launches Lima House," *Film Daily*, April 1, 1948, 2.
37. "Tacna Theatre Lima, Peru," 22.

38. "Ray Milland Helps Bally Par's New Lima Showcase," 15; and "Coming and Going," *Film Daily*, March 10, 1948, 2.
39. "Para. Launches Lima House," 2.
40. Empire and Ritz (MGM, 1928), the Warner West End (WB, 1938), Carlton and Regent (Fox, 1954), and Paramount (Plaza).
41. Paul W. Drake, "International Crises and Popular Movements in Latin America," in *Latin America in the 1940's: War and Postwar Transitions*, ed. David Rock (Berkeley: University of California Press, 1994), 111–17.
42. Ayumi Takenaka, "The Japanese in Peru: History of Immigration, Settlement, and Racialization," *Latin American Perspectives* 31, no. 3 (May 2004): 77–98.
43. Clement Crystal, "Foreign Theater Operation," *Journal of the Society of Motion Picture Engineers* 50, no. 4 (April 1948): 344–49.
44. LaKecia Shockley, "Paramount Theatre in Marshall Is Being Sold—On eBay," *KSLA News*, September 24, 2008, http://www.ksla.com/story/9065778/paramount-theatre-in-marshall-is-being-sold-on-ebay.
45. "Inside Stuff—Picures," *Variety*, July 20, 1949, 18.
46. T. A. Wise, "Loew's to Expand Independent Film Use, Open More Foreign Theatres," *Wall Street Journal*, December 23, 1955, 5; and "Loew's Profit at $5,311,733," *Motion Picture Daily*, January 17, 1956, 7.
47. Edwin Schallert, "More U.S. Film Gains Forecast at Parley Here," *Los Angeles Times*, February 7, 1956, A1.
48. Thomas M. Pryor, "Loew's to Widen Foreign Holdings," *New York Times*, February 7, 1956, 28.
49. Even today, the current operator, Tango Porteno, refers to the old Metro as "luxurious . . . the embodiment of refined ambience; a treasured Metro Goldwyn Mayer movie theater from bygone years." "The Location," Tango Porteno website, https://tangoporteno.com.ar/eng/.
50. Emmet John Hughes, "Who's Who in Struggle for Loew's," *Film Bulletin*, September 2, 1957, 27.
51. "O Cine Marrocos: Sob Nova Bande," *Cine-Reporter*, May 16, 1959, 1; and "Theatres," *Twentieth Century-Fox 1965 Annual Report*, New York: Twentieth Century-Fox, 1966, 1, New York Public Library for the Performing Arts.
52. Francisco Noriyuki Sato, "Cine Niterói," Cultura Japonesa website, n.d., http://www.culturajaponesa.com.br/index.php/historia/imigracao/cine-niteroi/.
53. Toho Paramount Theater Opening Program, August 26, 1960, Cinemateca Brasileira, São Paulo, Brazil.
54. William Gabel, "Toho La Brea Theatre," Cinema Treasures website, http://cinematreasures.org/theaters/2293; and Bryan Krefft, "Bijou Theatre, New York, NY," Cinema Treasures, website, http://cinematreasures.org/theaters/2932.
55. Program, Metro Boavista—Rua Do Passeio, January 23, 1969, Cinédia Archive, Rio de Janeiro, Brazil.
56. "Theatres," *Twentieth Century-Fox 1965 Annual Report*, 1.
57. "Metro's Panama Site," *Variety*, April 2, 1969, 35; and "Antiguo Teatro Metro Será Remozado," *La Estrella de Panamá*, March 22, 2013.
58. Over the next decade, Panama City would remain a viable hub for MGM and then CIC investment, as the consolidated global distribution and exhibition company bought two lots on Avenida Balboa in 1975 for $280,000 and opened another (CIC-managed) Cine Metro there in 1980. "Cine Metro Se Transforma," *La Prensa*, August 6, 2013.

59. "MGM Due to Split with EMI in Brit.; Distrib Via CIC," *Variety*, November 7, 1973, 4.
60. "CIC Puts All Brazil Activity under Fucs," *Variety*, September 1, 1976, 39.
61. "CIC Buys Condor, 11-Site Brazil Chain," *Variety*, August 25, 1976, 35.
62. Ira Lee, "Brazil Complains of Film Theatres Loss; Hurts Producers," *Variety*, March 2, 1977, 43.
63. Danúsia Bárbara, "Uma Questão de Progresso," clipping, MAM, Modern Art Museum of Rio de Janeiro, Rio de Janeiro, Brazil.
64. Hugo Sukman, "Transformação Na Sala Escura," *O Globo*, May 1, 1997, 1, 2.
65. "O Valioso Espaço das Salas De Projeção," clipping, July 13, 1978, 3, MAM, Modern Art Museum of Rio de Janeiro, Rio de Janeiro, Brazil. "O Metro Tem A Melhor Projeção Tela E Pipoca," *O Globo*, July 14, 1995.
66. Aydano André Morta, "Closing Threatens Rio's Best Cinema," *O Globo*, March 27, 1997; and "Boavista Metro Is the Ball of the Time," *Journal Do Brasil* (Rio), April 15, 1997.
67. Sukman, "Transformação Na Sala Escura," 1, 2.
68. "Bogotá Theatre MGM's Newest in So. America," *LO!*, August 1947, 12.
69. "The Week in Colombia," JAN 76, FM AMEMBASSY BOGOTÁ TO SECSTATE WASHDC 2622. AAD Files, NARA.
70. Talitha Ferraz, "Cine Centímetro: Memories and Cinemagoing Practices in an MGM Replica Cinema in the Rio de Janeiro Countryside," in *Rural Cinema Exhibition and Audiences in a Global Context, Global Cinema*, ed. Daniela Treveri Gennari, Danielle Hipkins, and Catherine O'Rawe (Oxford: Palgrave Macmillan, 2008), 340, 347.
71. Ferraz, "Cine Centímetro."

11. Caribbean Dreams, 1929–1973

1. "Central America Deal," *Variety*, December 14, 1917, 50.
2. "Paramount-Artcraft Expands in South," *Motion Picture World*, December 29, 1917, 1923.
3. Caribbean Film Company Advertisement, *Cine-Mundial*, January 1920, 57.
4. "Richards Is President of Saenger Theaters," *Film Daily*, March 19, 1929, 9.
5. Phil M. Daly, "Along the Rialto," *Film Daily*, December 22, 1931, 4.
6. "Saenger Link," *Variety*, June 5, 1929, 6.
7. Gil Péerez, "Los Grandes Teatros Modernos," *Cine-Mundial*, December 1928, 1036, 1059.
8. "Foreign Market Awake," *Exhibitors Herald-World*, June 15, 1929, 127.
9. "Leonard Grossman Discusses Merchandising in Cuba," *Motion Picture News*, July 5, 1930, 44.
10. "Warner Havana Theatre," *Motion Picture News*, February 22, 1930, 15.
11. Daly, "Along the Rialto," 4.
12. "British Film Rule Decried in Jamaica," *Christian Science Monitor*, January 31, 1928, 6.
13. Keith Q. Warner, *On Location: Cinema and Film in the Anglophone Caribbean* (London: MacMillan-Caribbean, 2000), 7; see also Dave Rodney, "The Golden Age of Cinema in Jamaica—Movie Theatres Doubled as Stageshow Venues," *Daily Gleaner*, August 25, 2019, http://jamaica-gleaner.com/article/entertainment/20190825/golden-age-cinema-jamaica-movie-theatres-doubled-stageshow-venues. Warner's analysis

426   11. Caribbean Dreams

here syncs up with Laura Fair's own estimation of foreign cinemas' influence on another British colony, Tanzania. Laura Fair, *Reel Pleasures: Cinema Audiences and Entrepreneurs in Twentieth-Century Urban Tanzania* (Athens: Ohio University Press, 2018).

14. "Paramount-Famous Lasky to Acquire Saenger Theatres," *Daily Gleaner*, August 14, 1929, 1; and "Notice," *Daily Gleaner*, August 31, 1927, 2. That move had instantly bumped Sanger's E. V. Richards, general manager of the Saenger chain, to a vice president role with Publix Theatres, the operating subsidiary of the Paramount Famous-Lasky Corp. "Paramount-Famous Lasky," 1.
15. "Saengers Expansion on in Panama and Jamaica," *Film Daily*, August 25, 1927, 4.
16. "Member of the Movie Co. on Visit Here," *Daily Gleaner*, April 9, 1930, 17.
17. "Taking Pictures of Jamaica to Show in Canada," *Daily Gleaner*, April 27, 1929, 3.
18. James Burns, *Cinema and Society in the British Empire, 1895–1940* (New York: Palgrave Macmillan, 2013), 153.
19. Primnath Gooptar, "Indian Influences in the Development of the Cinema Industry in Trinidad and Tobago (Excerpted from my Ph.D. Thesis. Impact of Indian Movies on East Indian Identity in Trinidad, 2013)." Gooptar's article was once available at https://primnathgooptar.com, but that website is no longer available. See also Burns, *Cinema and Society*, 154.
20. Gooptar, "Indian Influences." See also Burns, *Cinema and Society*, 154.
21. "Moving Pictures for Port-of Spain," *Daily Gleaner*, April 8, 1932, 9; "Big Film Fight Now on in Trinidad," *Daily Gleaner*, April 18, 1932, 4; and "Battle of the Films Starts in Trinidad," *Daily Gleaner*, June 20, 1932, 23.
22. "Moving Pictures for Port-of Spain," 9.
23. "Big Film Fight Now on in Trinidad," 4; and "Battle of the Films Starts in Trinidad," 23.
24. "Coming & Going," *Film Daily*, April 27, 1932, 6; "Trinidad Exhibs Here," *Film Daily*, April 27, 1932, 8; and "Anyhow, Trade Is Good in Trinidad Islands," *Variety*, May 3, 1932, 11.
25. "MGM in West Indies" *Motion Picture Herald*, June 18, 1932, 48.
26. "Building in Islands," *Variety*, June 28, 1932, 19.
27. "American Films for British West Indies," *Scotsman*, July 4, 1932, 11.
28. "Battle of the Films Starts in Trinidad," 23.
29. "Legal Battle over Lease of Building to Film Co. in Trinidad," *Daily Gleaner*, July 25, 1932, 16.
30. "West Indian News by Cable," *Daily Gleaner*, October 28, 1933, 16.
31. Gooptar, "Indian Influences."
32. Gooptar, "Indian Influences."
33. Gooptar, "Indian Influences."
34. Burns, *Cinema and Society*, 154–55.
35. Upon gaining control from the Spanish following the Spanish-American War, the United States Anglicized and renamed the island Porto Rico in 1898. It did not revert back to Puerto Rico until the U.S. Congress approved the change in May 1932. "'Foreign in a Domestic Sense': Hispanic Americans in Congress During the Age of U.S. Colonialism and Global Expansion, 1898–1945," History, Art & Archives, U.S. House of Representatives, https://history.house.gov/Exhibitions-and-Publications/HAIC/Historical-Essays/Foreign-Domestic/Introduction/.
36. "Cuban Film Situation Meeting Severe Test," *Film Daily*, July 5, 1931, 8.

37. Naida Garcia-Crespo, *Stateless Nation Building: Early Puerto Rican Cinema and Identity Formation (1897–1940)* (Ph.D. diss., University of Illinois at Urbana-Champaign, Urbana, Illinois, 2015), 310.
38. Nelson Denis, *War Against All Puerto Ricans: Revolution and Terror in America's Colony* (New York: Nation Books, 2015), 55, 56.
39. "Decree Sales Policy Without P. R. Effect," *Film Daily*, September 13, 1946, 1.
40. Jose Mendez, "Teatro Paramount, San Juan, Puerto Rico," Cinema Treasures website, http://cinematreasures.org/theaters/3835.
41. "All-Disney Show for Porto Rico," *Film Daily*, November 20, 1935, 2.
42. Garcia-Crespo, *Stateless Nation Building*, 310.
43. "Buy for West Indies Houses," *Motion Picture Herald*, August 17, 1935, 11.
44. Denis, *War Against All Puerto Ricans*, 37.
45. Denis, *War Against All Puerto Ricans*, 64–65.
46. José Ché Paralitici, "Imprisonment and Colonial Domination, 1898–1958," in *Puerto Rico Under Colonial Rule: Political Persecution and the Quest for Human Rights*, ed. Ramón Bosque Pérez and José Javier Colón Morera (Albany: State University of New York Press, 2006), 71.
47. Denis, *War Against All Puerto Ricans*, 54, 69, 73.
48. "Metro Plans 12 New Spots 'Round Globe Will Set Sites for Six Theatres by Fall," *Motion Picture Daily*, July 12, 1937, 1.
49. "Goldwyn-Mayer en Puerto Rico," *El Mundo*, August 9, 1938, 5.
50. "Metro's Extensive New Bldg. Around the World," *Variety*, February 9, 1938, 12.
51. Denis, *War Against All Puerto Ricans*, 70.
52. "Winston to Puerto Rico," *Motion Picture Herald*, December 17, 1938, 56.
53. "Opening Gives Metro 26 Foreign Theatres," *Motion Picture Herald*, January 13, 1939, 2.
54. "San Juan House Opens," *Film Daily*, January 18, 1939, 3.
55. "Inauguration of Luxe Coming Soon," *El Mundo*, January 7, 1939, 7.
56. "Llamas to Open Six New Theaters in Puerto Rico," *Film Daily*, September 20, 1939, 12.
57. "You Are Invited to Join Up," *Motion Picture Herald*, August 26, 1939, 90; and "Raul Barrera," *Motion Picture Herald*, June 22, 1940, 78.
58. Denis, *War Against All Puerto Ricans*, 71.
59. "Winston in Cobiân," *Film Daily*, February 14, 1941, 6.
60. Reuben D. Sanchez, "Using Subtitles in Puerto Rico," *Motion Picture Herald*, September 28, 1946, 39.
61. Garcia-Crespo, *Stateless Nation Building*, 310.
62. Sanchez, "Using Subtitles in Puerto Rico," 39.
63. "Decree Sales Policy Without P.R. Effect," 1.
64. "4 U.S. Film Firms Still in Deadlock on Terms in Havana," *Variety*, January 21, 1942, 13.
65. Mary Louise Blanco, "Forecast Post-War Cuban Theaters for Majors," *Film Daily*, April 18, 1944, 1, 6.
66. "M-G Joins WB, 20th In Cuban Exhib Peace; UA Only U.S Co. Out," *Variety*, March 11, 1942, 16.
67. "Chatter: Havana," *Variety*, September 30, 1942, 53.
68. "20th-Fox May Acquire Havana 'Show Window,'" *Film Daily*, November 6, 1942, 1, 2.
69. Mary Louise Blanco, "20th-Fox To Acquire National In Havana!," *Film Daily*, March 15, 1943, 1, 7.

70. "20th-Fox Drops Plans for "Show Window" In Havana," *Film Daily*, March 26, 1943, 2.
71. "Cuban Capers," *Motion Picture Herald*, May 8, 1943, 9.
72. Cobiân was also planning to build new cinemas in Santa Clara, Santiago, and Havana, while Fernandez planned to construct a new cinema despite the wartime constrictions. "WB, Fox in Cobiân Deal? May Join in Cuban Circuit Operation," *Film Daily*, September 20, 1944, 1; "Cuba Decorates Three Warners," *Film Daily*, September 27, 1944, 3; and "Cobiân Leases Smith, Ferenandez Circuits," *Film Daily*, September 18, 1944, 1.
73. "WB, Fox in Cobiân Deal?," 1.
74. "Paramount and Cobiân in Partnership Deal," *Film Daily*, October 30, 1944, 5; "Paramount and Cobiân Partners in Cuba," *Paramount International News*, November 3, 1944, n.p.; and "Chatter: Havana," *Variety*, November 22, 1944, 43.
75. "Mexican 'Freeze Out' in Cuba," *Film Daily*, November 10, 1944, 1, 6.
76. "Valcarce in Metro Deal," *Film Daily*, July 24, 1944, 13; and "Universal Signed with Smith, 'U' Pix on Smith Circuit," *Film Daily*, March 3, 1944, 6.
77. Quoted in Megan J. Feeney, "Hollywood in Havana: Film Reception and Revolutionary Nationalism in Cuba Before 1959" (diss., University of Minnesota, 2008), 246.
78. "Warners Buy Lima House, Theater Site in Sydney," *Film Daily*, March 16, 1943, 2; and "Bogotá Deluxe to WB; More SA Deals Pending," *Film Daily*, September 18, 1946, 1.
79. "'Show Window' for Warners in Havana," *Film Daily*, June 15, 1945, 1, 3; see also "Warners Dickering for Havana Theatre," *Motion Picture Daily*, June 15, 1945, 162.
80. Untitled Agreement, July 27, 1945, Box 2713, FO11185, WB-USC.
81. "Loew's Sets $9,008,000 Program for Theatres in Latin America," *Variety*, September 5, 1945, 7; and Mary Louis Blanco, "Loew's Building Two; WB Reported Leasing House Being Erected by CMQ," *Film Daily*, January 16, 1946, 1.
82. Mary Louise Blanco, "Cobiân out of Cuban Circuit," *Film Daily*, November 5, 1945, 1, 10.
83. "Havana Dress Rehearsal," *Variety*, December 25, 1946, 20. Had all been built, it would have put Havana on par with only London and Lima in terms of Hollywood's engagement in local exhibition.
84. "Havana Theater Workers Walk Out," *Film Daily*, July 8, 1946, 6.
85. Excerpt from *Cuba's Weekly Business Report*, April 5, 1947, in "CUBA-PAYROLL," Box 16671B, Cuba Labor Laws #2, WB-USC.
86. Motion Picture Association of America, Inc., "Important Local Offices and Personnel," in *Theatre Directory—Cuba* (New York: MPAA, 1947), 16, 18–20, 28–29, 90–91, 95.
87. "Global Activities Covered at Colorful Forum Luncheon," *Paramount International News*, July 21, 1947, 3, 4.
88. Feeney, "Hollywood in Havana," 30, 244.
89. "Personal Mention," *Motion Picture Daily*, November 26, 1946, 2; and "Kalmine to Inspect Havana, Mexico Houses," *Motion Picture Daily*, November 26, 1946, 2.
90. "People," *Motion Picture Herald*, September 27, 1947, 9.
91. Feeney, "Hollywood in Havana," 26; and "Warners Gets Prado as Havana Showroom," *Film Daily*, September 16, 1947, 1.
92. "Coming and Going," *Film Daily*, October 24, 1947, 2.
93. "The Warner Theatre," *Motion Picture Herald*, January 10, 1948, 11.
94. R. Hart Phillips, "Carnival in Havana: Parades and Other Spectacular Events Start This Week and Last into March," *New York Times*, February 1, 1948, X17; and "Cab Calloway to Cuba and Europe," *Washington Afro-American*, June 21, 1955, 17.

95. "Warner Theatre, Havana, Cuba, Translation of Lease," January 7, 1948, Box 16671A, F581, WB-USC; and Proposed Theatre, Havana, Cuba, Indemnity Bond to Radio Centro, S.A, July 3, 1949, Box 16671A, 581, WB-USC.
96. "The News of Radio: Teen-Agers to Be Featured on CBS Network on Saturdays in 'Accent on Youth,'" *New York Times*, March 4, 1948, 50.
97. "Notaro Set as Warner Havana Theatre Manager," *Film Daily*, March 19, 1948, 2.
98. John Jones to Wolfe Cohen, February 9, 1948, Box 16671B, WB-USC.
99. Feeney, "Hollywood in Havana," 245.
100. Pat Notaro to Herbert Copelan, April 19, 1949, 16671B, Julio Ponce Case, WB-USC.
101. Feeney, "Hollywood in Havana," 245, 246.
102. "Telephone Call from Herb Copelan—Havana," March 14, 1951, Box 16671B, Esnard Case, WB-USC.
103. Feeney, "Hollywood in Havana," 248.
104. Pat R. Notaro to John J. Glynn, May 12, 1950, Box 16671B, Cuba Labor Laws #2, WB-USC.
105. Wolfe Cohen to Gabriel Alarcon, June 15, 1950, Box 2713, FO11186, WB-USC.
106. Warner Bros. First National South Films, Inc. to Radiocentro, S.A., February 21, 1950, Box 2713, FO11185, WB-USC.
107. General Syndicate and Its Different Sections to Manager of Warner Bros. First National, February 8, 1951, Box 16671B, Cuba Labor Laws #2, WB-USC. Geza Polaty wrote to John Glynn that the company had tried to hide its selective bonus policy, but word had leaked out to other employees. Geza Polaty to J. J. Glynn, February 9, 1951, Box 16671B, Cuba Labor Laws #2, WB-USC.
108. "Report of Transfer of Lease of WARNER THEATRE, HAVANA at the Office of Goar Mestre, in Radio Centro Building, Havana, Cuba," January 10, 1952, Box 2713, Folder FO11188, WB-USC; and "Memorandum of Transfer," January 15, 1952, Box 2713, Folder FO11188, WB-USC.
109. Geza Polaty to J. J. Glynn, March 15, 1952, Box 16671B, 17-Misc., WB-USC.
110. Juan Falcon to Karl G. Macdonald, October 5, 1954, Box 16771B, 17-Misc., WB-USC.
111. Warner Bros. divested its theatre division in 1951, and the separated company was renamed the Stanley-Warner Corp., itself a prior merger of the Stanley Company of America and Warner Bros.
112. Peter Lev, *Transforming the Screen* (New York: Scribner, 2003), 114.
113. "Cinerama Quits Oklahoma," *International Projectionist*, February 1957, 36; and "Argentine Driver Released," *New York Times*, February 25, 1958, 14.
114. "15 Cuban Rebels Seized by Army," *New York Times*, July 2, 1957, 9.
115. Michael B. Salwen and Bruce Garrison, *Latin American Journalism* (Hillsdale, NJ: Erlbaum, 1991), 148.
116. "Theatres," *Twentieth Century-Fox 1965 Annual Report*, 1, New York Public Library for the Performing Arts; and Jose Mendez, "Metro Cinema in San Juan, PR," Cinema Treasures website, http://cinematreasures.org/theaters/3819.
117. "Reformado, Sin Perder Su Origen," *El Nuevodia*, May 31, 2009, https://www.elnuevodia.com/entretenimiento/peliculas-series/notas/reformado-sin-perder-su-origen/.
118. Metro Cinemas, Caribbean Cinemas website, https://caribbeancinemas.com/theater/metro-cinemas/.
119. Quoted in Annabel Jane Wharton, *Building the Cold War: Hilton International Hotels and Modern Architecture* (Chicago: University of Chicago Press, 2001), 1.

12. Buildings, Ballyhoo, and Boycotts in Egypt, 1925–1947

1. Mohamed Khan, "That Same Big Screen," *Egypt Today*, January 2006, https://web.archive.org/web/20100628080346/http://www.egypttoday.com/article.aspx?ArticleID=6232.
2. "Egypt," *Variety*, December 17, 1924, 2; Georges Clarriere, "Latest from France," *Bioscope*, May 7, 1925, 46; "Marcus Loew Buying in on 11 Big Theatres in France and Egypt," *Variety*, June 3, 1925, 5; and "Film Union, by French, Americans," *Los Angeles Times*, June 11, 1925, A1.
3. "Egypt," 2; and Maurice Ventura, "Egypt's Films 60% American," *Variety*, November 11, 1925, 40.
4. Roy Chandler, "American Equipment and Methods in Foreign Countries," *Motion Picture News*, December 2, 1927, 1731.
5. "U.S. Film Boom in Near East," *Variety*, January 9, 1934, 11.
6. "U.S. Film Boom in Near East," 11.
7. "Ufa Out to Spike Boycott in Egypt," *Jewish Daily Bulletin*, December 11, 1934, 6.
8. Mohannad Ghawanmeh, "Entrepreneurship in a State of Flux: Egypt's Silent Cinema and Its Transition to Synchronized Sound, 1896–1934" (Ph.D. diss., UCLA, Los Angeles, 2020), 60–63; and Edward Asswad, "Chatter: Egypt," *Variety*, June 6, 1933, 61.
9. John B. Christopher, "Egypt's Young Rebels: Young Egypt, 1933–1952," *International Journal of African Historical Studies* 9, no. 4 (1976): 692–94; and Anne-Claire Kerboeuf, "The Cairo Fire of 26 January 1952 and the Interpretations of History," in *Re-envisioning Egypt 1919–1952*, ed. Arthur Goldschmidt, Amy J. Johnson, Barak A. Salmoni (Cairo: American University in Cairo Press, 2005), 211. Ironically, an earlier 1921–1922 boycott against foreign businesses had been organized expressly by the Wafd party. Viola Shafik, *Popular Egyptian Cinema: Gender, Class, and Nation* (Cairo: American University in Cairo Press, 2007), 27.
10. Ghawanmeh, "Entrepreneurship in a State of Flux," 72–73.
11. Enclosure No. 1 to Despatch No. 33 of January 20, 1934, from the Legation at Cairo, January 20, 1934, 883.4061, Department of State Files, RG 59: General Records of the Department of State, 1763–2002, NARA, College Park, MD.
12. Robert Vitalis, "American Ambassador in Technicolor and Cinemascope: Hollywood and Revolution on the Nile," in *Mass Mediations: New Approaches to Popular Culture in the Middle East and Beyond*, ed. Walter Armbrust (Berkeley: University of California Press, 2000), http://ark.cdlib.org/ark:/13030/ft8k4008kx/.
13. Enclosure No. 1 to Despatch No. 33 of January 20, 1934.
14. Enclosure No. 1 to Despatch No. 33 of January 20, 1934.
15. Enclosure No. 1 to Despatch No. 33 of January 20, 1934.
16. Ghawanmeh, "Entrepreneurship in a State of Flux," 71, 73.
17. Bert Fish to The Honorable Secretary of State, Washington, "Agitation Against Foreign Motion Pioture Theatres," January 20, 1934, 883.4061, NARA.
18. "Fascists in Egypt," *Palestine Post*, March 14, 1934, 4.
19. "Nazi Refugees in New Cairo Studio," *Variety*, February 17, 1937, n.p.
20. "Old Cairo Undergoes Marked Transformation with Many New Buildings on Modernistic Lines," *Washington Post*, August 2, 1936, E1, E2.
21. Zoe R. Badre, "Progress Beside the Nile," *Christian Science Monitor*, December 7, 1938, WM9.
22. Arthur Settel, "Egypt's New Nationalism," *Variety*, January 5, 1938, 110.

23. Shafik, *Popular Egyptian Cinema*, 32; "Loew Draws Plans for Three Foreign Houses," *Boxoffice*, June 12, 1938, 8; and "25 Metro Foreign Units By End of Year," *Boxoffice*, February 25, 1939, 24.
24. "More Loew Theatre Prospects to South," *Boxoffice*, January 14, 1939, 28.
25. Cinema Metro Ad, *Egyptian Gazette*, February 2, 1940, 4.
26. Cinema Metro Ad, *Egyptian Gazette*, January 31, 1940, 2, 8; and Cinema Metro Ad, *Egyptian Gazette*, February 1, 1940, 3.
27. "Western Showmanship Goes East Again," *Showmen's Trade Review*, April 27, 1940, 34.
28. Cinema Metro Ad, *Egyptian Gazette*, February 1, 1940, 3; "Metro's Cairo Preem," *Variety*, February 7, 1940, 21; "Lewis Stone Specials," *Daily Variety*, July 18, 1939, 5; and Cinema Metro Ad, *Egyptian Gazette*, February 2, 1940, 8.
29. *Metro-Goldwyn-Mayer's Big Parade of Hits for 1940* (MGM, 1940), Viewed on Turner Classic Movies, https://www.imdb.com/title/tt5367084/.
30. "Cinema Luxury," *Egyptian Gazette*, February 3, 1940, 4; see also Anna Sudany, "A Protest from the Elite," *Egyptian Gazette*, February 3, 1940, 4.
31. Cinema Metro Ad, *Egyptian Gazette*, February 7, 1940, 3.
32. "General-Egypt," 1, 99AN/1F, Box 7, Folder 1, UA-WHS.
33. Cinema Metro Ad, *Egyptian Gazette*, February 9, 1940, 6.
34. George Lait, "Vaude Troupe Under Fire on Sahara; Show Biz Hot, Too; No Africa Closeup," *Variety*, January 20, 1943, 2.
35. "New Product," 6, 99AN/1F, Box 7, Folder 1, UA-WHS.
36. Samir Raafat, "Cinema Metro" (unedited version), *Cairo Times*, Thursday, May 15, 1997.
37. Raafat, "Cinema Metro."
38. Lowe, "Egypt," 2.
39. Raafat, "Cinema Metro."
40. Will Saphir, "Hollywood Leadership Threatened by Cairo's Film Rise, (Cairo Says So)," *Variety*, March 13, 1940, 14.
41. Lowe, "Egypt," 7.
42. Lait, "Vaude Troupe Under Fire," 2.
43. After its debut, *Variety* noted that "Biz" at the Cairo theater had remained "big since the opening." "Metro's New Deluxer," *Variety*, March 13, 1940, 14.
44. "Twenty Years Of M.G.M: World's Largest Film Unit, *Palestine Post*, June 23, 1944, 4.
45. Khan, "That Same Big Screen."
46. Khan, "That Same Big Screen."
47. Eva Dadrian, "The Golden Age of Cairo's Silver Screens," *RAWI Magazine*, 2 (2011). https://rawi-magazine.com/articles/artdecocinemas/.
48. Clément Dassa, Skype interview, July 5, 2013.
49. Dassa, Skype interview.
50. Khan, "That Same Big Screen."
51. Stellaa, "Cinema, Alexandria the 1960's," *OpenSalon* (blog), May 28, 2008. http://web.archive.org/web/20090315164553/http://open.salon.com/blog/stellaa/2008/05/28/cinema_alexandria_the_1960s.
52. Phineas J. Biron, "Strictly Confidential," *American Israelite*, July 16, 1942, 1.
53. Lowe, "Egypt," 7, 8.
54. "'Fantasia' Screening in San Juan, Cairo Today," *Daily Variety*, February 2, 1942, 11.
55. Lait, "Vaude Troupe Under Fire on Sahara," 2.
56. Lowe, "Egypt," 1.

57. "Buys Egyptian Theatre," *Daily Variety*, July 14, 1943, 11; and "Warner Executive Moves to E. 55th St.," *New York Times*, October 15, 1943, 32.
58. "Warners Expanding for Big Post War Foreign Biz," *Daily Variety*, September 2, 1943, 13.
59. "Broadway," *Boxoffice*, May 26, 1945, 58; and "Silverstone Views Vast Near East Expansion," *Boxoffice*, June 16, 1945, 16.
60. "Silverstone Views Vast Near East Expansion," 16. Films were not much delayed from their openings in New York. When *Prince of Foxes* opened there four years later, for instance, the film opened day and date with the Roxy Theatre in New York. "'Prince' Day-Dated in 15 Global Keys," *Daily Variety*, September 29, 1949, 1.
61. "20th-Fox to Open New Branches in Middle East," *Film Daily*, June 13, 1945, 1, 8.
62. Shafik, *Popular Egyptian Cinema*, 32; and "20th-Fox to Open New Branches in Middle East," 1, 8.
63. Telegram from Cairo, TUCK to Secretary of State, March 28, 1945, 883.4061/3-2845, NARA.
64. Joseph Rosthal to Carl E. Milliken, March 29, 1945, 883.4061/3-3045, NARA.
65. Carl E. Milliken (MANAGER) to Joseph Rosthal, March 30, 1945; and Carl E. Milliken (MANAGER) to George R. Canty, March 30, 1945, both 883.4061/3-3045, NARA.
66. "Minutes of a Third Meeting" and copies of telegrams, 1945, 883.4061/10-1545, NARA.
67. Tuck to Secretary of State, May 23, 1945, 883.4061/5-2345, NARA.
68. Tuck to Secretary of State, June 2, 1945, 883.4061/6-245, NARA.
69. Walter Collins, "Rioting Flares Anew in Center of Cairo," *Ogden* (UT) *Standard Examiner*, November 4, 1945, 1; and "Cairo Police Suppress New Anti-Zionist Riots; 6 Killed," *Portsmouth Herald*, November 3, 1945, 1.
70. Walter Collins, "Anti-Zionist Riots Flare Anew in Cairo," *Lowell Sun*, November 3, 1945, 3.
71. Collins, "Rioting Flares Anew in Center of Cairo," 1; "Cairo Police Suppress New Anti-Zionist Riots," 1; and *Encyclopedia of Jews in the Islamic World*, ed. Norman A. Stillman, Brill Online, http://referenceworks.brillonline.com/browse/encyclopedia-of-jews-in-the-islamic-world.
72. Collins, "Anti-Zionist Riots Flare Anew in Cairo," 3.
73. Collins, "Rioting Flares Anew in Center of Cairo," 1.
74. Vitalis, "American Ambassador in Technicolor and Cinemascope," 19.
75. Geo. Coussy [Geogoussky] to RKO Radio Pictures Inc. Export Division, March 11, 1946, 883.4061/3-1346, NARA.
76. Jacques Pascal, "Bombing in Cairo Affects Theatres," *Motion Picture Daily*, May 3, 1946, 8. See also Coussy to RKO.
77. Quoted in "Nationalism on Upbeat in Middle East; Holds Threat to Yank Films," *Variety*, March 27, 1946, 20.
78. *Variety* noted that one "peculiar factor in this self-imposed ban on showing British-mades in Egypt is that Palestine, from which the violence stems, is showing British pictures without any restrictions and doing okay biz." "British Films Withdrawn from Pix Houses in Egypt After Bomb Threat," *Variety*, December 11, 1946, 17.
79. "Anti-Brit. Drive Hurts All Far East Pix Biz, Sez RKOs Georgoussky," *Variety*, June 26, 1946, 18.
80. "Memorandum of Settlement: Rivoli Cinema," July 19, 1951, JE 1611/2, NA-UK.
81. "British Films Withdrawn," 17.
82. "U.S. Films Losing Ground to Arabic Product in Egypt, Golden Reports," *Variety*, April 30, 1947, 19.
83. Raafat, "Cine Metro."

84. "Bomb Blast Kills 4 in Cairo Movie," *San Antonio Express*, May 7, 1947, 1. See also "New Cairo Blast," *Winnipeg (Canada) Free Press*, May 6, 1947, 1; "Bomb Kills 4 in Theatre," *Boxoffice*, May 10, 1947, 58; and "German Linked to Cairo Bombing," *New York Times*, May 13, 1947, 16.
85. "Time Bomb Kills 4 In Cairo Theatre," *New York Times*, May 7, 1947, 8.
86. "New Cairo Blast," 1; "Cairo Bomb Kills 4," 2; "Bomb Kills 4 in Theatre," 58; and "German Linked to Cairo Bombing," 16.
87. Raafat, "Cine Metro."
88. "Global Activities Covered at Colorful Forum Luncheon," *Paramount International News*, July 21, 1947, 3, 4; and "Personalities," *Paramount International News*, July 21, 1947, 5.
89. Rivoli Cinema Opening Program, March 1948, Rivoli Cinema (Cairo) Files, CTA.
90. "Rank Organisation Inaugurates Luxurious Cairo Super," *Ideal Kinema*, March 11, 1948, 5.

13. No Meeting in the Middle, 1947–1956

1. Isaac R. Molho, "U.S. Pictures Have Head Start in Favor with Palestine Public," *Motion Picture Herald*, February 20, 1937, 70.
2. "Political Rift Splits Palestine's Recovery," *Motion Picture Herald*, February 19, 1938, 62.
3. "Murray Silverstone Named for New Post," *New York Post*, April 13, 1943, 30.
4. "20th-Fox to Open New Branches in Middle East," *Film Daily*, June 13, 1945, 1, 8.
5. "Sees Palestine as Best Potential Market," *Film Daily*, June 26, 1946, 1, 10.
6. "WB Acquires 4 More Foreign Outlets," *Motion Picture Daily*, May 17, 1944, 2; "Warner's Exclusive Deals in Australia, Palestine," *Boxoffice*, May 20, 1944, 52-B; and "Asia, Africa Rank Houses," *Motion Picture Daily*, April 25, 1945, 1, 5.
7. "Copy of Letter from High Committee of the Nile Valley for the Liberation of Palestine," Enclosure No. 1 to Despatch No. 171 of March 1, 1948, RG 59, 883.4061 MP/3-148, NARA.
8. Memorandum, Enclosure No. 1 to Despatch No. 171 of March 1, 1948, RG 59, 883.4061 MP/3-148, NARA.
9. Memorandum, Enclosure No. 1 to Despatch No. 171.
10. United States Department of State, *Foreign Relations of the United States Diplomatic Papers, 1944*, vol. 5, *The Near East, South Asia, and Africa, the Far East* (Washington, DC: U.S. Government Printing Office, 1944), 639, https://search.library.wisc.edu/digital/A2TWJOGYVBMSVQ82/pages/AWEJWWZ46RUAGJ8O. Pasha (and others) added that "no country in the world has suffered a greater injustice than Palestine. From time immemorial it has been an Arab country. Jews entered it as invaders and only occupied it for a short time; for they were constantly at war with the aborigines, and other invaders soon drove them out until the Arabs, more than thirteen centuries ago, finally liberated the country and settled it. Palestine is, by the will of God and the patriotism of its people, an Arab country and will forever remain so." Quoted in The Minister in Egypt (Tuck) to the Secretary of State, November 21, 1944, 867N.01/11-2144, NARA.
11. "Memorandum," Enclosure No. 1 to Despatch No. 171. Twentieth Century-Fox would, for example, later deny an application by the South African Zionist Federation to host an event at their Colosseum Theatre in Johannesburg during Israeli colonel A.

Yoffe's visit to the country because it was the equivalent of taking a political side. "Fox Theatres South Africa (Proprietary) Limited, Minutes of Meeting..." February 11, 1957, Box 50, Folder 10, Spyros P. Skouras Papers, Stanford University Special Collections, Stanford, Calif. (hereafter, SPS).

12. "Memorandum," Enclosure No. 1 to Despatch No. 171.
13. Tyler Brooke, "Hollywood Jewish Appeal Soars Beyond One Million Mark," *Chicago Sentinel*, July 3, 1947, 18.
14. "Clark Pledges D. P. Aid at UJA Luncheon," *Film Daily*, July 23, 1947, 1, 7. See also "Help Now to DPs Is Urged by Clark," *New York Times*, July 23, 1947, 8.
15. "Hadassah Will Hear Skouras and Nizer," *Film Daily*, December 4, 1947, 8.
16. "Name Nine Groups for UJA Campaign," *Film Daily*, April 20, 1948, 7.
17. "Youssef Wahby Dead at 82," *New York Times*, October 18, 1982, B8; State Information Services (Egypt), "Youssef Wahbi," https://www.sis.gov.eg/Story/1295/Youssef-Wahbi?lang=en-us; and Transmission of Editorial Attack on American Motion Pictures by a Representative of Local Producers, Cairo Despatch no. 470, June 5, 1948, RG 59, 883.4061 MP/6-548, NARA.
18. "Start Second in Egypt," *Motion Picture Daily*, August 10, 1934, 16; "At the Cinema," *Palestine Post*, August 16, 1944, 2; and "At the Cinema," *Palestine Post*, June 12, 1946, 2.
19. "Youssef Wahby Dead at 82," B8; and State Information Services (Egypt), "Youssef Wahbi." Wahbi had just directed *Darbit al-qadar* (Fate's stroke) with Egyptian-Jewish actress Layla Murad in 1947. Viola Shafik, *Popular Egyptian Cinema: Gender, Class, and Nation* (Cairo: American University Press in Cairo, 2007), 256.
20. "Transmission of Editorial Attack on American Motion Pictures."
21. Robert Vitalis, "American Ambassador in Technicolor and Cinemascope Hollywood and Revolution on the Nile," in *Mass Mediations: New Approaches to Popular Culture in the Middle East and Beyond*, ed. Walter Armbrust, ed. (Berkeley: University of California Press, 2000).
22. "Seek to Halt Arabic Dubs," *Film Daily*, March 29, 1948, 3; and Vitalis, "American Ambassador in Technicolor and Cinemascope."
23. Jacques Pascal, "Egypt," *Motion Picture Herald*, February 22, 1947, 50.
24. Vitalis, "American Ambassador in Technicolor and Cinemascope."
25. "Transmission of Editorial Attack on American Motion Pictures."
26. "Jews Uneasy as Tension Spreads over Palestine; Martial Law in Iraq, Egypt," *Jewish Telegraphic Agency*, May 16, 1948, 3.
27. Enclosure to Cairo Despatch No. 470, June 5, 1948, RG 59, 883.4061 MP/6-548, NARA.
28. "Egypt Curbs Film Coin Because of Zion War," *Variety*, June 2, 1948, 2; and Patterson to Secretary of State, June 15, 1948, RG 59, 883.4061 MP/6-1548, NARA.
29. "Egypt May Release Hwoods Frozen Coin—in Pounds," *Daily Variety*, January 20, 1949, 3.
30. "Egyptian Mobs Pierce Eyes of Jews, Kill Rabbis Savagely; Jewish Situation Alarming," *Jewish Telegraphic Agency Daily News Bulletin*, August 5, 1948, 1, 2.
31. "War's End Brings Pix Hypo to Israel; New Houses, Studios, Production Seen," *Variety*, March 23, 1949, 16.
32. David Shalit, *Projection Power: The Cinema Houses, the Movies, and the Israelis* (Tel Aviv: Resling, 2006), 45.
33. "Skouras & Co. in Israel, Get Official Welcome," *Variety*, July 27, 1949, 18.
34. Shalit, *Projection Power*, 46.
35. Shalit, *Projection Power*, 47.

36. "Social & Personal," *Jerusalem Post*, January 9, 1964, 2.
37. "Primate Lights Candle at Mt. Zion Memorial Publication," *Jerusalem Post*, January 8, 1964, 3.
38. Speech by Mr. Skouras in Atlantic City on Friday, November 25, 1949, for the United Jewish Appeal, Box 83, Folder 3, SPS; and "20th-Fox Plans 5 Israeli Theatres, Says Skouras," *Variety*, November 30, 1949, 22.
39. Nadia Lourie, "Theatres in Israel," in *Theatre Catalog*, 14th ed. (Philadelphia: J. Emanuel Publications, 1956), 14. See also "11 New Cinemas for Tel Aviv," *Jerusalem Post*, September 27, 1955, 3.
40. "Skouras Urges," *Variety*, August 31, 1949, 25; and "20th to Build 4 Cinemas in Israel, 1 in Alexandria," *Variety*, August 3, 1949, 13.
41. "Yank Films Boost Lead Abroad over Foreign Product, Says M-Gs Burger," *Variety*, December 21, 1949, 15.
42. "Para, Int. May Enter Exhibition in India," *Film Daily*, January 14, 1946, 5.
43. "Disney's New Musical Fantasy," *Palestine Post*, May 7, 1946, 4.
44. Nadia Lourie, "Early Habonim Days: Co-Founder of Habonim Writes About the Beginning," *Habonim Reunited*, March 21, 1990.
45. "Lourie Here to Set African House Deal," *Film Daily*, March 24, 1939, 1, 3; and "UA To Have 1st-Run House In Capetown," *Film Daily*, July 17, 1941, 1, 4.
46. A. A. Lowe, "Egypt," June 10, 1944, 99AN/1F, Box 7, Folder 1, UA-WHS.
47. "Israel's 1st Feature Film Due Soon, Plans for H'wood of Middle East," *Variety*, June 2, 1948, 2.
48. Enclosure to Cairo Despatch No. 470 dated June 5, 1948.
49. "Plans Large Scale Palestine Production," *Film Daily*, April 15, 1947, 1, 4.
50. "Israel's 1st Feature Film Due Soon," 2.
51. "Named as Consul General of Israel's Government," *New York Times*, May 30, 1948, 3.
52. "Physical Distribution of 'Israel Reborn' by Fox," *Film Daily*, July 7, 1948, 15.
53. David Brown, "Israeli Film Making," *Chicago Sentinel*, September 30, 1948, 121.
54. "UA Distribs 2d Israel Short, 20th Has 1st," *Variety*, August 11, 1948, 9; and "UA Set to Distribute Palestine's 'Israel Today,'" *Film Daily*, August 13, 1948, 2.
55. A. Edith Richards, "New York Community Shows What Real Interfaith Work Can Accomplish," *Chicago Sentinel*, December 29, 1949, 9.
56. "Dorothy Silverstone, A Philanthropist, 89," *New York Times*, March 23, 1993, B7; and "Colour Film of Children," *Palestine Post*, August 18, 1949, 2.
57. Mrs. Murray Silverstone to Mary Pickford, August 16, 1961, folder 1194, Mary Pickford Papers, Margaret Herrick Library, Academy of Motion Picture Arts and Sciences, Beverly Hills, Calif. (hereafter, MHL).
58. "The Magnetic Tide," *Variety*, November 29, 1950, 22.
59. Dorothy Silverstone to Mary Pickford, November 11, 1965, folder 1194, Mary Pickford Papers, MHL.
60. "Israel Short at Roxy," *Variety*, November 22, 1950, 9.
61. Arthur Krim to Norman Lourie, February 2, 1950, folder 1302, Fred Zinneman Papers, MHL.
62. "Israel's 1st Feature Film Due Soon," 2.
63. Owen T. Jones to Department of State, June 12, 1951, RG 59, 884A.452/6-1251, NARA.
64. "Movie Makers Salvage Frozen Foreign Profits; Shoot Pictures Abroad," *Wall Street Journal*, 12 September 1949, 1.

65. "Skouras Urges," 25; and "20th to Build," 4, 13.
66. "'FOX' Will Build Cinemas in Israel," *Al Hamishmar*, December 5, 1949, 4.
67. "Foreign Operations," *Twentieth Century-Fox, Annual Report* (New York: Twentieth Century-Fox, December 31, 1949), 4, 5.
68. Fox Company Ltd. Application, August 24, 1950, 21, Historical Archives of the Municipality of Tel Aviv-Yafo, Tel Aviv, Israel.
69. G. M. Koigen to Cities Construction Committee, August 24, 1950, 21, Historical Archives of the Municipality of Tel Aviv-Yafo, Tel Aviv, Israel.
70. Municipal Building and Cinema for Twentieth Century-Fox Import Corp. Jerusalem, Israel, (Arch) John and Drew Eberson, TD1991.154.36, John and Drew Eberson Architectural Records Archive, Wolfsonian-FIU, Miami Beach, Fla.
71. Cinema and Medical Arts Building for Twentieth Century-Fox, Tel Aviv, Israel, (Arch) John and Drew Eberson (Assoc.) G. M. Koigen, Project #1612. TD1991.158.1.1, Wolfsonian-FIU; and Cinema and Office Building for Twentieth Century Fox, Haifa, Israel, Project #1611, TD1991.155.37, Wolfsonian-FIU.
72. "'FOX' Company Will Build Cinemas in Jerusalem," *Heruth*, March 16, 1950, 4; and "Social & Personal," *Palestine Post*, March 16, 1950, 2.
73. "'Bor-Shiber' Will Not Be Delivered to 'FOX,'" *Heruth*, April 9, 1951, 4.
74. N. Lezter to Cities Construction Committee, January 4, 1951, Historical Archives of the Municipality of Tel Aviv-Yafo, Tel Aviv, Israel.
75. "Metro's 3 New Showcases in Egypt, Cuba, Argentina," *Variety*, May 12, 1948, 15.
76. Both of the Egyptian Metros would now be under the supervision of George Chasanas, MGM head in Egypt. "Metro Is Building New Egypt House," *Daily Variety*, May 2, 1949, 4.
77. "Loew's Building Theatre in Alexandria, Egypt," *Boxoffice*, May 7, 1949, 42.
78. "New Loew House," *Daily Variety*, August 1, 1950, 3; and "MGM Opens New Theatre in Alexandria, Egypt," *Boxoffice*, September 2, 1950, 16.
79. "'Mines' Soaring In Foreign Field," *Variety*, March 21, 1951, 13.
80. Shafik, *Popular Egyptian Cinema*, 32.
81. Quincy F. Roberts to Department of State, "Showing of An American Motion Picture in Alexandria Cancelled," January 9, 1951, 874.452/1-951, NARA.
82. "Pictures: Tighter Foreign Censorship," *Variety*, October 15, 1952, 19.
83. "Memorandum of Settlement: Rivoli Cinema," July 19, 1951, JE 1611/2, NA-UK.
84. "J. Arthur Rank's Theatre in Cairo," January 3, 1952, JE 1611/1, NA-UK.
85. R. Allen to A. N. Cumberbatch, January 5, 195[2], JE 1611/1, NA-UK.
86. "J. Arthur Rank's Theatre in Cairo."
87. "Aide Mémoire for Foreign Office Talks Odeon (Cairo) Ltd.," ca. January 1952, JE 1611/2, NA-UK.
88. "Aide Mémoire for Foreign Office Talks Odeon (Cairo) Ltd."
89. A. N. Cumberbatch to R. Allen, January 8, 1952, JE 1611/2, NA-UK.
90. "Aide Mémoire for Foreign Office Talks Odeon (Cairo) Ltd."
91. "Aide Mémoire for Foreign Office Talks Odeon (Cairo) Ltd."
92. Allen to Cumberbatch, January 23, 1952, JE 1611/2, NA-UK.
93. Allen to Cumberbatch, January 23, 1952.
94. Quoted in Anne-Claire Kerboeuf, "The Cairo Fire of 26 January 1952 and the Interpretations of History," in *Re-envisioning Egypt 1919–1952*, ed. Arthur Goldschmidt, Amy J. Johnson, Barak A. Salmoni (Cairo: American University in Cairo Press, 2005), 198.
95. Kerboeuf, "The Cairo Fire," 198.

96. John B. Christopher, "James P. Jankowski, *Egypt's Young Rebels: 'Young Egypt,' 1933–1952*," *International Journal of African Historical Studies* 9, no. 4 (1976): 692–94; "Egypt," *Corpus Christi* (TX) *Caller Times*, January 27, 1952, 12; "Loew's and 20th-Fox Hit in Cairo Riots," *Boxoffice*, February 2, 1952, 51; "Dead May Total 20," *New York Times*, January 27, 1952, 1; and "Caffery Seeks King," *New York Times*, January 27, 1952, 1.
97. James P. Jankowski, *Egypt's Young Rebels: Young Egypt, 1933–1952* (Stanford, Calif.: Hoovers Institution Press, 1975), 105, 106; and Foreign Office, JE 1611/4, A. N. Cumberbatch to Roger Allen, January 30, 1952, NA-UK.
98. Jankowski, *Egypt's Young Rebels*, 105, 106.
99. "American Citizens in Cairo in Peril as Mobs Go Wild," *Sheboygan (Wis.) Press*, 26 January 1952, 15.
100. Fred J. Zusy, "Egyptian Mobs Rioting in Cairo," *Kerrville (Tx.) Times*, 1.
101. Clément Dassa, Skype interview, July 5, 2013.
102. "Loew's and 20th-Fox Hit," 51; and "Cairo Mobs Vandalize Yank-Owned Theatres," *Daily Variety*, January 29, 1952, 1.
103. United Press, "Cairo Flaming After Day of Burning, Riots; Premier Pleads With People to Save Nation," *Sunday Press* (Binghamton, NY), January 27, 1952, 1, 4.
104. Kenneth Winckles to Selwyn Lloyd, February 25, 1952, Foreign Office, JE 1123/2, NA-UK.
105. British Embassy, Cairo to Anthony Eden, February 5, 1952, Foreign Office, JE 1123/1, NA-UK.
106. "UK Egypt—Report of Committee of Enquiry into Riots in Cairo, 26th January 1952," Ministry of Labour and National Service Overseas Department, 225/1952, LAB 13/740, NA-UK.
107. "UK Egypt—Report of Committee of Enquiry into Riots."
108. "UK Egypt—Report of Committee of Enquiry into Riots."
109. "Egypt Tense After Cairo's Mob Riots," *Advertiser* (Adelaide, SA), January 28, 1952, 1.
110. A. H. King, "Minutes," January 31, 1952, 10111/3/526, NA-UK.
111. Amany Aly Shawky, "Downtown's Department Stores: A Demolished History of a Bygone Era," *Egypt Independent*, January 10, 2013, https://egyptindependent.com/downtown-s-department-stores-demolished-history-bygone-era/.
112. "Cairo Mobs Vandalize Yank-Owned Theatres," 1; and "Riot-Hit Loew's House to Reopen in Cairo," 22. The American Embassy launched an official protest with the Egyptian government over the destruction of U.S. property. "Egypt," *Corpus Christi Caller Times*, 12; and "Loew's and 20th-Fox Hit in Cairo Riots," 51.
113. Clément Dassa, Skype interview, July 5, 2013; and "Dassa in MGM Egypt Post; Schmitt Goes to Austria," *Boxoffice*, May 24, 1952, 46-D.
114. Joel Beinin, *The Dispersion of Egyptian Jewry: Culture, Politics, and the Formation of a Modern Diaspora* (Berkeley: University of California Press, 1998), 38.
115. Beinin, *Dispersion of Egyptian Jewry*, 38.
116. Beinin, *Dispersion of Egyptian Jewry*, 21.
117. Beinin, *Dispersion of Egyptian Jewry*, 38.
118. Shafik, *Popular Egyptian Cinema*, 23.
119. Clément Dassa, Skype interview, July 5, 2013.
120. Clément Dassa, Skype interview, July 5, 2013.
121. "Amir," *1952 Theatre Catalog* (Philadelphia: J. Emanuel Publications, 1952), 17, 18.
122. Alex Cinema for Twentieth Century Fox Corp. Alexandria, Egypt, (Arch[itect]) John and Drew Eberson. Project #1610. TD1991.154.44, Wolfsonian-FIU.

123. "Amir," 17, 18.
124. "Cairo's Metro Reopens," *Variety*, December 3, 1952, 4; and "Rebuilt Metro in Cairo Opens With 'Quo Vadis,'" *Boxoffice*, December 6, 1952, 42.
125. Samir Raafat, "Cinema Metro" (unedited version), *Cairo Times*, Thursday, May 15, 1997.
126. "Rebuilt Metro in Cairo Opens with 'Quo Vadis,'" 42.
127. Annabel Jane Wharton, *Building the Cold War: Hilton International Hotels and Modern Architecture* (Chicago: University of Chicago Press, 2001), 46–47.
128. Raafat, "Cinema Metro."
129. Donald A. Robb to Cecil B. DeMille, August 8, 1953, Paramount Pictures, Folder 206, THE TEN COMMANDMENTS—production, MHL.
130. Shafik, *Popular Egyptian Cinema*, 22.
131. "H'wood Needs Near East's Market; Slow Native Adoption of Gear Primes Overseas Theatre Deals," *Variety*, September 29, 1954, 20. Architectural plans for the Amir Cinema were drawn up in August 1950 by John and Drew Eberson. Alex Cinema for Twentieth Century Fox Corp., Alexandria, Egypt, Wolfsonian-FIU.
132. Edwin Schallert, "More U.S. Film Gains Forecast at Parley Here," *Los Angeles Times*, February 7, 1956, A1, A2.
133. "Arab Boycott of Israel Extending to Leading American Film Producers," *Variety*, April 7, 1954, 1.
134. Vitalis, "American Ambassador in Technicolor and Cinemascope."
135. HARE to Secretary of State, November 14, 1956, RG 59, 874.452/11-1456, NARA; and HARE to Secretary of State, November 20, 1956, RG 59, 874.452/11-2056, NARA.
136. "Egypt Queries on Jewishness Not Taken Too Seriously by Yankees," *Variety*, December 12, 1956, 3.
137. "Obituaries," *Daily Variety*, July 25, 1955, 6.
138. "Egypt Too Emotional, Baldwin Not Going," *Variety*, January 2, 1957, 4.
139. Shafik, *Popular Egyptian Cinema*, 22, 35.
140. HARE to Secretary of State, November 20, 1956.
141. Philip E. Haring to Robert M. Carr, "Egyptian Controls Affecting Certain Foreign Motion Pictures," December 20, 1956, RG 59, 874.452/12-2056, NARA.
142. Quoted in Farah Montasser, "The Jewish Alley of Old Cairo," *Al Ahram*, June 21, 2015, http://english.ahram.org.eg/NewsContent/32/97/133308/Folk/Street-Smart/The-Jewish-alley-of-Old-Cairo.aspx.
143. Quoted in Montasser, "The Jewish Alley of Old Cairo."
144. Montasser, "The Jewish Alley of Old Cairo."
145. Philip E. Haring to Department of State, January 22, 1957, RG 59, 874.452/1-2257, NARA.
146. Walter Wanger and Joe Hyams, *My Life with Cleopatra: The Making of a Hollywood Classic* (New York: Vintage, 2013), 107.
147. Haring to Department of State, January 22, 1957.
148. Fathi Ibrahim to Spyros P. Skouras, April 29, 1961, Box 40, Folder 14, SPS.
149. Philip E. Haring to Robert M. Carr, "Egyptian Controls Affecting Certain Foreign Motion Pictures."
150. Raafat, "Cinema Metro."
151. "Cinema, Alexandria the 1960's," *OpenSalon*, May 28, 2008, http://web.archive.org/web/20090315164553/http://open.salon.com/blog/stellaa/2008/05/28/cinema_alexandria_the_1960s.
152. Vitalis, "American Ambassador in Technicolor and Cinemascope."

14. After the Revolution, 1957–1982

1. Herb Golden, "4-Year Doubling of Israel Population Finds Yank Pix Upped in Popularity," *Variety*, May 7, 1952, 4, 54.
2. David Shalit, *Projection Power: The Cinema Houses, the Movies, and the Israelis* (Tel Aviv: Resling, 2006), 46, 47.
3. S. Greenvald to Tel Aviv Municipality Construction Department, December 10, 1953, Historical Archives of the Municipality of Tel Aviv-Yafo, Tel Aviv, Israel.
4. "Cantor's 60th Birthday Spearheads Israel Drive," *Variety*, January 9, 1952, 2.
5. "Broadway," *Variety*, December 3, 1952, 62.
6. "Eban Declares Israel, Beset by Hostility, Will Press Culture and Security Goals," *New York Times*, January 6, 1955, 4.
7. American Fund for Israel Institution Dinner, January 5, 1955, Box 84, Folder 21, SPS.
8. "Wars End Brings Pix Hypo to Israel; New Houses, Studios, Production Seen," *Variety*, March 23, 1949, 16.
9. "Reds Stop U.S. Picture," *New York Times*, August 14, 1950, 6.
10. "Israeli Reds Slash Screens in Cinemas," *New York Times*, August 21, 1950, 7.
11. "Wars End Brings Pix Hypo to Israel," 16.
12. Acheson to AMEMBASSY, TEL AVIV, December 7, 1950, RG 59, 884A.452/12-750, NARA.
13. Spyros P. Skouras, "Skouras Sees Greater Global Markets for U.S. Films; Also as Potent Force vs. Communism," *Variety*, January 7, 1953, 15.
14. "H'wood Needs Near East's Market; Slow Native Adoption of Gear Primes Overseas Theatre Deals," *Variety*, September 29, 1954, 20.
15. HARE to Secretary of State, March 18, 1957, RG 59, 874.452/3-1857, NARA; and W. H. Weathersby to Department of State, "Communist Penetration of Egyptian Theatrical Film Market," April 11, 1956, RG 59, 874.452/10-2056, NARA.
16. Ibrahim Zein, "Palestine," *Motion Picture Herald*, March 15, 1947, 47.
17. "Israel Okays 'The Robe,'" *Variety*, January 19, 1955, 7.
18. Herb Golden, "4-Year Doubling of Israel Population Finds Yank Pix Upped in Popularity," *Variety*, May 7, 1952, 4.
19. "500G Yearly Bond Sale in Hollywood Is Hope of Israel's N. Lourie," *Variety*, March 2, 1955, 3.
20. "H'wood Needs Near East's Market," 20.
21. Shalit, *Projection Power*, 47.
22. Wolfsonian, Cinema and Medical Arts Building, Wolfsonian-FIU; David Stern to Messrs. Twentieth Century Fox Import Corp., July 27, 1955, Box 41, Folder 5, SPS; and I. Arnon to Messrs. Twentieth Century Fox Import Corp., July 27, 1955, Box 41, Folder 5, SPS.
23. "New Cinemas for Tel Aviv," *Jerusalem Post*, September 27, 1955, 3; and "Fox Builds New Theatre in Tel Aviv," *Motion Picture Herald*, April 23, 1955, 32.
24. "New Cinemas for Tel Aviv," 3.
25. "Stone Laid for Largest Cinema," *Jerusalem Post*, April 20, 1956, 3.
26. Fox Theatre Building Advertisement, *Jerusalem Post*, January 25, 1957, 2.
27. Nadia Lourie, "Theatres in Israel," in *Theatre Catalog*, 14th ed. (Philadelphia: J. Emanuel Publications, 1956), 14, 17, 18.
28. Shalit, *Projection Power*, 47.
29. Lourie, "Theatres in Israel," 14, 17, 18; see also Shalit, *Projection Power*, 82.
30. "'Fox' Engineer Came to Israel," *Maariv*, March 29, 1956, 3.

31. Philip Slomovitz, "David Idzal Introduces American Theatre Management Methods in Israel," *Southern Israelite*, December 6, 1957, 1.
32. "'Fox' Company Invests 1 Million Pounds (Israeli) in Israel," *Maariv*, January 22, 1950, 4.
33. "The Boycott Fear," *Maariv*, October 10, 1957, 2.
34. Paul Kohn, "'Tel Aviv,' Opens Tonight," *Jerusalem Post*, October 24, 1957, 4.
35. Quoted in Annabel Jane Wharton, *Building the Cold War: Hilton International Hotels and Modern Architecture* (Chicago: University of Chicago Press, 2001), 120.
36. Tel Aviv Theatre, Opening Program, October 26, 1957, Tel Aviv Cinematheque Library; see also "Israeli to Get Latest Type Cinema in Fall," *Variety*, May 29, 1957, 18; and "'Tel Aviv' Opens with Gala Benefit," *Jerusalem Post*, October 25, 1957, 3.
37. Tel Aviv Theatre, Opening Program.
38. Quoted in Shalit, *Projection Power*, 79.
39. "'Tel Aviv' Opens with Gala Benefit," 3.
40. Advertisement, *Jerusalem Post*, October 23, 1957, 1.
41. "'Tel Aviv' Opens with Gala Benefit," 3.
42. "At the Cinema," *Jerusalem Post*, October 28, 1957, 4.
43. Burt Halpern, "Israel: Merry, Moviegoing Mecca," *New York Times*, August 31, 1958, X5.
44. Uri Klein, "Before the Curtain Fell," *Haaretz*, September 22, 2010, http://www.haaretz.com/weekend/week-s-end/before-the-curtain-fell-1.315177.
45. "Rani," Tel-Aviv Theatre, *Cinema Treasures*, http://cinematreasures.org/theaters/23633. The Cinema Tel Aviv was demolished in 2011.
46. "Focus on Tel Aviv-Jaffa," *Jerusalem Post*, January 17, 2003, 10.
47. Slomovitz, "David Idzal Introduces," 1.
48. "Israeli to Get Latest Type Cinema in Fall," 18.
49. "190 Motion Picture Theaters in Israel Close; Protest Ticket Taxes," *Jewish Telegraphic Agency*, April 18, 1958, 1.
50. Investments, Egypt: Purchase of TV Sets for U.A.R. Govt, 53:2 March 22, 1960, Telegram from Skouras to Minister Hatem; Notes for discussion between Skouras and Abdel Kader Hatem, March 18, 1960; Letter from J. Kattan at Emerson to Skouras, March 22, 1960; Letter from Martin F. Bennett at RCA to Skouras, March 22, 1960; Letter from Skouras to Bennett, March 23, 1960; Telegram from Skouras to Hatem, March 24, 1960; Telegram from Skouras to Hatem, March 31, 1960; Telegram from Skouras to F. Ibrahim, April 13, 1960; Telegram from Skouras to F. Ibrahim, April 15, 1960; Telegram F. Ibrahim to Skouras, April 21, 1960; Telegram from Hatem to Skouras, May 2, 1960; Telegram from F. Ibrahim to Skouras, May 3, 1960; Telegram from F. Ibrahim to Skouras, May 31, 1960; F. Ibrahim to Skouras, June 10, 1960, all from Box 53, Folder 2, SPS.
51. Fathi Ibrahim to Spyros P. Skouras, May 18, 1960, Box 48, Folder 3, SPS.
52. "Memorandum—Egypt," undated, ca. 1960, Box 48, Folder 3, SPS.
53. Telegram, Spyros to Ibrahim, December 23, 1960, Box 48, Folder 3, SPS.
54. Slator C. Blackiston Jr. to "The Files," August 21, 1962, RG 59, Bureau of Near Eastern and South Asian Affairs, Office of Near Eastern Affairs, records of the United Arab Republic affairs desk, 1956–1962, Box 3, HM 1994, NARA.
55. Spyros Skouras to Gamal Abdel Nasser, July 25, 1963, Box 12, Folder 2, SPS.
56. David Lamb, "The Sorry Scenario of Egyptian Movies," *Washington Post*, May 31, 1984, B4.

57. Stellaa, "Cinema, Alexandria the 1960's," *OpenSalon* (blog), May 28, 2008, http://web.archive.org/web/20090315164553/http://open.salon.com/blog/stellaa/2008/05/28/cinema_alexandria_the_1960s.
58. "Memorandum—Egypt."
59. Fathi Ibrahim to Spyros P. Skouras, August 4, 1961, Box 50, Folder 7, SPS.
60. Ibrahim to Skouras, August 4, 1961.
61. Spyros Skouras to Fathy Ibrahim, August 22, 1961, Box 50, Folder 7, SPS.
62. "Agreement," ca. 1961, Box 50, Folder 7, SPS.
63. Telegram, Spyros Skouras to Fathi Ibrahim, April 4, 1961, Box 50, Folder 7, SPS.
64. Fathi Ibrahim to Murray Silverstone, July 28, 1961, Box 50, Folder 7, SPS.
65. Fathi Ibrahim to Murray Silverstone, July 28, 1961.
66. Telegram, Fathi Ibrahim to Spyros Skouras, August 13, 1961, Box 50, Folder 7, SPS.
67. Robert Vitalis, "American Ambassador in Technicolor and Cinemascope Hollywood and Revolution on the Nile," in *Mass Mediations: New Approaches to Popular Culture in the Middle East and Beyond*, ed. Walter Armbrust, ed. (Berkeley: University of California Press, 2000).
68. Fathi Ibrahim to Spyros P. Skouras, March 23, 1961, Box 40, Folder 14, SPS.
69. As *New York Jewish Week* observed in 2015, "During her lengthy career she worked hard for Jewish charitable causes and on behalf of the new state of Israel, which she visited frequently." "Marilyn Monroe, Liz Taylor Were Seriously Jewish, Exhibit Explains," *New York Jewish Week*, November 30, 2015, https://jewishweek.timesofisrael.com/marilyn-monroe-liz-taylor-were-seriously-jewish-exhibit-explains/.
70. Gabe Friedman, "Before Gal Gadot, Liz Taylor Sparked Debate as Jewish Actress Playing Cleopatra," *Times of Israel*, October 13, 2020, https://www.timesofisrael.com/before-gal-gadot-liz-taylor-sparked-debate-as-jewish-actress-playing-cleopatra/; and "Ask Nasser Okay for 'Cleopatra,'" *Variety*, July 27, 1960, 5.
71. Walter Wanger and Joe Hyams, *My Life with Cleopatra: The Making of a Hollywood Classic* (New York: Vintage), 2013, 42.
72. Wanger and Hyams, *My Life with Cleopatra*, 107.
73. Lloyd Shearer, "Hollywood's Biggest Gamble: Blockbusters," *Charleston* (WV) *Gazette-Mail*, July 22, 1962, 80; see also "Marilyn Monroe, Liz Taylor"; and Telegram, Spyros Skouras to Fathi Ibrahim, April 4, 1961, Box 50, Folder 7, SPS.
74. Wanger and Hyams, 207.
75. Carlo Curti, *Skouras: King of Fox Studios* (Los Angeles: Holloway House, 1967), 270.
76. Wanger and Hyams, *My Life with Cleopatra*, 208.
77. "Elizabeth Taylor Barred from Egypt; Is Blacklisted as Jewish," *Jewish Telegraphic Agency Daily News Bulletin*, July 20, 1962, 2.
78. Robert C. Strong to Mr. Grant, August 16, 1962, RG 59, Bureau of Near Eastern and South Asian Affairs, Office of Near Eastern Affairs, records of the United Arab Republic affairs desk, 1956–1962, Box 3, HM 1994, NARA.
79. Strong to Grant, August 16, 1962.
80. "Says Egypt Not Anti-Semitic Now; Wanna Make Pix," *Variety*, October 16, 1963, 1.
81. Spyros Skouras to Fathi Ibrahim, August 23, 1963, Box 50, Folder 7, SPS.
82. Haim Hanegbi, Moshe Machover, and Akiva Orr, "The Class Nature of Israeli Society," in *Israelis and Palestinians: Conflict and Resolution*, ed. Moshe Machover (Chicago: Haymarket Books, 2012), 81–82.
83. "G.U.S.-Rassco Widens Scope of Investments," *Jerusalem Post*, January 7, 1965, A2.

84. David B. Green, "A Knight with a Golden Touch, Who Liked Giving Away His Money, Is Born," *Haaretz*, September 17, 2015, http://www.haaretz.com/jewish/features/.premium-1.676172; and Allen Eyles, *ABC: The First Name in Entertainment* (London: Cinema Theatre Association, 1993), 20.
85. Spyros Skouras to Isaac Wolfson, March 30, 1961, Box 50, Folder 9, SPS.
86. Isaac Wolfson to Spyros P. Skouras, April 13, 1961, Box 50, Folder 9, SPS; Spyros Skouras to Isaac Wolfson, April 24, 1961, Box 50, Folder 9, SPS; and Isaac Wolfson to Spyros P. Skouras, May 10, 1961, Box 50, Folder9, SPS.
87. "Zanuck in Command; Postpones 3 Movies, Accepts Resignations," *Daily Press* (Utica, NY), August 28, 1962, 17.
88. Skouras kept up his political and financial support for Israel after his retirement and until his death in August 1971, continuing associations with the American Israel Public Affairs Committee, the American-Israel Chamber of Commerce and Industry, and the American Jewish Committee. Organizations and Charities, Commercial American-Israel Chamber of Commerce, Box 62, Folder 2, SPS; and "Obituaries: Spyros P. Skouras," *Variety*, August 18, 1971, 55.
89. Carl Alpert, "Big Screen Versus Little Screen," *Southern Israelite*, December 20, 1968, 7.
90. Alpert, "Big Screen Versus Little Screen," 7.
91. James Feron, "Bombs—a Hazard of Moviegoing; Jerusalem's Theaters a Favorite Target of Terrorists," *New York Times*, August 31, 1968, 8.
92. "Terrorist Incident in Tel Aviv Theater," December 1974, 1974TELAV07172 (NARA-AAD).
93. "Ushers Bid for 'Violence Bonus' Closes Cinema," *Jerusalem Post*, June 17, 1975, 3; see also Untitled, *Jewish Telegraphic Agency Daily News Bulletin*, June 20, 1975, 4.
94. "Warner Fox Shuts Tel Aviv Theatre Following Strike," *Variety*, July 2, 1975, 12; and "Ushers Bid for 'Violence Bonus' Closes Cinema," 3.
95. "Warner Fox Shuts Tel Aviv Theatre Following Strike," 12.
96. "A. D. Matalon to Handle Fox Product in Israel," *Boxoffice*, December 30, 1976, 1.
97. "Tel Aviv Cinema Sold by 20th-Fox to Local Investors for $1.7-Mil," *Variety*, January 10, 1979, 67.
98. Samir Raafat, "Cinema Metro," (unedited version), *Cairo Times*, Thursday, May 15, 1997.
99. "Egypt Finally Okays Liz & Fox's 'Cleopatra,'" *Variety*, March 20, 1968, 28.
100. "Houses Now Being Built Are Among MGM's Divestiture," *Daily Variety*, September 18, 1973, 115; and "MGM Due to Split with EMI in Brit.; Distrib Via CIC," *Variety*, November 7, 1973, 4.
101. Raafat, "Cinema Metro."
102. "Libyan Bombings Affect Egyptian Public," August 1976, 1976CAIRO11245, NARA-AAB.
103. Hank Werba, "Sadat Slaying, Paris Nyet, Meagre O'Seas Pix Hurt Cairo Fest; Will Re-Org," *Variety*, January 6, 1982, 7.
104. "Nasser, Sadat, and Now; Yanks' Interest in Egypt Is Varied," *Variety*, May 12, 1982, 390.
105. David Lamb, "Only the Peasants Go: Egypt's Film Industry: On Hard Times," *Los Angeles Times*, April 28, 1984, 20.
106. Lamb, "Only the Peasants Go," 1, 20.
107. Lamb, "Only the Peasants Go," 1, 20.
108. Raafat, "Cinema Metro."

109. "Cinema Metro Movie Theater," *Cityseekr* website, n.d., http://cairo.cityseekr.com/venue/196518-cinema-metro.
110. Klein, "Before the Curtain Fell."
111. "Focus on Tel Aviv-Jaffa," 10.

15. MGM and the "Uncrowned King of South Africa," 1932–1937

1. Allison K. Shutt and Tony King, "Imperial Rhodesians: The 1953 Rhodes Centenary Exhibition in Southern Rhodesia," *Journal of Southern African Studies* 31, no. 2 (2005): 362.
2. Thelma Gutsche, *The History and Social Significance of Motion Pictures in South Africa, 1895–1940* (Cape Town: H. Timmins, 1972), 232–76.
3. Neil Parsons, "Investigating the Origins of The Rose of Rhodesia, Part II: Harold Shaw Film Productions Ltd.," *Screening the Past*, January 2015, http://www.screeningthepast.com/2015/01/investigating-the-origins-of%C2%A0the-rose-of-rhodesia-part-ii-harold-shaw-film-productions-ltd/.
4. Keyan G. Tomaselli, *Ideology and Cultural Production in South African Cinema* (Johannesburg: University of Witwatersrand, 1983), ii, iii, vii, 38, 39.
5. Some of the key texts since that time include Keyan G. Tomaselli, *The Cinema of Apartheid* (Brooklyn, NY: Smyrna, 1988); and Johan Blignaut and Martin Botha, *Movies, Moguls, Mavericks: South African Cinema, 1979–1991* (Cape Town: Showdata, 1992).
6. Lawrence Mbogoni observed in 2013 that "the study of film as a medium of communication in colonial Tanganyika, like that of radio broadcasting, has [also] attracted little research attention" with "only a few pages" about "the film industry in colonial Tanganyika." Lawrence L. Mbogoni, *Aspects of Colonial History* (Dar es Salaam: Mkuki na Nyota, 2013), 81.
7. James Burns, *Cinema and Society in the British Empire, 1895–1940* (New York: Palgrave Macmillan, 2013).
8. Charles Ambler, "Popular Films and Colonial Audiences: The Movies in Northern Rhodesia," *American Historical Review* 106, no. 1 (2001): 83–84.
9. James R. Brennan, "Democratizing Cinema and Censorship in Tanzania, 1920–1980," *International Journal of African Historical Studies* 38, no. 3 (2005), 484–85.
10. Parsons, "Investigating the Origins."
11. Parsons, "Investigating the Origins."
12. "A Great Man, and a Great Friend Passes, I. W. Schlesinger, 1871–1949," *Paramount International News*, March 20, 1949, 31.
13. Parsons, "Investigating the Origins."
14. Parsons, "Investigating the Origins."
15. Arnold Shepperson and Keyan Tomaselli, "South Africa," in *The International Movie Industry*, ed. Gorham Kindem (Carbondale: Southern Illinois University Press, 2000), 141, 142.
16. "South Africa," *Times* (London), March 19, 1929, xiii. See also "South African Notes," *Billboard*, May 28, 1927, 39; and "South African Notes," *Billboard*, February 4, 1928, 86.
17. Parsons, "Investigating the Origins."
18. Parsons, "Investigating the Origins."
19. Arnold Shepperson and Keyan G. Tomaselli, "South African Cinema Beyond Apartheid," *Social Identities* 6, no. 3 (2000): 323.

20. "South African Notes," *Billboard*, May 28, 1927, 39; and "South African Notes," *The Billboard*, February 4, 1928, 86.
21. Gutsche, *History and Social Significance*, 185; and "Seeks Moving Pictures," *New York Times*, November 21, 1921, 24.
22. "I. W. Schlesinger, So. African Leader," *New York Times*, March 12, 1949, 17.
23. Shepperson and Tomaselli, "South Africa," 141, 142.
24. "South Africa," *Times* (London), March 19, 1929, xiii.
25. "South African Notes," *Billboard*, May 28, 1927, 39.
26. "South Africa," *Billboard*, September 3, 1927, 42.
27. "To Spend $5,000,000 on South African Theaters," *Film Daily*, July 24, 1927, 5; and "News in Brief," *Times* (London), July 5, 1927, 15.
28. "South African Notes," *Billboard*, May 28, 1927, 39.
29. "Broadcasting in South Africa," *Times* (London), January 21, 1927, 13; and H. Hanson, "Foreign: South Africa," *Variety*, July 27, 1927, 58.
30. C. J. North to C. Grant Isaacs, "Film Clippings," April 26, 1927, Bureau of Foreign and Domestic Commerce, Motion Pictures—United Kingdom, 1927, file no. 281, NARA.
31. Shepperson and Tomaselli, "South Africa," 142, 143.
32. "London," *Billboard*, July 13, 1929, 79. Schlesinger wasn't invincible. In April 1930, after the stock market crash and a declining global economic outlook, his United Pictures Theatres Ltd., which owned seventeen cinemas in the London suburbs, fell into "unsatisfactory financial condition." "Schlesinger's U. P. Cos Unsatisfactory Report," *Variety*, April 30, 1930, 6, 56.
33. "80 Kinemas Houses, So. Africa, First to Break Through Wall Built Up by African Trust," *Variety*, November 20, 1929, 3; and "South African Film Industry," *Times* (London), April 26, 1929, 14.
34. "80 Kinemas Houses, So. Africa," 3.
35. "South Africa," *Times* (London), March 19, 1929, xiii.
36. H. Hanson, "Protests Against Schlesingers' South African Rule Strike Snag," *Motion Picture Herald*, December 22, 1934, 19.
37. "Movie Theater Chain Started by Purchase of Johannesburg Site," *Chicago Daily Tribune*, April 17, 1931, 34.
38. Gutsche, *History and Social Significance*, 214.
39. Shepperson and Tomaselli, "South Africa," 144, 145.
40. "Loew Orders Carrier System for South African Theatre," *Motion Picture Herald*, August 8, 1931, 33.
41. H. Hanson, "South Africa," *Variety*, December 13, 1932, 11.
42. Hanson, "South Africa," *Variety*, December 13, 1932, 11.
43. Gutsche, *History and Social Significance*, 233, 234.
44. Over the following four decades, the Union's racial policies grew more and more draconian, limiting access to voting, social services, employment, public venues, and many other aspects of South African life. Apartheid eventually became official policy in 1948.
45. Untitled, *Motion Picture Herald*, July 16, 1932, 68; and "Off to So. Africa," *Variety*, October 11, 1932, 62.
46. Hanson, "South Africa," *Variety*, December 13, 1932, 11.
47. "Loew Quits Flying at Mother's Request—His Miraculous Escape," *Variety*, November 22, 1932, 2; and "Loew Back by Boat," *Variety*, November 29, 1932, 3.
48. H. Hanson, "South Africa," *Variety*, November 1, 1932, 44.
49. H. Hanson, "South Africa," *Variety*, March 21, 1933, 46.

50. Hanson, "Protests Against Schlesingers' South African Rule," 19.
51. "Metro Building in S. A.?," *Variety*, May 29, 1935, 15.
52. "Schlesinger Suit Won by Metro," *Variety*, February 19, 1936, 23.
53. "Carl J. Sonin Is Dead," *Motion Picture Daily*, January 3, 1935, 2.
54. "M-G-M Set to Build Two in South Africa," *Motion Picture Daily*, February 29, 1936, 1, 4; and "Loew-MGM Building Theatres Abroad To Insure Representation, *Motion Picture Herald*, June 27, 1936, 32.
55. "Attendance in South Africa," *Film Daily*, June 26, 1936, 22.
56. "Metro Plans 12 New Spots 'Round Globe," *Motion Picture Daily*, July 12, 1937, 1; and "Metro's African Theatre," *Wall Street Journal*, August 13, 1937, 9.

16. Fox Hunting on the African Continent, 1937–1956

1. "20th-Fox Will Have South Africa Branch," *Motion Picture Daily*, August 5, 1937, 6.
2. "UA-20th-Fox Unite in South Africa," *Motion Picture Daily*, October 31, 1938, 1.
3. Arthur W. Kelly to Edward G. Raftery, July 20, 1937, MSS 99an, Series 2a, O'Brien Legal File, 38–9, UA-WHS.
4. "Hutchinson to Africa," *Film Daily*, June 6, 1938, 1.
5. "20th-Fox Expanding in Southern Africa," *Film Daily*, March 14, 1938, 1, 6.
6. Keyan G. Tomaselli, *Ideology and Cultural Production in South African Cinema* (Johannesburg: University of Witwatersrand, 1983), 71; and Thelma Gutsche, *The History and Social Significance of Motion Pictures in South Africa, 1895–1940* (Cape Town: H. Timmins, 1972), 257, 258, 261.
7. "20th-Fox Expanding in Southern Africa," 1, 6.
8. "20th-Fox Investing in African Theater," *Film Daily*, June 1, 1938, 1, 10.
9. "South Africa Circuit Aims at 40 Houses," *Motion Picture Daily*, June 21, 1938, 1, 7; and "Hutchinson Sails Friday For S. A., African Tour," *Film Daily*, July 27, 1938, 1, 3.
10. "20th-Fox Expanding in Southern Africa," 1, 6.
11. "20th-Fox Investing in African Theater," 1, 10.
12. "Hutchinson Sails Friday for S. A., African Tour," 1, 3.
13. "U.S. May Build More Theatres in South Africa," *Variety*, June 1938, 233.
14. "UA-20th-Fox Unite in South Africa," 1.
15. Albert A. Lowe to Paul O'Brien, September 28, 1948, United Artists Corporation, MSS 99AN, Series 2A, O'Brien Legal File, 1919–1951, UA-WHS.
16. "A. Hutchinson of 20th Details Plan for Fox Co. and UA to Invade South African Field," *Variety*, December 28, 1938, 4; and "So. Africa Cautious About Over-Seating," *Variety*, December 28, 1938, 4.
17. Arnold Shepperson and Keyan Tomaselli, "South Africa," in *The International Movie Industry*, ed. Gorham Kindem (Carbondale: Southern Illinois University Press, 2000), 144.
18. "Foreign Sales Chiefs Conjecture at Large, but Hopefulness Is Their General Keynote," *Boxoffice*, September 9, 1939, 17; and Shepperson and Tomaselli, "South Africa," 144.
19. "So. Africa Building Boomed by 20th-Fox," *Motion Picture Daily*, March 6, 1939, 10.
20. 20th-Fox Invests $250,000 In South African Theater," *Film Daily*, April 10, 1939 (?), 8; "Launch Palestine Producing Co.," *Film Daily*, July 25, 1947, 1, 4; and "UA Sets Up Own So. African Distrib System," *Variety*, April 26, 1939, 3.
21. "20th-Fox Opens First South African House," *Motion Picture Daily*, March 18, 1940, 2.

22. "Lourie Sets $250,000 20th-Fox Deal, Sails," *Motion Picture Daily*, April 10, 1939, 7.
23. "Lange Sees U.S. Films Cut to 20% Abroad," *Motion Picture Daily*, July 31, 1940, 4; and "South African Building Boom," *Motion Picture Herald*, September 7, 1940, 38.
24. Gutsche, *History and Social Significance of Motion Pictures in South Africa*, 261.
25. "85 Outlets For UA-20th In So. Africa," *Variety*, April 23, 1941, 14; and H. Hanson, "Over-Building Hits Film Biz in S. Africa," *Variety*, January 7, 1942, 106.
26. Arthur Kelly to A. A. Lowe, October 20, 1939, United Artists Series 2A, Box 38, Folder 11, UA-WHS.
27. Kelly to Lowe, October 20, 1939.
28. "UA to Have 1st-Run House in Capetown," *Film Daily*, July 14, 1941, 1, 4.
29. "New 20th-UA House," *Variety*, August 1941, 16; and R. N. Barrett, "In Johannesburg," *Motion Picture Herald*, August 2, 1947, 42.
30. "Lourie, Boxer Guilty," *Variety*, April 8, 1942, 18; H. Hanson, "South Africa," *Variety*, June 17, 1942, 53; and J. Hansen, "South Africa," *Variety*, February 17, 1943, 45.
31. "UAs GM in So. Africa Cites Russia's Ambitions in the World Pix Market," *Variety*, August 1, 1945, 2.
32. "To Build, Alter 250 S. African Theatres," *Motion Picture Daily*, March 23, 1945, 12; and "UAs GM in So. Africa Cites Russia's Ambitions in the World Pix Market," 2, 38.
33. "Majors May Open Offices in Africa," *Motion Picture Herald*, November 11, 1944, 42.
34. "To Build, Alter 250 S. African Theatres," 12.
35. Barrett, "In Johannesburg," 42.
36. "Twentieth Century-Fox, Rank Set South African Deal," *Film Daily*, April 25, 1945, 1, 3.
37. "Universal-Rank Get South Africa Tieup," *Boxoffice*, March 29, 1947, 62.
38. "Rank-U-Schlesinger Finally Conclude South African Exhib-Distrib Deal," *Variety*, March 19, 1947, 16.
39. "Rank Dickers for So. Africa Chain," *Variety*, September 11, 1946, 11.
40. "Rank-U-Schlesinger Finally Conclude South African Exhib-Distrib Deal," 16.
41. R. N. Barrett, "South Africa," *Motion Picture Herald*, February 1, 1947, 45.
42. "S. Africa Market on Pix Upbeat," *Variety*, April 9, 1947, 13.
43. "News in Brief," *Times* (London), March 13, 1948, 7.
44. Barrett, "South Africa," 45.
45. "Metro In 10-Year Deal for Africa," *Motion Picture Herald*, July 26, 1947, 46.
46. "M-G Africa Pact Aimed at Rank," *Variety*, July 23, 1947, 6.
47. "Metro in 10-Year Deal for Africa," 46.
48. R. N. Barrett "20th-Fox Opens S. Africa Office," *Motion Picture Herald*, November 16, 1946, 34; and R. N. Barrett, "20th-Fox Acquires S. Africa Circuit," *Motion Picture Daily*, November 18, 1946, 6.
49. "20th-Fox Studying 16mm. for Africa," *Film Daily*, November 29, 1946, 8.
50. "Forms Company for Production in Palestine," *Motion Picture Herald*, August 2, 1947, 43.
51. United Artists Corporation (S.A.) (Pty.) (Ltd.) to Secretary of the Treasury, Government of the Union of South Africa Pretoria, South Africa, October 5, 1949, United Artists Corporation, MSS 99AN, Series 2A, O'Brien Legal File, 38-8, UA-WHS.
52. Garth Jowett, "Apartheid and Socialization: Movie-Going in Cape Town, 1943–1958," *Historical Journal of Film, Radio and Television* 26, no. 1 (2006): 13.
53. John S. Saul and Stephen Gelb, "The Crisis in South Africa: Class Defense, Class Revolution," *Monthly Review* 33, no. 3 (1981): 9, 10, 14, 15.
54. Nicoli Nattrass, "Controversies About Capitalism and Apartheid in South Africa: An Economic Perspective," *Journal of Southern African Studies* 17, no. 4 (December 1991): 654.

55. Gina Taylor, "South Africans Immersed in White Superiority," *Sun Reporter* (San Francisco), October 7, 1972, 44. The term "Asians" meant South Asians. It did not apply to Japanese people, for example, but to *darker-skinned* Asian people and is thus bound up in the racial hierarchies of apartheid.
56. Albert A. Lowe to Paul O'Brien, September 28, 1948, United Artists Corporation, MSS 99AN, Series 2A, O'Brien Legal File, 1919–1951, Wisconsin Historical Society, 38, 39; and "President's Message," *Twentieth Century-Fox, 1949 Annual Report* (New York: Twentieth Century-Fox, 1949), 4.
57. "A Great Man, and a Great Friend Passes, I. W. Schlesinger, 1871–1949," *Paramount International News*, March 20, 1949," 31.
58. Untitled, *Kalgoorlie Miner* (Western Australia), March 7, 1950, 2.
59. "South Africa Sees Big Screen T.V. First," *South Coast Times and Wollongong Argus* (New South Wales), July 31, 1950, 2.
60. "Max Schlesinger, Theatre Official," *New York Times*, February 26, 1953, 25.
61. "A Harvard Man in South Africa," *New York Times*, January 20, 1964, 82.
62. "A Millionaire Adds to His Empire," *Sunday Herald* (Sydney), July 19, 1953, 13; and "Odeon Cinema Deal," *Times* (London), July 14, 1953, 6.
63. "Review of Operations," *Twentieth Century-Fox, 1953 Annual Report* (New York: Twentieth Century-Fox, 1953), 12; and Arnold Hanson, "Schlesinger Org's Jubilee Fete Aids S. Africa's Prosperous Show Biz Year," Variety, December 30, 1953, 12.
64. "Review of Operations," *Twentieth Century-Fox, 1953 Annual Report*, 12.
65. "Fox Builds New Theatre in Tel Aviv," *Motion Picture Herald*, April 23, 1955, 32.
66. "Chatter: So. Africa," *Variety*, November 18, 1953, 78.
67. "More Building or Buying Abroad Plans of Both Metro and 20th-Fox," *Variety*, May 19, 1954, 5.
68. Charles S. Reed II to Department of State, "Negotiations for Acquisition of African Consolidated Theatres by Twentieth Century Fox Film Corporation," June 20, 1955, 845A.451/6-2055, NARA.
69. Reed to Department of State, June 20, 1955.
70. "Schlesinger Empire to Fox?" *Variety*, June 15, 1955, 3, 18.
71. "20th-Schlesinger Deal Is Finalized," *Motion Picture Daily*, July 8, 1955, 1, 7.
72. "Schlesinger Empire to Fox?," 18.
73. "See Protracted Talks On 20th-Fox Deal with Schlesinger," *Motion Picture Daily*, July 1, 1955, 1, 4; and "Fox-Schlesinger," *Motion Picture Daily*, July 5, 1955, 7.
74. "Ratify Fox Purchase of Schlesinger Circuit," *Motion Picture Daily*, July 2, 1956, 1.
75. "African Theatres," *Times* (London), November 7, 1955, 13.
76. "Wits Notes—1956," 1956/12/29, 13–14, Fox Theatres South Africa (Proprietary, Limited (Incorporated in the Union of South Africa) Balance Sheet And Accounts—29th December 1956 and on Consolidated Balance Sheet & Accounts—29th December 1956 of Fox Theatres South Africa (Proprietary) Limited and Its Subsidiary Companies and Directors Report, all from ZA HPRA A1724-F-Fd, Fox Theatres S.A. (Pty) Ltd, General Correspondence 1956–1966, Zebediela Citrus Estate, Historical Papers Research Archive, University of the Witwatersrand, Johannesburg, South Africa (hereafter, WITS); and E. F. Lomba to Spyros P. Skouras, September 26, 1957, Box 51, Folder 5, SPS.
77. "Excerpt from the 'Rand Daily Mail' Dated Nov. 3, 1955: *Schlesinger Explains Why African Theatres Is Selling to Skouras*," 845a.452/11-1055, NARA.
78. Peter Burnup, "Will Sign Fox-Schlesinger Deal Monday," *Motion Picture Daily*, July 21, 1955, 1, 3.
79. Charles S. Reed II to Department of State, July 21, 1955, 845A.452/7-2155, NARA.

80. Reed to Department of State, July 21, 1955.
81. Reed to Department of State, July 21, 1955.
82. "20th-Schlesinger Deal Is Finalized," 1, 7.
83. "Fox Theatres Group, Mr. S. P. Skouras—Conference," September 11, 1957, Spyros P. Skouras Papers, 1942–1971, Box 51, Folder 55, SPS.
84. "Whose Screen Is Biggest?," *International Projectionist*, December 1955, 28.
85. Edward Wailes to Department of State, June 29, 1955, 845A.452/6-2955, NARA.
86. Wailes to Department of State, June 29, 1955. See also "Skouras Clarifies Many Points," *Variety*, August 3, 1955, 4.
87. "Skouras Buys in Africa," *New York Times*, July 8, 1955, 14.
88. Wailes to Department of State, June 29, 1955.
89. Victor Von Lossberg to Department of State, November 10, 1955, 845A.452/11-1055, NARA.
90. "Comments on Operations," *Twentieth Century-Fox, 1956 Annual Report* (New York: Twentieth Century-Fox, 1957), 15; and Gwen Thompkins, "Curtain Call for Kenya's Last Outdoor Picture Show," *NPR*, March 23, 2009, http://www.npr.org/templates/story/story.php?storyId=102168350.
91. David J. Gainer, "Hollywood, African Consolidated Films, and "Bioskoopbeskawing," Or Bioscope Culture: Aspects of American Culture in Cape Town, 1945–1960." Master's thesis, University of Cape Town, January 2000.
92. "Comments on Operations," 15; and Thompkins, "Curtain Call."
93. "Twentieth Century-Fox Buys 144 South African Theatres," *Wall Street Journal*, July 2, 1956, 5; and "Skouras Report Range: Juve Bait, Oil, South Africa," *Variety*, October 3, 1956, 3, 28.
94. "Drive-In Theatres the World Over," *Boxoffice*, February 3, 1958, 58, 60; and "Climate Favors So. Africa Drive-Ins," *Variety*, April 15, 1959, 102.
95. "Wits Notes—1956."
96. Evelyn Levison, "Climate Favors So. Africa Drive-Ins," *Variety*, April 15, 1959, 102.
97. "Continuous Film Flow Vital Now," *Motion Picture Daily*, April 24, 1957, 1, 7.
98. Miscellaneous Scrapbook, 1957–1960s, General Correspondence 1956–1966, Zebediela Citrus Estate, WITS.
99. "Continuous Film Flow Vital Now," 1, 7.
100. "20th-Fox So. Africa Ozoner," *Variety*, August 6, 1958, 14.
101. "Filming Take-Over on Rand Cape Times Correspondent," Clipping, Miscellaneous Scrapbook, 1957–1960s, General Correspondence 1956–1966, Zebediela Citrus Estate, WITS.
102. African Film Productions Limited. (Incorporated in the Union of South Africa), Circular to Members, May 29, 1959, 11-18, General Correspondence 1956–1966, Zebediela Citrus Estate, WITS.

17. A "Royal" Mess

1. Stuart Cloete, *The Turning Wheels* (Boston: Houghton Mifflin, 1937); and "S. Africa Novelist Stuart Cloete Dies," *LAT*, March 21, 1976, A24; and "Cloete Banned," *Time*, January 24, 1938. http://content.time.com/time/magazine/article/0,9171,759007,00.html#ixzz2e8FxgTbq.
2. "Van Johnson Will Star in 'Steak for Connie,'" *Los Angeles Times*, June 2, 1952, B8; Thomas M. Pryor, "Metro Will Film 'Turning Wheels,'" *New York Times*, May 6,

1952, 34; and Philip K. Scheuer, "Africa Recalls Granger," *Los Angeles Times*, November 6, 1952, A9.
3. Jack Henry Stodel, *The Audience Is Waiting* (Cape Town: H. Timmins, 1962), 182–83.
4. "20th Bankrolling Stuart Cloete's S. African Novel," *Variety*, December 18, 1957, 7.
5. "Kidding-on-the-Square Letter from Skouras on 'So. Pacific' in So. Africa," *Variety*, March 2, 1960, 79.
6. Frederic Fox, "Nellie Forbush In Rhodesia: 'Very Much Lovely' Was One Boy's Reaction to 'South Pacific,'" *New York Times*, March 11, 1962, SM55.
7. "'Carmen Jones' Okay with South Africans," *Chicago Defender*, October 27, 1956, 9.
8. Allison K. Shutt and Tony King, "Imperial Rhodesians: The 1953 Rhodes Centenary Exhibition in Southern Rhodesia," *Journal of Southern African Studies* 31, no. 2 (2005): 362.
9. Clarence B. Randall to Eric Johnston, October 19, 1959, Desegregation of Cinemas Correspondence with Spyros Skouras, 1959–1961/3110D (hereafter, DCCSS), RG 59, NARA.
10. "Federal American Businesses and Race Relations," *African Daily News*, June 22, 1959, DCCSS.
11. Michael Oliver West, *The Rise of an African Middle Class: Colonial Zimbabwe, 1898–1965* (Bloomington: Indiana University Press, 2002), 113, 191.
12. Joseph Palmer to Joseph Satterthwaite, July 2, 1959, DCCSS.
13. Joseph Satterthwaite to Joseph Palmer, August 27, 1959, DCCSS.
14. "Rhodesian Group Fights Color Bar," *New York Times*, September 27, 1959, 37.
15. West, *Rise of an African Middle Class*, 62, 197; and Bizeck Jube Phiri, "The Capricorn Africa Society Revisited: The Impact of Liberalism in Zambia's Colonial History, 1949–1963," *International Journal of African Historical Studies* 24, no. 1 (1991): 65–68.
16. "Fortnightly Notes and Comments," clipping, September 6, 1959, DCCSS.
17. "'We Cannot Afford to Withdraw'—Red Cross," *Rhodesia Herald*, n.d., DCCSS.
18. "'Nationalise Cinemas,'" D. N. Staff Reporter, clipping, DCCSS.
19. "Rhodesian Group Fights," 37.
20. Fox, "Nellie Forbush in Rhodesia," SM55.
21. "'We Cannot Afford to Withdraw.'"
22. "Rhodesian Group Fights Color Bar," 37.
23. "Capricorn Protest at 'Royal' Colour Bar," *Rhodesia Herald*, n.d., DCCSS.
24. "A Wise Decision," *African Daily News*, September 5, 1959, DCCSS.
25. "Rhodesian Group Fights Color Bar," 37.
26. Leonard Ingalls, "Rhodesia Resists Anti-Bias Moves," *New York Times*, September 23, 1959, 5.
27. Alexandra Rema, "A Chance That Was Missed," *Rhodesia Herald*, n.d., DCCSS.
28. Jocelyn Alexander, "'Hooligans, Spivs and Loafers?' The Politics of Vagrancy in 1960s Southern Rhodesia," *Journal of African History* 53 (2012): 348–50.
29. A Correspondent in Washington, "Washington's Answer to the 'Royal Affair,'" *Central African Examiner*, October 10, 1959, 9, 10, DCCSS.
30. Joseph Palmer to Joseph C. Satterthwaite, September 17, 1959, DCCSS.
31. "A Correspondent in Washington," 9, 10.
32. Andrew J. DeRoche, "Frances Bolton, Margaret Tibbetts and the U.S. Relations with the Rhodesian Federation, 1950–1960," in *Living the End of Empire: Politics and Society in Late Colonial Zambia*, ed. Jan-Bart Gewald, Marja Hinfelaar, and Giacomo Macola (Boston: Brill, 2011), 322, 323.
33. Joseph Palmer to Joseph Satterthwaite, October 14, 1959, DCCSS.

34. Joseph Satterthwaite, "Memorandum of Telephone Conversation," October 16, 1959, DCCSS.
35. Clarence Randall to Eric Johnston, October 19, 1959, DCCSS.
36. J. C. Satterthwaite to Joseph Palmer II, October 29, 1959, DCCSS. Despite Satterthwaite's remarks, a letter from JFK to Skouras has not been located in Skouras's papers at Stanford University, the National Archives at College Park, or at the JFK Presidential Library.
37. Spyros Skouras, quoted in Clarence Randall to Joseph Satterthwaite, November 2, 1959, DCCSS.
38. Spyros Skouras to Clarence Randall, November 6, 1959, DCCSS.
39. Joseph Palmer to Joseph Satterthwaite, December 8, 1959, DCCSS.
40. Palmer to Satterthwaite, December 8, 1959.
41. Joseph Satterthwaite to Joseph Palmer, January 20, 1960, DCCSS.
42. Joseph Palmer to Joseph Satterthwaite, February 15, 1960, DCCSS; and Joseph Satterthwaite to Clarence Randall, March 2, 1960, DCCSS.
43. Spyros Skouras to Randall B. Johnson, March 9, 1960, DCCSS.
44. John K. Emmerson to Spyros Skouras, April 25, 1961, DCCSS.
45. Donald Lowry, "Whitehead, Sir Edgar Cuthbert Fremantle (1905–1971)," in *Oxford Dictionary of National Biography* (Oxford: Oxford University Press, 2004), http://www.oxforddnb.com/view/article/31828.
46. Emmerson to Skouras, April 25, 1961.
47. Hugh Ashton to John K. Emmerson, March 29, 1961, DCCSS. British Dominion status was dissolved in 1961 with the drafting of a new constitution for the Republic of South Africa that authorized a forced migration of the country's nonwhite populations into segregated areas.
48. Hugh Ashton to A. H. Stodel, "Race Harmony Committee," March 2, 1961, DCCSS.
49. Ashton to Emmerson, March 29, 1961.
50. Ashton to Emmerson, March 29, 1961.
51. Emmerson to Skouras, April 25, 1961.
52. John Emmerson to Olcott H. Deming, May 29, 1961, DCCSS.
53. Emmerson to Deming, May 29, 1961.
54. E. F. Lomba to Spyros Skouras, June 9, 1959, Box 48, Folder 1, SPS.
55. "Memorandum on TIE's TV Plans in Southern Africa," September 1, 1959, Box 48, Folder 1, SPS.
56. David Stirling to Donald A. Henderson, September 7, 1959, Box 48, Folder 1, SPS; and Richard Hughes, *Capricorn: David Stirling's Second African Campaign* (New York: I. B. Tauris, 2003), 286.
57. Donald A. Henderson to Spyros P. Skouras, September 2, 1959, Box, 48, Folder 1, SPS.
58. Spyros Skouras to Edward Lomba, June 17, 1959, Box 48, Folder 1, SPS.
59. "Agreement," August 28, 1959, Box 48, Folder 1, SPS.
60. Untitled, *Rhodesia Property & Finance*, September 1959, n.p., Ziebedela Citrus Estate, Scrapbook, 1957–1960, WITS.
61. "Abroad in Brief," *Broadcasting*, July 20, 1959, 85.
62. Untitled, *Rhodesia Property & Finance*, September 1959, n.p.
63. "Schlesinger May Be in TV Battle," *Daily Mail*, September 17, 1959, n.p., Ziebedela Citrus Estate, Scrapbook, 1957–1960, WITS.
64. "Abroad in Brief," 85; and "Schlesinger May Be in TV Battle," *Daily Mail*, September 17, 1959, WITS.
65. "Foreign TV Stations Increase by 50%," *Broadcasting*, October 26, 1959, 118, 119.

66. Keyan G. Tomaselli, *Ideology and Cultural Production in South African Cinema* (Johannesburg: University of Witwatersrand, 1983), 165, 168.
67. Quoted in Tomaselli, *Ideology and Cultural Production in South African Cinema*, 168. Through government negotiations with Fox, "certain monopolistic conditions" were "voluntarily remedied." Keyan G. Tomaselli, *The South African Film Industry*, 2nd ed. (Johannesburg: University of the Witwatersrand, 1980), 93, 94.
68. Fox and TIE's biggest success came through its investment in Kenya, where, by 1961, Fox held a 12 percent investment in the country's Television Network (Kenya) Ltd. while TIE held a 20 percent stake. Eddie Lomba to Spyros Skouras, October 13, 1961, Box 48, Folder 1, SPS; and "Television," *Twentieth Century-Fox 1961 Annual Report* (New York: Twentieth Century-Fox, 1962), 11.
69. "Foreign: T.V. Taboo in S. Africa," *Weekly Television Digest*, November 9, 1959, 23.
70. "International," *Sponsor*, June 20, 1960, 75.
71. "No TV in S. Africa Before Color Ready," *Motion Picture Daily*, May 12, 1960, 4.
72. "Foreign: T.V. Taboo in S. Africa," 23; and "International," 75.
73. E. F. Lomba to Spyros P. Skouras, August 2, 1961, Box 48, Folder 1, SPS.
74. Donald A. Henderson to E. F. Lomba, August 23, 1961, Box 48, Folder 1, SPS.
75. "Television," *Twentieth Century-Fox 1961 Annual Report*, 11.
76. J. R. T. Wood, *So Far and No Further! Rhodesia's Bid for Independence During the Retreat from Empire, 1959–1965* (Johannesburg: 30 South, 2005), 92, 93.
77. The *New York Times* noted that managers still insisted that their admissions policies were "voluntary" despite changes to the law. "Color Bar Is Lifted: Theatres Open to All Races in Southern Rhodesia," *New York Times*, October 5, 1961, 26.
78. Edward Lomba to Spyros Skouras, October 5, 1961, Box 51, Folder 2, SPS.
79. Arnold Hanson, "Fence Divides So. African Drive-In but New Theatres Despite Apartheid," *Variety*, January 10, 1962, 47.
80. Alan Cousins, "State, Ideology, and Power in Rhodesia, 1958–1972," *International Journal of African Historical Studies* 24, no. 1 (1991): 42.
81. David Gainer, "Hollywood, African Consolidated Films, and 'Bioskoopbeskawing,' or Bioscope Culture: Aspects of American Culture in Cape Town, 1945–1960" (master's thesis, University of Cape Town, 2000), 188–93; and Laura Fair, "Drive-In Socialism: Debating Modernities and Development in Dar es Salaam, Tanzania," *American Historical Review*, October 2013, 1086.
82. Leon Goldstein to Spyros Skouras, April 27, 1960, Box 50, Folder 11, SPS; Spyros Skouras to Leon Goldstein, June 7, 1960, Box 50, Folder 11, SPS; and Leon Goldstein to Spyros Skouras, June 20, 1960, Box 50, Folder 11, SPS.
83. Leon Goldstein to Spyros Skouras, July 27, 1960, Box 51, Folder 2, SPS; Leon Goldstein to Spyros Skouras, January 6, 1961, Box 51, Folder 2, SPS; and Leon Goldstein to Spyros Skouras, February 17, 1961, Box 51, Folder 1, SPS.
84. Gainer, "Hollywood, African Consolidated Films," 83.
85. Thomas Doherty, "Race Houses, Jim Crow Roosts, and Lily White Palaces: Desegregating the Motion Picture Theater," in *Going to the Movies*, ed. Richard Maltby, Melvyn Stokes, and Robert C. Allen (Exeter, UK: University of Exeter Press, 2007), 211.
86. Spyros Skouras to RFK, June 26, 1963, Box 11, Folder 8, SPS; and RFK to Spyros Skouras, July 22, 1963, Box 11, Folder 8, SPS.
87. J. L. Keith, File Minute, June 30, 1941, FO/44F/Colour Discrimination East Africa: Admission of Coloured Persons in Cinemas, East Africa: Admission to Cinemas etc., CO 859/80/15, NA-UK.

452   17. A "Royal" Mess

88. "Mau Mau Uprising: Bloody History of Kenya Conflict," *BBC News*, April 7, 2011, https://www.bbc.com/news/uk-12997138.
89. Spyros Skouras to Eric Johnston, June 1, 1960, Box 19, Folder 6, SPS; "Statement Issued by Mr. Eric Johnston, President of the Motion Picture Association of America, Inc., September 11, 1960, Box 19, Folder 6, SPS.
90. Skouras to Johnston, June 1, 1960, Box 19, Folder 6, SPS; Spyros Skouras to Julius Nyerere, June 1, 1960, Box 19, Folder 6, SPS.
91. Eric Johnston to Spyros Skouras, June 9, 1960, Box 19, Folder 6, SPS.
92. Spyros Skouras to Eric Johnston, August 9, 1960, Box 19, Folder 6, SPS; and "Skouras at Home Base Briefly Before Hollywood," *Variety*, August 10, 1960, 4.
93. "A Current Report on American Films in Africa" (Based on Information collected by Mr. Johnston and Mr. Hetzel in Africa, Motion Picture Export Association of America, Inc., December 1960), Box 19, Folder 6, SPS.
94. "Obituaries," *Variety*, February 26, 1975, 63.
95. Samba Gadjigo, *Ousmane Sembène: The Making of a Militant Artist* (Bloomington: Indiana University Press, 2010), 43.
96. Boubacar Boris Diop, "Ousmane Sembène Ou L'art De Se Jouer Du Destin / Ousmane Sembène or the Art of Playing with Fate," *Africultures* 76, no. 1 (2009): 16–27.
97. Gadjigo, *Ousmane Sembène*, 43, 44.
98. "Obituaries," *Variety*, February 26, 1975, 63.
99. "A Current Report on American Films in Africa," SPS.
100. Donald A. Henderson, March 8, 1962, Box 50, Folder 9, SPS; and Skouras to Marvyn Carton, March 9, 1962, Box 50, Folder 9, SPS.
101. "August 23, 1962, MPEA Meeting, Memorandum," Box 19, Folder 6, SPS.
102. Harris Peel to Eric Johnston, October 26, 1962, Box 19, Folder 6, NARA.
103. "Status of Proposal to Purchase West African Theatres," November 5, 1962, Box 19, Folder 6, SPS.
104. "Nigeria Slowly Improving Film Spots," *Variety*, December 5, 1962, 5.
105. "Chore: African Chain Purchase," *Variety*, June 26, 1963, 3, 24.
106. By 1965 Jack Labow noted that his AMPEC subsidiary was now "paying off in 'considerable profits' for its member companies" and had "realized both its primary and subsidiary aims . . . to improve Yank film earnings as well as to improve the overall U.S. image in that part of Africa." "MPEA's W. Africa Experiment Now Runs at Profit," *Variety*, August 18, 1965, 3.
107. *Variety* noted that "in East Africa distribution is shared largely by Indians and Americans." Gordon Kitchens, "Black Films for African Blacks," *Variety*, May 3, 1972, 199, 206.
108. Pierre Girard, "Maurice Jacquin: 'Les Américains en Afrique Risquent d'Avoir des Surprises,'" *Journal Du Show Business*, February 6, 1970, 1, 5.
109. Kitchens, "Black Films for African Blacks," 199, 206.
110. "A Current Report on American Films in Africa."
111. "MPEA's Vietheer Checks African Sales System," *Variety*, November 7, 1962, 4.
112. "Nigeria Slowly Improving Film Spots," 5.
113. "MGM Theatre, Nigeria, Africa," "Proposed Theatre of One Thousand Seats Located in West Africa," Job #2764, June 29, 1964, Drawings SK1-3, John J. McNamara A.I.A. Architect, Box 5, Folder 3, Avery Library, Columbia University.
114. "U.S. Makers Unite In AFRAM, Deal For 'French' Africa," *Variety*, January 21, 1970, 3; and Ikechukwu Obiaya, "A Break with the Past: The Nigerian Video-film Industry in the Context of Colonial Filmmaking," *Film History* 23, no. 2 (2011), 138.

115. "Push Kenya TV Plans," *Variety*, February 8, 1961, 72.
116. "British Staff for Kenyan TV," *East African Standard*, October 13, 1961, 13; and "TV in '62 Goal Set for Kenya," *Broadcasting*, December 25, 1961, 51.
117. "TV in '62 Goal Set for Kenya," 51.
118. "Television—Kenya," October 13, 1961, Box 48, Folder 1, SPS.
119. E. F. Lomba to Alan M. Silverbach, October 16, 1961, Box 48, Folder 1, SPS.
120. Ed Lomba to Spyros Skouras, October 20, 1961, Box 48, Folder 1, SPS.
121. R. S. Berry to J. J. Miller, October 16, 1961, Box 48, Folder 1, SPS.
122. Gwen Thompkins, "Curtain Call for Kenya's Last Outdoor Picture Show," *NPR*, March 23, 2009, http://www.npr.org/templates/story/story.php?storyId=102168350.
123. Seymour Poe, "The Wide World of Twentieth Century-Fox," *Twentieth Century-Fox 1964 Annual Report* (New York: Twentieth Century-Fox, 1965), n.p.; see also "Color Bar Is Lifted," 26; Hanson, "Fence Divides So. African Drive-In," 47; and Edward Lomba to Spyros Skouras, October 5, 1961, Box 51, Folder 2, SPS.
124. "20th Acquires 13 S. Africa Cinemas," *Variety*, May 12, 1965, 16.
125. Evelyn Levison, "Fox Chain Paces South Africa," *Variety*, April 26, 1967, 153.
126. David Wigston, "A South African Media Map," in *Media Studies: Institutions, Theories, and Issues*, ed. Pieter J. Fourie (Lansdowne: Juta, 2004), 85, 86.
127. Evelyn Levison, "Fox Chain Paces South Africa," 153.
128. Charles S. Reed II to Department of State, July 21, 1955, 845A.452/7-2155, NARA.
129. Evelyn Levison, "Old Hokum Bucket Full as South African Studios Busy," *Variety*, April 26, 1961, 109.
130. "Subsidies Help, Hurt South African Films," *Los Angeles Times*, March 24, 1972, G26.
131. "Subsidies Help, Hurt South African Films," G26.
132. "New Fox Western Opens Tomorrow," *Los Angeles Times*, June 19, 1956, 19.
133. Will, "The Cape Town Affair [1967]," *Silver Remulsion Film Reviews*, March 2, 2015, https://www.silveremulsion.com/2015/03/02/the-cape-town-affair-1967/.
134. "Tsonga and Venda," *South Africa: A Country Study*, ed. Rita M. Byrnes (Washington, DC: Government Printing Office, for the Library of Congress, 1996), http://countrystudies.us/south-africa/48.htm.
135. Laura Fair, *Reel Pleasures: Cinema Audiences And Entrepreneurs In Twentieth-Century Urban Tanzania* (Athens: Ohio University Press, 2018); Glenn Reynolds, "Playing Cowboys and Africans: Hollywood and the Cultural Politics of African Identity," *Historical Journal of Film, Radio and Television* 25, no. 3 (2005); Ch. Didier Gondola, *Tropical Cowboys: Westerns, Violence, and Masculinity in Kinshasa* (Bloomington: Indiana University Press, 2016); and Charles Ambler, "Popular Films and Colonial Audiences: The Movies in Northern Rhodesia," *American Historical Review* 106, no. 1 (February 2001): 81–105.
136. Joseph K. Heumann and Robin L. Murray, "Cape Town Affair: Right-wing Noir, South African Style," *Jump Cut* 47 (2004), https://www.ejumpcut.org/archive/jc47.2005/capetown/text.html.
137. This ruling was an influence on the creation of Neil Blomkamp's 2009 sci-fi film *District 9*, itself a global Hollywood–South Africa coproduction with Sony's TriStar Pictures, which also delves into the role of South African police, race relations, and politics.
138. "Ms Ex-TVers Chopped Up for Theatre Screens," *Variety*, September 27, 1967, 30.
139. Markone Advertisement, *Broadcasting*, October 9, 1967, 23.
140. Edwin Ngure Nyutho, *Evaluation of Kenyan Film Industry: Historical Perspective* (Mauritius: Lambert Academic, 2018), 151.

141. See Fair, *Reel Pleasures*.
142. Nyutho, *Evaluation of Kenyan Film Industry*, 209.
143. "Gazette Notice No. 2820," *Kenya Gazette*, August 4, 1967, 832; and Skouras to Johnston, June 1, 1960.
144. Nyutho, *Evaluation of Kenyan Film Industry*, 209; see also Robert M. Maxon and Thomas P. Ofcansky, *Historical Dictionary of Kenya* (Lanham, Md.: Rowman & Littlefield, 2014), 218–19.
145. Nyutho, *Evaluation of Kenyan Film Industry*, 210.
146. Nyutho, *Evaluation of Kenyan Film Industry*, 151–52.
147. "East African Theaters to Close Doors," *Los Angeles Times*, December 30, 1967, 12.
148. Nyutho, *Evaluation of Kenyan Film Industry*, 209.
149. "MPEA Recognizes Kenya Film Corp," *Variety*, September 18, 1968, 5.
150. "Bellfort to Kenya to Reopen Fox Offices," *Variety*, October 16, 1968, 24.
151. "Algeria Seizes U.S. Distribs," *Variety*, June 4, 1969, 5.
152. Aubrey Tarbox, "20th's Profit Is $14.6-Mil," *Variety*, May 7, 1969, 5.
153. Evelyn Levinson, "Fox Exits and Theories Rife," *Variety*, May 7, 1969, 5.
154. Robert E. Dallos, "Twentieth Century Fox '70 Loss Triples to $77.35 Million," *Los Angeles Times*, March 17, 1971, F8; and "Fox Film Plans to Sell South African Units," *Wall Street Journal*, May 1, 1969, 14.
155. "S. African Interests Sold by 20th-Fox," *Boxoffice*, May 5, 1969, E1; Tarbox, "20th's Profit Is $14.6-Mil," 5; and Levinson, "Fox Exits and Theories Rife," 5.
156. "S. African Interests Sold by 20th-Fox," E1.
157. Evelyn Levinson, "What Follows Fox After Exit from So. Africa?" *Variety*, January 7, 1970, 5.
158. "Raphel, 20th's Foreign Topper Specifies Exec Role of V.P. Livingstone," *Variety*, June 18, 1969, 4, 30.
159. "Twentieth Century-Fox Promotes Stephen Roberts to V-P," *Boxoffice*, May 20, 1974, 4; and "Fox's Van Ewijk for East Africa," *Variety*, September 3, 1975, 3.
160. "Twentieth Century-Fox Promotes Stephen Roberts to V-P," 4; and "Fox's Van Ewijk for East Africa," 3.
161. "Cinema Intl. Corp. Sanguine on Potential Earnings from Former Metro Global Theatres," *Variety*, January 16, 1974, 5.
162. "Cinema Intl. Corp. Sanguine on Potential Earnings," 5; "CIC Names Hoare Theatre Op Veep," *Variety*, September 11, 1974, 5; and "CIC Appoints Hoare to Top Theatre Post," *Independent Film Journal*, September 1974, 12.
163. "WB-CIC Team in So. Africa to Test Lock on Local Film Biz," *Variety*, December 31, 1975, 23.
164. Arnold Shepperson and Keyan Tomaselli, "South Africa," in *The International Movie Industry*, ed. Gorham Kindem (Carbondale: Southern Illinois University Press, 2000), 146–47.
165. Roger Watkins, "CIC Sights A $235-Mil Global Windfall," *Variety*, April 29, 1981, 3, 34.
166. "CIC Status Update," *Variety*, October 14, 1981, 5, 28; and "United Intl Staffing Up," *Variety*, October 21, 1981, 53.
167. "CIC FACT FILE," Cinema International Corporation Files, CTA.
168. "CIC FACT FILE—Case Study," Cinema International Corporation Files, CTA.
169. Secstate Washdc to Amembassy Pretoria, "Subject: The Janeth Rudolph Incident," October 23, 1976, 1976STATE263486, D760398-1154, STATE, THE JANETH RUDOLPH INCIDENT, PRETORIA, NARA-AAD, https://aad.archives.gov/aad/createpdf?rid=306999&dt=2082&dl=1345.

170. Dennis C. Stanfill to Dick Clark, November 15, 1976, Twentieth Century Fox Film Corporation, 95th Congress, Senate Foreign Relations, Subcommittee on African Affairs, Investigation Files, U.S. Corporations-Survey; 00761850725, NARA, Washington, DC.
171. "Warner Communications to Divest Some S.A. Assets," *Baltimore Afro-American*, November 1, 1986, 8.
172. Keyan G. Tomaselli and Arnold Shepperson, "Transformation and South African Cinema in the 1990s," in *Critical Approaches to African Cinema Discourse*, ed. Nwachukwu Frank Ukadike (Lanham, Md.: Lexington, 2014), 117–19.
173. Wigston, "A South African Media Map," 85, 86.
174. Lucia Saks, *Cinema in a Democratic South Africa: The Race for Representation* (Bloomington: Indiana University Press, 2010), 59–62.
175. Philip Mwaniki, "Kenya: Fox Claws for Lion's Share of Cinema Pie," *Nation* (Nairobi), December 20, 2005, https://allafrica.com/stories/200512200618.html.
176. John Kamau, "Kenya: Why Nairobi Is a Cemetery of Cinema Halls," *Nation* (Nairobi), July 15, 2018, https://allafrica.com/stories/201807150008.html.
177. Shepperson and Tomaselli, "South Africa," 147.
178. "Ster-Kinekor Theatres, The Largest Cinema Chain in Africa," *Supple Magazine*, September 4, 2011, http://www.supplemagazine.org/ster-kinekor-theatres-the-largest-cinema-chain-in-africa.html.
179. Thompkins, "Curtain Call."

18. *Benshi* and Ballyhoo, 1927–1973

1. Oswald Wynd, "East Meets Western," *American Heritage* 36, no. 5 (August/September 1985), http://www.americanheritage.com/articles/magazine/ah/1985/5/1985_5_98.shtml.
2. "Famous Players in Japan," *Wall Street Journal*, July 7, 1922, 9.
3. "T. D. Cochrane Saw Japanese Mountains Topple," *New York Times*, September 8, 1923, 1.
4. "News Weeklies Show 'Quake Views,'" *Motion Picture News*, October 6, 1923, 1631.
5. "American Motion Pictures Help Japanese in Reconstruction Work," *New York Times*, April 20, 1924, X4.
6. "Tom D. Cochrane Dies Here at 65," *Motion Picture Daily*, November 10, 1937, 15.
7. Yuko Itatsu, "Japan's Hollywood Boycott Movement of 1924," *Historical Journal of Film, Radio and Television* 28, no. 3 (August 2008): 353.
8. "Rioters in Tokio Stop Foreign Dance; Ban American Films," *New York Times*, June 8, 1924, 1.
9. "Rioters in Tokio Stop Foreign Dance," 1.
10. Izumi Hirobe, *Japanese Pride, American Prejudice: Modifying the Exclusion Clause of the 1924 Immigration Law* (Cambridge: Cambridge University Press, 2001), 14; Itatsu, 355.
11. Itatsu, "Japan's Hollywood Boycott Movement," 355–56.
12. Quoted in Itatsu, "Japan's Hollywood Boycott Movement," 358.
13. Itatsu, "Japan's Hollywood Boycott Movement," 359–62.
14. Itatsu, "Japan's Hollywood Boycott Movement," 364.
15. "Hogaku-Za Starts a Permanent Movie Theater," *Yomiuri Shinbun*, Morning Edition, March 13, 1927, 5; and "Japan Hails the De Luxe Cinema," *Motion Picture News*, July 1, 1927, 2530, 2532.

16. "Paramount in Tokio," *Film Daily*, July 24, 1927, 5.
17. Wynd, "East Meets Western"; "Hogaku-Za Introductory Lineup," *Yomiuri Shinbun*, Morning Edition, April 5, 1927, 5; "Movies at Hogaku-Za," *Yomiuri Shinbun*, Morning Edition, April 26, 1927, 5; and "Price of Hogaku-Za," *Yomiuri Shinbun*, Morning Edition, April 28, 1927, 5.
18. "Japan Hails the De Luxe Cinema," 2530, 2532.
19. "Japan Hails the De Luxe Cinema," 2530, 2532.
20. "Movies, Dance, and Music," *Yomiuri Shinbun*, Morning Edition, May 11, 1927, 5.
21. "Japan Hails the De Luxe Cinema," 2530, 2532.
22. "Movies, Dance, and Music," 5.
23. Wynd, "East Meets Western."
24. Donald Kirihara, *Patterns of Time: Mizoguchi and the 1930s* (Madison: University of Wisconsin Press, 1992), 44.
25. Wynd, "East Meets Western."
26. "Hogaku-Za Finally Becomes a Talkie Movie Theater," *Yomiuri Shinbun*, Morning Edition, January 17, 1929, 10; "First Soundies in Japan," *Hollywood Filmograph*, June 22, 1929, 32; and "Paramount Sound Pictures in Japan," *Film Daily*, June 7, 1929, 5.
27. Kirihara, *Patterns of Time*, 44; and "Paramount Sound Pictures in Japan," 5.
28. Wynd, "East Meets Western."
29. "Hogaku-Za Fires All Gakushi," *Asahi Shinbun*, Morning Edition, June 11, 1929, 7; and "Film Notes," *Billboard*, June 22, 1929, 25.
30. "Freelancing Musicians Appear," *Yomiuri Shinbun*, Morning Edition, July 2, 1929, 10; and "Old World Jottings," *Hollywood Filmograph*, July 13, 1929, 28.
31. "Around the World with Paramount," *Variety*, August 7, 1929, 6, 66.
32. "Hogaku-Za as Long Term Theater," *Yomiuri Shinbun*, Morning Edition, October 7, 1930, 10; Donald Crafton, *Talkies: American Cinema's Transition to Sound* (New York: Scribner's, 1997); and "La Paramount Por El Mundo," *Mensajero Paramount*, March 1931, 30.
33. Markus Nornes, *Cinema Babel: Translating Global Cinema* (Minneapolis: University of Minnesota Press, 2007), 135.
34. Kirihara, *Patterns of Time*, 44.
35. "Talkies Shown Without Benshi," *Yomiuri Shinbun*, Morning Edition, May 20, 1930, 6.
36. Kirihara, *Patterns of Time*, 45.
37. "Paramount and Shouchiku Merge," *Asahi Shinbun*, Morning Edition, May 30, 1931, 7.
38. "Embodiment of the Modern," *Yomiuri Shinbun*, Morning Edition, September 5, 1931, 11.
39. "Foreign Picture Houses Show Increase in Osaka," *Film Daily*, January 24, 1932, 8.
40. "Par's Japanese Theatre Pool Ended, Show Quality Off, Attendance Drops," *Variety*, June 27, 1933, 17.
41. "M-G-M-Fox Japanese Circuit," *Film Daily*, November 29, 1932, 2.
42. Untitled, *Asahi Shinbun*, Morning Edition, June 1, 1933, 11. Reviewing published lists of Paramount cinemas from 1933 to 1934 confirms the loss, for example, of the Hogaku-Za and the Denki Kan. "36 of Par's Foreign Theatres and Nearly All to Profitable Trade," *Variety*, February 7, 1933, 17; and "Paramount Theatre World Activities," *Paramount International News*, June 1, 1934, 10.
43. Kirihara, *Patterns of Time*, 45.
44. Untitled, *Asahi Shinbun*, Morning Edition, June 1, 1933, 11.
45. "Kobayashi Rises," *Motion Picture Herald*, July 6, 1935, 9.

46. Unknown, *St. Petersburg Times*, August 10, 1932.
47. "Metro's Air-Conditioned Tokyo Bldg. and Theatre," *Variety*, February 5, 1936, 15.
48. "Melniker Made MGM Foreign Theatres Head," *Motion Picture Daily*, June 9, 1936, 7; and "More Foreign Houses Are Planned by Loew," *Film Daily*, July 8, 1936, 1, 12. By the end of July 1937, the Metro had still not broken ground, doomed now by growing geopolitical issues. "Metro Planning House For Tokyo, If Possible," *Variety*, July 28, 1937, 20.
49. "Theatre Attendance Drops 20 Per Cent," *Boxoffice*, May 14, 1938, 18.
50. "Foreign Theatres Holding Their Own," *Boxoffice*, May 14, 1938, 19.
51. "Picture Companies," *Production Encyclopedia 1952* (Hollywood, Calif.: The Hollywood Reporter, 1952), 583.
52. "Recap on Gone' Shows Big B.O. Abroad," *Variety*, July 17, 1940, 7.
53. "War Again Upsets Overseas Business," *Motion Picture Herald*, December 20, 1941, 18, 19.
54. Four months later, MGM shipped him off again to its offices in Trinidad. "Cohen Back as MGM Philippine Manager," *Motion Picture Daily*, November 2, 1945, 3.
55. "Noble and Ever Loyal City," *Urban Historian* (blog), n.d., http://theurbanhistorian.tumblr.com/post/43978723581/the-ideal-theater-designed-during-the-1930s-is-a.
56. "Distributors' Business Was $5,600,000 in Far East," *Motion Picture Herald*, January 31, 1942, 43.
57. "The Defense of Leadership in the World," *Motion Picture Daily*, April 17, 1942, sec. 2, 156, 159.
58. "Distributors' Business Was $5,600,000 in Far East," 43.
59. "The Defense of Leadership in the World," 156, 159.
60. "M-G's Cohen, Berman in Japanese Hands," *Variety*, June 24, 1942, 16; and "Metro and Para. Execs. Released by Japanese," *Film Daily*, October 15, 1943, 1, 8.
61. Four months later, MGM shipped him off again to its offices in Trinidad. "Cohen Back as MGM Philippine Manager," 3.
62. "'U' Philippine Manager Safe," *Showmen's Trade Review*, March 3, 1945, 17; "Core Liberated from Japanese," *Showmen's Trade Review*, March 3, 1945, 17; and "WB Philippine Manager Rescued," *Showmen's Trade Review*, March 3, 1945, 17.
63. "National Newsreel: Picture People," *Showmen's Trade Review*, December 7, 1946, 12.
64. Isidra Reyes, "From Palaces to Ruins: The Story of Manila's Dearly Missed Cinemas Cum Architectural Wonders," *ANCX*, February 3, 2020, https://news.abs-cbn.com/ancx/culture/spotlight/02/03/20/from-palaces-to-ruins-the-story-of-manilas-dearly-missed-cinemas-cum-architectural-wonders.
65. "Only 3 Theatres in Manila Usable After Jap Defeat," *Motion Picture Herald*, March 31, 1945, 37.
66. Reyes, "From Palaces to Ruins"; see also "Japs Set Torch to 10 Manila Theaters," *Film Daily*, February 9, 1945, 1.
67. "Only 3 Theatres in Manila Usable After Jap Defeat," 37.
68. "'U's' 'Phantom of Opera' Re-opens Ideal in Manila," *Film Daily*, June 4, 1945, 2.
69. "Philippine Theatres Reopen," *Showmen's Trade Review*, July 21, 1945, 8, 44.
70. "Regional," *Showmen's Trade Review*, July 28, 1945, 24; "Regional," *Showmen's Trade Review*, September 8, 1945, 26; "Cohen Back as MGM Philippine Manager," 3; and Phil M. Daly, "Along the Rialto," *Film Daily*, December 13, 1945, 2.
71. William Kadison, "Prices Double Pre-War," *Film Daily*, August 13, 1945, 7.
72. "Philippines Need 30 Houses: Almy," *Motion Picture Daily*, October 22, 1945, 8.
73. Tina Santos, "Manila Then Was Classy, Entertaining, Grand," *Philippine Daily Inquirer*, n.p. Quoted in comment 60, "The Families of Old Santa Cruz, Manila," *Remembrance of Things Awry*, June 2, 2010, https://remembranceofthingsawry.wordpress.com/2010/06/02/the-families-of-old-santa-cruz-manila/.

74. "Mayer Goes to Tokyo," *Motion Picture Daily*, May 2, 1960, 2.
75. "Old Filipino Cinema Destroyed in Blaze," *Variety*, April 26, 1978, 45.

19. Joining the Global Metro Cub Club, 1936–1973

1. "Indian Cinemas for American Syndicate?," *Bioscope*, April 28, 1927, 22.
2. "Mooser in India for M.-G.-M. Specials," *Variety*, September 21, 1927, 10.
3. "India Is Alarmed Over American Invasion," *Billboard*, December 1, 1928, 3.
4. "Calcutta Critics Aid Crasto's Campaign," *Motion Picture Daily*, November 24, 1934, 76.
5. Michael Hoffay, "With RKO Radio Overseas: Foreign Theatre Managers Aided by Executives of Branch Offices Exhibit Interesting Showmanship," *Motion Picture Herald*, May 16, 1936, 85.
6. Reginald Armour, "Window Displays Now Accepted by Indian Merchants," *Motion Picture Herald*, June 13, 1936, 129.
7. "Foreign Theatres Planned by MGM," *Motion Picture Herald*, November 30, 1935, 42.
8. "Loew-MGM Building Theatres Abroad to Insure Representation," *Motion Picture Herald*, June 27, 1936, 32.
9. "Foreign Theatres Planned by MGM," 42.
10. "Two More Cinemas Planned in Calcutta," *Variety*, March 25, 1936, 12.
11. *Kinematograph Year Book 1938* (London: Kinematograph Publications, 1938), 32.
12. "Another New Cinema for Bombay: An Exclusive M.G.M. House," *Times of India*, December 14, 1935, 9.
13. "Construction of the New Cinema," *Times of India*, June 8, 1938, A8.
14. "Protest Against Erection Of 'Metro' Theatre," *Malaya Tribune*, June 16, 1938, 19.
15. "Ben Cohen to Calcutta," *Motion Picture Herald*, March 5, 1938, 22; "To Manage the 'Metro': Mr. Adolph Beuhrig," *Times of India*, April 23, 1938, 9; and "Metro Cinema Fulfils a Modern Need," *Times of India*, June 8, 1938, A2.
16. "Construction of the New Cinema," A8.
17. David Vinnels and Brent Skelly, *Bollywood Showplaces: Cinema Theatres in India* (Cambridge: E & E Plumridge, 2002), 102, 104.
18. "Broadway Melody of 1938," *Times of India*, June 11, 1938, 7; and Advertisement, *Times of India*, June 8, 1938, 5.
19. "Bombay Daily Hits M-G; Lashes U.S. Film Interests, Too, as Harmful to Local Theatres," *Variety*, July 4, 1938, 11.
20. Wallace Murray to Frederick L. Herron, MPPDA (Foreign Department), MPPDA Record #3051, Letter, February 11, 1939, Reel 12, Frame 12-2426 to 12-2427, MPPDA Digital Archive, Flinders University Library Special Collections, https://mppda.flinders.edu.au/records/3051.
21. "Judas" [Baburao Patel], "Bombay Calling," *filmindia*, August 1938, 7.
22. Sidharth Bhatia, *The Patels of filmindia: Pioneers of Indian Film Journalism* (Mumbai: Indus Source Books, 2015), 9. See also Debashree Mukherjee, "Creating Cinema's Reading Publics: The Emergence of Film Journalism in Bombay," in *No Limits: Media Studies from India*, ed. Ravi Sundaram (Oxford: Oxford University Press, 2013), 177.
23. Judas, "Bombay Calling," *filmindia*, August 1938, 7.
24. "Bombay Benefit Show," *Times of India*, March 2, 1940, 13.
25. "Film Premiere in Aid of War Fund," *Times of India*, September 14, 1940, 4.
26. "English Dialogue in Bombay Movie," *New York Times*, October 6, 1941, 13.
27. Judas, "Bombay Calling," *filmindia*, July 1946, 11, 12.

28. "Blackmailing a National Industry," *filmindia*, August 1946, 7.
29. "Loew's in Overseas Kid Show Promotion," *Film Daily*, June 3, 1947, 1, 7.
30. "New MGM Manual out on Kiddies Shows," *Boxoffice*, October 16, 1948, 26.
31. "New MGM Manual out on Kiddies Shows," 26.
32. "Metro Cub Club in India Is Model for Loew International Theatres," *Boxoffice*, October 23, 1948, 33–34.
33. "Metro Cub Club in India," 33–34.
34. Salman Rushdie, *Midnight's Children* (New York: Knopf, 1981), 206–7.
35. Anvar Alikhan, "Around Midday, from Mt. Sinai," *Outlook*, May 2, 2011. http://www.outlookindia.com/magazine/story/around-midday-from-mt-sinai/271499.
36. Quoted in Chandrima Pal, "My Family Is Full of Terrifying Women: Salman Rushdie," *Mumbai Mirror*, January 30, 2013, https://timesofindia.indiatimes.com/entertainment/hindi/bollywood/news/My-family-is-full-of-terrifying-women-Salman-Rushdie/articleshow/18251230.cms.
37. Sanji Kripalni Mukherjee, "The Sindhis of Calcutta," in *Calcutta Mosaic: Essays and Interviews on the Minority Communities of Calcutta*, ed. Himadri Banerjee, Nilanjana Gupta, Sipra Mukherjee (New Delhi: Anthem Press, 2012), 105.
38. "Pictures in Making," *filmindia*, May 1948, 69.
39. "Editor's Mail," *filmindia*, January 1948, 27.
40. "Vanishing Newsreels of India!," *filmindia*, June 1949, 9.
41. "Compulsory News!," *filmindia*, June 1949, 71, 72.
42. "Vanishing Newsreels of India!," 17.
43. Baburao Patel, "India Has No Stars," *filmindia*, December 1937, 5, 6.
44. "Editor's Mail," *filmindia*, March 1946, 25.
45. "Rehearsing Wife-Murder," *filmindia*, March 1946, 33; and "Be Warned," *filmindia*, March 1946, 33.
46. "Power of Films," *filmindia*, December 1945, 43.
47. Robert E. Herzstein, *Henry R. Luce, Time, and the American Crusade in Asia* (Cambridge: Cambridge University Press, 2005), 29.
48. "At Home and Abroad," *filmindia*, December 1948, 63.
49. Abbas is quoted in Bhatia, *The Patels of filmindia*, 15. See also "Editor's Mail," *filmindia*, October 1948, 31
50. Judas, "Bombay Calling," *filmindia*, June 1949, 8, 9.
51. "Woes & Echoes," *filmindia*, July 1949, 68–70.
52. "Premiere of 'Quo Vadis,'" *Times of India*, November 15, 1952, 5.
53. "Milestone in Motion Picture History: Arthur Loew on New Screen," *Times of India*, August 28, 1953, A1.
54. "'Quo Vadis' to Inaugurate New Metro Screen, Normal Admission Rates," *Times of India*, August 28, 1953, A1; and "'Quo Vadis' Packing Metro Theatre," *Times of India*, September 10, 1953, 3.
55. Spyros Skouras to Murray Silverstone and Donald A. Henderson, December 28, 1959, Box 17, Folder 15, SPS.
56. "Eros, Bombay to WB," *Variety*, January 15, 1958, 13; and Skouras to Silverstone and Henderson, December 28, 1959.
57. Spyros P. Skouras to W. C. Michel, January 4, 1960, Box 17, Folder 15, SPS.
58. Keki Modi to Mr. Spyros Skouras, January 5, 1960, Box 17, Folder 15, SPS.
59. P. V. Prabhu to Murray Silverstone, August 3, 1961, Box 17, Folder 15, SPS.
60. Seymour Poe, "Our World Inventory," *Twentieth Century-Fox 1965 Annual Report* (New York: Twentieth Century-Fox, 1966), 5–7.

61. Twentieth Century-Fox, "Theatres," *Twentieth Century-Fox 1965 Annual Report* (New York: Twentieth Century-Fox, 1966), 1.
62. "MGM's Petition Against Tax Order Dismissed," *Times of India*, June 23, 1976, 4.
63. "Govt, to Probe into Metro Cinema Remittances," *Times of India*, March 13, 1973, 1.
64. "Govt, to Have a Role in Joint-Sector Units," *Times of India*, March 22, 1973, 11.
65. "India Dickers Takeover of Metro's Two Theatres," *Variety*, June 12, 1974, 27.
66. "India Acquires 2 Metro Houses In $1.3-Mil Deal," *Variety*, July 24, 1974, 3.
67. "Metro Cinema, Calcutta, Taken over by India's FFC from Swiss Outfit," *Variety*, March 2, 1977, 43.
68. Jonah Blank, "Lashkar-e Taiba and the Threat to the United States of a Mumbai-Style Attack," Testimony presented before the House Homeland Security Committee, Subcommittee on Counterterrorism and Intelligence on June 12, 2013 (Santa Monica, Calif.: RAND Office of External Affairs, June 2013), http://docs.house.gov/meetings/HM/HM05/20130612/100964/HHRG-113-HM05-Wstate-BlankJ-20130612.pdf.

20. China as Hollywood's Final Frontier, 1946–2013

1. Alexander Krisel to Captain Dennis O'Brien, May 29, 1922, UAC China Agreements and Misc., 1922, MSS 99AN, Series 2A, O'Brien Legal File, 58-4, UA-WHS.
2. Nitin Govil and Eric Hoyt, "Thieves of Bombay: United Artists, Colonial Copyright, and Film Piracy in the 1920s," *BioScope* 5, no.1 (2014): 5–27.
3. Ting Wang, "Hollywood's Pre-WTO Crusade in China," *Jump Cut* 49 (Spring 2007), http://www.ejumpcut.org/archive/jc49.2007/TingWang/text.html.
4. "Metro-Goldwyn-Mayer's Window Display," *China Press*, November 12, 1930, 5; and "Nanking Theatre to Show Big List of Fox Movietone Films in the Near Future: The Sea Wolf," *China Press*, October 25, 1930, 10.
5. "Nanking Theatre to Show Big List," 10.
6. "Metro-Goldwyn-Mayer's Window Display," 5.
7. Poshek Fu, *Between Shanghai and Hong Kong: The Politics of Chinese Cinemas* (Redwood City, Calif.: Stanford University Press, 2003), 32–33, 36.
8. Fu, *Between Shanghai and Hong Kong*, 32–33, 36.
9. "Paramount Publix in Foreign Exhibition," *Motion Picture Herald*, August 8, 1931, 95.
10. Memorandum from Bureau of Foreign and Domestic Commerce, August 30, 1935, MSS 99AN/1F, 4-4, UA-WHS; and Excerpt from General Report of 12/2/35, December 2, 1935, MSS 99AN/1F, 4-4, UA-WHS.
11. Fu, *Between Shanghai and Hong Kong*, 34–35.
12. "Shanghai Theatres," *Motion Picture Herald*, September 25, 1937, 9; and "Tension on Theatre Business and Other Lines Eases at Shanghai," *Motion Picture Herald*, September 25, 1937, 33.
13. "500G Shanghai Theatre," *Variety*, June 15, 1938, 12. Burger foreclosed the possibility of building in North China but expressed a desire to open additional MGM cinemas in Hong Kong and Canton. "M-G-M Plans Big Theater for Shanghai: Confidence Expressed in Future of Film Business Here," *China Press*, May 5, 1938.
14. "Conditions in Philippines Cited by Metro Manager," *Boxoffice*, September 24, 1938, 19; and "220 Films to Japan Planned by Majors," *Boxoffice*, October 29, 1938, 18.
15. Fu, *Between Shanghai and Hong Kong*, 35–36.
16. "China and the Motion Picture," *Mercury* (Hobart, Australia), August 21, 1937, 5. A decade later, patrons who were unable to follow the English soundtrack of a given

film "could also rent earphones which carry a running Chinese translation of the movie dialogue!" "Loew's on the International Front," *LO!*, July 1947, 3.
17. Fu, *Between Shanghai and Hong Kong*, 102, 106.
18. Fu, *Between Shanghai and Hong Kong*, 107.
19. "Dunn Named EL Assistant General Sales Manager," *Showmen's Trade Review*, December 27, 1947, 9.
20. "Loew's (Nearly) Lost Battalion!" *LO!*, January 1, 1945, 13.
21. "Loew Men 'Stay Put,'" *LO!*, April 15, 1945, 11.
22. "Loew's Fox Hole Battle Front Circuit," *LO!*, October 1, 1944, 6, 7.
23. Wang, "Hollywood's Pre-WTO Crusade in China."
24. "China Film Biz's Marked Upbeat," *Variety*, December 25, 1946, 165, 3, 20.
25. "New York," *Showmen's Trade Review*, January 5, 1946, 24; and "Silverstein to Far East for Loew International," *Motion Picture Herald*, January 12, 1946, 28.
26. "The Largest Movie Theater in Far East Will Appear in Shanghai," *Shen Bao*, August 28, 1946; "MGM Is Building the Largest Movie Theater in Far East: The Interior Space Includes Offices, Dorms and Apartments," *Shen Bao*, September 2, 1946; and "MGM Theater Will Start Construction Work: The Architecture Style Is Extravagant And Comfortable," *Shen Bao*, September 5, 1946.
27. "Telephone Company Will Build a 17-Story New Building, the Survey of the Location Is Work in Progress; According to the Public Works Bureau Policy, It Must Be Built Near the Bund," *Shen Bao*, November 14, 1946.
28. "MGM Shanghai Branch Manager Will Go Back to Hollywood Next Week to Negotiate Issues on Building the New Theater," *Shen Bao*, March 2, 1947.
29. While *Film Daily* reported that Loew's had bought the Roxy, the *South China Morning Post* reported that "the theatre has not been purchased by MGM, but through a special agreement reached as of January, it is being fully operated by MGM." "Loew's International in Shanghai Theater Buy," *Film Daily*, January 15, 1947, 3; "Shanghai Cinema," *South China Morning Post*, March 15, 1947, 2; and "MGM Gets Shanghai's Roxy as First-Run," *Motion Picture Daily*, January 15, 1947, 6.
30. "China Film Biz's Marked Upbeat," 20.
31. Eagle Lion Distributors Ltd. Manager of North China to W. G. Graham Esq., Counsellor, British Embassy, Peking, August 15, 1950, FC2031/5, Foreign Office 371/83573, NA-UK.
32. Mr. Hutchison, Peking to Far Eastern Department, February 28, 1950, FC2031/1, Foreign Office 371/83573, NA-UK; and Peking to Foreign Office, March 2, 1950, FC2031/1, Foreign Office 371/83573, NA-UK.
33. British Consulate General Shanghai to F. E. Dept., May 9, 1950, FC2031/2, Foreign Office 371/83573, NA-UK.
34. Included in "Translation by R.V. Tchoo of Eagle-Lion in Peking, from 'People's Daily News,'" July 12, 1950, FC2031/5, Foreign Office 371/83573, NA-UK.
35. "Translation from 'People's Daily News,' Peking—July 12, 1950," FC2031/5, Foreign Office 371/83573, NA-UK.
36. David Platt, "Hollywood," *Daily Worker*, October 12, 1950, 12.
37. "Banning of British and United States Films in Shanghai & Canton," November 14, 1950, FC2031/9, Foreign Office, NA-UK; and Peking to Foreign Office, November 17, 1950, FC2031/3, Foreign Office 371/83573, NA-UK.
38. Wang, "Hollywood's Pre-WTO Crusade in China."
39. Wang, "Hollywood's Pre-WTO Crusade in China."
40. Wang, "Hollywood's Pre-WTO Crusade in China."

41. Philip Turner, *Warner Cinemas*, (St. Paul's Cray, Kent, UK: Brantwood, 1997), 12, 16, 17.
42. Time Warner, "Warner Bros. and Village Roadshow Open Their First Multiplex in Taiwan to Blockbuster Attendance," February 12, 1998.
43. Turner, *Warner Cinemas*, 8, 17.
44. Michael Curtin, *Playing to the World's Biggest Audience: The Globalization of Chinese Film and TV* (Berkeley: University of California Press, 2007), 85. As Michael Curtin notes, Warner Bros. distributors had "no special deals" with Warner Village, and each film was negotiated picture by picture as each did with their other partners. It was, then, Time Warner that profited most from these kinds of investments, rather than the individual divisions, which competed for yearly profits and internal reputation (101).
45. Time Warner, "Warner Bros. and Village Roadshow."
46. Curtin, *Playing to the World's Biggest Audience*, 85.
47. James M. Zimmerman, *China Law Deskbook: A Legal Guide for Foreign-Invested Enterprises*, vol. 1 (Chicago: American Bar Association, 2010), 175, 176.
48. Wang, "Hollywood's Pre-WTO Crusade in China."
49. Wang, "Hollywood's Pre-WTO Crusade in China."
50. Penelope B. Prime, "China Joins the WTO: How, Why, and What Now?" *Business Economics* 37, no. 2 (April 2002): 28–29.
51. Zimmerman notes that foreign ownership could be "up to 75 percent in some pilot city markets including Beijing, Shanghai, Guangzhou, Chengdu, Xian, Wuhan, and Nanjing." Zimmerman, *China Law Deskbook*, 175, 176.
52. Zimmerman, *China Law Deskbook*, 176.
53. Redwood Capital, *Cinema Operator Industry Sector Review*, May 2014. https://web.archive.org/web/20160103102806/http://www.redcapgroup.com/media/1035a448-73ff-4295-b83d-46d24aee8a73/Sector%20Reports/2014-05-07_Cinema%20Operator%20Industry%20Report%20May%202014_pdf.
54. Quoted in Wang, "Hollywood's Pre-WTO Crusade in China."
55. "Warner Bros. Lands in China; Opens First Phase in Pirate War," *Taipei Times*, July 21, 2003, 10, http://www.taipeitimes.com/News/biz/archives/2003/07/21/2003060268.
56. Prime, "China Joins the WTO," 28–29.
57. "Time Warner Announces Strategic Alliance With CETV," June 15, 2000; and "Warner Music International Opens Warner Music China," September 27, 2000.
58. "President Jiang Zemin Reaffirms China's Welcome to Foreign Business at 2001 Fortune Global Forum," May 8, 2001.
59. "Warner's First Cinema in China Operational," *People's Daily Online*, July 13, 2003, http://english.peopledaily.com.cn/200307/13/eng20030713_120100.shtml.
60. Time Warner, "Warner Bros. International Theatres to Open Multiplex Cinema in Shanghai with Local Partners," March 4, 2002; and Time Warner, "Chinese Government Approves Warner Bros. International Cinemas' Multiplex in Shanghai," July 10, 2003.
61. Time Warner, "Warner Bros. International Theatres to Open Multiplex Cinema"; and "Warner's First Cinema in China Operational."
62. "Warner's First Cinema in China Operational."
63. Time Warner, "Chinese Government Approves."
64. "Warner Bros. International Theatres to Open Multiplex Cinema." Millard Ochs later recalled that "we assisted Shanghai Paradise from the early stages with the complex's

design and technical specifications, as well as with training of management and operations personnel." Time Warner, "Chinese Government Approves."
65. "Warner Bros. International Theatres to Open Multiplex Cinema."
66. Leon Forde, "UK's Warner Village Cinemas sold to SBC for $402m," *Screen International*, May 13, 2003, http://www.screendaily.com/uks-warner-village-cinemas-sold-to-sbc-for-402m/4013294.article.
67. Time Warner, "Chinese Government Approves."
68. "Warner Bros. Taps China's Cinema Market," Xinhua News Agency, October 15, 2003. http://www.china.org.cn/english/international/77335.htm.
69. "Warner Brothers Marches into China's Cinema Market," Press Release, Consulate-General of the People's Republic of China in Houston, January 18, 2004; and Zhang Rui, "Warner Bros. Pulling Out from China's Cinema Business," *China.org*, November 8, 2006, http://www.china.org.cn/english/entertainment/188323.htm.
70. "Warner Brothers Marches into China's Cinema Market."
71. National Association of Theatre Owners, "Number of US Movie Screens," http://natoonline.org/data/us-movie-screens/; and National Association of Theatre Owners, "Number of US Cinema Sites," http://natoonline.org/data/us-cinema-sites/.
72. "Wanda Group and Warner Bros. International Cinemas to Build Some 30 Multiplexes in China," WBIC Press Release, *Cinema Treasures* website, January 21, 2004, http://cinematreasures.org/blog/2004/1/21/wanda-group-and-warner-bros-international-cinemas-to-build-some-30-multiplexes-in-china.
73. Time Warner, "Warner Bros. International Cinemas Becomes First Western Cinema Investor Approved to Hold Majority Ownership in Chinese Cinemas Under New SARFT Guidelines," January 30, 2004.
74. Rui, "Warner Bros. Pulling Out from China's Cinema Business."
75. "Warner Brothers to Build Digital Cinema in Beijing," *China.org*, December 26, 2005, http://www.china.org.cn/english/features/film/153221.htm.
76. Levent Ozier, "Warner Bros. Moves Cinema Design Center to Shanghai," *Dexigner*, January 7, 2006.
77. "Time Warner Inc.: Cinema Building-Design Center Will Be Relocated to Shanghai," *Wall Street Journal*, January 9, 2006, A8; and Josh Friedman and Don Lee, "Time Warner Quits China Cinema Deal, Citing Rules," *Los Angeles Times*, November 9, 2006.
78. 彭侃 迈克李 (Peng Yu Mike Lee), "外资可控股电影院,将对国内电影市场有何影响? (What Impact Will Foreign-Owned Cinemas Have on the Domestic Film Market?)," *Sina Finance AFP* (China), July 14, 2019, https://finance.sina.com.cn/roll/2019-07-14/doc-ihytcerm3526680.shtml.
79. Zhang, "Warner Bros. Pulling Out from China's Cinema Business."
80. Gao Ming, quoted in Zhang, "Warner Bros. Pulling out from China's Cinema Business"; and Friedman and Lee, "Time Warner Quits China Cinema Deal, Citing Rules."
81. Geoffrey A. Fowler, "Time Warner Decides to End Theater Run in China,' *Wall Street Journal*, November 9, 2006, B2.
82. Zhang, "Warner Bros. Pulling out from China's Cinema Business"; and Friedman and Lee, "Time Warner Quits China Cinema Deal, Citing Rules."
83. Quoted in Friedman and Lee, "Time Warner Quits China Cinema Deal, Citing Rules."
84. "Warner Brothers Marches into China's Cinema Market."
85. Friedman and Lee, "Time Warner Quits China Cinema Deal, Citing Rules."

86. Quoted in Pen Densham, "An In-Depth Illumination into the Chinese Film," *Studio System News*, December 17, 2013.
87. "Warner Brothers Exits from China's Movie Theatre Mkt," *Economic Times*, November 10, 2006.
88. Time Warner, "China Film Group Taking Over Three WBIC Cinemas in China," March 1, 2007; and Li Fangfang, "Warner Bros Offloads Theaters," *China Daily*, February 3, 2007, 13, http://english.peopledaily.com.cn/200703/02/print20070302_353671.html.
89. Time Warner, "Shanghai Film Group Taking Over Two WBIC Cinemas in China," April 10, 2007.
90. Lee, "What Impact Will Foreign-Owned Cinemas Have on the Domestic Film Market?"
91. Scott Rosenberg, "Plex Drive: Asian Multiplexes Celebrate a New Era of Success," *Film Journal International*, November 30, 2007.
92. Quoted in Time Warner, "Warner Bros. Entertainment to Become First Studio to Offer Films on Demand Nationally via Television Sets in the People's Republic of China, June 15, 2011.
93. Wayne Ma and Laurie Burkitt, "American Movies Lose Market Share in China; Local Filmmakers Step Up Their Game in Fast-Growing Market," *Wall Street Journal*, October 23, 2013, http://online.wsj.com/news/articles/SB10001424052702304682504579153241399905968.
94. Clifford Coonan, "China's Box Office Surges 36 Percent in 2014 to $4.76 Billion," *Hollywood Reporter*, January 1, 2015, http://www.hollywoodreporter.com/news/chinas-box-office-surges-36-760889.
95. Coonan, "China's Box Office Surges"; and Jean Noh, "CJ CGV to Open 19 More Cinemas in China," *Screen Daily*, January 9, 2014, http://www.screendaily.com/news/cj-cgv-to-open-19-more-cinemas-in-china/5065190.article.
96. Amol Sharma and Melodie Warner, "Time Warner Invests $50 Million in China," *Wall Street Journal*, June 6, 2013, http://online.wsj.com/news/articles/SB10001424127887324299104578529594007840524.
97. "Aeon Buys Out Warner Mycal Cinemas," *Film Business Asia*, December 20, 2012; and Mark Schilling, "Warner Exits Japan Exhib Market," *Variety*, December 19, 2012. http://variety.com/2012/film/news/warner-exits-japan-exhib-market-1118063823/.
98. Jeremy Kay, "Millard Ochs, Warner Bros.," *Screen Daily*, June 20, 2013, http://www.screendaily.com/features/millard-ochs-warner-bros/5057576.article.
99. Tom Brueggemann, "China's Box Office Is Now Bigger Than North America: It's Time to Start Worrying," *Indiewire*, April 6, 2018, https://www.indiewire.com/2018/04/chinas-box-office-is-now-bigger-than-north-america-its-time-to-start-worrying-1201949453/.
100. Patrick Brzeski, "China Opens Door for Foreign Movie Theater Chains, But Will They Enter?," *Hollywood Reporter*, July 9, 2019, https://www.hollywoodreporter.com/news/china-opens-door-foreign-movie-theater-chains-but-will-they-enter-1223076; see also Rebecca Davis, "China to Open up Cinema Sector To Foreign Entities," *Variety*, July 2, 2019, https://variety.com/2019/film/asia/china-cinema-foreign-investment-1203257940/.
101. Lee, "What Impact Will Foreign-Owned Cinemas Have?"
102. Brzeski, "China Opens Door for Foreign Movie Theater Chains, But Will They Enter?" See also Davis, "China to Open Up Cinema Sector."
103. Patrick Brzeski, "China Shutters Nearly 70,000 Movie Theaters in Response to Coronavirus Outbreak," *Hollywood Reporter*, January 23, 2020, https://www

.hollywoodreporter.com/news/chinas-cinemas-officially-close-response-coronavirus-outbreak-1272566; and Rebecca Davis and Patrick Frater, "Will China's Movie Industry Recover from Coronavirus?," *Variety*, February 12, 2020, https://variety.com/2020/film/features/china-coronavirus-movie-industry-box-office-1203501046/.

104. Patrick Frater, "China's Wanda Opens First Movie Theme Park in Wuhan," *Hollywood Reporter*, December 19, 2014, http://variety.com/2014/biz/news/chinas-wanda-opens-first-movie-theme-park-in-wuhan-1201384159/.

105. Dade Hayes, "Warner Bros & Universal Bosses Say No Movie Theater Buyouts in the Works, But 'We're Rooting for Them,'" *Deadline*, October 15, 2020, https://deadline.com/print-article/1234598176/?KeepThis=1.

Epilogue

1. National Amusements—Viacom's parent company and Sumner Redstone's original exhibition company—has retained a small number of cinemas in the United Kingdom.
2. Daniel Loria and Rebecca Pahle, "A Guide to Studios' Shifting Stances on Theatrical Exclusivity," *BoxofficePro*, January 8, 2021, https://www.boxofficepro.com/a-guide-to-studios-shifting-stances-on-theatrical-exclusivity/.
3. Kirsten Acuna, "China's Wanda Group Purchases Debt-ridden AMC," *Business Insider*, May 21, 2012, https://www.businessinsider.com/wanda-group-buys-amc-2012-5; and Terril Yue Jones and Denny Thomas, "China's Wanda to Buy U.S. Cinema Chain AMC for $2.6 Billion," Reuters, May 20, 2012, https://www.reuters.com/article/us-amcentertainment/chinas-wanda-to-buy-u-s-cinema-chain-amc-for-2-6-billion-idUSBRE84K03K20120521.
4. J. Sperling Reich, "A Closer Look at Wanda's Acquisition of Hoyts," *Celluloid Junkie*, June 3, 2015, https://celluloidjunkie.com/2015/06/03/closer-look-wanda-acquisition-hoyts/.
5. David Lieberman, "AMC Entertainment's Acquisition of Odeon & UCI Clears European Commission," *Deadline*, November 16, 2016, https://deadline.com/2016/11/amc-entertainment-acquisition-odeon-uci-approved-european-commission-1201855798/.
6. David Lieberman, "AMC Theatres Becomes World's No. 1 Chain as Odeon & UCI Deal Closes," *Deadline*, November 30, 2016, https://deadline.com/2016/11/amc-theatres-closes-odeon-uci-cinemas-deal-1201861948/.
7. Ryan Faughnder, "China-Owned AMC Seals Deal to Buy Carmike Cinemas, Making It the Largest Theater Chain in U.S.," *Los Angeles Times*, November 15, 2016, https://www.latimes.com/business/hollywood/la-fi-ct-amc-carmike-20161114-story.html.
8. Echo Huang, "AMC Theatres' Chinese Boss, Wang Jianlin, Has a Delusional Plan to Infiltrate American Culture," *Quartz*, September 13, 2016, https://qz.com/773508/asias-richest-man-wants-his-worlds-biggest-theater-line-to-screen-more-chinese-films/.
9. Robert Cain, "Wanda's Real Reasons for Acquiring AMC Theatres," *ChinaGoAbroad*, ca. May 2012, http://www.chinagoabroad.com/en/commentary/wanda-s-real-reasons-for-acquiring-amc-theatres.
10. "AMC Theatres to Acquire Odeon & UCI Cinemas Group," Press release, *Businesswire*, July 12, 2016, https://www.businesswire.com/news/home/20160712005791/en/AMC-Theatres-to-Acquire-Odeon-UCI-Cinemas-Group.

11. Ana Swanson, "Shadowy Forces Are Fighting for Control of Your Local Movie Theater," *Washington Post*, December 5, 2016, https://www.washingtonpost.com/news/wonk/wp/2016/12/05/inside-the-shadowy-campaign-to-control-your-local-movie-theater/.
12. "Dalian Wanda Buys AMC Movie Exhibitor," *South China Morning Post*, May 22, 2012, https://web.archive.org/web/20170421062205/https://www.scmp.com/article/1001659/dalian-wanda-buys-amc-movie-exhibitor.
13. Kenji Kawase, "Sale of AMC Cinemas Closes Curtain on Dalian Wanda's Global Dream," *Nikkei Asia*, May 25, 2021, https://asia.nikkei.com/Business/Markets/China-debt-crunch/Sale-of-AMC-cinemas-closes-curtain-on-Dalian-Wanda-s-global-dream.
14. Patrick Frater, "South Korean Exhibition Giant CJ-CGV Aggressively Expands Empire," *Variety*, January 24, 2014, https://variety.com/2014/biz/asia/south-korean-exhibition-giant-cj-cgv-aggressively-expands-empire-1201066384/.
15. Jean Noh, "South Korea's CJ CGV Pushes Past 400 Theatres," *ScreenDaily*, June 19, 2017, https://www.screendaily.com/news/south-koreas-cj-cgv-pushes-past-400-theatres/5119199.article.
16. Frater, "South Korean Exhibition Giant CJ-CGV."
17. "CJ CGV to Open Third U.S. Theatre and First in San Francisco in Early 2020," CJ CGV Press release, *Celluloid Junkie*, April 17, 2019, https://celluloidjunkie.com/wire/cj-cgv-to-open-third-u-s-theatre-and-first-in-san-francisco-in-early-2020/.
18. Patrick Frater, "Reliance Forms U.S. Theater Chain," *Variety*, March 26, 2008, https://variety.com/2008/scene/asia/reliance-forms-u-s-theater-chain-1117982984/; and Anita Watts, Phoenix Rising: Phil Zacheretti Oversees 97 Screens in Eight States," *Film Journal International*, December 2, 2014, http://fj.webedia.us/features/phoenix-rising-phil-zacheretti-oversees-97-screens-eight-states.
19. Frater, "Reliance Forms U.S. Theater Chain."
20. Frater, "Reliance Forms U.S. Theater Chain."
21. Watts, "Phoenix Rising."
22. Nyay Bhushan, "India's Reliance, China's Wanda Group to Explore Cinema Projects in India, U.S.," *Hollywood Reporter*, December 14, 2012, https://www.hollywoodreporter.com/news/reliance-wanda-group-exploring-us-402435.
23. Watts, "Phoenix Rising."
24. Pam Kragen, "New Carlsbad Luxury Cinema Puts the Focus on Food," *San Diego Union-Tribune*, January 31, 2020, https://www.sandiegouniontribune.com/communities/north-county/carlsbad/story/2020-01-31/new-carlsbad-cinema-to-put-the-focus-on-food-rather-than-movies.
25. Juan Llamas-Rodriguez, "A Global Cinematic Experience: Cinépolis, Film Exhibition, and Luxury Branding," *Journal of Cinema and Media Studies* 58, no. 3 (Spring 2019): 53.
26. Maryam Farooqui, "Confident About Bengali Content and Movie Buffs in Bengal, SVF Cinemas to Add 15 Screens in 2021," *Money Control*, January 11, 2021, https://www.moneycontrol.com/news/trends/entertainment/confident-about-bengali-content-and-movie-buffs-in-bengal-svf-cinemas-to-add-15-screens-in-2021-6330091.html.
27. Bruce Haring, "CMX Files Chapter 11, Asks Studios, Landlords for 'Industry Rebalancing,'" *Deadline*, April 25, 2020, https://deadline.com/2020/04/cinemex-chapter-11-studios-rebalancing-1202917844/.
28. "About Maya Cinemas," Maya Cinemas, https://www.mayacinemas.com/about-maya.

29. Anna Marie de la Fuente, "Mexico's Cinepolis Launching New Arthouse Distributor with 'Parasite,'" *Variety*, October 21, 2019, https://variety.com/2019/film/festivals/mexico-cinepolis-launching-new-arthouse-distributor-parasite-1203376960/.
30. Sylvain Estibal and Yussel Gonzalez, "Mexican Directors Dazzle Abroad—in Mexico, Not So Much," *Dawn*, March 4, 2018, https://www.dawn.com/news/1393066.
31. Kragen, "New Carlsbad Luxury Cinema Puts the Focus on Food"; and "About Us," Cinépolis India, https://www.cinepolisindia.com/about-us.
32. Jill Goldsmith, "Theater Chain Cinepolis of Mexico Takes Stake in Cinemark," *Deadline*, May 20, 2020, https://deadline.com/2020/05/cinepolis-of-mexico-takes-stake-cinemark-1202939667/.
33. "Our History," Cineworld, https://www.cineworldplc.com/en/about-us/our-history; and Paul Moore, "The Empire Strikes Back? The Sale of Canadian Cineplex to a British Company Is Just a Sequel of an Old Story," *Globe and Mail*, December 17, 2019, https://www.theglobeandmail.com/opinion/article-the-empire-strikes-back-the-sale-of-canadian-cineplex-to-a-british/.
34. Moore, "The Empire Strikes Back?"
35. David Friend, "Canadian Filmmakers Worry Cineworld's Takeover of Cineplex Signals New Hurdles Ahead," *Canadian Press*, December 18, 2019, https://www.ctvnews.ca/business/canadian-filmmakers-worry-cineplex-takeover-signals-new-hurdles-ahead-1.4735771.
36. Friend, "Canadian Filmmakers Worry."
37. Friend, "Canadian Filmmakers Worry."
38. Haring, "CMX Files Chapter 11."
39. Dave McNary, "Cineplex Taking Cineworld to Court over Failed $2.1 Billion Takeover Deal," *Variety*, June 15, 2020, https://variety.com/2020/film/news/cineplex-court-cineworld-takeover-deal-1234635356/.
40. Jeremy Fuster, "Why Pixar's 'Luca' Skipping Theaters Is a Double Blow to the Box Office," *The Wrap Pro*, June 21, 2021, https://www.thewrap.com/pixar-luca-box-office-test/.
41. Dade Hayes, "Warner Bros & Universal Bosses Say No Movie Theater Buyouts in the Works, But 'We're Rooting for Them,'" *Deadline*, October 15, 2020, https://deadline.com/2020/10/warner-bros-universal-bosses-movie-theater-buyouts-covid-19-1234598176/.
42. James Hatton, "Wanda's AMC Facing Imminent Default as COVID-19 Empties Movie Theatres," *Mingtiandi*, April 14, 2020, https://www.mingtiandi.com/real-estate/outbound-investment/amc-facing-imminent-default-as-covid-19-empties-theatres/; Wolf Richter, "Cinema Chains Near Collapse: The Problem Beyond the Pandemic," *Wolf Street*, October 5, 2020, https://wolfstreet.com/2020/10/05/cinemas-approach-collapse-as-movies-thrive-online-the-problem-beyond-the-pandemic/; and Wolf Richter, "After 17 Years of Falling Ticket Sales, Movie Theaters Got Annihilated in 2020," *Wolf Street*, January 10, 2021, https://wolfstreet.com/2021/01/10/movie-theater-ticket-sales-after-falling-for-years-got-annihilated-in-2020/.
43. Millard Ochs, "Chapter Eight," comment on LinkedIn, ca. December 2020, https://www.linkedin.com/feed/update/urn:li:activity:6740992607280857088/.
44. "The Producer-Exhibitor 'Menace,'" *Bioscope*, October 22, 1925, 21.

INDEX

Page numbers in *italics* refer to figures.

20th Century Theatre: Cape Town, 232, 280, 282; Durban, 280, 286; Johannesburg, *9*, 232, 252, 280, 286; Maritzburg, 279, 282; Nairobi, 291; Pietermaritzburg, 386; Pretoria, 282
4DX, 387

AAT. *See* African Amalgamated Theatres (AAT)
Abbas, Kwaja Ahmed, 356
ABC Cinemas. *See* Associated British Cinemas (ABC Cinemas)
Abdulaziz Al Saud, Prince Talal bin, 237
Abeles, Arthur, 83
Abrahams, K. C., 97, 113
ACF. *See* African Consolidated Films (ACF)
ACIC. *See* African Consolidated Investments Corp. (ACIC)
Acland, Charles, 3, 4, 15, 89
ACT. *See* African Consolidated Theatres (ACT)
Adams, Brian, 105, 106, 110, 114
Adlabs, 387
Adventures of Huckleberry Finn (1939), 352
Adventures of Robin Hood, The (1938), 62
AEON Group. *See* Mycal (AEON)

Aetna Insurance, 141–42
Afamal Advertising, 306
Affair to Remember, An (1957), 254
AFP. *See* African Film Productions (AFP)
Africa, 2, 4, 13, 22, 25, 90, 271; CIC, 84, 327; Fox/ACT, 284–87, 315–18, 322–24, 329; Fox/ACT's dominance, 5, 289–90, 322–23; Fox/ACT's troubled racial history, 2, 25, 269, 305, 310, 316–17, 324, 329; nationalism, 297, 303, 314; sub-Saharan, 270–72, 276, 284, 285, 292, 295. *See also* East Africa; Egypt; Kenya; North Africa; Northern Rhodesia; South Africa; Southern Rhodesia; West Africa
African Affairs Society of America, 296, 299
African Amalgamated Theatres (AAT), 273
African Broadcasting Company, 274
African Consolidated Films (ACF), 279, 289
African Consolidated Investments Corp. (ACIC), 288–89
African Consolidated Theatres (ACT), 108, 176, 276, 285; MGM and, 276–77, 279, 280, 284, 287; Rank and, 284; Sanlam's purchase of, 318, 325, 329

African Consolidated Theatres (ACT), Fox-owned, 17, 25, 270–71, 288–92, 318–19, 325–26, 383; Fox's promise to produce films in Afrikaans, 290, 319; Fox's whites-only cinemas, 2, 25, 309
African Film Productions (AFP), 273–74, 292
African Films Trust, 271
African Films United, 289
African National Congress, 303, 322
African Theatres Ltd., 98, 273–76. *See also* African Consolidated Theatres (ACT)
Ai Lin Chua, 18
air-conditioning, 15, 173, 184, 224, 257, 265; Cairo Palace, 220; Cinema Tel Aviv, 251; MGM cinemas/Metros, 13, 157–58, 165, 192, 198, 276–77, 343, 366; MGM cinemas/Metros (Cinema Metro, Cairo), 214, 216, 243; MGM cinemas/Metros (Roxy Theatre, Shanghai), 363, 364, 366; Paramount cinemas, 199
Aitken, Barbara, 82
Alamo Drafthouse, 380
Albee Theatre, Cincinnati, 398n95
Albert, Don, 46
Alexander Kann, Finch & Partners, 138
Alexandria, Egypt, 210, 211, 213, 222, 223, 266; antisemitism, 221, 229; boycott against foreign-owned cinemas, 211, 229; Egyptian government's construction of cinemas, 256; Fox, 10, 244; Fox (Amir Cinema), 243, 244, 247, 264; Fox (Semiramis), 256; MGM, 216, 217; MGM (Cinema Metro), 24–25, 178, 218–19, 235, 242, 243, 264; Mohamed Aly Cinema, 210, 216, 235; Paramount, 235; Royal Cinema, 216, 235, 250, 254; Soviet films, 250; terrorism, 264; Ufa, 211; Warner Bros., 63, 219, 223
alfrescos. *See* drive-ins
Algeria, 23, 48, 312, 324
Alhambra Theater, Amsterdam, 60
Ali, Shawky Abu, 265
Alikhan, Anvar, 353–54
Allen, Sir Roger, 237–38
Allied Artists, 291
Almeida Saltes, F. L. de, 176
Almy, Cliff, 344, 345
Alpert, Carl, 262
Amalgamated Theatres Ltd., 118–19; CinemaScope, 132–33; Exhibitors Association/Film Industry Board, 123, 126; Fox and, 93, 94, 120–24, 126–28, 134–44, 279, 292, 383; Fox and Chase National Bank's role in the purchase of, 24, 94, 122, 141; Hoyts and, 119–20, 139, 141–42; Kerridge and, 121, 126–28, 139; local branding of, 94, 123, 144; television's impact on, 135–36; Urban Diversified's purchase of, 141, 142; xenophobic attacks on, 121–22
Ambler, Charles, 21, 271–72, 320
AMC Cinemas/AMC Entertainment, 85, 89, 178, 381, 390; Dalian Wanda–owned, 368, 379, 381–86, 392
AMC Empire 25, New York, 384
America: capitalism in, 15, 148, 175, 270, 354–55; Coca-Cola, 81, 141, 217, 218, 243, 354, 355; consumerism in, 10–11, 181, 346, 354–55, 357, 358; cosmopolitanism in, 346, 354; cultural imperialism of, 178, 359; democracy in, 10, 17, 148, 170, 175, 181, 202, 210, 249, 270, 357; as exotic, 3, 16, 20, 339, 348; modernity of, 15, 244, 276; philo-Americanism, 333, 357; rags to riches archetype in, 157, 277; showmanship of, 30, 41, 47, 157, 214; technology in, 4, 10, 15, 192–93, 243, 358. *See also* anti-Americanism; cultural embassies; United States
American Motion Picture Export Co. (Africa) Inc. (AMPEC), 315, 452n106
American Seating Company, 184, 252
Amir Cinema, Alexandria, 243, 244, 247, 264
AMPEC. *See* American Motion Picture Export Co. (Africa) Inc. (AMPEC)
Amsterdam, Netherlands, 59–61; CIC headquarters, 313–14; Fox, 3, 14, 60; Fox (Rembrandtpleintheater), 81; Loew's/MGM, 59–61, 178; MGM (Alhambra Theater), 60; MGM (Corso Theater), 60; MGM (Royal Theater), 60; NBB protectionism in, 60–61, 81; Tuschinski (Roxy Theater), 59; Tuschinski (Tuschinski Theater), 59, 60, 68, 404n30; Ufa, 61
Angels of Mercy (1939), 351
Anglo-EMI Film Distributors, 326
Angola, 321, 322
Anschutz, Philip, 384
anti-Americanism, 12, 162; in Cuba, 183, 204; in Egypt, 25; in England, 34, 46; in India, 333; in Japan, 335–37, 339; NBB and, 60; *NZMPEB* and, 120; in São Paulo, 151; in Southern Rhodesia, 328

anticommunism, 161, 206; in *Cape Town Affair*, 321–22; Hilton as promoting, 16–17; Skouras's, 17, 25, 210, 249, 266
antisemitism, 250; in Birmingham, against the Levys, 45, 122; in Brazil, 161; in Egypt, 221, 235–36, 246, 260; in *filmindia*, 355–57; in Germany, 58; at *Time*, 356
Antongiorgi, Angel Esteban, 192
Antonio, Pablo, 343
Apollo Théâtre, Paris, 62
Arab League, 244–45, 252–53, 259, 263
Arab-Israeli War, 210, 228, 229, 235, 250
Archibald Nettlefold Productions, 275
architecture. *See* cinema architecture
Argentina, 3, 149, 163, 164–65, 171, 194; film industry, 182, 189, 195; MGM, 24, 154, 158, 159, 166, 171, 177; military dictatorship, 205; Nazi Germany and, 160, 162, 167; UA, 167. *See also* Buenos Aires
Arjun, Anil, 388
Aron, Adam, 382, 383
art deco, 123–24, 155, 190, 343, 360
Ashton, E. H. (Hugh), 303–4
Asia Theater Group, 364
Assad, Hagg, 246
Associated British Cinemas (ABC Cinemas), 63, 306, 316, 328, 352
Associated British Picture Corp. Ltd., 63
Associated Cinemas of South Africa, 281
Associated Television Ltd. (ATV), 306, 316
Associated Theatres of South Africa Ltd., 285
Astaire, Adele, 45
Astaire, Fred, 45, 223
ATV. *See* Associated Television Ltd. (ATV)
Auckland, New Zealand, 116–19; Amalgamated, 117–19, 126, 135, 140, 141; Amalgamated (Civic Theatre), 118, 123, 132, 133, 139; Capitol Theatre, 126; Embassy Theatre, 119; Fullers, 116; Haywards, 116; Rank, 127; television, 135–36; Warner Bros., 63
Auschwitz concentration camp, 68, 76
Australasia, 2, 13, 23–24, 90, 93–95, 334; banks' control of film industry, 101, 120, 141; Fox/Hoyts, 93, 99, 101, 137, 140–41, 142, 143–44; MGM, 93, 107, 143–44, 155; Paramount, 93, 143–44; U.S. exhibition dominance, 93–94, 142, 143–44; Warner Bros., 93, 129, 143–44
Australasian Films, 95

Australia, 4, 23–24, 93–95, 186, 210; Adelaide, 10, 63, 95, 105, 125, 134; banks' role in exhibition expansion, 94–95, 99–102, 105, 115, 141, 144; Canberra, 96; CIC, 85, 327; Dalian Wanda, 382, 384, 385; drive-ins, 133–34; Fox/Hoyts (*see* Hoyts Theatres Ltd., Fox-owned); Fox's dominance, 4, 5, 13, 14–15, 93–94, 263; indigenous film production, 94, 102, 110, 114; MGM, 10, 15, 23, 93–94, 96, 102, 107–15, 131–32, 134; Paramount, 57, 93, 95–97, 102, 103–5, 113, 115, 125; Perth, 95, 103, 105, 125, 134; protectionism, 103, 110, 112, 114, 124, 131; racial segregation, 136–37; Rank, 283–84; television, 132, 133, 136; Village Roadshow, 88, 93, 143, 369, 372, 376, 386, 389; Warner Bros., 88, 93, 129–31, 143, 369, 372. *See also* Brisbane; Melbourne; New South Wales; Sydney
Austria, 74, 81, 85, 88, 240; Vienna, 81
Auto Theatres Pty. Ltd., 133–34
AVCO Embassy Pictures, 326

Bachman, Charles J., 200
Baez, E., 157
Bahri, Deepika, 26
Balaban, A. J., 233
Balaban, Barney, 74–75, 227, 248–49
Balcombe, Gordon, 98, 104
balconies, 60, 82, 147, 216; bombs in, 204, 223; in Peruvian cinemas, 172, 174; in Rio cinemas, 156, 420n39; separation of patrons, 156, 174, 218, 302; site of protest, 213
banks. *See* Chase National Bank; English, Scottish and Australian Bank (ES&A); investment banks
Barbados, 188
Barrera, Raul, 193
Barrett, Franklin, 96
Barros, Luiz de, 151
Batista, Fulgencio, 198, 203, 204
Batout, Ibrahim al-, 217
Bavetta, J. Carlo, 157, 162
Baxter Cox, Alfred, 125
BCFEC. *See* British Colonial Film Exchange Company Ltd. (BCFEC)
Bechet, Ernest, 66, 69, 70–75, 71, 73, 405n56
Beery, Wallace, 215, 223
Beijing (Peking), China, 362, 371, 372–73, 376, 384, 462n51; ban on American and British films in, 367; Warner Bros./WBIC, 372–73, 376

Beinin, Joel, 241
Belasco, Lionel, 188
Belgium: Antwerp, 77; Charleroi, 50, 54; Ghent, 50, 54, 58; Liege, 54, 58, 65, 77; Loew's/MGM, 46, 48, 50, 54, 64–65, 77, 210; Nazi occupation, 64–65, 66; Paramount, 31, 35, 65, 67, 69. *See also* Brussels
Ben-Gurion, David, 228
Ben-Hur (1959), 345
Benavides, Óscar, 156
Benefico, Amerigo, 366
Bénites, Nena, 203
Berlin, Germany: Hilton, 17; Kracauer on moviegoing in, 54; MGM, 80–81; Ufa (Ufa-Palast am Zoo), 53–54; Universal, 53; Universal (Mercedes Palast), 53
Berman, Julian, 343, 365
Berman and Co., 384
Bernhard, Joseph, 197
Bernstein, Harry, 150
Bernstein, Sidney, 39, 47, 63, 74
Berry, Roger, 316
Beverley, S.: Paramount cinemas, 56, 57, 80, 82
Bewkes, Jeff, 376–77
Bey, Imam, 239
BFO (British Foreign Office). *See under* Britain
BIG Cinemas, 360, 387–89, *388*
Big Clock, The (1948), 173
Birch Carroll & Coyle, 408n3
Birmingham, England: Paramount (Futurist Theatre), 43–44, 45, 57, 63, 80; Paramount (Scala Theatre), 41, 43–44, *43*, 63, 80; "Battle of Birmingham," 23, 41, 42–45, 56, 60, 61, 122; UA, 37
Bjeike-Petersen, Joh, 140
block-booking, 38–39, 106–7, 114, 152–53
blockbusters, 88, 390–91
Blomkamp, Neil, 453n137
Blow-Up (1966), 263
Bluhdorn, Charles, 83
Blum, David, 352
Bluysen, Auguste, 50
Boardman, Dixon, 106
Bogart, Humphrey, 372
Bogotá, Colombia: Fox cinema, 166, 167; MGM, 79, 167, 170; MGM (Teatro San Jorge), 158; MGM (Cine Metro-Teusaquillo), 170; MGM (Teatro Astral), 167, 170; UA (Teatro Astral), 167; Warner (Teatro San Jorge), 86, 169–70, 197, 200
Bolle, Otto, 279, 281
Bombay (Mumbai), India, 3, 347–48; Fox, 14, 359; MGM (*see* Metro Cinema, Bombay); Reliance MediaWorks, 387–88, 389; Warner (Eros Theatre), 358, 359
Botha, Martin, 20, 443n5
Botha, Pik, 327
Bowes, Edward, 42, 49
Boxer, William, 281, 282, 317–18
boycotts, 10, 22, 37, 58, 59, 118, 196, 298, 314, 375, 385; anti-Nazi, 211, 225; Arab League, of Israel, 244–45, 252–53, 259, 261, 263; British/CEA, of Paramount/PPL, 12, 22, 23, 34–35, 36, 44–45, 61; Chinese, of American films, 367; Dutch/NBB, of MGM, 60–61; Egyptian/Misr al-Fatat/Wahbi, of foreign-run cinemas, 209, 211–13, 228–29, 235, 430n9; Japanese, of American films, 336–38; PAMECA, of South African businesses in Kenya, 310–11
Brazil, 147–52, 178; Art-Palacio, 178; Bahia, 169; Brazilian Portuguese, 151, 157, 158; CIC, 177–78; Condor, 84, 178; Fox, 148, 166–67; Japanese population, 176; MGM, 155, 156, 159, 160, 169, 171, 177; MGM/Empresas Reunidas Metro-Goldwyn-Mayer Ltda., 24, 50, 147–48, 150–52, 159, 347, 419n12; MGM/Metro-Goldwyn-Mayer do Brasil Ltda., 150; MGM's wartime expansion, 163–66; military dictatorship, 178, 205; multiplexes, 178; Nazi Germany and/Nazi films screened in, 157, 160–62, 166; Paramount, 5, 147, 148, 150, 153, 160, 178, 418n2; protectionism, 168; racial division, 157, 161; Recife, 162, 171; television, 177; UA, 159, 160; UCI, 85, 178; Ufa, 160; United States and, 157, 162, 163–64, 166–67; Warner Bros., 168. *See also* Rio de Janeiro; São Paulo
Brennan, James, 272
Brett, Homer, 44
Briggate Picture House, Leeds, 37
Brisbane, Australia: Hoyts, 95, 125; Hoyts (Regent Theatre), 105, 140; MGM (Cine Metro), *8*, 58, 107, 125; Paramount, 105; Warner Bros., 63
Britain: ban on British films in China, 367; BFO, 367; BFO inquiry into the Cairo

Fire, 239–40; BFO response to the attack on Smeeden, 236–37; British Mandate Palestine, 225–26, 228; colonial rule in India, 346, 347, 351; colonial rule in Jamaica, 24, 148, 183, 185, 189; colonial rule in Kenya, 284, 310–11, 316, 323; colonial rule in Trinidad, 24, 148, 183, 188–89. *See also* Birmingham; London
British & Dominion Films, 96, 275
British Capital Ltd., 178
British Colonial Film Exchange Company Ltd. (BCFEC), 187–89
British Empire Films, 139
British Foreign Office (BFO). *See under* Britain
British Guiana, 188
British International Films, 275
British International Pictures, 275
British Lion Films, 291
British United Film Producers, 187
Brittenden, Wayne, 126, 128, 139
Broadband Investment Ltd., 371
Broadway, New York, 19, 54, 68, 151, 155, 254
Brock, Louis, 150–51
Brody, Richard, 100
Broglie Theater, Strasbourg, 57
Brolin, James, 321
Bruce, Stanley, 96
Brussels, Belgium: Loew's/Fox, 50, 54, 58; MGM (Cinéma Caméo), 58, 64, 65, 77; MGM (Queen's Hall), 64, 65, 77; Paramount, 39, 57, 75; Paramount (Colosseum Theatre), 67
Bryman, Harry, 195
Buchenwald concentration camp, 71–74
Budapest, Hungary: MGM (Kamara Theater), 58; MGM (Metro-Scala), 58, 59; MGM (Radius Theatre), 58, 59; Ufa, 58, 59
Buehrig, Al, 348
Buenos Aires, Argentina: Fox, 150; MGM, 10, 169, 171, 175; MGM (Cine Metro), 171, 176, 424n49; Nazi "outlets," 162
Burger, Samuel, 163, 169, 188, 192, 364, 46on13
Burma (Myanmar), 347, 386
Burns, James, 4–5, 21, 271
Bustamante y Rivero, José, 173, 175

Cain, Robert, 383, 385
Cairo, Egypt, 210–13, 222–23, 266; anti-British attacks, 220, 222–23, 239, 245; anti-Jewish attacks, 221–22, 230, 238; Cairo Fire, 238–40, 243, 437n112; Diana Theatre, 235; Fox, 243, 244, 246, 255–56, 264; Fox (*See* Cairo Palace); Gaumont Palace, 210; MGM (*See* Cinema Metro, Cairo); Miami Theatre, 250; Misr al-Fatat boycott, 211–13; Misr Theatre, 228; Nile Hilton, 16, 244, 253; Paramount, 210, 223; Rank, 236–37; Rank (Rivoli Theatre), 222–24, 230, 239, 240, 284; Soliman Pasha Street, 214, 221; terrorism, 264; Wahbi Cinema, 211; Warner Bros., 63, 223
Cairo Palace, 7, 24–25, 220–21, 244, 246, 256, 263–65; Cairo Fire and, 239; Egyptian government's demands on, 221; forced fundraising, 226–27, 235; opening, 220; symbol of Western influence, 25, 209
Calcutta (Kolkata), India, 3; Fox, 359; Fox (Elphinstone Picture Palace), 359; MGM (*See* Metro Cinema, Calcutta); nationalism, 351–52, 355; Paramount, 347; RKO (Elphinstone Picture Palace), 347
Calderon, Jose, 155
Cali, Colombia: Fox (Cine Colon), 168, 172; MGM (Cine Metro), 169, 171, 179
Calloway, Cab, 200
Campos, Pedro Albizu, 191–92
Canada, 104, 127, 169, 186; Cineplex Odeon, 178, 390, 391–92; Famous Players, Paramount's stake in, 85, 88, 380; IMAX, 376, 378; Montreal, 150, 190, 391, 395n4. *See also* Toronto
Canty, George R., 220
Cape Town, South Africa, 323; ACT (Colosseum Theatre), 309; Bioscopes, 309; District Six, 322; Fox, 279, 292; Fox (Van Riebeck Theatre), 286; Fox (20th Century Theatre), 232, 280, 282; MGM, 287; MGM (Metro Cinema), 58, 78, 309; as overseated, 277–78; Schlesinger/AAT, 273, 274; segregated cinemas, 309; Ster, 318
Cape Town Affair (1967), 319–22
Capitan Theatre, El, Los Angeles, 380
Capitol Theatre: Auckland, 126; Dublin, 45, 57; Madrid, 58; Melbourne, 56, 57, 96, 104–5, 115, 125, 400n66; New York, 38, 49, 53; Rotterdam, 60; Sydney, 96
Capricorn Africa Society, 297–98, 305
Cardiff, Wales, 32, 57

Caribbean, 2, 24, 90, 147–49, 178, 182–83, 186, 189, 196, 205–6; anti-U.S. sentiment, 183; Cobiân as key player, 191, 194; Colonial Film Exchange Company Ltd., 187; Hollywood's departure from, 203–5; Loew's/MGM, 182, 183, 189; role of politics, 148, 205; Paramount, 4, 24, 57, 148, 182–87; Warner Bros., 24, 169–70, 182, 199. *See also* Cuba; Jamaica; Puerto Rico; Trinidad
Caribbean Cinemas, 205
Caribbean Film Co. (CFC), 183–84
Carlton Theatre: London, 24, 39, 50, 55–56, 57, 80; Shanghai, 362
Carlton Theatre Company Ltd., 55–56
Carmel Films, 233–34
Carmen Jones (1954), 294–95
Carmike Cinemas, 382–85
cartoons, 10, 125, 215, 247; *Art Gallery*, 214; at Metros/Metro Cub Clubs, 158, 181, 214, 215, 216, 217, 218–19, 352; *Tom & Jerry*, 158, 165, 181, 217, *218*, 355, 360
Castro, Fidel, 204, 206
Casuso, Jorge, 201
CEA. *See* Cinematograph Exhibitors Association of Great Britain and Ireland (CEA)
censorship, 72, 308, 384; Chinese, 367; Egyptian, 211, 216, 229, 230, 235, 243, 263, 265; Israeli, 250; Japanese, 340; South African, 293, 294
Centra-Film, 65
Central African Federation, 291, 295, 296, 298, 306
Central African Television, 306
Central America: MGM, 177; Paramount/Paramount-CFC, 154, 184; Warner Bros., 169
Century Heroes, 372
Ceravolo, Lucidio, 176
Ceylon (Sri Lanka), 342, 347
CFC. *See* Caribbean Film Co. (CFC)
CGV, 386. *See also* CJ CGV
Chan, Jackie, 372
Chandler, Roy, 210
Chaplin, Charlie, 356
Chargeurs, 88, 89
Chasanas, George, 220–21
Chase, Stanley, 195
Chase Group of Companies of N.Z., 142
Chase National Bank, 23–24, 95, 101, 113, 115, 141, 142; Fox's stake in Amalgamated, 24, 94, 122, 141; Fox's stake in Gaumont-British, 23; Fox's stake in Hoyts, 23–24, 94, 98, 101, 110, 120, 141; GTE's acquisition of William Fox's shares, 100–101
CheilJedang (CJ). *See* CJ CGV
Chevalier, Maurice, 67
Chile, 160, 163; Fox, 148, 172; Loew's/MGM/Metros, 24, 155, 159, 166, 169, 177, 352; Nazi Germany and/pro-Nazi films in, 160, 162–63; U.S. loan to, 172; Valparaiso, 166, 169, 172, 352. *See also* Santiago
China, 25–26, 361–64; ban on American and British films, 367–68; civil war, 367; Japanese occupation, 342, 364, 365–66, 371; MGM, 342–43; multiplexes, 369–70, 371–74, 379, 386; number of screens in, 376, 377; piracy, 362, 371; revolution, 361, 383; SARFT/SAPPRFT laws encouraging foreign investment, 370, 372–74, 376; Warner Bros./WBIT/WBIC, 5, 26, 333, 361, 365, 368–79, 380, 386; World Trade Organization, 333, 361, 371; Wuhan, 369, 372–73, 378, 462n51. *See also* Dalian Wanda; Guangzhou (Canton); Nanjing; Shanghai
China Entertainment Television, 371
China Film Corp., 368
China Media Capital, 376
China National Production Importation and Exportation Corp., 371
China Theatre, Stockholm, 23, 55, 57
Christchurch Cinemas Ltd., 122
CIC. *See* Cinema International Corp. (CIC)
Cine Bella Vista (Fox), Panama City, 177
Cine Capitólio Rio de Janeiro, 56
Cine Coliseum, Barcelona, 23, 35, 57
Cine Colombia, 167
Cine Colon, Cali, 168, 172
Cine Excelsior, Lima, 3, 14, 166–67, 168, 172, 173
Cine Ideal, Manila, 58, 334, 343–45
Cine Império, Rio de Janeiro, 56
Cine Ipiranga, São Paulo, 166
Cine Marrocos, São Paulo 176
Cine Metro: Barranquilla, 169, 170–71, 179; Brisbane, 8, 58, 107, 125; Buenos Aires, 171, 176, 424n49; Cali, 169, 171, 179; Lima, 10, 24, 58, 155–56, 166, 173, 352; Medellín, 169, 179, 353; Montevideo, 58, 155, 157–58, 352; Santiago, 58, 155, 156, 352; São Paulo, 158–59, 162, 353
Cine Metro-Boavista, Rio de Janeiro, 177–78

Cine Metro-Copacabana, Rio de Janeiro, 147, 162, *163*, 165, 178, 179
Cine Metro-Passeio, Rio de Janeiro, 164, 165, 177, 179
Cine Metro-Teusaquillo, Bogotá, 170
Cine Metro-Tijuca, Rio de Janeiro, 3, 58, 152, *163*, 163–66, *179*, 181, *181*; closing and demolition, 178, 179; opening, 165, 194; replica, 26, 179–81, *180*, 206
Cinema Palace, Angers, 49
Cine Palácio, Rio de Janeiro, 166, 168, 172
Cine Rialto, Rio de Janeiro, 152
Cine Tacna, Lima, 10, 24, 148, 172–75
Cine-Theatro Broadway, Rio de Janeiro, 162
Cine-Theatro Paramount, São Paulo, 10, 13, 57, 147, 152–54, *153*, 162, 176–77
Cine-Ufa Palácio, São Paulo, 161
cinema architects: S. Beverley, 56, 57, 80, 82; Drew Eberson, 129, 156, 234, 243, 250; John Eberson, 16, 96, 129, 234, 243, 250; Thomas W. Lamb, 16, 38, 125, 214, 235, 347, 348, 398n95; James McNamara, 135, 235; Robert Prentice, 156–57, 158; Ben Schlanger, 156, 172; Frank Verity, 41, 50, 55, 56, 57, 80, 82
cinema architecture: American exteriors, 16, 348; art deco, 123–24, 155, 190, 343, 360; glocal/hybrid, 42, 86–88, 155, 156–57, 243; locally inflected/indigenous interiors, 16, 156–57, 214, 348; modernity, 156, 213, 244, 276, 347, 364
Cinema Astória, Rio de Janeiro, 158
Cinema Avenida, Rio de Janeiro, 150
Cinéma Caméo: Brussels, 58, 64, 65, 77; Lille, 49, 54
Cinema City International, 390
Cinema de Lux, 88
Cinema International Corp. (CIC), 82–85, 139, 177–79, *179*, 326–29; CIC-Film Trust, 83, 326; CIC Theatre Group, 85, 327; CIC-Warner/Nu Metro, 85, 326, 328–29; MGM's sale of cinemas to, 83–85, 138, 179, *179*, 205, 263–64, 326, 327, 345; UCI, 82, 85, 88, 89, 178, 368, 382, 390
Cinema Metro, Alexandria, 24–25, 235, 242, 243; CIC, 178, 264; Metro Cub Club, 218–19; symbol of Western influence, 25
Cinema Metro, Cairo, 7, 10, 24–25, 178, 214–17, *215*, 218, 221, 243–44, 245–46, 263–65, 266; 1947 attack on, 25, 226, 235; air-conditioning, 216; *Blow-up*, 263; Cairo Fire and, 238–39, 240; cartoon screenings, 217, 265; decline, 264–65; forced fundraising, 226–27; governmental demands and protectionism, 221, 246; Nasser and, 247; opening, 214, 215, 264, 431n43; popularity, 24, 216, 247, 263, 431n43; *Quo Vadis?*, 243; renovation, 265; reopening, 240, 243–44; symbol of pro-Western acquiescence, 209; *Valley of the Kings*, 16, 244
Cinema Opera, Reims, 57
Cinema Tel Aviv, 231, 234–35, 248, 250–55, 253, 261, 265–66; boycott fears and, 252; construction delays, 234–35, 248; demolition, 265–66, 440n45; labor and tax issues, 255, 262–63; opening, 253–55; sale of, 263; Skouras and, 14–15, 25, 234, 250–51; terrorist attack near, 262
Cinema Theater Investments (Pty.) Ltd., 280, 282
Cinemark, 89, 178, 390
CinemaScope, 247, 387; in Africa, 286–87; in Australia, 132–33; Cinema Tel Aviv, 251, 253; as driving force for exhibition expansion, 13, 80; in England, 80; in New Zealand, 132–33; as response to television, 133; *The Robe*, 250; in South Africa, 287, 290
Cinemas Investment Corp., 232
Cinematograph Exhibitors Association of Great Britain and Ireland (CEA), 34, 37, 39, 43–46
Cinemex, 389–91
Cineplex Odeon, 178
Cinépolis, 381, 389–90
Cinerama, 139, 204, 318, 387
Cinesa, 382
Cineworld, 381, 390–91, 392
Cintrust, 326
Circuito Cobián of Cuba, S.A., 196–97
Circuito Teatral Radiocentro, S.A., 202
City Theatre, Rotterdam, 60
Civic Theatre, Auckland, 118, 123, 132, 133, 139
CJ CGV, 376, 378, 381, 386–89; China; "Cultureplex"
Clark, Kenneth, 301
Clarke, Harley, 98, 100, 102
Clarriere, Georges, 52
class, 10, 156, 250, 269, 285, 295, 299, 389; American "rags to riches"/class mobility, 36, 157, 175, 277; division, in Brazil, 157; division, in China's cinemas, 363, 364; division, in cinemas, 41, 52; division, in Peru, 174; division/status, at

476 Index

class (*continued*)
    the Hogaku-Za, 338, 341; middle-class moviegoers, 219, 265, 354, 369
Cleopatra (1963), 254, 258–61, 263
Cloete, Stuart, 293–94
Coad, Stuart, 137
Coates, Joseph Gordon, 118
Coca-Cola, 81, 141, 217, 218, 243, 354, 355
Cochrane, Tom D., 334–35, 336, 337
Cohen, Charles, 380
Cohen, Isadore, 343–45
Cohen, Wolfe, 168, 169, 199–200
Cohen Media Group, 380
Colbert, Stephen, 384–85
Cold War, 11, 14, 17, 270, 290, 291; exhibition expansion in Israel amid, 25, 210, 249; Hilton Hotels amid, 11, 15–17. *See also* anticommunism
Colli, Peter, 196
Colombia, 148, 178; Cine Colombia, 167; FARC, 179; Fox, 148; Fox shop window, 168, 172; MGM, 158–59, 169, 170–71, 177, 179; MGM (Cine Metro, Barranquilla), 169, 170–71, 179; MGM (Cine Metro, Cali), 169, 171, 179; MGM (Cine Metro, Medellin), 169, 179, 353; Warner Bros., 24, 86, 148–49, 368. *See also* Cali; Bogotá
Colonial Film Exchange Company Ltd., 187
colonialism, 148, 149, 182, 183; British fears of American cultural, 33; British in India, 346, 347, 351; British in Jamaica, 24, 148, 183, 185, 189; British in Kenya, 284, 310–11, 316, 323; British in Palestine, 225–26, 228; British in Trinidad, 24, 148, 183, 188–89; French in West and North Africa, 25, 312, 313; Hollywood as "colonist," 12, 182, 186; U.S. in Puerto Rico, 169, 184, 189–90, 426n35. *See also* independence movements
Colosseum Theatre: Brussels, 67; Cape Town, 309; Johannesburg, 277–78, 433–34n11
Columbia Pictures Corp. Ltd., 83, 157, 202, 283; ACT and, 291; CIC and, 85; Havana, 185, 195; London (Columbia Theatre), 80, 81; Shochiku Youga Koukousya and, 342; Smith-Valcarce and, 195; Sony's acquisition of, 89, 379, 385; Ster and, 318
Columbia Theatre, London, 80
COMACICO. *See* Compagnie Marocaine Cinématographique et Commerciales (COMACICO)

communism, 148, 179, 199, 319, 356, 384; Brazilian-Nazi "agreement" to combat the spread of, 161; Chinese Communist Revolution, 361, 383; in India, 357–58; in Israel, 230, 249; in South Africa, 321; U.S. efforts to combat the spread of, 175, 270. *See also* anticommunism; Cold War
Compagnie Marocaine Cinématographique et Commerciales (COMACICO), 311–15
Companhia Cinematográfica Brasileira, 150
Companhia Constructora Nacional, 150
Condor, 84, 178
Conner, Lindsay, 377–78
Consolidated Drive-Ins, 134
Conspirator, The (1949), 249
Cooper, Robert A., 191–92
Copelan, Herbert, 199–200, 204
Copernie, 312
Corban, Assid Abraham, 117
Core, Charles, 344
Corrêa de Araujo, Luciana, 151
Corso Theater, Amsterdam, 60
Cosens, Spencer, 95
Cosmopolitan Productions, 36
Cossel, Hans Henning von, 160
Costa Rica, 56
coups d'état, 161, 175, 203, 241, 257
Court Dancer (1941), 351
Cousins, Alan, 308
Covered Wagon, The (1923), 36
COVID-19, 75, 378, 379, 381, 385–86, 391
Corvin Cinema, Budapest, 59
Crasto, J. Remi, 347
Credit Lyonnais, 89
Crick, Stanley S., 98, 99, 102, 120–22
Criterion Theatre, New York, 36
Crystal, Clement, 173–75, 231
Csaznik, Fred, 233
Cuba, 148, 182, 189, 194–97; anti-U.S. building embargo, 195; under Batista, 198, 203, 204; Camaguey, 196–97; under Castro, 205, 206; Cobiân, 190, 194, 196–98, 428n72; Fox, 148, 194, 195–96, 198, 199; independence, 184; labor issues, 197–98, 200–203; MGM, 194–97; nationalization of the film industry, 204; Paramount, 24, 56, 148, 183–87, 194–99, 201, 205, 401n74; political unrest, 183, 203–4; Smith-Valcarce, 185, 195–96; U.S. involvement

and anti-Americanism, 148, 183, 184, 204; Warner Bros., 5, 24, 86, 148, 185, 194–95, 197–98, 203–5, 368. *See also* Havana

cultural embassies, 3, 9–10, 16, 26, 30–31, 90, 148, 173, 206, 329, 356; Cinema Tel Aviv, 254; MGM Metros, 158, 162, 165, 171, 173, 181, 205–6, 345, 357; Paramount cinemas, 57, 75, 105, 173; as a term, 18, 19–20

Cumberbatch, Arthur N., 237–38
Curti, Carlo, 259
Curtin, Michael, 369, 462n22
Curzon Cinemas, 318, 380
Cyprus, 242

Dabadie, Suzy, 70
Daff, Alfred E., 313
Daini Sumiyoshi, Osaka, 342
Dalian Wanda, 143, 368, 378–39, 381–86, 387, 389, 390, 392; AMC's sale to, 379, 381–84; Reliance pact with, 389; Wanda Cinema Line, 381, 382; Warner Bros./ WBIT and, 26, 334, 372–74, 374
Daly, Len, 167
Daly Theatre, London, 62, 275
Dandridge, Dorothy, 294–95
Darweesh, Mustafa, 263
Darwish, Youssef, 246
Dassa, Clément, 217–18, 238
Dassa, Maurice, 217–18, 238, 240–43, 242, 245
Daumer, W. A., 103
Davies, David, 34
Davis, John H., 126, 127, 237
Davis, Marvin, 141, 142
Davis, Morris, 293–94
Day, John L., 149
Delaney, William B., 310–11
Delmaur Ltd., 420n49
DeMille, Cecil B., 244
Deming, Olcott, 304–5
Denis, Nelson, 190, 191
Denmark, 55, 56, 57, 88, 89; Copenhagen, 55
DeRoche, Andrew, 300
D'Errico, Bruno, Lopes and Figueiredo, 150
desegregation, 305, 311, 328; of Peruvian cinemas, 174; Skouras on, 175, 301, 309–10; of Southern Rhodesian cinemas and other public venues, 175, 209, 303–9, 316–17, 451n77; of U.S. cinemas, 174–75, 309
Deutsch, Oscar, 62–63

Devi, Sabita, 355
Diana Theatre, Cairo, 235
Dick Clark Productions, 838
Dickinson, A. R., 139
Dillane, Tom, 143
Dimension 150, 177
Diop, Boubacar, 312
diplomacy. *See* U.S. Department of State
DiPrida, Larry, 344
Disney. *See* Walt Disney Company
distribution revenues, repatriation of, 12, 103–4, 171, 230, 234, 251, 366
distribution vs. exhibition, 12
District 9 (2009), 453n137
Dobson, Peter, 370
Doherty, J. A., 314
Dominican Republic, 194
Dored, John, 72
Dowd, Tommy, 49
Doyle, Stuart Frank, 96–98, 104–5, 109, 112–13, 408n3
Drake Theatre, Plymouth, 80
Drafthouse Films/NEON, 380
drive-ins: ACT, 291, 292, 318; in Australia, 133–34; in Egypt, 244, 256, 260; Fox, 25, 214, 218, 256, 260, 291, 316, 318, 329; Hoyts, 133–34, 141–42; in Kenya, 25, 214, 218, 291, 316, 329; Kinekor, 325; MGM/ Loew's, 81, 128, 134, 291; in New Zealand, 128, 134; popularity of, in Africa, 318; in South Africa, 291, 292; in South Africa, segregated, 285, 309; in Southern Rhodesia, 291, 318; Ster, 318
Drott Biograf, Malmö, 55, 57
dubbing: in Brazil, 157, 161; in Egypt, 213, 228–29, 235, 250; in Latin America, 171; in Puerto Rico, 190, 194; subtitling vs., 52, 171, 194; in West Africa, 312
Dublin, Ireland: Paramount (Capitol Theatre), 45, 57; La Scala Theatre, 45
Dunn, Harold, 365
duopolies: Amalgamated/Kerridge-Odeon, 121, 121, 127–128, 131, 134; COMACICO/SECMA, 311–14; Fullers-Hayward/Williamsons, 121; Hoyts/Greater Union, 15, 97, 102, 112, 113, 134; WAP/Farrah, 314
Durban, South Africa: African Theatres, 274, 279; Fox/ACT, 318; Fox/ACT (20th Century Theatre), 280, 286; Fox/ ACT (Royal Cinema), 286; MGM (Metro Cinema), 58, 278, 279; as overseated, 277–78

Dutch Motion Picture Federation (Nederlandschen Bioscoop-Bond; NBB). *See under* Netherlands

East Africa, 322, 452n107; CIC, 85; "Dutch East Africa," 293; Fox, 289, 291, 311, 315; Fox subsidiary, 311, 323; PAMECA calls for boycott, 310–11; Portuguese, 289, 291; Schlesinger, 306
East African Newspapers Ltd., 316
Eberson, Drew, 156; Fox cinemas, 234, 243, 250; Warner Bros., 129
Eberson, John, 16; Capitol Theatre, Sydney, 96; Fox cinemas, 234, 243, 250; Warner Bros. cinema, 129
Eckman, Samuel, Jr., 46, 49–50
Eden, Barbara, 258
Efftee Film Productions, 99, 110
Egypt, 12, 24–25, 95, 209–10, 263–65, 355, 375, 383; anti-Americanism, 25; anti-British sentiment, 239, 432n78; antisemitism, 221, 235–36, 246, 260; censorship, 211, 216, 229, 230, 235, 243, 263, 265; Company Law (1947), 241; drive-ins/open-air cinemas, 210, 213, 216, 244, 256–57, 260, 264; Fox, 2, 4, 24–25, 209–10, 220; Fox, and television and loans for the UAR, 255–58; Fox's *Cleopatra*, 254, 258–61, 263; Heliopolis, 257, 264; MGM/Gaumont-Loew-Metro, 10, 11, 23, 24–25, 48, 83, 178, 226–27, 231, 240–46, 263–64, 265, 436n76; Misr al-Fatat, 209, 211–13, 220, 238, 385; nationalism, 25, 211–13, 220, 222–23, 228–28, 240–41, 246; nationalization of the film industry, 247, 256–57; Port Said, 210, 211, 221, 223; revolution, 241; Soviet Union and, 250, 256; Studio Misr, 213, 221; Suez Canal, 238; Suez crisis, 245, 246; terrorism, 12, 222–23, 226, 230, 235, 264, 375, 432n76; UAR, 255–56, 258, 259–60, 263; Wahbi's anti-Zionist campaign against MGM and Fox, 209, 228–30, 232, 257. *See also* Alexandria; Cairo
Egyptian Theatre, Los Angeles, 40, 42
Einstein, Oskar, 53
Eisenhower, Dwight, 75, 300–301, 303
El Atrash, Farid, 221
Electric Theaters, 95
Elgin Theater, Toronto, 395n4
Elite Cinema, 355, 359
Elmasri, Essam, 259
Elms, J. D. "Jack," 150–51

Elphinstone Picture Palace Calcutta, 347, 359
Embassy Theatre: Auckland, 119; Melbourne, 131; Port Elizabeth, 279, 286
Emmanuelle series, 84
Emmerson, John K., 304–5
Empire Films, 291–92, 318
Empire of the Sun (1987), 371
Empire Strikes Back, The (1980), 140
Empire Theatre, London, 36, 38–39, 45–46
Empire Theatre, London (MGM), 23, 38–39, 45–46, 49, 54, 57–58, 61, 76, 347; CIC/UCI ownership and operation, 83–85, 89; opening/launch, 46, 152; popularity and success, 61, 79; renovation, 81–82
Empresas Cinematográficas Reunidas Ltda., 150
Empresas Ramos Cobián. *See* Ramos Cobián, Rafael
England, 4, 31, 54; American exhibition expansion as threat to, 32–34, 186, 383; CIC, 84, 178; Cosmopolitan Productions, 36; Fox, 23, 61, 62, 63, 79–80, 279, 325; Granada Theatres, 39, 47, 56, 63, 74; industry boycotts, 10, 12, 23, 34, 44–45, 375, 383, 385; "kinema mind," 47; Liverpool, 32, 44, 63, 80; Loew's/MGM, 3, 4, 31, 37–38, 57, 64, 79, 81, 84, 125, 131; National Amusements, 88; Odeon Cinemas, 62–63, 80, 286; Paramount, 22, 23, 32–34, 43–45, 55–57, 60, 61–64, 78, 79, 84, 104, 186; Rank, 121, 127, 226; Schlesinger, 274–75, 278; Warner Bros., 61–62, 79, 86. *See also* Birmingham; Britain; Leeds; London; Manchester; Newcastle-on-Tyne; Plymouth
Englander, Fred S., 53
English, Scottish and Australian Bank (ES&A), 112, 113, 114, 141; Hoyts relationship with Greater Union, 97–98, 105–6, 112–15, 124, 141; Hoyts sale to Fox, 23–24, 101, 102, 103–4, 141
Equitable Insurance Company, 272
ES&A. *See* English, Scottish and Australian Bank (ES&A)
Esparza, Moctesuma, 389–90
Espino, Francisco, 201
Ethiopia, 242, 311, 315
Europe, 2, 3, 13, 19, 22, 23, 30–31, 33, 36–37, 53–54, 90, 280, 334; CIC, 82–85, 327; Cineworld, 381, 390–91, 392; Dalian Wanda, 382–85; film exports, 149, 273, 362; Fox, 54–55, 81, 281, 289; Grauman's tour of cinemas in, 12–13, 36; Loew's/

MGM, 36, 37, 49–50, 54, 58, 64, 155, 263, 351, 395n4; National Amusements, 88; Nazism, 58–59, 64, 66, 225; Paramount, 32, 35, 36, 37, 55–57, 62–63, 64, 76, 81–82, 104; Paramount/CIC, 82–85; refugees from, 226, 227, 250; UA, 59; Ufa, 59; Universal, 53; Warner Bros./WBIT, 61–62, 63, 86, 88, 370, 373, 377. *See also specific countries*
European Union, 370
Evans, William, 35
Ewijk, Wim van, Jr., 326
Eyles, Allen, 47, 62, 80

Fabello, Phil, 151
Fair, Laura, 20, 309, 320, 426n13
Familia Theater, Lille, 57
Famous Players Films (FPL), Paramount and, 32–33, 35, 85, 88, 96–97, 380; Famous-Lasky Paramount Films Ltd., 334; Famous Players-Lasky British Producers Ltd., 32–33, 35; London (Plaza), 19, 40–41, 45, 82
FARC (Fuerzas Armadas Revolucionarias de Colombia). *See under* Colombia
Farmer, James, 174
Farnham, Johnny, 140
Farouk I, 223, 244; Cairo Metro and, 24–25, 216; overthrow of, 240–41
Farrah Ltd., 314
Farrell, Tommy, 366
fascism, 11, 148, 158, 161, 211
Fatah, 262
Feeney, Megan, 201
Ferraz, Talitha, 180–81
Film Finance Corp., 360
Filmes Lusomundo, 88
First National Pictures, 96, 347, 362; Warner Bros. and, 62, 130, 198, 199
Fish, Bert, 213
Fisher, Carrie, 140
Fisherman, The (1968), 177
Fitzpatrick, James, 156
Flaherty, Robert, 233
Flint, Carl, 170
Florez & Costa, 172
Flyger, Alan, 142
Foch, Marshal Ferdinand, 50
Forbes, Ralph, 46
Forum, Le, Liege, 54, 58, 65, 77
Fourie, Bernardus Gerhardus, 327
Fox, Frederic, 294
Fox, William, 36, 54, 100, 102, 272

Fox Film Corp. *See* Twentieth Century-Fox
FPL. *See* Famous Players Films (FPL)
France, 10, 31, 54, 312, 383; Angers, 49; Fox, 81; Le Havre, 49, 54; liberation, 72; Lille, 49, 54, 57; MGM/Gaumont, 4, 23, 48–50, 54, 58, 77, 131, 150, 152, 347; Nazi occupation, 65–66, 68–69; Paramount, 5, 35, 50, 57, 67, 75, 84; Resistance (*see* Le Paramount, Paris); Strasbourg, 54, 57; V-E Day, 74. *See also* Le Havre; Paris; Reims; Rouen; Toulouse
Franklin, Harold, 52
Frankovsch, M. J., 80
Frater, Patrick, 386, 388, 389
Freeman, Herbie, 135
Freeman, Sir Nathaniel Bernard, 107, 142; MGM expansion into New Zealand drive-ins, 132–33, 134; MGM cinemas, 107–12, 124, 132; National Films Council, 125; retirement, 138
Friend, David, 390–91
Froude, Tony, 123–24, 135
Fu, Poshek, 363–64, 365
Fucs, Paulo, 177–78
Fuerzas Armadas Revolucionarias de Colombia (FARC). *See under* Colombia
Fugitive, The (1993), 368
Fuller, Benjamin, 123
Fuller, John, 116, 124
Fuller, Samuel, 319–20, 321
Fuller, W. R., 44
Fuller-Seeley, Kathy, 4–5
Fullers' Pictures Ltd., 108, 116, 411n2; Fuller-Hayward Theatre Corp., 116, 118, 121, 122–23
FunAsia, 387
Futurist Theatre, Birmingham, 43–44, 45, 57, 63, 80

Gaafar, Moustafa and Mohammed, 220, 223, 236–38, 256, 257, 263
Gable, Clark, 372
Gadjigo, Samba, 311–12
Gaiety Theatre, Kingston, 57, 186–87
Gainer, David, 309
Gainsborough, 106, 119, 275
Gamal, Samia, 16
Gance, Abel, 50
Gandhi, Mahatma, 355
Gao Jun, 385
Garcia-Crespo, Naida, 190, 191, 194
Garcia-Moreno, Sergio, 155
Gaston, Enrique, 199

Gaulle, Charles de, 74
Gaumont, 42, 176; Gaumont-Franco-Film Aubert, 58; Gaumont Graphic, 106; Gaumont-Loew-Metro, 13, 48, 152, 210; Gaumont-Metro-Goldwyn, 48–50, 58; Gaumont Opera, Paris, 75; Gaumont Palace, Paris, 13, 32, 36, 49, 50; Gaumont-Ufa, 106, 176. *See also* Gaumont-British Picture Corp.
Gaumont, Leon, 49
Gaumont Palace, Cairo, 210
Gaumont Palace, Paris, 13, 32, 36, 48–50
Gaumont-British Picture Corp., 56; Amalgamated and, 119, 127; Fox's stake in, 23, 54, 61, 62, 63, 99–100, 106, 110, 115, 279; Kinemas and, 275; Montevideo shop window, 420n50; Rank and, 283
Gawler, Fred, 96
Geach, Edwin, 98
Geisel, Ernesto, 178
Gelb, Stephen, 285
General Film Company of Australasia, 95
General Theatres Corp. of Australasia Ltd. (GTC), 106–13, 124
General Theatres Equipment Inc. (GTE), 100–101, 134
Georgoussky, Georg, 222
Germany, 52–54, 211; antisemitism in, 58; East Germany, 263; Hamburg, 80, 81; Paramount, 52–53, 66; Parufamet, 52–53; Tobis, 61, 65; UCI, 85; Universal, 52–53; Warner Bros./WBIT, 88; West Germany, 80, 85. *See also* Berlin; Nazi Germany and Nazism; Ufa
Gerö, Stephen, 59
Gerschtanowitz, Max, 404n30
GFFPL. *See* Golden Films & Finance Private Ltd. (GFFPL)
Ghana, 315
Ghawanmeh, Mohannad, 212
Gibbons, Cedric, 157
Gigi (1958), 80
Gilad, Ephraim, 262–63
Gilbert, Morris, 50–52
Glasgow, Scotland: Paramount, 57, 63, 80; PPL, 32–33
Glass, John, 136
globalization, 3, 10, 89, 123, 342
Glücksmann, Bernardo, 158
Glücksmann, Max, 158
Godard, Jean-Luc, 312
Godowicz, Yisrael, 254
Goebbels, Joseph, 58
Gokool, N. M. "Meah," 188–89

Golden, Herb, 250
Golden Films & Finance Private Ltd. (GFFPL), 360
Golden Harvest, 368, 376, 386
Goldenson, Leonard, 175
Goldsmith, Charles, 188
Goldstein, Leon, 309
Goldstein, S., 157
Goldwyn Pictures, 49
Goldwyn-Cosmopolitan, 35
Gondola, Didier, 20
Gong Li, 372
Gonzaga, Alice, 157
González Videla, Gabriel, 172
Goodman, Gene, 173
Gooptar, Primnath, 187, 188–89
Gore, Robert Hayes, 191
Gould, David, 192, 193
Gould, Walter, 159
Gouvêa, Oswaldo, 161
Govil, Nitin, 362
Graham, John Cecil (J. C.), 32, 37, 40, 42, 45, 55–56
Granada Theatres, 39, 47, 56, 63, 74
Granada TV Network, 306, 315
Grant, Cary, 254
Grant, James P., 259–60
Grauman, Sid, 40–41; Egyptian Theatre, 40, 42; tour of European cinemas, 12–13, 36
Grau San Martín, Ramón, 198, 200
Greater J. D. Williams Amusement Company, 95
Greater Union Theatres, 130, 132, 408n3; Brazil, 178; ES&A's financing of, 105–6; Hoyts and, 15, 94, 106, 108, 110, 112–15, 124, 125, 134, 141–42, 352; Hoyts and/drive-ins, 134, 141–42; MGM and, 125, 138–39, 352; Sixteen Millimetre, 139
Greenvald, Simha, 234, 248, 250
Greidinger, Mooky, 390–91
Griffith, G. F., 98, 102, 133–34
Grossman, Leonard, 185
Groves, John, 344
GTC. *See* General Theatres Corp. of Australasia Ltd. (GTC)
GTE. *See* General Theatres Equipment Inc. (GTE)
Guangzhou (Canton), China, 367, 372, 373, 460n13, 462n51
Guangzhou Performance Co., 373
Guatemala, 140, 154
Guggenheim, Jack, 78–79
Gujral, I. K., 360
Gulf + Western Inc., 83

Guoming, Yu, 374
Gutsche, Thelma, 20, 271–72, 277, 281
Gyles, H. J. W., 113

Hadassah, the Women's Zionist Organization of America, 227, 232
Hague, The, Netherlands, 50, 59, 61, 81
Haifa, Israel, 225, 248; Fox, 231, 234, 250, 254, 261; Louries in, 232; MGM, 231; Paramount, 231; Rank, 226
Hajime Sakai, 176
Halsey, Stuart & Co., 100, 101
Hammerstein, Oscar, II, 269, 294
Hansen, Lulu, 375
Hanson, H., 278
Harley, Robert, 230
Harris, Norman F., 315–16
Hassanein, Salah, 5–7, 22, 86–88, 368–69
Havana, Cuba, 428n83; Columbia Pictures, 185; Fox, 150; Fox (Teatro Nacional), 195–96, 198; labor conflicts/strike, 183, 197–203, 205; Loew's/MGM cinemas, 169, 183, 196, 198; Paramount, 199; Paramount-Cobián, 196–97, 198, 428n72; Paramount (Teatro Encanto), 56, 184–85, 195–95, 197, 199, 202; Paramount (Teatro Fausto), 55, 154, 184–85, 194–95, 197, 199, 202; Saenger, 184; Smith-Valcarce, 195, 196; UA, 201; Warner Bros., 5, 10, 86, 183, 185; Warner Bros.'s Christmas bonus policy, 201–2; Warner (Plaza Theatre), 199–200, 202, 203, 205; Warner (Warner Theater/Teatro Radio Centro/Cine Yara), 197–200, 202–3, 203, 204, 205
Hayden, Sidney, 275, 276
Hayward, Bruce, 135
Hayward, Henry, 116
Hayward, Phil, 116
Hayward, Selwyn, 135
Haywards' Enterprises/Haywards' Pictures Ltd., 116; Fuller-Hayward Theatre Corp., 116, 118, 121, 122
HBO Max, 381, 392
Hearst, William Randolph, 36, 72, 158
Hecht, Ben, 356
Heggie, O. P., 46
Henderson, Donald, 288, 305, 308
Herbert, Bert, 82
Hertzog, A. A., 307
Herzstein, Robert E., 356
Heumann, Joseph K., 321
Hicks, John W., Jr., 57, 67, 196
Higginson, Stanley, 129, 130
Highet, Alan, 135

Hill, Arthur, 137
Hilton, Conrad, 16–17, 206, 253
Hilton International Hotels, 11, 15–18; Arab League boycott and, 252–53; Nile Hilton, 16, 244, 253; Ramses Hilton, 265
Hippodrome Pictures Ltd., 117–19. *See also* Amalgamated Theatres Ltd.
Hitchcock, Alfred, 74
Hitler, Adolf, 59, 113, 125, 161, 162, 225
Hoare, Victor, 83–84, 177
Hogaku-Za, Tokyo, 25, 55, 152, 333–34, 338–41, 356n42, 364; anti-Americanism and, 339–40; *benshi*, 334, 338–41; conversion to sound, 340–41; *Paramount on Parade*, 341
Holland. *See* Netherlands
Hollinshead, C. N., 125
Hollywood: "colonization," 12, 182, 186; exotic allure, 3, 144, 157, 165, 173, 177, 339, 348, 357. *See also* cultural embassies; shop windows
Holmes, Jeffrey, 328
Hometown (1930), 341
Hong Kong: box office boom, stalling of, 363; Broadband Investment Ltd., 371; CGV headquarters, 386; Golden Harvest, 368, 386; Hong Kong Disneyland, 378; MGM, 342, 460n13; Paramount (King's Theatre), 363; Salon Films, 372; UACC, 369
Hongkong Amusement Company, 362
Hongsen, Zhang, 376
Hoover, Herbert, 54, 101
Horowitz, David, 230, 250
House of Wax (1953), 128
Hove, Masotha Mike, 296
Howe, W. J., 103
Hoyt, Eric, 362
Hoyts Theatres Ltd.: Amalgamated and, 119–20, 139, 141–42; drive-ins, 133–34, 141–42; Capitol Theatre, Melbourne, 125; Fox's stake in, 12, 14, 23–24, 94, 98, 101, 110, 120, 131, 140–44; Fox's stake in, Chase National Bank's role in the purchase, 23–24, 94, 98, 101, 110, 120, 141; Fox's stake in, ES&A's role in the purchase, 23–24, 101, 102, 103–4, 141; Greater Union and, 15, 94, 106, 108, 110, 112–15, 124, 125, 134, 141–42, 352; Hoyts America, 143; multiplexes, 140, 178; Paramount and, 105, 125; Regent Theatre, Brisbane, 105, 140; Regent Theatre, Melbourne, 96, 132; segregated cinemas, 136; television and, 136–37; UA and, 96.

Hughes, Charles Evans, 100
Humphrey, William Pettigrew, 187–89
Hungary, 58, 59
Husan, Jack, 246
Husayn, Ahmad, 209, 211, 213, 216, 238, 240, 243
Hutchinson, W. J., 120, 280

Iakovos (archbishop), 231
Ibrahim, Fathi, 246, 255–58, 260
Idzal, David, 252, 254
IFC Films, 380
IMAX Corp., 265, 376, 378, 382
immigrants and immigration: German, in Brazil, 160; moguls, 101, 272; to Palestine/Israel, 230, 233, 249; U.S. Immigration Act (1924), 334, 335–37
independence movements, 10, 272, 322; Cuba, 184; Egypt, 11; India, 11, 346, 348, 351, 353–55; Israel, 228; Jamaica, 185; Kenya, 316, 322; Peru, 155–56; Senegal, 312
independent cinemas: in Australia, 102; in Cuba, 195; in Japan, 336, 337; in New Zealand, 126, 127; in South Africa, 274, 283, 292, 328; in South Korea, 386
Independent Picture Palaces Ltd., 279–80
India, 25, 344, 346–48, 361, 374, 387–90; anti-Americanism, 333; Bollywood, 387–88; British colonial rule, 346, 347, 351; communism, 357–58; Dalian Wanda, 389; film industry, 346, 350; Fox, 358–59; independence, 11, 346, 348, 351, 353–55; Indian films abroad, 182, 189, 312, 324, 387; Loew's, 347; MGM, 342, 355–60, 366; MGM India's sale, 360; MGM's Metro Cub Clubs, 10, 11, 346, 352–55, 360; nationalism, 351–57; New Delhi, 359; philo-Americanism, 333; Reliance, 388–89; Soviet Union and, 357–58; *Thief of Baghdad*'s unlicensed distribution in, 362; Universal, 347. *See also* Bombay (Mumbai); Calcutta (Kolkata)
indigenous film production, 272, 315, 324; in Australia, 94, 102, 110, 114; in China, 361, 363; in Egypt, 220; in India, 346, 350
Indonesia, 386
Industrial and Commercial Development Corp., 324
Inkay Film Distributors, 263
Inmobiliaria San Martín, S.A., 172

insurance companies, 94; Aetna, 141–42; Sanlam, 141, 318, 325, 329; Schlesinger and, 272, 273, 286
investment banks, 4, 24, 94, 99–102, 235, 259
Iran, 242, 255; Tehran, 226
Iraq, 228, 233, 242, 255, 258; Baghdad, 226
Ireland, 34; Cineworld, 391; Dalian Wanda, 382; Paramount, 45, 56, 57, 85; Rank, 127, 283; UCI, 85. *See also* Dublin
Irizarry, Luis, 192
Isaza, Jorge, 155, 167
Isis Theater, Shanghai, 362
Israel, State of, 25, 95, 391; Arab-Israeli War, 210, 228, 229, 235, 250; Arab League boycott, 244–45, 252–53, 259, 263; Beersheba, 261; communism, 230, 249; films about, 232–33, 253; Fox, 4, 25, 209–10, 230–32, 234–35, 248–55, 260–63, 266; Histadrut, 252, 262; immigration to, 230, 233, 249; independence, 228; Israel Film Bureau, 251; Natanya, 231, 234, 261; Patel's attacks on, 356–57; Russian films in, 230, 249; Silverstone's support for, 227–28, 229, 232; Six-Day War, 262; Skouras's support for, 227–28, 229, 231, 232, 233, 236, 245, 248–49, 252, 258, 259, 442n88; Suez crisis, 245, 246; Elizabeth Taylor's visits to/support for, 258, 259, 441n69; television, 254–55, 262. *See also* Haifa; Jerusalem; Palestine; Tel Aviv
Italy, 391; fascist, 113, 161, 162, 211; Dalian Wanda, 382; Loew's/MGM, 80–81, 131; UCI, 85; Warner Bros./WBIT/WBIC, 88, 374
Itatsu, Yuko, 335–37

Jackals, The (1967), 319–20
Jackman, Terry, 140–42
Jackson, Jesse, 327
Jacquin, Maurice, 311–12, 314
Jamaica, 148, 182, 185–87; British colonial rule and pushback, 24, 148, 183, 185, 189; independence, 185; law requiring inclusion of British and Jamaican films (1928), 185–86; Paramount, 24, 56, 57, 148, 183, 184, 185, 186–87, 401n74; Warner Bros., 85. *See also* Kingston
Japan: AEON Group, 377; American prisoners of war, 66, 333, 344, 365; Brazil and, 162, 176–77; Great Kanto Earthquake, 335, 337; invasion of China, 342,

364, 365, 371; invasion of the Philippines, 343–45, 365; MGM, 342–43; Paramount, 25, 57, 333, 334–35, 337–42, 344, 347, 401n74; Pearl Harbor, 162, 165, 343; Shochiku Kinema Ltd., 336, 341–42; silent film and *benshi*, 334, 337, 338–41; Sony, 89, 379, 385, 453n137; surrender in World War II, 365; UCI, 85; U.S. Immigration Act (1924) and anti-American backlash, 334, 335–37; Warner Bros., 344; Warner-Mycal, 26, 88, 333, 343, 361, 369, 377; Warner/WBIT/WBIC, 88, 369, 373–74. *See also* Osaka; Tokyo

Jarvie, Ian, 2, 15

J. C. Williamson (New Zealand) Films Ltd./J. C. Williamson Films Ltd./J. C. Williamson Picture Corp. Ltd., 117, 118, 121, 122, 127, 411n2

Jenkins, William Oscar, 169

Jennings, R. P., 418n2

Jerusalem, Palestine/Israel, 217, 225; cinemas, as sites of terrorism, 262; Fox, 231, 234, 250, 254, 261; Hilton, 17, 252–53; Louries, 232; Rank, 226

Jesus, Luiz Carlos de, 179–89

Jiang Zemin, 371

Johannesburg, South Africa, 3, 62; drive-ins, 309; Fox/ACT, 279–80, 286, 295; Fox/ACT (Cinerama franchise), 318; Fox/ACT (Colosseum Theatre), 277–78, 433–34n11; Fox/ACT/ACF, 288–91, 318; Fox/ACT/Killarney, 319; Fox/ACT (20th Century Theatre), 9, 232, 252, 280, 286; Independent Picture Palaces Ltd., 279–80; Kinemas, S.A., 274, 275; MGM (Metro Cinema), 5, 58, 152, 163, 276–78, 347; Schlesinger/AAT/AFP/ACT, 272–75, 286; Ster, 318, 327; television, 286

Johnson, Van, 170

Johnston, Eric, 295, 296, 300, 301, 303, 311, 313; tour of/report on Africa (1960), 311, 314–15

Johnston, William A., 50

Jordan, 228, 244

Jordi, M. K., 325

Judel, A., 157

Kahn, Henry, 278
Kalmine, Harry M., 199–200
Kamara Theatre, Budapest, 58
Kamau, John, 328

Kann, Red, 50
Kaplan, Eliezer, 230
Kaufman, Al, 40–41, 42, 52
Kaye, Danny, 230
Kazan, Elia, 247
Kearney, Eric, 118–19
Kefer, Pierre, 52
Keith, J. L., 310
Kelly, Arthur, 281–82
Kelly, Grace, 24
Kelsoum, Om (Umm Kulthum), 221
Kennedy, John F., 301, 303, 309, 313
Kennedy, Robert F., 309
Kent, Sidney R., 106
Kenworthy, G. N., 129
Kenya, 270–71, 322–24, 329; African Theatres Ltd., 273; British Capital Ltd., 178; British colonial rule, 284, 310–11, 316, 323; desegregation of cinemas, 299, 304, 305, 316; drive-ins, 25, 214, 218, 291, 316, 329; Fox, 284, 291, 292, 308, 311, 323–26, 328, 359; Fox's acquisition of ACT, 14, 17, 25, 270, 279, 288–89, 291, 292, 310, 318; Fox's segregated cinemas, 2, 25, 269, 305, 310–11, 316; Fox's stake in Kenya's TV network, 308, 315–16, 325, 451n68; independence, 316, 322; Indian-owned cinemas in Kenya, 324; Kenya Broadcasting Corp., 316; Mau Mau Uprising, 310, 311; MGM/ACT, 284; nationalization of the film industry/KFC, 323–24; Nu Metro, 328; PAMECA boycott, 310–11; television, 308, 315–16, 325, 451n68; TIE, 451n68. *See also* Nairobi

Kenya Film Corp. Ltd. (KFC), 323–24
Kenya Theatre Building, Nairobi, 323
Kerboeuf, Anne-Claire, 238
Kerkorian, Kirk, 89, 138
Kerr, Deborah, 254
Kerridge, Robert, 126–37, 133, 135, 139
Kerridge-Odeon, 128, 133, 134; Amalgamated and, 121, 127–28; Odeon Holdings (New Zealand) Ltd., 127; Rank, 283; Williamson's sale of cinemas to, 411n2
Kerridge Theatres, 126–27. *See also* Kerridge-Odeon
Kessler-Howes, H. F., 42
KFC. *See* Kenya Film Corp. Ltd. (KFC).
Khan, Mohamed, 10, 209, 217, 218
Khrushchev, Nikita, 358
Kilar, Jason, 392
Killarney Film Studios, 273, 292, 318–22, 325

Kinekor Organisation, 325; Ster-Kinekor, 326–29
Kinema Palace, Osaka, 342
Kinemas, S.A., 274
Kinemas Ltd., 274–76, 277
King, A. H., 240
King, Tony, 295
King, W. Gavazzi, 37, 392
Kingston, Jamaica: Paramount (Gaiety Theatre), 57, 186–87; Paramount (Movies Theatre), 57, 186–87; Paramount (Palace Theatre), 57, 186–87
Kinshasa, Democratic Republic of the Congo, 320
Kirihara, Donald, 339, 342
Kissinger, Henry, 327
Kitchens, Gordon, 314
Kiyashi Yamamôta, 176
Klarsfeld, Henri, 67
Klein, Dave S., 295
Klein, Uri, 254, 265
Klinov, I., 230
Knight, Reginald, 298
Kobayashi, Ichizo, 342
Koigen, George M., 234, 250
Kokas, Aynne, 385
Kolkata, India. *See* Calcutta (Kolkata), India
Kollek, Teddy, 250
Korean War, 249
Kracauer, Siegfried, 54
Krefft, Vanda, 100
Krim, Arthur, 233
Krisel, Alexander, 362
Kunieda, Kanzi, 338
Kurtz, Gary, 140

Laborde, Jean de, 404n44
Labow, Jack, 452n106
Lady Hamilton (1941), 163
Laemmle, Carl, 36, 37, 52, 53
Lait, George, 217, 219
Lamb, David, 265
Lamb, Thomas W., 16; Albee Theatre, 398n95; Loew's theaters, 38, 125, 214, 235, 347, 348
Landmark Theatres, 380
Lange, Fred W., 67
Langley, Donna, 379, 392
Latin America, 2, 24, 90, 147–49, 189, 195, 206; CIC, 84–85, 327; Cinemark, 390; cinemas during World War II, 166–67; Fox, 13, 24, 166–67, 168, 172; "Good Neighbor" policies, 164; Loew's/MGM's focus on and dominance in, 13, 24, 147–49, 154–55, 159, 168, 170–71, 172, 177, 194, 198, 202; market's rapid growth in the 2010s, 370; National Amusements, 88; Nazi Germany and, 157, 160, 162; Paramount, 13, 24, 55, 148, 154, 171–72, 175; UA, 159; Warner Bros., 24, 148–49, 166, 199, 200. *See also* Argentina; Brazil; Chile; Peru; Puerto Rico; Uruguay; Venezuela
Lattre de Tassigny, Jean de, 74
Lazar, Lou, 175
Le Havre, France: MGM (Select Cinéma), 49, 54
Leasin, H. W., 278
Lebanon, 117, 233, 244; Beirut, 226, 245, 261; Fox, 255, 258; MGM, 242; television, 255
Lebreton, Rene, 67, 69, 71, 72, 75
Lee, S. Charles, 3
Leeds, England: British Odeon, 62; Paramount (Paramount Theatre), 56, 57, 63, 80; Universal (Briggate Picture House), 37; Universal (Rialto Theatre), 53
Legendary Entertainment, 383
Leighton, William, 125
Leopold III, 64
Lesquen, P., de, 312
Letsch, Jan, 65
Levi, Rino, 161
Levin, Gerald, 370
Levy, Alfred, 43, 44–45, 122
Levy, Bert, 107
Levy, Sol, 43, 44–45, 122
Liberman Family Group, 141
Liberty Theatres, 109, 110, 111, 131
Libeskind, Nat, 157
Libya, 264
Lichtman, Al, *288*
Lima, Peru, 63, 86, 199, 200, 428n83; cinemas, 14, 24, 166, 172, 173; Fox (Cine Excelsior), 3, 14, 166–67, 168, 172, 173; MGM (Cine Metro), 10, 24, 58, 155–56, 166, 173, 352; Paramount (Cine Tacna), 10, 24, 148, 172–75; Plaza San Martín, 155, 156; racial division, 174–75; Warner (Teatro Central), 10, 63, 86, 166, 173, 197, 200
Llamas, T., 193, 194
Llamas-Rodriguez, Juan, 389
Locke, F. W., 44–45
Loew, Arthur, 46, 77, 107, 131, 155, 157; cinemas in South Africa/ACT and, 276,

278, 284, 287; cinemas in Switzerland, 78–79; cinemas in the Netherlands, 59–60; on exhibition expansion, 30–31, 154, 168; plane crash, 277; retirement, 176; on selling America and American democracy overseas, 17, 155, 170
Loew, Marcus, 13, 14, 35, 49, 395n4; on British boycott threats, 37–38; Lower East Side origins, 272; vaudeville, 31
Loew's 7th Avenue Theatre, New York, 151
Loew's Inc.: Gaumont-Loew-Metro, 13, 48, 152, 210; Lamb as architect for, 38, 125, 214, 235, 347, 348; Loews Cineplex, 89, 370, 381; Loew's International and Puerto Rico, 169, 183, 189–90; Loews Theatres, 385; MGM's split from (1959), 78, 80, 149, 175; New York (Capitol Theatre), 38, 49, 53; New York office, 107, 125, 150, 214; New York (Loew's 7th Avenue Theatre), 151. *See also* Metro-Goldwyn-Mayer (MGM)
Logan, Joshua, 1
Lomba, Eddie, 288, 290, 294, 302, 305, 308, 316, 399
London, England, 3, 24, 30, 46–47, 163, 173, 428n83; "American invasion of London" and backlash, 33, 37–39; CIC, 83, 85; Columbia (Columbia Theatre), 80; Cosmopolitan (Empire Theatre), 36; Fox, 81; Fox's Cinemascope, 80; Fox (Palace Theatre), 14, 36; Fox's subsidiary in, 311, 323; Hilton, 17; Loew's/Metro (Tivoli Theatre), 35–36, 38; Marble Arch Pavilion, 41; MGM (Empire Theatre) (*see* Empire Theatre, London); MGM (Ritz Cinema), 61, 82, 83; Odeon (Odeon Leicester Square), 223; Paramount, 23, 57, 63, 152, 338; Paramount-Astoria-Theatres-Ltd., 56, 57, 62, 63; Paramount/Famous Players-Lasky British Producers Ltd., 32–33, 35; Paramount/Odeon, 63; Paramount/Picture Playhouses, 32; Paramount (Carlton Theatre), 24, 39, 50, 55–56, 57, 80; Paramount (Pavilion Theatre), 36–37; Paramount (Plaza Theatre) (*see* Plaza Theatre, London); Paramount (Tottenham Court Road), 57; Paramount/UT, 95–96; RKO, 61; Schlesinger, 275; Schlesinger (Daly Theatre), 275; Shepherd's Bush Pavilion, 32, 41; UA, 42–43, 61; Universal (Empire Theatre), 36; Universal (Rialto Theatre), 53; Warner Bros., 42; Warner (Daly Theatre), 62; Warner (Warner Theatre/Warner West End Theatre), 5, 7, 24, 61–62, 82, 86, 87, 368; Warner/WBIT/WBIC, 368–69, 373
Los Angeles, California: BIG Cinemas, 388; El Capitan Theatre, 380; Century City, 139; Chevalier's visit to, 67; CJ CGV, 387; Egyptian Theatre, 40, 42; Toho La Brea Theatre, 177, 342
Lotte, 376
Lourie, Arthur, 233
Lourie, Harry, 280
Lourie, Jeanette Leibel, 232
Lourie, Nadia, 251–52
Lourie, Norman, 233, 250; arrest, 282–83; Associated Theatres, 2085; Cinemas Investment Corp., 232; Fox/20th Century Theatre and, 227, 232, 251–52, 280–82, 286; fundraising for Palestine/Israel, 231–32; Habonim, 232; Palestine Films/documentaries, 232–33
Lourie & Katz, 280, 281
Louw, Eric, 293–94
Low, Sidney, 33
Luce, Henry, 356
Lumley, Sir Roger, 351
luxury, 11, 18, 103, 153, 184; ACT's "luxury theatres," 284; CIC's "luxury multiplex concept," 85; Cinépolis's luxury cinemas, 389, 390; Fox (Amir Cinema), 243; Fox (Cinema Tel Aviv), 251, 266; Hilton, 15; MGM cinemas/Metros, 151, 181, 216, 348, 424n49
Lyra, Carlos (Carlos Eduardo Lyra Barbosa), 147

Maas, Irving, 196
Macdonald, Karl, 169, 197
Madan Theatres, 347
Madeleine Cinéma, Paris, 48, 49
Madru, Gaston, 72
Magnetic Tide, The (1950), 233
Magnusson, Charles, 55
Maier, Herman R., 62, 199
Maingard, Jacqueline, 20
Majestic Theatre, Ghent, 50, 54, 58
Malaysia, 386
Mali, 312
Maltby, Richard, 2, 3–4, 36–37
Manchester, England: British Odeon, 62; Paramount (Paramount Theatre), 30, 32, 56, 57, 62, 63, 80; PPL, 32
Mangan, Francis, 40–41

Manila, Philippines, 3; Japanese attack on, 343–45, 365; MGM (Cine Ideal), 58, 334, 343–45
Mann Theatres, 85, 380
Manuel Ramon Fernandez, 196, 428n72
Marble Arch Pavilion, London, 41
Marden, C. F., 108–9
Marks, F. W., 110–11, 114
Martin, David N., 109–11, 131
Martin, Germain, 58
Masilela, Ntongela, 20
Mason, J. H., 122–23
Master Pictures, 96
Matiba, Kenneth Stanley Njindo, 323
Matrix Reloaded, The (2003), 372
Maxwell, Catherine, 63
Maxwell, John, 63
Mayer, Louis B., 101
Mayer, Seymour, 345
Mayo, Virginia, 319
Mbogoni, Lawrence, 443n6
MCA Inc., 83
McCoy, Howard, 186
McDonald, G. F., 44
McIntyre, Robert, 335
McNamara, John, 315; Cinema Metro, Alexandria, 235
Megabox, 376
megaplexes, 88, 390
Megastar, 386
Melbourne, Australia: drive-ins, 133–34; Greater Union, 114; Hoyts/Fox, 3, 95, 113, 114, 125; Hoyts (Capitol Theatre), 125; Hoyts (Regent Theatre), 96, 132; MGM, 58, 107–8, 134; MGM (Capitol Theatre), 96; MGM (Embassy Theatre), 131; MGM (Metro Theatre), 124–25; Paramount (Capitol Theatre), 56, 57, 104–5, 115, 125
Melniker, William, 157, 158, 176, 192, 280–81
Mercedes Palast, Berlin, 53
mergers, 150, 381; CIC, 82–83; CIC/MGM/UA, 85, 327; Colonial Film Exchange Company Ltd., 187; Films Paramount, 67; Foxmeric, 81; Hoyts, 95; Hoyts/UT, 98; Kinemas/African Theatres, 276–77; Kinemas Ltd., 274; Metro-Goldwyn, 38; NZ Picture Supplies, 116; Shochiku Paramount, 25, 341; Ster-Kinekor, 326, 328; Twentieth-Century Fox, 101, 115; UCI, 85; U-I, 283; UT, 95
Merman, Doc, 259
Mestre, Abel, 197–98, 199, 202

Mestre, Goar, 197–98, 199, 200, 202, 204
Metro Cinema, Bombay (MGM), 3, 25, 334, 348–55, *350*, 357–58; benefit screenings, 351; Metro Cub Club, 26, 346, 353–55; nationalism and, 25, 350, 355–57; "panoramic screens," 358; *Quo Vadis?*, 358. *See also* Metro Cinema, Mumbai
Metro Cinema, Calcutta (MGM), 10, 58, 334, 347, *349*, 351, 355; Metro Cub Club, 346, 353, 354–55, 360; nationalization of, 360; opening, 25, 347–48; "panoramic screens," 358; Tramarsa's purchase of, 359–60
Metro Cinema, Mumbai: as BIG Cinema, 360, 387, *388*; Lashkar-e Taiba's attack on, 360
Metro Crows Nest, Sydney, 132
Metro-Goldwyn-Mayer (MGM): Alexandria, 24–25, 178, 216–19, 235, 242, 243, 264; Amsterdam, 59–61, 178; anti-Zionist campaign against, 209, 228–30, 232, 257; Argentina, 24, 154, 158, 159, 166, 171, 177; Australasia, 93, 107, 143–44; Australia, 10, 15, 23, 93–94, 96, 102, 107–15, 131–32, 134; Belgium, 46, 48, 50, 54, 64–65, 77, 210; Berlin, 80–81; Bogotá, 79, 158, 167, 170; Bombay, 3, 25, 26, 334, 346, 348–60, *350*, 387, *388*; Brisbane, 8, 58, 107, 125; Brussels, 64, 65; Budapest, 58–59; Buenos Aires, 10, 169, 171, 175, 176, 424n49; Cairo, 7, 10, 16, 24–25, 178, 209, 214–17, *215*, *218*, 221, 226–27, 235, 238–40, 243–47, 263–66, 431n43; Calcutta, 10, 25, 58, 334, 346–48, *349*, 351, 353–55, 358–60; Cali, 169, 171, 179; Cape Town, 58, 78, 287, 309; Caribbean, 182, 183, 189; Chile, 24, 155, 159, 166, 169, 177, 352; CIC's purchase of cinemas, 83–85, 138, 179, *179*, 205, 263–64, 326, 327, 345; Colombia, 158–59, 169, 170–71, 177, 179, 353; Cuba, 194–97; drive-ins, 81, 128, 134, 291; Durban, 58, 278, 279; Egypt, 10, 11, 23, 24–25, 48, 83, 178, 209, 226–32, 240–46, 257, 263–64, 265, 436n76; England, 3, 4, 31, 37–38, 57, 64, 79, 81, 84, 125, 131; Europe, 36, 37, 49–50, 54, 58, 64, 155, 263, 351, 395n4; France, 4, 23, 48–50, 54, 58, 77, 131, 150, 152, 347; Ghent, 50, 54, 58; Hamburg, 80; Haifa, 231; Havana, 169, 183, 196, 198; Hong Kong, 342, 460n13; India, 10, 11, 342, 346, 352–60, 366; Italy, 80–81, 131; Japan, 342–43; Johannesburg, 5, 58, 152, 163, 276–78,

347; Kenya, 284; Latin America, 13, 24, 147–49, 154–55, 159, 168, 170–71, 172, 177, 194, 198, 202; Lebanon, 255, 258; Liege, 54, 58, 65, 77; Lille, 49, 54; Lima, 10, 24, 58, 155–56, 166, 173, 352; London, 23, 24, 35–36, 38–39, 45–46, 49, 54, 57–58, 61, 76, 79, 81–85, 89, 152, 347; Manila, 58, 334, 343–45; Melbourne, 58, 96, 107–8, 124–25, 131, 134; Mexico City, 419n29; Montevideo, 58, 155, 157–58, 352; Netherlands, 50, 59, 60–61, 65, 77, 78; Panama City, 177, 424n58, 425n65; Paris, 13, 32, 36, 48–50; Peru, 24, 156, 159, 175; Port of Spain, 183, 187–89; Puerto Rico, 24, 183; Rio de Janeiro, 3, 26, 58, 147, 152, 163–66, *163*, 177–81, *179*, *180*, *181*, 194, 206; San Juan, 183, 190, 192–94, 200, 205, 206; Santiago, 58, 155, 156, 352; São Paulo, 150–52, 158–59, 162, 353; Shanghai, 25–26, 334, 361–62, 364–67; South Africa, 276–77, 279, 280, 284, 287, 293–94, 309, 322, 327, 328; South America, 5, 83, 151, 152, 155, 158–59, 169, 170, 177, 178, 180, 205, 352; Strasbourg, 54; Sydney, 58, 96, 105, 107–8, 111–12, 124, 131, 132, 134, 138; Syria, 23, 48, 210, 242; Tel Aviv, 10, 231; Tokyo, 58, 342; Trinidad, 24, 183, 187–89, 457n54, 457n61; widescreen cinema, 133, 177, 358

Metro-Goldwyn-Mayer (MGM), partnerships and subsidiaries: ACT, 276–77, 279, 280, 284, 287; CIC/MGM/UA, 83, 237; Empresas Reunidas Metro-Goldwyn-Mayer Ltda., 24, 50, 147–48, 150–52, 159, 347, 419n12; Gaumont-Loew-Metro, 13, 48, 152, 210; Gaumont-Metro-Goldwyn, 48–50, 58; Greater Union Theatres, 125, 138–39, 352; Loew's-MGM, divorcement (1959), 78, 149, 175; Metro-Goldwyn-Mayer do Brasil Ltda., 150; Metro-Goldwyn-Mayer Films of India (MGM India), 360; Metro-Goldwyn-Mayer International Cinemas, 2, 89, 175; Metro-Goldwyn-Mayer Manila Co., 343; Metro Goldwyn Mayer Pty. Ltd., 138; MGM Film Trust, 326; MGM India, 360; MGM-Nordisk, 89; MGM-Pathé, 89; Nikkatsu, 342

Metro-Goldwyn-Mayer (MGM), productions: *Adventures of Huckleberry Finn*, 352; *Ben-Hur*, 345; *Conspirator*, 249; *The Fisherman*, 177; *Gigi*, 80; *Metro-Journal*,

215; *Metro News Gazette*, 277; *The Mortal Storm*, 351; *News of the Day*, 72, 158; *Quo Vadis?*, 243, 358; *Red Danube, The*, 249; *The Secret of Dr. Kildare*, 351; *Tale of Two Cities*, 352; *Thrill of a Romance*, 77, 170; *Traveltalks*, 156, 158, 214; *The Turning Wheels*, 293–94; *Valley of the Kings*, 16, 244; *The Wizard of Oz*, 352, 354; *The Yearling*, 352; *Ziegfeld Follies*, 366

Metro-Goldwyn-Mayer (MGM), cinemas/Metros: air conditioning, 13, 157, 165, 198, 214, 216, 243, 276–77; combination theater-office buildings, 198, 342, 348; as cultural embassies, 158, 162, 165, 171, 173, 181, 345, 357–58; as "foreign," 357; Metro Cub Clubs, 11, 26, 181, 218–19, 346, 352–55, 360

Metro-Goldwyn-Mayer (MGM), cinemas, locations: Alexandria, 24–25, 178, 218–19, 235, 242, 243, 264; Barranquilla, 169, 170–71, 179; Bombay (see Metro Cinema, Bombay); Brisbane, 8, 58, 107, 125; Budapest, 58, 59; Buenos Aires, 171, 176, 424n49; Cairo (see Cinema Metro, Cairo); Calcutta (see Metro Cinema, Calcutta); Cali, 169, 171, 179; Cape Town, 58, 78, 309; Durban, 58, 278, 279; Johannesburg, 5, 58, 152, 163, 276–78, 347; Lima, 10, 24, 58, 155–56, 166, 173, 352; London, 23, 24, 38–39, 45–46, 49, 54, 57–58, 61, 76, 79, 81–85, 89, 152, 347; Manila, 58, 334, 343–45; Medellin, 169, 179, 353; Melbourne, 124–25; Milan, 81; Montevideo, 58, 155, 157–58, 352; Paris, 13, 32, 36, 48–50; Rio de Janeiro (Cine Metro-Boavista), 177–78; Rio de Janeiro (Cine Metro-Copacabana), 147, 162, *163*, 165, 178, 179; Rio de Janeiro (Cine Metro-Passeio, Rio de Janeiro), 164, 165, 177, 179; Rio de Janeiro (Cine Metro-Tijuca), 26, 163–66, *163*, 179–81, *179*, *180*, 194, 206; San Juan, 183, 190, 192–94, 200, 205, 206; Santiago, 58, 155, 156, 352; São Paulo, 158–59, 162, 353; Shanghai, 25–26, 334, 361, 364–67; Sydney (Liberty Theatre), 131; Sydney (Metro Crows Nest), 132; Sydney (Metro Twin Drive-In), 134; Sydney (Minerva Theatre), 131; Sydney (Prince Edward Theatre), 96, 105, 107–8, 111–12; Sydney (St. James Theatre), 124, 131, 132, 138; Tokyo, 58, 342; Valparaiso, 166, 169, 352

Metro Liberty, Sydney, 131
Metronome, 88
Metro Pictures and Screen Classics, 34, 35
Metro Theatre: Cape Town, 58, 78, 309; Durban, 58, 278, 279; Johannesburg, 5, 58, 152, 163, 276–78, 347; Melbourne, 124–25
Metro Twin Drive-In, Sydney, 134
Metro-Scala, Budapest, 58, 59
Mexico, 194; Cinemex, 389–90, 391; Cinépolis, 381, 389–90; Fox, 148, 166, 168, 172; Loew's, 169; Paramount, 148; Warner Bros., 169–70
Mexico City, Mexico: MGM, 419n29; Paramount (Teatro Olimpia), 55, 154, 396n24, 418n2; Warner Bros., 63, 166, 199, 200
MGM. *See* Metro-Goldwyn-Mayer (MGM)
Miami Theatre, Cairo, 250
Michael Strogoff (1926), 53
Michalove, Dan, 166
Michaud, Henri, 83
Middle East, 2, 16, 24–25, 32–33, 90, 209; Fox's focus on, 226, 249–50, 252, 255; political turmoil, 175, 222, 264; refugees from, 250; Skouras's aspirations for, 249, 266; Wahbi's fame throughout, 228. *See also* Egypt; Israel; Palestine
Miggins, Ben, 281
Milder, Max, 63
military dictatorships, 148, 175, 204, 205–6
Milland, Ray, 173
Miller, Arthur, 259
Miller, Toby, 4
Milliken, Carl E., 220
Minerva Theatre, Sydney, 131
Ming, Gao, 374
Minter, Clifford, 98, 102, 111
Misr Theatre, Cairo, 219, 228
Mitchell, J. W., 120
Mizoguchi, Kenji, 341
Mizrahi, Togo, 244
Modi, Keki, 358, 359
Mohamed Aly Cinema, Alexandria, 210, 216, 235
Mondini, Gisèle, 70, 71, 74
monopolies, 77, 112, 186, 280; ACT, 276, 278, 296; Cine Colombia, 167; Fox, 280, 307, 309, 323, 451n67; GTC, 109, 111; KFC's attempted, 324; Schlesinger/ACT, 271, 274–76, 278, 283, 296. *See also* duopolies
Monroe, Marilyn, 247, 258–59

Montasser, Farah, 246
Montevideo, Uruguay: Delmaur, 420n49; Fox, 150; Gaumont-British (Teatro Urquiza), 420n50; MGM (Cine Metro), 58, 155, 157–58, 352; United Cinema, 158
Moodabe (Moudabber), Elizabeth, 117
Moodabe (Moudabber), Ferris, 117
Moodabe (Moudabber), Joseph (M. J.'s brother), 117, 118, 132, 135, 137, 142–43
Moodabe, Joe (M. J.'s son), 137, 141–43
Moodabe, Michael (M. J.'s son), 142; family memoir, 107, 117–18, 120, 121, 133, 134–36, 137, 412n7
Moodabe (Moudabber), Michael Joseph (M. J.), 117–19, 132, 142, 412n10; Elizabeth and, 117–18, 412n7; Fox and, 120, 121, 137
Moodabe, Royce, 141–43
Moodabe family, 24, 66, 117–18, 120, 121–22, 137; anglicized name change, 117; Kerridges and, 128; Lebanese origins, 117; protectionism, 133–35; xenophobic attacks on, 122
Moore, Owen, 46
Moore, Paul, 4–5, 390
Moorhouse, H., 44
Mooser, George, 347
Morais, Audley, 186
Moren, Pax, 319
Morgan Creek, 88
Morris, Sam, 62
Mortal Storm, The (1940), 351
Moskowitz, Harry, 125, 155, 156, 342
Motion Picture Association of America (MPAA), 197, 199, 234, 246, 270, 295, 296, 301
Motion Picture Distributors Association of Australasia, 122
Motion Picture Export Association (MPEA), 311–15, 324
Motion Picture Producers and Distributors of America, 220
Mourad, Leila, 221
Movies (Theater), Kingston, 57, 186–87
Movietone, 153
Mozambique, 279, 318, 321, 322
MPAA. *See* Motion Picture Association of America (MPAA)
MPEA. *See* Motion Picture Export Association (MPEA)
Mukherjee, Sanji Kripalni, 354
Mullen, Joseph, 196

Muller, Hilgard, 327
Multiplex Cinemas, 88
multiplexes, 3, 75, 178, 376; CGV, 387; in China, 369–70, 371–74, 379, 386; Cinépolis, 390; homogeneity of, 378; Hoyts, 140, 178; MGM as "pioneer" of, 85; Paramount/Parafrance, 84, 88, 178; Warner Bros./WBIT/Shanghai Paradise, 14, 86–88, 368–69, 371–74, 379, 462–63n64
Mumbai, India: MGM (Metro Cinema), 359–60, 387, 388. *See also* Bombay (Mumbai)
Munro, Charles, 98, 99, 102, 112–13, 120, 122
Munshi, Kanaiyalal Maneklal, 348
Murad, Layla, 434n19
Murdoch, Rupert, 136, 143
Murray, Robin L., 321
Murray, John, 297
Musashinokan, Tokyo, 340
Music Box Films, 380
Myanmar (Burma), 347, 386
Mycal (AEON): Warner-Mycal Cinemas, 26, 88, 333, 343, 369, 377

NABIO. *See* Nationale Bio-scoopondernerming N.V. (NABIO)
Nader, George, 260
Naguib, Muhammed, 241, 243–44
Nahas Studio, 228
Nairobi, Kenya, 304, 328; Fox, 3, 284, 292, 324, 325; Fox (20th Century Theatre), 291; Thika/Fox Drive-In, 25, 291, 324, 328, 329; Fox (Kenya Theatre Building), 323; *Mogambo* filming in, 293; segregated cinemas, 25, 310; television, 316, 325
Nakuru Press Ltd., 316
Namibia, colonial. *See* South West Africa
Nanjing, China, 365, 462n51; Japanese attack on, 342; Warner Bros./WBIT, 372, 373, 375
Nanking Theatre, Shanghai, 362–64
Napoleon (1927), 50
Nasser, Gamal Abdel: antisemitism, 245–46; attempted ouster by British, French, and Israelis, 245; Cairo Metro and, 24–25, 247; *Cleopatra* and, 258, 263; Free Officers (Movement), 241, 243; Misr al-Fatat, 211; nationalization of the Egyptian film industry, 247, 256, 257; Skouras/Fox and, 256, 258

National Amusements, 88–89, 143, 384, 465n1
Nationale Bio-scoopondernerming N.V. (NABIO), 81
nationalism, 12, 76, 109; African, 303, 314, 322; Chinese, 367, 375; Egyptian, 25, 211–13, 220, 222–23, 228–28, 240–41, 246; Indian, 351–57; Japanese, 336–37; Kenyan and decolonization, 322–324; protectionism and, 112, 113, 124, 135
Nattrass, Nicoli, 285
Nazario, Luiz, 160–61, 162
Nazi Germany and Nazism, 76, 113, 342–43; Argentina and, 160, 162, 167; Auschwitz, 68, 76; boycotts against, 211, 225; Brazil/Vargas government and, 157, 160–62, 166; Buchenwald, 71–74; Chile and, 160, 162–63; films, 58–61, 67, 211; Le Paramount and the Resistance, 23, 66–72, 74, 344; occupation of Belgium, 64–65, 66; occupation of France, 65–66, 68, 72; occupation of the Netherlands, 65, 66, 68, 76, 77; Operation Lila, 404n44; removal of Jewish officials, 59; Sturmabteilung Braunhemden, 211; Ufa/German film industry under the control of, 59, 160, 166, 205, 211, 225; United States and, 148, 157, 205; Westerbork, 68, 76
NBB (Dutch Motion Picture Federation; Nederlandschen Bioscoop-Bond). *See under* Netherlands
Nell Gwynn (1934), 40, 41, 46
Netflix, 380
Netherlands (Holland), 31, 59; CIC, 84, 326; Fox, 81; Loew's/MGM, 50, 59, 60–61, 65, 77, 78; MGM International Cinemas, 89; Nazi occupation, 65, 66, 68, 76, 77; NBB, 60–61, 65, 77, 81, 401n91; Philips Radio Ltd., 306, 307; RKO, 65; Tobis, 61, 65; Ufa, 61, 65; Warner Bros./WBIT, 88. *See also* Amsterdam; Rotterdam
Newbould, A. E., 34
Newcastle-on-Tyne, England: Odeon, 62; Paramount, 56, 57, 63
New Center, 85, 327
Newmar, Julie, 258
News Corp., 143
New South Wales (NSW), Australia, 96, 103, 108–9, 112, 136; inquiry into the local film industry (1934), 110–15; Quota Act, 114

490   Index

newsreels, 3, 42, 61, 162, 222, 247, 251, 290, 291, 352; *The African Mirror*, 273, 319, 320, 322, 325; *Fox Movietone News*, 99, 106, 115, 362; *Indian News Review*, 355; Madru's footage from Buchenwald, 72–74; *Metro-Journal*, 215; *Metro News Gazette*, 277; *Metrotone*, 61; *News of the Day*, 72, 158; Ufa (Wochensau), 161; *United Newsreel*, 345; U.S.-produced, 10, 11, 125, 158, 249, 277, 345

New York, 151; AMC Empire 25, 384; Broadway, 19, 54, 68, 151, 155, 254; Fox (Roxy Theatre), 233; Fox head office/board, 121, 257, 298; Loew's office, 107, 125, 150, 214; Loew's 7th Avenue Theatre, 151; Loew's Capitol Theatre, 38, 49, 53; Lower East Side, 272; Netflix (Paris Theater), 380; Paramount (Criterion Theatre), 36; Paramount (Paramount Theatre), 50–52; Paramount (Rialto Theatre), 32, 35, 36; Paramount (Rivoli Theatre), 32, 35, 36; Radio City Music Hall, 198, 200, 254; Roxy Theatre, 233, 364; Schlesinger, 62, 274; Toho Theatre, 177, 342

New Zealand, 4, 31, 94–95, 116–17, 210; Dalian Wanda, 382; drive-ins, 128, 134; Fox/ACT, 289–90, 325; Fox/Amalgamated Theatres (*see under* Amalgamated Theatres Ltd.); Fox's dominance, 4, 5, 13, 14, 23–24; *NZMPEB*, 119–20, 122–23, 126–27; MGM's efforts to expand into, 128, 134–35; Rank, 121, 126–27; television, 135–36, 139; Wellington, 119, 122, 135. *See also* Auckland

New Zealand Motion Picture Exhibitors' Bulletin (*NZMPEB*). *See under* New Zealand

New Zealand Theatres Ltd., 122

Niger, 312

Nigeria, 312, 314–15; Lagos, 315

Niichi, 88, 369

Nikkatsu, 336, 342

Nordisk Film, 89

Nornes, Markus, 341

North, C. J., 45, 274

North Africa, 4, 25, 250, 312

Northern Rhodesia (colonial Zambia), 310, 323; Central African Federation, 291, 295, 296, 298, 306; Copperbelt Cowboys, 320; desegregated cinemas, 305; Fox, 279, 289; multiracial partnership, 294, 297–98, 304

Nosseir, Abou, 256–57

Notaro, Pat, 200, 201, 204

N. V. Niger Co., 60

Nyasaland, 305; Central African Federation, 291, 295, 296, 298, 306

Nyerere, Julius, 310–11

Nyutho, Edwin Ngure, 322–24

NZMPEB (New Zealand Motion Picture Exhibitors' Bulletin). *See under* New Zealand

NZ Picture Supplies, 116

O'Brien, Thomas, 116–17, 118

Ochs, Millard, 85, 377, 392; selling off of Warner Village Cinemas, 88, 372; Warner Bros.'s expansion into China, 369, 371, 373, 377, 462–63n64

Odeon (Cairo) Ltd., 222–23, 236

Odeon Cinema Holdings Ltd., 286

Odeon Cinemas (UK), 129, 328, 352; Leicester Square, London, 223; Marble Arch Pavilion, London, 80; Paramount and, 62–63; Rank, 226, 283, 286; Dalian Wanda's acquisition of, 368, 382

Odeon Holdings (New Zealand) Ltd., 127

Odeon Leicester Square, London, 223

Odría, Manuel A., 175

Olympia Theater, Shanghai, 362

Olympia, L', Paris, 58

Olympic Kinematograph Laboratories Ltd., 56

Omnia Cinema, Rouen, 49

open-air cinemas: in Egypt, 210, 213, 216, 256–57, 264; in Nigeria, 314; Rialto Theatre, Dakar, 311, 312. *See also* drive-ins

Orbeta, Enrique de, 192

orchestras, 19, 36, 46, 52, 54, 55, 63, 186, 224; Gaumont Palace, Paris, 49, 50; Hogaku-Za, Tokyo, 338, 340–41; Plaza Theatre, London, 40–42; Theatro Santa Heleña, São Paulo, 151

Osaka, Japan: Daini Sumiyoshi, 342; Kinema Palace, 342; MGM, 342; Osaka-Za, 342; Shichiko-Za, 342; Universal, 336

Osaka-Za, Osaka, 342

Ospina Pérez, Mariano, 170

Osserman, Jack, 168

Oumansky, Alexander, 53–54

Out West (1918), 162–63

Overseas Cinematograph Theatres Ltd., 127, 222–23, 236

Packer, Frank, 136
Pakistan, 351
Palace Theatre, Kingston, 57, 186–87
Palace Theatre, London, 14, 36
Palace Theatre, Sydney, 95
Palestine, 95, 225–26, 231–32, 356, 432n78; anti-Nazi boycotts, 225; Arab-Jewish conflict, 221–23, 226–27; British control of/Balfour Declaration, 221, 225–26, 228; Children to Palestine, 233; Gaumont-Loew-Metro, 23, 48, 210; "High Committee of the Nile Valley for the Liberation of Palestine," 226–27; Jewish immigration to, 227, 233; Jewish statehood, 221–22, 226, 232; Lourie's documentaries on, 232–33; Wahbi's fame in, 228. *See also* Israel, State of
Palestine Films Inc., 232–33, 280
Palestine Liberation Organization, 262
Palmer, Joseph, II, 296, 300–303
Palladium Biograf, Malmö, 55, 57
PAMECA. *See* Pan-African Movement for East and Central Africa (PAMECA)
Pan-African Movement for East and Central Africa (PAMECA), 310–11
Panama, 56, 177, 184, 186. *See also* Panama City
Panama City, Panama: CIC, 177–78, 424n58, 425n65; Fox (Cine Bella Vista), 177; MGM, 424n58, 425n65; MGM (Teatro Metro), 177; Paramount, 154
Paraliticí, José Ché, 191
Paramount: Australasia, 93, 143–44; Australia, 57, 93, 95–97, 102, 103–5, 113, 115, 125; bankruptcy reorganization, 57, 148, 171, 186, 195; Barcelona, 23, 35, 55, 57; Belgium, 31, 35, 65, 67, 69; Birmingham, 23, 41, 42–45, 56, 60, 61, 122; block-booking, 39, 152–53; Brazil, 5, 147, 148, 150, 153, 160, 178, 418n2; Brisbane, 105; Brussels, 39, 57, 67, 75; Cairo, 210, 223; Calcutta, 347; Camaguey, 197; Caribbean, 4, 24, 57, 148, 182–87; Cuba, 24, 56, 148, 183–87, 194–99, 201, 205, 401n74; Dublin, 45; England, 22, 23, 32–34, 43–45, 55–57, 60, 61–64, 78, 79, 84, 104, 186; Europe, 32, 35, 36, 37, 55–57, 62–63, 64, 76, 81–85, 104; France, 5, 35, 50, 57, 67, 75, 84; Germany, 52–53, 66; Glasgow, 57, 63, 80; Haifa, 231; Havana, 55, 56, 154, 184–85, 194–95, 197, 199, 202; Hong Kong, 363; Ireland, 45, 56, 57, 85; Jamaica, 24, 56, 57, 148, 183, 184, 185, 186–87, 401n74; Japan, 25, 57, 333, 334–35, 337–42, 344, 347, 401n74; Kingston, 57, 186, 187; Latin America, 13, 24, 55, 148, 154, 171–72, 175; Leeds, 56, 57, 63, 80; Lille, 57; Liverpool, 63, 80; London, 23, 24, 32–33, 36–37, 39–43, 45–46, 50, 55–57, 59, 62–63, 79, 80–82, 84, 85, 95–96, 152, 338; Malmö, 55, 57; Manchester, 30, 32, 56, 57, 62, 63, 80; Melbourne, 56, 57, 104–5, 115, 125; Mexico City, 55, 154, 396n24, 418n2; Newcastle-on-Tyne, 56, 57, 63; *Paramount Around the World*, 55; *Paramount International News*, 67, 68, 70, 71, 72, 73, 75; Paris, 6, 13–14, 23, 30, 39, 48, 50–52, 51, 55, 57, 66–75, 76, 80, 95, 152, 344; Rio de Janeiro, 56, 150, 152–54, 153; São Paulo, 10, 13, 57, 147, 152–54, 153, 162, 176–77; Shanghai, 362; Spain, 57; Stockholm, 23, 55, 57; "super cinemas" 47, 48; Sydney, 57, 105–6; Tokyo, 10, 13, 25, 55, 95, 152, 333–34, 334, 337, 338–41, 340, 356n42, 364; Viacom's purchase of, 88, 379, 380
Paramount, partnerships and subsidiaries: CFC, 183–84; Cobiân/Circuito Teatral Paramount, 198; Famous Players, 85, 88, 380; Filmaktiebolaget Paramount (Film AB. Paramount), 55; Films Paramount, 67; Hoyts and, 105, 125; Odeon, 62–63; Parafrance, 84; Paramount-Astoria-Theatres Ltd., 56, 57, 62, 63; Paramount Europe, 74; Paramount Films, S.A., 65; Paramount Films of Cuba Inc., 199; Paramount-Film Service Ltd., 56; Paramount International Films Inc., 196; Paramount International Theatres Corp., 173; Paramount Publix, 67, 363; Parufamet, 52–53; Peliculas D'Luxe Da America Do Sul, 150; Picture Play-houses Ltd. (PPL), 32–35; Saenger and, 183, 184–87; Siritzky family and, 68, 84; Société Anonyme Française des Films Paramount, 35, 67
Paramount, productions: *The Big Clock*, 173; *Nell Gwynn*, 40, 41, 46; *Out West*, 162–63; *Paramount on Parade*, 341; *The Patriot*, 154; *Wings*, 55
Paramount, cinemas: Dublin, 45; Havana (Teatro Encanto), 56, 184–85, 194–95, 197, 199, 202; Havana (Teatro Fausto), 55, 154, 184–85, 194–95, 197, 199, 202; Hong Kong, 363; Kingston, 57, 186, 187; Lima, 10, 24, 148, 172–75; London

Paramount, cinemas (*continued*)
(Carlton Theatre), 24, 39, 50, 55–56, 57, 80; London (Plaza Theatre) (*see* Plaza Theatre, London); Manchester, 30, 32, 56, 57, 62, 63, 80; Melbourne, 56, 57, 104–5, 115, 125; Mexico City, 55, 154, 396n24, 418n2; Paris (*see* Paramount, Le, Paris); Rio de Janeiro, 152–54, *153*; São Paulo, 10, 13, 57, 147, 152–54, *153*, 162, 176–77; Tokyo (*see* Hogaku-Za, Tokyo)
Paramount, Le, Paris, 6, 13–14, 30, 39, 48, *51*, 55, 57, 76; Nazi occupation and Resistance base, 23, 66–71, 344; opening, 50–52, 75; Paramount's New York theater and, 50–52; reopening after liberation, 72–75
Paramount, Le, Toulouse, 57
Paramount Theatre: Glasgow, 57, 63, 80; Leeds, 56, 57, 63, 80; Liverpool, 63, 80; London (Tottenham Court Road), 57; Manchester, 30, 32, 56, 57, 62, 63, 80; New York, 50–52
Paris, France: Fox, 54; Gaumont-Loew-Metro (Gaumont Palace), 13, 32, 36, 48–50; Gaumont-Loew-Metro (Madeleine Cinéma), 48, 49; liberation, 71, 72; MGM (L'Olympia), 58; Paramount, 80, 95, 152; Paramount shop window (*see* Paramount, Le, Paris); Warner (Apollo Théâtre), 62
Paris Theater, New York, 380
Parker, Eleanor, 16, 244
Parkhouse, Archie, 277
Parsons, Neil, 271, 272
Pascal, Jacques, 222
Pasha, Mohamed Aly Allouba, 226–27, 433n10
Patel, Baburao, 350–52, 355–57
Pathé, 96; British Pathé, 42; Cannon-Pathé/MGM-Pathé, 89; *Pathé Gazette*, 273; Pathé-Natan, 403n22
Patriot, The (1928), 154
Patton, George S., 72
Pavilion Theatre, London, 36–37
Payet, Guillermo, 155, 166
Peking, China. *See* Beijing (Peking), China
Pelegrine, Lou, 166–67
Peliculas D'Luxe Da America Do Sul, 150
Pereira, Margarete, 156, 157
Perez, Paul, 69–70, 72, 74
Perkins, James E., 344
Perkins, Robert, 345
Peron, Juan, 175

Peru, 148, 173, 204; class stratification, 174; Fox, 24, 148; MGM, 24, 159, 175; MGM *Traveltalks* on, 156; Paramount, 10, 24; political turmoil/military dictatorship, 173, 175, 305; racial division, 174, 175; Warner Bros., 24, 85, 148, 368. *See also* Lima
Peter, Bruce, 57
Phantom of the Opera (1943), 345
Philippines, 25, 333, 342, 346, 361. *See also* Manila
Pickford, Mary, 233, 337
Picturehouse, 390
Pierson, David, 376
Pieterse, Andre, 139
Pimin, Zhang, 373
Pinero, Sir Arthur Wing, 46
piracy, 362, 371
Pitcairn, R. A., 34
Platt, Abe, 173, 175
Plaza (MGM), Toulouse, 77
Plaza Theatre, Havana, 199–200, 202, 203, 205
Plaza Theatre, London, 39–42, 43, 45, 55, 57, 79, 80; CIC's ownership of, 84, 85; female ushers, 40; Le Paramount and, 59; manager, 56; name, 39–40; *Nell Gwynn*, 40, 41, 46; opening, 40, 42; Paramount Manchester and, 56; reconstruction and reopening, 81–82; Tiller Girls, 40–41, 56, 82; Wurlitzer, 40, 42
Plymouth, England: Fox (Drake Theatre), 80
Poe, Seymour, 137, 262, 317
Poelmans, Rene, 64, 77
Poincaré, Raymond, 50
Polis, Alfred, 65
Pollack, F. W., 357
Ponce, Julio, 201
Pons, Lily, 65
Portman, Henry (Harry), 46, 49–50
Portugal, 5, 85, 88
Potter, S. R., 281
Pow, Rance, 378
Prabhu, P. V., 359
Pratchett, A. L., 173
Prentice, Robert: MGM cinemas, 156–57, 158
Pretoria, South Africa, 327; Fox, 279; Fox (20th Century Theatre), 282; Ster, 318
Price, L., 157
Price, Vincent, 319

Priestley, J. B., 46
Primedia Unlimited, 328, 329
Prince Edward Theatre, Sydney, 57, 96, 105, 107–8, 111–12
Prince of Foxes (1949), 432n60
Prío Socarrás, Carlos, 203
Pro Patria, 275
protectionism, 11, 12, 30, 171, 173, 183; Australia, 103, 110, 112, 114, 124, 131; Brazil, 168; China, 366, 367, 386; Egypt, 220, 221, 257; England, 30, 34, 61; Netherlands/NBB, 59–61; New Zealand, 135
Puerto Rico, 148, 183–84, 185, 189–93, 195; CFC, 183–84; Cobián's dominance in, 191, 194, 196; as commonwealth, 169, 184, 189–90; Loew's International and, 169, 183, 189–90; MGM, 24, 183; Nationalist Party of Puerto Rico, 190–92, 193; Paramount, 183; Ponce massacre, 192, 193, 206; as U.S. colony, 169, 184, 189–90, 426n35; U.S. involvement in, 148, 191–92, 193, 206; Warner Bros., 199–20. *See also* San Juan
Pynchon & Co., 101
Pyramid Saimira, 387

Queen Elizabeth (1912), 31–32
Queen's Hall, Brussels, 64, 65, 77
Quo Vadis? (1951), 243, 358

Raafat, Samir, 16, 216, 223, 243–44, 247, 263–65
race: Capricorn Africa Society, 297–98, 305; "color bar," 217, 285, 298–99, 305; "economic segregation," 304–5, 308; "Europeans only"/whites-only cinemas, 2, 25, 277, 294, 297, 298, 301, 309; Fox's troubled racial history in Africa, 2, 25, 269, 305, 310, 316–17, 324, 329; interracial romance, 269, 293, 294; "multiracial partnership," 2, 269, 270, 295, 297, 299; racial division in Brazil, 157, 161; racial division in Peru, 174, 175; racial segregation in Australia, 136–37; racial segregation in the United States, 174, 309–10. *See also* desegregation; South Africa, apartheid; *South Pacific*
radio, 105, 273, 274, 443n6
Radio City Music Hall, New York, 198, 200, 254
Radio-Keith-Orpheum (RKO), 7, 157, 168, 196, 202, 227, 263, 278, 280, 291; Calcutta (Elphinstone Picture Palace), 347–48;

Egypt, 210, 222; London, 61; Mexico City, 419n29; Nazi-occupied Holland, 65; RKO-Radio Pictures of Cuba, 199; Uruguay, 158
Radius Theatre, Budapest, 58, 59
Raiyu, Ikoma, 338–39
Ramos Amusement Company, 362
Ramos Cobián, Rafael, 190–91; in Cuba, 190, 194–95, 196–97, 198, 428n72; in Puerto Rico, 190, 191, 194–95, 196
Randall, Clarence, 301–3
Ranjit Studios, 355–56, 358
Rank, J. Arthur, 126, 222, 223, 237, 283, 286, 306
Rank Organisation, 176, 283–86, 306, 326; ACT and, 283–86, 291, 318; Cairo (Rivoli Theatre), 222–24, 236–38, 239; Israel, 226; Kerridge and, 121, 126–27; New Zealand, 121, 126–27; Ster-Kinekor and, 326; television, 285–86, 306; *The Turning Wheels*, 293; U-I, 283; United World Pictures, 283
Rapee, Erno, 53–54
Raposo, Ivo, 26, 179–81, *180*, *181*, 206
Raymond, Charles, 277
Rayner, Frederick John, 117, 118, 412n10
Recife, Brazil, 162, 171
Red Cross, 1, 245, 297, 298, 300, 301, 351
Red Danube, The (1949), 249
Redstone, Sumner, 143, 465n1
Reed, Charles, 287–90
refugees, 226, 227, 233, 250
Regal Entertainment Group, 359, 370, 381, 384, 390–91
Regent Theatre, Brisbane, 105, 140
Regent Theatre, Melbourne, 96, 132
R. E. Hall & Company, 50
Reich, J. Sperling, 382, 383
Reims, France: Paramount (Cinema Opera), 57
Reliance MediaWorks, 387
Rema, Alexandra, 299
Rembrandtpleintheater, Amsterdam, 81
Republic Pictures, 287, 291
Reyes, Isidra, 344–45
Rhodesia Television Ltd., 307–8
Rhodesian Theatres Ltd., 289, 306
Rialto Theatre: Dakar, 311, 312; Leeds, 53; London, 53; New York, 32, 35, 36; Sydney, 109
Rich, Mervin, 136
Ridley, R. G., 316
Riefenstahl, Leni: *Olympia*, 161, 312

Riesenfeld, Hugo, 12–13, 36
Riggs, Elisha Francis, 191–91
Rio de Janeiro, Brazil, 3; Cinelandia, 156, 161–62; Fox distribution office, 150; Fox (Cine Palacio), 166, 168, 172; MGM (Cine Rialto), 152; MGM (Cine Astoria), 158; MGM/Empresidas Reunidas MGM, 150; MGM (Cine Metro-Boavista), 177–78; MGM (Cine Metro-Copacabana); 164, 165, 177, 179; 164, 165, 177, 179; MGM (Cine Metro-Passeio), 164, 165, 177, 179; MGM (Cine Metro-Tijuca), , 26, 163–66, *163*, 179–81, *179*, 180, 194, 206; multiplex operators, 178; Paramount (Cine Capitólio), 56; Paramount (Cine Império), 56; Paramount (Cinema Avenida), 150; Paramount (Cine Theatro Paramount), 152–54, *153*; Ribeiro chain, 150, 178; Ufa (Cine-Theatro Broadway), 162; Warner Bros., 168
Ritz Cinema: Bloemfontein, 286; London, 61, 82, 83
Rivoli Theatre: New York, 32, 35, 36; Cairo, 222–24, 230, 239, 240, 284
RKO. *See* Radio-Keith-Orpheum (RKO)
Roach, Hal, 277
Robb, Donald A., 244
Robe, The (1953), 132, 250
Roces family, 343–45
Roces-Paterno, Regina, 345
Roces, Rafael "Liling," 344–45
Rodgers, Richard, 269, 294
Rokach, Israel, 234
Rooney, Mickey, 214, 230
Roosevelt, Franklin, 226; "Good Neighbor" policies, 164; Puerto Rico and, 191–92, 193
Rose, David E., 62
Rosen, J., 292
Rosenberg, Scott, 376
Rosenberger, Salo, 214
Rosenthal, George, 187
Rosenvald, A., 157
Rosthal, Joseph, 220
Rothafel, Samuel "Roxy," 40–42, 364
Rotterdam, Netherlands: Fox, 81; MGM (Capitol Theatre), 60; MGM (City Theatre), 60; Tuschinski, 59; MGM (Tuschinski Theatre), 60; Ufa, 61
Rouen, France: Fox, 54; Loew's/MGM (Omnia Cinema), 49
Rowland, Richard A., 34
Roxy Cinema, Shanghai, 25–26, 334, 361, 364–67

Roxy Theater: Amsterdam, 59; New York, 233, 364
Royal Cinema: Alexandria, 216, 235, 250, 254; Durban, 286
Royal Cinema, Salisbury: segregated premiere of *South Pacific*, 1–2, 269, 270, 295, 296–99; segregated premiere of *South Pacific*, fallout, 300, 305, 306, 308, 316, 322, 329
Royal Theater, Amsterdam, 60
Rubin, J. Robert, 48
Rubin, Nat, 365
Rudolph, Janeth, 327
Rui, Zhang, 374
Rushdie, Salman, 26, 353–54; *Midnight's Children*, 10, 26, 353
Rusk, Dean, 313
Russell, Arthur, 95
Rutledge, Eric, 135
Ryan, Robert, 319
Rydge, Norman B., 124, 283

Sadat, Anwar, 211, 242
Saenger Amusements, 154, 183–87, 426n14
Sagar Movietone, 355
Saif, Salah Abou, 264–65
Saks, Lucia, 20, 328
Sala de Arte Distribución, 390
Salisbury, Southern Rhodesia: MGM Drive-in, 291; Royal Cinema's segregated premiere of *South Pacific*, 1–2, 269, 270, 295, 296–99; Royal Cinema's segregated premiere of *South Pacific*, fallout, 300, 305, 306, 308, 316, 322, 329; segregated hotels, 299; television, 308
Salon Films, 372
Salván, Marta Hernández, 4
Samkange, Stanlake, 298
San Juan, Puerto Rico: Cobiân, 190, 194; MGM (Teatro Metro), 183, 190, 192–94, 200, 205, 206; Paramount and Teatro Paramount, 190–91, 205; Ponce massacre, 192, 193, 206
Sanlam, 318, 325, 329
Santiago, Chile, 156, 428n72; MGM (Cine Metro), 58, 155, 156, 352; Nacional/Nazi films at, 162–63
São Paulo, Brazil: Fox (Cine Ipiranga), 166; Fox distribution offices, 150; Fox (Cine Marrocos), 176; MGM (Theatro Santa Heleña), 150, 151–52; MGM (Cine Metro), 158–59, 162, 353; MGM/Empresas Reunidas MGM, 150–51; multiplex operators, 178; Paramount

(Cine-Theatro Paramount), 10, 13, 57, 147, 152–54, *153*, 162, 176–77; pro-Nazi films/sentiment in, 161, 166; Serrador, 150–52, 159, 161; Toho (Cine-Theatro Paramount), 176, 342; UA, 159; Ufa (Cine-Ufa Palácio), 161; Warner Bros., 168
Saphir, Will, 216
Sapir, Pinchas, 250
SARFT/SAPPRFT (State Administration of Press, Publication, Radio, Film and Television). *See under* China
Sarnoff, Ann, 379, 392
Satterthwaite, Joseph C., 296, 299–303, 450n36
Saul, John S., 285
Savage, M. J., 122–23
Sayvant, Arain S., 355
SBC International Cinemas, 372
Scala Theatre, Angers, 77
Scala Theatre, Birmingham, 41, 43–44, *43*, 63, 80
Scala Theatre, La, Dublin, 45
Schaap, Philip de, 65, 76–77
Schary, Dore, 227
Schenck, Joseph, 37, 42–43
Schiller, E. A., 38, 48–49
Schiwy, Freya, 4
Schlanger, Ben, 156, 172
Schlanger, Hoffberg, Reisner and Urbahn, 172
Schlesinger, Isidore William, 62, 98, 271–74, 276, 277, 284, 285, 326, 381; death of, 285; executives' fear of, 281; Lower East Side origins, 272; other businesses, 273. *See also* African Consolidated Theatres (ACT)
Schlesinger, John, 286, 288, 289, 306, 325
Schlesinger, Julian, 289
Schlesinger, M. A. (Max), 62, 274, 282, 286, 289
Schlesinger Organisation. *See* African Consolidated Theatres (ACT)
Schless, Robert, 74–75
Schmitt, Robert, 238, 240
Scotland, 33, 56, 57
Scottish Television and Northern Broadcasting Company of Toronto, 316
ScreenX, 387
SECMA. *See* Société d'Exploitation Cinématographique Africaine (SECMA)
Secret of Dr. Kildare, The (1939), 351
Seddon, J. A., 34

Seidelman, Sam, 167
Select Theatre, Le Havre, 49, 54
Selzer, Al, 157
Sembène, Ousmane, 311–12
Semiramis theater, Alexandria 256
Senegal, 311, 312; Dakar, 311
Seo Jung, 386–87
Serrador, Francisco, 150–52, 159, 161
Sethna, Sir Phiroze, 348
Severiano Ribeiro, Luiz, 150
Severiano Ribeiro, Jr., Luiz, 176, 178
Shafik, Viola, 235
Shah, Chandulal, 355–56, 358
Shaheen, Yousef, 256
Shalit, David, 230–31, 248, 250, 251
Shand, J. W., 113
Shanghai, China, 362–78; boycott of American and British films, 367; CGV, 386; Dalian Wanda, 373; Disneyland, 378; First National, 362; Fox (Nanking Theatre), 362–64; Isis Theater, 362; Japanese occupation, 364, 365; MGM (Carlton Theatre), 362; MGM (Roxy Cinema), 25–26, 334, 361, 364–67; Paramount, 362; Ramos Amusement Company, 362; UACC, 369; Warner Bros./WBIT/WBIC (Shanghai Paradise), 371–72, 373–76, 462–63n64; Zhonghua (Roxy Cinema), 365
Shanghai Film Group, 375
Shanghai Paradise, Shanghai, 371–72, 373–76, 462–63n64
Shanghai Paradise Co. Ltd., 371;
Shanghai Paradise Warner Cinema City Co., 371–72, 375, 462–63n64
Shanghai United Circuit, 373
Sharett, Moshe, 230–31
Sharma, P. N., 355
Sharp, Martha, 233
Shauer, Emil (E. E.), 32, 39
Shauer, Melville, 55
Shaw, Harold, 273
Shaw Bros., 366
Shawky, Amany Aly, 240
Shearer, Lloyd, 258–59
Shearer, Norma, 46
Sheehan, Clayton, 102
Sheehan, Winfield, 102
Shepard, M. Simeon, 50
Shepherd's Bush Pavilion, London, 32, 41
Shepperson, Arnold, 273, 274, 276, 328
Shichiko-Za, Osaka, 342
Shirley, Graham, 105, 106, 110, 114
Shirou, Otsuji, 338

Shochiku Kinema Ltd., 336; Shochiku Paramount, 25, 334, 340–42; Shochiku Youga Koukousya, 342
Shochiku-Za, Osaka, 342
Shochiku-Za, Tokyo, 340
shop windows, 3, 11, 12–14, 22–23, 36–38, 47; boycotts of, 59; chain ownership vs., 14; as exotic and foreign, 20, 357; MGM's shop windows, Freeman's role in, 107–11; Paramount's Plaza as the first, 39–42; as a term, 18–19, 40. See also under Metro-Goldwyn-Mayer; Paramount; Twentieth Century-Fox; Warner Bros.
Showcase Cinemas, 88, 384
Shutt, Allison, 295
silent era: *benshi*, 334, 338–41; intertitles, 52; musical accompaniment, orchestras (*see* orchestras); musical accompaniment, organs, 40–42, 50, 82, 223, 277; stage shows, 19, 41, 42, 151, 195
Silverstone, Dorothy, 227, 233
Silverstone, Murray, 133, 225–26, 255, 287, 359; boycott fears, 252; Cairo Palace and Cairo drive-in, 220, 256; Cinema Tel Aviv, 250–51, 252, 266; Fox cinemas in Palestine/Israel, 226, 230, 232–33, 234, 261, 266; Fox exhibition expansion, 176, 260–61; Fox's Middle East aspirations, 225–26, 249–50; fundraising/support for Israel, 227–28, 229, 232; retirement, 262; Skouras's hiring of, 225–26
Simmel, Ed, 222
Sinclair, Upton, 100
Sinder-Dean, 125
Singapore, 342, 344
Siritzky, Jo, 84
Siritzky, Leon, 68
Siritzky, Sam, 404n29
Siritzky family, 84, 404n29
Sixteen Millimetre Australia Pty. Ltd., 139
Skinner, Tom, 128
Skouras, Charles, 166
Skouras, George, 86
Skouras, Siroula, 137
Skouras, Spyros, 86, 133, 135, 137, 196, 229, 288, 292; Anglo-American Film Distributors Ltd., 311, 323; anticommunism, 17, 25, 210, 249, 266; *Cleopatra* and, 258–59, 261; Fox/ACT cinemas in South Africa, 288–89, 290, 299, 316; Fox cinemas in Egypt, 246, 256–57, 260; Fox cinemas in Ethiopia, 311, 315; Fox cinemas in India, 359; Fox cinemas in Israel, 210, 230–31, 234, 249–50, 261, 266; Fox cinemas in Kenya, 291, 299, 315; Fox cinemas in Southern Rhodesia, 299; Fox cinemas in West Africa, 312; Fox exhibition expansion, 176, 260–61; Fox's Cinema Tel Aviv, 14–15, 25, 250–51, 266; Fox's segregated cinemas/"Salisbury incident," 175, 299–305, 309–10; Fox's UAR expansion/loans, 255–56, 258, 259–60; Fox television, 305, 306, 315–16; Greek ties/Greek Orthodox heritage, 227, 231; M. J. Moodabe and, 121, 132, 137; Nasser and, 256, 258–59; retirement, 261–62, 316; Silverstone and, 225; support for Israel/UJA, 227–28, 229, 231, 232, 233, 236, 245, 248–49, 252, 258, 259, 442n88; Ernest Turnbull and, 137, 138
Skouras Theatres, 86
SkyCity Cinemas, 143
Skyline Cinemas, 128, 133, 134
Slomovitz, Philip, 254–55
Smart, Charles, 82
Smith, Ernesto P., 185, 195
Smith, Frederick James (F. J.), 112–14
Smith-Valcarce, 195–96
Smoodin, Eric, 4–5
Sociedade Cinematográfica Paulista, 150
Société des Grands Cinémas Français, 67
Société d'Exploitation Cinématographique Africaine (SECMA), 311–15
Société Générale des Films, 50
Société Immobilière du Vaudeville, 67
Sogecable Corp., 88
Solot, Steve, 22
Sonin, Carl, 276, 278
Sony, 89, 379, 385, 453n137
Sorrentino, Ugo, 157
sound film, 55, 152; Movietone, 153; six-channel stereo sound, 177; synchronous sound, 13, 116, 154, 186, 334, 340, 341, 387; Vitaphone, 153; Western Electric sound systems, 154, 158, 340
South Africa: African National Congress, 33, 303; Bloemfontein, 274, 279, 286; censorship, 293, 294; communism, 321; drive-ins, 285, 291, 292, 309; Fox/ACT (*see* African Consolidated Theatres (ACT), Fox-owned); global trade sanctions against, 328; Habonim, 232; Maritzburg, 279, 282; MGM/ACT, 276–77, 279, 280, 284, 287; MGM/CIC, 326–27; PAMECA boycott, 310–11;

Pietermaritzburg, 274, 286; Port Elizabeth, 274, 279, 286; Republic of South Africa, founding of, 303, 307, 450n47; television, 306–7, 326; Union of South Africa, founding of, 277, 444n44. *See also* Cape Town; Durban; Johannesburg; Pretoria; South Africa, apartheid

South Africa, apartheid, 25, 270, 290, 307, 320, 327–29, 444n44, 447n55; *Cape Town Affair* and, 321–22; codification of, 277, 285, 307, 309, 444n44; "Europeans only"/"whites-only" cinemas, 2, 25, 277, 294, 297–98, 301, 309; Fox's facilitation of, 2, 25, 299, 309, 311, 317, 319, 322, 324, 326; MGM's facilitation of, 277, 309, 322, 327, 328; multiracial partnership vs., 295

South African Broadcasting Corp., 285–86, 307

South African Screen Productions (Pty.) Ltd., 292, 319

South America, 4, 22, 148, 149, 166–67, 168, 175, 178–79, 334; anti-Nazi efforts in, 148; CIC, 85, 327; "Good Neighbor" policies, 164; Loew's, 214, 395n4; MGM (Metros/cinemas), 5, 83, 151, 152, 155, 158–59, 169, 170, 177, 178, 180, 205, 352; National Amusements, 88; Nazi films, 160, 167; Ufa, 160; Warner Bros., 168. *See also* Brazil; Argentina; Uruguay

South Korea, 376, 378, 386–91

South Pacific (1958), 294–95, 297–98; interracial romance and multiracial tolerance, 1, 269, 294, 329; Royal Cinema's segregated premiere, 1–2, 269, 270, 295, 296–99; Royal Cinema's segregated premiere, fallout, 300, 305, 306, 308, 316, 322, 329; viewing of, in Northern Rhodesia, 294, 297–98; viewing of, in South Africa, 294

South West Africa (colonial Namibia), 284, 289, 291, 318

Southern Rhodesia (colonial Zimbabwe): Bulawayo, 295, 303, 307, 308; Central African Federation, 291, 295, 296, 298, 306; desegregation of cinemas, 175, 209, 303–9, 316–17, 451n77; Fox/ACT and indifference to segregation, 25, 270, 289, 291–92, 300, 305–7, 317–18; Fox/TIE television deal, 305–8, 315; "multiracial partnership," 2, 269, 270, 295, 297, 299; segregated cinemas, 270, 295–98, 307. *See also* Salisbury

Soviet Union, 321; Egypt and, 250, 256; India and, 357–58; U.S.-operated cinemas abroad and struggle against, 17, 249

Spain, 190, 259, 343; Barcelona, 23, 35, 55, 57; Dalian Wanda, 382; Madrid, 58; Paramount, 57; screen quota system, 391; Spanish Civil War, 57, 61; UCI, 85; Warner Bros./WBIT, 88

Spanish-American War, 184, 189, 426n35

Specterman, Edith, 261

Specterman, Ralph, 261

Spencer Pictures, 95

Spielberg, Steven, 371

Spring, Morton, 220–21

Springbok Film Company, 273

St. James Theatre, Sydney, 124, 131, 132, 138

St. John, Earl, 56, 63

Standard Bank of South Africa, 316

Stanfill, Dennis C., 140–41, 142

Star Cinema Grill, 389, 391

Star Wars (1977), 81, 139, 140, 254

Stardawn Investments, 141

Stark, J. Albin, 55

State Administration of Radio, Film and Television (SARFT/SAPPRFT). *See under* China

Steel, Barbara, 258

Ster Films, 318, 319, 325; Ster-Kinekor, 326, 327–29

Stern, Mordechai, 261

Stirling, David, 297, 305, 316

Stodel, A. H. "Harry," 273, 293, 299, 303–4

Stodel, Jack, 293–94

Stone, E. A., 62

Stone, Lewis, 214, 215

Strand, Curt, 252–53

streaming, 381, 385, 392

Streit's Filmtheater, Hamburg, 81

Strengholt, F. L. D. "Fritz," 59–60, 65, 77

Strijdom, Johannes, 290, 319

Strong, Robert C., 259–60

subtitling, 219, 221, 264, 312, 364; *benshi*'s interpretation of, 338; dubbing vs., 52, 171, 194; in Egypt, 217, 219, 220, 221, 247; multiple, 217, 220, 247, 250

Sudan, 212, 242, 255

Suisei, Matsui, 341

Sulatycky, Warren, 391

"super cinemas," 38, 47, 48, 309

SuperLux, 88

Svensk Filmindustri, 55

Swanson, Ana, 384, 385

Sweden: Malmö, 55, 57; Stockholm, 23, 55, 57, 63
Switzerland, 48, 77–79, 210; Geneva, 77, 79, 360; Lausanne, 77, 79
Sydney, Australia: Fox, 103; Hoyts, 95–98, 139, 140–41; MGM, 58, 107–8; MGM (Metro Crows Nest), 132; MGM (Metro Twin Drive-In), 134; MGM (Metro Liberty), 131; MGM (Minerva Theatre), 131; MGM (Prince Edward Theatre), 96, 105, 107–8, 111–12; MGM (St. James Theatre), 124, 131, 132, 138; Palace Theatre, 95; Paramount, 57, 105–6; Paramount (Prince Edward Theatre), 57, 105; Universal (Rialto Theatre), 109; UT, 97–98; UT (Capitol Theatre), 96; Warner Bros., 63
Syria, 233, 244–45; Arab-Israeli War, 228; Fox, 258; MGM, 23, 48, 210, 242; UAR, 255–56, 258, 259–60, 263

Tait, E. J., 9, 95
Tait, John, 95, 98, 102
Taiwan: Taipei, 369; UCI, 85; Warner Bros./WBIT, 14, 88, 361, 369
Takenaka, Ayumi, 174
Tale of Two Cities (1935), 352
Tallis, George, 95, 98
Tanganyika, 279, 284, 289, 311, 320, 426n13, 443n6
Tanzania, 320, 322, 323. See also Tanganyika)
Taylor, Elizabeth, 258–60, 441n69
Taylor, Robert, 16, 244
Teatro Alcazar, Havana, 197
Teatro Astral, Bogotá, 167, 170
Teatro Central, Lima, 10, 63, 86, 166, 173, 197, 200
Teatro Encanto, Havana, 56, 184–85, 195–95, 197, 199, 202
Teatro Fausto, Havana, 55, 154, 184–85, 194–95, 197, 199, 202
Teatro Metro: Panama City, 177; San Juan, 183, 190, 192–94, 200, 205, 206
Teatro Nacional, Havana, 195–96, 198
Teatro Olimpia, Mexico City, 55, 154, 396n24, 418n2
Teatro San Jorge, Bogotá, 86, 158, 169–70, 197, 200
Teatro Urquiza, Montevideo, 420n50
Teatros Modernos, 193, 194
Technicolor, 358
Tel Aviv, Israel, 225, 266; cinemas, as sites of political protest and terrorism, 249, 262; Fox (*see* Cinema Tel Aviv); Hilton, 17; Louries in, 232; MGM, 10, 231; Paramount, 231; Rank, 226; Warner (Orion), 63, 226
television: Australia, 132, 133, 136; Brazil, 177; CIC, 83, 84, 326; CinemaScope as response to, 133; Fox and, in the Middle East, 255; Fox and, in the UAR, 255–56; Fox/TIE and, in southern and Central African Africa, 305–8, 315–16; Hoyts and, 136–37; Israel, 254–55, 262; Kenya, 308, 315–16, 325, 451n68; Mestre and, 204; New Zealand, 135–36, 139; Rank and, in South Africa, 285–86; Schlesinger/ACT and, in South Africa and Southern Rhodesia, 286, 289, 306–7; South Africa, 306–7, 326; Warner Bros./Time Warner, 371, 376; worldwide rollout of, 81
Television International Enterprises Ltd. (TIE), 305–6, 316
Television Network (Kenya) Ltd., 316, 451n68
Television Wales and West of England, 316
Temple, Shirley, 24
terrorism, 148; Colombia, 179; Cuban cinema, 204; Egypt and Egyptian cinemas, 12, 222–23, 226, 230, 235, 264, 375, 432n76; Israeli cinemas, 262; Mumbai cinema, 264; Universal offices, Osaka, 336
Theater Tuschinski, Amsterdam, 59, 60, 68, 404n30
Theatro Santa Heleña, São Paulo, 150, 151–52
theme parks, 10, 11, 370, 378–79
Thief of Baghdad, The (1940), 228, 362
Thika/Fox Drive-In, Nairobi, 25, 291, 324, 328, 329
Thomas O'Brien Theatres Ltd., 117, 118
Thompkins, Gwen, 316
Thompson, Kristin, 2, 15
Thompson, Roy, 307
Thorne, Ross, 125
Thornicroft, Gaston, 297–98, 302, 303, 305
Thornley, J. L., 104
Thrill of a Romance (1945), 77, 170
Thring, F. W. "Frank," 95, 98–99, 102, 110, 114
TIE. *See* Television International Enterprises Ltd. (TIE)
Time Warner, 369–71, 374, 376–77, 462n44
Tivoli Theatre, London, 35–36, 38
To, Johnnie, 372
Tobis, 61, 65

Todd, Garfield, 297, 303
Toho, 176–77, 342
Tokyo, Japan: anti-American boycott, 336; Great Kanto Earthquake, 335, 337; MGM (planned Metro cinema), 58, 342; Paramount, 10, 13, 95, 334, 337; Paramount (Hogaku-Za) (*see* Hogaku-Za, Tokyo); *ronin*, 335–36; Paramount (Musashinokan), 340; Shochiku Paramount (Shochiku-Za), 340
Tokyo-Takarazuka Theater Company. *See* Toho
Tomaselli, Keyan, 20, 271, 273, 274, 276, 328, 451n67
Toronto, Canada, 316, 391; Loew's, 150, 190, 395n4
Toulouse, France: Fox, 54; MGM (Plaza Theater), 77; Paramount (Le Paramount), 57
Tours, Frank, 40, 42
Tramarsa, S.A., 359–60
Transjordan, 233
Trelawney of the Wells (1916), 46
Trinidad, 148; British colonial rule and pushback, 24, 148, 183, 188–89; Indian films in, 189; MGM, 24, 183, 187–89, 457n54, 457n61; Port of Spain, 24, 148, 183, 188–89
TriStar Pictures, 453n137
Trumpbour, John, 2, 15
Trussart, G., 64–65
Tunisia, 23, 48, 210
Turkey, 35, 242, 387
Turnbull, Dale, 12, 14, 66, 99, 121, 133, 136, 137–38
Turnbull, Ernest, 66, 125, 137–38, 288
Turner, Philip, 3, 88
Turner Broadcasting System Asia Pacific, 371
Tuschinski, Abraham, 59, 60, 65, 68, 76, 404n30
Twentieth Century-Fox: Africa, 2, 5, 25, 269, 284–87, 289–90, 305, 310, 315–18, 322–24, 329; Alexandria, 10, 243, 244, 247, 256, 264; Amsterdam, 3, 14, 60, 81; anti-Zionist campaign against, 209, 228–30, 232, 257; Australasia, 93, 99, 101, 137, 140–41, 142, 143–44; Australia, 4, 5, 13, 14–15, 93–94, 263; block-booking, 106; Bogotá, 166, 167; Bombay, 14, 359; Brazil, 148, 166–67; Brussels, 50, 54, 58; Buenos Aires, 150; Cairo, 7, 24–25, 209, 220–21, 226–27, 235, 239, 243, 244, 246, 255–66, 263–65; Calcutta, 347, 359; Cali, 168, 172; Cape Town, 232, 280, 282, 286, 309; Chile, 148, 172; CinemaScope, 13, 80, 132–33, 247, 250, 251, 253, 287, 290, 387; circuit power/chain ownership, 14. 102, 347; Colombia, 148, 168, 172; debt, 24, 94, 99–101, 126, 325; drive-ins, 25, 214, 218, 256, 260, 291, 316, 318, 329; Durban, 280, 286, 318; Egypt, 2, 4, 24–25, 209–10, 220, 228–30, 232, 254–61, 263; England, 23, 61, 62, 63, 79–80, 279, 325; Europe, 54–55, 81, 281, 289; France, 81; Haifa, 231, 234, 250, 254, 261; Hamburg, 81; India, 358–59; Israel, 4, 25, 209–10, 230–32, 234–35, 248–55, 260–63, 266; Jerusalem, 231, 234, 250, 254, 261; Johannesburg, 9, 232, 252, 277–80, 286, 288–91, 295, 318, 319, 433–34n11; Kenya, 2, 14, 17, 25, 269, 270, 279, 284, 288–89, 291, 292, 305, 308, 310–11, 315–16, 318, 323–26, 328, 359, 451n68; Latin America, 13, 24, 166–67, 168, 172; Lebanon, 255, 258; Lima, 3, 14, 166–67, 168, 172, 173; London, 14, 36, 80, 81, 311, 323; Mexico, 148, 166, 168, 172; Middle East, 226, 249–50, 252, 255; Montevideo, 150; Nairobi, 3, 25, 284, 291, 292, 323–25, 328–29; Netherlands, 81; Northern Rhodesia, 279, 289; Panama City, 177; Paris, 54; Peru, 24, 148; Pretoria, 279, 282; Rio de Janeiro, 150, 166, 168, 172; São Paulo, 150, 166, 176; Shanghai, 362–64; South Africa, 2, 17, 25, 270–71, 288–92, 309, 318–19, 325–26, 383; Southern Rhodesia, 1–2, 269, 270, 295, 296–99; Strasbourg, 54; Sydney, 103; Syria, 258; Tel Aviv, 14–15, 25, 231, 234–35, 248, 250–55, 253, 261–63, 265–66; troubled racial history in Africa, 2, 25, 269, 305, 310, 316–17, 324, 329; The Walt Disney Company's purchase of, 143, 379, 381; Vienna, 81
Twentieth Century-Fox, cinemas: Bogotá, 166, 167; Cairo (*see* Cairo Palace, Palaca); Calcutta, 347; Cali, 168, 172; Cape Town (20th Century Theatre), 232, 280, 282; Cape Town (Colosseum Theatre), 309; Havana, 195–96, 198; Johannesburg, 9, 232, 252, 280, 286; Lima, 3, 14, 166–67, 168, 172, 173; London, 14, 36; Panama City, 177; Plymouth, 80; Rio de Janeiro, 166, 168, 172; São Paulo, 176; Tel Aviv (*see* Cinema Tel Aviv). *See also specific 20th Century Theatres*

Twentieth Century-Fox, partnerships and subsidiaries: Anglo-American Film Distributors Ltd., 311, 323; Chase National Bank and, 23–24, 94, 98, 101, 110, 120, 141; Cinema Theater Investments (Pty.) Ltd., 280, 292; Fox Film Corp. Pty. Ltd., 123; Fox Filmes do Brasil, 176; Fox Films de Cuba, 199; (Fox) International Theatres of Australasia, 141; Foxmeric, 81; Fox Television, 255, 322; Fox Theatres South Africa (Pty.) Ltd., 288–89, 291–92, 316; Gaumont-British, 23, 54, 61, 62, 63, 99–100, 106, 110, 115, 279; Independent Picture Palaces Ltd., 278–80; Loew's/MGM, 54, 99; South African Screen Productions (Pty.) Ltd., 292, 319; Twentieth Century-Fox Film Corp. (N.Z.) Ltd., 122–23, 139; Walt Disney, 264, 291, 318. *See also* Amalgamated Theatres Ltd. (Hippodrome); Hoyts Theatres Ltd.

Twentieth Century-Fox, productions: *An Affair to Remember*, 254; *Cape Town Affair*, 319–22; *Carmen Jones*, 294–95; *Cleopatra*, 254, 258–61, 263; *The Empire Strikes Back*, 140; *Fox Movietone News*, 99, 106, 115, 290, 340, 362; *The Jackals*, 319–20; *The Magnetic Tide*, 233; *Prince of Foxes*, 432n60; *The Robe*, 132, 250; *South Pacific* (see *South Pacific*); *Star Wars*, 81, 139, 140, 254; *Viva Zapata*, 247

UA. *See* United Artists (UA)
UACC. *See* United Artists Cinema Circuit (UACC)
UAR. *See* United Arab Republic (UAR)
UCI. *See* United Cinemas International (UCI)
Ucko, Luis, 170
Ufa. *See* Universum-Film Aktiengesellschaft (Ufa)
Ufa-Palast am Zoo, Berlin, 53–54
UGC. *See* Union Generale Cinématographique (UGC)
U-I (Universal International). *See under* Universal
UJA. *See* United Jewish Appeal (UJA)
Ullmann, Andre, 67–70, 72, 74–75
Union Generale Cinématographique (UGC), 390
Union Theatres (Pty.) Ltd., 276

United Arab Republic (UAR), 255–56, 258, 259–60, 263
United Artists (UA), 7, 89; Amsterdam, 61; Bogotá (Teatro Astral), 167, 170; Brazil, 159, 160, 162, 168; Budapest (Corvin Cinema), 59; CIC merger with MGM and UA/UCI, 85, 327; Cobiân and, 191, 194; Cuba, 195, 196, 201; England, 22, 37, 42–43, 61; Hoyts and, 96; Latin America, 147, 148, 159; Lourie and, 232; piracy of, in China, 362; Puerto Rico, 191, 194; Skouras Theatres, 86; Smith-Valcarce and, 195, 196; South Africa/ACT and, 22, 280, 283, 285, 286, 291, 318; United Artists Communications Inc., 85, 86; United International Pictures, 85, 327
United Artists Cinema Circuit (UACC), 369–70
United Artists Theatres, 86, 89, 159
United Cinemas International (UCI), 82, 85, 88, 89, 178, 368, 382, 390
United International Pictures, 85, 327
United Jewish Appeal (UJA), 227–28, 231–32, 245, 249
United Pictures Theatres Ltd., 444n32
United States: Civil Rights Act (1964), 309, 322; Commerce Department, 11, 30, 211; distribution revenues, repatriation of, 12, 103–4, 171, 230, 234, 251, 366; "Good Neighbor" policies, 164; Immigration Act (1924), 334, 335–37; MPAA, 197, 199, 234, 246, 270, 295, 296, 301; -produced newsreels, 10, 11, 125, 158, 249, 277, 345; Production Code, 217; segregated cinemas, 174–75, 309; stock market crash, 100, 444n32. *See also* America; anti-Americanism; cultural embassies; U.S. Justice Department; U.S. State Department; *and specific cities*
United World Pictures, 283
Universal, 7, 38, 85, 90, 96, 157, 158, 344, 379; Australia, 96, 109–11, 114; Berlin (Mercedes Palast), 53; Brazil, 161, 177, 178; British boycott threats, 37–38; CIC/UCI, 82–84, 85, 89, 139, 264, 326, 382; Cintrust, 326; Cobiân and, 194, 197; Egypt, 244; Fox/ACT, 283, 284, 291, 318; Havana, 195, 197, 199; India, 347; Japan, 334–37; Leeds (Rialto Theatre), 37, 53; London (Empire Theatre), 36; London (Rialto Theatre), 53; *Michael Strogoff*, 53; Neukölln-area cinema, 53; Peacock, 381;

Phantom of the Opera, 345; Ufa and, 52; U-I, 283–84; United International Pictures, 327, Universal Filmed Entertainment Group, 379
Universal-International (U-I). *See under* Universal
Universum-Film Aktiengesellschaft (Ufa), 52, 176; Argentina, 162; Berlin (Ufa-Palast am Zoo), 53–54; Brazil, 157, 161–62; Budapest, 58; Budapest (Ufa-Urania), 59; Chile, 162–63; Egypt, 211, 250; Gaumont-Ufa, 106; Nazi control of, and backlash against, 58–59, 160, 166, 205, 211; Netherlands, 61, 65; Parufamet, 52–53; São Paulo (Cine Ufa-Palácio), 161, 166; South Africa, 275; Universal and, 52
Urban Diversified Properties, 141
Uruguay, 24, 85, 158, 159, 177. *See also* Montevideo
ushers, 3, 19, 277, 297, 363, 364; Cinema Metro, Cairo, 209, 217; Cinema Tel Aviv, 251, 262–63; Hassanein's start as, 86; Le Paramount's, role in the Resistance, 69–70, 71, 74; Plaza Theatre, London, 40; Tel Aviv, protests by, 255, 262–63
U.S. Justice Department: consent decree (1948), 5, 7–8, 79–80, 131, 172, 289, 381; Fox's short-lived acquisition of Loew's/MGM (1929), 54, 101, 172
U.S. State Department, 313; British protectionism, 38–39, 44; Cinema Tel Aviv, 254, 266; Egyptian protectionism, anti-Americanism, and antisemitism/Cairo Fire, 213, 220, 226–29, 238, 245–47, 258, 264, 437n112; Fox's acquisition of ACT, 270, 287–90, 327; Fox's acquisition of ACT and Royal Cinema (Salisbury) controversy 1–2, 25, 269–71, 287, 290–91, 295–305, 306, 308, 316, 322, 327–29; Israel, 249, 266; MGM in Brussels, 64–65; MGM's Bombay and Calcutta shop windows, 357–58; MGM's Cine Metros, 158, 162, 165, 170–71, 173, 181, 205–6; MGM's Manila shop window, 345; myth of American social and racial equality, 36, 270; Paramount shop windows, 57, 75, 105, 162, 173; Swiss protectionism, 78–79; UAR loan, 256, 259–60; U.S. anti-communist efforts, 148, 175, 270, 357–58; U.S. anti-Nazi efforts, 148, 162, 205; U.S. cinema expansion and cooperation with local governments, 12, 19–20, 30, 315; U.S.-owned cinemas as embassies/soft power catalysis, 4, 9–10, 19–20, 30–31, 46–47, 90, 148, 155, 162, 170–81, 206, 233, 266, 357–58

Valcarce, Jose, 195–96, 197
Valencise, João Miguel, 152–53
Valley of the Kings (1954), 16, 244
Valparaiso, Chile, 166, 169, 172, 352
Van Riebeck Theatre, Cape Town, 286
Vargas, Getúlio, 157, 161, 162, 164
Vasey, Ruth, 36–37
Venezuela, 24, 159, 177–78, 184, 204
Verity, Frank, 41; Paramount cinemas, 41, 50, 55, 56, 57, 82; renovation of Rialto Theatre, London, 80, 82
vertical integration, 5, 34, 271, 273, 381, 392; Dalian Wanda, 382; Gaumont-Loew-Metro, 48; Loew's/MGM, 52, 78, 131
Verwoerd, Hendrik, 321
Viacom, 88, 379, 380, 384, 465n1
Victoria Theater, Shanghai, 362
Vieira, João Luiz, 147, 156, 157, 180
Vietheer, George, 315
Vietnam, 374, 386, 387
Village Force Cinemas, 143
Village Roadshow: Golden Harvest and, 376, 386; Priya Cinemas and, 386; Warner Bros./WBIT/WBIC and, 88, 93, 143, 369, 372
Virgin Cinemas, 89
VistaVision, 133
Vitalis, Robert, 212, 222, 228, 245, 257
Vitaphone, 153
Viva Zapata (1952), 247

Wagdi, Anwar, 221
Wahab, Mohamed Abdel, 221
Wahbi, Youssef, 209, 228; anti-Zionist campaign against Fox and MGM, 209, 228–30, 232, 257; "Committee on the Projection of Arabic Film in High Class Motion Picture Houses," 221; *Darbit-al qadar*, 434n19; Egyptian Syndicate, 283; Nahas Studio, 283; Ramses City, 213; Wahbi Cinema, 211
Wahbi Cinema, Cairo, 211
Wai Ka-fai, 372
Wailes, Edward, 290–91
Walberg and Udassim, 251
Wall, Ed. J., 97

Wallace, Walker, 373
Waller, Gregory, 4–5
Walt Disney Company, The, 134; Disney+, 381, 392; El Capitan Theatre, 380; Fox's distribution of Disney films, 264, 291, 318; Fox's sale to, 143, 379, 381; Pixar, 392; Ster-Kinekor and, 326; theme parks, 11, 30, 378–79
Wanda Group. *See* Dalian Wanda
Wang, Ting, 362, 366, 368
Wang Jianlin, 383, 385
Wang Jingwei, 365
Wanger, Walter, 246, 258–59
WAP. *See* West African Pictures Ltd. (WAP)
Warner, Albert, 37
Warner, Keith Q., 185–86
Warner Bros.: Alexandria, 63, 219, 223; Auckland, 63; Australasia, 93, 129, 143–44; Australia, 88, 93, 129–31, 143, 369, 372; Beijing, 372–73, 376; Bogotá, 86, 169–70, 197, 200; Bombay, 358, 359; Brazil, 168; Brisbane, 63; Cairo, 63, 223; Caribbean, 24, 169–70, 182, 199; China, 5, 26, 333, 361, 365, 368–79, 380, 386; Colombia, 24, 86, 148–49, 368; Cuba, 5, 24, 86, 148, 185, 194–95, 197–98, 203–5, 368; England, 61–62, 79, 86; Europe, 61–62, 63, 86, 88, 370, 373, 377; Germany, 88; Havana, 5, 10, 86, 183, 185, 197–205, *203*; Italy, 88, 374; Jamaica, 85; Japan, 26, 88, 333, 343–44, 361, 369, 373–74, 377; Latin America, 24, 148–49, 166, 199, 200; Lima, 10, 63, 86, 166, 173, 197, 200; London, 5, 7, 24, 42, 61–62, 82, 86, *87*, 368–39, 373; Mexico, 63, 166, 169–70, 199, 200; Nanjing, 372, 373, 375; Netherlands, 88; Paris, 61–62; Peru, 24, 85, 148, 368; Puerto Rico, 199–20; Rio de Janeiro, 168; São Paulo, 168; Shanghai, 371–72, 373–76, 462–63n64; Spain, 88; Sydney, 63; Taiwan, 14, 88, 361, 369; Tel Aviv, 63, 226
Warner Bros., cinemas: Bogotá, 86, 169–70, 197, 200; Havana (Plaza), 199–200, 202, 203, 205; Havana (Warner/Teatro Radio Centro/Cine Yara), 197–200, 202–3, *203*, 204, 205; Lima (Teatro Central), 10, 63, 86, 166, 173, 197, 200; London, 5, 7, 24, 61–62, 82, 86, *87*, 368
Warner Bros., parent companies, partnerships, and subsidiaries: ABC Cinemas, 63; CIC-Warner/Nu Metro, 85, 326, 328–29; Dalian Wanda, 26, 334, 372–74, 374; HBO Max, 381, 392; Nanjing SFG-Warner Cinema City, 375; Shanghai Paradise Warner Cinema City Co., 275, 371–72; Stanley-Warner Corp. (SWC), 204, 429n111; Time Warner, 369–70, 374, 376–77, 462n44; Warner Bros. First National Pictures Pty. Ltd., 130; Warner Bros. First National South Films Inc., 198, 199; Warner Bros. Home Entertainment Group, 376; Warner Bros. Pictures Inc., 197–98; Warner Bros. Pictures Ltd., 63; Warner Communications, 327–38; Warner-Fox, 262, 263; Warner Music Asia Pacific, 371; Warner Music China, 371; Warner Music International, 371; Warner-Mycal Cinemas, 26, 88, 333, 343, 369, 377; Warner Village Cinemas, 87, 88, 93, 369, 372, 462n44. *See also* Warner Bros. International Cinemas (WBIC); Warner Bros. International Theatres (WBIT)
Warner Bros., productions: *The Adventures of Robin Hood*, 62; *Angels of Mercy*, 351; *Empire of the Sun*, 371; *The Fugitive*, 368; *House of Wax*, 128; *The Matrix Reloaded*, 372; *Turn Left, Turn Right*, 372
Warner Bros. International Cinemas (WBIC), 373–78, 386, 390
Warner Bros. International Theatres (WBIT), 14, 82–83, 86, 88, 89, 368–73
Warner Theatre (Teatro Radio Centro/Cine Yara), Havana, 197–200, 202–3, *203*, 204, 205
Warner Theatre (Warner West End Theatre), London, 5, 7, 24, 61–62, 82, 86, *87*, 368
Wasserman, Lew, 83
Waterloo Theatre, Hamburg, 80
Waxman, Clive, 107
WBIC. *See* Warner Bros. International Cinemas (WBIC)
WBIT. *See* Warner Bros. International Theatres (WBIT)
Webb, Robert D., 319–20, 321–22
Week-end (1967), 312
Weiner, Steve, 86
Weinzeile Theatre, Vienna, 81
Welensky, Roy, 299
Wellman, William, 319
Weltner, George, 74–75, 173
West, T. J., 95

West Africa, 25, 310, 311–15
West African Pictures Ltd. (WAP), 314
West Coast Theatres, 54
West Germany, 80, 85
West's Pictures, 95
Westerbork transit camp, 68, 76
Western India Theatres Ltd., 348, 359
Western Suburb Cinemas, 126
westerns, 319–21, 323
Wharton, Annabel, 15–18, 20, 244
White, Walter, 248
Whitehead, Edgar, 298, 299, 303
widescreen cinema, 387; Cinerama, 139, 204, 318, 387; Dimension 150, 177; IMAX, 265, 376, 378, 382; MGM, 133, 177, 358; ScreenX, 387; VistaVision, 133. *See also* CinemaScope
Wiggin, Albert, 101, 102
Wigmore, Barrie, 100, 101
Wigston, David, 318, 328
Williams, Billy Dee, 140
Williams, Esther, 170, 223
Williams, Fritz, 53
Williamson, J. C., 117. *See also* J. C. Williamson (New Zealand) Films Ltd.
Willocq, Gisèle, 70, 71, 74
Winckles, Kenneth, 239
Wings (1927), 55
Winship, Blanton, 191–92, 193, 206
Winter Garden Theater, Toronto, 395n4
Wizard of Oz, The (1939), 352, 354
Wolf, David, 375
Wolfson, Isaac, 261
World Trade Organization, 333, 361, 371
World War I, 32–33, 35, 50, 149, 361–62; Freeman in, 107; Ullmann in, 67, 69
World War II, 11, 16, 26, 79, 125, 196, 270; Battle of the Lys, 64; in China, 365; Japanese attack on the Philippines, 343–45; Japanese surrender, 365; Le Paramount under Nazi occupation/role in the Resistance, 66–75; "Loew's Rice Paddy," 365; MGM expansion in Latin America during and after, 163–66, 168–69, 198; Operation Lila, 404n44; Paramount after, 171–72; Pearl Harbor, 162, 165, 343; Siritzky family after, 404n29; V-E Day, 74; Warner Bros. expansion during, 166. *See also* Nazi Germany and Nazism
World's Films, 32
Wuthrich, Jim, 376
Wynd, Oswald, 333, 334, 338–39, 340

xenophobia, 122

Yamada, Kosaku, 338, 340
Yan, Xing, 375
Yearling, The (1946), 352
York, Carl P., 55
Yu Aihong, 373
Yun Ik-jun, 386

Zacheretti, Phil, 387, 388
Zakkai, David, 263
Zambia, colonial. *See* Northern Rhodesia
Zanuck, Darryl, 137, 236, 261–62, 323, 325, 356
Zanuck, Dick, 137
Zelnick, Gustave, 243
Zhonghua, 365
Zhou Liming, 385
Zhu Rongji, 370
Ziegfeld Follies (1945), 366
Zimbabwe, colonial. *See* Southern Rhodesia
Zimbalist, Sam, 293
Zimmerman, James, 370, 462n51
Zoufoukal, Salah, 265
Zukor, Adolph, 31–32, 45, 56, 74, 107, 272

FILM AND CULTURE

A series of Columbia University Press

Edited by John Belton

What Made Pistachio Nuts? Early Sound Comedy and the Vaudeville Aesthetic
HENRY JENKINS

Showstoppers: Busby Berkeley and the Tradition of Spectacle
MARTIN RUBIN

Projections of War: Hollywood, American Culture, and World War II
THOMAS DOHERTY

Laughing Screaming: Modern Hollywood Horror and Comedy
WILLIAM PAUL

Laughing Hysterically: American Screen Comedy of the 1950s
ED SIKOV

Primitive Passions: Visuality, Sexuality, Ethnography, and Contemporary Chinese Cinema
REY CHOW

The Cinema of Max Ophuls: Magisterial Vision and the Figure of Woman
SUSAN M. WHITE

Black Women as Cultural Readers
JACQUELINE BOBO

Picturing Japaneseness: Monumental Style, National Identity, Japanese Film
DARRELL WILLIAM DAVIS

Attack of the Leading Ladies: Gender, Sexuality, and Spectatorship in Classic Horror Cinema
RHONA J. BERENSTEIN

This Mad Masquerade: Stardom and Masculinity in the Jazz Age
GAYLYN STUDLAR

Sexual Politics and Narrative Film: Hollywood and Beyond
ROBIN WOOD

The Sounds of Commerce: Marketing Popular Film Music
JEFF SMITH

Orson Welles, Shakespeare, and Popular Culture
MICHAEL ANDEREGG

Pre-Code Hollywood: Sex, Immorality, and Insurrection in American Cinema, 1930–1934
THOMAS DOHERTY

Sound Technology and the American Cinema: Perception, Representation, Modernity
JAMES LASTRA

Melodrama and Modernity: Early Sensational Cinema and Its Contexts
BEN SINGER

Wondrous Difference: Cinema, Anthropology, and Turn-of-the-Century Visual Culture
ALISON GRIFFITHS

Hearst Over Hollywood: Power, Passion, and Propaganda in the Movies
LOUIS PIZZITOLA

Masculine Interests: Homoerotics in Hollywood Film
ROBERT LANG

Special Effects: Still in Search of Wonder
MICHELE PIERSON

Designing Women: Cinema, Art Deco, and the Female Form
LUCY FISCHER

Cold War, Cool Medium: Television, McCarthyism, and American Culture
THOMAS DOHERTY

Katharine Hepburn: Star as Feminist
ANDREW BRITTON

Silent Film Sound
RICK ALTMAN

Home in Hollywood: The Imaginary Geography of Cinema
ELISABETH BRONFEN

Hollywood and the Culture Elite: How the Movies Became American
PETER DECHERNEY

Taiwan Film Directors: A Treasure Island
EMILIE YUEH-YU YEH AND DARRELL WILLIAM DAVIS

Shocking Representation: Historical Trauma, National Cinema, and the Modern Horror Film
ADAM LOWENSTEIN

China on Screen: Cinema and Nation
CHRIS BERRY AND MARY FARQUHAR

The New European Cinema: Redrawing the Map
ROSALIND GALT

George Gallup in Hollywood
SUSAN OHMER

Electric Sounds: Technological Change and the Rise of Corporate Mass Media
STEVE J. WURTZLER

The Impossible David Lynch
TODD MCGOWAN

Sentimental Fabulations, Contemporary Chinese Films: Attachment in the Age of Global Visibility
REY CHOW

Hitchcock's Romantic Irony
RICHARD ALLEN

Intelligence Work: The Politics of American Documentary
JONATHAN KAHANA

Eye of the Century: Film, Experience, Modernity
FRANCESCO CASETTI

Shivers Down Your Spine: Cinema, Museums, and the Immersive View
ALISON GRIFFITHS

Weimar Cinema: An Essential Guide to Classic Films of the Era
EDITED BY NOAH ISENBERG

African Film and Literature: Adapting Violence to the Screen
LINDIWE DOVEY

Film, A Sound Art
MICHEL CHION

Film Studies: An Introduction
ED SIKOV

Hollywood Lighting from the Silent Era to Film Noir
PATRICK KEATING

Levinas and the Cinema of Redemption: Time, Ethics, and the Feminine
SAM B. GIRGUS

Counter-Archive: Film, the Everyday, and Albert Kahn's Archives de la Planète
PAULA AMAD

Indie: An American Film Culture
MICHAEL Z. NEWMAN

Pretty: Film and the Decorative Image
ROSALIND GALT

Film and Stereotype: A Challenge for Cinema and Theory
JÖRG SCHWEINITZ

Chinese Women's Cinema: Transnational Contexts
EDITED BY LINGZHEN WANG

Hideous Progeny: Disability, Eugenics, and Classic Horror Cinema
ANGELA M. SMITH

Hollywood's Copyright Wars: From Edison to the Internet
PETER DECHERNEY

Electric Dreamland: Amusement Parks, Movies, and American Modernity
LAUREN RABINOVITZ

Where Film Meets Philosophy: Godard, Resnais, and Experiments in Cinematic Thinking
HUNTER VAUGHAN

The Utopia of Film: Cinema and Its Futures in Godard, Kluge, and Tahimik
CHRISTOPHER PAVSEK

Hollywood and Hitler, 1933–1939
THOMAS DOHERTY

Cinematic Appeals: The Experience of New Movie Technologies
ARIEL ROGERS

Continental Strangers: German Exile Cinema, 1933–1951
GERD GEMÜNDEN

Deathwatch: American Film, Technology, and the End of Life
C. SCOTT COMBS

After the Silents: Hollywood Film Music in the Early Sound Era, 1926–1934
MICHAEL SLOWIK

"It's the Pictures That Got Small:" Charles Brackett on Billy Wilder and Hollywood's Golden Age
EDITED BY ANTHONY SLIDE

Plastic Reality: Special Effects, Technology, and the Emergence of 1970s Blockbuster Aesthetics
JULIE A. TURNOCK

Maya Deren: Incomplete Control
SARAH KELLER

Dreaming of Cinema: Spectatorship, Surrealism, and the Age of Digital Media
ADAM LOWENSTEIN

Motion(less) Pictures: The Cinema of Stasis
JUSTIN REMES

The Lumière Galaxy: Seven Key Words for the Cinema to Come
FRANCESCO CASETTI

The End of Cinema? A Medium in Crisis in the Digital Age
ANDRÉ GAUDREAULT AND PHILIPPE MARION

Studios Before the System: Architecture, Technology, and the Emergence of Cinematic Space
BRIAN R. JACOBSON

Impersonal Enunciation, or the Place of Film
CHRISTIAN METZ

When Movies Were Theater: Architecture, Exhibition, and the Evolution of American Film
WILLIAM PAUL

Carceral Fantasies: Cinema and Prison in Early Twentieth-Century America
ALISON GRIFFITHS

Unspeakable Histories: Film and the Experience of Catastrophe
WILLIAM GUYNN

Reform Cinema in Iran: Film and Political Change in the Islamic Republic
BLAKE ATWOOD

Exception Taken: How France Has Defied Hollywood's New World Order
JONATHAN BUCHSBAUM

After Uniqueness: A History of Film and Video Art in Circulation
ERIKA BALSOM

Words on Screen
MICHEL CHION

Essays on the Essay Film
EDITED BY NORA M. ALTER AND TIMOTHY CORRIGAN

The Essay Film After Fact and Fiction
NORA ALTER

Specters of Slapstick and Silent Film Comediennes
MAGGIE HENNEFELD

Melodrama Unbound: Across History, Media, and National Cultures
EDITED BY CHRISTINE GLEDHILL AND LINDA WILLIAMS

Show Trial: Hollywood, HUAC, and the Birth of the Blacklist
THOMAS DOHERTY

Cinema/Politics/Philosophy
NICO BAUMBACH

The Dynamic Frame: Camera Movement in Classical Hollywood
PATRICK KEATING

Hollywood's Dirtiest Secret: The Hidden Environmental Costs of the Movies
HUNTER VAUGHAN

Chromatic Modernity: Color, Cinema, and Media of the 1920s
SARAH STREET AND JOSHUA YUMIBE

Rewriting Indie Cinema: Improvisation, Psychodrama, and the Screenplay
J. J. MURPHY

On the Screen: Displaying the Moving Image, 1926–1942
ARIEL ROGERS

Play Time: Jacques Tati and Comedic Modernism
MALCOLM TURVEY

Spaces Mapped and Monstrous: Digital 3D Cinema and Visual Culture
NICK JONES

Anxious Cinephilia: Pleasure and Peril at the Movies
SARAH KELLER

Film Studies, 2nd Edition
ED SIKOV

Hollywood's Artists: The Directors Guild of America and the Construction of Authorship
VIRGINIA WRIGHT WEXMAN

Absence in Cinema: The Art of Showing Nothing
JUSTIN REMES

Bombay Hustle: Making Movies in a Colonial City
DEBASHREE MUKHERJEE

Music in Cinema
MICHEL CHION

GPSR Authorized Representative: Easy Access System Europe, Mustamäe tee 50, 10621 Tallinn, Estonia, gpsr.requests@easproject.com